W9-AUO-764

Brief Contents

Contents

Preface

As in previous editions, anonymous reviewers have suggested ways to improve *Close Relations: An Introduction to the Sociology of Families*, and we have, in almost every instance, followed their helpful suggestions. This meant that first the book got very long, then we brought it down to size again—a process of editing somewhat like playing the accordion.

In particular, we resolved in this edition to talk more about cultural variations among families (including cultural influences on mate selection, attitudes toward marriage and family, relations between parents and children, and so on). We also set out to talk more about media and its impact on the family and the effects of population aging; to include more on feminist theory; and of course, to update all statistics and references. We also tried to increase the number of graphics, figures, and tables throughout the book to make it more visually appealing.

As you can imagine, talking about the general features of Canadian family life and its variations has proven a challenge. That said, our text has remained the same in its essentials. Readers have agreed with our approach, which is to stress family process over structure, diversity over uniformity, and reality over myth. This is a Canadian book, rooted in sociological research from around the world, and reflecting concerns of the twenty-first century. It continues to cover all the most important topics in the family literature and, as before, ends with a look at the future of families.

THE APPROACH OF THIS BOOK

As recently as 30 years ago, books on the family were often simple "how-to" guides to family life. Sometimes called "matching, hatching, and dispatching" books, they often had chapters such as "Dating and Courtship" and "Family and You." This approach seemed reasonable a few decades ago since the ways in which people lived in families tended to be less diverse than now, and the diversity that did exist was neither portrayed nor celebrated in family texts. There are still books like this today, which tend to "sell" the traditional family way of life. But, of course, shifting patterns and demands of work in postmodern societies create new kinds of family relations and forms, as we explore in this fifth edition.

Far more interesting than the regularities in close relations are the variations in family processes, forms, and structures. Twenty-first-century families are remarkably diverse. It is largely in response to this reality that we wrote the first edition of this text, and then revised it substantially with updated data and new insights about families in the second, third, and fourth editions, and again in this edition. This text sets itself the task of being different from other family books in use today. Its focus is on applications and theory: what works for families, for us as individuals, and for society. Several themes characterize our text:

- Families are immensely varied and characterized more by processes than by the forms they take.

- Family is becoming more, not less, important to us as individuals and to society as a whole. Recent research and theory have clearly shown that family health affects individual health and longevity and the population health of entire countries.

- Old expectations about family may no longer work. New solutions to family problems, based on what is known from family research, are offered here.

- There is a constantly changing interplay among families, school, and work. Family is both part of the problem and part of the solution, as shown in this text in a variety of ways.

- Historical changes and cross-national comparisons help us to better understand and interpret families today.

Throughout this text, we look at families as plural and diverse. We focus on families in terms of what they do rather than the shape they take.

CANADIAN CONTENT

Speaking of diversity, this is a Canadian book intended primarily for Canadian students and classrooms. While some generalizations based on American, European, or Asian data apply to Canadian situations, others do not. Our laws and policies are different, as are our histories, traditions, values, norms, and customs relating to family and marriage. At the same time, it is difficult to write a text based entirely on the findings of Canadian research. It must be noted, however, that both the volume of research on families in Canada and the scope of the topics covered have expanded enormously in recent years. A Canadian text, to be useful, should rely on the Canadian research and then incorporate findings from abroad. Thus, we attempt here a careful triangulation, using research from Canada, the United States, and the world. We try to offer international comparisons wherever we feel they are important. On the other hand, we do not draw attention to the nationality of a finding if we think that doing so adds nothing to understanding the research on families.

BRIEF OVERVIEW

Chapter 1 begins with an exploration of the variety of interesting shapes and processes of families and family-like relationships. We explore competing definitions of family and how families are seen through theoretical lenses. We also consider different research approaches to family work and what they enable us to see.

From here, we move on to Chapter 2, which opens the door to what we now know about families in the past. It offers an exciting glimpse of family diversity from a historical perspective. This discussion provides context for today's debates.

Chapter 3 then explores how families begin by taking a look at dating and mating. A renewed emphasis on ethnic and other cultural differences is offered here; attention is also paid to same-sex dating.

In Chapter 4 we examine the different ways couples form and live, including cohabitation, marriage patterns, and same-sex partnerships.

There follows in Chapter 5 a discussion of ways of being close, in which we consider points of satisfaction and dissatisfaction, particularly in relation to communication, trust, and sex.

People sometimes think of real family life as beginning with the entry into parenthood—a time fraught with many new changes and challenges. That is the subject of Chapter 6. In this chapter we also propose several approaches to parenting that are supported by research and offer some solutions to parenting problems.

In Chapter 7 we discuss work and family life, including the division of both domestic work and paid work. Domestic work is a known source of family conflict, while paid work in relation to the family is a topic of strong interest, as most adult members of families must balance family life with paid employment.

An understanding of violence and stress in families, the topic of Chapter 8, is crucial if we are to solve or even ameliorate these problems. We describe some of the contexts in which stresses occur for families, including poverty, racism, alcoholism, and the particular challenges faced by First Nations families. We also give attention to policies that attempt to reduce the negative situations with which families must cope.

In Chapter 9, the trends, myths, causes, and consequences of relationship dissolution and divorce are considered.

If couples divorce, some people remarry, and some experience step-parenthood. Other families, over the life course, go through the stages of children growing up and leaving home. Second (or subsequent) families, in all their diversity, are the topic of Chapter 10.

Chapter 11 takes a glimpse at families of the future, emphasizing how families create their own futures, influenced by both the opportunities and the constraints of society.

CHAPTER FEATURES

Each chapter of the text begins with a chapter outline with learning objectives

Throughout the chapters, figures, tables, and boxes cover key current data on the topics, erroneous beliefs, international findings, major Canadian findings, and key statistics. The most important new feature is a series of boxes in each chapter that contain interesting facts and observations drawn from other studies.

Study tools at the end of each chapter include a chapter summary, key terms with definitions, critical thinking questions, and an annotated list of relevant internet sites.

SUPPLEMENTS

The Instructor's Manual, Test Item File, and PowerPoint slides can be downloaded by instructors from a password-protected section of Pearson Education Canada's online catalogue. Navigate to the catalogue page for your textbook to view the list of those supplements that are available. Contact your local sales representative for further information.

Instructor's Manual. An instructor's manual is available with this fifth edition. Its features include chapter outlines, key terms and concepts, motivational activities, answers to critical thinking questions in the text, critical thinking exercises, debate suggestions, group activities, project suggestions, and film and video suggestions.

Test Item File. This carefully prepared test bank in Word format contains over 600 multiple-choice questions that correspond to the text. Designed to test students' comprehension of the material, this supplement contains the relevant page numbers from the textbook along with the correct answer for each question.

PowerPoint Slides. This supplement provides a comprehensive selection of slides highlighting key concepts featured in the text. The slides have been specifically developed for clear and easy communication of themes, ideas, and definitions.

CourseSmart for Instructors. CourseSmart goes beyond traditional expectations—providing instant, online access to the textbooks and course materials you need at a lower cost for students. And even as students save money, you can save time and hassle with a digital eTextbook that allows you to search for the most relevant content at the very moment you need it. Whether it's evaluating textbooks or creating lecture notes to help students with difficult concepts, CourseSmart can make life a little easier. See how when you visit *www.coursesmart.com/instructors*.

CourseSmart for Students. CourseSmart provides instant, online access to the textbooks and course materials you need at an average savings of 60 percent. With instant access from any computer and the ability to search your text, you'll find the content you need quickly, no matter where you are. And with online tools like highlighting and note-taking, you can save time and study efficiently. See all the benefits at *www.coursesmart.com/students*.

Learning Solutions Managers. Pearson's Learning Solutions Managers work with faculty and campus course designers to ensure that Pearson technology products, assessment tools, and online course materials are tailored to meet your specific needs. This highly qualified team is dedicated to helping schools take full advantage of a wide range of educational resources by assisting in the integration of a variety of instructional materials and media formats. Your local Pearson Education sales representative can provide you with more details on this service program.

Pearson Custom Library. For enrollments of at least 25 students, you can create your own textbook by choosing the chapters that best suit your own course needs. To begin building your custom text, visit www.pearsoncustomlibrary.com. You may also work with a dedicated Pearson Custom editor to create your ideal text—publishing your own original content or mixing and matching Pearson content. Contact your local Pearson Representative to get started.

peerScholar. Firmly grounded in published research, peerScholar is a powerful online pedagogical tool that helps develop your students' critical and creative thinking skills. peerScholar facilitates this through the process of creation, evaluation, and reflection. Working in stages, students begin by submitting a written assignment. peerScholar then circulates their work for others to review, a process that can be anonymous or not, depending on your preference. Students receive peer feedback and evaluations immediately, reinforcing their learning and driving the development of higher-order thinking skills. Students can then re-submit revised work, again depending on your preference. Contact your Pearson Representative to learn more about peerScholar and the research behind it.

ACKNOWLEDGMENTS

The decision to prepare a new edition of this text, though welcome, came when both authors were deeply involved in other projects. So, 2012 and 2013 were not the relaxed years we might have imagined or planned for. Instead, they demanded intense work, for we resolved to continue improving the text even though our time was limited.

In this edition, we wanted to improve the text in ways both small and not so small, and we think you will enjoy the improvements (though, if we have done our job properly, they will be stitched seamlessly into earlier text). To achieve this goal we relied on a team of research assistants to help, and we were lucky to get excellent support from them. So, our first thanks go to two outstanding undergraduate assistants at the University of Toronto—Anita Feher and Nina Gheihman—who helped us update and upgrade the fifth edition by collecting and drafting new materials for inclusion. These fine assistants gave us a huge leg-up in the revision, and we thank them for helping so enthusiastically. We thank Leanne Little at the Prentice Institute for Global Population and Economy, University of Lethbridge, who fought through illness to tenaciously help with this edition. We thank her greatly and with enthusiasm.

Second, we want to thank the people at Pearson for their wonderful support from beginning to end—starting first with Cheryl Finch, who oversaw the revision and repeatedly shepherded us back towards efficient completion. Thank you, Cheryl, for your help and patience. We want to thank Sally Glover, who expertly edited this book into its current form and Sapna Rastogi, who ably oversaw the formatting of this manuscript and its translation into an actual book. Your help is much appreciated. Finally, we are grateful to those colleagues who acted as reviewers for this edition, including Barbara Baker (Georgian College), René R. Gadacz (Grande Prairie Regional College), and Duane Seibel (Thompson Rivers University).

We hope our readers, new and old, will enjoy this version of the text. Please let us know what you think about it.

Susan McDaniel, University of Lethbridge
Lorne Tepperman, University of Toronto

Chapter 1
Families and Family-Like Relationships
Definitions, Theories, and Research

Monkey Business/Fotolia

Chapter Outline

Learning Objectives

1 Learn different ways to define family.

2 Identify the three key relationships in a nuclear family.

3 Understand the connection between household and census family.

4 Learn the advantages of a process-based definition of family.

5 Define the common processes-based elements of family life.

6 Recognize the importance of intimacy and dependency.

7 Recognize how sexuality is regulated and protected in families.

8 Compare different theoretical approaches to family life.

9 Examine the contributions to theory after functionalism.

10 Consider the life course approach to family life.

INTRODUCTION

Among our deepest and most enduring human needs is to have someone close who understands and loves us and in whom we can confide and trust. In an uncertain and insecure world, we seek solace and hope in close relations, whatever form they might take.

Families belong to a group of relationships we characterize as "close," including intense friendships, love affairs, and long-term social or work relationships. These relationships are characterized by a strong attachment or bonding between the individuals. Not all family members feel strongly attached or bonded to each other. However, what people commonly imagine when they think of the word *family*—what the word *family* evokes in our culture—is attachment, sentiment, and emotional intensity. For most of us, families provide our most important relationships, our first connection to the social world, and one that remains important throughout our lives.

This text explores the changing dimensions of family relations and the ways in which they affect and are affected by school, work, society, and, perhaps most importantly, social changes. We examine the diversity of close relations and consider how families may be becoming more rather than less important in our lives.

THE IMPORTANCE OF FAMILY

Some people point to the upsurge in lone-parent households, increases in the number of children born outside legal marriage (Statistics Canada, 2012), and high but declining divorce rates (Kelly, 2010) as evidence the family is in trouble. At the same time, public opinion polls consistently find that family life is important to Canadians (Angus Reid, 1999; Vanier Institute of the Family, 2004)—perhaps increasingly important. Since the legalization of same-sex marriages in Canada in 2005, there have not been many polls asking Canadians about their views of families. Nonetheless, it is clear that despite negative trends in marriages, the majority of young Canadians still consider having a spouse and children an important aspect of their lives (Bibby, 2009).

People continue to value families because they provide emotional support and economic security in sharing resources. Perhaps most importantly, families give us grounding in an increasingly uncertain and chaotic world. The familiarity of family can be reassuring and, throughout our lives, gives us the confidence to explore new things.

WHAT IS FAMILY?

Many people think of families as groups of people related through marriage, blood, or adoption. Yet is that description contemporary enough? Is it inclusive enough?

To some people, the answer seems obvious. They propose the word "families" should be used only to describe "traditional families." Fifty-eight percent of Canadians feel that a traditional family—with one husband, one wife, and children—is the ideal (Bibby, 2004c). Yet families have varied in form throughout history, still vary from one society to another, and are different in societies like Canada and the United States. There is, in this sense, no traditional family.

In this text we shall examine the ways in which families are now viewed and lived. We will see that family changes are closely tied to events in society and to what is seen as a social problem or concern.

DEFINING THE FAMILY

People tend to think when they talk about family that everyone is talking about the same thing. "How's the family?" someone might ask, referring perhaps to one's spouse and possibly children. "I'm taking time now to have a family," says a woman to her co-worker. "My family came from the Ukraine," says another. An HIV/AIDs survivor says, "My family are those around me now who support me." Immigration policy refers to "family reunification," where the concept of family has shrunk to include only close blood relatives and spouses, and now includes fewer relatives. What do these images of family have in common? How differently do we see family?

What Is Family?

Other things may change us, but we start and end with family.

—Anthony Brandt

Families are like fudge—mostly sweet with a few nuts.

—Author Unknown

To us, family means putting your arms around each other and being there.

—Barbara Bush

We cannot destroy kindred: our chains stretch a little occasionally, but they never break.

—Marquise de Sévigné

The family. We were a strange little band of characters trudging through life sharing diseases and toothpaste, coveting one another's desserts, hiding shampoo, borrowing money, locking each other out of our rooms, inflicting pain and kissing to heal it in the same instant, loving, laughing, defending, and trying to figure out the common thread that bound us all together.

—Erma Bombeck

Family life is a bit like a runny peach pie—not perfect but who's complaining?

—Robert Brault

What greater thing is there for two human souls than to feel that they are joined—to strengthen each other—to be at one with each other in silent unspeakable memories?

—George Eliot

A family is a unit composed not only of children but of men, women, an occasional animal, and the common cold.

—Ogden Nash

Source: www.quotegarden.com/family.html.

Answers to questions about family are far from only academic. How family and other close relations are defined matters to us personally—to our values, our dreams, our hopes as individuals, and our identities.

Definitions are important also for our rights under the law and to our claims to pensions, schools, child support, and many other social resources.

Debates rage about whether cohabiting spouses should have the same rights as married spouses, about parental rights for gays and lesbians, and about the financial responsibilities and the rights (to custody, access, and so on) of divorced people. Let's look now at some definitions of family.

MURDOCK: THREE RELATIONSHIPS

For many years, sociologists used as a benchmark George Murdock's (1949: 1) definition of family as

> a social group characterized by a common residence, economic cooperation and reproduction [including] adults of both sexes, at least two of whom maintain a socially approved sexual relationship, and one or more children, own or adopted, of the sexually cohabiting adults.

By this definition, three basic relationships—co-residence, economic co-operation, and reproduction—must all be present to qualify a social group as a family. Murdock's definition excludes many groups that most of us consider families: childless married couples, for example, and single parents and their children. Same-sex unions are excluded, as are married couples that are separated. Celibate couples, according to Murdock, cannot be a family even if they have children, live together, and share other kinds of intimacy. (This means questioning a couple about their sex life to find out whether they and their children make up a family.) Two sisters who live together cannot be a family, according to Murdock. Thus, Murdock's definition does not seem to allow for the variability that exists among families living in Canada today.

Census Family

Because the approach to defining family discussed previously is so limiting, Statistics Canada (2011), the official census and survey agency for Canada, takes a much more inclusive approach. Statistics Canada defines family, for the Census, as comprising a married or a common-law couple (a couple can be opposite sex or same sex) with or without children, or a lone parent living with at least one child in the same dwelling. Married or common-law couple families with children refer to a family with at least one child aged 24 and younger who is present in the home. This definition also includes children from either a current or previous union, but excludes children who might have a permanent residence other than that of their parents at the time of the Census.

This definition is better, since it includes a wider variety of people. However, it still misses many groups that consider themselves families and are considered families by others outside of their household. This being so, many researchers have changed their focus to households for practical purposes.

Household versus Family

Market researchers and census-takers often try to sidestep difficulties of definition by focusing on "households" as though they were "families." Doing so allows us to talk about changes in households and imply changes in close relations without necessarily addressing changes in families or family life. Yet this approach also presents problems. As pointed out by Eichler (1997), many families live in separate households but maintain ongoing family relationships. The prime example is divorced families in which custody is joint or shared (Smart and Neale, 1999); the divorced parents and their child(ren) form at least one family and maybe more. For other trends in Canadian families, see "Six Trends for Canadian Families" on page 7.

A "household" may contain only one person or many unrelated members—roommates, boarders, or residents in a group home. Or it may contain a **nuclear family**, an **extended family**, or multiple families (for example, co-ops, group homes, or families sharing living space to save money). Sharing living accommodations among generations is, as we shall see, a growing trend in Canada. Occasionally, these arrangements involve multiple families—parents, for example, with their parents or with their adult children's families. Conversely, a family may spread across many households, even households located in different countries. However, usually it is thought, whether true or not, that families and households coincide, resulting in "family households."

In the United States, family households are officially defined by the Bureau of the Census as married couples with or without children younger than 18 years or one-parent families with children younger than 18. As we shall discover, this definition may be problematic in that it excludes growing numbers of cohabiting couples. Family households also comprise other households of related individuals (for example, two sisters sharing a household or a parent living with a child older than 17). Non-family households contain unrelated individuals or people who live alone. Canadian definitions from Statistics Canada and other official data-gathering organizations are similar but tend to be broader and more inclusive.

Process-Based Definitions

The United Nations (1991) prefers to define family by the important **socio-economic functions** it performs, such as emotional, financial, and material support to its members; care of each other; transmission of cultural values; and personal development. In doing so, the UN is defining families in terms of their main shared processes, rather than in terms of structural features that they may not—and increasingly do not—share. The Vanier Institute of the Family (2013) uses this function- or process-based definition of family in Canada.

In Canada, serious consideration has been given to the question of what family is and what families are. The question has been taken up by family researchers, the Vanier Institute of the Family, and the Canada Committee for the International Year of the Family, on which one of the authors of this book (McDaniel) served. The conclusion is that ultimately families are defined not by the shape they take but by what they do (Vanier Institute of the Family, 2013). As Moore Lappé (1985: 8) puts it:

> Families are not marriages or homes or rules. Families are people who develop intimacy because they ... share experiences that come ... to make up their uniqueness—the mundane, even silly, traditions that emerge in a group of people who know each other ... It is this intimacy that provides the ground for our lives.

Over the past few decades, a broad process-based definition of family has become accepted by most Canadians (see Angus Reid, 1999; Vanier Institute of the Family, 2000; 2004; 2013). Much of current Canadian family law and policy reflects the move toward inclusion of families that are diverse but similar in their processes, if not their structures (Kronby, 2010).

For example, in 2003, Alberta passed the Adult Interdependent Relationships Act. The law redefines relationship as "a range of personal relationships that fall outside of the traditional institution of marriage" (Alberta Justice, 2002). By doing so, it amends several statutes as they relate to people in non-conjugal relationships and recognizes financial and property benefits and responsibilities attached to these relationships.

Governments as well as various other organizations are trying to keep up with societal changes in the family. However, some groups continue to actively oppose inclusive definitions. The diversity of families is controversial and has become a highly political issue, with some "family values" groups pushing to have these issues placed at the forefront of the national agenda or some provincial agendas (see Baker, 2005a; Stacey, 1996, for examples). The family values proponents have been visible in recent U.S. election campaigns. Gay and lesbian families, for example, have become a touchstone in the United States in many contemporary debates about what is and is not a family and what rights and entitlements those who are deemed family ought to have. Remember that Statistics Canada, in its recently modified definition of Census family mentioned earlier, includes same-sex families. Same-sex couples have had the option of legal marriage across Canada since 2005 and in several provinces prior to that. Similarly, immigration and growing ethnic diversity have challenged the ways we define family forms and maintain and connect in close relations. Definitions of "the family" matter greatly when policies and legislation are being planned, and these definitions may differ by cultural group.

How family is defined and thought about is a weathervane for social ideas and ideologies. The kind of research done in the study of families reflects the concerns of the day. We shall explore this idea in more detail later in this chapter.

Six Trends for Canadian Families

- The number of common-law couple families increased 18.9 percent between 2001 and 2006, more than five times the increase for married-couple families. And from 2006 to 2011, the number of common-law couples rose again by 13.9 percent, more than four times the 3.1 percent increase for married couples (Statistics Canada, 2012a).

- In 2011, there were more census families that consisted of couples without children (44.5 percent) than with children (39.2 percent; Statistics Canada, 2012a).

- Lone-parent families headed by men increased by 16.6 percent since 2001.

- In 2011, young children aged four and younger were more likely to have a mother in her forties than in 2001.

- The proportion of children aged 14 and under who lived with common-law parents increased from 12.8 percent in 2001 to 16.3 percent in 2011.

- More young adults aged 20 to 29 in 2011 were living in the parental home compared to 2001.

Source: Statistics Canada. 2012. *Family Portrait: Continuity and Change in Canadian Families and Households in 2006*. Ottawa: Statistics Canada. Catalogue Number 97-553-XIE.

COMMON ELEMENTS OF FAMILY LIFE

The social groups we think of as families typically share many features, and that commonality can help us begin to understand the nature of families. Because families are extraordinarily diverse in the twenty-first century, it is difficult to generalize about them. However, it is possible to focus our attention on some common processes.

Dependency and Intimacy

All close relations have in common attachment and some dependency or interdependency. This is not unique to families; most close friendships and social or work relationships also include a degree of emotional dependency, based on familiarity and expectations of reciprocity. However, family relations are special in that they tend to include long-term commitments, both to each other and to the shared family.

Sexuality

Adult partners within families typically have, or are expected to have, a long-term, exclusive sexual relationship, whereas among circles of friends or co-workers, sexual relations are expected to be either absent or of short duration. In families, sexual relations are allowed and expected between spouses but banned between other family members (for example, parents, children, and extended family members). Norms of sexual propriety are much stronger in families than they are in friendship or work circles. Taboos against sexual exploitation of children exist to prevent sexual relations with a family member other than a spouse. Nevertheless, sexual abuse of children and elders does occur within families, as we know.

Protection

Effective families keep their members under guard against all kinds of internal and external dangers. There is a clear cultural expectation that families will try to protect their members. Parents and relatives are supposed to keep children safe from accidents and household dangers, and away from drugs, alcohol, predators, and other forms of harm. As well, spouses are supposed to protect one another, and adult children are supposed to protect and help their parents. All this is an ideal. In reality, family members often fail to protect each other enough, and worse, some people neglect, exploit, or abuse family members. Others overprotect, hovering over children so the child has little independence. However, those who break the cultural rules face criticism and disapproval.

Power

Households and families are small social groups whose members spend time together and depend on each other to fill both economic and social needs. There are large differences in power, strength, age, and social resources among members. Ideally, the more powerful family members protect the less powerful ones. However, it is this imbalance in power that makes **patriarchy**—control of the family by a dominant male (typically, the father)—a central fact in the history of family life in most known societies. Simply put, men have dominated because they possessed and controlled more of the resources. And, in much of family law and policy, this domination over family by men was seen as a right, occasionally even a duty.

Families have been seen historically in practice and occasionally in law as men's places of domination and control. The often heard phrase, "A man's home is his castle," reflects this. As we will see in this text, feminist scholarship and theory have taken us a long way in understanding the multiple ways patriarchy has shaped, and continues to shape, families.

Violence

Likewise, families—though idealized as peaceful and loving—are also marked by violence, perhaps to a higher degree than any other groups based on close relations. Violence has always existed in families, but in the past few decades there have been growing reports of violence within families. The increase is likely the result of more reporting rather than an increase in violent acts. In fact, domestic violence against women has decreased since 1999 (Statistics Canada, 2013). Usually the assailant is a spouse or boyfriend. As well, researchers estimate that one girl in four and one boy in ten is sexually abused before the age of 16, often by friends or relatives. Perhaps violence is more common in families than in other close relations precisely because, for many, the family is a place of intense emotions. Its patriarchal structure also is a contributing factor. Also, proximity makes it easy to inflict behind closed doors, and some family members are young or otherwise vulnerable and cannot easily escape.

KINSHIP, CLAN, AND COMMUNITY

So far we have focused on families as they exist normatively in our own dominant culture. However, families vary from one society to another, just as they vary within our own society. In many societies, families exist within larger social networks—in kinship groups and clans—and we cannot understand how nuclear families function unless we also understand their place in these larger networks and in the community at large. The members of the household—the husband and wife, parent and child, brother and sister—are thoroughly integrated into a larger web of kin—uncles, aunts, cousins, grandparents, grandchildren—and their lives cannot be understood without reference to this larger web.

A **kinship group** is a group of people who share a relationship through blood or marriage and have positions in a hierarchy of rights over the property. The definition of a kin relationship varies between societies; kin relationships may also influence where the members must live, whom they can marry, and even their life opportunities.

Some societies count relationships through the male line, so that any individual's relationships are determined by his or her father's relationships; we call such kinship systems **patrilineal**. Others count relationships through the female line; these are **matrilineal** systems. Still others count relationships through both lines; they are **bilateral kinship systems**.

The Canadian system is mildly patrilineal. For example, a woman has historically taken her husband's family name, not the reverse, and this name is the one that passes to the children. However, this is not the case everywhere in the West. In Quebec, for example, the law prevents women from taking their husband's name on marriage. And some couples invent new names by hyphenating their names or choosing a new last name that everyone takes. There are also examples of men taking their wives' last name on marriage.

Our family system follows the Western pattern, in which property is also typically inherited along the male line. Where families settle down is traditionally determined by the husband's job, not the wife's, although this is changing as more women in families become the main earner. However, our society also has certain matrifocal characteristics. Because women have been defined as the primary **kin-keepers**—the people who maintain family contacts—children tend to have stronger ties with their mother's kin than with their father's kin (Rosenthal, 1985; Thomson and Li, 1992: 15). Children also tend to preserve closer contacts with their mothers when the parents grow old (Connidis, 2001). When parents of grown children live separately, fathers are less often visited, called, and relied on than are mothers.

NEW WAYS TO UNDERSTAND FAMILY DIVERSITY

In this text, we will propose repeatedly that some of the older ways of understanding family life do not serve us well in a diverse, fluid, and increasingly global society. As a result, we have adopted some new approaches to studying family life. We did not invent these new approaches, however; they enjoy wide currency among many sociologists.

The life course approach is one way of studying family change. The pioneering study by Elder of children in the Depression (Elder, 1992) opened the door to this approach to studying families. This life course perspective follows families and individuals over time, studying a variety of social and interpersonal dynamics of close relations (linked lives) and how these change throughout lifetimes (Bengston, Biblarz, and Roberts, 2002; Thomson, Winkler-Dworak, and Kennedy, 2013). Over time, families change—change is the nature of families—to meet new needs, such as the arrival, care, or departure of children; aging; and other life course changes. These changes have effects on the entire family system: on relations between spouses, parents and children, and siblings; and on the family's relations with the "outside world," such as parents' changing relations with their employers and their careers (Kruger and Levy, 2001; Martinengo, Jacob, and Hill, 2010; McDaniel and Bernard, 2011; McDaniel et al., 2013). More on this later in the chapter.

Another "new" approach is to look at family relations from the perspectives of different family members. This approach recognizes that, within any given family, different members have different interests and experiences. Smart and Neale (1999) use this approach, for example, to study post-divorce families. Because different family members often have different interests, it is often inappropriate to speak of "the family" as though it has a single interest and acts in a unified way. Gazso and McDaniel (2010; 2014) have used a similar approach by interviewing multiple members of families living in low income by choice.

Much family research in the past was done from a male perspective (Eichler, 2001; Giddens, 1992; Luxton, 1997). A popular phrase of the time that has stuck is "bedroom communities," which describes suburban communities in which families lived and women often worked at home. These were living communities and could be seen as bedrooms only from the point of view of men who worked elsewhere. Many other examples exist. What do family life and changes in close relations among adults look like from the viewpoint of children, for example? Markedly different, as we are now discovering (Marcil-Gratton, 1993; Mason, Skolnick, and Sugarman, 2003). Children live in many and varied kinds of families while still dependent, and changes in family are happening earlier in their lives than those of children in times past. Looking at the changes in close relations among adults from the viewpoint of children gives us a new and important vantage point on families. For example, adults tend to worry that divorce is negative for children, and it can be, but some children see advantages of having more than two parents.

Another way to study family diversity is by exploring different groups in society in order to better understand how they function as families. This text, for instance, examines the way immigrant, rural, Aboriginal, and gay and lesbian families work and the way historical and societal changes have shaped and influenced their family life. Consider Aboriginal families. Because of changes imposed on them by the Canadian government though the Indian Act, many Aboriginal children were separated from their families involuntarily and shipped off to residential schools or to live with other Canadian families in an effort to integrate them into what was then seen as mainstream society. It was a long-standing policy of forced assimilation (see King, 2012). In doing so, generations were disrupted, and many parents were unable to pass on important Aboriginal traditions to their children or be the loving and caring parents they would have liked to be. This, as it will be seen in the following chapters, has had lasting negative effects for Aboriginal families.

By studying differences in families, we learn that families may look different today, but it is essentially the process of family life that is important to the health of the family and its members. For one, gay and lesbian families may not be structured like the "typical" heterosexual family, but more and more research shows that they provide security, love, and other fundamental family supports to their children and partners (Sullivan, 2012).

Another approach is to collect data in new ways so family diversity can be studied over time. This is consistent with the life course perspective on families. Instead of studying families at one point in time, the interest with longitudinal data is to follow families over a longer span of time. Example are Statistics Canada's National Longitudinal Survey of Children and Youth (NLSCY; Willms, 2002) and the Survey of Labour and Income Dynamics (SLID; Statistics Canada, 1996a), which build a picture of the changes in people's work and family lives over time. Many important discoveries about families and children have been found with analyses of these data. Cheal (1997), as one example, relies on SLID to examine the longer-term effects of being in a financially dependent family while young or at various life course stages. He finds the effects of both dependence and poverty of youth increase intergenerational inequities over time. Thus, families have different "life histories," and as these histories develop and change, they shape the prospects of their members, especially the youngest members. The NLSCY follows individual children as they grow, interviewing them and their families every two years. Data were collected[1] on family changes, schooling, health, and a whole range of variables that affect children's lives. A wealth of new insights is emerging about children's lives and how families and society can best benefit in the long run. Findings from this survey have already taught us that the effect on children of living with a lone parent is more than the result of the low incomes often faced by these families. The good news for both lone parents and for society from this longitudinal research is that good parenting can, largely, overcome these harmful effects. Much more is learned by following the same people (children or adults) over time and seeing whether they can, eventually, escape the disadvantages of a low-income childhood, and if so, how.

All families change, and the times change families. For example, Whitehead (1990: 1) reminds us that "Today's stay-at-home mother is tomorrow's working mother." Or, as Swedish social policy sees it, every married woman with children today is potentially a divorced or separated lone mother tomorrow. Whitehead (1990: 1) points out that families change with the times: "One day, the Ozzie and Harriet couple is eating a family meal at the dining room table; the next day, they are working out a joint custody agreement in a law office." Studying families in a context of change reminds us to stay away from simple definitions of family, or theories about family life and change that assume that all families are the same and stay the same, regardless of their socio-historical context.

THEORETICAL APPROACHES TO UNDERSTANDING FAMILIES

A theory puts things together in a way that helps us understand the social world. Theories may be only speculation about how things might work, although some are based more on evidence than others. Each theoretical approach is different, and each one may have a different insight to contribute to our understanding. In the following section, we discuss how the thinking about families and research on families has changed over time. These changes in thinking are closely tied to the events and climate in a society. Second, we highlight some basic theoretical approaches to understanding families. However, these are not all the theoretical approaches. Each one of the approaches presented will allow you to begin to see aspects of families that you might not have seen without the use of the theoretical lens. Theories offer a kaleidoscope of possibilities.

Theories of Family over Time

Thinking about families over time is challenging for sociologists for three linked reasons. First, there is new information, not only about families now but also about families in the

---

[1] The NLSCY has now been discontinued.

past and how they lived. This new information challenges our understandings and shakes our beliefs about families and family change. Second, new ways to view families, socially and politically, are connected to new theories about families. If you think theories are only academic, think again! Feminist and gay and lesbian theories of family (often called "queer theories" in the literature) have been hotly contested by some interest groups and politicians. And the debate goes beyond family theory. New sociological and cultural studies theories and their proponents were blamed in part for the lack of simple political agreement on the causes of the terrorist attacks of September 11, 2001. Americans, and at times Canadians, too, were asked not only to denounce terrorists and terrorism but also to avoid postmodern social theorizing—theorizing that implied that societies are complex, with many factors leading to the taking up of terrorism. More recently, Prime Minister Stephen Harper said publicly that discussing the "root causes" of terrorism was inappropriate, that we should simply condemn terrorism. He then added that we should not "commit sociology." Theories are much alive and part of public debate. Third, changing family lives and changing ways to see families have risks and concerns that make us constantly question and revise our theories. Keep these challenges in mind as we outline how families have been viewed over time.

"The family" as we currently imagine it is a surprisingly recent social idea. Before the eighteenth century in Europe, for example, the term *family* was not used at all (Flandrin, 1979), even when people lived in groups that today we see as nuclear families—parents with their children. More important then was the larger social grouping or the community. The focus was on how people lived, how they produced food and other necessities, and how they shared them. Therefore much of the study of communities, and indirectly of families, has focused on sustaining life.

Anthropological, intensive studies of small, simply organized communities have found that in foraging societies—which gathered food such as roots and berries—child-bearing was more often postponed to later in life than in early agricultural societies (Fox and Luxton, 2001). There were few assets to inherit in societies that foraged, so it was proposed that, in theory, there were fewer restrictions on how children were viewed in relation to their parents. Families *per se* may not have been seen to "own children." Rather, children may have been seen as belonging to the community.

A well-known theory developed by Friedrich Engels ([1884] 1972), the theoretical collaborator of Karl Marx, in the late nineteenth century paints a picture of people living in a group without giving much importance to whose spouse was whose or which children belonged to which parents. The children were "parented" by the entire community, Engels asserts. All children were welcomed, and even though their biological parents may have been known, it didn't change how people lived. There was some evidence that communities like this did, in fact, exist. Some still live much like this, especially in poor urban neighbourhoods (see Edin and Kissane, 2010; Stacey, 1990), with entire communities raising children and little focus on nuclear family structures.

Once agricultural development began to yield a food surplus, people no longer consumed their food immediately but could save and store it. This led to the idea, according to Engels, of private property and new ideas about the organization of family life. Then, Engels says, it mattered much more who a child's parents were, as inheritance was to follow bloodlines. How these bloodlines were decided is unclear, according to Engels's theory. Men began to control the food surplus, it was theorized. Women were expected to be sexually faithful to their husbands, to ensure the children they had were their husband's. Monogamy was born, this theory proposes, not because it was more moral than any other system of family or because living in families was a natural way to live. Monogamy was related to the economics of life at the time.

In part, many contemporary controversies about family life are efforts to wrest the family away from the effects of economic factors and forces. For example, some conservative groups propose the family is more natural and fundamental than any economic change. Families, they propose, should respond to economic pressures and shifts by *not* changing. In fact, it is proposed that it is family change that is the problem (see Popenoe, 1988). In this way, we are still engaging theories about family from the late nineteenth century.

Another theory of family and family change parallels Engels's theory but follows a different thread at a different historical moment. The theory of Le Play proposes that families in feudal times were large and extended, with blood relatives and members of the community of the castle largely undifferentiated from each other. Large, extended families were not always happy. Some, for example, had many children not because they wanted them or could afford them. As a result, some large families lived in poverty with a mother worn down by childbearing. However, with the development of towns and trades and markets, this kind of community "family" became awkward. It was not easily mobile. So, the smaller "stem family" emerged, a family that ran the farm or small shop while the rest moved on. It was this development that led, in large part, to a massive out-migration from Europe to North America in the 19th and the early 20th centuries, as more people without access to family enterprises sought opportunities in the "new world" of North America.

Prior to the 1850s, sociology was only in its infancy, as was thinking about family. Family theory consisted largely of Judeo-Christian religious belief. The Biblical "begats" of the Old Testament characterized a patriarchal theory that saw an elder male as head of a community, clan, extended family, or even realm. In many ways, monarchies are remnants of this system. It is only rarely, in the absence of a male heir, that women become the heads of state and spiritual leaders of the realm. It was as recently as 2013 that the law was changed in the United Kingdom to eliminate male preference in the line of succession, a custom already in place in most other European monarchies. The system of male headship was more than familial and private; it was a system of governing before public systems of law and democracy were invented. In fact, the parliamentary system of government in Canada still parallels democracy with a ruling monarch who is Head of State. The extended-kin headship system was presumed to be natural and unchanging in both theory and practice. It was also, theoretically at least, presumed as a model for the emerging urban working class to follow.

In the middle of the nineteenth century, debates in society started to challenge old religion-based theories about family. This does not mean that religious beliefs or theories about family disappeared. In fact, they have continued to this day, some say even more actively as the twenty-first century began (Bibby, 2011).

The emerging debate in the 1850s occurred as societies were changing rapidly with industrialization and the beginning of capitalism. Social unrest was apparent, as were social movements that challenged prevailing beliefs. One belief actively challenged at that time was the role of women in family and society. New kinds of societies were springing up, based not on patriarchal authority, but on communal living arrangements where women and men were more equal and children could be raised collectively (Luxton, 2001: 34). This experimental approach continued with the kibbutz or collective farming settlement in Israel; many there are still communal. Elsewhere, people lobbied for women's rights in both marriage and society. Married women at that time were not entitled to own property or to vote, or to have many other citizenship rights that women today take for granted.

Paralleling these changing social attitudes were changing sociological theories. Émile Durkheim, known as one of the founders of sociology, saw family as a social creation, not as something given by nature or religion. His theories about family had two aspects, and the two did not fit together well. First, he argued in favour of "the law of contraction," or that families were, in the middle of the nineteenth century, being reduced in size at the same time as family ties were being intensified. Second, he then theorized that relations between husbands and wives were organized by society as monogamous and "near perfect" (Sydie, 1987: 19–20). Durkheim saw the marriage relationship as permanent, unequal, highly regulated by society, and, crucially, the means of moral organization of all of society. Family was theorized as both less and more important than in earlier times. It was less important in that family sizes were reduced, but more important in that families' ties were strengthened. Key to Durkheim's contribution was his understanding of family as a social creation, not as something given by nature or religion.

As industrialization continued in the nineteenth century, family and work became more separate. Work, which had been an integral part of family life, was moved out of the family and into the marketplace. As work became separated from family, specialization of men in work and women in family began to emerge, creating the notion of separate spheres in which women were seen as being naturally suited to home life and raising children (private sphere) and men to the outside world (public sphere). Social theorists like Durkheim saw the bond between husband and wife as strengthened by this increasing specialization (Sydie, 1987: 22). The search began for biological differences between men and women to parallel the growing social differences in family and society. In hindsight, some of these searches were amusing. A Dr. Lebon is quoted by Durkheim as reporting, "The volume of the crania of men and women, even when we compare subjects of equal age, of equal height and equal weight, show differences in favour of man . . ." (quoted in Sydie, 1987: 22). We now know that this difference does not exist (McGlone, 1980), and many historians and sociologists are now recognizing that even during this period of separate spheres and biological determinism, women still held a great amount of independence and autonomy in running their own households, employing and managing servants, and being involved in charity work. Regardless, that social theories about family were linked to presumed biological differences between men and women was significant to later theories. It is also important to observe that sociological theories of the day were in response to the push in society for social change.

Most of the sociological theorists of the nineteenth century were white, middle-class men. Many, it has been proposed since, were keen to defend or promote the new capitalism and the new way to view marriage and family (Mandell, 2011). Some insisted the birth rate would fall if marriage were changed and if women were more equal to men. This way of thinking persists into the twenty-first century in some conservative circles, evidenced most clearly in U.S. election campaigns. The argument is further made that the gender-unequal marriage is natural and based on both biology and God's will. Other theorists—for example, Herbert Spencer—see this kind of family as a social construction that supports (and should support) capitalism. The patriarchal family was seen as the peak of social evolution (Luxton, 2001; Sydie, 1987). Had these social theorists been women, or working-class or Aboriginal or ethnic minorities, they might have viewed family differently. Writings from some social movements of that time seem less content with the patriarchal family (Dua, 1999; Eichler, 2001; Luxton, 2001; Sydie, 1987).

The 1950s are occasionally seen as the "golden age" of the nuclear family, when suburbs were settled and the standard North American family (SNAF) was born.

Black And White Retro Snd Nostalgia/Mark Skyes/Alamy

As society changed, so did the preoccupations of family researchers. For instance, in the 1920s when the Roaring Twenties overtook the Victorian era, sociologists turned their attention to dating and courtship. Women, previously so guarded in their appearance, dress, and behaviour, were dancing the Charleston in public, no longer wearing corsets, and showing not only ankles but also knees as they kicked up their heels! Speakeasy clubs became popular, where men and women could drink, socialize, dance, and listen to music and entertainers. Society worried, caught up as always in concerns about social and family change. So, sociologists studied these changes by looking at relations among young people and changed dating practices.

The 1950s saw what many still consider the "golden age" of the nuclear family. The suburbs were created and nuclear families thrived, or at least seemed to. Moms did the child rearing and Dads commuted to work. Television programs such as *Father Knows Best, Leave It to Beaver*, and *The Adventures of Ozzie and Harriet* reflected the ideal in family life. The standard North American family (SNAF) was born. As in previous eras, this kind of family had the support of family theory. The 1950s can be better seen as a response to a time of political insecurity and uncertainty after World War II that was, in general, an unusual decade in the twentieth century. This will be further discussed in Chapter 2.

In terms of family theory, the basic concept was that the family was an essential social institution, well adapted to fit into society. Further, the nuclear family differentiated by gender was seen as a universal, something good for everyone. Earlier work by Malinowski among the Australian Aborigines lent credibility to the North American nuclear family form (Luxton, 2001). His views and assumptions about biological differences between men and women found their way into later theories of structural functionalists such as Talcott Parsons, a giant of twentieth-century sociology. Key to Malinowski's theory was that the nuclear family specialized by gender was essential for societies to function smoothly.

The advent of the structural functional theory (see page 20) led to research on men as breadwinners and less so on women as housewives. Research viewed families with a resolutely happy face. Until the late 1960s, there was nothing in the sociology of the family on family violence or on women's dissatisfaction with their families or their family roles. This is surprising, given what we know now of the "mad housewife" of the 1950s, the high teen pregnancy rate, and the unhappiness of many men with the breadwinner role of that time. But, so it was.

Structural functional theories of family were not used only to study families; the same theories shaped workplace policies. If women, for example, were theorized to specialize in family and men in work, then women were presumed not to be good workers. Married women were often fired from paid employment upon marriage since it was thought that they were now to be housewives and dependent economically on their husbands. Women, who were, according to family theory at the time, emotional and centred on caring, were not thought to be appropriate candidates for jobs that required judgment or supervision. They were also excluded from jobs that involved risk, such as pilots, miners, soldiers, and much blue-collar work. That women had done a lot of this kind of work during World

War II while the men who usually worked in these jobs were at war didn't seem to matter. Women were viewed as family specialists, unsuited by nature to working for pay, and certainly not suited to working for pay in high-paying jobs! Some of this thinking lingers in the twenty-first century.

Research using this theoretical approach was intensely focused on family dynamics and interactions and on how families around the world were becoming more similar and more like the U.S. ideal. Not surprisingly, other theories developed that let us look at these aspects of family more clearly. One of these was *symbolic interactionism*. While not fully disputing structural-functionalist theory, symbolic interactionists looked at how people interpret social organization and expectations. They focused on how we change our behaviours depending on how others behave and treat us. This is an "in the face" look at family interactions. Mothers' interactions with children was a favourite subject of research.

The concept of "roles" became a central part of the vocabulary of sociology of family. Society assigned the roles, but all the roles were not the same in all aspects of our lives. So, a woman could play the mother role with her kids and then the wife role with her husband. Increasingly, both were "scripted" by self-styled marriage and parenting experts who based the expertise they marketed on social theories of family. The role of the mother, for example, was scripted as caring, selfless, unassertive, always there for the child. It became an ideal, something to be carefully worked toward by women, no matter what their individual inclinations might be. In its demands, the mother role also overshadowed everything else.

Beginning in the 1970s and then in the 1980s, there was what Cheal (1991) and others have called a "big bang" in sociological theories on families. So big was this "bang," proposed Cheal (2002), Giddens (1992), Fox and Luxton (2001), among others, that there was no turning back to previous ways of viewing families. All subsequent theories, states Cheal (2002), can be traced to this "big bang"—the feminist theories of families.

There is no single feminist sociological theory of family or of any other aspect of society: there are many. What is so different about feminist sociological theories of family is the opening of fresh new ways to regard families. Feminist theories, like family theories before them, grew out of the times. After the 1960s, there was increased political unrest in women's lives. The political push for daycare; for reproductive rights; for equal access to jobs, promotions, and benefits; for rights in marriage; for rights *not* to marry; for gays and lesbians; for older women; for the disabled; for children; and for the poor and disenfranchised led to the posing of "why" questions. Why are all of these groups disadvantaged relative to straight, white, middle-class men with jobs? The answers called for new ways to see, new lenses through which to view the social and political landscape.

Feminist theories have several dimensions in common. For example, they all note discrimination and unequal advantage: Even in families, we find gendered social inequalities. They agree that no particular family form is God's will or written into our biology. There is a feeling that things we create, we can uncreate and recreate. Family, proposes much of feminist theory, is an ideology as much as a way to live. We owe concern and respect to the larger community, as well as to the members of our household. So, the nuclear family should not—cannot—be the extent of our social responsibility and affection.

A key insight of feminist theories of family is that the family is not private, but an important public social institution. Feminist theories reveal how families are power-based. There are hierarchies of who has the money, who gets listened to, and who is more likely to be abused. The list is a long one, and we will explore many of these in this text.

Perhaps most fundamentally, feminist sociology opened new ways of thinking about sociological research on families. As a result, researchers now look through the feminist lens at the multiple ways to live in families, for example. Gay and lesbian families were studied for the first time as families, whereas previously they had been studied only by the sociology of deviance. Families were seen not as given but as in constant change. People began to explore the ideology of the nuclear family and the denial of other ways to live. It is easy to see why so many see this theorizing as a "big bang."

For Canadian sociologists especially, immigration theories have become popular and an important part of understanding a large segment of our society. Every year, more than 250 000 immigrants and refugees come to Canada, seeking a new home and a new life (McDonald et al., 2010). Much of the research on the topic of immigrant families is concerned with acculturation—the "process by which ethnic and racial groups learn and begin to participate in the cultural traditions, values, beliefs, assumptions, and practices of the dominant or host culture" (Lee and Edmonston, 2013), or simply the adoption of a foreign culture. Most importantly, acculturation is a gradual process that often occurs more quickly for immigrant children than parents, since immigrant youth must adopt the language and culture of their new country quickly in order to succeed in school and social relations among peers. Also, children have an easier time learning languages and cultural habits than do older people.

Meanwhile, immigrant parents, facing considerable pressure to integrate successfully into the new country, often turn to their own cultural communities in search of knowledge about ways to start life anew and for financial and emotional support. Also, many immigrants live in extended family households and rely on kinship ties to face life challenges (Bastida, 2001).

As a result, over time an **acculturation gap** often emerges within immigrant families, meaning there is distance between immigrant children and their parents in their language ability and cultural values, in which parents tend to rely more heavily on their former cultural views. According to Hwang (2006), this situation increases the risk for family dysfunction and potential health problems (see also Boyce and Fuligni, 2007).

Immigrant families are increasingly becoming part of the Canadian population, so their challenges and experiences are of essential importance to our society. The effects of acculturation and related topics on immigrant families will be further discussed throughout the text.

Lastly, in the latter part of the twentieth century and now in the twenty-first century, *postmodern* and *post-structural* theories of families have emerged (Cheal, 2002; Klein and White, 1996). With globalization, the spread of international capitalism, and the development of new, more controlling technologies, new theories of the family were needed. A central dimension of postmodernism and post-structuralism is the notion of flux or constant change. Families today may live in multiple families and households that change in response to the changing circumstances around them. But we also change our families and households and our ways of being women and men in big ways—for example, globalization, immigration, economic depression, and surges in unemployment. Topics researched from the point of view of these theories include sexuality, body images, cultural images, and representations, including theories and ideologies of families.

BASIC THEORETICAL APPROACHES TO THE FAMILY
Structural Functionalism

As shown in Table 1.1, there are various theoretical approaches to studying family life, and they proceed from somewhat different assumptions about the organization of social life more generally. Structural functionalism proposes that everything in society has a structure and purpose. It is up to us to see and understand those purposes. Structural functionalism is a theoretical approach developed in the first half of the twentieth century and applied to families by a variety of North American sociologists.

This approach directs us to view families in the light of how they benefit society, and how each member of a family fits in with the purposes that families serve. Why have nuclear families? From this standpoint, nuclear families are seen as useful because they are small, versatile, and mobile; when social change occurs, families can change easily. What purpose does a gender division of labour at home serve where women nurture children and men work for pay? Well, again the answer is simple and compelling. Women specialize in family and emotional relationships, while men specialize in work and relationships based on order and merit. Combining the two roles in a family makes the family stronger, structural functionalists propose, since women and men complement each other. Competition between women and men, it is thought by this reasoning, is not beneficial to families or to work.

The theoretical approach of structural functionalism has dominated family research for decades. Although much criticized in recent times, structural functionalism is and has remained the dominant theoretical approach to understanding families in North America. Its semblance of common sense captivates even those who criticize it. Everything about families has a structure and a function. Family relations are orderly and neat. This approach inspires us to find out how and why families act the ways they do.

The trouble with this approach is that it may be too captivating. It doesn't allow for conflict and social change. When women work in the paid labour market like men, what, then, for families? Do they fall apart because there are no longer complementary roles in family and society? Some might respond, "Yes, this could be a problem." Others might

Table 1.1 Sociological Theories on the Family

Structural Functionalism

- Elements in society have a structure and function (or purpose).
- Study of the family examines how family members fit together, given the purpose families have within a society.
- Gender division in the family is universal and probably inevitable.

Symbolic Interactionism

- Society is a product of face-to-face interactions between people.
- Understanding of the family requires studying the symbols and meanings shared among members.
- People depend on the labels of their roles to guide them.

Marxist

- The family exists in relation to economic systems.
- The family is a way to ensure inheritance is passed down to the proper people; namely, rightful children.

Feminist

- Men and women negotiate with the resources and power they have.
- Women suffer more because they have fewer resources when they enter the family.
- Women take responsibility at home because society needs their unpaid labour, while men focus their efforts on paid work.

Postmodern

- Family is a social creation and changes are expected.
- Examination of family requires teasing apart the various components.
- Family members are aware of, and reflect on, family changes.
- Convergence theory (a branch of structural functionalism) presents a rosy picture of family modernization, as though families and individuals are choosing to change and are all changing effectively.
- Changes in society are part of a universal progress that will result in a single world-wide culture of modernity.
- Economic development requires specific kinds of families and family roles.

Life Course

- Human development is lifelong.
- People construct their own life courses.
- History shapes lives.
- Timing of events matters.
- Lives are linked, especially in families.

say, "Wait a minute. Societies change. Women and men change. Where is that change allowed for in structural functionalism?"

This theoretical approach dominated family research through much of the twentieth century and is still important today because it tries to answer one important question: Why is gendering so common throughout the world?

Symbolic Interactionism

Symbolic interactionism depends not on structure or function but on sharing. The key to understanding families, this theory proposes, is that family members share symbols and meanings. So, for example, the word "dad" is not something that you alone understand, but is a symbol shared by others. The shared meaning makes family experience more universal, and more understood by others whose experience may be a little different than yours.

People are not passive recipients of social meanings, but work to make those meanings their own. They then interact with others on the basis of their own meanings. For example, the meaning of "dad" is changing. In this way, meanings become new realities in families.

Marxist Theory of Family

Many readers know Karl Marx as a political theorist or activist. In fact, Marx was a great thinker, a sociological theorist who conceptualized family in relation to economic systems. His thinking led him to see the nuclear family as specialized so that women would have to be faithful to their husbands to benefit economically. Originally, Marx and his collaborator, Friedrich Engels, imagined women and men living together freely in groups. They would have sex and children but not worry much about whose children they were. Then, with agricultural surpluses, the notion of private property developed. Men had to know who their own children were so that only those children could inherit their rightful surplus of food (dried root crops, dried animal meat, and so on). The only way men could know who their own children were was to demand sexual faithfulness from women. Thus, it is theorized, women traded free and open sexual relations for economic benefit for themselves and their children. The notion of women's sexual faithfulness to men in monogamous marriage was born in this way. Notably, it was not individual preference or religion or anything other than economics that created this system.

Feminist Theory

Feminist sociological approaches view family as a place of discussion and negotiation. Men and women come to family with different resources and power. Therefore, they negotiate from different places.

Women, feminist theorists propose, do not enter family with resources comparable to men's. They therefore suffer inequality in close relations and, if the relationship breaks down, are more likely to be in poverty. In fact, lone mothers with children have the highest family poverty rate in Canada, something we discuss in subsequent chapters. The following chapters will describe in more detail the major issues that mothers confront in negotiating the relationships among employment, domestic work, child and elder care, and family life. Important to these discussions will be the idea that women's decision-making processes in each of these domains are not isolated to an individual family but, instead, are embedded in a social context and a political ideology.

Feminist theories propose that women are taught to see family work as based on love and social expectation. It may be based as much or more on the need of society and of men for cheap labour to keep society going. So, women take on the major responsibilities for child and elder care as well as for housework, thus freeing men to focus more fully on paid work. Similarly, women's preoccupation with child rearing and unpaid housework compromises their capacity to work for pay outside the home.

With respect to housework, as an example, feminist theories reveal how women's lower pay at work is linked to the domestic division of labour—why they do more work at home and men do less. Recognition of the unpaid work done largely by women in families has led to inclusion of unpaid work on the Census of Canada and to policies that increasingly recognize the importance of unpaid work.

Postmodern Theory

Postmodernists see that numerous ways of understanding and viewing family coexist. The new social, economic, and political dimensions of a globalized world reveal new identities (active disabled, transgendered, immigrant, and so on) and new ways to live in families. This is not a crisis in any way, but something natural and vital to understanding life and society in the twenty-first century.

Key to the postmodernist theoretical approach to family is that nothing can be taken for granted. Instead, all must be subject to being taken apart, or deconstructed, in order to be explained. Families and men's and women's relations to families are seen as social creations, subject to constant change and re-examination. Family members become part of the process. They re-create themselves and their ways to relate as they examine and re-examine what they are doing and why. Their senses of self form in response to this constant process of reflecting, responding, and re-examining.

When applied to the study of families, postmodern theories look at the meanings of mothering, both individual and social. They look at body images and at sexuality in relation to family. Nothing is taken as given by postmodern theory.

VARIATION DESPITE CONVERGENCE

As we have seen throughout the chapter, changing economies and societies, as well as changing approaches to seeing family, play a major role in changing the form and content of family life, both in countries just becoming industrialized and in the Western world, where economic change continues. Many social scientists see these changes as part of an inevitable and universal progress toward a single worldwide culture of modernity, in which families have a distinct and different form compared to traditional families. This approach has several pitfalls. First, it assumes that all modern families are similar to one another and different from all traditional families. Second, and equally important, it assumes that all modern families "choose" their new forms, and that these forms are necessarily better.

Convergence theory presents a rosy picture of family modernization, as though families and individuals are choosing to change and are all changing effectively. In fact, modernization forces families to change. William Goode (1982: 57–58), a structural functionalist, proposes that families change when societies industrialize precisely because industrialism "fails to give support to the family." He gives several reasons for this conclusion:

1. The industrial system fires, lays off, and demands geographical mobility by reference to the individual, ignoring the family strains these actions may cause.

2. The economy increasingly uses women in the labour force, and thus puts a still larger work burden on them, but few corporations have developed programs for helping women with child care or making it easier for men to share in these tasks.

3. The industrial system has little place for the elderly, and the neolocal, independent household, with its accompanying values in favour of separate lives for each couple, leaves older parents and kin in an ambiguous position.

4. The family is relatively fragile because of separation and divorce, but the larger system offers little help in these crises for adults and their children.

Industrialization produces not only great opportunities but also great perils for families and family life. Some societies, and some families, respond better than others. Some industrial states provide much more support for the family than others. By its laws and policies, a state influences the costs associated with marriage, divorce, child-bearing, child rearing, and elder care. In this way, the state influences the patterns of family life in that society. That is, in part, why industrial societies do not have identical family forms.

Major forces of change like industrialization, urbanization, and education certainly affect family life; yet the relationships are not simple, nor are the outcomes predictable. In two of the most industrialized countries, Japan and Sweden, we find different family forms. In Japan, traditional family and gender norms persist. In Sweden, by contrast, there are high rates of cohabitation and of women working in the paid work force (although mostly in traditional female sectors). Throughout this text we propose that many family forms are not only possible but also desirable and that they work well—in Canada and throughout the world.

No simple conclusions can be drawn about what a family is, what causes families to change, or whether family life is getting better or worse. Those who want simple answers may find this ambiguity disappointing. Those who want to understand the modern family will find that the many open questions make for an exciting and intellectually challenging area of sociology.

LIFE COURSE THEORY

The life course perspective is commonly used to understand families and family change. This was not always the case, however. Life histories and connections between individuals and history used to be neglected in studies of family.

The life course perspective consists of five principles. First, human development is seen as occurring throughout life. In families, this matters because adults as well as children are part of family change. Second, people construct their own lives through choices and actions. In families, choices matter greatly to outcomes and happiness. Third, people's life courses are shaped by the times in which they live. Good economic times shape our families, as do wars, depressions and recessions, and tough times. Fourth, the same events affect individuals and families differently depending on when they occur in the life course. For example, having a baby at age 18 is different in terms of the rest of a woman's life than having a baby at age 28 or 38. Fifth, and importantly for the understanding of family lives, is that lives are linked. Nowhere is this truer than in families. Transitions in one person's life in a family can affect all members of the family, as well as the family itself. These five principles of the life course perspective, taken together, lead to a focus in family studies on social contexts as well as life change and choice (Elder, Johnson, and Crosnoe, 2004; McDaniel and Bernard, 2011). It is a powerful theoretical lens.

CONCLUDING REMARKS

It seems that everywhere, family relationships are in flux. Around the world, industrialization and urbanization are transforming extended kinship networks and drastically changing the nature of family obligations. In North America, people value family life, but they are spending a smaller fraction of their lives in anything resembling whatever might be viewed as a traditional family. North American families today show signs of stress and conflict as well as greater freedom and happiness. How are these observable realities connected to one another?

Current family trends are the result of long-term worldwide changes in social life. New laws and new contraceptive technology have given rise to new sexual permissiveness. Fertility has continued to fall for more than a century. Divorce rates, once at historically high levels, have now stabilized and declined, while legal marriage rates have continued to drop. These long-term trends have been boosted by rapid increases in the labour force participation of mothers of young children. In turn, women's behaviour is the culmination of a struggle for equality with men that began in earnest two centuries ago.

As we will see, the process of industrialization has set in motion irresistible, irreversible social forces that have transformed, and continue to transform, the content of close relations in everyday life. These social forces include the development of a consumer culture, market economy, welfare states, and a mobile, urban, global social structure. As well, new technologies prolong life, prevent unwanted births, and can create life outside the womb. In future, many scientists expect that it will even create new sentient creatures through genetic engineering and artificial intelligence.

CHAPTER SUMMARY

In this chapter, we discussed what families are and how they are viewed. We explored how defining families is a challenge because both families and how they are seen are constantly changing. Families, for most of us, are our most important social relationships, defining who we are and providing emotional attachment.

This chapter examined the complexity of what families are, why they are interesting to study sociologically, and how they have changed and are still changing. Family is as important to people as ever, but it has changed. Even the Census of Canada has broadened its definition of family to include common-law unions, including same-sex unions, and adult children living with parents.

We have seen that sociologists are moving away from defining families by the shape they take. This is a recurring theme throughout the text, as we will see when we explore the ways Aboriginals, gays and lesbians, and immigrant families, to name a few, function and care for their family members. In doing so, it will be clear that families are more often now defined by what they do for us and for society. The common elements of family living—dependency and intimacy, sexuality, protection, and power—are explored.

The key to understanding families is how families are theorized. This chapter followed a brief journey through the major changes in theorizing families from the early days of human living to postmodern media imagery.

We have the stage for an in-depth examination of family change and family diversity in subsequent chapters.

Key Terms

acculturation gap The gap between immigrant children and their parents with regard to language ability and cultural values. Parents tend to rely more heavily on their former cultural views, while immigrant children adapt more easily to the values of the new country.

bilateral kinship system Kinship through both the male and female lines.

extended family A family system in which three or more generations of family members live together and have social rights and obligations.

kin-keeper The family member who maintains and nurtures family contacts.

kinship group A set of people who share a relationship through blood or marriage and have positions in a hierarchy of rights over property.

matrilineal kinship system Kinship through the female line.

nuclear family A family group that consists only of spouses, or spouses and their children.

patriarchy A system in which family decision-making is dominated by males, most typically by fathers.

patrilineal kinship system Kinship through the male line.

socio-economic functions Functions that offer emotional, financial, and material support to members of a group.

Critical Thinking Questions

1. Why is studying the family so complicated in society today?

2. What are the benefits of a function-based definition of the family and a structural-based definition? What are the drawbacks of each?

3. In this chapter we discussed what the Canadian Census defines as a family. What would you add or remove from this definition and why?

4. Why have feminist theories become so prominent in recent decades? Do feminist theories improve our understanding of family life?

5. Predict some future changes that will likely occur for Canadian families in the next five years.

6. We discussed some theoretical approaches to family in this chapter. Which theoretical approach do you think is the most useful for studying the family today? Which do you think is the least useful?

7. Why are gay and lesbian families of particular interest for sociologists studying family?

8. People often refer to the increase in divorce, delaying marriage, and common-law unions as proof the value of family is decreasing in our society. Do you think these trends prove the family is becoming less important, or even unimportant?

Weblinks

The Vanier Institute of the Family
www.vifamily.ca
This Ottawa-based independent organization has a wealth of information, new studies, and data on families in Canada. The site has many links to other sources of information on families.

Institute of Marriage and Family Canada
www.imfcanada.org
This site offers a variety of resources about family life, including some interesting articles and press releases on recent debates such as same-sex marriage, the "value" of marriage today, and issues facing aging families, to name a few.

Childcare Resource and Research Unit
www.childcarecanada.org
This site focuses on providing up-to-date resources that deal specifically with child-care issues and family policy in Canada and internationally.

First Nations Child & Family Caring Society of Canada
www.fncfcs.com
This is an incredible site for academic information regarding the issues facing Aboriginal families today. It provides links to community projects that focus specifically on Aboriginal youth and children's rights, along with numerous volunteer opportunities for anyone interested in getting involved.

Citizenship and Immigration Canada
www.cic.gc.ca
This site provides new Canadian immigrants with a location-specific list of resources to assist in settling into Canada and information such as how to set up a business.

Services for Youth
www.youth.gc.ca
This site focuses on a variety of youth issues facing Canadian teenagers. One of the best features of the site is that it targets unemployed, immigrant, and disabled youth issues and provides easy-to-understand tips on how to find jobs and earn an education.

Chapter 2
Historical Perspectives on Canadian Families
Demographic, Social, and Economic Origins and Trends

Lebrecht Music and Arts Photo Library/Alamy

Chapter Outline

Learning Objectives

1 Identify and discuss key historical factors that influence Aboriginal families in Canada.

2 Understand the impact of the "mechanization" of housework on families.

3 Distinguish the role of immigration in Canada's past, present, and future families.

4 Analyze how past patterns of courtship, marriage, and divorce have affected present family patterns.

5 Identify the key aspects of an aging population and assess how an aging society may change Canadian families.

6 Explain how the definition of family has changed over time.

7 Describe how resources affect individual and family transitions.

8 Define and evaluate the role of social policy for families, both at individual and societal levels.

In this chapter, we look at families through a sociological lens. We emphasize the big changes in society, such as contact and ongoing relations between Aboriginals and settlers, industrialization, large-scale immigration waves, and wars. We consider how families in the past connect to some of today's patterns and how contemporary socio-economic changes have altered families and our views of them. We also focus on the multicultural families that have been part of Canada since its beginnings. Historical dimensions of families are explored more specifically in the chapters that follow.

A HISTORICAL, CROSS-CULTURAL PERSPECTIVE
Aboriginals and Settlers: Contact and Conflict

Aboriginal families in what was to become Canada have always been diverse. First contacts between Aboriginal peoples and foreigners were with male explorers, followed by fur traders and missionaries, and lastly women and families who settled in Canada. Such contacts changed Aboriginal family practices, as they did the family practices of some of the settlers. Early settlers in Canada developed strong relationships of mutual aid with their Aboriginal neighbours. Blood First Nations women helped homesteading women on the prairies with childbirth and with building houses that would help them stay warm and survive the harsh winters. The settlement of New France (now Quebec) and Upper Canada (now Ontario) brought together the families of the Aboriginal groups and the colonists. In the early days, children born to unmarried settler women were often adopted by Aboriginal families.

The relationships in those days between settlers and Aboriginals cannot be characterized as simply good or bad. Some explorers and fur traders married or cohabited with Aboriginal women (Van Kirk, 1980). Some of these relationships were committed and long-lasting, while others were short-term and exploitative, with men from afar taking advantage of differences in culture and status between themselves and the local women (Brown, 1980). This is a common story of colonialism, occurring throughout the world and leaving a legacy of combined racism and sexism toward indigenous women.

Not sanctioned by church or society, the unions were also disapproved of by fur trading companies, notably Hudson's Bay Company, which banned these men from taking their "country wives" and families back home with them upon retirement (Van Kirk, 1980). Some of the men simply abandoned their Canadian families. Others, however, remained in Canada with their families, adapting to Aboriginal societies. One couple, William Hemmings Cook and his wife, Agatha, made a fresh start by marrying after living together according to the "custom of the country" for years (Van Kirk, 1992: 79). Still others provided for their country wives in their wills or organized to find them new husbands to ensure that they would be provided for.

Unlike the Europeans, relatives of the Aboriginal women often did support the relationships. The Huron, for example, saw ties between French men and Huron women as a way to develop kinship alliances. Many thousands of Canadians today can trace their ancestry to the British and French fur traders and Aboriginal women of the seventeenth to nineteenth centuries.

However, the children of unions between European men and Aboriginal women suffered a significant strain. Some, especially boys, left their familiar lives at a young age, sometimes going abroad to their father's relatives to be educated. Daughters more often stayed with their mothers and the mother's culture (Brown, 1992). Efforts were made at various times, notably in the 1820s, to organize and to "civilize" what were seen as mixed-race families and communities. This resulted in officials making new laws and in missionaries working to sanction relationships. One outcome was a sense of *in loco parentis*, whereby family life was controlled by others who regulated and governed the Aboriginals as children who needed discipline and order.

Other family issues that arose with early contact between Aboriginal peoples and Europeans have to do with kinship ties. For hundreds of years, Aboriginal cultural beliefs and practices around family and family issues had been developing and changing, and were widely divergent throughout Canada. Aboriginals viewed kinship, the basis for assigning rights and duties, more flexibly than did European settlers. Kinship regulated relations with others without courts and states per se. Decisions about justice and about compensation were often filtered through kinship rules, with different outcomes than might have resulted from following European rules. Some of the conflicts that resulted are continuing to this day.

Another large difference between the early Europeans and Aboriginals was in gender roles. Though societies always seem to organize rights and responsibilities by gender, they differ significantly in the way gender is employed. Bradbury notes that "[i]n most Aboriginal societies women appear to have been able to exercise greater power than their European counterparts ... " (2001: 72). This system led some European observers to shocked reactions.

Finally, Aboriginal peoples and early Europeans had divergent views on the relationship of family to its community, and of both to property. To the colonial settlers, property, whether it was land, money, or goods, was private and to be traded in a market economy. Assets belonged to individuals and nuclear families. This was not the case with Aboriginal groups, whose extended kinship groups often determined who would be eligible for the benefits of a hunt, for example. These different viewpoints created a clash of values, posing some difficulty in the fur trade. The concept of furs for sale was a new one to many Aboriginal peoples. Ritual exchanges among Aboriginal family groups, such as the potlatches of the peoples of the West coast, were seen as dangerous by the colonials, both to their economic values and to their sense of righteousness. In fact, potlatches were outlawed by authorities, and in some villages all the goods to be exchanged were symbolically burned (Dickason, 2002).

English and French Settlers

Interestingly, the conflicts between colonists and Aboriginal peoples over family and kinship relations parallel the conflicts between British and French settlers. English Common Law, from which many of the modern understandings of marriage, family, inheritance, and property rights came, tended to concentrate power, authority, and property in male heads of households. For women, marriage meant the "suspension of independent existence" (Bradbury, 2001: 74).

For a long time (until the early part of the twentieth century), married women could not own property, sign a contract, or sue. Like children, they had no rights under law. In contrast, in New France, which became Quebec, rules governing marriage and family were guided by the Custom of Paris (Bradbury, 2001: 75). This set of legal codes was much more egalitarian than English Common Law. Property was seen as shared between husbands and wives, even if controlled by husbands. And children, regardless of gender, could share inheritances.

After the Battle of the Plains of Abraham in 1760, known in Quebec as the Conquest, the English tried to impose their version of family law and practice on the French. This attempt failed immediately and has never succeeded for political reasons. As early as 1774, it was agreed that Quebec would have its own legal code regarding family matters, though all criminal law would follow the English practice. Even today in Quebec, we see different approaches to family than in the rest of Canada. One major family difference is that the Québécois/Québécoise (Quebec men and women) are significantly more likely to live in common-law unions than other Canadians. Another difference is that a Québécoise does not take her husband's name on marriage. Both of these points will be discussed in the chapters that follow.

Also after the Conquest, there was a significant gender imbalance in New France, with a much higher proportion of men than women. The low birth rate in the new colony threatened the success of territorial expansion. In response, about 770 young women were imported to New France from the streets of Paris between 1663 and 1673 (Landry, 1992). These women were called *les filles du roi* (daughters of the King). Many were orphans, some were illiterate, all were poor, and, despite their name, none were even remotely related to royalty. The *filles du roi* were expected to find marriage partners quickly, and most did. Out of the whole group, only 15 percent of the marriages were annulled, the equivalent of divorce in Catholic New France at the time (Huck, 2001: 14). Of those, most remarried, and seven even married for a third time. Many Quebeckers today can trace their ancestry to the unions of original French settlers and the *filles du roi*.

The Transition to Industrialism

Before Canada industrialized and urbanized, families were the primary unit of production. Most families were rural, and work and family were found in the same space. Therefore, the two were inseparable. Each person, old or young, had a role to play as defined by society.

In this way, agricultural work depended on the formation of extended families. Farmwork—based on land and animals—could not be moved, so people mostly stayed in one place. Exceptions were non-inheriting children, who often migrated or emigrated in search of their own land. People who stayed formed strong bonds among neighbours and generations. This led to the formation of a **gemeinschaft** type of community typical of pre-industrial rural life: that is, one in which everyone knows everyone else and people share common values. Since limited social safety nets existed, families largely had to create their own. Aging grandparents helped busy parents to care for the many children and often provided housing and money when needed (McDaniel and Lewis, 1998).

When many of the Europeans migrated to Canada and established an agricultural way of life, the conventional division of labour was altered. Even though most early settlers to Canada preferred a strict division of labour at home (as in their native countries), they often could not manage this divide. As a result, land was sometimes owned and worked by unmarried women, for example, a practice unheard of in the "old country." This change was motivated less by an interest in gender equality than by a desire to increase agricultural output. At the same time, men's and women's work was still largely separate in pre-industrial times. The husband was usually responsible for representing the family in public. However, men also had domestic responsibilities such as farmwork, child discipline, and some provisioning. The wife, on the other hand, was mainly responsible for the private domain. Besides doing housework and taking responsibility for child care, women at this time also took care of farm animals, manufactured needed household items, and provided social services to those in their community (Cross and Szostak, 1995). When, often, men had to leave their farms and shops to work at other jobs, women would often supplement household income with home-based businesses.

This provided a small source of income for women that contributed to the family and to their pride. It also gave some women considerable power and autonomy both in their families' enterprises and in the wider society. However, with industrialization many women could not continue such work. For instance, zoning bylaws might prohibit non-family establishments in some neighbourhoods, and in this way they would prevent separated, divorced, and widowed women from taking in boarders to make ends meet (Bradbury, 1984).

With the advent of industrialization, the agricultural family and way of life drastically changed. First, industrialization drove many individuals and families out of the countryside and into the new towns and cities. Some families became migratory, moving where work was available. Since this was almost impossible to do with an extended family, the smaller, compact nuclear family became the more common family form. It was also more specialized. Everyone had a role to fill, although the roles were different from those in an extended family.

A new image of childhood emerged as many nuclear families couldn't survive with only one or two people working for wages. Children worked in factories or on the street selling papers, shining shoes, or looking after younger children so mother could work. Children often sought to keep some or all of their wages, moving out of their home and staying poor to gain their independence. Clearly, children in an industrializing society were more independent. Thus, a significant change occurred in relations between older and younger generations, and a new image of childhood emerged. Increasingly, children became a liability. So, parents started to have fewer children.

As well, the Industrial Revolution, which only began in Canada in the mid-1850s, moved the productive activity of men outside the household. Increasingly, people began to work *with* strangers and *for* strangers. Family life was their own private business, and work life was, if they wished, outside the family's purview. A clear line between work and family life, in the way that we perceive them today, only appeared with the coming of industrialization.

Then, in the beginning of the twentieth century, industrialization of household technology brought new and unexpected dimensions to family life, especially changing what families expected of women. Vacuum cleaners, for example, brought the possibility of cleaning a house more readily than by sweeping or taking heavy area rugs out to the yard to be beaten with brooms or paddles. Yet expectations about cleanliness also rose, so there was no reduction in the housework to be done. Similarly, refrigerators replaced wells, cold storage areas, and iceboxes. Fridges saved the worry and the trouble of food storage in homes but created the necessity to shop longer and with greater care because meals were expected to be more complex and elegant than they had been before.

Thus, the growing availability of new "labour-saving devices" raised standards of living and increased the time women spent shopping. Homes quickly shifted from small-scale production units into showplaces of consumer goods. In the new domestic division of labour, women were no longer producers of goods to sell on the market, but rather specialists in the consumption of goods aimed at making houses "homey." This shift sharpened the domestic division of labour by gender. It was the precursor to the modern "domestic goddess" movement, spearheaded by Martha Stewart.

Campaigns to promote new household technologies stressed the "love" part of housework out of fear that women might abandon their domestic work with the **"mechanization" of housework** (Fox, 1993: 151). Home economists worked to raise the esteem of homemakers by promoting the idea that the new home technologies required skilled operators. Health came to be associated with extreme standards of cleanliness. Homemakers were therefore expected to master household technology and promote family health—complex but unrewarded increases in responsibility. The scientization of housework was complete, and women were cast into the role of preserving the home as their central life work, with limited access through their homemaking skills to the markets they had enjoyed before industrialization. They had been transformed into domestic engineers, responsible for all things related to family and the household.

The History of Immigration in Relation to the Family

People often think of family change and family transitions as recent occurrences. In reality, family changes are nothing new. Immigration has been a significant part of Canada since before Confederation. Early immigrants, mainly from the colonizing countries of Britain and France, arrived in search of opportunities for work, land ownership, and a new life. These goals were pursued, in part, as the means to start or support a family. Despite the notable change in other aspects of recent immigration—such as changed countries of origin—many immigrants continue to see economic advancement as a means to ensuring family welfare.

In the eighteenth century, the American Revolution brought to Canada the United Empire Loyalists, including significant numbers of African Americans. The latter settled largely in Nova Scotia and southern Ontario. Many black families did not fit the expected family model. For instance, black women often worked outside the home to earn enough money to get by. "[F]or African-Nova Scotian men in the early 1800s, many families practised gender interdependence and reversals of traditional gender roles in the division of labour" (Calliste, 2001: 402). This reflects, in part, need that resulted from discrimination. But it may also be reflective of the West African cultural tradition where women are both more economically and sexually independent of men and families.

Later, in the early twentieth century, African American families settled as homesteaders in central Alberta. In *The Keystone Legacy: Recollections of a Black Settler* (1997), author Gwen Hooks, daughter of original homesteaders in that area, describes how settlers banded together in families and communities to make a new and happy life on the prairies. Hooks also states that homesteaders of all ethnic origins banded together to build community facilities such as schools. Later immigrants to the West of Canada have included people from all regions of the world, seeking a better life and bringing along rich family traditions and strong values and beliefs. With time, some of these family practices have changed or even disappeared, while others influenced the practices of other people with whom they came in contact.

Immigration from Europe has also had a long history in Canada, beginning with colonialism and expansion. Canada continued to receive European immigrants from strife-torn, and sometimes poverty-stricken, countries throughout the first half of the twentieth century. Immigrants and refugees from Europe are still coming, as strife and economic difficulties recur, and have now been joined by people from Africa, Asia, and Latin America fleeing an old life or seeking new opportunities.

Today, South Asian families form a large portion of new immigrants in Canada. As such, they experience unique difficulties in their immigration experiences. South Asian women in particular face significant problems in adjusting after immigration because of the rigid gender roles in their home countries (Samuel, 2010). A study by Ahmad, Shik, Vanza, Cheung, and Stewart (2004) found that South Asian women face stress-inducing factors that include the loss of social support, economic uncertainties, downward social mobility, and health problems associated with climatic and food changes. Equally important, these women feel they cannot turn to professional health workers for help with these concerns for fear of disgracing their families. This inability to seek help is aggravated by the fact that immigrant women already face a lack of resources with the loss of family and friends from the homeland.

The isolating experience of South Asian women migrants highlights the need for health-care professionals to provide and understand the specific challenges and needs of recent immigrants in order to offer necessary support and care for this vulnerable population. Inevitably, life in the new country forces families—both parents and children—to live in new ways. These family changes are demanded by the process of immigration and the contact with new ways of living in close relations.

The History of Immigration Policies

As Canadians, we like to imagine that our country helps people in need, and occasionally these imaginings prove justified. However, Canada's past immigration policies undermine this idealistic point of view. For example, during the early periods of Chinese immigration to Canada, racially discriminatory laws such as the head tax were imposed in the period of 1885–1923 (Man, 2001). As well, the Chinese Exclusionary Act strictly prohibited Chinese workers (including those who built the railroads and worked in the early mines) from bringing in their wives and children. In this way, their harsh, impoverished lives were made even harder by Canadian immigration laws.

This example reminds us that Canadian immigration laws were not, and are still not, primarily philanthropic or immigrant-focused: They were intended to supply needed labour power and little more (Green and Green, 2004). The labourers were admitted into Canada historically specifically to build the Canadian Pacific Railway (Comeau and Allahar, 2001). Then, in the 1920s, in the 1950s, and again in the 2000s, immigration was used to meet demands for labour in resource sectors. In the 1960s and 1970s, increasing skill level among occupational workers was the goal. In the 1980s, immigrant labour was sought to compensate for the large population of aging baby boomers in the native-born population. And in the 2000s, the belief is that immigrants are filling skills shortages in Canada. The large inflows of immigrants at these times were permitted mainly to fill shortages of specific kinds of labour.

At other times, immigration inflows were significantly cut back, and entry restrictions ensured that groups that were not needed were turned away (McLean, 2004).

This method of controlling immigration reflects a concern with Canada's absorptive capacity—that is, "only accepting the number of immigrants that the Canadian economy [can] easily absorb" (Green and Green, 2004: 135). Yet through the 1980s, 1990s, and 2000s, this short-term focus on labour demand shifted to a long-term one that considered immigration as essential to longer term economic growth and prosperity. This policy allows for immigration inflow even during economically difficult times, which has inevitably helped immigrant families start new lives in Canada. However, in the second decade of the twenty-first century, short-term economic objectives have returned to centre stage in immigration policy, with various programs such as the Temporary Foreign Workers Program and the explicit stating of labour needs by employers who can then request suitable immigrants.

Along with changes in policy, the source countries of Canada's immigrants have changed. In 2011, 19.1 percent of Canadians (one in five) were visible minorities (what Statistics Canada used to refer to as non-white; Statistics Canada, 2013). This compares to 12.4 percent in 1971. Among the G8 countries (the most advanced countries in the world), Canada had the highest proportion of foreign-born population in the early 2010s (20.6 percent), well above the shares in Germany (13.0 percent) and the United States (12.9 percent; Statistics Canada, 2013).

Asia, including the Middle East, remains the most significant source of immigrants to Canada, accounting for 56.9 percent of all immigrants arriving between 2006 and 2011 (Statistics Canada, 2013). In the 2011 National Household Survey (NHS), more than three-quarters of the immigrants who reported coming to Canada before 1971 were from Europe. The share of European-born immigrants from subsequent periods of immigration has declined steadily. The 2011 NHS showed a slight increase in the share of immigration from Africa, the Caribbean, and Central and South America during the past five years. The Philippines was the leading country of birth among people who immigrated to Canada between 2006 and 2011.

With the development of feminist theory in the 1970s to 1990s, strong efforts have been made to understand the unique experiences of immigrant women. This has signalled a shift away from the initially male-focused experience of migration that deemed women largely invisible and their experiences the same as those of men. Previously, when women's motives for immigration were taken into account, they were seen as based on family responsibilities, rather than on independent choice or labour opportunities in the receiving country. Today, scholars are more likely to examine female migration as a complex and gender-specific experience based on a complex set of factors, including the gendered restrictions that often exist in a women's home culture that either encourage or inhibit immigration and family change (Boyd and Grieco, 2003; Nesteruk and Gramescu, 2012; Samuel, 2010).

The immigration policy of a home country can affect migrants in various ways. For one, migration policies sometimes assume a "dependent" status for women and an "independent" status for men (Boyd and Grieco, 2003: 4; Tastsoglou and Dobrowolsky, 2006). Women, therefore, are more likely to be classified in relation to their family and husbands, rather than independently (Samuel, 2010). Second, the differences between dependent and independent status can automatically place women within a family role and men in a market role. This can reinforce patriarchal relations between spouses and also shut women out of important economic roles and a chance for bargaining power within the home. More important, this power imbalance accounts for much of the social vulnerability of migrant women (Samuel, 2010). Thus, although immigration policy may be seen as "gender neutral," the entry status of men and women can have important implications for the experience of new immigrants, especially of women.

The mid-1850s created a paradigm shift from agriculture to industrialism. Families were driven into urban settings, where men left the house to work in factories.

Brand X Pictures/Jupiter Images

Wars

The two world wars of the twentieth century had profound impacts on families. They also had an influence on women's social roles and responsibilities. World War II brought an influx of women into the labour force, as men were sent away to fight. Women were employed in jobs that they had previously been excluded from due to their gender, such as work involving manual labour (Coontz, 2005: 221). More important, the government supported and encouraged both single and married women to join the labour force, and many women even earned men's wages.

However, upon the return of the men, women had to give up their jobs and resume a domestic way of life.

But families did not effortlessly pick up where they left off before the outbreak of war. For one, marriage experts worried that women had become too independent during wartime and would subsequently demand more autonomy and authority within the household (Ravanera, Rajulton, and Burch, 1998: 223). This would threaten the male breadwinner model of the nuclear family.

Moreover, the experience of families during the 1950s was not as simple or happy as has been believed and portrayed in some media. Although some women willingly embraced domesticity and were pleased to revert back to more traditional gender roles within the household, others resented their exclusion from the labour force and missed the independence they enjoyed during the war years (LaRossa, 2004: 50).

For men, the changing role of the father came to emphasize children's socialization more than in the past. Popular sitcoms such as *Leave It to Beaver* and *Father Knows Best* also reflected the role of the father within the household and as a participant in raising children. However, the "father" that was popularly promoted during the 1950s was a traditional, patriarchal version of the role demanding clear gender lines. In fact, the popular image of a nuclear family during this time—particularly rigid and stereotypical—reflected the need many people felt for stability and clarity during an insecure, fearful Cold War period.

World War II had profound effects on Canadian families who had come from Axis power countries (that is, Germany, Italy, and Japan), Canada's opponents during combat. For instance, between 1941 and 1949, approximately 27 000 Japanese Canadians were forced to leave their homes, deprived of possessions and civil rights, such as the right to vote. Some were even deported to Japan, even if they were Canadian citizens (Kobayashi, 1992). The Canadian government committed these acts under the pretense that Japanese Canadians posed a threat to national security during World War II, despite claims to the contrary by the military and the RCMP (Sunahara, 1981). The geographic dispersal of these people was meant to distribute them across the country in such a way that they could be easily assimilated into Canadian culture, undermining the likelihood that they would retain traces of their own traditions and culture (Sugiman, 1983). These actions had a deep impact on the attitudes of Japanese Canadians growing up in those times, and the effects of World War II policies continue to be felt by the older generations today.

The effect of these actions is shown in a study by Sugiman and Nishio (1983), which examined the attitudes of aging (51 to 67 years old) Japanese Canadians in Toronto toward old age and dependency of the aged. In traditional Japanese culture, care of the elderly by their children or grandchildren is viewed positively as it is considered a repayment of the older individual's life work. Yet, though it is the norm in traditional Japanese culture, Japanese Canadian aging persons prefer not to rely on younger generations for care. In their study, Sugiman and Nishio find the values of aging Japanese Canadians somewhat ambiguous. They report detecting traces of the Japanese upbringing in the participants, but also attitudes that coincide with Anglo Canadian views. Much like their

Anglo Canadian counterparts, the Japanese Canadian respondents dislike the prospect of growing dependent on their children and demonstrate a preference for living alone in old age (Sugiman and Nishio, 1983).

Wars and the experiences associated with them directly affect entire generations and their families, but also affect future generations indirectly, by influencing beliefs and attitudes. Currently, there are many Canadians in the Canadian Forces serving overseas in various roles, including combat roles. Large numbers of Canadian families are affected by this military service, even though Canada does not see itself as a military power. Deborah Harrison (2002), along with colleagues (see Harrison et al., 2011) has extensively studied the effects of military deployments in the Canadian Forces on families and children.

VARIATION IN THE FAMILY LIFE COURSE

In the past century, families have changed significantly, as we can see by examining changes in the timing and sequencing of major life course events. People born between the two world wars married younger, and most married over a narrow spread of ages. For these cohorts, the transition to adulthood was compressed into a relatively short period of completing formal education, entering the labour force, leaving home, setting up a nuclear household, and having a first child.

In contrast, later cohorts have experienced a lengthening of this time sequence. In addition, the events themselves are less clearly defined and their sequencing is more diverse. This timing of transitions involves trade-offs. Waiting longer to have children allows greater investment in oneself before investing in reproduction. However, delay may mean having no children at all. Later transitions enable more transfers from parents to children, allowing recipients to benefit more from resources, but this may reduce the potential for the parents to invest in their own retirement. Thus these children enter work life later but better equipped.

As well, couples in the past spent a much longer period of time having and raising children than they do now. When we look at a woman's age at last birth across **cohorts**, we see a fundamental change in family lives. Women having children in the 1950s had their last birth at the same age as women a hundred years before had their first birth! Even more striking is the huge difference in the timing of last births: at age 40 in the mid-nineteenth century compared with age 26 one hundred years later. Over a hundred-year period, families reduced the time they spent having and raising children by over 10 years! Recall that this happened at a time when life expectancy was increasing substantially. The result is that the portion of life spent as a parent with dependent children has been sharply reduced. By contrast, the portion of life spent married with no children at home, or at least no juvenile children, has sharply increased from 0 to almost a quarter of a century. (We shall see in Chapter 10 that in the 2000s there is a significant difference between when children become adults and when they leave home.) See Figure 2.1 for more detailed information about recent changes in the number of families with and without children.

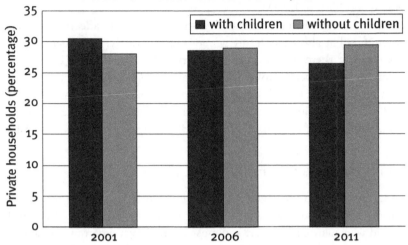

Percentage of private households containing a couple with[1] children or without[2] children Canada, 2001 to 2011

Figure 2.1 Percentage of private households containing a couple with children or without children Canada, 2001 to 2011.

[1]With at least one child aged 24 years and under.

[2]Without at least one child aged 24 years and under; includes families with all children aged 25 and over (Statistics Canada, 2011).

Source: Statistics Canada census of population 2011. Catalogue No. 98-315-XWE. Retrieved January 2013 from www12.statcan.gc.ca/census-recensement/2011/dp-pd/vc-rv/index.cfm?LANG=ENG&VIEW=C&TOPIC_ID=3&GEOCODE=01&CFORMAT=jpg#f3_1.

Given these trends, it may not be surprising that having second or even third families was more characteristic of families in the past than we sometimes admit today. In some ways, widows in the past were similar to single mothers today, both in the economic vulnerability they and their children faced and in the social challenges they experienced (Gordon and McLanahan, 1991). Widows often fell into poverty and had to rely on charity or the generosity of the state or family members to survive. In Chapter 9, we will see the differences in children's lives between the loss of a parent to death and the loss of a parent to divorce.

In the past, people expected a certain sequencing of family-related events. They expected, for example, young people to complete their education before marrying, to marry before having children, to get old before becoming a grandparent, and so on. So predictable were the patterns that sociologists spoke confidently about a normal life cycle of family events. Today, the timing and sequencing of events are too varied to be easily categorized. A woman can be a grandmother and a mid-career professional at the same time, or a new mother at midlife while starting a career. Patterns of family life have evidently become more complex—even "individualized."

The Impact of Modernization on Family Changes in Canada and Worldwide

Many changes in close relations accompany modernization. Struggles to define and redefine families continue throughout the industrialized world (Baker, 1995). Indeed, industrialization, as we have seen, has had a huge impact on family living. In addition to industrialization, urbanization has also had a great effect on family life (see Finlay, Velsor, and Hilker, 1982). That is mainly because households—or who lives with whom—are determined by property ownership arrangements, which vary between urban and rural areas. Typically, households are larger (that is, extended) and family life is more psychologically important to people in rural than in urban areas—or so we usually think. In many parts of the world, people still spend substantial parts of their lives in extended households, though they increasingly spend significant parts of their lives in nuclear families.

Along with industrialization and modernization, women's roles and responsibilities are changing. Most significantly, women increasingly seek higher education and careers (Divale and Seda, 2001). By means of their higher education and job participation, women are now more able to control their child-bearing and to support themselves economically and they may also delay marriage. Marriages are showing more egalitarianism than in the past, meaning that family power is shared between spouses. Not that all are equal, but more men are seeking wives who are educated and nearer their own age. This trend is occurring throughout the world. In Brazil, for example, there are more women than men seeking job opportunities in cities rather than living the traditional rural life. This is in part because of patriarchal norms still in place that prevent women from inheriting land. Because they have fewer job prospects at home, many women move to urbanized centres (Brumer, 2008).

As in the Brazil example, these and other societal changes can be observed in other parts of the world, wherever modernization has affected social and cultural life. In many modern Arab societies, modernization is associated with smaller family sizes, a higher literacy rate, and better economy (Ajrouch et al., 2013; El-Ghannam, 2001). Moreover, Milikian and Al-Easa (1981) have noted that in Qatar (in the Persian Gulf), a modern industrial economy means that young people, including women, earn wages that their families cannot control. Better-educated young people today, exposed to higher standards of living, can come into conflict with parents and other institutions of power as they seek to change their lives. These changes may be especially challenging in countries where the state and religion are not separate, such as Iran or Israel. Yet outcomes are not preordained; there is no certainty, for example, that the family in a modernizing Muslim region will be identical to the modern Christian, Hindu, or Jewish family.

Some of the impacts of modernization on other cultures can be predicted since, along with industrialization and individualism, modernization alters traditional customs and norms in foreseeable ways. For instance, in Asian countries where filial piety is a traditional value, massive and sudden modernization in recent years (Quach and Anderson, 2008) has also resulted in negative experiences for families with older relatives

(Chappell, 2013; Ding, 200). The family remains the main support for aging relatives, but providing for them is becoming increasingly difficult, especially because children are pursuing higher education and are influenced by individualistic notions of the West. Families in many parts of the world are experiencing similar challenges (McDaniel and Zimmer, 2013).

As another example, consider the effects of modernization in India. Here, modernization has arguably had a very significant impact on society, or at least on parts of the society. And, of course, families are hugely affected by this social and political shift. Before modernization, even over its expansive history and countless societal changes, the family as a unit in India has remained fairly stable. With industrialization and urbanization, however, as well as the growing influence of Western markets and ideologies, the traditional customs of marriage, family, and kinship have changed significantly. Some of the changes are viewed as positive, yet this is so only for a small percentage of the population. Many more people have been marginalized as a result of modernization and have experienced suffering (Kashyap, 2004). Women in particular have been impacted in both good and bad ways. As more jobs open, women have many more opportunities. Yet, these very opportunities can clash with older cultural values, leading to increased violence against women who are seen as stepping away from traditional values and patriarchy (Chibber et al., 2012; Kimuna et al., 2012).

Another factor that changes family life is political will and ideology. China, for example, has mobilized families and citizens in support of social and economic development. State planning of family life has gone hand in hand with dramatic economic and political change. In research by Kejing (1990), both hardship and progress as a result of this are apparent. Conditions of life in China for many, particularly in rural areas, remain difficult, yet for some, quality of life has been hugely enhanced. And there are indications that family life is improving, especially for women. State efforts to regulate marriage, fertility, and the rights of women are starting to pay off with smaller families and increased gender equality, though at the expense of personal liberty (Attané, 2012). And of course, smaller families are more amenable to urban living, as has been true of every modernizing society.

Moreover, even in the smaller, more isolated rural areas of the world, where traditional family forms persist most strongly, parent–child relations are changing with modernization (Caldwell, Reddy, and Caldwell, 1984). Children, on average, are gaining more autonomy and power in interactions with parents. These changes show the pervasive influence of Western cultural notions, specifically notions about childhood and adolescence, but also, more generally, notions about the life cycle. They also show the growing importance of education and media even in rural areas, and the socialization of new generations in preparation for an urban, industrial lifestyle.

Changes in Sexual Attitudes and Courtship

As sociologists have known since the founding works by Durkheim, there is an important connection between population size, population diversity, specialized roles, and changing attitudes. So, let us begin this section by noting, as shown in Figure 2.2, that Canada's

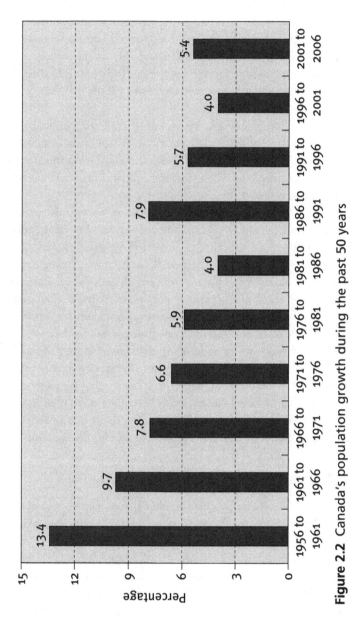

Figure 2.2 Canada's population growth during the past 50 years

Source: Statistics Canada censuses of population, 1956 to 2011. Retrieved January 2013 from www12.statcan.gc.ca/census-recensement/2011/dp-pd/vc-rv/index.cfm?LANG=ENG&VIEW=C&TOPIC_ID=1&GEOCODE=01&CFORMAT=018&CFORMAT=jpg#f1_1.

population has grown continuously and dramatically over the past 100 years. For that and other reasons, family forms and practices have changed, diversified, and specialized as well.

Before the nineteenth century, sex was strongly associated with the wedding night and virginity was hugely valued. Then, newlyweds had no privacy. They were accompanied into the matrimonial bedroom by relatives and friends and, of course, rude jokes. In some cultures, the bloodied sheets of a virgin "deflowered" would be tossed from the window to the cheers of crowds of relatives and friends below. However, in the nineteenth century, the Victorians "de-sexed" the honeymoon. Isobel March, a newly married young woman in 1871 in Niagara Falls, cited by Dubinsky (2001: 30), "did all she could to avoid the horror of being an 'evident bride.'"

In the Victorian era, the banishing of sex from public view reached its peak. Legs on tables were covered for fear that, in their naked state, they would make people think of sex! Pregnancy was disguised, hidden, or denied. Nonetheless, during this period a world of men's pubs and clubs flourished, as did a thriving prostitution trade as well as lurid romance novels. Sex did not cease to exist.

By the late nineteenth century, sex began to be seen as a central part of marriage and sexual attraction a crucial part of courtship. Sex is considered to have "come out" in the 1920s (Dubinsky, 1999)—heterosexuality in a married relationship, that is. Soon, sex experts and romance filmmakers invented the sexual honeymoon. Sexuality and sexual attraction began to occupy a more central place in modern ideas of personality and identity, and sexual happiness came to the fore as a primary purpose of marriage (Dubinsky, 2001).

At the beginning of the twenty-first century, marriage is seldom considered rationally by sentimental youth, who are often engaged not in planning lives together, but in planning romantic—and increasingly costly—white weddings. Interestingly, in weddings today, all but the most ultra-modern brides still look like fairy princesses, and grooms remain one step short of riding in on white horses (but, of course, in some ethnic groups, that is exactly what grooms still do). Brides are still "given away" by their fathers (or both parents) to their husbands. And the important ritual of uniting the couple sexually—sending them on the expected honeymoon—as well as socially is shared by families brought together for the wedding.

Changes in Attitudes toward Marriage

Traditionally, marriage was viewed largely in terms of rights, duties, and obligations to each other's families. Throughout the West, a major attitude shift has placed greater emphasis on the personal or emotional side of close relations.

Why, then, do so many people still keep up the old forms? Why do so many still get married, many of them in churches or religious places, dressed in hugely expensive white bridal gowns and formal black tuxedos, or in all the glitter and gold of the Hindu wedding? We shall discuss these questions in detail in Chapter 4. In short, formal weddings and the legal ceremony have more to do with marking a life transition or gaining social approval than with emotional commitment. Many people still find the idea of legal marriage compelling, despite what they know about the realities of marriage and divorce (Vanier

Changes in the Marriage Rate in the Twenty-First Century

■ In 1986, with amendment to the divorce law, the percentage of those married over age 15 decreased to 61.4 percent. Married couples made up 80.2 percent of all Census families. Lone-parent families accounted for 12.7 percent, and cohabiting couple families for only 7.2 percent, rates that both increased substantially in 2006 (Statistics Canada, 2006a).

■ By 2011, married couples remained the predominant family union at 67 percent, while those cohabiting rose 13.9 percent since 2006, an increase more than four times that of married couples. These couples, in the 2011 Census, counted for 16.7 percent of all families (Statistics Canada, 2011).

■ The number of same-sex married couples nearly tripled between 2006 and 2011, reflecting the first five-year period for which same-sex marriage was legal across the country. Of all same-sex couples, 32.5 percent were married and those in cohabiting relationships accounted for 67.5 percent (Statistics Canada, 2011).

■ For the first time, in 2006, the number of unmarried people (meaning never married, divorced, separated, or widowed) over age 15 surpassed the number of married people, at 51.5 percent (see Figure 2.3; Statistics Canada, 2006a).

■ In 2011, those who were single, as defined above, were difficult to assess as the Census did not isolate that portion of the population as a discernible group. The number of respondents who declared being single, and not living common-law, was 39.8 percent; however, there is no way to determine if they had ever been married or not (Statistics Canada, 2011).

■ Canada's declining marriage rate is similar to that in other Western countries, including the United Kingdom, Australia, and the United States. In the United States in 2001, the number of married-couple families was 70 percent, down from 83 percent in 1981, and common-law families increased from 6 percent to 14 percent in the same period (Statistics Canada, 2006a).

Institute of the Family, 2004). Enormous numbers of North Americans are neither rejecting the family or other long-lasting, close relationships nor accepting family in a traditional form. Most are hoping to revitalize and reinterpret family (Scanzoni, 2000; Vanier Institute of the Family, 2004), making families suited to themselves and their needs.

Although many people still get married, one significant change in family life in the Western world has been an increase in cohabitation—people living together without being legally married. Cohabitation, or the "common-law union" as it is also called, used to be more prevalent among working-class people. It also used to be seen as a lesser form of relationship than marriage—the practice was sometimes referred to as "living in sin" or "shacking up." Now, however, cohabitation has lost some of its stigma and is much more accepted. In Quebec, cohabitation has become the norm for younger couples, while legal marriage is decidedly less preferred (Vanier Institute of the Family, 2004). These trends are discussed further in Chapter 4.

It may be coincidental that the growth in cohabitation has coincided with later marriage (since the 1960s and 1970s), higher divorce rates, and lower rates of child-bearing.

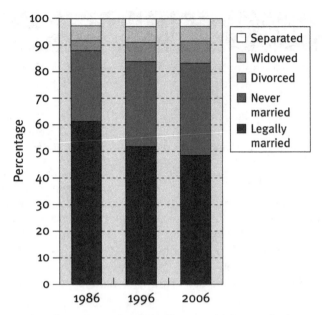

Figure 2.3 For the first time, the legally married population aged 15 and over fell below 50 percent in 2006.

Source: Statistics Canada, censuses of population 1986 to 2006. Retrieved from www12.statcan.ca/census-recensement/2006/as-sa/97-553/figures/c7-eng.cfm.

More and more often, people think of spousal relations as being about love and sexual attraction, not about child-bearing and creating family alliances. People have come to expect more satisfaction of their emotional and psychological needs in their close relationships. Women, particularly, are less economically dependent on their partners than they used to be. These shifting norms, opportunities, and expectations have all contributed to a decline in the stability of married and cohabiting life. But both continue and for the majority seem to work and work happily.

DECLINING FERTILITY AND THE VALUE OF PARENTHOOD

There can be no denying the dramatic changes that have occurred in family life—especially, in the size, structure, and composition of Canadian families—even in the last 20 to 30 years (on this, see the data in Table 2.1 below). However, it is important to note that these recent changes are rooted in dramatic changes that began over a century ago and took place, at differing rates, in all modern industrial societies.

One of the most marked changes in family life has been a change in family size over the past century or so. Since the 1870s, fertility in the West has declined steadily.

Table 2.1 Selected Trend Data, 2011, 2006, 2001, and 1996 Censuses

	Census Year			
	2011	**2006**	**2001**	**1996**
% of couples (married & common-law) with children (of any age)	n/a	54.3	56.7	59.3
% of couples (married & common-law) with at least one child under 24 years of age	39.2	49.2	51.7	54.7
% of one-person households	27.6	26.8	25.7	24.2
% of households containing a couple with children	26.5	28.5	30.5	32.9
% of households containing a couple without children	29.5	29.0	28.0	26.8
Average household size	2.5	2.5	2.6	2.6

Source: Statistics Canada website. Census Trends for Canada, Provinces and Territories, census population 2011, Statistics Canada Catalogue No. 92-596-XWE and Catalogue No. 98-312-X-2011001. Retrieved April 15, 2009 and January 2013, from www12.statcan.ca/english/census06/data/trends/Index.cfm and http://www12.statcan.gc.ca/census-recensement/2011/as-sa/98-312-x/98-312-x2011001-eng.cfm.

Birth rates in Canada hit a record low in 2000, after 10 straight years of decline. A total of 327 882 babies were born in 2000, down 2.8 percent from 1999 and the lowest number since 1946 (Statistics Canada, 2002e). Today, most European and North American countries are at, or just below, population replacement levels. While Canada is still showing some population growth, it is steadily decreasing, and growth is due more to immigration than to births. This means that unless there is a radical shift in fertility or immigration in the future, Western populations will get smaller and older during the next century. This process is already well underway in Sweden, France, and Japan. Whether this is a problem—for families and for societies—depends on who is deciding and how the situation is defined. It is a topic to which we will return.

A significant blip on this downward fertility curve was the post-war "baby boom." The baby boom, however, was only a temporary reversal of the long-term trend and was largely confined to North America. The "boom" was also misnamed. Higher birth rates were the result not of increasing family size alone but also of compressing two decades of births into a decade and a half (roughly 1947–1962). In other words, while fertility did increase somewhat, the boom was more the result of postponed fertility due to World War II. Several different age groups then had their desired number of children within a short time frame, leading to a dramatic increase in birth rate for those years. Largely, the long-term downward trend in fertility over the course of the twentieth century never really ceased (see Figure 2.4). Married-couple families with children aged 24 and under is no longer the largest family structure.

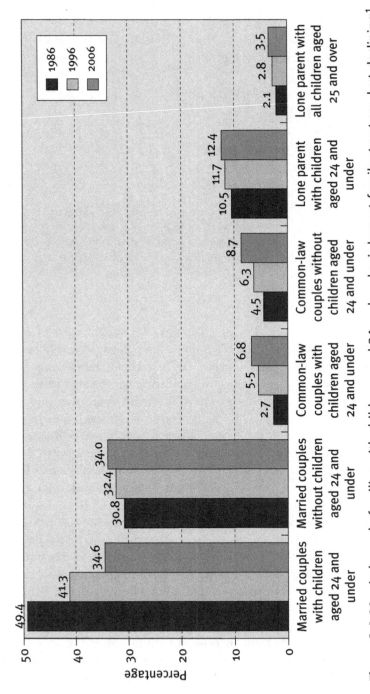

Figure 2.4 Married-couple families with children aged 24 and under is largest family structure, but declining[1]

[1]Historical comparisons for Census families, particularly lone-parent families, must be interpreted with caution due to conceptual changes in 2001.

Source: Statistics Canada, censuses of population, 1986, 1996, 2006 and 2011 Statistics Canada Catalogue No. 98-312-X2011001. Retrieved May 2013 from http://www12.statcan.ca/census-recensement/2006/as-sa/97-553/figures/c1-eng.cfm and http://www12.statcan.gc.ca/census-recensement/2011/as-sa/98-312-x/2011001/fig/fig1-eng.cfm.

Changes in the Birth Rate and Age of First-Time Mothers

- At the start of the Great Depression in 1931, women were having fewer than three children. During the baby boom of 1946 to 1965, however, alongside a higher percentage of married people, the number of children born increased to three children per woman on average. Most of these children were born to young mothers in their early twenties (Statistics Canada, 2006a).

- With the legalization of contraception in 1969, the number of children born decreased and has continued its decline over the past half-century. In fact, 1971 marked the last year during which the birth rate was at replacement level (Statistics Canada, 2006a).

- There are now more couples without children than with children. For the first time, in 2006, there were slightly more couples without children than with children (less than 1 percent). In 2011, this trend became more firmly entrenched, with the gap between the two groups widening.

- Women today are having children at increasingly older ages. Number of births by women in their thirties rose from 23 percent in 1982 to 44.8 percent in 2002 (Statistics Canada, 2004b). Whereas in 2001 7.8 percent of children aged four and younger had a mother aged 40 to 49, in 2006 this percentage increased to 9.4 percent (Statistics Canada, 2006a).

Family size and birth rates in Canada have always been political issues, as we mentioned earlier. The term used to describe Quebec's historically high birth rates (before they fell sharply from the late 1950s on) was "the **revenge of the cradle**," reflecting the belief that Quebec's long-standing sense of political injustice might be countered by having more Quebec (French-speaking) citizens (see Henripin and Peron, 1971). Early birth-control promoters, such as A. R. Kaufman of Kitchener, Ontario, were concerned about the French in Canada "outbreeding" the English (see McLaren and McLaren, 1986: 124).

The Quebec government awarded prizes in the 1930s and 1940s to women who bore many children. Their photos would appear in newspapers. Both the church and the government encouraged families to have more children. This policy was formalized with baby bonuses, which increased with each extra child born. The shift from large to small families in Quebec has occurred rapidly indeed, leaving many Quebec families with older and younger generations of vastly different sizes. Quebec's birth rate remains a political issue in the 2000s. Family researchers who study birth rates—known as **demographers**—are household names to Quebeckers; not so in the rest of Canada.

Aboriginal peoples in Canada also had high birth rates in the past. In the 1970s and into the 1980s, births to Aboriginals peoples started to decline. Recently, however, First Nations birth rates have since increased and are now the fastest growing in Canada (Vanier Institute of the Family, 2004). The current fertility rate among

Recent Statistical Trends in the Aboriginal Population

We should start by noting that Aboriginal peoples are variously located in different Canadian provinces and territories (see Figure 2.5): In some, they are a tiny minority, while in others they are a large minority or even majority. Moreover, Aboriginal bands vary quite markedly in size and prosperity. So it is difficult to generalize about Aboriginal peoples in Canada, but we will venture a few generalizations nonetheless.

- The number of Aboriginal peoples in Canada—including the First Nations, Métis, and Inuit—is now almost 1.5 million. Aboriginal peoples make up 4.3 percent of Canada's total population, compared to 2.8 percent in 1996. The population has been increasing significantly and grew by 20.1 percent between 2006 and 2011, compared with 5.2 percent for the non-Aboriginal population (Statistics Canada, 2013a).

- Eight in ten Aboriginal people lived in Ontario and the western provinces in 2011 (Manitoba, Saskatchewan, Alberta, and British Columbia). Aboriginal people made up the largest shares of the population of Nunavut and the Northwest Territories (Statistics Canada, 2013a).

- By 2017, the number of Aboriginal young adults aged 20 to 29 years ready to enter the labour market is projected to increase by more than 40 percent, compared to the 9 percent of the same age group from the general population (Statistics Canada, 2005b).

- The percentage of Aboriginal peoples in Canada is similar to that of New Zealand, Australia, and the United States. Canada's Aboriginal population is second to New Zealand's, where the Maori population accounts for about 15 percent of the total population (Statistics Canada, 2006a).

Aboriginals is around 1.5 times the overall rate among Canadians (Statistics Canada, 2005d), with 10.5 percent of the Aboriginal population being in the youngest age group (0–4 years old) compared to only 5.3 percent of the Canadian population at large (Statistics Canada, 2005c).

Although Canadians are having fewer children than before, expectations of marrying and having children remain strong. When asked by family researchers, most young people say that they expect to get married and have children (Vanier Institute of the Family, 2004). Interestingly, few expect ever to be divorced, despite the high divorce rate in modern society. Moreover, in the late nineteenth century and the early part of the twentieth century, many more people than now never married at all, a fact contrary to the common assumption that everyone in the past got married. For example, Gee (1986: 266) finds from historical records that in 1911, 12 percent of Canadians had never married. This compares with only 5.8 percent in 1981. Today, fewer than 2 percent of Canadians are likely to remain single their whole lives (neither marrying nor cohabiting). Not marrying in the past generally meant not entering parenthood. So, in fact, parenthood in the past

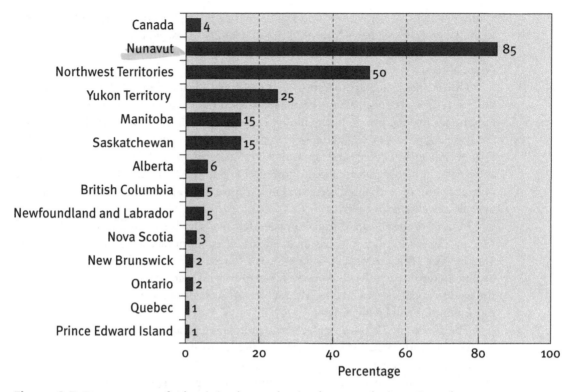

Figure 2.5 Percentage of Aboriginal peoples in the population, Canada, provinces and territories, 2011

Source: Statistics Canada, National Household Survey, 2011. Retrieved May 2013 from http://www12.statcan.gc.ca/nhs-enm/2011/as-sa/99-011-x/2011001/tbl/tbl02-eng.cfm.

was not part of as many people's lives as it is now. In the past, a lower percentage of the population got married, but those who did had many more children, on average, than couples do today.

The First and Second Demographic Transitions

The **demographic transition** from high mortality and fertility to low mortality and fertility transformed the social meaning of children, child rearing, and women's place in the family. The transition to low fertility in the West, which began around 1870, is called the *first demographic transition*. It brought births into line with a sharply reduced death rate. Since 1965, we have seen a new force for lower fertility in the West. Demographers have called this new phase the *second demographic transition* (Van de Kaa, 1987). This contemporary transition brought birth rates into line with new lifestyle goals and family practices. Wherever we find the second demographic transition well advanced, we find a profusion of new ("non-traditional") family styles, women working in the paid labour force in large numbers, and people seeking autonomy and fulfillment in their personal lives.

The second demographic transition is especially advanced in Northern and Western Europe. Renewed concerns have been expressed in these regions about depopulation and a shortage of young people in the future. In Europe, the fertility rates needed to replace the population—about 2.1 lifetime births per woman—are found only in Ireland, Malta, Poland, Albania, Turkey, and some new countries in Eastern Europe. None of these countries is a highly industrialized, Protestant country. All of them have made a virtue of large family size or limited access to birth control. It must be remembered that Canada did this as well until recently.

In most Protestant industrial countries, fertility rates hover around 1.5 children per woman. Japan's fertility rate has dropped too, from an annual level of 2.1 in 1973 to 1.29 in 2004 (BBC News, 2005, June 1), the lowest ever recorded there. A continuing decline in fertility will leave Europe's population with a growth of only 6 percent while the world's population overall nearly doubles. As a result of low fertility, by 2025 one in five Europeans will be 65 or older.

The effects of this transition are both profound and subtle. A long decline in fertility, together with increased life expectancy, has led to an aging population. On the other hand, people today are much more likely to have many generations alive at once than at any previous time in history, with some families having as many as five or even six living generations (McDaniel, 1996a). Remarried, step-, and blended families also expand our kin networks into stepchildren and stepgrandchildren, as well as larger extended families. And, largely because of urbanization and industrialization, more people today live alone or outside conventional families than their parents or grandparents would have done. Domestic lives are becoming more varied and complex.

Several explanations exist for these recent fertility declines. For one, women have been taking advantage of more access to education and employment. Another factor is that couples have delayed marrying. When people delay marriage, they are likely to have fewer children. At the same time, the costs of raising children, both economic and social/personal, rose dramatically during the twentieth century. Children are especially expensive if they need daycare by someone other than the mother (whose child care in the past was presumed to be costless), or if caring for them means forgoing a parent's income and career aspirations for several years. Moreover, parents usually spend increasing amounts of money on children's lessons, camps, and education. As well, children today remain in a state of economic dependency for longer than in the past, sometimes for surprisingly long times, as we shall see in later chapters. Finally, children often contribute less to the family economy than they used to in pre-industrial times and in the early part of the twentieth century. We will discuss these issues further in Chapter 6.

Contraception, Child-bearing Choice, and Abortion

In the past, women found a major source of identity in having children and being mothers. This was the case in such different situations as urban Quebec in the seventeenth century and the early frontier societies in the West of Canada. Silverman (1984: 59) explains that giving birth and raising children was the answer often given to the question "What are women for?"—an answer given by women as well as by men (also see Mitchinson, 2002). Until recently, both women and men agreed that child-bearing and child rearing gave women's lives meaning. Entering parenthood was also vital to populate Canada, especially in settling the West and, as we have seen, in the earliest settlements in Quebec.

However, there have always been attempts, some of them successful, to regulate pregnancy and births. Although it was officially illegal in Canada until 1969, some couples tried to use birth control to choose how many children they would have and when they would have them. Among the most common birth control methods in the past were abstinence and prolonged breast-feeding. Other popular birth control methods used in the past included barrier methods, timing or rhythm approaches, withdrawal, abortion, and, as one wise adviser to young married women suggested in her 1908 marriage manual, "twin beds" (McLaren and McLaren, 1986: 19–20).

Abortion was also common in previous centuries, with methods of "bringing down the menses" routinely advertised in daily newspapers and early magazines (McLaren and McLaren, 1986: 33–35). It is only in recent decades that abortion has come to be seen as an important public and moral issue. Interestingly, several of the well-known nineteenth-century **abortifacients** (herbs or potions that brought on a miscarriage) are still in use today for inducing labour.

During the 1960s, however, safe, reliable, and easily available contraception methods were invented. This technological shift significantly changed the concept of birth control and so contributed to the decline in fertility rate. Therefore, the first demographic transition was accomplished through a combination of strategies including late marriage, abstinence from sex, awkward methods of birth control, and dangerous, illegal abortion. The second demographic transition has occurred in the midst of a liberalizing sexual revolution and new, accessible means of contraception. The pill and other relatively readily available forms of contraception—including IUDs (intrauterine devices), spermicidal gels and foams, and higher-quality condoms—allow women and couples to choose if and when to become pregnant.

Contraceptive devices, for example, were generally scarce in Eastern Europe under Communism. As a result, the average woman in the former Soviet Union and Romania in the mid-1960s would have had seven abortions during her lifetime. Van de Kaa (1987) notes the dramatic rise in third and higher-order births after the repeal of legal abortion legislation in Romania, while the Ceausescu regime maintained an iron-fisted stance against birth control in a deliberate effort to increase the birth rate. What this shows is that, before the ruling of abortion, this method had been playing a large role in controlling fertility where other means of birth control were unavailable. Consequently, many people abandoned their babies to the care of the state. The net result was a huge number of Romanian babies and children crammed into orphanages under appalling conditions.

Up to the 1890s, abortion was tolerated in many jurisdictions, including Canada. Women who wanted to end their pregnancies could do so with the assistance of surgeons, herbalists, or midwives. Abortion was in fact legal in most North American states until the 1890s. Then it became illegal for 70 years, as a result of pressure exerted by social purity movements. Legalizing abortion once again made the process safer and more medically controlled. The (legal) abortion rate rose briefly after the mid-1960s, with a more liberal interpretation of the laws, but the rate soon tapered off (McLaren and McLaren, 1997). The most important factor promoting a decline in the incidence of abortion is the use of contraception, which enables avoidance of unwanted pregnancies. As contraceptive knowledge and use have spread, abortion has become a less often relied-upon means of limiting fertility. Yet, there is a renewed focus on women's reproduction and reproductive rights and access, particularly apparent in the United States, where many states have sharply limited women's access to abortion and simultaneously reduced their access to contraception. These changes have also influenced people's ideas about love, sex, and intimacy in ways that would have been hard to imagine.

Family and Household Size

As fertility has declined, so has the number of people in the average Canadian household. It has shrunk by 50 percent, from around six people in 1961 to now two or even one today. In addition, complex family households, containing people not part of a traditional nuclear family, had almost vanished by 2001, but now it seems that those multi-generational households are on the rise, perhaps as a result of tough economic times (McDaniel, Gazso, and Um, 2013).

Decrease in Family Size

- The size of families in Canada is continually decreasing. Whereas in 1961, 32.3 percent of all families were made up of five or more persons, half a century later the percentage is only 8.4 percent (Statistics Canada, 2012a).

- Along with the size of families, the size of households has been declining over the past half-century. The average size of the Canadian family decreased from 3.9 people in 1961 to 2.5 in 2011 (Statistics Canada, 2012a).

- One-person households are more common. The percentage rose from 9.3 percent in 1961 to 25.7 percent in 2001. In 2011, it was at 27.6 percent, three times that of those households consisting of five or more people (Statistics Canada, 2012a).

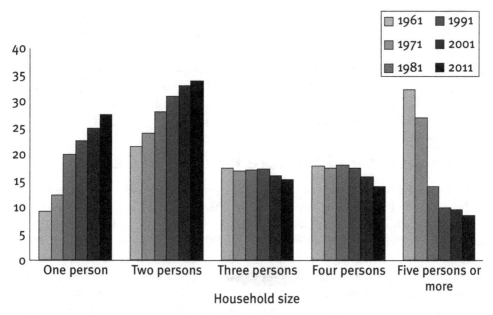

Figure 2.6 Distribution, in percent, of private households by household size, 1961 to 2011

Source: Statistics Canada censuses of population, 1961 to 2011, Statistics Canada Catalogue No. 98-312-X-2011003. Retrieved January 2013 from http://www12.statcan.gc.ca/census-recensement/2011/as-sa/98-312-x/2011003/fig/desc/desc3_1-4-eng.cfm.

A major change in family life is a rise in the proportion of single-person households (Statistics Canada, 2012)—this more than tripled from 1931 to 2011, to 13.5 percent of the population aged 15 and over, while the proportion of people overall living in families declined since 1981 (Vanier Institute of the Family, 1994: 29). In 2011, there were more than three times as many one-person households as those with five or more people (see Figure 2.6; Statistics Canada, 2012a). Curiously, while households have been growing smaller, houses have been growing bigger. Victorian-era single family houses, where as many as 15 people lived at the peak of immigration, today are often occupied by couples with fewer than three children or no children at all (Iacovetta, 1992).

SOCIAL SUPPORT AND REGULATION: THE ROLE OF THE STATE IN FAMILIES

As families have changed and evolved with respect to meeting people's needs for support, state support also changed and has now shrunk significantly. For example, state support in Canada for lone mothers changed from being largely supportive of widows with dependent children, enabling them to be "stay-at-home" mothers, to encouraging today's lone mothers (who are more often never married, divorced, or separated) to work for pay while their children are young (Gazso and McDaniel, 2010a; 2010b; Baker, 2005b). In the second decade of the twenty-first century, there is little doubt that Canada has become less supportive of families overall (Vanier Institute of the Family, 2006), despite words to the contrary. Major cycles of change in state support for families have occurred through recent times, with sharp reductions occurring at the present.

Child Support and Welfare Reforms in Canada

At the beginning of the twentieth century and especially during the Great Depression, child poverty and support for low-income mothers remained a low priority on the political agenda. Instead, legislation of the 1930s tended to reverse earlier progress toward a universally protected childhood (Strong-Boag, 2000). Change began after World War II under the Mackenzie King government, which recognized the state's role in supporting its young citizens and introduced **family allowances**. These monthly payments, based on the number of children at home, went to all women with children—but only to women, never to men. For many women who worked solely at home, this was their only independent income. In a way, family allowances were given to women as a way to compensate for and recognize their important role in child rearing.

During the 1980s, the publication of Lenore Weitzman's book *The Divorce Revolution* sparked widespread concern that rising divorce rates together with inadequate child support were responsible for poverty among single mothers and their children. One of the most notable findings was that "a woman's standard of living decreases by 73% after divorce, while a man's increases by 42% on average" (Millar and Gauthier, 2002: 140). This led to a re-evaluation of child support guidelines in Canada and the United States. In 1989, the Canadian government announced its mandate to erase child poverty by the year 2000 (Crossley and Curtis, 2006). That said, there was almost no change in the proportion of children under age 18 living in a low-income family from 1989 to 2004, despite government interventions and a strong economy since 1990/1992 (Fleury, 2008).

What followed was a number of tax and benefit policy changes. In 1990, parental benefits were added to the unemployment insurance (UI) benefits. The federal program of family allowances was discontinued in 1992 and was replaced by the Child Tax Benefit program, which aimed to provide relief for low- and middle-income families in Canada (although Quebec adopted its own guidelines; Millar and Gauthier, 2002). Finally, the National Child Benefit program was established in 1998 to support low-income families that move from welfare into the labour market (National Child Benefit, 2009). Despite these state interventions, child poverty increased from about one in seven in 1989 to one in five in 1999 (Strong-Boag, 2000).

Critics argue that these reforms do little to relieve child and women's poverty (Williamson and Salkie, 2005; Gazso and McDaniel, 2009). Rather, they fuel the privatization of social benefits, increase economic stratification, and are not responsive enough to changing family circumstances (Millar and Gauthier, 2002). Today, only Quebec continues with some form of family allowances in Canada (LeBourdais and Marcil-Gratton, 1996). The Quebec program of baby bonuses is intended both to increase the numbers of births and to provide support for women raising children. The amounts paid, however, in no way compensate for the costs involved in raising a child.

It is important to note that child poverty is not equally distributed in society. Poverty rates are consistently higher among young, single-parent, immigrant, and Aboriginal families (Prentice, 2007; Statistics Canada, 2012). For example, in 1997 only 13.7 percent of *all* children lived with a single mother, compared to 41 percent of *income poor children* and 49.8 percent of children in *deep poverty* who lived in this family type (Kerr and Beaujot, 2003: 327). The rates among Aboriginal populations are as high as 52 percent, and roughly 43 percent of visible minority children experience child poverty (Strong-Boag, 2000: 125).

The rise in lone-parent households, neoliberal economic reforms, and the retrenchment in the welfare state may contribute to the persistence of child poverty (Kerr and Beaujot, 2003). There are interesting patterns found when low income is examined among groups at risk of social exclusion: seniors, children, lone parents, Aboriginals,

The Imbalance of Aboriginal Poverty

Ongoing socio-economic struggles among the Canadian Aboriginal population continue to go unrecognized by the general population and solutions are limited and unsatisfactory. The negative impacts of extreme poverty, which is experienced by disproportionately high numbers of indigenous children, encompass far more than hunger. These impacts are extensive and pervasive. Statistics Canada, 2006, finds over half of First Nations children live in low-income families. Compare this with 21 percent of non-Aboriginal children. Most Canadians are not aware of the extreme poverty these children, especially those living in remote areas, are subjected to. Growing up in a system that clearly does not understand how to deal with their needs, these children can expect to experience a number of impacts: family violence, family structure breakdown, lower educational attainment, high suicide rates, widespread alcohol and solvent abuse, undiagnosed mental health issues, and low chance of improving socio-economic situation. "Aboriginal children are one of the most marginalized and oppressed populations with in Canada. Their rights ... are regularly being violated and they are extremely overrepresented in the child welfare system. Allowing communities to take on [self-governing child welfare] responsibility ... is a step in the right direction." (Jones, 2010, pp. 21, 27)

Melanie Jones. (2010) Systemic/Social Issues Aboriginal Child Welfare, *Relational Child & Youth Care Practice* 23(4)17–30.

http://encore.uleth.ca:50080/ebsco-web/ehost/pdfviewer/pdfviewer?sid=b97fd556-b536-460a-beef-cc17aa7bac1e%40sessionmgr114&vid=2&hid=123

immigrants, unattached non-elderly people, and people with activity limitations. In the past few decades, measures have improved somewhat for seniors and lone parents; however, low income was still high relative to the other groups (Statistics Canada, 2012c). As children comprise nearly all groups, their situation is the most desperate. Debates on how to define and measure child poverty make it difficult to evaluate the efficacy and success of government policies.

"Welfare-to-work" initiatives of the 1990s added a new dimension to the plight of low-income families and their children. Prior to the 1990s, single mothers across Canada "could provide full-time care to their children and receive social assistance until their youngest child was at least school age" (Williamson and Salkie, 2005: 56). However, in the mid-1990s, Canadian policy-makers sought to reduce the proportion of welfare recipients by mandating them to find work or take part in employment-related programs (for example, job training). Contrary to original goals, these welfare reforms did not improve children's well-being (Gazso and McDaniel, 2010a; 2010b).

Instead, impoverished children are now more likely than before to have parents who are trying to balance work with employment, and they are more likely to live in families that secure income from the labour market rather than social assistance. Therefore, elimination of child poverty will likely entail the integration of several carefully planned and evaluated social policies—not only child support benefits and welfare-to-work initiatives, but also those associated with social assistance incomes, higher minimum wages, affordable housing, and more accessible and universal child care (Lloyd, 2008).

Changing Nature of Elder Support by the State and the Family

Traditionally, support of older individuals was provided by what is sometimes referred to as the "three-legged stool" of responsibility—namely, government, employers, and families (Salisbury, 1997). However, efforts to reduce government spending, the precarious nature of employment markets, and changes in family life have altered the support received by the elderly (Kemp and Denton, 2003).

The Canadian welfare state, developing during and immediately after World War II, underwent a progressive expansion, culminating into a full-blown Canadian social security system in the 1970s (Li, 1996). Given its supply of economic, medical, and social assistance, the system was especially important for older people, who were now supported by the government. Two other main sources of support were available in later life—the market and the family (Esping-Andersen, 1999). The financial services market provided plans such as life insurance and private pension policies, while the family, often mainly through the efforts of women, provided care for infirm older adults.

The post-industrial society, however, brought with it changes to the traditional sources of support for the aging portion of society. Due to changes in the labour market and demographic transformations, the state, the market, and the family started limiting their provision of welfare compared to their contribution in the past (Esping-Andersen, 1999).

Beginning in the 1980s, a concern with the overextension of the welfare state and with the public expenditure implications of an aging population took over in the political realm. This lead to decreased spending, terminated social programs, and streamlining of services (Baines, Evans, and Neysmith, 1998; Brotman, 1998). Such changes caused a greater responsibility for late-life provisions to fall on the shoulders of the family and the market.

However, high levels of unemployment that have characterized the past two decades have forced many into early retirement or unemployment, often with not enough financial resources (Kohli, Rein, Guillemar, and Van Gunsteren, 1991). The trend toward early retirement in Canada has recently turned around, however, with people working longer (Statistics Canada, 2012c). Further, the new face of the labour market, which included interrupted employment patterns, contract work, and part-time employment, also began limiting the support of employers through private pension plans and insurance programs (McDaniel, 1997).

The socio-demographic changes during this time, mentioned earlier in the chapter, reduced the availability of relatives able to provide support for older family members. Such changes included a rise in single-parent families, substantially increasing female participation in the labour force, as well as the geographical dispersion of family members. Thus, overall, the post-industrial society and the changes it brought with it have translated into a shift in responsibility for the care of the elderly from the state, market, and family to the elderly trying to take care of themselves.

These circumstances become evident when examining the attitudes and beliefs of today's middle- and old-age population. Kemp and Denton (2003) investigated the way in which mid- and late-life Canadians discuss and allocate responsibility for the provision of social, financial, and medical supports in later life. The answer was clear—care for the elderly is the responsibility of the elderly. Recall the example of the Japanese Canadian and Canadian seniors discussed previously. Their reports were similar to those of the participants in this study. Most respondents in this study assumed personal responsibility for later life, citing individual planning and preparation as necessary tasks to secure against the perceived risks associated with becoming or being old. Furthermore, most participants rejected the notion that family members should provide housing, financial support, or personal care and were generally seen as a source of emotional support (Kemp and Denton, 2003).

Even though studies have shown the senior population is not responsible for escalating health-care costs or depletions of the Canadian pension fund (see Barer, Evans, and Hertzman, 1995), the shift to greater individual responsibility for societal and personal social security remains significant today. It has been argued that this can lead to increased social and financial risks in old age (e.g., Esping-Andersen, 1999).

Due to aging population, the payments for Old Age Security and Guaranteed Income Supplement for low-income seniors are expected to quadruple (or double, accounting for inflation) between 2009 and 2036. There is pressure to improve these programs soon. One idea is to implement a penalty for those receiving benefits early and create a bonus if delaying payments until 70 years of age. Bigger challenges include individual preparedness for retirement and the cost of federal public service pensions. The challenges of seniors and health care that need to be addressed will depend on things external to the aging population per se: Economic growth, innovations in health care delivery that improve cost effectiveness, individual health status, and trade-offs among coverage, taxation, and debt-financing are some of the issues facing the future of Canadian health care in general (Echenberg, Gauthier, and Léonard, 2011).

The Regulation of Divorce

Marriage dissolution is of great interest to the state. In fact, at the turn of the twentieth century, divorce in Canada could only be granted by an Act of Parliament. Marriage was considered a crucial part of the social fabric, not to be tampered with by the parties involved.

However, marriage failure and divorce did not, as some might think, begin recently. There have always been men who deserted their families (some women deserted, too) and couples who agreed mutually to separate (Gordon and McLanahan, 1991). Some Canadians went to the United States to seek divorce when it was not attainable in Canada (Bradbury, 1996: 72–73). In some provinces, such as Quebec, where divorce was almost impossible to obtain until well into the mid-twentieth century (and was frowned upon strongly), some women slipped into Ontario and declared themselves widows.

In 1968, greater access to divorce was made possible under the Divorce Act. This led to a fivefold increase in divorce between the late 1960s and the mid-1980s. Immediately following the revised 1985 Act, divorces again rose sharply, but much of this increase appears to have been accounted for by people who put off divorcing in 1984 and 1985, in anticipation of the revised legislation, and then initiated proceedings once the new law was enacted. By the late 1980s, the rate was declining.

These changes did not come to all parts of the Western world at the same time. For example, divorce remained illegal in Ireland until 1995. A referendum on the topic in that year defeated existing laws by a narrow margin. The pressure to liberalize Irish divorce laws contributed to a wide-ranging discussion of **secularization** (a move away from religion as an organizing principle of society) and the nature of social and familial change. People have also begun to reconsider the connection between moral and constitutional matters, or the church and state. Ireland is not yet a secular society (Wills, 2001). However, it is more pluralistic and tolerant than it was a decade ago. Individual Catholics, in Ireland as elsewhere, no longer completely embrace all the doctrines of the Church (though it may well be that, in practice, they never did so entirely).

CONCLUDING REMARKS

A long and complex process has marked efforts to reform government policies concerned with family life. One reason that government policies often do not meet the needs of Canadians is that most are based on the outdated assumption that all families are alike. Canadian sociologist Margrit Eichler (1997) argues that there are increasingly complex ways to live in families and for family life to connect with work life. Thus, her starting point is to recognize the fact that families and work–family relationships vary widely. So must models of the family and state responses to family life.

Further, the Canadian family is not a static entity; rather, it is a product of a unique history of ethnic relations, transition to industrialism, wars, and demographic changes. The historical analysis outlined in this chapter showed how broad cultural, social, and economic changes can redefine traditional notions of courtship, marriage, family, parenthood, and gender relations. Informed by the successes and oversights of the past, we may begin to develop more effective policies and interventions to suit the changing nature of families in modern society. No doubt, the changing social and political landscape of the twenty-first century will have its own influence on the future of the family. The following chapters will discuss in detail the trends in our modern understanding of family norms, structures, and processes.

What the reader should take away from this chapter is the sense that family forms and structures have always varied. They have varied throughout history, and they vary today, cross-nationally and cross-culturally. They vary because different circumstances call on families to perform different social tasks, often with different kinds and amounts of support. As a result, families have always had to adapt—to be almost infinitely flexible and resourceful. Keep this in mind when, in the chapters that follow, we examine the ways that different "kinds" of families—legally married and cohabiting, one-parent and two-parent, single-earner and dual-earner, same-sex and opposite-sex, and so on—try to grapple with their changing circumstances.

CHAPTER SUMMARY

Historically, families have been important bases for identity and for resource allocation. In many cultures, broader family structures, such as kinship groups and clans, have played a large role in determining relationships and social positions.

We have seen in this chapter that families are always and have always been changing in response to societal shifts, changing attitudes and expectations of women and men, and altering roles and views of and toward children. We have seen that contact with new cultures, either through colonization or immigration,

brings about inevitable change that has both micro and macro implications.

Immigration has been part of Canada since its beginning, and changing immigration policies reflected Canada's position toward new people coming to live in this country, positions that, as we saw, were not always admirable. We have also seen how politics, economic circumstances, state regulations and reforms, wars, and consumerism shape families and family change, and the long-term impacts of these changes. We will explore the effects and significance of such changes in more detail in later chapters.

Key Terms

abortifacients Herbs or potions that bring on a miscarriage.

cohort A group of people who experience some major demographic event, typically birth, migration, or marriage, within the same year or period.

demographic transition The transition to low fertility in the West, which began around 1870, is called the first demographic transition. This brought births into line with a sharply reduced death rate. A second demographic transition, more contemporary, has brought birth rates to a low level and, it is theorized, into line with new lifestyle goals and family practices.

demographers Those who study population changes such as births, deaths, and migrations.

family allowances Monthly payments started in Canada after World War II as a way to give women compensation as well as recognition for child rearing. They were based on the number of children at home and went to all women with children, but not to men.

gemeinschaft A type of community typical of pre-industrial rural life; that is, one in which everyone knows everyone else and people share common values.

"mechanization" of housework The introduction of new home technologies. Home economists worked to elevate the esteem of homemakers by promoting the idea that the new home technologies required skilled operators.

revenge of the cradle An expression reflecting the belief that Quebec's long-standing sense of political injustice might be countered by having more (French-speaking) citizens.

secularization A move away from religion as an organizing principle of society.

Critical Thinking Questions

1. Families adapt when societies change as they come into contact with other cultures through colonization or immigration. The Aboriginal peoples of Canada and their families have been greatly impacted by colonization. What is the significance of the original contact and conflict between English and French colonizers and the Aboriginal peoples on today's Aboriginal families? How do social policies affect Aboriginal families?

2. As we have seen, immigration has been part of Canada since its founding and is still an important aspect of our country. However, some of Canada's past policies do not cast our country in a favourable light. In recent years, these policies have improved, shifting to a long-term perspective that considers future growth and prosperity. Is it likely that future circumstances can alter this perspective? Do you think Canada may revert to its previous position? How important is immigration to Canada's present and future families? Can you identify some of the issues recent immigrant families may experience?

3. Courtship, marriage, childbirth, and divorce have all experienced changes in the past decades. From definition to legality, our close relations are quite different than those of our grandparents. Increases in cohabitation and childless unions, as well as legalization of same-sex marriage, are a few of the changes we have experienced. In the past, the primary reason for lone motherhood was widowhood; at present, it is divorce. Why? Why is this important when considering social support in families? What other examples of changing relationships can you think of?

4. In order to make good policy decisions, governments need to have good data and understanding of society as it changes and ages. What changes has our society experienced and what can we expect to experience in the future?

5. The typical life course of an individual is less predictable than in the past. What are the implications for families? What must be considered when developing definitions, generalizations, and predictions about families?

Weblinks

Library and Archives Canada
www.collectionscanada.gc.ca/index-e.html
Library and Archives Canada has an incredible amount of resources, primary and secondary, about the history of Canada and its people. It features publications, photographs and other images, audio, and internet resources. It provides links to other Canadian government websites. Also visit www.archivescanada.ca for the Archives Canada portal, "your gateway to Canada's past."

Our Roots
www.ourroots.ca
This site features a search system on information about local communities and the histories of specific Canadian families. It also provides a search engine for Canadian books that is frequently updated with new and rare material. For students, several interactive educational resources are available. The collection has both French and English information and documents.

The Peopling of Canada 1946–1976
www.ucalgary.ca/applied_history/tutor/canada1946/index.html
This site is a research project by the Applied History Research Group at the University of Calgary. It provides information about the history of Canada's demographic changes, government and policy changes, and other topics significant to families in the past. It covers history from after World War II to the mid-1970s.

Multicultural Canada
www.multiculturalcanada.ca
This site contains a wealth of information about the history of immigration to Canada and how it has affected people from diverse backgrounds. It includes newspapers, photographs, book references, legal documents, audio files, pamphlets, and other materials, most of which are in languages other than English.

Multicultural History Society of Ontario (MHSO)
www.mhso.ca
MHSO is a "not-for-profit educational institution and heritage centre" founded by Professor Robert F. Harney in 1976. Ontario has had a rich history of multiculturalism, and this site provides information about cultural issues and links to publications and exhibit information at the Oral History Museum in Toronto.

Quebec History
http://faculty.marianopolis.edu/c.belanger/QuebecHistory/index.htm
This site is intended for a post-secondary school course in Montreal. It covers the history of Quebec people and culture from the mid-eighteenth century (after the fall of New France) to the present. It includes supplementary sections on important issues, biographies, statistics, documents, and images. It is updated on a regular basis.

The Global Gathering Place
www.mhso.ca/ggp
Related to the MHSO, the Global Gathering Place is an interactive site with an aim to educate Canadians about the diversity of Canadian people through documents, images, videos, and audio material. It has information about immigration, ethnicity, community and family life, labour, and Canadian citizenship.

First Peoples' Heritage Cultural Council
www.fphlcc.ca
The First Peoples' Cultural Council is an organization based in British Columbia that works to promote Aboriginal culture and language and to improve the well-being of Aboriginal peoples. It works in conjunction with the First Peoples' Cultural Foundation as well as First Voices, organizations that "raise awareness and funding for Aboriginal language revitalization." Both also have interactive and informative sites. Visit www.fpcf.ca and www.firstvoices.com for more information.

Chapter 3
How Families Begin
Dating and Mating

Nataliia/Fotolia

Chapter Outline

Learning Objectives

1 Describe the historical evolution of love.

2 Differentiate between the various theories of mate selection.

3 Identify the social influences affecting how people seek and meet potential mates.

4 Analyze how modern technologies have revolutionized the dating process.

5 Describe how the forming of intimate relationships is different for older adults.

6 Develop a multicultural viewpoint of dating and mating practices.

7 Apply knowledge of homogamy to dating and mating practices with concern to educational status, age, ethnicity, and religious background.

8 Differentiate between the mate preferences of men and women.

9 Argue against seeking an optimal mate, and argue for satisficing.

10 Describe various forms of dating violence.

Dating and mating are important elements of our social lives. Émile Durkheim, one of the founders of sociology, discovered in the earliest sociological research that close social ties make a difference to personal survival (married people are less likely to commit suicide, for example). In this context, ceremonies and symbols, such as weddings and wedding rings, bring people together for common purposes (Durkheim, 1951[1915]). We will talk more about the importance of symbols and rituals in the following chapters, when we focus on the effects of close relations on individual and social well-being.

Max Weber, another founder of sociology, revealed the centrality of marriage in his exploration of feudalism (Sydie, 1987: 73–77). In feudal times, marriages were the means to cement clans or family groups. When a man married a woman who owned a fiefdom, he sometimes took the woman's name on marriage. Women of feudal nobility were often the managers of estates and huge feudal households in partnership with their husbands.

Yet another founder of sociology, Friedrich Engels, outlined a theory of marriage (Sydie, 1987: 96) that says that as people accumulated private property in the past, women and men became **monogamous** (i.e., married to only one partner for life). The reason was to protect their family's property in the event of childbearing and inheritance. Monogamy increased the likelihood that a parent could identify his or her offspring; in other words, men could pass their wealth to their offspring with some certainty about their status as fathers. As a result, women's fidelity in marriage became part of an economic system. Here, says Engels, we find the origin of modern marriage—as well as a material basis of inequality between men and women in marriage, and one way that marriage gives men power over their wives.

LOVE: A RECENT INVENTION?

Courtly love, the likely origin of **romantic love** as we know it today, emerged in Europe in the Middle Ages. Many images of romantic love in the late twentieth century still preserve aspects of this period. The idea of romantic love is therefore the product of a particular culture in a particular historical period, although some propose that it also has an evolutionary basis (Fisher, 1992). Many people today think that love and marriage have always gone together, but there is nothing natural about this connection. In fact, traditionally, most people thought the purpose of marriage was to benefit the family group, not the individual spouses. Through most of history, marriages were arranged in ways that were mutually profitable for families.

Historically, this mattered more than whether the couple loved each other romantically in the way we think of love today. But, as we shall see, neither marriage for love nor marriage by arrangement is certain to produce happiness and a durable union.

Morton (1992) explains how the idea of love as a basis for marriage grew out of questioning the traditional social and economic grounds for marriage. As feudalism ended and the market economy began to grow around the fifteenth century, Western European households, which had previously included many unrelated people, began to shrink. Households containing *only* family members increased rapidly, and people began to question the traditional basis of marriage—the melding of households for economic or political reasons. Marriage was gradually transformed, and love came to be the basis on which families began. A division of labour developed between marriage partners, including different sexual norms for men and women, and gendered inheritance patterns. At home, power differentials sharpened between the sexes, since they were no longer equal partners in work.

The emergence of the idea of romantic love changed social roles, especially for women. In relationships, women became less valued for their position as partners in work and more valued as passive decorations (Abu-Laban and McDaniel, 2004). As such, their adornment and appearance mattered more than their contributions to the family's overall well-being. The social differences between men and women were exaggerated, as men gained more social and economic power—a process that reached its peak with industrialization in the nineteenth and twentieth centuries.

Under the ideas of courtly love, the woman was seen as an object of male affections and placed on a pedestal. She was to be pursued and won, though she remained pure and (therefore) unattainable. These ideas persist in some present-day thinking about love and sex. They continued to support the well-entrenched idea of a **sexual double standard**, which places a high value on women's virginity before marriage and fidelity afterward. Men's sexual experience before marriage and fidelity afterward is seen as less important. Our sexual attitudes have changed in the past two generations, but remnants of the double standard persist.

We can see this persistence in the language used to describe sexually experienced males and females. Terms used to describe women who have had many sexual partners have negative connotations: for example, "slut," "promiscuous," "loose," and "easy." Compare these to the terms used for men with many sexual partners—"stud," "stallion," and "playboy," for example—and it is clear that more positive connotations are associated with male sexual promiscuity. The sexual double standard is weaker today, as more young people are sexually active before marriage, but there is still gender inequality in this realm (see Figure 3.1).

Other cultures, by contrast, still condemn female sexual experience before marriage. For example, among Sunni and Shiite Muslim American families, the need for Muslim women to preserve modesty in their interactions is highly valued and strongly enforced (Carolan, 1999).

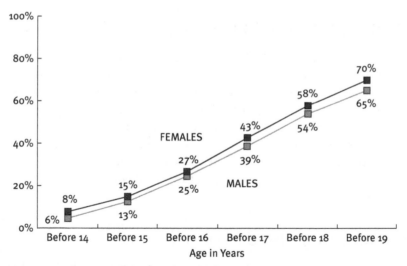

Figure 3.1 Cumulative Percentage of Never-Married Teens Having Sexual Intercourse, by Age and Gender, 2002

Source: Abma et al. (2004). *Teenagers in the United States: Sexual Activity, contraceptive use, and childbearing, 2002.* Hyattsville, MD: National Center for Health Statistics.

MATE SELECTION

The term *mate selection* may seem odd, given all the constraints on our choices, both logistical and social. Our own society is permissive, but traditional societies have a great many specific rules about who can marry whom. Some societies practice **endogamy, which is the requirement common in small, traditional societies that people marry within their own social group** (such as their own class, caste, or ethnic group). Other societies practice **exogamy, which means marrying outside one's social group.**

In traditional societies, marriage rules aim to ensure a kin group's survival. Wherever land or other immovable property might be lost through marriage, the pressure toward endogamy is strong. Endogamy is also likely when a group is suffering discrimination by outsiders and has to strengthen its social bonds by strengthening group boundaries in marriage. On the other hand, exogamy has value for particularly small societies, such as hunter-gatherers: It gives the members more chance of surviving by increasing the size of the group they can call on in the event of famine, war, or other trouble. Exogamy is a good survival strategy where group resources are few and the group does not feel threatened by (all) outside groups, or where there are few, if any, family properties to be lost (or gained) through marriage.

Our own society has no clear rules of endogamy or exogamy. That said, most people end up marrying outside their extended kin group and, increasingly, outside their own ethnic, racial, and religious group. And, owing to the great deal of geographic mobility in our society, many people end up marrying people from another community entirely.

THEORIES OF MATE SELECTION

Whether we examine heterosexual or same-sex couples, a central feature of couple relationships in Canada is commitment to the ideals of romantic love. In our society, the arrangements—geographic and economic—of marriage are framed through the ideological rhetoric of romance. Practical concerns always play some part, more so in some relationships than in others, but most people marry because they believe they love each other. Often people feel they have discovered the best—even the perfect—mate. That said, mate selection cannot be described simply as the result of two people falling in love. It is a more complex process, and various theories have been developed to explain it.

Complementary Needs Theory

Robert Winch (1962) proposed that, in mating, a person is typically drawn to someone whose needs are opposite and complementary to his or her own. This is commonly referred to as the "opposites attract" phenomenon. For example, a person who wants to provide care would be attracted to someone who needs care. Needs are also complementary if the partners have the same needs but at different intensities—for example, if one partner has a stronger need for physical intimacy than the other (Knox, 2005). According to this theory, people choose mates different from themselves in hopes of filling in the "missing pieces" in their own lives or personalities.

Exchange Theory

Exchange theory, in a sense, describes the mechanism that makes such mating work— namely, the process of continuing interaction and exchange of benefits between partners. The exchange perspective sees marriage as give-and-take, where each partner both gives and gets. The stability of a relationship is thought to depend on how well a balance is maintained in exchanges between partners; that is, how well what is given matches what is received.

Expressive exchanges in marriage are exchanges of emotion between spouses. They include hugs and kisses, sexual pleasure, friendship, a shoulder to lean on, empathy, and understanding. Expressive exchanges affirm the affection and love each spouse has for the other, and presumably each spouse gets the amount and kind of affection that is needed. By contrast, **instrumental exchanges** involve tangible or material support (Muncer, Burrows, Pleace, Loader, and Nettleton, 2000). These include contributions of domestic labour, with couples sharing household duties and tending to practical matters such as housework, paying the bills, and looking after the children.

Evolutionary Perspective

Developed from Darwin's theory on the evolution of species, the evolutionary perspective sees human mating as guided by principles that maximize survival advantages. Presumably, people mate in ways that ensure the production and survival of offspring, since this gives their genes the best chance of surviving over generations. However, genetic survival strategies differ for men and women, because their reproductive potential differs. Men, who can easily father many children, seek women who appear to be fertile, as shown by their youth and sexual attractiveness. However, giving birth to each child represents a major investment for a woman, so women are more interested in the social and economic advantages that men can offer and pass on to their children. They seek a mate who would make a good provider and stay faithful in his support of the family. As such, women, in the evolutionary perspective, are thought to base their preference for mates on men's social and economic status (Doosje, Rojahn, and Fischer, 1999).

Social Role Theory

Not surprisingly, this gives rise to and maintains gendered differences in mating and dating, reflecting those in public and private life. Over the past few hundred years of Western society, traditional roles of men have differed from those of women. Men's roles were more related to the public domain and women's roles to the private. According to social role theory, men and women are thus socialized to prefer partners whose attitudes are congruent with those stereotypic roles (Doosje et al., 1999). The mate selection process is guided by these preferences.

Today, most families need two incomes to support a middle-class lifestyle that one income would have supported in the past; nonetheless, traditional role expectations are still central to mate selection for most members of society. This persistence of a commitment to traditional social roles and expectations has created stress for many members of society, and especially for women. There have been huge increases in the proportion of women working for pay, yet there is a lag in the adjustment of household work and childcare to this new reality. Men's contributions to domestic labour have increased, but we still find inequality in dual-earner families (Hook, 2006). Modern marriages therefore continue to struggle with traditional social roles.

This creates a contradiction: Men may look for ambitious and career-oriented women when they are choosing a mate, but because of the influence of traditional social roles, they will also expect the same women to fit into stereotypical housewife roles. This often creates role conflict at home. In large part, it is the idealization of marriage as a romance-driven dream world versus the reality of social roles and domestic duties that leads to conflict between ideal and real family lives, and between men and women. This often leads to high rates of frustration, divorce, and even violence.

Gender Equality

The level of gender equality in a society has a profound influence on mate selection. In traditional societies, patriarchal ideologies support male dominance and control over women (Lupri, Grandin, and Brinkerhoff, 1994). Within such societies, women prefer mates who are older and have good financial prospects, while men prefer mates who are young, fertile, and good housekeepers (Eastwick et al., 2006). These practices tend to keep women in the private sphere—the household—and men in the public sphere. In this way, they support the evolutionary and social role theories of mate selection.

In more gender-equal societies, people tend to favour different qualities in mate selection. There, women follow less traditional patterns (Moore, Cassidy, Smith, and Perrett, 2006). In particular, women, being more educated and with access to good jobs, are less likely to look for men who are good providers and put less importance on earning potential in a mate (Koyama, McGain, and Hill, 2004). Women with high control over their resources also tend to prefer partners who are nearer in age to themselves (Moore, Cassidy, Smith, and Perrett, 2006). And, given their own economic and social independence, women are even likely to engage in short-term sexual relationships without fearing it will harm their marriage chances (Stanik and Ellsworth, 2010). In this and other respects, women take on more male-typical mate preferences and place a bigger emphasis on physical attractiveness during mate selection (Moore and Cassidy, 2007).

In general, a high level of gender equality reduces sex differentiation in mate preferences, with men and women looking for similar qualities during mate selection—for example, focusing on personality and value compatibility. In a recent study, Zentner and Mitura (2012) assessed mate preferences in 10 countries. They found that societies with the most gender equality, such as Finland, Sweden, and Norway, had correspondingly higher gender equality in mate selection. In other words, men and women put a similar emphasis on the importance of qualities like physical appearance and financial prospects during mate selection, as well as on social and education similarity. Countries with slightly lower levels of gender equality, like Canada, had slightly less gender parity in mate selection; countries that scored lowest in gender equality, like Iran, had the lowest levels of gender parity and, conversely, the greatest difference in how men and women chose mates.

MEETING AND MATING

Meeting a potential mate is not what it used to be. Some old traditions remain, but new traditions have also emerged. The range of ways to meet one's life partner has widened in recent years. Many couples meet in the usual places of shared activities—schools and universities, workplaces, religious places, neighbourhoods, sporting groups, or events. Others meet through common friends or relatives. Cyberspace is a hugely popular setting for singles in search of partners. Others are still put together by relatives in arranged or semi-arranged marriages.

Arranged Marriages and Love Matches

A society that practises arranged marriage puts parents or kin in the centre of making matches between people. In most societies for most of history, marriages have been arranged in this sense, based not on love but on the needs, beliefs, or desires of the couple's relatives. In Western Canada, for example, there were a large number of arranged marriages in the period between 1860 and 1945 (Millar, 1999), when partners were scarce. Today, arranged marriage remains popular among certain ethnic communities, including some South Asians and some Orthodox Jews (see Howell, with Albanese and Obosu-Mensah, 2001; Weinfeld, 2001).

Arranged marriages are most common in pre-industrial or developing societies where people are organized around close extended families. Unmarried people whose daily lives revolve around school or work are likelier to choose their own partners, whether in Japan, China, Europe, or India—or Canada. School and work are important to mating, because they offer young people a place to meet and become acquainted, often across ethnic, racial, and class lines. It is here, in situations of social discovery, that themes of romantic love and dating are most important for mating (Ghimire, Dirgha, Axinn, Yabiku, and Thornton, 2006).

Reasons for arranged marriages vary from culture to culture. Some people with an interest in this practice want to ensure a certain religion is carried on through generations. Others want to ensure that land is passed from one generation to the next within

- Children of South Asian and Chinese immigrants to Canada show a greater preference for chastity in a mate than their European Canadian peers. The views of South Asian Canadian youth fall between what they believe their South Asian parents view as appropriate and what they believe their Canadian peers approve of. This shows that young adults from some Eastern cultures are caught between local and traditional norms about dating and marriage choices (Lalonde and Giguere, 2008).

- Traveller communities, or Gypsies, as they are known in Britain, commonly practise "grabbing," a dating ritual at weddings where women are physically grabbed by men and forced to kiss them (McDonald, 2011). In other cultures, women are literally kidnapped and raped, then married afterward to legitimize the relationship.

- In Western cultures, physical attractiveness and passionate feelings are valued characteristics in partners. In Eastern cultures, family values and wishes have more significant influence on mate selection (Zhang and Kline, 2009).

- Urbanization and new media technologies have led to the emergence of a dating culture in previously traditional cultures, as in Nepal (Regmi, van Teijlingerm, Simkhada, and Acharya, 2011). In the past, the transition from childhood to adulthood was marked by early marriage and childbearing. Recently, adolescents are waiting longer to get married, staying in school longer, going on dates, and likelier than in the past to engage in premarital sexual behaviours.

the extended family. Since marriage is an economic arrangement between families, it makes sense to arrange marriages in a way that protects family assets such as land, grazing rights, or animals. Parents also want to minimize potential conflict between the families that will be joined by the marriage. For these reasons, the choice of marriage partners is considered far too important to be left to the whims of youth. Spouses are chosen by the family because the union is economically valuable or because of friendship or kinship ties.

In Chinese cultures, Confucian ideology stresses the importance of family perseverance. This means that arranged marriages are prevalent in China, with two-thirds of marriages arranged in urban areas and even more in rural areas. However, recent trends show steep declines in arranged marriages in that country. Friends and colleagues have taken over the matchmaker role formerly played by parents. This is consistent with the idea that close extended families can be connected through arranged marriages. Chinese families used to be known for close-knit, three-generation households. Family remains the main pillar of the support network, but the nuclear family has become more popular. As well, consistent with findings that will be discussed later in the chapter, a high value on a partner's education has replaced the value on a partner's family background among the educated in China (Xu, Xie, Liu, Xia, and Liu, 2007).

Among South Asians, arranged marriage remains prevalent. Key characteristics to be considered in a marriage include language, caste, religion, and fairness or lightness of skin (Ternikar, 2004). In Japan, so called *go-betweens*—matchmakers who help out informally—are sought because of their networks. With their familiarity and knowledge of both parties, go-betweens can bring suitable couples together (Abe, 2005).

Sometimes people marry people they have never met. Today, however, few marriages are "arranged" in the traditional sense. Arranged marriage candidates are becoming more active participants and have more say in the process (see page 91, "Dating and Mating Trends").

Personal Ads and Internet Dating

Many people today are bypassing the traditional methods of dating in favour of a technology-oriented approach. The search for compatibility has extended to the online population by means of internet dating (see Table 3.1). Personal ads have grown both in popularity and acceptability. What used to be called "lonely hearts ads" for the desperate are now mainstream, used by respectable people searching for real relationships. Brym and Lenton (2001) assert the following reasons for the growth of internet dating:

- As career and time pressures increase, people look for more efficient ways of meeting potential intimate partners.
- Growing sensitivity about workplace sexual harassment has led to a decline in workplace romance.
- Due to job market demands, single people are becoming more mobile, making it harder to meet dating partners.

Table 3.1 Dating-Related Activities Online

Most online Americans who are single and looking for dates have used the internet to pursue their romantic interests, and millions more Americans know people who have tried and succeeded at online dating.

At the same time, most internet users believe online dating is dangerous because it puts personal information online, and they also think that many online daters lie about their marital status.

While some stigma persists, most do not view online dating simply as a last resort.

One in ten internet users say they have personally gone to dating websites.

A majority of online daters report good experiences with the sites.

Online daters believe dating websites help people to find a better match because they can get to know a lot more people.

There are uses of the internet beyond dating websites that have woven themselves into the world of romance.

Source: From Pew Internet and American Life Project Survey, September-December 2005. "Online Dating." Mary Madden and Amanda Lenhart, March 5, 2006. Reprinted with permission.

According to a study by Ward and Terence (2004), many people prefer online dating to traditional dating because it allows them to develop a relationship in a safe and comfortable setting; in particular, it allows people to establish communication and awareness before meeting face-to-face. The internet also provides a larger pool of people to choose from.

The internet enlarges the pool of potential mates within socially preferred categories by reducing the factor of distance. As Sprecher (2009) puts it, people are likelier to find their perfect mate online than offline. Later in this chapter we talk about the impossibility of finding the "ideal" mate. Online dating potentially challenges this impossibility by introducing people to a massive database of potential mates. By giving each user a profile of potential partners, it allows daters to search and match based on these ideal traits. Internet dating also increases the potential for cross-cultural (i.e., inter-ethnic, inter-racial, and inter-religious) romance (Yum and Hara, 2005).

When people go online to find a mate, they are usually looking for qualities that could be found through traditional dating. The only difference is that these traits are revealed through the computer screen, not over dinner. Similarity remains the major predictor of early attraction for internet daters, as it does for face-to-face daters (Baxter and West, 2003). Participants online most often assess one another according to traits that have always been important to them for long-term relationships, such as physical attractiveness, income and occupation, hobbies, smoking status, and desire for children (Sprecher, 2009). These are the same traits that are important to traditional daters. There are, however, certain factors that are unique to online dating—notably, a different emphasis on response time, writing style, and honesty (Baker, 2007).

Men prefer ads where women claim intrinsic values—honesty, integrity, and the like—but they also emphasize looks and physical features (weight, height, ethnicity, even eye and hair colour) more than women do. In their advertisements, men use terms such as "attractive," "slender," "petite," or "sexy" much more often to describe the person they are seeking (Coltrane, 1998: 47; Smith, Waldorf, and Tremblath, 1990). In this sense, this method of mate-seeking may play to gender stereotypes even more than conventional mating practices. Sev'er (1990: 76) concludes, "Even in this unconventional market, the rules of the mating game have remained traditional. Women (especially older women) are at a disadvantage, both as choosers and as potential chosen. The personal ads market seems to be a traditional market in disguise, a new bottle for the same old wine." Or it could be that people placing personal ads are especially "consumer" oriented: They want to be assured of a good "product."

This is not to say that people insist on the qualities they initially look for; often, whatever their mating strategy, they settle for something else. For example, one study that found that men valued physical attractiveness more than women and women valued earning prospects more than men in their ideal romantic partner. But when the researchers followed up with participants to find whether these were the characteristics of the people they actually dated, they found that participants met and went on dates with people who differed from the stated ideals (Eastwick and Finkel, 2008). As we will see shortly, this is how reality works: We state ideals of perfection but act in ways that satisfy us, however imperfectly.

Myth: Older couples are likelier than other couples to express negative views about their partner, since they have lived together for a longer time and are well past the early infatuation stage of a romantic relationship.

- Reality: Older couples are likelier to view their partners positively and seem to develop an automatic response to handle negative traits in their partner. Older adults are therefore biased toward highlighting the positive aspects of their partner and their relationship (Story, Berg, Smith, Beveridge, Henry, and Pearce, 2007; Perunovic and Holmes, 2008).

Myth: Meeting people online is more dangerous than meeting people in the "real world."

- Reality: There are potential dangers associated with meeting people online, but Dr. Saltz, a relationship expert, has reported that online dating is no riskier than dating

people in the "real world" and that taking safety precautions are just as important in both situations (Mock, 2011). For example, some have counselled always meeting in a public area on the first few dates, and letting a friend know about your plans for the date.

Myth: People with disabilities are not interested in activities of a romantic or sexual nature.

- Reality: A Dutch study found that most young adults with cerebral palsy were interested in sex and fantasized about love-making (Wiegerink, Roebroeck, Van, Stam, and Cohen-Kettenis, 2010). They had fewer romantic relationships or sexual experiences than other young adults of the same age. However, they valued these things nonetheless and sought romantic and sexual experience by participating in peer groups.

Online personal ads have also become a popular method for gays, lesbians, and bisexuals to connect with one another. Due to their smaller total numbers, these groups often use the internet as a meeting space. A 2008 study found that gays, lesbians, and bisexuals are even likelier than heterosexuals to meet in person, have sex with, and have a long-term relationship with someone they meet online (Lever, Grov, Royce, and Gillespie, 2008).

SOCIAL ASPECTS OF FINDING A MATE

The term *marriage market* may seem too rational or cold-blooded a description of a process we tend to view as largely emotional. And yet, there is much that is market-like about finding a mate. We can think about mating in terms of exchanges, as discussed earlier. Each potential partner brings to the potential relationship something that is of value to the other: personality, skills, physical attractiveness, earnings potential, and so on.

Whether participants admit it or not, rating and ranking is part of the mate market. Meeting, mating, and marrying involve a giant sorting process whereby our "market values" are matched with the market values of others. It can be a cold calculation, as when, for example, a man seeks a wife who will "look good on his arm." We call such women "trophy wives," for their purely decorative value in the relationship. Interestingly, we do not have a name for the men who seek them. Sometimes their husbands match them well in terms of appearance and style, but sometimes they do not. The husband's allure in such relationships is typically his earning power, not his good looks.

A central part of the mate market is the politics of attractiveness. Good looks make a difference—for men and women, heterosexuals and gays—in getting attention in the mate market. Immense amounts of time, effort, and money go into the construction of attractiveness. Many women pluck, wax, and shave unwanted hair, and carefully groom the wanted hair. Through workouts and other unnatural processes, they shape and flatten unwanted bulges and enhance wanted ones. Men increasingly focus on their appearance as well, and the recently coined term *metrosexual* is used to describe a straight young man (typically city-dwelling and wealthy) who takes great interest in his image. Interestingly, the term was coined by advertisers looking to motivate men with money to shop. It has increased in popularity and become part of pop culture and a self-identification of many males who take pride in grooming.

People often use personal decoration as a means of communicating their status on the mate market. The engagement ring is one common example. A woman wears the ring as a symbol with dual meanings: She is desirable on the mate market, her intended mate makes sufficient money (or comes from sufficient family money), and she can be decorated well. This suggests that she will be "kept well" during their married life, and announces to all who see her ring that she has made a "good catch." This idea is supported by research on the amount men spend on engagement rings. A study found that men marrying younger women spent more. The same was true for men who earned more money and whose fiancées earned more money (Cronk and Dunham, 2007). This is consistent with the theory that the engagement ring is a symbol of mate quality.

In the mate market, flirting matters. It is still an important part of the meeting and mating scenario. Women in the past were expected to flirt with a blend of innocence and interest; the mix had to be exact, so as not to send unintended messages. However, the flirting script, like the dating market, has been considerably updated. Flirting before the 1990s was heavy on the innocence, light on the sexual suggestion. Now, the content is reversed, with women expected to be sexual in flirting, though not too aggressive (Coltrane, 1998: 34). Men tend to report that women display more sexual interest in cross-sex interactions than women admit to displaying. This has been explained by findings that behaviour that men view to be sexually motivated is attributed different motivations by women (Henningsen, Dryden, Braz, and Davies, 2008). So, it seems that flirting has a lot to do with views that are not always agreed upon by everyone involved.

Where people meet potential mates is also an important factor in mate selection. Lampard (2007) studied trends in where couples report having met. He notes that a decreasing number of couples report meeting in settings such as restaurants, bars, and clubs, while an increasing number of met at places of work and education (Lampard, 2007).

Dating Scripts, Double Standard, and Sexual Practices

A traditional sexual double standard was the premise for dating rituals (or "scripts") that existed in North America from about the 1920s through the 1950s and most of the 1960s (despite popular images of that decade as the era of "free love"). **Sexual scripts** saw boys as initiators, calling girls for dates and often paying for the date. Some of these expectations persist today; however, patterns of meeting and dating have changed over time. With greater equality between men and women, women are less likely to wait for the man to ask her out, although some women still wait for men to initiate dating. Often, also, the man still picks up the woman and pays for the first date (Serewicz and Gale, 2008). This persistent expectation is part of a traditional dating script.

The question remains whether wooing is more equal today than it was in the past. In some ways it is, since both sexes take initiative in singling out the person they especially like. However, a gender imbalance remains. Studies of first-date initiation still find that men are likelier than women to view a woman who asks a man out as showing sexual interest, or even being sexually forward (Mongeau and Carey, 1996; Serewicz and Gale, 2008). Women who initiate dates are also seen as being more sociable and more liberal, but less physically attractive than the person being asked. Despite a growing tendency toward more equality in dating initiatives, women who initiate dates are still viewed differently from men, who are expected to do the asking.

The media is included among the cultural factors that may play a role in the age of first sexual activity. There is constant alarm of the increasingly sexually overt nature of all types of media, specifically the manner in which women are represented. A recent longitudinal study found that media consumption matters when it comes to adolescent sex. The study found that, controlling for other factors, white teens who watched the most television when they were aged 12 to 14 were more than twice as likely to have had sex when they were 14 to 16 than those who watched the least television. The relationship was not significant for black youth. This was explained by more parental disapproval of teen sex and viewed permissive peer sexual norms (Brown, Bulanda, and Lee, 2005). Media influence sexual attitudes and behaviours among adolescents, but parents may serve to mediate that connection.

Fingerson (2000) discovered that parents, too, affect their teens' sexual behaviour (see Figure 3.2), but in terms of the teens' perceptions of parental beliefs about sexual behaviour, not the parents' own reported beliefs. In addition, having a good relationship and open communication with their mothers is associated with a lower likelihood of teens having sex and having fewer partners if they choose to have it. In contrast, Regnerus (2006) finds that among adolescents in intact, two-parent biological families, closeness of daughters to fathers rather than mothers postpones coital debut and reduces risky sexual behaviour. Nevertheless, the findings support the notion that parental monitoring, adolescents' *perception* of their parents' disapproval, and adolescent sexual attitudes

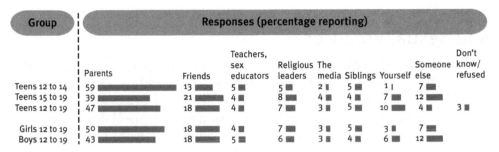

Group	Parents	Friends	Teachers, sex educators	Religious leaders	The media	Siblings	Yourself	Someone else	Don't know/ refused
Teens 12 to 14	59	13	5	5	2	5	1	7	
Teens 15 to 19	39	21	4	8	4	4	7	12	
Teens 12 to 19	47	18	4	7	3	5	10	4	3
Girls 12 to 19	50	18	4	7	3	5	3	7	
Boys 12 to 19	43	18	5	6	3	4	6	12	

NOTE: The percentages, as reported in *With One Voice 2007*, do not total 100 percent.

Figure 3.2 Parents remain influential regarding teens' decision about sex.

When asked, "When it comes to your decisions about sex, who is the most influential?" about half of high schoolers surveyed identified their parents. Older teens were likelier to be influenced by their friends.

Source: Albert, Bill. 2007. *With One Voice 2007: America's Adults and Teens Sound Off About Teen Pregnancy.* Washington, D.C.: The National Campaign to Prevent Teen Pregnancy. Retrieved from www.thenationalcampaign.org/resources/pdf/pubs/WOV2007_fulltext.pdf.

(mediated by parent–child communication) are important predictors of later age of sexual initiation (Regnerus, 2006). Overall, teens report that their parents are the biggest influence on their decisions about sex.

Men and women often differ in how they view sexual activity. These differing views, in turn, may affect how couples engage in sexual behaviour, which has important implications for dating. Knox, Zusman, and McNeely (2008) conducted surveys of undergraduate students in the United States. Among other findings, men and women disagreed about whether oral sex was sex, with men less likely to think so and women thinking the opposite. These findings were consistent with opinions of Canadian youth indicating that (only) 25 percent considered oral genital behaviour to be sex (Bersamin, Fisher, Walker, Hill, and Grube, 2007: 182).

The threat of AIDS and venereal diseases has a large influence on sexual practices. In the latter part of the twentieth century, sexually transmitted diseases (STDs) were widely known and reported to be a serious threat. The importance of using protection was emphasized during this period. Many young people mistakenly believed that heterosexuals were not vulnerable to AIDS. Perhaps this is part of the reason why a new wave of adolescents in the twenty-first century has been contracting HIV/AIDs at increasing rate.

Certain social groups (for example, low-income African American and Puerto Rican young adults in the United States) continue to engage in risky sexual behaviour despite the high prevalence of HIV/AIDS and STDs in their populations (Singer, Erickson, Badiane, Diaz, Ortiz, Abraham, and Nicolaysen, 2006). Interviews with a sample of these young adults uncover an underlying cultural logic being followed in their dating and mating lives. In particular, participants said their assessment of risk for STDs, and therefore their viewed need to use condoms, was based on beliefs about "who is safe" rather than "which behaviors are risky" (Singer et al., 2006: 1018).

Also, because of living in poverty, and fear and doubt about the future, women value having a relationship with a man who can provide access to essential resources more than they value being risk-free. So, the decision not to ask the partner to use a condom is sometimes based on a rational choice specific to an economic and cultural context. Yet sexual behaviour cannot be reduced to individual decision making based solely on health risks. Economic conditions, aspects of the social environment (neighbourhood disadvantage, class, or ethnic inequality), and psychosocial factors (internalized racism, living in fear) all play an important role in shaping group sexual behaviour.

Dating and Aging

Most sociological research focuses on the dating lives of adolescents and young adults, but a growing number of older adults are also dating these days. Clearly, however, adults and seniors are at a different point in their lives than adolescents, so different rules and priorities shape their dating activities.

Increasingly, seniors (65+ years of age) are a large segment of society and, therefore, a large part of the dating market. However, seniors face particularly pressing problems in relation to dating. As people age, they find it much harder to develop new relationships. Some obstacles include smaller social networks, retirement, relocation, and death of friends or loved ones (Alterovitz, Sheyna, and Mendelsohn, 2011). For women, the problems are even more pressing, as the pool of eligible dates shrinks considerably more than for men, since women live longer. This leaves a shortage of men at every age over forty. For people over 65 years of age, the sex ratio is roughly one man for every three women (Thies and Travers, 2006). Additionally, seniors are usually less willing to date outside their culture, race, or religion (Bulcroft and Bulcroft, 1991), thus eliminating even more potential partners. On the other side, seniors are reportedly more willing to travel substantial distances to meet a date (McIntosh et al., 2011).

We all know the qualities younger people look for in their mates (physical attractiveness, for example), and research shows that seniors look for many, though not all, of the same things. A study by Bulcroft and Bulcroft (1991) found that the main factor attracting seniors to one another was health and mobility. Age preferences of seniors, however, reflected youthful patterns: Men preferred younger women, and women preferred older men (though they preferred younger men after the age of 75) (Alterovitz, Sheyna, and Mendelsohn, 2011). The reason women preferred younger men after 75 was because they did not want to end up as caregivers.

A big difference between young daters and senior daters is the reversal of traditional dating roles. Among younger people, typically men tend to want casual relationships and women want serious ones. By contrast, among older people, men tend to approach dating with intentions of marriage, since they have grown accustomed to the stability and comfort that comes with it (Buss and Schmitt, 1993). By contrast, older women want to avoid these responsibilities and seek more casual relationships.

Dating in a Multicultural Society

As Canada and other countries become increasingly diverse, any discussion of meeting and mating must recognize the different habits of the cultures within a country. In Canada especially, immigrants make up a large part of modern society, and children of immigrants, whether born in Canada or in their home country, are one of the fastest-growing populations. According to King and Harris (2007), since this demographic shift is so recent, researchers today know little about the social development of these youth during the critical life stage when dating and mating occur. Most of the sociological research on ethnic romantic interactions focuses on sexual behaviour (Raffaelli and Ontai, 2001, for example).

Many factors are associated with the dating practices of immigrants in their new country. To date people of a different culture, language competence is a precondition. Other factors include the interrelationship of a person's cultural background, family beliefs and values, and the expectations of peers in their school or community in shaping romantic relationships. This is because norms of the cultural tradition may be at odds with the norms of Canadian society regarding the ways young people date and select partners (Howell et al., 2001: 135). Research shows that first-generation adolescents are less likely to enter romantic relationships than adolescents in native-born families (King and Harris, 2007).

There are many reasons why immigrant youth date less often than their peers. Many new immigrant families have less money or many dependent relatives and are isolated from society for linguistic reasons (King and Harris, 2007). All of these factors increase the likelihood that an immigrant teenager will have more household responsibilities than his or her peers and therefore less time for dating. However, those immigrant adolescents who do decide to engage in romantic relationships do so as readily as any host-country youth, most likely because they are more integrated in the culture of their new country.

Many immigrants come from cultures in which youth have little say in choosing their dating partners and long-term mates. Even if their families are not as traditional as others in the same culture, they are likely to be more rigid in their beliefs than are families of North American adolescents. For many immigrants, attitudes toward women and dating are seen as indicators of a successful transmission of culture (Dasgupta, 1998). Many young women, such as those in the study by Espiritu (2001) of Filipino immigrants, believe that abstaining from casual intercourse is declarative of their moral superiority over the dominant culture of the West. However, this study also shows that this outlook may be enforced by a patriarchal society to restrain girls from seeking autonomy.

Sometimes, children follow the cultural rules and practices taught to them by their parents. In one study, groups of Chinese and European Canadians were asked to respond to a scenario in which a young adult was having a conflict with his parents over inter-racial dating. In reviewing this scenario, Chinese Canadian respondents gave much more support to the parents than European Canadians, who gave more support to the choice of the young adult (Uskul, Lalonde, and Cheng, 2007).

In other cases, some parents who control or oversee their children may be increasing the likelihood that the children will go against their family's wishes and engage in unwanted romantic relations (King and Harris, 2007). If immigrants have close friends that date, they are much likelier to do so as well. One study found that Russian immigrant girls in Israel with many immigrant friends were likelier to date Israeli boys (Eisikovits, 2000). Another study found the same for girls with Israeli friends (Remennick, 2005).

Increased immigration and ethnic diversity in Canada and other countries predicts that we will see even greater shifts in dating and mating practices in the future (Zhenchao and Lichter, 2007). One effect of growing up in a multicultural society and an ever-growing change in dating and mating is the rise of interracial dating. Increasing acceptance of interracial dating (see Figure 3.3) may also be contributing to this trend. Overall, interracial marriage is rare. In the United States, only 4 percent of marriages are between couples of different races (Fisman and Iyengar, 2008). It is likely that this indicates a general tendency for people to seek mates within their own race, but marriage is the result of a lengthy search that may involve several interracial potential partners.

In many cultures, parents are concerned about the background of their children's partner and try to exert some influence over their choice. This parental tactic is sometimes successful. In general, groups that are especially concerned about their ethnic community's survival place a premium on dating others from within the same ethnic group. For example, this is the case among Jews in Canada (Weinfeld, 2001). Similar findings can be found across most ethnic groups.

However, not all children respond to their parents' wishes, and intergenerational conflicts can occur. A comparison of women born and raised in India with women of Indian descent raised in the United States finds that some believe Indian women raised

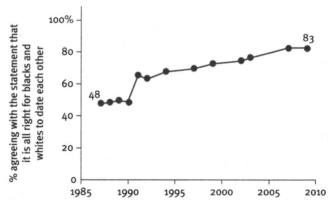

Figure 3.3 Change in Acceptance of Interracial Dating, United States, 1987–2009

Source: PEW Research Centre-Social and Demographic Trends, "The Rise of Intermarriage: Rates, Characteristics Vary by Race and Gender," February 16, 2012. http://www.pewsocialtrends.org/files/2012/02/SDT-Intermarriage-II.pdf.

in the United States are "not Indian enough" on issues regarding marriage and dating, because of their assimilation of U.S. beliefs (Srinivasan, 2001). Similarly, among Asian American college students, intergenerational conflicts about dating and marriage are more common among immigrant families than U.S.–born families (Gim Chung, 2001). Growing up in a multicultural society widens the number of available cultures in which one can find dates.

A 1995 study of black, Latino, and white people found interracial dating in more than 50 percent of each ethnic group (Tucker and Mitchell-Kernan, 1995). More recently, it seems that younger, more educated, more popular people are engaging in interracial dating (Fleras and Elliott, 2003). A study of student dating at one U.S. university found that 66 percent of students interviewed had been involved in an intercouple (that is, inter-faith, intercultural, or interracial) relationship at some time. This practice is increasing in most in university towns and large cities where diverse populations come together.

Same-Sex Dating

Much like interracial dating, same-sex dating is becoming more mainstream and accepted. One instance was even covered by the media extensively, leading to the production of a TV movie about the case: *Prom Queen: The Marc Hall Story*. Marc Hall, a student at Monsignor John Pereyma Catholic high school in Oshawa, Ontario, was prohibited from bringing his 21-year-old boyfriend to the prom. Officials from the Durham Catholic District School Board admitted that Hall had a right to be gay, but proposed that allowing the date would send a message that the Church supported his "homosexual lifestyle." On May 10, 2002, Ontario Superior Court Justice Robert McKinnon ruled that a gay student had the right to take his boyfriend to the prom. Hall went to the dance (CBC News, 2005).

Where gays and lesbians meet and mate has changed over time. In 1990, gay bars were the most common first meeting place, regardless of whether people were looking for a short- or long-term relationship (Berger, 1990). Today, there are many other avenues open to gay and lesbian youth, including well-established subcultural institutions (bars and nightclubs, theatres, comedy clubs, gay travel tours, and so on), and internet dating.

However, so far, little research has been done comparing same-sex and opposite-sex dating practices.

Homogamy

The theory of **homogamy** proposes that people tend to fall in love within their own social group, as defined by class, educational level, religion, and race or ethnicity. This tendency of like marrying like—also referred to as *assortative mating*—is found for a wide variety of characteristics: age, geographic location, various physical traits and overall physical attractiveness, and mental traits, including attitudes, opinions, and personality (Buss, 1985).

There are good reasons people tend to be homogamous. First, **propinquity (closeness) theory** states that people are likelier to find a mate among those with whom they associate.

Given the social circles within which we move, we are likelier to meet others who are (at least socially) like ourselves than to meet people unlike ourselves. Second, we like people who think the way we do and act the way we expect them to; indeed, we feel comfortable in their presence. Third, instrumental and expressive exchanges are easier to balance when like is marrying like. That's because people are bringing similar, therefore more equal, qualities and resources to the marriage.

Educational and Other Status Homogamy

Some characteristics of prospective mates are more important than others in determining mate selection. For example, in our society, education—an achieved status—is a more important criterion in the selection of marriage partners than social class origins, which

There is an increasing prevalence of people who marry spouses of the same or similar educational attainment, most likely because of extended education and post-graduate programs.
Gina Smith/Shutterstock

are ascribed (that is, inherited at birth). Educational homogamy has become the most relevant aspect of homogamy in Canada and the United States. Since 1960, educational homogamy has continued to increase. There is an especially strong decline in the odds that someone with low levels of education will "marry up" educationally—that is, marry someone with more education.

Educational intermarriage continues to decline for those with "some college education" and those with more. Instead, college graduates are much likelier to marry each other, rather than others with less education (Schwartz and Mare, 2005). There may be several explanations for this, including the increased importance of educational attainment for upward mobility, and the increased numbers of young people who prolong their education through secondary school, college, or university, and even post-graduate programs. These young people who spend a longer period of time within these institutions are likelier to meet and date people in the same settings who often have similar interests.

Age Homogamy

In the days when marriage meant financial security, women tended to look for a financially secure man who could provide for them. That meant that it was the older, more established, and more mature men who were deemed suitable as marriage partners by younger women. This age difference persists even today. It could be said that with the gender gap in earnings potential, marriage is still a matter of security for many women who cannot earn as much by their own labours in the market as they can by marrying someone with higher earning power. However, this is not likely the best explanation.

Age difference can reflect different power and experience. This difference can mean that men exercise greater financial leverage in marriage. The younger partner may be in a weaker bargaining position. It is also probable that if the man is a little older, his career is more established, and that sets the course for the marriage in terms of who is likely to follow whom for a job, promotion, or transfer.

Research finds that when people remarry after divorce, there is less age homogamy in the remarried relationship. Findings show that both men and women tended to remarry someone younger than themselves (Gelissen, 2004).

Whatever reasons there may be for marrying someone of older, younger, or similar age, in Canadian society today, people do not tend to have strong preferences one way or another. Age plays less of a determining role in a relationship than in the past. This marks a major difference worth noting in marriage patterns: the decline of a marriage gradient. First proposed by sociologist Jessie Bernard (1973), the **marriage gradient** meant that people sorted themselves into couples not only by age but also by differential status. Men, on average, married women with a little less education or a lower occupational status than their own, following this pattern.

Today, the marriage gradient is much less marked, but it persists in some societies and in some more-traditional ethnic groups; and there, it often gives rise to difficulties. The world comprises men and women of all statuses, so there are bound to be some men

- Little more than half of Canadian couples (58 percent) are three years apart or less in age, and just over 40 percent are four or more years apart (Boyd and Li, 2003).

- The average age for first marriages in Canada has increased over the past two decades. In 1980, women and men were 25.9 and 28.5 years old, respectively (CBC News, 2005). However, in 2000, it was reported that the average age for first-time marriage was 31.7 and 34.3 for women and men, respectively.

- Interracial marriage in Canada is on the rise. In 2006, there were 289 420 married and common-law mixed-race couples in Canada. This is one-third more than in 2001, when these data were first collected. In most of these interracial couples (85 percent), one partner is white and the other is from a visible minority group. The remaining 15 percent are couples in which both partners are from *different* visible minority groups (e.g., black and Asian).

- Common-law relationships have increased over the past few decades, but marriages still account for the majority of Canadian unions (CBC News, 2005). Specifically, in 2002, Canadian families consisted of 84 percent of married couples.

- In Canada, Japanese people are most likely to enter mixed-race unions (75 percent). Next are Latin Americans (47 percent) and blacks (41 percent). South Asian and Chinese people are least likely to form a union with a partner outside their own ethnic or racial group (Statistics Canada 2006a; CBC News, 2008).

and some women who are prevented from making marriage matches. But they are not the same kinds of people. Men left out of marriage by the marriage gradient are those at the bottom of the socio-economic ladder, for whom there is no one of lower status to marry. Women left out of marriage by the marriage gradient are those at the top of the ladder, for whom there is no one of higher status to marry.

This is currently causing significant problems in parts of East Asia, where woman are rapidly attaining high levels of education and high occupational status. Many lower-status men solve the problem of mate shortage by importing mail-order brides from poorer Asian countries.

When men and women pair off unequally by status and age, the impression is created that differences between men and women are larger than they are. It works like this: We see couples in which she is younger and lower in status than he is. Some people might conclude from this that there is a natural sex difference. In fact, social choices in marriage partners tend to exaggerate existing sex differences. By the marriage choices we make, we reproduce cultural prejudices about the natural abilities of women compared with men, in relation to education, wealth, and status.

Despite this marriage gradient, research shows great age and educational homogamy. This points to increasing age homogamy among people in their first marriages, and a parallel, though smaller, increase in the same direction in later marriages. The increasing age homogamy hints at a decline in women's reliance on men as "breadwinners."

Ethnic Homogamy

At the turn of the century, endogamy was strong for all North American ethnic groups. Ethnic homogamy was strongest for new immigrants from southern and eastern Europe, with weaker endogamy in the second generation (Pagnini and Morgan, 1990). Today, ethnic intermarriage is more common for all groups (see Figure 3.4). Second-generation European Canadians and Americans marry increasingly out of their ethnic group, and the ethnic boundaries that separate potential mates have weakened over time (Kalmijn, 1993). That's likely because people from different ethnic backgrounds are, during adolescence and early adulthood, attending educational institutions together. There, they meet and mate with others of similar educational status, typically regardless of ethnicity.

Between 1970 and 2000, the number of interracial marriages rose tenfold, with many saying that this signifies increasing status equality between Caucasians and minorities (Fu, 2008).

Between groups of equal status, people in interracial marriages tend to be from the higher strata of their group (Fu, 2008). This pattern of individual status matches results in the perpetuation of income and poverty inequality among ethnic groups. "Low-status minority families that carry on their racial and ethnic heritages through endogamy tend to have lower status within their group, while those with higher status tend to marry out and no longer carry the sole racial and ethnic heritage to the next generation. If this pattern persists, underprivileged minorities may suffer from low family resources across generations." (Fu, 2008: 152). In this way, intermarriage poses a social dilemma. On the one hand, it can foster greater acceptance between ethnic and racial groups, while at the same time preserving ethnically and racially defined social classes.

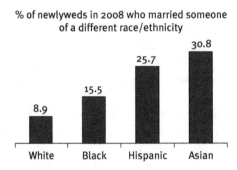

% of newlyweds in 2008 who married someone of a different race/ethnicity

White 8.9 Black 15.5 Hispanic 25.7 Asian 30.8

Note: "Newlyweds" refers to people who got married in the 12 months before the survey. All groups (other than Hispanic) are non-Hispanic single races.

Figure 3.4 Intermarriage Rates, by Race and Ethnicity

Source: Pew Research Center. Analysis of 2008 American Community Survey (ACS), based on Integrated Public-Use Microdata Series (IPUMS) samples.

Religious Homogamy

Sociological data also reveal weak and dwindling barriers to religious outmarriage (see Figure 3.5). Even among the Jews, a group that is especially concerned about its group survival, the high degree of homogamy is achieved largely by selection but also by increasing acceptance of religious conversion, before or after marriage (Weinfeld, 2001: 154–160).

Intermarriage between Protestants and Catholics has increased dramatically since the 1920s (Richard, 1991), showing that the social boundaries separating educational groups are stronger than religious or ethnic boundaries. In addition, interfaith marriages

CST	Interreligious unions less likely among Muslims, Hindus and Sikhs				
	1981	**1991**	**2001**		
Religious group			**Both sexes**	**Men**	**Women**
	% of population in couples who are interreligious unions				
Total	15	17	19	19	19
No religion	38	27	25	32	17
Catholic	12	14	16	15	17
Protestant	14	17	21	19	23
Mainline Protestant[1]	15	19	23	21	25
Conservative Protestant[2]	9	11	13	11	15
Other Protestant	15	22	25	23	27
Orthodox Christian	23	25	26	27	24
Christian n.i.e	19	18	18	15	20
Muslim	13	11	9	11	6
Jewish	9	12	17	19	16
Buddhist	19	16	19	16	22
Hindu	11	10	9	9	8
Sikh	4	4	3	4	3
Other Eastern Religions	26	24	27	25	29
Other Religions[3]	41	41	46	40	50

1. Mainline Protestant includes Anglican, Lutheran, Presbyterian, United Church.
2. Conservative Protestant includes Baptist, Pentecostal, Nazarene, Evangelical Free, Mennonite, Salvation Army, Reformed, Christian and Missionary Alliance and other smaller groups.
3. Other religions includes New Age, Aboriginal Spirituality, Pagan, Scientology, Satanist, Wicca, Gnostic, Rastafarian, Unity, New Thought, Pantheist and other small religious groups.

Note: Protestant breakdown is based on definitions by Nock, David A. 1993. "The organization of religious life in Canada," in *The Sociology of religion– A Canadian Focus*, edited by W.E. Hewitt, Toronto: Butterworths; and Bibby, Reginald W. 1987. " Fragmented Gods, The Poverty and Potential of Religion in Canada." Toronto: Stoddart Publishing Co. Ltd.

Figure 3.5 Interreligious Unions in Canada

Source: Statistics Canada, Census of Population. "Interreligious unions in Canada" by Warren Clark, 2006, Statistics Canada Catalogue No. 11-008.

have become increasingly homogamous with respect to education, showing that education has replaced religion as a key factor in spouse selection (Kalmijn, 1991). However, the freedom to marry a partner of a different faith often depends on how conservative the religion is. Again, using the example of Protestants, there is a much stronger preference for religious homogamy among conservative Protestants in comparison to mainline Protestants (Logan, Hoff, and Newton, 2008). The same principle probably applies to Catholics, Jews, and Muslims. Conservative or pious members of a religion are likelier to prefer religious homogamy and push their children in that direction.

The research on religious homogamy and its affect on marital satisfaction is mixed. However, in general, the link between religious homogamy and marital satisfaction seems to have weakened over the past 50 years. There has been an overall decline in perceptions of religious authority among younger generations, causing less importance to be placed upon religion and its traditions (Myers, 2006).

Similarity and Couple Happiness

The literature consistently shows that social similarity of partners promotes marital satisfaction. Homogamous couples are significantly more satisfied than dissimilar couples (Gaunt, 2006). This applies not only to age and religion but also to attitudes. A study of long-term committed couple relationships finds that agreement on a wide variety of issues is one factor that contributes to the longevity of the marriage, marital satisfaction, and overall happiness (Lauer, Lauer, and Kerr, 1990). Men and women whose attitudes diverge from those of their spouses are less satisfied with their marriages (Lye and Biblarz, 1993).

Different aspects of couple similarity may become more important depending on time and place. For example, studies have found that congruent religious beliefs are no longer significant predictors of marital satisfaction (Myers, 2006). This is a general finding, but we must be cautious about its applicability. More conservative members of religions would probably be likelier to highlight the importance of religious beliefs.

The Ideals of Mate Selection

Some believe that mating and marriage are about the capture and possession of "erotic property" (Collins, 1975). This view is consistent with what we have said so far about the role of romance in the mating process and can account for the complicated and unreal beliefs people hold about mating.

Experts who provide premarital counselling note a variety of unrealistic beliefs commonly held by people when choosing mates. They include the beliefs that

- people will find the perfect partner;
- there is only one good partner for each person;
- love is enough to smooth over the rough patches in a relationship;

- when all else fails, the mates will try harder and succeed; and
- opposites complement each other (that is, heterogamy is better than homogamy).

People tend to hold such beliefs because, for many, mate selection is the capture of erotic property, and people's ability to reason is often clouded by passion.

GENDER DIFFERENCES IN ATTRACTION

The gender difference is larger in self-report data than in observed social behaviour, yet men's preference for physical attractiveness, youth, and reproductive value in a mate is documented in many studies (Feingold, 1995). The results are similar no matter how we obtain the data: Whether by survey, experiment, or otherwise, findings consistently show the emphasis men place on physical attractiveness. A study examining speed-date behaviour found that women put greater weight on intelligence and race of a partner, while men respond more to physical attractiveness. Further, they found that men do not value women's intelligence or ambition when it exceeds their own (Fisman and Iyengar, 2006).

Both men and women may value inexperienced marriage partners, regardless of their own experience (Jacoby and Williams, 1985; Williams and Jacoby, 1989). However, Oliver and Sedikides (1992) found strong evidence of a double standard. For men, permissive partners may be attractive as dates but are less attractive as potential marriage partners.

Women prefer low levels of sexual permissiveness for both low- and high-commitment partners, rating permissive potential mates lower than non-permissive ones on both dating and marriage desirability. In casual mating opportunities, and when considering how to choose a long-term partner, undergraduate women are more selective than men overall. Especially important are status-linked variables and the anticipated investment of a partner in a relationship.

In a study of strategies used to attract mates, women tried to attract "investing" mates, who are willing to consider eventual parenthood, by acting chaste and stressing their fidelity. Men who showed more interest in eventual parenthood than other men attracted women by highlighting their own chastity, fidelity, and ability and willingness to invest (Cashdan, 1993). By contrast, non-investing men, and women who expected non-investing men as partners, flaunted their attractiveness and sexuality to draw in as many partners as possible.

Some of this gender difference may be a matter of mere self-presentation. An experiment by Hadjistavrolous and Genet (1994) found that women intentionally under-report the impact of physical attractiveness on their preferences. Connected to a lie detector–like apparatus, women undergraduates admitted being more strongly influenced by the physical attractiveness of potential male dating partners and gave lower desirability ratings to physically unattractive men. So, some of this gender difference is cultural, a result of what we are taught to say that we want, and not a biological difference between men and women.

One might expect that women's attainment of higher education—and more direct access to their own economic resources—would reduce such gender-based differences in mate choice, but survey results point to the opposite. Rather, consistent with what we've said about the strength of educational homogamy, higher education increases women's socio-economic standards for mates, thereby reducing their pool of acceptable partners (Townsend, 1990).

WHY PEOPLE DO NOT OPTIMIZE

Despite the ideals many hold about marriage, people do not seek an ideal or **optimal mate**. They do not try to optimize; rather, they satisfice. That is, they seek a "good enough" mate within the constraints life has handed them (March and Simon, 1958). The difference between optimizing and satisficing is the difference between searching a haystack for the sharpest needle and merely searching for a needle that is sharp enough to sew with. For most purposes, whatever satisfies us is ideal.

Suppose that, as an idealistic teenager, you had listed 10 qualities you felt you absolutely must have in a mate. If we assume that one in five people has each of these qualities, and the qualities you are looking for in a mate are uncorrelated, only one person in five to the 10th power—one in 9.8 million—will meet all your requirements. That may be less than one adult person of the right sex, aged 20 to 60, in all of Canada. Equally, there is only one chance in 9.8 million that your "perfect mate" will consider you the perfect mate. So, by this scenario, the chances of meeting and marrying the perfect mate are one in 9.8 million squared (or nearly zero).

Even more modest goals cannot be optimized. Suppose that, instead of needing your perfect mate to be among the top fifth in attractiveness, you need him or her to be only in the top half. You similarly lower your standards for your other requirements. This makes your mating problem more manageable: Now, you only need to look for that one "perfect" person in a thousand (that is, two to the 10th power).

With this in mind, you may try to solve the problem by reducing the number of qualities you look for in a mate. Suppose your potential mate has to excel in only one respect and satisfy you in four others. Now you and your perfect mate are each looking for someone who is in the top fifth in one quality and in the top half in just four other qualities. The likelihood of finding a person with the qualities you seek is one in 1250. The likelihood that you will satisfy his or her needs is also one in 1250. Even so, the chance of meeting and mating is still well below one in a million (that is, one in 1250 squared).

However you revise the list and extend your range and number of contacts, the chance of finding the perfect mate this way is nearly zero. Most people cannot and do not find a mate in this way. Rather, people fall in love with those who are close at hand. As in so many areas of life, we come to value what we know best and have available: people like ourselves. We become satisfied with the possible, not the ideal; and then we come to love the person who satisfies us.

It is also important to note that over the life course, as people face new experiences and life transitions, they tend to change their views about what constitutes a satisfactory mate. The man who was good for a teenage girl in high school would most likely not be considered good when that same woman is older and looking to start a family. To form good long-term relationships, people need to search for someone who will satisfy them across the life course and not just be satisfactory for a specific point.

Whether we choose homogamous or heterogamous (intermarriage) mates depends on what kinds of people are available nearby. That explains why our chances of mating with people of other religious, ethnic, and racial groups increase when we have more contact with them. People marry others who are socially and geographically near, even if "better" mates can be found much farther away.

DATING VIOLENCE

Unfortunately, every discussion of dating and mating must include a discussion of interpersonal violence. This is ironic because, as we said at the beginning of this chapter, dating in our society is charged with romantic illusion and emotional intensity.

Dating and Mating Trends

- The term *hooking up*, commonly used by young adults, is deliberately left ambiguous, telling us little about what sort of intimate activity it describes (Bogle, 2008). This ambiguity allows young adults to adhere to the traditional sex roles of our society. Girls can use the term to downplay their sexual experience while boys can use it to pretend greater sexual expertise.

- In seeking mates, men tend to put the highest priority on facial attractiveness in long-term relationships while putting the highest priority on bodily attractiveness in short-term relationships (Confer, Perilloux, and Buss, 2010). Women, on the other hand, tend to show no preference for facial or bodily attractiveness in their choices.

- College/university students reportedly use cigarettes as part of their mating strategy (Jones, Figueredo, and Aurelio, 2007). Specifically, students who are actively looking for a mate are likelier to smoke—or at least try to smoke—cigarettes in social settings.

- Both men and women use conspicuous consumption as a mating strategy, as it gives them an opportunity to show off their wealth, status, and taste (Sundie, 2003). Indeed, people seeking a short-term sexual partner—men particularly—are most likely tend to engage in conspicuous consumption, compared with people seeking a long-term marriage partner.

- Compared to men, women are more likely to want to be asked for consent before sexual involvement (Humphreys and Herold, 2007).

- Men and women typically have different mating goals when they use online dating websites. Research shows that women mainly use online dating in search of a long-term partner, while males more often use it to build casual relationships (Alam, Yeow, and Loo, 2011).

- As adolescents grow older, they are likelier to engage in sexual intercourse but also likelier to use a condom when they do so (Saewyc, Taylor, Homma, and Ogilvie, 2008).

The U.S. National Violence Against Women Survey has been conducted several times in the past few decades. The survey asks 8000 female and 8000 male participants detailed questions about experiences of violence in intimate relationships (Tjaden and Thoenness, 2000). The most recent findings stem from the survey conducted in 2000, showing that partner violence is pervasive, especially for women: 25 percent of women and 7.5 percent of men reported being raped or physically assaulted by a partner.

Estimates from the survey show nearly 1.5 million women in the United States are raped or physically assaulted annually. This, however, is not consistent with findings from the National Family Violence Survey, which consistently reports that men and women are equally likely to be physically assaulted. A survey by sociologists Walter DeKeseredy and Katharine Kelly (1995) conducted on 44 college and university campuses across Canada found four women in five saying they had been abused by a dating partner, with nearly as many men admitting having done so. This shows the importance of recognizing that women also commit acts of physical violence, a fact often ignored by popular conceptions of abuse.

We will have more to say about domestic violence, in Canada and elsewhere, in a later chapter. As will then become apparent, research on this topic is significantly hindered by disputes about the definition and measurement of domestic violence.

Unfortunately, emotional abuse is often accompanied by physical violence. The survey found that women whose partners were jealous, controlling, or verbally abusive were significantly likelier to be raped, physically assaulted, or stalked. These findings show that education and treatment should target emotional abuse just as seriously as physical abuse.

The survey also examined violence among gay and lesbian dating partners, finding that lesbian couples were significantly less likely to experience violence, while the opposite was true for gay men. Men in homosexual couples experienced more partner violence than men in opposite-sex partnerships. This would support the findings that dating violence is perpetrated mainly by men. However, more research is needed on same-sex relationships.

Young people are beginning their sex lives at much earlier ages, which increases the general susceptibility to dating violence. People who are dating, not married or in a committed relationship, are also especially vulnerable to partner violence. There is a gap in the willingness of boys and girls, men and women, to report dating violence. Girls are much likelier to report physical violence and psychological abuse in dating relationships than boys (Swahn, Simon, Arias, and Bossarte, 2008). This is related to general social views about male and female roles and ideas surrounding violence.

Men are most often the perpetrators of violence in dating relationships (see Figure 3.6), but girls are sometimes also perpetrators of violence, a fact that must not be ignored in education on violence prevention and coping.

Where violent abuses are concerned, women are more than twice as likely as men to admit their occurrence. Where less violent abuses are concerned, men and women admit

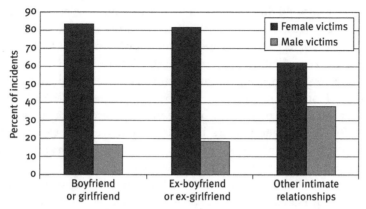

Figure 3.6 Females most likely victims of dating violence, 2008.

Source: Statistics Canada, "Police-reported dating violence in Canada, 2008. By: Tina Hotton, Mahony, 2010.

them equally often. The 2004 General Social Survey (Statistics Canada, 2005c), the most comprehensive survey on family violence in Canada, found a clear inconsistency in the reports by women and men. This consistent difference leads to one of three possible conclusions: (1) Violent and abusive men date a lot more women than gentle, non-abusive men; (2) women tell a lot of lies about their dates; or (3) many men are ashamed to admit the things they have done to their dates and therefore lie. The third option seems the most probable based on what we know as sociologists.

These disturbing findings reveal that violent abuse on dates is not only physical but also sexual. Date rape is a growing concern among sociologists. But in this area of research, getting good data is difficult, because young men and women disagree about what happens on dates. Bear in mind, too, that most instances of forced sexual activity occur between people who know each other, so there may sentiments of liking as well as fear attached to these experiences.

The result is, too often, that women blame themselves for the experience. Since they know the assailant, they often react passively to the sexual assault and thus blame themselves for not reacting more forcefully. A few even continue the dating relationship. Some girls tolerate sexually coercive behaviour because non-physical coercive tactics are seen as socially acceptable. For example, many girls find it hard to deal with being verbally pressured into unwanted sex because verbal pressure is not identified as overt abuse. However, the results are real. Verbal sexual coercion is associated with relationship dissatisfaction and troubles with sexual functioning that each lead to further negative consequences (Katz and Myhr, 2008).

Social position plays a factor in dating violence. Foshee and colleagues (2008) found that adolescents from minority families, single-parent families, or whose parents have lower educational attainment report significantly more experiences of physical dating violence. Typically, this also connotes an acceptance of dating abuse and gender stereotyping in less-educated, minority populations (Foshee et al., 2008).

Research on the effect of low socio-economic status on the risk of dating violence is divided (see O'Keefe, 1998; Lavoie et al., 2002). There is some evidence that good parenting (satisfactory supervision, fostering a sense of closeness, and provision of support) can reduce the risk of dating violence by promoting self-esteem in the adolescent. These relationships, in turn, are conditioned by parental socio-economic status (Pflieger and Vazsonyi, 2006). Low-income families have fewer resources and experience more life stressors, which lead children to experience low levels of self-esteem and externalize their feelings by venting their frustrations outside the home.

Adolescents with low self-esteem may interpret their dating partner's actions more negatively or as a personal rejection. Poor relationships with their parents, especially lack of closeness to their mothers, may also result in an inability to effectively deal with complex emerging emotions and conflicts. So, the likelihood of endorsing dating violence beliefs and acting on them is greater among low-income families.

CONCLUDING REMARKS

Mating, and especially marriage or a long-term, committed relationship, gives people the chance for both greater life satisfaction and deeper dissatisfaction than single life normally does. If you marry, you will probably increase your standard of living and longevity, especially if you are a man. Marriage has riskier, less predictable outcomes for women, especially when there are children involved or when women lack skills that would allow them to earn a living. Men gain the most from a marriage that works, and women—especially mothers and poorer women—lose the most when a marriage fails.

Deciding whether to marry should mean assessing your relationship realistically. If you think there is too much fighting and not enough hugging in your relationship, marriage will not solve the problem. As we will see in a later chapter, the "enchanted newlywed" period is normally followed by many years of declining marital satisfaction, especially if children are present. The typical marriage may worsen before it starts to improve. Most important, flee a relationship that is marked by physical or emotional violence. The violence is likely to recur. You are not to blame, and your partner is not likely to change.

Do people get what they want from mating and marriage? On the one hand, the range of possible choices is wider than ever: People are increasingly free to marry or not to marry, to have the kinds of relationships they want, and to choose their own mate. On the other hand, what we want is patterned by our social experience. People learn to want marriage as the preferred form of adult life. We mate with people who are nearby and socially like ourselves, not with "ideal" mates. However, we can grow to think our partner is, in fact, the "perfect" mate.

CHAPTER SUMMARY

The way we choose a mate has changed from when romantic love emerged during the Middle Ages. As we look at our dating and mating rituals in the courtly love tradition, we see the origins of the sexual scripts of men and women. These dating rituals contributed to a sexual double standard in which boys were the initiators and girls were the receivers of romantic attention. Love is the ideal basis of a marriage in the Western tradition, but in other traditions a material exchange is more important. What happens during the process of arranging a marriage is different from what happens to those in the marriage market looking for a love marriage; however, in both cases an exchange takes place.

We compare our marketability on the basis of physical features, earning potential, and personality; we search for "the one" on campus, in workplaces, among friends, on the internet, or on holiday. As we select our mates, it is clear there are rules about whom we may date and whom we are most likely to date and mate with.

Like marrying like, or homogamy, is one way the exchange process of dating becomes apparent. Similarity seems to play a large role in whom we choose to mate with. Educational homogamy has increasingly become an important factor in dating. Couple happiness is deeply connected to the social similarity of the partners.

Dating and mating sometimes end in violence. Sociologists face many problems in getting reliable data about violence, because men and women are unlikely to report it, whether as perpetrator or as victim. Sexual harassment is a too common experience for many Canadian women.

Key Terms

endogamy Marriage to a member of one's own tribe or social group.

exogamy Marriage outside of one's own tribe or social group.

expressive exchange An exchange of emotional and sexual benefits.

homogamy The selection of a mate with similar social attributes, such as class, education level, religion, race, or ethnicity.

instrumental exchange An exchange of practical and useful benefits, such as unpaid work or financial support.

marriage gradient A systematic difference between mates, such that men are typically older and of higher social or economic status than their female partners.

monogamous Married to one person for life.

optimal mate One's theoretical ideal mate.

propinquity (or closeness) theory A theory of mate selection that people are likelier to find a mate among those who are geographically nearby.

romantic love An idea of love that is influenced by idealistic concepts of mating, like chivalry and a search for one's soul mate.

sexual double standard The application of different rules, or standards of sexual behaviour, to men and women.

sexual scripts Attitudes and activities that a culture links to each gender, or that are typically expected of members of a particular gender in regard to dating.

Critical Thinking Questions

1. What two forms of exchange occur between spouses according to the exchange theory of mate selection?

2. Why do some people choose to participate in mate selection online instead of through more traditional methods? Is it possible to form a serious relationship using the internet?

3. In what ways do parents influence the sexual behaviour of teenage children?

4. What are some obstacles facing older adults who wish to find new intimate relationships?

5. What are the different types of homogamy? Specifically, discuss educational homogamy and the effect it may have on social inequality and social segregation.

6. What unrealistic beliefs do people possess about choosing mates? Why do these beliefs persist, despite evidence to the contrary?

Weblinks

New Directions
www.newdirections.mb.ca
This non-profit agency funded by the United Way provides information on families and parenting.

Second Wives Club
www.secondwivesclub.com
This site provides an array of articles, information, and discussion for remarried women and stepmothers, as well as links to other family- and woman-oriented advice and information sites.

Match.com
www.match.com
This dating site caters to all types of singles in many areas, including lesbian and gay people.

Matchmaker.com
www.matchmaker.com
This fun, less traditional dating service allows you to participate in a trial match without spending money or giving away personal information. The site categorizes its participants by gender, sexual orientation, expected level of commitment, and ethnic and religious backgrounds. Ironically, it does not sort its participants by occupation or interests/hobbies.

Do Something
www.dosomething.org
This site encourages teens to become empowered agents of change in their own communities and includes a large section on dating violence aimed at adolescents. The Teen Dating Bill of Rights and Pledge encourages respect and responsibility in relationships.

Family Violence: A Fact Sheet from the Department of Justice Canada
http://canada.justice.gc.ca/eng/pi/fv-vf/facts-info/fv-vf/fv2-vf2.html
This site provides information on various topics related to family violence, including spousal abuse and dating violence. It also provides suggestions on preventing family violence and links to resources.

About: People and Relationships
http://about.com/people
This site provides a vast array of information, including data on dating and relationships, marriage, divorce, homosexual life, and senior life.

Chapter 4
Types of Intimate Couples
Marriage, Cohabitation, Same-Sex Relationships, and Other Forms

Inti St Clair/Blend Images/Getty Images

Chapter Outline

Learning Objectives

1 Describe what constitutes close relationships.

2 Assess how important intimacy is, or is not, in achieving and maintaining a healthy life.

3 Identify different intimate relationships and evaluate their impact on Canadian society.

4 Analyze data to determine the trends in various types of close relationships.

5 Identify changing social perceptions toward what constitutes a partnership or family.

6 Examine the legal implications of divorce and separation on family relations.

7 Define important family and relationship issues for older Canadians.

8 Explore the effect of Canada's immigration policies on families and family reunification.

Intimacy and the changing trends in intimate unions is one of the fastest-growing areas of theory and research in sociology (see Giddens, 1992; Smart, 2007). In intimate couple relations, sociologists argue, the family is being redesigned. Intimacy involves a mix of emotion, caring, and often interdependency—none of which are well understood by sociology. We will have much more to say about this in the next chapter. In this chapter, we explore whether it matters what form intimacy takes.

The importance of having a long-term intimate relationship may be both greater and lesser than it was historically (see Bawin-Legros, 2004). Personal need and social pressures continue to push us to find a close intimate partner with whom to share our lives. Most young people consider this a top- (or near-the-top-) priority life goal (Bibby, 2001; Vanier Institute of the Family, 1994), and 90 percent of Canadian teens plan to marry, have children, and stay with the same partner for the rest of their lives (Bibby and Wayne, 2004). People are very interested, as we have seen, in finding a long-term intimate relationship. Less emphasis, however, is placed on helping the partnerships work well once matches are made, as we saw in Chapter 3.

We live longer now than in the past, so a lifetime commitment involves a much longer period than it did for your grandparents. When marriage for life often meant 20 to 30 years, most of which were spent having and raising large families, couples had a different kind of intimate relationship. Now, couples may spend years childless, then have children, and find that they still have a lifetime together after the children leave home. Being a close couple for a lifetime is a different prospect now in an aging Canada, and it continues to change (see Katz, Peace, and Spurr, 2012).

Today, more people live in families without an ongoing close personal relationship. Long life expectancy and family changes increase the likelihood of spending a significant portion of one's life, perhaps at different periods, outside a couple relationship.

Official definitions of family, as discussed in Chapter 1, rely on some concept of an ongoing intimate relationship. Despite the immense changes that have occurred, governments still define families in terms of legal or semi-legal relationships and shared residence, not in terms of what they share and what they do for each other. This, however, is contested by some sociologists (see Smart, 2007; or Vanier Institute of the Family, n.d.).

Twenty-five years ago, the Tax Guide for Canada had no definition of "spouse"; none was needed to guide people in preparing their tax returns. By the end of the 1990s, a full page in the guide was devoted to defining *spouse*. In 2013, the Canadian government developed clear definitions of marital status, with "spouse" being a partner to whom you are legally married, while "common-law" partner refers to a person *who is not your spouse* with whom you are living in a conjugal relationship and to whom at least one of the following applies. He or she is someone who

1. has been living with you in such a relationship for at least 12 continuous months
2. is the parent of your child by birth or adoption
3. has custody and control of your child (or had custody and control immediately before the child turned 19 years of age), and your child is wholly dependent on that person for support (Canada Revenue Agency, 2013)

The definition of *spouse* has expanded to incorporate different types of unions in which the members are not traditionally classified as "partners." This reflects society's adaptability and malleability in recognizing and catching up with the changing nature of intimate relationships in Canada.

INTIMATE RELATIONSHIPS: MORE DIVERSE AND MORE COMPLEX TOO

Rates of traditional marriage are declining. Married couples dropped from 70.5 percent of all Census families in 2001 to 67.0 percent in 2011 (Statistics Canada, 2012a). That is not to say, however, that the proportion of people who are in intimate relationships is also declining. In fact, the number of common-law-couple families rose from 13.8 percent to 16.7 percent in the same decade (Statistics Canada, 2012a). These are significant changes from two decades ago, when common-law-couple families accounted for only

7.2 percent of all Census families, while married-couple families represented 80.2 percent (Statistics Canada, 2007a). In 2011, for the first time, the number of common-law couples in Canada surpassed the number of lone-parent families (Statistics Canada, 2012a). Deviance from past trends in intimate unions is further exemplified by the inclusion of same-sex married couples for the first time in the 2006 Census.

The 2011 Census represented the first five-year period during which same-sex couples could legally marry. A total of 64 575 same-sex-couple families were reported in that year, up 42.4 percent from 2006. In 2006, 16.5 percent of same-sex couples were married, while by 2011 this number had nearly doubled to 32.5 percent (Statistics Canada, 2012a).

Further highlighting the diversity of close relations in Canada is the variation of marriage rates in communities, For example, more than half of the total Aboriginal population has never married, while more than one-third is married (Frideres, in Cheal, 2007). More interestingly, the rates of divorce and separation in this population are comparable to that of non-Aboriginal Canadians (Frideres, in Cheal, 2007). These findings point to the role of cultural specificity of marital status among Canadians. As well, Canada's Aboriginal population is younger than its non-Aboriginal counterpart, a fact that partially accounts for these differences (Trovato, 2013; Statistics Canada, 2013).

Close relations are becoming more complex, too. There are many more households in Canada than in the past, for example, but fewer are family households (Statistics Canada, 2012a). This means that more Canadians live alone or with others in what they, and the 2011 Census, see as non-family households. For instance, since 2001, there has been a large increase in one-person households. In 2011, 27.6 percent of the total number of private households were one-person households, while only 8.4 percent were households of five or more persons (Statistics Canada, 2012b). Many of those living in non-family households maintain close relationships with someone not in their household; they may have a commuter marriage/relationship, for example, or (especially for young adults or older people) a significant other who does not share their home.

RELATIONSHIP TRENDS AND PATTERNS

Two seemingly contradictory trends characterize present-day marriage: growth in popularity of alternatives to marriage and the continuing popularity of marriage. Since the 1970s, there has been a persistent decline in rates of legal marriage in Canada. This trend continues (Statistics Canada, 2012a; 2012b) and data show that a lesser proportion of all families are married families. The crude marriage rate was 4.7 for every 1000 population in 2003, compared to the most recent peak of 7.0 in both 1988 and 1989 (Statistics Canada, 2004c). Further, the 2006 Census found that, for the first time ever, unmarried people aged 15 and older outnumbered legally married people in Canada. According to the 2011 Census, single people comprised 51 percent of those 15 years and older (see Figure 4.1; Statistics Canada, 2012c). While these are large changes, the fact remains that most men and women, even in Quebec where cohabitation rates are very high, do marry

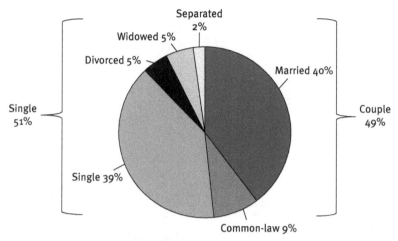

Figure 4.1 Population by Marital Status, 2011.

Source: Statistics Canada, 2012c. CANSIM, Table 051-0042. www.statcan.gc.ca/tables-tableaux/sum-som/101/cst01/famil01-eng.htm. Retrieved January 2013.

at some point. And when asked, most Canadians value marriage and want to get married (Vanier Institute of the Family, 2004). "From a longer-term perspective, Canadians are still hooked on legal marriage" (Vanier Institute of the Family, 2004: 23). No more recent information is available about the attitudes of Canadians. We need to consider, however, what else is happening in the formation of couple unions.

Age at Marriage

People marry later now than they did in the 1960s and 1970s. Even though those decades were supposedly a time of "free love," the age at marriage during that period was much lower than it had been for a long time, and lower than it has been since (about 22 years for women, 25 years for men; Ram, 1990: 80). The long-term trend toward postponement of marriage continues; by 2011, the latest data available, women were 29.1 years old on average at first marriage, and men were 31.1, as shown in Figure 4.2 (Statistics Canada, 2012).

The reasons for later marriage are complex and are related to social and economic opportunities and expectations as well as values. One factor is today's uncertain job prospects for young people. Compared to young people in the 1980s, young people in the 1990s and 2000s have lower cumulative earnings (Statistics Canada, 2002c), leading to speculation that postponement of union formation may be, in part, economic. Another factor seems to be people's desire to pursue non-family interests such as education, travel, or work, and the greater value placed on these options. Although young people still value marriage and family, as we have seen, they value marriage per se considerably less than older people. Younger people seem to prefer not to jump into marriage too early in their adult lives.

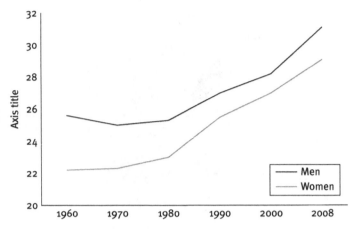

Figure 4.2 Average age at first marriage, by gender, 1960–2008

Note: Since 2003, the definition of marriage has been changed in some provinces and territories, and since 2005 for all of Canada, it includes the legal union of two persons of the same sex. Age at first marriage for same-sex couples has been higher than for opposite-sex couples.

Source: For 1921 to 1987: Statistics Canada. *Marriage and conjugal life in Canada.* Ottawa: Statistics Canada, 1992. (Cat. No. 91-534E); for 1988 to 1999: Statistics Canada, Demography Division; for 2000 to 2004: Statistics Canada. *Mean age and median age of males and females, by type of marriage and marital status, Canada, provinces and territories, annual* (CANSIM Table 101-1002). Ottawa: Statistics Canada, 2008; and for 2005-2008: Statistics Canada. Canadian Vital Statistics, Marriage Database and Demography Division (population estimates), Ottawa: Statistics Canada, 2012. http://www4.hrsdc.gc.ca/.3ndic.1t.4r@-eng.jsp?iid=78#M_2.

Types of Marriage

Broadly defined, **marriage** across the world is a socially approved sexual and economic union between two or more people that is expected to last for a long time. People often enter this union with public formalities or a ceremony, such as a wedding.

In Canada, traditional forms of marriage and the family are experiencing dramatic change. Because the family is such a basic institution, and marriage is such an intimate relationship, change can seem threatening. Yet there is no single universal or necessary form of couple relationship. In order to understand the change in our own society and what it may predict for the future, we will take a larger view of the institution of intimate couples and the many ways societies organize marriage-like arrangements.

In some societies, people wed more than one mate at a time. **Polygamy** is the generic name for this arrangement. Within this general category, **polyandry** is the marriage of one woman to more than one man, and **polygyny** is the marriage of one man to more than one woman. Polygamy was common in many pre-industrial societies and is still permitted in a few. But polygamy is banned in all industrial societies. That said, it is practised still, most notably among some fundamentalist isolated religious groups and among some recent immigrants from countries where polygamy is accepted (Bala, 2009).

Polyandry, on the other hand, has always been a rare form of marriage. It occurs in societies like Nepal, where living conditions are harsh, and few men are able to support a wife and children on their own (see Suwal, 2003). A woman is therefore "shared" by a group of men—usually, brothers—and she is a wife to all of them. Female infanticide is practised, justified by the argument that the number of women "needed" in such a society is much less than the number of men. Anthropologist Marvin Harris (1997) suggests that societies with low population pressure (the relation between population density and arable land) favour polygyny; societies with high population pressure favour polyandry. Policies and laws on polygamy in Canada are being considered in light of the open practice in a small southern community in British Columbia and the possibility that refugees or immigrants to Canada may have foreign polygamous marriages (Bala, 2009; Beeby, 2006).

Monogamy—marriage between one woman and one man—is the form most familiar in Canada. However, variations on monogamy are also becoming more common, such as **cohabitation**, or non-marital couples, and same-sex couples. Another form is what sociologists have called **serial (sequential) monogamy**. Serial monogamy is the marriage of a person over the life course to a series (or sequence) of partners, though only one at a time. In a society with high rates of divorce and remarriage, a growing number of people practise serial monogamy.

Is Marriage Still Valued?

Despite changes in timing and permanence, marriage continues to be central to interpersonal life in North America. See, for example, the popular book *The Case for Marriage: Why People Are Happier, Healthier, and Better Off Financially* by Linda J. Waite and Maggie Gallagher (2001). Cultural stereotypes and supports favouring traditional family life have not changed. Beaujot (2000) reports that Canadians typically see marriage as "natural" and believe it to be the foundation of family, as seen in Table 4.1. Also, the vast majority (85 percent) feel that marriage provides more advantages than singlehood (Beaujot, 2000: 108–9).

Yet, in the early 1990s, David Popenoe (1993) wrote a widely discussed article on the alleged "decline" of the family between 1960 and 1990. He attacked the devaluation of marriage and noted the increased acceptability and rates of divorce. He claimed that the psychological character of marriage had changed over the years; whereas before it was understood as a social obligation for economic stability and procreation, it was now seen as a path to self-fulfillment where couples enjoy a true companionship (Popenoe, 1993: 533). Popenoe claimed this led to a deinstitutionalization of marriage and expressed his concern about the impact of the relative fickleness of marriage today and the breakdown of the nuclear family on children.

Other sociologists have argued that the shape of marriage is simply changing, not declining. Stephanie Coontz (2005), for example, writes that today we are pioneers "picking our way through uncharted and unstable territory" (282–83). Further, she writes

Table 4.1   Top reasons why people marry and choose partners (2004)

Top 8 reasons people marry

Feeling that marriage signifies commitment

Moral values

Belief that children should have married parents

The natural thing to do

Financial security

Religious beliefs

Pressure from family

Pressure from friends

Top 10 characteristics people want in a partner

Honesty

Kindness

Respect

Compatibility

Humour

Dependability

Love

Values

Religious Community

Communication

Source: The Vanier Institute, 2012, "Families Count: Profiling Canada's Families IV, p. 48-49. http://www.vanierinstitute.ca/families_count_-_profiling_canadas_families_iv#.UaUlsdjm98G.

that marriage or other intimate relationships today are carried out within an economy and culture that allows for more individualistic choices than in the past and, thus, more based on respect and companionship (313).

Therefore, it may be the case that people today still value marriage enough to consciously make the choice to enter or stay in marriages even though divorce and cohabitation are socially accepted. This leads us to ask whether couples actually value marriage *more* than couples did in the past—couples who stayed together out of social duty rather than true happiness, love, and respect for each other.

Zheng Wu's (2000) study of cohabitation and marriage in Canada reveals that "there is clear evidence that people now place less emphasis on marriage than they did a decade ago ... The centrality of marriage seems to have weakened" (71). For example, the Statistics Canada 2001 General Social Survey found about one-half of mature singles (single men between the ages 30 and 55 and single women between ages 28 and 55) in Canada did not expect to marry. Among these groups, either the option of marriage was not seen as real, or love, marriage, and family did not have high priority (Statistics Canada, 2005d). Wu (2000) also notes that Canadians have become more accepting of non-marital sexual behaviour and non-marital cohabitation. As mentioned, common-law unions in the 2011 Census represented 16.7 percent of all Census families, up 13.9 percent since 2006, and up from 6 percent in 1981 (Statistics Canada, 2002g, 2007a, 2012a). In Quebec, the proportion of cohabiting relationships in 2011 was 31.5 percent of all Census families, comparable to levels in northern Europe.

People have individual reasons for choosing to live common-law rather than getting married, but the question remains whether the chosen difference ceases if law and policy make the two equivalent. A recent court decision in Quebec (the *Eric vs. Lola* case) ruled that cohabiting couples are not eligible for alimony (spousal support) when they separate (CBC, 2013). Their children, however, are expected to be provided child support. It should be noted that Quebec is governed by a different legal system and so this decision does not apply in the rest of Canada, A similar question occurs with respect to gay and lesbian unions. The differences between gay and straight relationships that may be valuable to some gay and lesbian partners could be seen as either diminished or enhanced now that the option of legal marriage exists (Canada, Department of Justice, 2005b). It is important to society to make gay and lesbian relationships equivalent to heterosexual relationships in terms of responsibilities and benefits. However, equivalence could lessen ways in which heterosexual relationships might benefit from being more like gay and lesbian couples, especially in partner equality. In this and subsequent chapters, we will consider gay and lesbian couples in various ways as vital family forms.

Changing Attitudes That Affect Marriage

In the 1960s, marriage was a social ritual by which young people were expected to declare their adulthood. Parents of baby boomers (children born between 1946 and 1964) epitomized this sentiment. These couples married in their early twenties and had lots of children—about twice as many as the generation before and the generation after!

The sexual revolution and the women's movement paved the way for changes in attitudes to sexuality and to women's place in the family and the economy. This shift in attitudes is reflected in changes in the timing, structure, and permanence of marriage. Marriage rates began to decline in the 1960s, declined rapidly in the 1970s, and have continued to decline at a slower rate since 1980. A slight recent decrease is currently seen across Canadian provinces, though not in British Columbia, Ontario, or the Yukon, where marriage rates have gone up (see Table 4.2). The proportion of adult years spent outside marriage has also changed, and it is higher than ever before. It began to rise as the average age at first marriage increased after 1960, a trend that continues today, as noted above.

Table 4.2 Marriage Rates by Province and Territory

	2002	2003	2002–2003	2003	2008
				crude marriage rate per 1,000 population	crude marriage rate per 1,000 population
	number		% change		
Canada	**146 738**	**147 391**	**0.4**	**4.7**	**4.4**
Newfoundland and Labrador	2959	2876	−2.8	5.5	5.3
Prince Edward Island	901	823	−8.7	6.0	6.8
Nova Scotia	4899	4742	−3.2	5.1	4.9
New Brunswick	3818	3724	−2.5	5.0	4.9
Quebec	21 987	21 138	3.9	2.8	2.9
Ontario	61 615	63 485	3.0	5.2	4.7
Manitoba	5905	5659	−4.2	4.9	4.7
Saskatchewan	5067	4977	−1.8	5.0	5.3
Alberta	17 981	17 622	−2.0	5.6	5.3
British Columbia	21 247	21 981	3.5	5.3	5.2
Yukon	143	158	10.5	5.2	4.0
Northwest Territories	144	139	−3.5	3.3	2.7
Nunavut	72	67	−6.9	2.3	2.5

Source: Statistics Canada website. 2007. Marriages. *The Daily.* Retrieved May 12, 2009, from www.statcan. gc.ca/daily-quotidien/070117/dq070117a-eng.htm, and Statistics Canada, 2011. Canadian Vital Statistics, Marriage Database and Demography Division (population estimates). http://www4.hrsdc.gc.ca/.3ndic.1t.4r @-eng.jsp?iid=78.

Many people still find the idea of legal marriage compelling, despite what they know about the realities of marriage and divorce. Enormous numbers of North Americans are neither rejecting the family or other long-lasting, close relationships, nor accepting family in a traditional form. Most are hoping to revitalize and reinterpret family (Baker, 2009; Beaujot, 2000; Scanzoni, 2000, 2001), suiting their families to themselves and their needs.

Efforts to reinterpret the family are reflected in the recent legalization of same-sex marriage. Reactions to the legislation, which had been proposed for some time before passing, reflected the clash between traditional and non-traditional conceptions of marriage. Those who view marriage as a sacred arrangement whose main purpose is procreation were upset initially by the use of marriage vows to legitimate same-sex relationships. Those who view marriage as an enduring close bond, the goal of which is love, companionship, and sex, were pleased to see the ceremonial forms made available to a wider range of people who care for each other deeply. Interestingly, now that same-sex marriage has been legal throughout Canada since 2005, these debates are seldom heard.

Living Solo

Most North Americans today postpone marriage or establishment of a long-term committed relationship until they have completed their education. For a small minority, this is high school. For most, it is something beyond high school, such as technical training, college, or university. This means that most people marry in their mid-twenties or later. In both Canada and the United States, many young people come to marriage with much experience with dating and sexual experimentation; many have lived with someone, either the marriage partner or someone else, prior to marriage.

Moreover, marriage is not a choice everyone makes, as we have seen. Over the past few decades, one-person households have increased substantially in Canada. Of the population 15 years and older, 13.5 percent live alone, according to the most recent census data (Statistics Canada, 2012d). Interestingly, older Canadians most often live alone, while more and more young adults tend to live at home with their parents for longer periods (Statistics Canada, 2012d). In part, the growth in living alone is because of an aging population with more widowed people. It is also the result of capability to live alone as a preference achieved. In the past, it may have been that some older people wished to live alone rather than with their families, but it was not possible due to either financial challenges or lack of availability of housing for one person. The economic recession of 2008 has, however, resulted in more multi-generational living arrangements than were seen earlier, including families moving in with older relatives (McDaniel, Gazso, Um, 2013)

To live without a life partner is not new, nor is it more common now than it was in the early part of this century, though more concerns are expressed about it now. Alone, however, need not mean lonely. Many who live solo are not isolated from their communities or circles of friends.

People who are devoted to their work may prefer not having a life partner; many great artists and writers have remained unmarried and unattached in any permanent way. And the need for marriage for security and acceptability for women has declined, although not entirely.

Commuter/LAT Relationships

Many people still feel a strong urge to marry. Indeed, some people would prefer (or decide) to marry and live apart than postpone or avoid marriage. Consider so-called **commuter marriages**, or what is also called a **living apart together (LAT) relationship**. A LAT is a marriage or other intimate relationship between partners who live in two separate

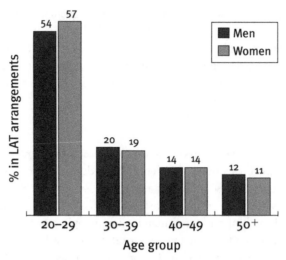

Figure 4.3 Living Apart Together Arrangements by Age Group, 2001

Source: Adapted from the Statistics Canada. 2003. Couples living apart. *Canadian Social Trends.* Retrieved May 13, 2009, from www.statcan.gc.ca/pub/11-008-x/2003001/article/6552-eng.pdf.

households (Borell and Karlsson, 2002; Turcotte, 2013). Based on data from the 2011 General Social Survey, it is estimated that 7 percent of Canadians who have a partner live separately from him or her (Turcotte, 2013). LAT relationships are increasingly tracked by statistical agencies around the world to get a more complete sense of people's living arrangements. More often now, couples live in two different homes from the beginning of their relationship, which is why some European sociologists call this arrangement "living together apart." In Canada, LAT couples were mostly concentrated among young adults, with 31 percent of individuals aged 20 to 24, and 17 percent of those aged 25 to 29, in a LAT relationship in 2011. LAT relationships among older people is increasing, too (see Figure 4.3), with over 2 percent of those age 60 and older living in a LAT couple (Turcotte, 2013). There are many plausible reasons for older people to live in LAT relationships—among them, wishing to keep one's own home and patterns of life and concern by adult children of a new relationship. Among those who are younger, the common explanation seems to be the difficulty of finding jobs in the same place or the expense of maintaining their own domicile.

Nault and Belanger (1996) describe committed long-term relationships in which both partners live with their parents as an aspect of the growing "cluttered nest" phenomenon that occurs when adult offspring return to the family home or never leave it.

For some couples, a LAT relationship is only a short-term arrangement. This is particularly the case for younger people, 80 percent of whom anticipate living together at some point in the future (Turcotte, 2013). For others, it becomes a long-term lifestyle preference. This is more true for older people and professional couples in LAT relationships (Turcotte, 2013). Though LAT relationships remain a minority among intimate unions, nothing illustrates so well people's continued commitment to close involvement with a partner despite enormous odds and the conflict between the cultural values of living together versus pursuing career success. LAT relationships force couples to create intimacy differently than couples who see each other every day. While couples living in LAT relationships tend to have an enhanced appreciation for their spouse or family, it remains a complicated way to live (Groves and Horm-Wingerd, 1991; Forsyth and Gramling, 1998; Borell and Karlsson, 2002; Turcotte, 2013).

Divorcees sometimes opt for this arrangement when entering a new relationship (Levin, 2004). After experiencing an unsuccessful marriage, people may be more careful with new relationships. Choosing to live apart from their partners may be a strategy to avoid another painful separation. As well, some may fear that moving in together could change the current dynamics in the relationship or the sharing of assets. Others simply may not find jobs in the same area, so living apart is the only option.

Economic, cultural, or even policy pressures may explain why couples choose LAT relationships. Today, more women and men in committed relationships are in professional careers that make it hard for them to move when their spouses move. Laws and policies also make relocating to another country as a couple challenging. At the same time, tight job markets are forcing more people to relocate. In addition, people travelling because of work may meet a partner abroad. If relocation is not an alternative, they may form a long-distance relationship (Levin, 2004). Technology makes staying in touch easier for couples living apart, making LAT relationships more workable.

The Falling Marriage Rate

Fewer people than ever are marrying, and those who do are spending a smaller proportion of their lives married. Marriages last a shorter average time than in the past (Wilson, in Baker, 2005). These trends inevitably lead to a decline in the numbers of those experiencing marriage. Let's examine two theories to explain this: an economic explanation and a demographic explanation.

A leading economic argument is that marriage rates have fallen in recent decades because marriage is less necessary for both men and women, and the alternatives to marriage are more attractive. For women, financial independence and reproductive control have begun to tip the balance to cohabitation or singlehood. Women have less to gain from marriage and more to gain from paid work than in the past. Combining marriage, parenthood, and labour force participation is hard work, especially for women.

Despite marriage rates being currently in decline, we cannot conclude that people are avoiding stable, emotionally committed relationships. In fact, when we look at the increased numbers of cohabiting couples, we realize that North Americans are still inclined to have intimate couple relationships and commitments, even if they are taking slightly different forms.

COHABITATION

One significant change in family life in the Western world has been a sharp increase in cohabitation—people living together without being legally married. In the past, cohabitation, also called **common-law union**, used to be more prevalent among working-class people. It also used to be seen as a lesser form of couple relationship than legal marriage. Now, however, cohabitation has become more common among all social classes and all age groups and is much more accepted.

Cohabitation is, however, a less stable form of union than legal marriage. A gradual movement into cohabitation occurs without clear communication between partners about the meaning of the transition (Manning, Smock, and Majumdar, 2005). Research shows that for many individuals, beginning to cohabit "just happened." With such a slide into cohabitation many couples are at risk for later distress due to a lack of a stable foundation of mutual commitment (see Stanley, Rhoades, and Markman, 2006).

Cohabitation has also been associated with fewer advantages than marriage, which may or may not be true as cohabitation becomes much more accepted. Cohabitating couples tend to have less involvement with extended families and less responsibility to the other partner during crisis; moreover, the union is rejected by some religious institutions (Waite, 1999, 2000). Domestic violence rates are also higher in cohabitating relationships, and levels of psychological well-being are lower. That said, the evidence on the well-being effects of cohabitation versus marriage is changing, and the numbers of long-lasting, happily cohabitating couples are growing rapidly. The 2006 Census revealed a large growth in cohabitation among Canadians (Statistics Canada, 2007a), and the 2011 Census found a 13.9 percent growth in cohabitation since 2006, compared with a growth of 3.1 percent of married couples (Statistics Canada, 2012a). Recent U.S. evidence reports that those who cohabit may have a slight health advantage (Musick and Bumpass, 2012).

Like all other relationship forms, cohabitation is not a homogeneous category. For instance, Canadian residents who are immigrants are less willing to cohabit than Canadian-born residents, the English-speaking less than the French, and women less than men (Milan and Peters, 2003). Recently, for a significant proportion of couples, cohabitation has replaced dating relationships, which do not necessarily involve any long-term commitment and least of all marriage (Rhoades, Stanley, and Markman, 2009). Under these circumstances, one would expect very high rates of eventual dissolution, much like a short acquaintanceship leads to an increased likelihood of divorce among the married.

For couples who move in together to split expenses, cohabitation is economically advantageous, simple, and generally not a long-term commitment. Divorced adults may also find economic advantages in cohabitation. For instance, splitting expenses with a partner may benefit many divorced men who have to support a child who lives elsewhere. Interestingly, despite the advantages that come with splitting expenses, overall cohabiters are far less likely than married couples to pool their finances (Heimdal and Houseknecht, 2003). In concert with the previous finding, cohabitation is more common

The Prevalence of Cohabitation in Canada

- In 2011, married couples made up the largest portion of couples, at 67 percent. However, this number has been in steady decline over the past two decades, falling 3.5 percent since 2001 (Statistics Canada, 2012a).

- As the percentage of married couples decreases, the percentage of couples cohabiting increases. The number of common-law-couple families increased a substantial 18.9 percent from 2001 to 2006. This number rose five times faster than that of married-couple families and twice that of lone-parent families (Statistics Canada, 2006a). The year 2011 saw an increase of 13.9 percent, more than four times the increase for married couples, and for the first time, numbers of cohabiting couples surpassed the number of lone-parent families (Statistics Canada, 2012a).

- The proportion of visible-minority women among those living common-law was 3.6 percent in 2011. For visible-minority men, it was 4.0 percent. This compares with 11.7 percent for women not of a visible minority, and 12.4 percent for men in the same group (Statistics Canada, 2011a).

- Of recent immigrants, 3.6 percent of women and men lived with a common-law partner in 2011. The proportions for all immigrants were 3.8 percent for women and 4.6 percent for men. These figures contrast with those of non-immigrant women at 12.5 percent and of men at 13.1 percent (Statistices Canada, 2011a).

- Starting conjugal life in a common-law relationship increases the probability of this first union ending in separation, regardless of whether the common-law partners eventually marry (Statistics Canada, 2004d). This, too, may be changing (James and Beattie, 2012).

- Average length of cohabitating relationships in Canada is about five years (Bibby, 2004a).

- Canadians who have experienced divorce tend to opt more often for cohabitation for their second union rather than remarrying (Statistics Canada, 2012a; Wu and Schimmele, 2005a).

- In Quebec, where the proportion of cohabiting couples has been on the rise for half a century, growth slowed slightly in 2011. That year, one-third of couples (31.5 percent) lived in a common-law union, a level more than double that in the other provinces and slightly more than in the territories, except Nunavut, where the rate is 32.7 percent (Statistics Canada, 2012a).

- The number of common-law-couple families in Quebec accounts for 31.5 percent of the province's total families. About one-third (32.7 percent) of census families in Nunavut were common-law couples in 2011, with 28.7 percent and 25.1 percent of couples being common-law in the Northwest Territories and Yukon, respectively (Statistics Canada, 2012a).

- In the territories, about one-third (32.7 percent) of census families in Nunavut were common-law couples in 2011, with high shares also found in the Northwest Territories (28.7 percent) and Yukon (25.1 percent; Statistics Canada, 2012a).

- Ontario had the lowest proportion of common-law-couple families in 2011 (10.9 percent), and Prince Edward Island had the highest proportion of married-couple families (72.3 percent) in Canada (Statistics Canada, 2012a).

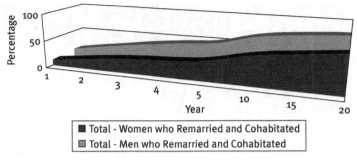

Figure 4.4 Repartnering after Marital Dissolution

Source: Reprinted with permission from Vanier Institute of the Family.

among working women than among women who stay at home (Wu, 2000). This suggests that marriage sometimes is a less attractive option for women who are financially independent.

For others, cohabiting unions constitute a "prelude to marriage" or a "trial marriage"—that is, a period in which to test the solidity of the relationship without the legal commitment. For instance, Bianchi and Casper (2000) have found that nearly 50 percent of American couples who cohabit do so as a precursor to marriage. Such cohabiters are committed to each other and plan on getting married. Nevertheless, the Bianchi and Casper study illustrates that after five years, only 52 percent of these couples had married, 31 percent had separated, and 17 percent were still cohabiting.

The majority of Canadians repartner following divorce or separation (see Figure 4.4). Research from the Vanier Institute reveals that 26 percent of women and 37 percent of men are in a new conjugal relationship within three years of marital dissolution. After five years, these numbers rise to 36 percent of women and 51 percent of men; after 20 years, they rise to 69 percent of women and 82 percent of men. Many second partnering relationships are cohabitation unions.

More than 40 percent of women cohabitants have previously been married (Statistics Canada, 2001a). These women have their own reasons for living together instead of marrying. Some are separated but not yet divorced, so they cannot legally remarry. Some often wish to avoid forgoing their newly acquired independence. Religious beliefs prevent others from divorcing and remarrying. Some widows do not want their pension benefits reduced by remarriage (Connidis, 2001). They may also be afraid that a marriage will force on them the role of a nurse for an ailing husband (Davidson, 2001).

For older adults who have already been married, cohabitation seems to carry far fewer risks than it does for younger adults. Thus, higher levels of happiness and stability have been found among older cohabiters when compared to their younger counterparts (King and Scott, 2005). This can be explained by the fact that for these people, cohabitation becomes a substitute to marriage with a similar level of commitment, not just the road

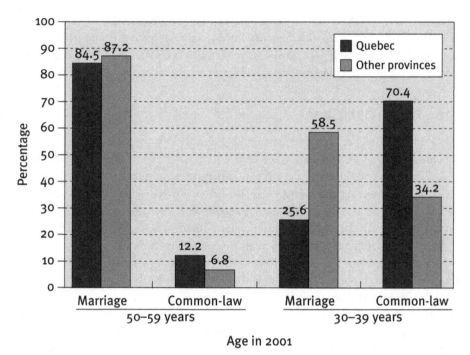

Figure 4.5 Probability for Women of Experiencing Marriage or a Common-law Union as a First Union, Quebec and Other Provinces, 2001

Source: Statistics Canada website. 2002. Changing conjugal life in Canada. *General Social Survey*. Retrieved on May 13, 2009 from www.statcan.gc.ca/pub/89-576-x/89-576-x2001001-eng.pdf.

to an eventual marriage. Much more research is needed in Canada on intimate unions among older people.

In the past 20 years, cohabitation has become a long-term alternative to marriage. In this form, cohabitation is a marriage-like commitment without the wedding and with obligations to each other, often spelled out in law. Cohabitation gives people many of the expected benefits of family life—emotional and sexual satisfaction, mutual dependency, and support, for example—while they retain (or at least perceive) a greater degree of choice. Cohabitation may be a personal "vote" against the restrictions, legal and often religious, of traditional marriage.

Despite, or perhaps because of, Quebec's history of strict Catholicism, cohabitation is much more common there than in any other Canadian province (see Figure 4.5). Compared to several countries where common-law couples comprise a large share of all couples, such as Sweden (29.0 percent in 2010), Finland (24.7 percent in 2010), and Norway (23.9 percent in 2011), the proportion of all couples who were common-law in Quebec in 2011 was higher (31.5 percent; Statistics Canada, 2012a, USA: National Health Statistics Reports, 2012). In the United States, the percentage of cohabiting couples is much lower, at 11.2 percent in 2010. The percentage in Canada outside Quebec (16.7 percent; Statistics Canada 2012a) falls far below these other countries, except the United States. By age 35, 44 percent of Quebec men and 40 percent of Quebec women have cohabited, compared to only 28 percent for either sex in the rest of Canada.

Legal Implications

The major difference between marriage and cohabitation is that the former is an explicit legal commitment and the latter is not—or not in quite the same way. In some provinces, such as Ontario, cohabitation may mean differences in rights to spousal support or property acquired during the relationship. In other provinces, such as Alberta, the law regarding common-law relationships was changed with the introduction of *adult interdependent relationships*. The Adult Interdependent Relationships Act, applied in Alberta since June 2003, provides some but not all the rights and benefits of marriage to "adult interdependent partners" (Renaud, 2004). The term includes same-sex couples and people sharing committed, responsible relationships, such as adult siblings who live together or an adult child sharing a home with an aging parent.

Even so, law and policy increasingly regard a long-term cohabiting relationship as a legally binding partnership. Most provinces in Canada treat common-law unions that last for some specific period, typically more than two years, the same as married unions; the obligations of the partners to their children are the same. The split of property if the union ends may be the same as it would be for married couples, although this varies. Long-term cohabitants are legally expected, in most jurisdictions in Canada, to support each other during the relationship and after a breakup. The degree of this expectation varies from province to province, and from state to state in the United States. As mentioned above, a 2012 court case in Quebec found that spousal support was not binding after the end of a common-law relationship, as it would be on marital dissolution. One thing is clear, however: The difference between marriage and cohabitation is blurring.

Births and Children in Common-Law Unions

Increasingly, couples in cohabiting relationships are having children, another indicator of their degree of commitment and permanence. In 1993–94, 20.4 percent of all Canadian children were born to women living in common-law unions with the child's father. This is considerably different from the picture in 1963, when fewer than 5 percent of children were born to cohabiting parents (Marcil-Gratton, Le Bourdais, and Lapierre-Adamcyk, 2000; Vanier Institute of the Family, 1994). In Quebec, 44 percent of births were to common-law couples in 1997, more than twice the percentage in 1990 (Statistics Canada, 2004d). This trend can also be observed in the United States. In 2001, 37 percent of all births in the United States occurred outside marriage; more than half those births (52 percent) were to cohabiting couples (Mincieli, Manlove, McGarrett, Moore, and Ryan, 2007). The old stigma of births "out of wedlock," once known as illegitimate births, is largely gone,

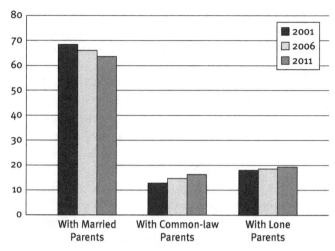

Figure 4.6 Percentage of Children under Age 14 Living with Parents

Source: Statistics Canada, 2012a. Censuses of population, 2001 to 2011. Retrieved September 2012.
http://www12.statcan.gc.ca/census-recensement/2011/as-sa/98-312-x/2011001/fig/fig3-eng.cfm.

especially when the parents are in a stable, caring relationship. This attitude change is captured in Figure 4.6, which shows an increasing number of children younger than age 15 who live with parents in a common-law relationship and in lone-parent families.

According the 2011 Census, about 16.4 percent of all children younger than age 15 lived with common-law couple families that year. The rate in Quebec in 2011 was 30 percent (Statistics Canada, 2012e). This suggests clearly a change in the historical assumption that baby carriages follow marriage and not the other way around.

Effects of Cohabitation on Marriage

Some common-law partnerships are a prelude to marriage, with just under one-half of the people ever in a common-law union ending up marrying their common-law partner.

Cohabitation is no better a "screening device" for mates, or preparation for marriage, than traditional courtship. Prior cohabitation is found to be positively related to marital disagreement (Wu, 2000). For instance, it has been shown that in the first two years of their marriage, couples who have cohabited have less positive problem-solving behaviours and are generally less supportive of each other than those who have not cohabited (Cohan and Kleinbaum, 2002). Surprisingly, the probability of divorce is greater, on average, for couples who marry after having lived together than for couples who marry without first living together (Statistics Canada, 2004d). Estimates suggest the chance of marital dissolution is two to three times higher among couples who lived together before marriage (Le Bourdais, Neil, and Turcotte, 2000; Marcil-Gratton et al., 2000; Wu, 2000).

Serial cohabitation has also been associated with higher likelihood of divorce. A study by Bumpass and Lu (2000) found that the percentage of cohabiting unions ending in marriage declined from 60 percent to 53 percent from the early 1980s to the 1990s. Furthermore, recently, marriage rates have been low, especially among disadvantaged and minority couples (Lichter, Qian, and Mellott, 2006), with less than one-third of poor cohabiting couples ending in marriage. The inclination of these relationships toward dissolution sets the stage for forming new cohabiting relationships. Serial cohabitation may therefore precede an increasing proportion of all first marriages and represent an overlooked but important risk factor for divorce.

So can we conclude that if a particular couple wants to ensure a long relationship, they would do better to get married right away rather than to cohabit first? Not necessarily. The reasons for the increased level of divorce may be complex and even contradictory. It may be that it is not cohabitation per se that relates to the higher risks of splitting up, but the social risk factors that people bring into the relationship. First, people who cohabit may be already divorced once. If so, the difference in divorce rates may be not a result of cohabitation but a reflection of the characteristics of a self-selected group.

Moreover, the data hints that people who are willing to cohabit may also be more open to divorce. Along these lines, Canadian sociologist Zheng Wu states that "people who cohabitate tend to have less conventional views towards marriage or see themselves as poor risks in terms of a long-term relationship" (2000: 3). People who cohabited prior to marriage are generally less religious and conventional; they are probably less hesitant to end marriages when they face marital problems than people who did not cohabit before marriage. Moreover, the experience of living together may itself be a factor. Living together without marriage can change a couple's views of marriage and divorce, and foster less conventional attitudes about marriage and family life. (James and Beattie, 2012; Wu, 2000: 3)

Overall, the evidence shows a weaker commitment to the institution of marriage among those who cohabit and then marry (Bennett, Blanc, and Bloom, 1988; James and Beattie, 2012). Yet some research has found positive effects of cohabitation on marriage. Work by Manning et al. (2004) illustrates that marriage following a cohabiting birth is associated with greater union stability. Some studies find that cohabitation leads to a more egalitarian household division of labour and less traditional gender ideologies among married individuals who cohabit premaritally, as compared to those who do not (Le Bourdais, Lapierre-Adamcyk, and Pacaut, 2004).

Teachman and Polonko (1990) argue that the effect of cohabitation on marriage duration must be assessed more carefully. The durability of the relationship should be considered not in terms of the length of the marriage alone but in the total length of the relationship. When this is done, there is no difference in marital duration between those who cohabit and those who do not before marriage.

In short, we have no sociological evidence that cohabitation itself causes a decline in the quality of a later marriage; but neither is there any clear evidence that cohabitation improves mate selection or prepares people for marriage. What is certain is that couples

Lone Parent Families on the Rise

- Along with cohabiting-couple families, the percentage of lone-parent families is also increasing. From 1986 to 2001, the proportion surged by 58 percent, while that of two-parent families only increased by 10 percent. The number rose by another 8.0 percent from 2006 to 2011 (Statistics Canada, 2012a). Most lone parents were separated, divorced, or widowed.

- Although lone-parent families are still usually headed by women (80 percent in 2011), the number of those headed by men increased 16.3 percent from 2006 to 2011, well more than double the rate of those headed by women (6 percent; Statistics Canada, 2012a).

- While the proportion of lone-parent families did not change significantly throughout the twentieth century, the reason people were parenting alone did. In the 1950s, single parents were usually widows or widowers. In the 2000s, most single parents are separated or divorced (Statistics Canada, 2006a).

- The percentage of children age 14 and younger living with married parents declined by 15.5 percent from 1986 to 2006. In 2001, the count was at 68 percent; in 2006, it was at 65.7 percent; and in 2011, it was at 64.1 percent (Statistics Canada, 2012f).

are opting more for bypassing the legal strictures of marriage in favour of cohabitation at some point in their lives.

Young People's Attitudes

Reginald Bibby's 2001 study of Canadian youths found that the vast majority—86 percent—approve of cohabitation. Further, about 63 percent of teenagers feel it is okay for a couple who are not legally married to have children together, and fully three-quarters think that homosexual couples should be entitled to the same legal and human rights as other Canadians.

Other studies also show an increased acceptance of cohabitation by young people. Dating and sexual experience, as well as parental influence, affect adolescents' attitudes toward union formation. Sexual activity is associated with positive views about cohabitation. Cunningham and Thornton (2004) find that 18-year-olds with more sexual partners are more positively inclined toward cohabitation. Virgins may be more conventional and more oriented toward the traditional marriage pathway that excludes cohabitation. Teens who experience parental divorce may be especially hesitant to marry and may view cohabitation as a way to avoid divorce and to test the relationship (Smock, Huang, Manning, and Bergstrom, 2006). Similarly, adolescents living with cohabiting parents may be more likely to cohabit as a result of modelling the behaviour to which they were exposed.

A study by Manning, Longmore, and Giordano (2007) finds that adolescents are less certain about their cohabitation than their marriage expectations. Furthermore, the authors find that not all adolescents consider cohabitation and marriage as mutually exclusive, with one-half of the respondents expecting both to cohabit and to marry sometime in the future. While the study illustrates a general support for cohabitation among the American teenagers interviewed, this support is not unequivocal, with 25 percent of teens ever expecting to cohabit.

Older Couples

As the first edge of baby boomers passes age 65, more attention should be paid to older couples. Légaré, Martel, Stone, and Denis (2000) found that 40 percent of Québécois seniors are involved in mutually supportive relationships, most often with their partners.

Many older couples do not live alone—they live with extended families, especially children. This further contributes to the "cluttered nest" phenomenon. Older couples live with their children for many reasons: illness, limited income, loneliness, or unsuitable housing. Though many older people might prefer more independent living, shrinking social services make this independence difficult.

For instance, when examining whether Canada's public pensions—Old Age Security and Canada Pension Plan—provide enough income to seniors living in Nova Scotia in 2005 for a basic nutritious diet, Green, Williams, Johnson, and Blum (2008) found that single-person households could not meet basic food expenses. Moreover, although living with a partner protected against inadequate financial resources, the disposable income left over for that household after subtracting basic non-food and food expenses was negligible: roughly $300 (Green et al., 2008). Such shortcomings in Canada's retirement systems to ensure adequate financial resources for the basic needs of seniors contribute to the formation of multigenerational households (LaRochelle, Myles, and Picot, 2012).

Cluttered nests are more common among older immigrants than Canadian-born seniors. Some studies have attributed such discrepancies to differences in cultural values between immigrant and Canadian families. For instance, strong family values and norms of filial piety have been quoted as reasons for the choice of most older Chinese immigrants to live with their family members (Liu, Ng, Weatherall, and Loong, 2000). Recent studies have found, however, that there is an increasing tendency for older couples to live alone. This phenomenon has been linked to acculturation—the process by which culturally diverse groups become more homogeneous through changes in identity, values, beliefs, even physical, political, and economic adjustments (Greenland and Brown, 2005). For instance, in a study examining the preferred living arrangements of Chinese Canadians age 55 and older, just over one-half of the older Chinese Canadians reported a preference for not living with children (Lai, 2005). This preference was influenced by a longer residence in Canada, older age, having received income from government programs, and having higher levels of social support (Lai and Leonenko, 2007).

Other studies suggest that acculturation is not the reason for changing preferences in living arrangements. Research by Wilmoth, Dejong, and Himes (1997) points toward immigration policies—and not economic resources, functional limitations, or acculturation—as an influence on the decision of older couples to move in with their children.

A 1998 study showed that because older immigrants arriving in Canada are not eligible for government transfer payments or welfare benefits for up to 10 years, there is an 18 times greater chance that they will live with family than seniors born in Canada (Basavarajappa, 1998). Moreover, in April 2005, Joe Volpe, then minister of citizenship and immigration, announced measures to speed up the processing of sponsorship applications for parents and grandparents coming to Canada as family-class immigrants. With these measures, the number of parents and grandparents immigrating to Canada is increasing (Government of Canada, 2005), contributing to more cluttered nests. Recently, a halt has been put on family reunification immigrants, so the flow of older immigrants may lessen. That said, the pressures on immigrant families to care for elder relatives at long distances will increase.

The 2011 Census revealed that more seniors now live with their spouse or partner (56.4 percent) than previously (Statistics Canada, 2012b). This is not surprising, since

It was estimated that by the years 2005 and 2006, the number of older immigrants to Canada would increase substantially, creating cluttered nests and contributing to caregiving needs.
Asiaselects/Getty Images

Close Relations of Older Couples

- Although more seniors are living with their partners, men are far more likely than women to spend their senior years with a spouse or partner because of their lower life expectancy and tendency to marry younger women. Among the population aged 65 and over, the majority (56.4 percent) lived as part of a couple in 2011, a higher proportion than a decade earlier in 2001 (54.1 percent). More than 7 in 10 senior men (72.1 percent) and over 4 in 10 senior women (43.8 percent) lived with a spouse or partner in 2011 (Statistics Canada, 2012b).

- As among their younger counterparts, alternative relationships are popular among older adults. Eight percent of women age 50 to 59 in Canada are in a common-law relationship as their first union. Eventually, 20 percent of women age 50 to 59 will be involved in a common-law relationship (Statistics Canada, 2002h).

- While the majority of people in LAT relationships are young adults, in 2001, 44 percent of people in such unions were age 30 and older. About 19 percent of those were in their thirties, 14 percent were in their forties, and the remaining 11 percent were age 50 and older (Statistics Canada, 2003b).

- Cohabitation among older adults has been associated with poorer health when compared with the married elderly. In the United States, older cohabiting men report more depressive symptoms than do married men (Brown, Bulanda, and Lee, 2005). Finnish cohabiters age 65 and older also have poorer health outcomes, with an excess mortality of 35 to 40 percent, compared with married couples (Koskinen, Joutsenniemi, Martelin, and Martikainen, 2007).

- Other studies have shown that for older adults who have already been married, cohabitation becomes a substitute to marriage—a relationship in its own right with a similar level of commitment. At least one study found that older cohabiters experience higher levels of happiness and stability than younger ones (King and Scott, 2005).

there has been an extension in healthy life expectancy among Canadians, enabling them to live independently and in an intact couple for a longer period of their lives. More men than women now live with spouses until late in life. Men die earlier and also often marry younger women; thus, they more often leave widows. The 2011 Census also found a growing tendency for seniors, especially women, to live alone: 31.5 percent of women aged 65 and older lived alone in 2011 compared to 16.0 percent of men. Those aged 85 and older who lived alone consisted of 36.6 percent of women and 21.8 percent of men (Statistics Canada, 2012b). This trend has much to do with the longer life expectancy of women; in 2011, there were 4870 women aged 100 and older in Canada, compared to 955 men (Statistics Canada, 2012b).

Day-to-day caring for one's partner becomes an important factor in older couples, as they become more prone to illness. Caring for one's spouse in old age is a key issue for current debates about Canada's aging society. This task can put extra pressure on the relationship (Keating, Fast, Frederick, Cranswick, and Perrier, 1999). For instance, when deciding to place their partner in a chronic care hospital, 48 percent of spouses associate the institutionalization of their husband or wife with the ending of their marriage, due to a loss of companionship—sometimes preceded by non-responsiveness of the partner due to cognitive impairments (Gladstone, 1995).

Providing care can also undermine the caregiver's emotional and physical health through feelings of guilt, not enough personal time, increased stress, social isolation, and poor sleeping patterns. For example, Rosenthal and Dawson (1991) found that women who chose to institutionalize their spouse are ridden by feelings of ambivalence: relief, on the one hand, since they know their husband is receiving good care, and sadness and loneliness, on the other, since their husband no longer shares their home.

Women are usually more likely than men to experience these effects and suffer from "caregiver burnout" (Keating et al., 1999; McDaniel, 1999). Gendered roles and expectations may explain why older women find caring for ailing partners more distressing than do men, who report more positive experiences (Davidson et al., 2000; McDaniel, 1999). We will discuss gender roles and wellness further in the next chapter.

Same-Sex Couples

Recent media attention and increasing social acceptance of same-sex couples may lead some readers to believe that these arrangements are new ways to live in intimate relationships; it is not so. As stated by the Vanier Institute of the Family, "The growth in the number of same-sex couples may in part reflect an emerging social acceptance of same-sex unions and a greater ease and willingness among same-sex couples to self-identify in the Census" (2012). Gays and lesbians have formed and lived in couples since the beginning of families. However, it is difficult to know how many gay and lesbian couples there are.

In looking clearly at how lesbians live in close relations, Dunne (1997a) says we can learn about the links of intimate relationships to economic and social systems. In a different study, Dunne (2001) suggests that the exploration of non-heterosexual experience also provides an opportunity to consider alternative ways of parenting, gender, and close relations. For instance, she argues that gay men who become fathers construct parenting identities and practices beyond the borders of heterosexuality. Dunne claims that by observing lesbian and gay people, we notice the construction of more innovative and egalitarian approaches to work and family life and not a mirroring of the polarized division of tasks that characterizes heterosexual arrangements.

Coming out of the theoretical tradition known as queer theory, Michelle Owen (2001) argues that "families headed by same-sex couples signal both a 'normalization of the queer' and a 'queering of the normal'" (97). On one hand, many same-sex families want to be recognized as just like heterosexual families. On the other, the very situation of being a same-sex couple raising children resists the dominant model of family because the dominant model operates on the premise of gender difference.

Since conventional family norms do not apply in the same way, gay and lesbian couples must renegotiate and re-create for themselves how roles, responsibilities, and the balance of power will be distributed in their family. Thus, same-sex couples "normalize the queer" by forming families, raising children, and struggling to be recognized as being just like heterosexual families in their abilities to parent, provide stability, and be self-sufficient. At the same time, they "queer the normal" because their very existence signals that families are defined as being heterosexual.

The use of heterosexuality as a point of reference is also evident in research on lesbian parenthood. Some authors have argued that research on lesbian mothering practices is conducted on the basis of comparisons between lesbian and heterosexual mothers to determine whether lesbian mothers' practices can be characterized as forms of assimilationism or resistance (Hequembourg, 2007). When trying to legitimize lesbian-headed families, many researchers and civil rights activists accentuate the similarities in lesbian and heterosexual mothering practices, while undermining the role of sexuality plays in influencing mothering abilities. On the other hand, those who wish to discredit lesbian-headed families rely mainly on pointing out differences between lesbian-headed mothers and heterosexual mothers.

Same-Sex Couples in Canada

- The 2006 Canadian Census enumerated same-sex married couples for the first time since gay and lesbian marriage was legalized in July 2005. The 2011 Census numbered same-sex married couples at 21 015, or 0.3 percent of all couples in Canada. This is an increase of 181.5 percent, which is triple the number of married couples from 2006 (Statistics Canada, 2012a). Of course, it could be that more married same-sex couples are now willing to be counted than in 2006.

- Same-sex couples represented 0.8 percent of all couples in Canada in 2011 (Statistics Canada, 2012a). Of those, 45.6 percent lived in Toronto, Montreal, and Vancouver, compared to 33.4 percent of opposite-sex couples. This is slightly lower than in 2006, when 50 percent of same-sex couples lived in these three census metropolitan areas. Ontario, Quebec, and British Columbia were the first provinces to legalize same-sex marriage (Statistics Canada, 2012a).

- Most same-sex married spouses are men (54.5 percent in 2011). This proportion is similar among same-sex cohabiting partners (Statistics Canada, 2012a).

- There were 9.4 percent of same-sex couples who had children (age 24 and younger) living with them in 2011. This is more common among women couples (16.5 percent) than men (3.4 percent; Statistics Canada, 2012a).

- The percentage of same-sex couples in Canada in 2011 was consistent with recent data from Australia (0.7 percent in 2011) and the United Kingdom and Ireland (0.4 percent for each country in 2011). Although not directly comparable, 0.6 percent of households in the United States were comprised of same-sex couples in 2010 (Statistics Canada, 2012a).

Such dichotomous analyses of the parenting skills and outcomes of children raised in lesbian- and gay-headed families are thought to lead to an inaccurate image of lesbigay couples. Judith Stacey and Timothy Biblarz (2001), for example, claim that a majority of family research emphasizes lesbian mothers' similarities with other mothers while overlooking the small but interesting differences that arise in day-to-day parenting practices. In this way, even sympathizers of lesbigay couples risk unintentionally constructing an image of lesbigay families that does injustice to their essence. This suggests that, for practical and theoretical purposes, lesbigay relationships and families should be accepted as another alternative to the many existing family forms and not considered an extension or opposition to heterosexual close relations. Therefore, same-sex families force us to examine in new ways how we think of family, what we do as families, and what we want the family to be. We discuss this further in Chapter 10.

POLICY CHALLENGES AND DEBATES

In July 2002, an Ontario court ruled to allow same-sex marriage, finding that prohibiting gay couples from marrying is unconstitutional and violates the Charter of Rights and Freedoms. In 2005, federal legislation made same-sex marriage legal across the country. Both opposite-sex and same-sex partners can now choose to marry, and even if they do not, after a period of cohabitation they may still be granted spousal status.

Some argue that legalized same-sex unions are helpful to the institution of marriage, for they erase stereotypical gender roles that produce sexist legal treatments when dealing with heterosexual couples. As well, assumptions about the assumed complementary nature of female and male roles, and their importance in relation to the socialization of children, are eliminated. Fiona Nelson (1996), in her study on lesbian parenting in Canada, argues that because lesbian families need to redefine who a mother is and what she does, they throw into question the very idea of motherhood. Forcing us to rethink our understanding of motherhood and families in this way is, according to Nelson (1996: 137), a revolutionary turn that "has implications for family-focused policies and programs." From an economics standpoint, Christopher Portelli (2004) argues that same-sex

Legalizing Same-Sex Marriage

Canada was the third country in the world to legalize same-sex marriage, following the Netherlands and Belgium. Same-sex marriage is now also legal in Spain, South Africa, Norway, Sweden, Portugal, Iceland, Argentina, and Denmark. Some jurisdictions within other countries, such as parts of the United States (12 states) and Mexico, have legalized same-sex marriage. (Statistics Canada, 2012a, p. 7)

At the time of publication, France, New Zealand, and Uruguay had legalized same-sex unions.

Source: Statistics Canada. 2012a. "Portrait of Families and Living Arrangements in Canada" (from the 2011 Census of Canada short form) http://www12.statcan.gc.ca/census-recensement/2011/as-sa/98-312-x/98-312-x2011001-eng.cfm#a1 (accessed 29-05-2013)

marriage would strengthen the incentive to marry, increase the efficiency of marriage markets, provide for more children to be raised in two-parent environments, and benefit economies overall.

On the other hand, some argue that the terms on which recent same-sex legal struggles have advanced in Canada have led to the reinforcement of conservative and heteronormative discourses on marriage and family (Young and Boyd, 2006). In particular, the authors argue that the focus on feminist voices on various issues related to the family and economic security has diminished, leading to the survival of conservative discourses on marriage and family, despite the legal recognition of same-sex relationships (Young and Boyd, 2006).

Generally, the involvement of policy or the state (with all its agents and agencies) in marriage has been limited to laws about who cannot marry whom. The reality is that the state and state policies have actively shaped the ways in which we form and live in families, as well as our sense of family. Ideas about individual responsibility, the vulnerable dependent, sex and morality, and life chances and choices are all reaffirmed through our laws and policies. Therefore, it is not surprising that changes to these basic ideas cause concern and debate about family policies.

Two factors propelling the re-evaluation of policies on marriage and mating are recent concerns about family poverty, especially the poverty of children in mother-headed lone-parent families, and the rapid growth in women's labour force participation.

Are Policies Making Marriage Less Attractive?

It has been suggested that marriage laws may be a disincentive to marriage. Laws may discourage couples from marrying if aspects of legal marriage are seen as bringing major, and possibly unwanted, changes in a couple's relationship. On the other hand, if legal marriage is seen as changing nothing much, they may not find it attractive as an alternative to living common-law.

A strong argument is emerging from the family economy literature that many tax policies are based on an outdated view of what families are. Increasingly, Canadian family policy is delivered through the income tax system. Thus, it does make a difference what model of family is used. Men are defined much more often as the economically dominant partner in a marriage or common-law union and women as the subordinate partner. "Our tax system cannot achieve the modern social welfare and equity goals claimed for it so long as we continue to base policy decisions on an image of family that belongs to old reruns" (Phillips, 1995: 31).

Another policy debate involves the question of who should be entitled to the workplace benefits that marriage allows. Groups have lobbied for a broad definition of "spouse" in spousal rights. Access to such benefits, including health care, is especially important in the United States. In Canada, public health-care insurance makes the issue less pressing, but an incentive for being declared a spouse remains.

Alternative ways have emerged for gay, lesbian, and heterosexual couples to form intimate couple bonds. One is the *pacte civil de solidarité* (**PACS**), or civil solidarity pact, available only in France (Daley, 1999). The PACS began as an effort to legalize gay and lesbian unions and was instituted into law in early 2000 after intense debate and public protests. A PACS officially recognizes non-married couples, either gay or heterosexual (Johnston, 2008). In a PACS, each partner is responsible financially for the other, in both support and debts. It is easier to dissolve than a marriage and can be done without a lawyer. In the first four months, more than 14 000 couples had made PACS unions. Interestingly, many were heterosexual.

Perspectives of Low-Income Groups on Marriage and Cohabitation

Marriage among low-income groups has been declining since the mid-1900s. Whereas in the past, marriage rates were similar for the rich and the poor, today those living in poverty are only about half as likely to marry as those whose incomes are three or more times above the poverty level (Edin and Reed, 2005). These trends have raised concerns among policy-makers about the well-being of children born out of wedlock and living in poor, single-parent households.

As we learned in Chapter 2, the 1990s was a decade of welfare reforms in both the United States (Kissane and Krebs, 2007) and Canada (Williamson and Salkie, 2005). In the United States, in particular, welfare reform was closely tied to promotion of traditional marriages as a way to relieve poverty among single mothers and their children.

The real impact of these reforms was to simply shift women and families from the rank of poor welfare recipients to that of the working poor. Women living in poverty are still more likely to get pregnant out of wedlock, remain unmarried, and thus work in low-paying jobs (Kissane and Krebs, 2007). While it is true that married women fare better economically, what the policies failed to take into account was that non-marital birth mothers are less likely than other women to marry "economically attractive" men after welfare reforms (Graefe, Roempke, and Lichter, 2007). Their husbands are more likely to have lower levels of education, more likely to be unemployed, and thus unable to earn a family wage. Therefore, for low-income women, marriage is not necessarily a route to upward social mobility. Rather, socio-economic differences and mate selection patterns maintain class boundaries and increase family income inequality.

Low-income men and women still value and aspire to marriage; however, "they believe they are currently unable to meet the high standards of relationship quality and financial stability they believe is necessary to sustain a marriage and avoid divorce" (Edin and Reed, 2005: 117). Therefore, instead of promoting marriage, governments should provide people with tools that would enable stable marriage formation. Increasing job stability, improving male earnings, and providing affordable housing and child care are among some possible initiatives. Another way to alleviate poverty among single mothers is to promote education. Research shows that post-secondary education "is the single most important factor with potential for breaking the cycle of poverty and is most promising in reducing poverty and reliance on public assistance" (Pandey and Kim, 2008). In addition, there is a positive relationship between education and marriage prospects. Women with post-secondary education are more likely to marry educated men (Graefe and Lichter, 2008), who, in turn, are more able to earn a family wage and support a middle-class lifestyle.

Cohabitation is another important family form to consider in the discussion of changing marriage patterns among low-income groups. In Quebec, where cohabitation is socially accepted and almost equivalent to marriage, cohabitation is not strongly related to socio-economic characteristics (Kerr, Moyser, and Beaujot, 2006). In fact, cohabiting men and women have similar and, in some cases, even slightly higher incomes than their married counterparts. In contrast, data from the rest of Canada resembles the broader North American pattern, "whereby persons with less education, lower incomes and more uncertain economic prospects are more likely to be in a cohabiting type of relationship and less likely to marry" (Kerry et al., 2006: 86). Therefore, cultural attitudes and norms play a role in controlling the extent to which family structure predicts the economic well-being of families. It appears that where cohabitation is widespread, the characteristics of cohabiters do not differ greatly from those of married individuals. Elsewhere, marriage seems to be, to an extent, selective of higher status.

Perspectives of Immigrants on Marriage and Cohabitation

Even after acculturation into the new country in terms of language and some social views, many immigrants (usually older people) hold on to traditional cultural values regarding marriage. In part, this is due to a social stigma attached to intimate unions outside of marriage.

Therefore, most immigrant parents prefer traditional union formations and often go out of their way to influence their children to adopt the same perspective. For instance, De Valk and Liefbroer (2007) studied to what extent immigrant parents of Turkish, Moroccan, and Dutch descent in the Netherlands influenced romantic partnerships of their youth. Those children with a Turkish or Moroccan background, especially those who identified most strongly with their cultural background, preferred marriage. On the other hand, cohabitation was most popular among Dutch adolescents. Further, there is evidence that a close family relationship between immigrant youth and their parents predicts the likelihood that children will share cultural values with their families. According to Hynie, Lalonde, and Lee (2006), who studied Chinese immigrants in North America, this occurs through a transmission of values.

Marriage Policy and Canadian Immigrants

There may be a difference emerging between recent immigrants and the Canadian-born in terms of marriage policy. Immigration policy in Canada has long highlighted, along with market forces, family reunification. The definition of family is, of course, critically important in carrying out family reunification.

Who exactly counts as family and is thus eligible for immigrant status in Canada has narrowed over recent years. The shrinking definition of family has excluded adult children of a couple, for example. A paradox emerges. Although in Canada, as we have seen, more couples are living common law, for purposes of immigration a person does not qualify as a spouse unless there has been a formal, binding, traditional marriage. Thus policy preserves a wide and widening gap between new and other Canadians.

With the increasing diversity of immigrants and refugees come other policy and legal challenges. One is polygamy, typically foreign marriages of one man to several wives. A 2006 study for the federal Justice Department (Beeby, 2006) argues that Canadian law does not well serve women immigrants in polygamous marriages. This will no doubt continue to be debated and discussed.

CONCLUDING REMARKS

There can be no doubt that people worldwide are redefining what it means to be an intimate couple. The family remains the arena in which personal, emotional, and psychological growth can take place. But more than ever, couple relationships have come to be voluntary acts—choices made freely by individuals. As well, there is a sense that what's done can be undone. Intimate partners are not as closely dependent on each other economically as they once were, and they can opt out of couple relationships that do not meet their personal expectations.

In Western countries, people are less inclined to marry legally than in the past; more people view singlehood positively. Cohabitation offers many of the benefits of marriage, without the same social and religious constraints.

Yet, where marriage and divorce are concerned, variations persist among industrialized countries. For example, in Sweden reforms have removed many of the traditional incentives to marry. Marital-type property rights of married couples were extended to cohabiting couples in 1987. So, legal marriage offers no direct economic policy benefits to Swedish women or men. Even spousal support after divorce is uncommon, having been abandoned as early as 1973 (Fawcett, 1990). It appears that all Western countries are moving in the same direction, toward diversity of ways to form intimate couple unions.

From the data we have examined in this chapter, we see a continued increase in the acceptance of varied intimate partner forms, without a decrease in the strength of commitment overall toward exclusive intimacy within a spousal relationship.

CHAPTER SUMMARY

Close relations in couples have become much more diverse and individualized, especially in the past few decades. At the same time, debate over who can be a couple and how couples should (or should not) be legitimized has intensified. In this chapter, we looked at the variety and types of intimate couples. We examined how couples are changing, and why, and what the differences are, if any, in family experiences with different forms of couplehood. We saw that, around the world, cohabitation is becoming much more common, and couples are redefining what they mean by a "close relationship."

Now, more than ever before, the decision to be a couple and the decisions of what kind of couple to be are left to the individuals. Also, there is an increasing sense that one can separate from one's partner and start again. Legal marriage is less popular, and singlehood is seen as more respectable and positive. When we look at marriage as an exclusive contract of intimacy between two people, we see that marriage in all its forms is still a popular arrangement.

Living together or cohabiting has gone mainstream; it is more popular and much more often leads to a lifelong union. Ironically, the chance of divorce is greater for couples who lived common law before legally marrying.

We discovered that first marriages are taking place later in Canada and that many people wait to begin a committed relationship until after they finish their education. Most Canadians marry in their mid-twenties or later. Homogamy, or like marrying like, is visible in marriages as well as in dating. However, men still tend to marry younger women and women with less education and slightly lower occupational status than their own.

Many Canadians live alone, some as widowers or widows, some as divorcees, some as single persons by choice. The reasons for this vary; interestingly, one way some women solve their conflict between career and family is to choose career and independence by living alone. A commuter marriage, when partners live in separate homes, often for career-oriented reasons, comes about for similar reasons. Commuter marriages/relationships are not common but may increase for practical reasons, such as the scarcity of good jobs.

Common-law relationships affect our ideas about families. For example, births in common-law arrangements are increasing, and the stigma attached to children of such unions has almost disappeared. Despite its increased social acceptability, in places where cohabitation is rare, it is more likely associated with lower socio-economic groups.

Another change that is occurring is greater societal acceptance of same-sex couples. Increasingly, same-sex couples are being granted rights and duties similar to heterosexual couples, including the right to marry legally.

Key Terms

cohabitation A sexual relationship in which two people live together without being legally married.

common-law union A valid and legally binding marriage entered into without civil or religious ceremony, resulting from a cohabiting relationship that lasts for more than three years.

commuter marriage (also called living apart together, or LAT) A marriage between partners who live in two separate households for any of a variety of reasons.

living apart together (LAT) relationship An intimate relationship between partners who live in two separate households for any of a variety of reasons.

marriage A socially approved sexual and economic union between two or more people that is expected to last a long time.

monogamy A form of marriage in which one is allowed only one partner.

***pacte civil de solidarité* (PACS, civil solidarity pact)** An alternative form of couplehood in which a partnership is legally recognized and each member is financially responsible for the other, but that is easier to dissolve than a marriage.

polyandry The marriage of one woman to more than one man.

polygamy The marriage of one person to two or more partners at the same time.

polygyny The marriage of more than one woman to one man.

serial (sequential) monogamy The marriage of one person to two or more partners in a lifetime, though only one at a time.

Critical Thinking Questions

1. Marriage as an institution has been deemed an agency of social control through its contribution to the emotional stability and overall well-being of adults and children. To what extent can alternatives to marriage serve the same purposes? Do you think it is possible for "polyandry" and/or "polygyny" to replace "serial monogamy" in Canadian society? Why or why not?

2. In the past, couples who moved in together often had been in a long-term relationship and were planning on marrying. How have the nature and goals of cohabitation changed? In most, but not all, provinces in Canada, cohabiting couples are given rights similar or equal to married couples and the same responsibilities in the case of separation. In view of this, does cohabitation still constitute an alternative to marriage?

3. In the past, lesbians and gays rejected parenthood as well as traditional family values. Yet the movement toward integration within the mainstream family culture and a focus on stable couple formation and family life emerged when marriage was no longer considered a traditional heterosexual institution. How can we explain this apparent contradiction—a desire for mainstream integration and a rejection of heterosexual norms?

4. With increased life expectancy, older couples live together for longer. However, with aging comes chronic illness for some, which leads to seniors becoming caregivers for their partners. What is the role of formal and informal supports for these caregivers?

Weblinks

Citizenship and Immigration Canada
www.cic.gc.ca/English/immigrate/sponsor
/spouse-apply-who.asp
This site provides information about sponsorship programs and eligibility of spouses, common-law or conjugal partners, or dependent children who may immigrate to Canada as permanent residents.

Equal Marriage for Same-Sex Couples
www.samesexmarriage.ca
This site documents the journey toward the legal recognition of gay marriage rights in Canada and around the world. It provides links to articles in the media that document the efforts, stories, and successes of activists in their feat to legalize gay marriage.

Loving More
www.lovemore.com
The Loving More site provides information for people of all orientations who are interested in exploring relationship options, including group marriage, open couples, intimate networks, and expanded families. It provides information about annual conferences, retreats, and seminars aimed at familiarizing people with polyamory.

The Vanier Institute of the Family— Fascinating Families
www.vanierinstitute.ca/fascinating_families# .UI9GkFPoy9I
Fascinating Families is a regularly updated web feature of the Vanier Institute of the Family that highlights current family-related facts and trends. The information helps to understand the strengths of Canadian families and the challenges they face by discussing the implications of recent trends for families in Canada through a "family lens."

Seniors Canada
www.seniors.gc.ca
This site provides general information about different areas of Canadian seniors' lives, such as marriage, divorce, family violence, health and wellness, and care facilities.

Chapter 5
Happy and Healthy Relationships

Veronika Vasilyuk/Fotolia

Chapter Outline

Learning Objectives

1 Explain how intimate relationships and individual health are related.

2 Differentiate between the types of intimate unions that people engage in.

3 Describe how relationship quality is affected by the relationship status of a person.

4 Argue for the benefits of homogamy in a relationship.

5 Identify the stages of the life cycle of marriage, as well as the characteristics that define each of these stages.

6 Describe what is necessary in a relationship for it to be considered satisfying for the people involved.

7 Show how gender roles affect the experience of a close relationship.

8 Describe how the different styles of communication relate to relationship satisfaction.

9 List the rules for successful communication.

10 Describe what factors make marital and family therapy (MFT) successful.

The world can be a cold, lonely place for people who are on their own, without a close intimate relationship. That may be why, over the course of their lives, most people enter one or more intimate relationships. Despite the benefits, no relationship is perfect, and no long-term relationship is easy to preserve. Close relations can be frustrating, boring, irritating, exhausting, and disappointing. People in close relations can feel just as alone as single people. Yet, most people continue to enter and remain in these relationships and, if they end, seek new ones.

This chapter is about why people enter and stay in close intimate relations—what benefits they receive by doing so—and how some manage to "succeed" better than others do. We will also study the reasons people in committed long-term relationships are, on average, happier and healthier than unattached people—despite the many difficulties associated with setting up and preserving intimate relations.

SOCIOLOGICAL FINDINGS ON MARITAL QUALITY

Sociologists have measured the link between marriage and well-being for more than a century. In fact, they have gone about this in at least three different ways: (1) by examining the suicide rates of attached and unattached people; (2) by asking people to report their feelings of happiness or satisfaction with life; and (3) by looking at the mental or physical health, and any changes from previous healthfulness, of people in relationships. Interestingly, these different methods have yielded similar results.

One of the earliest sociological studies, Émile Durkheim's classic work *Suicide*, looked at the patterns of French suicide rates in the late nineteenth century. Durkheim found that socially integrated—that is, socially attached—people are less likely to kill themselves. The more attached they are—as spouses or parents, for example—the less likely people are to commit suicide.

People who are isolated and unregulated often suffer from rootlessness and aimlessness that Durkheim called **anomie**, a condition that increases the risk of suicide. Close relations reduce the risk by providing attachment and care. Close relations also provide order. They set healthy limits on people's hopes and ambitions. Emotional ties connect people to those they live with. Duties to protect and support these people regulate their lives.

On the other hand, unattached people—especially people with no partner, children, or other close family (for example, dependent parents, brothers, or sisters) to care for—can go where they want, when they want, with whom they want. Paradoxically, with less integration and order, these people are likelier to commit suicide than attached people. Thus, having fewer limits imposed on them carries risks as well as benefits for people.

Today's statistics support Durkheim's theory. Suicide rates remain higher among unmarried than among married people, just as they were a century ago. As Durkheim's frame of analysis states, people will always experience limited fulfillment and satisfaction unless they involve themselves with others, in close relations.

However, researchers rarely rely on suicide statistics to measure people's well-being. Suicide may be a sign of unhappiness, but few people who are unhappy commit suicide. Besides, divorce and singlehood are not the only causes of suicide. Therefore, sociologists have developed other ways to measure health, happiness, and satisfaction in relationships. As the reasoning runs, good marriages should provide more benefits than bad close relations or good distant relations. This reasoning can be subjected to empirical analysis.

Close Relations, Good Health

Research consistently shows that marriages—despite the effort they take and the conflict they often breed—*are* healthy for people. Committed marriages can do people a lot of mental and physical good, though bad ones can do them much harm. Best of all, most of the time people can *choose* the people they want to join in close relations and can act to improve their relationship if it starts to produce unhealthy results.

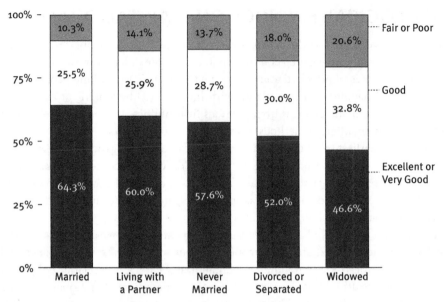

Figure 5.1 Age-adjusted Current Health Conditions by Marital Status

Source: National Center for Health Statistics, National Health Interview Survey, 2011.

Other things being equal, married people are healthier and happier than unmarried people are (see Figure 5.1). Compared with married people, separated, divorced, and unattached people are, on average, less happy, less healthy, more disturbed, and run a higher risk of early death (Keyfitz, 1988). Cohabiting people are typically less stable and satisfied than married people. However, other things being equal, people in long-term committed cohabiting relations are happier and better off than unattached people.

High divorce rates in North America may cause people to have more skeptical ideas surrounding marriage, but most people still marry, and it continues to have strong benefits for those people. Research has found the benefits of marriage for some groups have increased over the past several decades. During this time, there has been a dramatic rise in inequalities in health among men, such that unmarried middle-aged men are about one-third likelier than married men to die in any given year. This study included causes ranging from cancer to respiratory disease to suicide (Jaffe, Dena, Manor, Eisenbach, and Neumark, 2007).

Findings such as these show the strong associations that consistently link marriage and health. The link between marriage and health is mediated by the quality of the relationship, however—that is, how a couple gets along. The higher the quality of the relationship, the stronger is its positive effect on health.

Because a good marriage produces happiness and health, we can gauge the quality of a marriage from the partners' mental and physical health. In fact, we may be able to make a better guess about the quality of a marriage by looking at the health of the people in it than by listening to what the same people tell us about the marriage. To give an extreme example, a battered wife may give all the "right" answers on a survey about marital happiness. Yet, signs of poor health such as depression, lack of sleep, and poor eating—not to mention, signs of physical violence—will reveal the marriage is in trouble.

Marital stressors are related to both mental and physiological problems (Kiecolt-Glaser and Newton, 2001). The cause-and-effect relationship goes both ways: for example, psychiatric symptoms can lead to marital difficulties, or marital difficulties can aggravate psychiatric symptoms. People in unhappy marriages often show signs of psychological difficulty. The symptoms include a weaker will to live, less life satisfaction, and reported poorer health, compared with people in happy marriages (Shek, 1995).

Marriage quality affects the mental health of wives more than it affects husbands (Horowitz, McLaughlin, and White, 1998). Women tend to respond in a more directly emotional manner to adverse marital experiences. Under conditions of stress, men tend to act out—to drink or act violently, for example—while under the same conditions, women are likelier to suffer depression—that is, to drive the anxiety inward. A happy marriage can improve every part of a person's life, including health and parenting skills, especially if the mother is satisfied with the marriage (Feldman, Fisher, and Seitel, 1997). But a bad marriage is far worse, especially for women, than singlehood or divorce.

What Makes a "Good Marriage" Work

- Men tend to report higher marital satisfaction and benefit more from marriage than women do. Marital satisfaction generally predicts life satisfaction, but more so for women than men (Ng, Teik-cheok, Gudmunson, and Cheong, 2009).

- Similarities in cognitive style may increase the chance of a successful marriage, where *cognitive style* refers to the strength of a person's desire for structure when confronted with change (Skinner and Iaboni, 2009). For example, couples in which both members are "adaptors" (i.e., compliant, cautious, dependable, and structured) will have a higher marital success rate than if only one member is an "adaptor".

- Humour is important in helping a marriage to work. However, the *style* of humour employed makes a huge difference in whether the relationship is successful or not (Saroglou, Lacour, and Demeure, 2010). Relationship satisfaction (and with it, low divorce rates) is related to constructive, self-enhancing humour. Self-defeating or self-deprecating humour corresponds to normal levels of marital satisfaction but also to a higher risk of divorce. The worst humour style for a relationship is antisocial, or aggressive, humour; it predicts low levels of relationship satisfaction and a higher risk of divorce.

- Sharing of all kinds—including ideas, thoughts, worries, and dreams—with one's partner leads to more marital satisfaction and intimacy (Duffey, Wooten, and Lumadue, 2004). Partners who share on a regular basis are usually more able to resolve conflicts effectively (Knee, Lonsbary, Canevello, and Patrick, 2005).

A good marriage is especially important to people who are sick, weak, or vulnerable in other ways. For example, pregnant women benefit from being in a good marriage with a kind and understanding partner. The quality of the attachment between a pregnant woman and her partner increases the woman's sense of well-being (Zachariah, 1996). Intimacy gives both partners health protection within a stable and caring family environment. Intimacy may also promote coping strategies in dealing with stressful life events (Ren, 1997).

Recent studies have shown the positive effects of marriage are not only found among married heterosexual couples, but also among gay and lesbian married couples (Wienke and Hill, 2009). Many people cannot handle stress all by themselves. A partner or family can provide support during difficult times.

The likeliest explanation for the link between marriage and health is that a good marriage provides economic and emotional support. Emotional stability in turn strengthens the immune system, making partners more able to avoid or recover from illness. It also increases the will to live and promotes prudence and self-care. As well, marriage provides economic support. Married people who live together can pool their funds to avoid economic hardship. This increases their access to health care and also permits them to focus on healthy lifestyles. These two factors are likely the best explanation for the good health of people in good marriages.

A Continuum of Closeness

Imagine, first, that there are four (and only four) kinds of relationship statuses: single, dating, cohabiting, and married. Let us take "dating" to mean being involved in an intimate relationship with someone who lives in another household, while "cohabitation" means being involved in an intimate relationship with someone who lives in the same household. Together, these create a continuum of closeness, where legal marriage is at one end and single or non-dating status is at the other.

How does being in one of these statuses compare, for example, in health terms, with being in another of these statuses? In addition, does it matter how a person got into one of these statuses? These are questions that sociologist Edward Laumann and his team at the University of Chicago (1994) addressed to data collected from adults aged 18 to 59 who were part of the National Household Survey of Life Styles (NHSLS). The team cross-tabulated answers to questions about health, happiness, and physical and emotional satisfaction with each respondent's most recent partner against information about the respondent's relationship history and status (see Table 5.1).

The findings for women were clear-cut and convincing. On every dimension, women currently in their first marriage were better off—healthier, happier, more physically satisfied, and more emotionally satisfied with their partner—than any other women. After women who are in their first marriage, women who had never married or were cohabiting were the next healthiest, happiest, and most satisfied women.

Table 5.1 Percentage Distribution of Quality of Life Outcomes by Marital, Cohabiting, Dating, and Single Status: American Adults 18–59

Men	Excellent or very good health	Very or extremely happy	Very or extremely physically satisfied with partner	Very or extremely emotionally satisfied with partner
		Percentages		
Never married, single	90.6	44.8	71.7	46.2
Never married, dating	95.3	60.7	81.7	72.6
Never married, cohabiting	88.3	55.0	82.8	84.5
Currently in first marriage	91.5	70.4	89.1	88.4
Divorced/separated/ widowed, single	87.5	31.4	67.5	47.5
Divorced/separated/ widowed, dating	85.9	42.7	84.3	69.5
Divorced/separated/ widowed, cohabiting	79.0	63.2	97.4	92.1
Currently remarried	87.1	68.3	89.2	84.9

Women	Excellent or very good health	Very or extremely happy	Very or extremely physically satisfied with partner	Very or extremely emotionally satisfied with partner
		Percentages		
Never married, single	88.5	54.2	65.3	56.0
Never married, dating	87.8	51.3	83.9	74.2
Never married, cohabiting	90.4	61.1	84.5	73.2
Currently in first marriage	90.9	68.8	86.2	83.6
Divorced/separated/ widowed, single	86.8	36.7	50.0	38.2
Divorced/separated/ widowed, dating	83.5	41.1	84.1	67.5
Divorced/separated/ widowed, cohabiting	76.8	50.9	85.5	74.6
Currently remarried	80.3	66.2	85.2	80.1

Source: Edward O. Laumann, Jenna Mahay, and Yoosik Youm. "Sex, Intimacy and Family Life in the United States," Presented at the ISA Conference, Brisbane, Australia, XV World Congress of Sociology, July 8–13, 2002, Plenary Session, Symposium III, Table 4. Reprinted with permission.

On almost every dimension, the opposite was true for women who, after divorce, separation, or widowhood, were single. They were least likely to report being happy and physically or emotionally satisfied with their most recent partner. The only women in poorer health than these single women were cohabiting women who had previously divorced, separated, or been widowed. In short, close intimate relations are good for women's health and happiness.

The survey data demonstrate that relationships stretch along a continuum of closeness. This has been well supported by other research. Dush and Amato (2005) also examined this continuum of closeness. They included additional types of relationships, including married and cohabiting, as well as steady dating, dating multiple people, and, finally, not dating.

Consistent with Laumann's (1994) research, well-being was highest among married people, followed by cohabiting people, followed by steady daters and lowest for non-daters. Well-being decreased from first marriage, down through cohabitation, dating, to singlehood. First marriages were reported to be more valuable and satisfying than later marriages; and people who had ever gone through a marriage breakup were less happy and healthy than people who had not.

Bear in mind, these are only correlations, not proof of a causal link. Therefore, we cannot be certain from the data that good marriages confer good health and happiness. It is also possible that good health and happiness produce good marriages. Another possible interpretation is the psychic injuries associated with marriage breakdown (that is, divorce or separation) or widowhood make it difficult for people to experience the same high levels of satisfaction in second or later marriages. That said, this study by Laumann and his colleagues (1994) supports the findings of dozens of other researchers.

TYPES OF UNION AND RELATIONSHIP QUALITY

There are several explanations for the trends discussed in relation to relationship quality. What constitutes a "good" relationship is something people define uniquely in each relationship, because people have different needs and different ideas of what they are looking for. Good marriages should manage to achieve a good fit between the partners' individual needs, wishes, and expectations, a fit they regard as unique and irreplaceable (Wallerstein, 1996).

As we have seen, reported well-being varies from one sort of relationship to another—for example, from marriage to cohabitation to dating. Likely, people in different kinds of relations bring different standards to bear when evaluating their relationship and their lives within them.

For example, cohabiting marriages typically last a shorter time and yield less satisfaction than legal marriages. Studies comparing marital quality between three types of marriage—long-term cohabiting, married, and remarried—reveal that cohabiting couples have the least happiness (Skinner, Bahr, Crane, and Call Vaughn, 2002). Couples who cohabited before marriage were less happy than those who had not. In addition, long-term cohabiters were reportedly more violent (Stafford, Kline, and Rankin, 2004).

Research has shown that couples in marriages are more satisfied with their lives than cohabiting couples on average, but this difference is even larger in collectivistic cultures than in individualistic cultures like our own (Diener et al., 2000). In collectivistic societies, more value is placed on gaining social approval. Since cohabiting as a relationship type often goes against the normative expectations of such cultures, it is often met with disapproval. Cohabiters who have internalized the society's dominant values will feel that disapproval more keenly than those living in individualistic cultures and will thus rate their cohabiting relationships more unsatisfactory.

People in different kinds of relationships may also draw satisfaction from different things. Cohabiting couples place more emphasis on spending time together and enjoying physical intimacy, while married couples place more emphasis on emotional stability (Cannon, 1999). For (on average) longer-lived marriages, physical intimacy has become less significant.

Cohabiters reported less commitment than married people as well as a greater conflict frequency (Stafford et al., 2004). The greater stability of married couples is particularly important for their well-being. As a result, less instability and more happiness are found among cohabiters who eventually marry than among those who continue to cohabit (Brown, 2004). Brown also noted that cohabiters expressing plans to marry enjoy levels of relationship quality similar to those who did marry.

Cohabitation has a different effect on older couples, however. In recent years, cohabitation among even middle-aged and older adults has become increasingly popular, with rates of cohabitation doubling in the past decade.

First, cohabitation provides people with companionship without the formalities of marriage and the accompanying legal responsibilities. Second, even though they are living together, cohabiting people can still maintain financial autonomy if they wish, to protect their offspring's inheritance. Third, cohabitation avoids the commitment demands of marriage, since there is no risk of divorce—a rigorous and tiresome procedure. Fourth, studies show that there is no difference between cohabiting relationships and marriages in terms of emotional satisfaction, pleasure, openness, time spent together, and overall relationship quality. Fifth and finally, since the elderly tend to be less desirable partners due to their deteriorating health, cohabitation may be the most suitable option for both partners in the relationship.

There is a common belief (highlighted by those who reject same-sex marriages) that homosexual marriages are markedly different from their heterosexual counterparts. However, sociological evidence implies the same kinds of marriage dynamics are found in all couples, regardless of sexual orientation. Gays and lesbians show selection patterns similar to heterosexuals—they also tend to find partners who match them in age, race, education, and income (Jepson and Jepson, 2002).

"Coming out" is relevant to the marital quality of same-sex couples. Evidence shows that it is essential for the health of the marriage the partners reveal their sexual orientation to their families. Gay men who come out to friends and family are likelier to engage in a long-term marriage than men who do not (Eaton, 2000). Similarly, lesbians who come out to a wide group of people report more satisfaction in their marriage than those who do not (Jordan and Deluty, 2000).

If one partner is openly gay to friends and family but the other is still hiding his or her sexuality, conflict can result and marital quality can decrease (Haas and Stafford, 1998). One partner may not feel he or she is getting the needed social support or may feel insulted by the other partner's refusal to openly admit the legitimacy of the marriage.

The same holds true for heterosexual marriages: For any partners, declaring the importance of the marriage to friends and family marks a turning point in the relationship. It signals a commitment and invites support. Both commitment and support strengthen couple closeness and satisfaction with the marriage.

HOMOGAMY

Most research findings show there is a strong connection between spousal similarity and marital satisfaction. Gaunt (2006), for example, found that for both men and women similar personality traits and values were strongly and consistently associated with happiness and marital satisfaction. Gaunt found that similarity in self-direction, conformity, and achievement values were most important for wives' satisfaction and affect. Similarity on values around goodwill and charity were important for men's satisfaction and affect. In general, according to Gaunt's findings and consistent with other research, marital satisfaction showed the strongest and most consistent associations with couple similarity in almost all domains.

Homogamy increases marital satisfaction by reducing the number of issues on which the couple may disagree. As a result, other things being equal, partners who think they are a lot alike voice more satisfaction with their marriage. In fact, sometimes it is merely a belief in similarity that provides satisfaction. Research has found that an *assumed* similarity between partners may sometimes be just as important for marital satisfaction as *real* similarity (Blackmon, 2000; Hassebrauck, 1996; Yaffee, 2003).

Marital Satisfaction among Immigrant Couples

The experience of immigration is a stressful one, and stressful situations strain close relations. Current sociological research readily addresses the impact of migration on a person's well-being but scarcely examines how immigrant couples adapt to the environment in their new country. This is a significant research limitation, since couples and families—not individual people—usually migrate (Ataca and Berry, 2002).

According to Hyman, Guruge, and Mason (2008), there are many negative effects of immigration on marital satisfaction. Most significant of these is conflict related to gender roles and responsibilities. As we will see in a later chapter, this is an important point given the high rates of spousal violence in immigrant marriages. At the same time, immigration is a mutual challenge that can strengthen the bonds of marriage by increasing interdependence, improving communication and intimacy, and simplifying joint decision making (Hyman et al., 2008).

So, what is needed in a marriage to survive immigration? Most essential are communication and trust, as in all marriages. Also, satisfaction depends on the couple's ability to adjust to changing gender roles and responsibilities in the new society, increased intimacy and sexuality, and conflict management (Hyman et al., 2008; Cheung, 2008; and Huang and Akhtar, 2005). Some external factors are also significant, including a good balance between old and new cultures and the availability of support networks, whether formal or otherwise (Cheung, 2008).

THE LIFE CYCLE OF A MARRIAGE

In many marriages, the expected sequence of events is dating, cohabiting or legal marriage, children, and then possibly grandchildren. This "typical" sequence of events characterizes long-term, stable marriages (Ravanera and Rajulton, 1996). Note, however, that this characterization of the "typical" life cycle is limited by the evident range of cross-cultural variation. Some cultures do not allow for dating or cohabiting stages, for example, and as soon as people reach marrying age, they are thrust into the heart of the cycle—marriage itself. For example, the Yanomamo, a tribal subculture in Venezuela, view marriage as a political process of creating marriage alliances (Buunk, 2010). Similarly, arranged marriages are common in Western societies when immigrants, especially South Asian immigrants, continue to follow the marriage traditions of their home cultures (ibid).

Many couples expect that their marriage will become even more satisfying as they enter each stage of life. However, here people's expectations may be unrealistic. In fact, marital satisfaction does not increase, or decrease, linearly over time. Marriages have some predictable difficulties.

Marriage Beginnings

In the beginning, sex is especially important for close relations. The quality and frequency of sexual intercourse becomes an important indicator of couple satisfaction and relationship quality. Previous experiences play a role here; the choices couples make about their sexual behaviours are as much a result of earlier sexual experiences as they are of later ones. Preconceived notions about sex and proper sexual behaviour can also enable or constrain sexual activity. As discussed in Chapter 3, social beliefs (i.e., the sexual double standard) often have an influence over the sexual activities of couples in the beginning stage of a relationship.

Nevertheless, both men and women tend to report satisfaction. That is because sex is important for both men and women in new relationships.

For gay and lesbian couples, as well as for heterosexual couples, the frequency and importance of sexual intercourse declines with the passage of time in a relationship.

Around this central fact, different kinds of couples have different sexual expectations. Studies find that in the beginning gay male couples have more sex than other couples do, while lesbian couples have less (Peplau and Fingerhut, 2007). This may be due to learned attitudes toward sexuality and openness.

The Introduction of Children Into a Marriage

In general, the transition to parenthood is associated with less sex and steeper declines in marital satisfaction, compared to couples who remain childless (Lawrence, Rothman, Cobb, Rothman, and Bradbury, 2008).

That said, much of the effect of children on marital satisfaction depends on timing and planning. Not surprisingly, husbands and wives who plan the pregnancy experience less decline in marital satisfaction than those whose pregnancy is unplanned and unexpected (and possibly unwanted).

The same trend is found in lesbian couples. Shortly after the birth of a child, lesbian couples report less love and more conflict in their marriage (Peplau and Fingerhut, 2007). Therefore, despite the more egalitarian division of labour in lesbian homes, children are nonetheless stressful.

There are many explanations for this near-universal decline in marital satisfaction following childbirth. Four models have been proposed to explain this decrease (Twenge, Campbell, and Foster, 2003):

1. Role conflict model: The arrival of children often leads to changes in social roles, bringing them closer to the traditional ones—wives providing child care and husbands being the breadwinner.

2. Restriction of freedom model: Children drastically reduce the time wives have for their husbands or themselves. The presence of a pre-school-age child reduces significantly the activities wives do alone, or parents do as a couple or with non-family members. This radical shift from spousal (adult-centred) activities to parenting (child-centred) activities creates an emotional distance the partners find hard to bridge.

3. Sexual dissatisfaction model: With the presence of children, sleepless nights increase. Privacy, and often romance, disappears. It is more difficult to have sexual relations.

4. Financial cost model: Children are expensive, and the costs involved in raising them often constrain family resources.

Mothers, usually the main providers of child care, have to change their time use much more than fathers after the birth of a baby. According to the role conflict model, mothers may have to give up previous jobs in exchange for household and caregiving duties. Their happiness decreases if they resent the fact that they had to give up their careers. Fathers, on the other hand, may be spending more time at work to meet increased financial needs. Many studies point to the importance of men sharing child-care and household responsibilities in determining the effect children will have on a marriage. As well, access to and ability to afford daycare is significant.

Bonnie Fox (2001) points out that the transition to parenthood often increases gender inequality in the marriage. Many women put their jobs on hold to stay home with the newborn (even if it is just during maternity leave). Child care is difficult and time-consuming work, so typically, mothers have to devote more time to their infant and less time to their husband. Fox's study found that husbands often resent this change in marital attention. In order to appease their husbands and keep the family together, many wives end up catering to their husband's needs at the expense of their own needs for rest and leisure.

> In short, how a woman experiences mothering is largely a product of negotiation with her partner. Because intensive mothering requires considerable support, it is contingent upon the consent and active cooperation of the partner, which makes for all sorts of subtle inequalities in the relationship (Fox, 2001: 11–12). As well, partners with young children are often too busy to spend even limited "quality time" with each other. Sexual activity falls off dramatically and may never return to its original level. Researchers report that with preschoolers present in a household, sexual inactivity is likely and prolonged.

New sources of conflict emerge for the couple (Wadsby and Sydsjoe, 2001). Both husbands and wives become concerned with troubles associated with financial matters, family relations, work, and friendship.

Having children also affects the mental and physical health of a couple; however, the findings on the effects are mixed. Children younger than age 18 take time and work, create feelings of overload, and lower marital quality—all of which can cause depression (Bird and Rogers, 1998). However, Helbig, Lampert, Close, and Jacobi (2006) found that parenting decreased the likelihood of depressive disorders and substance abuse for both men and women. As well, an absence of partnership was associated with increased rates of all common mental disorders (Helbig et al., 2006).

A good marriage can decrease postnatal depression in first-time parents and can decrease couple morbidity. Many couples come to rely on their parents—especially their mothers—for practical help and emotional support (Matthey, Barnett, Ungerer, and Waters, 2000).

As mentioned, a husband's participation in pregnancy and parenthood is essential in helping keep the marriage healthy. Wives in strong, supportive marriages are likelier to view the fetus in a loving, warm, and joyful way, for example. These mothers are also likelier to report better marital adaptation and less likely to feel abandoned by their husbands in pregnancy (Sitrin, 2001).

Infertility

Having young children has been shown to increase stress and marital problems, but a lot of other research has focused on the couples who don't have children, either voluntarily or involuntarily. Recently, this has become a more prevalent issue. Women are waiting longer to have children as they complete their education and work toward establishing careers. When couples wait too long, they can find themselves in situations in which it is difficult to have children due to age and infertility. This has been associated with stress, anxiety, and sexual problems in both men and women. Women often experience high levels of depression because of this inability.

In recent times, there is a built-in biological life course discord. Biologically, women and men are in their prime child-bearing stages in young adulthood, but culturally, they are now expected to wait longer in order to ensure they are "ready." As a result, infertility is an increasingly prominent cause of marital strain. This further becomes exacerbated when we consider the financial strains that often hit couples who pursue expensive infertility treatments, as is made clear when we consider that the infertility treatment market was worth more than $1 billion in 2006 (BioPortfolio, 2006).

As with other strains, there are many ways couples may cope with the stress brought about by infertility, some more effective than others. *Active confronting coping* means asking for advice, trying to solve the problem, and discussing feelings about infertility. *Meaning-based coping* involves trying to grow as a person in other ways and redirecting life goals. Both have been linked to short- and long-term forms of adaptation to infertility (Peterson, Pirritano, Christensen, and Schmidt, 2008). Facing infertility is a unique experience and can cause intense feelings of powerlessness; however, as with all other marital stressors, coping abilities are key.

The Midlife Marriage

Midlife couples face unique difficulties in their lives often due to the many transitions they are likely to face at this stage. For one, couples may be dealing with parenting their children and also taking care of their elderly parents, although it is debatable if this has a negative impact on couple health. Menopause and parental death may also put strain on the marriage. In general, midlife married couples are more likely to report problems with financial matters, sexual issues, and ways of dealing with children. Problems are least reported in areas of values, commitment, spiritual matters, and violence (Henry and Miller, 2004: 405, 407–408, 413). Thus, the midlife couple faces unique challenges that are different from couples of a newborn baby and, as we will see, couples in later life.

Later in the Marriage

Marital satisfaction, which decreases with the arrival of children, typically reaches an all-time low when the children are teenagers. Then, as children approach late adolescence and eventually leave home, marital satisfaction usually starts to increase.

Once the children leave home, creating what is often called an "empty nest," many marriages improve nearly to newlywed levels of satisfaction. Parental and work responsibilities decline around that time, partly explaining this return of marital satisfaction (Orbuch, House, Mero, and Webster, 1996).

Many couples rediscover each other because they have more leisure time to get reacquainted. Compared with younger married couples, older couples report much less distress, less desire for change in their marriage, and a more accurate understanding of the needs of their partners (Rabin and Rahav, 1995).

Unfortunately, the experience of positive changes is not universal. Sometimes the absence of children has the opposite effect, resulting in feelings of loneliness. In particular, many senior adults in relationships report moderate or strong feelings of loneliness. Emotional loneliness is especially prevalent among women in second marriages; by contrast, social loneliness is especially prevalent among older men who care for spouses with health problems (Gierveld, van Groenou, Hoogendoorn, and Smith, 2009).

Married couples enjoy more relationship satisfaction during their retirement years than unmarried couples (Price and Joo, 2005). According to the so-called resource perspective, the amount of psychological well-being they experience depends on how they assess their personal resources after retirement as compared to before retirement (Wang, 2007). In this respect, meaningful social relationships are particularly important (Solinge and Henkens, 2008). Because social networks tend to shrink over the life course, marriages increasingly become a source of well-being in post-retirement years (Kupperbusch, Levenson, and Ebling, 2003).

Within marriages, couples tend to have more time to share activities after retirement, leading to greater social cohesion in the relationship (Fitzpatrick and Vinick, 2003). Also after retirement, husbands generally involve themselves more in household tasks (Kulik, 2001). That said, many aspects of the marriage do not change after retirement, and marital quality remains more or less the same (Fitzpatrick and Vinick, 2003). For example, power relations tend to remain similar before and after retirement, although spouses have somewhat more independence in how they use their time (Kulik, 2001). And some aspects of a marital relationship may even decline. In one study, many wives living with a retired spouse reported feeling that their husband now impinged on (or disrupted) the world they had occupied before retirement (Bushfield, Fitzpatrick, and Vinick, 2008).

The need for companionship in later life is strong for both men and women. For instance, in a qualitative, exploratory study of a sample of middle-class Jewish seniors who entered a new union after the age of 65, Schlesinger and Schlesinger (2009) found the main reason for entering a union after the death of a spouse for senior men is to alleviate loneliness. Women, on the other hand, enter into a new marriage for more reasons than companionship, such as sexuality, friendship, intellectual interests, and support for children and grandchildren. Regardless of the reasons behind them, the new unions are positive in a variety of ways for both senior men and women. So, in the third stage, couplehood is an experience of wellness (Schlesinger and Schlesinger, 2009).

WHAT MAKES A MARRIAGE SATISFYING?

There are many aspects of a marriage that lead to relationship satisfaction. However, a lot of the causes of relationship dissatisfaction can be predicted and avoided. We will now discuss separately, and in turn, several factors that affect marital satisfaction.

Love

People vary culturally in the qualities they look for when selecting mates (Rothbaum, Pott, Azuma, Miyake, and Weisz, 2000). For their part, North Americans consider love an essential part of the mating choice; to marry without love seems almost immoral. Traits they look for when forming a relationship typically include personal attraction, trust, and romantic love. By contrast, the Japanese consider loyalty and compassion just as important as love when choosing a mate. Accordingly, they look for unconditional loyalty, commitment, and compassion in a potential marriage partner.

What, then, of marriages that are not based on romantic love? In many societies, arranged marriages are the norm. Arranged marriages in China, the Indian subcontinent, and the Arab world are often built on parents' views about important qualities in future partners. In arranging the marriage, parents usually choose carefully—and homogamously— for their children. Arranged marriages tend, as a result, to be stable and sometimes happy. But are they happier than love marriages?

Westerners tend to assume that they cannot be. Cultures that support arranged marriages say that arranged marriages become, over time, even more satisfying than love marriages. Allegedly, arranged marriages "heat up" with time, while love marriages "cool down." Research on this idea is mixed. In China, where the arranged marriage has a long history, a survey by Xiaohe and Whyte (1990) found that love marriages are more satisfying at every stage or duration.

In Canadian society, as we have said, most people marry for love. They see love as the basis of their union, without which the marriage would not satisfy either partner. According to our ideology about marriage, people are not supposed to think about other things when assessing a partner for romantic compatibility. This is not to say, however, that people completely ignore practical considerations, like the earning power or social status of a potential mate. People who must live hand-to-mouth especially cannot afford to think as much about love; often, they have to be more practical. Therefore, the more financially secure people feel, the more willing they are to indulge romantic impulses: They can afford to indulge their emotions.

Typically, people who assign the most importance to love as a basis for happiness also have the highest divorce rates (Levine, Sato, Hashimoti, and Verma, 1995). They are likely to look for and find flaws in their love marriage. As well, a marriage based on romantic ideals may not be able to weather the often-harsh realities of the situations couples must face together.

In close relations, feelings of passion and companionship usually continue throughout life, yet some types of love are more common than others at particular stages of a marriage (Noller, 1996). What some consider **immature love**—exemplified by **limerence**, love addiction, and infatuation—is characteristic of the first year or two of a marriage. As anyone who follows Hollywood marriages will know, this love is not always the best base for a lasting marriage and family.

Another kind of love called **mature love**, though less euphoric and less chaotic, supports marriage and family life, and can continue throughout life. It creates an environment in which both the lovers and those who depend on them can grow and develop. Mature love is more common later in a romantic marriage. It is, without a doubt, central to the marital satisfaction and life satisfaction of present-day Western people—enacting current notions of intimacy.

Sexual Satisfaction

Sex may be most important in the early years of marriage; however, it is still important in middle age and beyond. Longitudinal research finds that, in middle-aged couples, sexual satisfaction serves as a reward and makes an important contribution to couples' continued positive evaluations of their marriage. And though there is evidence that sexual satisfaction increases marital satisfaction, there is little firm evidence to support the reverse effect (i.e., marital satisfaction affecting sexual satisfaction; Elder, Kirkpatrick Johnson, and Crosnoe, 2004). That said, it is probable that marital satisfaction also has some effect on frequency and satisfaction of sex.

With respect to age, the frequency of sexual behaviour in men and women was believed to decline into older age, often accompanied by a decrease in sexual desire. However, more and more studies point toward the importance of sexual activity and sexual satisfaction in middle age and later. With increased life expectancy, couples now live together longer and remain sexually active longer. The association between sexual activity and marital satisfaction is weaker for seniors than it is for younger couples, but there is still a positive relation between sexual frequency and happiness for older adults (Karraker, DeLamater, and Schwartz, 2011). It is not a lack of desire that typically causes a decline in the frequency of sexual interaction in older adults. For older women, the decline is typically due to a lack of opportunity: As they age, women are more likely (than men) to be widowed and often have a hard time finding a sexual partner. For older men, the decline in sexual activity is typically due to a decline in physical health.

An authoritative international study of men and women age 40 to 80 found that sexual well-being is strongly related to overall happiness. The study, by Laumann, Mahay, and Youm (2002), surveyed 27 500 people on their health, happiness, relationships, and

Table 5.2 Percentage of Respondents Who Report Sexual Satisfaction

The Top 10		The Bottom Five	
Austria	71.4	Thailand	35.9
Spain	69.0	China	34.9
Canada	66.1	Indonesia	34.0
Belgium	64.6	Taiwan	28.7
United States	64.2	Japan	25.8
Australia	63.6		
Mexico	63.2		
Germany	62.0		
Sweden	60.5		
United Kingdom	59.8		

Source: Edward O. Laumann, Jenna Mahay, and Yoosik Youm. "Sex, Intimacy and Family Life in the United States," Presented at the ISA Conference, Brisbane, Australia, XV World Congress of Sociology, July 8–13, 2002, Plenary Session, Symposium III, Table 4. Reprinted with permission.

attitudes to sex. Most middle-aged and older respondents with partners remained sexually active. The study found that people in countries with the most gender equality were likeliest to report being sexually satisfied. Of the 29 countries surveyed, Canada ranked third, behind only Spain and Austria (see Table 5.2). The lowest rankings were for Japan and Taiwan, possibly because in male-centred cultures where reproduction is seen as the main purpose of sex, there is less emphasis on pleasure, especially for the woman.

Intimacy

Most people would agree that feelings of intimacy are also important in making people feel satisfied with their marriage. *Intimacy* comes from the Latin word meaning "inward" or "inmost." To become intimate with someone else means allowing them access to our private world and trusting them with the things that are important to us, whether that be valued material possessions or property of a more emotional nature. Building this intimacy with a partner is the key to a mature, surviving marriage.

Intimacy is *not* mainly about sex. Many sexually active couples are not truly intimate with each other, and many who are intimate have no sexual relations. Consider the odd status of friendship—especially same-sex friendship—in our culture; friendships are sometimes far more intimate (in the original sense of the word) than marriages.

Men and women experience sexual intimacy differently. They want, need, and expect different things. This gendered difference has consequences in every aspect of a marriage, including sex. For example, wives typically report less sexual satisfaction than do husbands. As well, the predictors of sexual satisfaction are different for husbands and

The Importance of Intimacy

- Size matters: As the size of a family household increases, intimacy between the partners typically decreases and sexual pleasure declines (de Munck and Korotayev, 2007).

- Equality matters: In societies where men and women are of equal status (or of almost equal status), male–female romantic relationships are likelier to be intimate and satisfying (de Munck and Korotayev, 2007).

- Trust matters: In romantic relationships, most people seek and desire a partner with qualities that inspire confidence and (thereby) facilitate intimacy (Cann, 2004).

- Patriarchy matters: Traditional gender ideologies generally result in lower levels of couple intimacy by inhibiting self-disclosure, which hinders the development of intimacy (Marshall, 2008).

wives (Song, Bergen, and Schumm, 1995). For women, sex occurs within a gendered or gender-unequal society. Many women have to find sexual pleasure within a marriage that also provokes feelings of powerlessness, anxieties about contraception, and exhaustion from child care and outside employment.

There are many reasons why a loving, committed couple can have problems establishing and maintaining emotional intimacy. For example, one or both partners may have never learned how to express their feelings and respond to a partner's expression of feelings. Couples can also have problems with sexual intimacy when they have different levels of desire. Usually, the partner with less sexual desire is the wife (Trudel, Landry, and Larose, 1997). This can be a problem since North American culture places a high premium on sex, both as a source of pleasure and as an indicator of trust and intimacy.

As we have seen, sexual satisfaction contributes significantly to marital satisfaction (Kumar and Dhyani, 1996). Couples in which sexual activity is rare and one or both partners show little sexual desire may have problems getting along together.

Problems with intimacy sometimes lead to marital infidelity. Typically, men consider cheating by their partner to mean sexual interaction with another man. Women may consider cheating by their partner to mean *emotional* intimacy with another woman, whether sexual relations occurred or not. In good marriages, we find intimacy of both kinds, sexual and emotional. Satisfied partners are more sexually intimate with each other, as measured by how often they display affection physically, touch each other, kiss each other, cuddle, and have sex. These loving behaviours are mutual. Shows of affection by one partner in a good marriage usually prompt loving behaviour by the other partner. Intimacy grows naturally in a sympathetic marriage.

A new obstacle to intimate fidelity is posed by internet chat rooms and other online forums, such as MySpace and Facebook (Hoffner, 2008). These have made it easier than ever to enjoy the stability of marriage and the thrills of the dating scene at the same time (Mileham, 2007). Often this infidelity comes in the form of anonymous online interactions of a sexual nature. The anonymity makes the internet a "safe place" for infidelity for married people. Sometimes people turn to these online forums to satisfy emotional needs that their current partner is not fulfilling, and sometimes, despite initial intentions, such communications transform into close and intimate relationships (Hoffner, 2008).

Research shows that online relationships can be just as rewarding and intimate as face-to-face relationships. As a result, even though a person may participate with pure intentions, unexpected intimacies may evolve nonetheless (ibid).

Research finds that married people tend to rationalize this behaviour as innocent and harmless. Even people who report happy marriages have joined chat rooms for these purposes, researchers find (Heiman et al., 2011).

Coping and Conflict Management

How well a couple manages the conflicts that arise in their marriage shapes their marital satisfaction, and these conflicts and stresses come in many forms.

Less satisfied couples are likelier to avoid discussing important aspects of their marriage, such as their financial situation and their children, and they are likelier just to make small talk (Nielsen, 2002). When talking about important issues, they do so more negatively than couples with high marital satisfaction (Nielsen, 2002).

Health-induced strains also reduce marital satisfaction. Taking care of a severely ill partner puts an enormous chronic strain on a marriage. This leads to dissatisfaction, especially for the caregiving partner. Dissatisfaction is even more likely if a caregiver feels the ill partner brought on his or her own health problems, or has other reasons for feeling cheated in the marriage (Thompson, Medvene, and Freedman, 1995).

Traumatic events in the course of a marriage lead to distress, which has effects on marriage. For example, the death of a child reduces marital satisfaction by straining emotional and sexual intimacy for years afterward. Often, marriages fall apart after a child's death. Partners have a hard time thinking and talking about their suddenly changed lives, with their child missing. The grieving parents often need help reorganizing the ways they think and talk about themselves and their family (Riches and Dawson, 1996).

When strains are chronic or traumatic, they are distressing and increase the likelihood of marital conflict. It is clear that married people cannot avoid conflicts, whatever their cause, and trying to avoid disagreements altogether is unwise. Research has shown that marital well-being is affected less by the presence or absence of hardship than by marital skills and beliefs, or coping abilities. With the passage of time, many couples figure out how to defuse and laugh at their disagreements. In older couples, conflict resolution is usually less hostile and more loving than in middle-aged couples. However, styles of conflict resolution vary by gender, and this difference causes more conflict. Wives tend to be more emotional than husbands are; husbands tend to be more defensive and less expressive (Carstensen, Gottman, and Levenson, 1995).

Which is better—making a fuss or refusing to say anything at all? Research implies that becoming quiet and withdrawn does the most to keep the peace and preserve marital happiness, providing this is not just a means of avoiding the discussion of problems. Many new parents cope (effectively) with the increased stress that accompanies childbirth by adopting this strategy of quiescence (Crohan, 1996). However, this is only a short-term coping strategy and is only effective temporarily while the couple decides how to address their problem in a more useful way.

An important process affecting marital well-being is forgiveness. Forgiveness is strongly related to conflict resolution in marriages. Studies have found that retaliation and avoidance are ineffective strategies of conflict resolution. Unresolved conflicts due to ineffective communication spill over into future conflicts and create a negative cycle of continuing—and even worsening—conflict (Fincham, Beach, Vangelisti, and Perlman, 2006).

It is important to remember that, as tempting as this may seem, walking away from issues and troubles is not a good practice in the end. Neither is hostile argument a good practice. It neither makes the disagreement disappear nor improves the marriage. Partners who lack the skill to argue usefully (see "Rules for Successful Communication" later in the chapter) may fall into a pattern where both partners assert control but neither accepts the other's control (Sabourin, 1995). Each responds to the other's comments with one-upmanship, and the argument escalates, sometimes even resulting in violence. Violence, as we will learn in Chapter 8, is *never* a satisfactory way to deal with marital conflict.

In short, some mixture of emotional expression and emotional restraint is called for under conditions of stress. In the end, everything has to be discussed in a calm, friendly way. Most important, the partners should understand that each has his or her own way of dealing with the stress, and they need to show patience and sympathy for each other.

Gender Roles in Marriage

People are more satisfied with a marriage that meets their expectations of what a marriage should be and how a partner should treat them. Increasingly, this means that, in our society, people, especially women, are much more satisfied when their partner treats them as an equal in the marriage.

Women, as a group, have less power than men. Even if close relations yielded women as much mental, emotional, and financial benefit, women would still profit less than men because they invest more in the relationship. This is especially true where the partners have children to care for. As we will see in Chapter 7, women still do most of the

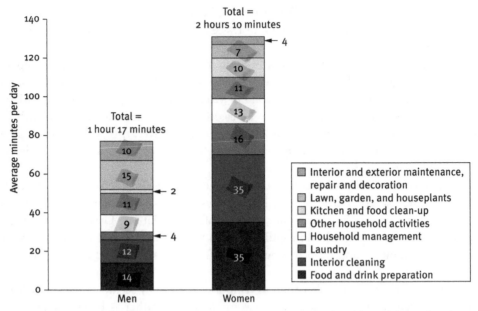

Note: Data include all noninstitutional persons age 15 over. Data include all days of the week and are annual averages for 2012. Travel related to these activities is not included in these estimates.

Figure 5.2 Average Minutes per Day Men and Women Spent in Household Activities, 2010.

Source: Bureau of Labor Statisitics, American Time Use Survey 2010, charts by topics: household activities. www.bls.gov/tus/charts/household.htm.

housework (see Figure 5.2), even if they also work outside the home. Not surprisingly, when the household division of labour is unequal (favouring husbands), wives—especially employed wives—are likelier to become unhappy and depressed (Pina and Bengston, 1995).

The most dissatisfied wives today are younger mothers who do most of the household work—often, far more than their husbands do—as well as work outside the home (Stohs, 1995). It is not just the objective reality of wives doing more housework that is the problem, but the subjective perception that the wife feels she is under-rewarded and undervalued (DeMaris, 2007). Despite being labour intensive, housework is not regarded as "real work" by most people in our society. Household labours are therefore not recognized and rewarded the way workplace labours are—for example, they are generally unpaid when done by a family member. Increasingly, this gender inequality leads to marital conflict. (We return to the division of household labour in more detail in Chapter 7.)

Couples today argue more about household work than about paid work or anything else. Conflicts about paid work often revolve around the husbands' working hours, with most wives preferring their husbands to spend less time at work (Kluwer, Heesink, and van de Vliert, 1996). Child care is an area of particular conflict when household work is discussed.

Whisman and Jacobson (1989) report an inverse relationship between marital satisfaction and power inequality. That is, happy couples more often share the power. Equality brings couples closer together, so partners are better able to see accurately the other's wishes and emotional state (Kirchler, 1989; DeLongis and Lehman, 1989). Equal partners are more satisfied with their marriage, better adjusted, and report using fewer power strategies in trying to get their way (Aida and Falbo, 1991; Diez-Bolanos and Rodrigues, 1989). Non-traditional gender attitudes, and husbands' approval of their wives' careers, promote higher marital satisfaction (Ray, 1990).

The division of labour in heterosexual marriages is more unequal than the division of labour in same-sex marriages. Research finds that in same-sex marriages the tasks are divided more equally, though lesbian partners tended to share tasks, while gay men tended to specialize in different tasks. Remember that most gay men and lesbian women are in dual-earner marriages. Largely as a result of this, most same-sex couples tend to highly rate power equality in terms of what they value in a marriage (Peplau and Fingerhut, 2007).

Summing up to this point, are marriages more beneficial for men or for women? In our society, close relations are still better for men (Keyfitz, 1988)—despite findings cited earlier that women are likelier to acknowledge these benefits. Indeed, men and women often have different experiences of marriage. Conflicts in close relations can have a greater toll on women, especially when coupled with conflicts at work. This may be because women are likelier to blame themselves for marital conflict. Husbands are also likelier to blame wives for marital conflict (Simon, 1995). In addition, the greater loads of child care and domestic labour are stressful for women, and stronger pressures to marry—from society, family, and personal expectation—increase the likelihood that women may form an unsatisfactory marriage.

We noted earlier that married people are, on average, healthier than unmarried people. Significantly, this is more true for men than it is for women. As a result, Canadian married men have a life expectancy five years longer than do single men, while married women live only one and a half years longer than unmarried women (Keyfitz, 1988). Men also gain more satisfaction from a marriage because men and women hold different positions in society.

Work, Money, and Marital Quality

With more women entering the workforce and the subsequent rise of dual-earner families, the influence of work and money on marital quality deserves a more detailed discussion. As researchers Dakin and Wampler (2008: 300) point out, "because money is woven into many parts of the family and marital fabric, it is essential to better understand this family financial phenomenon." They contend that disagreements over finances are among some of the top reasons for divorce.

Financial stress can include cognitive, emotional, and behavioural responses that can lead to spousal hostility (see Figure 5.3) and a decrease in spousal warmth (Dakin and Wampler, 2008). It also increases the likelihood of depression in both partners. Depression leads partners to withdraw their social support and undermine each other. These behaviours, in turn, reduce marital satisfaction and intensify the depression

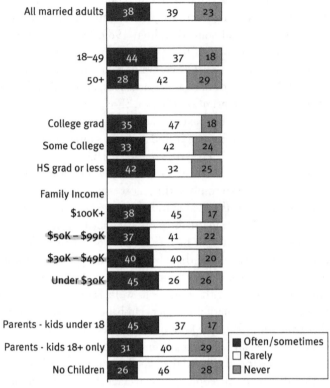

How often do you and your spouse disagree about money?

	Often/sometimes	Rarely	Never
All married adults	38	39	23
18–49	44	37	18
50+	28	42	29
College grad	35	47	18
Some College	33	42	24
HS grad or less	42	32	25
Family Income			
$100K+	38	45	17
$50K – $99K	37	41	22
$30K – $49K	40	40	20
Under $30K	45	26	26
Parents - kids under 18	45	37	17
Parents - kids 18+ only	31	40	29
No Children	26	46	28

Notes: Don't know responses not shown.

Figure 5.3 Marital Discord and Money Matters

Source: "What Americans Pay For—and How 'Information Age' Bills Keep Piling Up" February 7, 2007.

(Vinokur, Price, and Caplan, 1996). For families living in poverty, financial problems constitute one of the most significant stressors, as they find it difficult to meet their basic economic needs (Dakin and Wampler, 2008).

Researchers studying marital quality among low-income married couples in America find that religiosity can buffer some of the negative effects of economic stress on married couples if they share similar beliefs, pray together, or attend religious services together (Lichter and Carmalt, 2009). These results show that social institutions, shared beliefs, and engagement in common activities may have the capacity to enhance and strengthen marital bonds independent of financial circumstances.

The stresses of work can also reduce marital satisfaction. Often, conflicts resulting from a partner's employment cause distress and, in turn, produce hostility and reduce warmth and encouragement between partners (Matthews, Conger, and Wickrama, 1996).

Unemployment because of job loss is known to marital conflict, either from the loss of ordinary ways of family living or an unwanted role reversal (especially for males).

A good illustration of this comes from studying couples in which the husband was diagnosed with multiple sclerosis (MS), a debilitating neurodegenerative disease. Job loss because of MS is nearly inevitable and, out of necessity, results in wives becoming the main breadwinners, which many couples cite as the hardest thing to adjust to (Courts, Newton, and McNeal, 2005). The wives often find themselves with greater caring and financial responsibilities, whereas husbands diagnosed with MS feel that they have become a burden to their wives and have lost their independence and manhood in the face of the disease and unemployment (Edmonds, Vivat, Rubman, Silber, and Higginson, 2007; McCabe, 2006). This puts considerable strain on the marriage, as new ways of dividing responsibility within the household must be negotiated. The couples who successfully adjust to role reversal and experience a strengthening of their marriage cite open and honest communication as the key coping strategy (Courts et al., 2005).

Retirement from work can either increase or decrease marital satisfaction. Leaving a high-stress job normally increases satisfaction. However, poor health and other changes that often cause or go with retirement reduce satisfaction (Myers and Booth, 1996). Retirement, like unemployment, may also reverse gender roles or reduce social support.

In general, people need to prepare for retirement and, often, adjust their marriages to handle their new situation.

COMMUNICATION

The most important influence on marital satisfaction is good communication. Think of good communication as the scaffolding of a relationship. Every attempt to solve problems—for example, reorganizing the household division of labour or choosing a mate wisely—relies on effective communication.

Both the quantity and quality of communication are important in a marriage. The quality of spousal communication includes (1) how open partners are; (2) how well they listen; (3) how attentive and responsive they are; (4) whether do it at all; and (5) to what extent they confide in each other. These are all important to establishing a good, satisfying marriage.

Quantity means how often partners talk with each other. Successful couples talk a lot, even if they have tight schedules and little time to spend together, and even if the topics of conversation are trivial. Satisfied couples engage in much more communication than dissatisfied couples, who engage in little communication on most of the topics commonly discussed by satisfied couples (Richmond, 1995). This is true of same-sex couples, too: Lack of communication proves to be the most significant factor breaking up gay men in long-term marriages (Alexander, 1997).

Satisfied couples chitchat; they make small talk, banter, and joke around. Dissatisfied couples talk less, or mainly talk about weighty matters when they talk at all. Couples do not all have to communicate at the same rate to be successful; however, it is the couples' *sensed* quality of communication that contributes most to marital satisfaction.

The sensed accuracy, appropriateness, and effectiveness of communication contribute more to satisfaction than how much a couple may talk to each other (Glick, 1997).

A word, phrase, or even type of body language can have intensely different meanings for different people. It is partly to avoid these problems, and partly to separate themselves from others, that many couples develop their own private **idioms**. These idioms take a variety of forms: special pet names for each other, inside jokes, and words or phrases for intimate activities, special activities, or places. Couples in the earliest stages of marriage report using the most idioms, and those in later stages use the fewest, for various reasons. One is the arrival of children. When teaching children to speak, you want to teach them words that will help them in the outside world. Family idioms will not do that.

At the beginning, however, the use of idioms improves communication because the couple has defined their meanings together. As a result, satisfied couples use more idioms than couples who report lower levels of marital satisfaction. For interracial couples who may have grown up in different cultures, the use of idioms can reduce conflict and increase openness by creating a language with which both parties are now familiar (Shi, 2000).

Demand/Withdrawal Pattern of Communication

A common style of communication that increases marital conflict is the "demand/ withdrawal pattern." In this pattern, one party—the demander—tries to establish communication by nagging, bullying, or criticizing the other partner. Partners with more power in the marriage are likelier to be "the demander." The withdrawer, on the other hand, tries to avoid such discussions through silence, defensiveness, or withdrawal (Walczynski, 1998).

Like any behaviour that can reduce marital satisfaction, the demand/withdraw pattern of communication has health outcomes. Among married couples age 23 to 71 years old, withdrawers—nagged spouses—had higher blood pressure and heart rate reactivity than the other groups. Husbands of withdrawer wives had even higher blood pressure than the husbands of demander wives. Demander (that is, nagging) husbands with withdrawer wives experienced the highest blood pressure of all the groups (Denton, Burleson, Hobbs, Von Stein, and Rodriguez, 2001).

This implies that neither nagging nor being nagged is a recipe for good communication. Partner communication patterns must be effective and similar enough to uphold marital quality and couple happiness. If partners discuss this problem and what both parties want, their commitment to their marriage will increase.

Non-verbal Communication

Another important part of successful communication is the encoding and decoding of non-verbal information. Non-verbal communication includes all forms of communication that do not use verbal speech. This includes posture, the direction of the gaze, and hand position, for example. Researchers find that dissatisfied couples are especially prone to misunderstanding each other's non-verbal cues. This lack of understanding can cause problems, especially when a person's non-verbal cues contradict the speaker's verbal cues.

For example, if one partner is apologizing sincerely and the other partner misreads the non-verbal signals as insincerity, a simple miscue can turn into a full-blown argument. Long-term couples may also ignore each other's verbal cues and rely mostly on non-verbal ones, causing more misunderstanding. Older long-married couples display lower frequencies of responsive listening than younger couples, which can increase conflict in a situation where a partner uses verbal cues (Pasupathi, Carstensen, Levenson, and Gottman, 1999). Non-verbal accuracy increases over time in marriages, but it increases more for people who are satisfied with their marriages.

Communication and Gender

Communication is a gendered marital challenge, in that women sense more communication problems than men do and are likelier to see men as the source of these problems. Men, on the other hand, view the communication problem, if it is a problem at all, as shared (Eells and O'Flaherty, 1996). Some supposed gender differences in language are stereotypical and have not been empirically confirmed. However, researchers *have* found gender differences in such dimensions as how much women and men talk, length of utterance, use of qualifying phrases, swearing, breaking of silences, and compliment styles (O'Donohue and Crouch, 1996; Tannen, 1993). There are also differences in the emotional content of the talk, with women typically expressing more emotions than men do.

Communication Differences between Genders in Marriages

Studies show that women, more than men, are sensitive to the interpersonal meanings that lie "between the lines" in the messages they exchange with their mates. That is, societal expectations often make women responsible for regulating intimacy, or how close they allow others to come. For that reason, women pay more attention than men do to the underlying meanings about intimacy that messages imply. Men, on the other hand, are more sensitive than women are to "between the lines meanings" about status. For men, societal expectations are that they must negotiate hierarchy, or who's the captain and who's the crew (Tannen, 1993).

Women tend to be the marriage specialists and men tend to be task specialists. Women are typically the experts in *rapport talk* which refers to the types of communication that build, maintain, and strengthen marriages. Rapport talk reflects skills of talking, nurturing, emotional expression, empathy, and support. Men are typically the experts in task accomplishment and addressing questions about facts: They are experts in *report talk*, which refers to the types of communication that analyze issues and solve problems. Report talk reflects skills of being competitive, lacking sentimentality, analyzing, and focusing aggressively on task accomplishment. These differences can create specific, and commonly experienced, misunderstandings (Torppa, 2002).

Marriage Myths

Myth: Love marriages are bound to be happier than arranged marriages.

■ Reality: The evidence is mixed on this. Some studies have shown no difference in marital satisfaction between love/choice and arranged marriages (Myers, Madathil, and Tingle, 2005). In one study, Asian Indians who lived in North America were more maritally satisfied in their arranged marriages than North American counterparts in their love marriages (Madathil and Benshoff, 2008).

Myth: Intimate relationships in which the woman is older than the man don't work out well.

■ Reality: Relationships in which the woman is older have the highest level of romantic satisfaction, equality, and commitment (Lehmiller and Agnew, 2008). Perhaps, given the stigma associated with women-older relationships, this is because couples only enter into such relationships if they plan to be committed and feel confident the benefit will outweigh the cost (Lehmiller and Agnew, 2008).

Myth: Financial troubles won't hinder marital satisfaction, if the people involved love each other enough.

■ Reality: Research shows that poor people have more and worse marital conflicts because they are more stressed about problems caused by lack of sufficient income. The shortage of money leads to hostile emotions and thoughts of divorce, for example (Grable, Britt, and Cantrell, 2007).

Therefore, men and women speak differently, and this difference can become a problem. Consider an important form of marital communication called *debriefing*—conversation about what happened during the day. Men view their debriefing talk as having an informative report role: that is, to bring their partner up to speed on current events. In women's view, the talk may be about current events at home or at work, but the real purpose is downloading grievances, receiving and providing support, and renewing contact with the mate.

Rules for Successful Communication

Good communication is hardly ever the automatic result of a good marriage. Couples who love each other intensely and are committed to each other may still have trouble learning to talk effectively. Like all our other social skills, communication is something we learn, and continue to learn, throughout our lives.

What counts as good, effective communication varies over time and across cultures. In our own society, however, most people agree that forms of communication harm the marriage if they undermine the listener's self-esteem. For example, personal insults, ridicule, questioning a person's authority or competence, or dismissing or belittling the person's achievements are negative, hurtful, even emotionally abusive, forms of communication. Giving a partner the cold shoulder can sometimes hurt even more than a personal insult.

Some rules of successful communication emerge from sociological research on families. One purpose of communication is to send information of either a factual or an emotional nature. The first rule then is that communication must be clear if it is to be effective. Both partners should say what they mean and mean what they say. The second rule of communication is to be willing to hear and to respond to your partner's comments, complaints, and criticisms. This involves being an effective listener. A key to beginning and continuing good communication in a marriage is recognizing our own defects and trying sincerely to work on correcting them.

Communication is important at all stages of a marriage, but it can be especially important in the beginning. During the "honeymoon period," there is an increased sensitivity to the communication of a partner, as well as a strong wish to please and understand the other person. It is during this period that couples set up the basic interactional patterns of the marriage. Indications of marital quality are often first evident at this time.

The third rule of communication is to let your behaviour speak for you (and be sure to "listen to" your partner's behaviour, too). Often, we have trouble putting our thoughts and feelings into words. That is why actions can be meaningful in communicating feelings and desires.

Establishing family rituals can help a couple build and express stability. Among couples with small children, marriage satisfaction is highest for people who have created family rituals and believe that these rituals are important. In lesbian marriages, family routines are of utmost importance for increasing and expressing couple happiness. Caron and Ulin (1997) found that openness with a partner's family and friends is associated with the quality of the couple's marriage.

For example, the couple's presence at family events and participation in the family ritual strengthens the marriage. Family involvement also increases marital quality for gay men (Smith and Brown, 1997), but only if the family confirms the partners as a couple. Otherwise, extra stress is introduced into the marriage.

Ways to Increase Marital Well-Being

Close relations are emotionally satisfying only if they are "good," which is to say the partners *feel* the marriage is giving them something they value (see Figure 5.4). Throughout the chapter, we have discussed the many benefits of being involved in close relations that are high in quality. A marriage must increase and preserve both partners' sense of well-being if it is to survive. Social science evidence shows that marriages that fail to satisfy—whether because of differences between the partners, absence of love, too little intimacy, too much conflict (or abuse or violence), or poor communication—are less likely to survive.

Marital quality also depends on a couple's ability to adapt effectively in the face of stressful events, given their own enduring vulnerabilities (Karney and Bradbury, 1995). All couples face vulnerabilities and stressful events, and must find ways of adapting or coping. From this perspective, there are three ways to increase marital well-being:

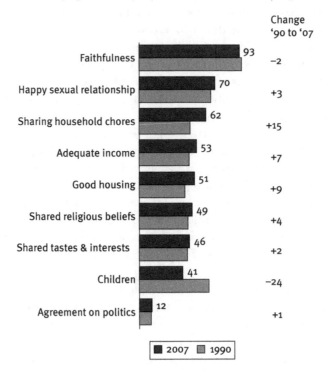

Percent saying each is very important for a successful marriage

Change '90 to '07

	2007	Change '90 to '07
Faithfulness	93	−2
Happy sexual relationship	70	+3
Sharing household chores	62	+15
Adequate income	53	+7
Good housing	51	+9
Shared religious beliefs	49	+4
Shared tastes & interests	46	+2
Children	41	−24
Agreement on politics	12	+1

■ 2007 ▪ 1990

Question wording: Here is a list of things which some people think make for a successful marriage. Please tell me, for each one, whether you think it is very important, rather important, or not very important.

Figure 5.4 What makes a marriage work?

Source: "Modern Marriage." July 18, 2007. Pew Research Center: Social and Demographic Trends. http://pewresearch.org/pubs/542/modern-marriage.

(1) by better adapting to stressful events; (2) by better avoiding stressful events; and (3) by reducing the couple's stock of vulnerabilities.

Many couples try to improve their marriage on their own and do so successfully. Others seek help from family and friends, or advisers such as priests/ministers/rabbis/mullahs, family doctors or lawyers, or teachers. Sometimes people talk with strangers who are there to listen: bartenders, cabbies, dental assistants, and hairdressers. Others, or sometimes the same people, consult specialized advisers, including psychologists, psychiatrists, and marital and family therapists.

Speaking to an outsider gives a person a chance to air his or her views to an objective listener in an unemotional setting. Sometimes, just doing this is enough to help a person see the source of problems and the possible solutions. Talking to an objective third party also gives people an impartial outsider's view of the problems they are experiencing. Other times, something more is needed. Then, a professional therapist with many hundreds of past clients and many thousands of hours of listening may be better able to help.

Marital Therapy

Many couples do not know how to handle the unexpected negative feelings they experience in their marriages. After all, the overwhelming majority of couples begin with true love and great hopes, yet divorce still claims more than one-third of all first marriages. Many researchers have decided that, instead of therapy, unhappy couples need to learn psychological skills, called "psychoeducation," to help them avoid intensifying conflict (Marano, 1997).

However, no marriage can avoid conflict altogether. Sometimes for reasons of cost, immediacy, or tolerance of partner(s), couples reduce the conflict without solving (or even recognizing) the underlying problem that is causing the conflict. This is bad for the relationship. If the underlying problem is spousal inequality, family poverty, or alcohol addiction, for example, helping a couple to avoid escalating its conflicts may merely mask the problem temporarily. In the long term, therapy—if it is to succeed—has to address the underlying issues that produce conflict: the issues we discuss throughout this text.

Marriage counselling has changed over the years, both with an increase in therapists' knowledge and with the ongoing development of new theories in the field. Therapy was once seen as the last resort for couples wishing to fix their marital problems, but now couples therapy is seen as the preferred method of treatment (Johnson and Lebow, 2000: 23). Furthermore, there have been significant developments in couples therapy in recent decades. Initially, feminist writers in the 1990s claimed that therapists promoted and maintained patriarchy within the marriage, in which the husbands were dominant and the wives were deferential and subordinate (Johnson and Lebow, 2000: 30). Therapists are now beginning to understand the importance of rebalancing power within the marriage and are trying to understand the gender meanings assigned to controlling money and allocating the division of labour within the household (Johnson and Lebow, 2000: 30).

Also, in light of same-sex marriage, therapists have begun to understand and appreciate the diversity of families and couples. Issues of ethnicity, class, and culture can have implications for the ways couples view their own marriages and each other (Johnson and Lebow, 2000: 32). For instance, this has led therapists to develop ways in which they can better understand the differing gender roles between African American partners (Johnson and Lebow, 2000: 32).

Whether a marital and family therapy (MFT) program is effective depends on the treatment goal. Thus, therapists must decide whether to apply psychological theories to help individual clients in a troubled marriage or to apply sociological theories to help improve the marriage itself. Some partner-aided therapy with depressed patients leads to reduced depression and thinking that is more productive. However, there is no evidence that this treatment affects marital satisfaction or communication and expressed emotion between the partners (Emanuels-Zuurveen, and Emmelkamp, 1997).

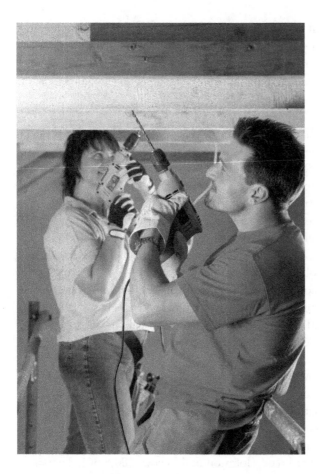

Couples therapy may help resolve issues when the well-being of a relationship is threatened.
Kzenon/Shutterstock

For some, couples therapy improves both individual psychological functioning and marital satisfaction. This shows that it can accomplish both goals simultaneously, while individual therapy cannot (Hannah, Luquet, and McCormick, 1997). Vansteenwegen (1996a) found that seven or more years after completing couples therapy, the individual changes were longer lasting than changes in the marriage itself.

A couple's expectation of their therapist can affect success rates as well. Couples expect marriage therapists to be active, directive, and focused. Couples identify poor therapists as those who waste time or are unclear in therapy. Both successful and unsuccessful couples think that therapy needs a safe environment and proper structure (Estrada and Holmes, 1999).

Many of the successes of marriage counselling are partial successes in the sense that some goals are accomplished while others are not. Ideally, both partners will be satisfied with the outcome of therapy. However, in two-fifths of the couples who receive therapy, one partner is more satisfied than the other. In only one-third of cases are both partners satisfied (Follette et al., 2000).

Also, helpful therapy does not always ensure the survival of the marriage. Sometimes, open discussion reveals that a marriage is deeply and irrevocably flawed, or that two people are unsuited to each other and may be wiser to break up. In a comparison of couples who divorced and those who stayed together after therapy, the divorced couples reported finding therapy just as useful as those who stayed together. In fact, these couples viewed the divorce as a positive result of therapy (Vansteenwegen, 1998).

The findings on the effectiveness of MFT vary widely. In a survey by the Ontario Association for Marriage and Family Therapy, 83 percent of clients reported that they had achieved their goals completely (Ontario Association for Marriage and Family Therapy, 1996). Another survey found moderate but significant effects (Shadish, Ragsdale, and Glaser, 1995). Recent studies have found that more than half of couples claim to have benefitted from marriage counselling, and about 60 percent of those couples stayed in treatment during the follow-up period (Follette et al., 2000). These numbers may seem small, but rates of relapse into old behaviour are low, and couples are usually satisfied with the treatment.

In short, therapy does help couples. Counselling can provide important insights that can be used to learn about each other and aid in effective communication.

CONCLUDING REMARKS

There are no guarantees in life and no fixed rules we can follow to ensure a satisfying marriage. Yet one reason we place so much importance on our marriages and family lives is that these are areas over which we can have a good deal of control. We may divorce if we no longer want to be married to our partner, remarry, perhaps encourage adult children to leave the house, adopt children, and so on. We assume that satisfaction will result if only we make the right decisions.

However, conflict is bound to arise, and a successful marriage is one in which conflict is managed well. Long before forming a marriage, couples should start to discuss what they expect from it, what they want from life, what they are willing to give up, and what they are not. A marriage is, in the end, a plan to try to solve problems together. People who can't solve problems together won't be married for long or, if married, they will be miserably unhappy.

CHAPTER SUMMARY

This chapter showed that relationships are complicated. Some factors make marriages highly successful while other factors can cause the whole relationship to collapse. In order to navigate through close relationships success-

fully, it is important to anticipate the inevitability of conflicts, and learn how to manage them successfully.

Life means dealing with the unexpected. Negotiation is key to working out problems in marriages. Interestingly, the fairer the distribution of power seems to the partners, the more satisfied they will be.

As we have seen, married people—and others in enduring close relations—tend to live longer, happier lives. Satisfaction in a marriage means different things to men and women. Men value emotional independence in their wives, while wives feel happiest when their husbands are "there for them," or emotionally available.

The life cycle of a family is full of difficulties; for example, planning to have a child and then setting out to produce one increases marital happiness. Yet marital happiness usually decreases once the child arrives or if that goal is unable to be met, as in the case of infertility.

Intimacy is an important part of a good marriage. Sexual intimacy is a reliable sign of happiness throughout a marriage, although after children appear, sexual activity typically decreases, often for extended periods of time.

One cause of increased marital satisfaction is homogamy—similarity in attitudes, interests, and behaviours. Not only do people tend to date people like themselves, they usually end up happier after marrying people like themselves. If partners disagree on a woman's role, the marriage is often less happy.

Communication is the key to a successful marriage but, like many skills, it is easier to applaud than to acquire. Good communication may seem irrelevant to couples who choose to divorce and start afresh. Others face their problems squarely, with the help of counsellors who may help them communicate and solve their troubles.

Key Terms

anomie According to Durkheim, a lack of control, or a lack of norms.

idioms Various verbal forms, including pet names and inside jokes, that couples use to separate their relationship and define themselves as a couple.

immature love A type of love typified by limerence, love addictions, and infatuation; characteristic of the first year or two of an intimate relationship.

limerence Infatuation or preoccupation with a relationship partner that is characteristic of the early stages of intimacy.

mature love Love that allows the lovers and those who depend on them to grow and develop; provides constraint, stability, and certainty.

Critical Thinking Questions

1. How do Western and Eastern cultures differ in what a marriage has to fulfill in order for it to be considered satisfying?

2. Why does cohabitation tend to lower life satisfaction even more in collectivistic societies than in individualistic societies?

3. What is the greatest source of marital conflict for immigrant couples?

4. At what stage of raising children is marital satisfaction the lowest, and when does it start to increase again?

5. What is the difference between immature and mature love, and when does each tend to develop in the marriage?

6. What are some factors that make marital and family therapy an effective form of relationship treatment? Does therapy always improve the couple's relationship and prevent divorce?

Weblinks

Relationship Information Online
The American Communication Association (ACA)
www.americancomm.org
The ACA was created to promote academic and professional research, criticism, teaching, practical use, and exchange of principles and theories of human communication. This is a resourceful educational site offering up-to-date information on communication.

Professor's House: Marriage Advice
www.professorshouse.com/relationships/marriage-advice
This link provides information on marriages and includes various articles that cover a wide range of phenomena related to marriage.

Ask the Internet Therapist
www.asktheInternettherapist.com
This resource provides a new and original form of marriage counselling. For people with time constraints or who are unwilling to physically visit a therapist, a new option is online counselling. For a fee, the site offers on-the-spot counselling from an array of medical professionals. The professionals also offer phone and video counselling.

Pew Internet: Dating
www.pewInternet.org/topics/Dating.aspx
This website presents numerous articles that provide information about online dating and relationships.

Service Canada: Getting Married
www.servicecanada.gc.ca/eng/lifeevents/marriage.shtml
This link provides a step-by-step guide to getting married, as well as information concerning other life events associated with close relations.

Chapter 6
Parenting
Childbearing, Socialization, and Parenting Challenges

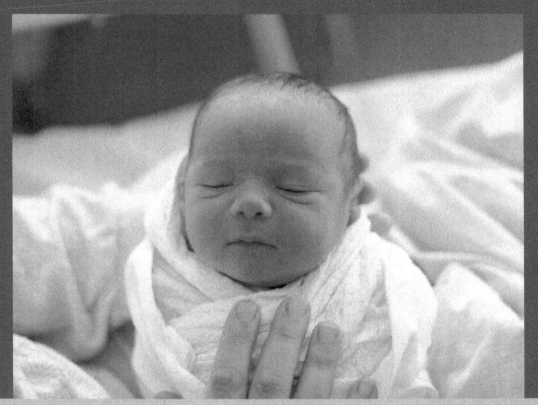

ZouZou/Shutterstock

Chapter Outline

- Gender Socialization
- Ethnic Socialization
- Parenting Processes
  - Love and Attachment
  - Emotional Stability and Family Cohesion
  - Protectiveness and Control
  - Fair and Moderate Discipline
  - Caring for Sick Children
- Variations on a Theme
  - Single Parents
  - Parenting in Poverty
  - Gay and Lesbian Families
  - Aboriginal Families
  - Custodial Grandparents
  - Cultural Variation
- Information Communication Technology
- Concluding Remarks

Learning Objectives

1 Sequence a brief and general history of fertility rates and their causes in Canada.

2 Relate the statistics of single parenting and childless couples to the changed social role of women.

3 Compare the issues that arise with infertility treatments, early entry into parenthood, and adoption.

4 Prioritize the factors that influence marital satisfaction after entering parenthood.

5 Provide three examples of how roles and expectations in close relationships are related to age, gender, and generational differences.

6 Distinguish between socialization, gender socialization, and ethnic socialization, and identify one way in which they overlap.

7 Discuss love and attachment, as well as emotional stability and family cohesion, including their benefits, how to provide them, what prevents parents from providing them, and the consequences of not providing them.

8 Identify the variables of control and acceptance that correspond with authoritarian, authoritative, unengaged, and permissive parenting, and explain why authoritative parenting is the most effective.

9 Define the three basic types of discipline techniques and explain why induction is most effective.

10 Explain how the role of family dysfunction differs in families with runaways and sick children.

11 Compare the possible effects of single parenthood and poverty on children.

12 Recognize the value of gay/lesbian parents and custodial grandparents.

13 Relate historical events to the obstacles facing Aboriginal families today.

14 Explain how the immigration and cultural policies of a country influence the family functions of immigrant families in an international and the Canadian context.

15 Evaluate the effect of mobile phones on communication and authority in the parent-child relationship.

In the days of your great-grandparents and before, it was assumed that people would marry and—as soon as it was affordable—start producing children. Marriages without children were considered to be scarcely marriages at all. Today, we think differently about these matters. We do not assume that everyone will want to have children or start to have children soon after marrying. Similarly, we do not assume that, in important ways, a family without children is no family at all.

As we shall see, there are many reasons for this dramatic change—a change that has accompanied dramatic changes in family life and, especially, dramatic changes in women's social roles. Today, with the availability of good contraception, people are better able to decide whether and when to have children, and the reasons they should or should not do so. And with good educational and occupational opportunities open to them, parenting is less attractive than it once was to many women. Though most women want to have at least one child, few women seem to want four, five, or six children.

ENTERING PARENTHOOD
Decisions about Entering Parenthood

Researchers have proposed several theories to explain why and when people enter parenthood. One theory proposes that child-bearing reflects deep and lasting beliefs. In traditional, high-fertility societies, everyone is raised to believe that parenthood should be a central part in their lives and the life of society. Another theory proposes that couples behave in economically rational ways, assessing the costs and benefits of childbearing. Into the equation go things like the costs of raising children, lost income opportunities for the main caregiver, and other goods (new house, car, travel, and so on) the couple may have to forgo.

Likely, deciding to enter parenthood combines both rational choices and non-rational (or irrational) longings—lifelong hopes for parenthood, self-realization, social and cultural influences, and estimated costs and benefits. No simple theory of the parenting decision covers all cases.

Entering Parenthood in the Past

Childbearing today is much less common than it was in the past, the result of a slow and (almost) consistent decline that took more than a century. Historical records show a marked, gradual decline in the Canadian **birth rate** from the mid-nineteenth to the mid-twentieth century in average numbers of children borne. Women born in Canada between 1817 and 1831, for example, had about 6.6 children, whereas women born between 1947 and 1961 had 1.7 children—less than one-third as many. And for the past 50 years, the numbers of births has continued to fall, especially among native-born, highly educated women.

The improvement of birth control has played an important role in this fertility decline but not as large a role as is often thought, compared with significantly changed views about the value of children. The numbers of children born into families declined largely because of the changing social and economic circumstances in which families lived. As Canadian society industrialized, fewer people needed children to work on the farms. Children cost more to raise in towns and cities than they did on farms, and they brought fewer economic benefits. As such, children in cities changed from an economic benefit to an economic liability.

So, a downward trend in childbearing continued from about 1871 with only a brief interruption—the so-called "baby boom" between 1947 and 1967. In 2008, the average number of births per woman was roughly 1.68, a slight increase from recent years (Statistics Canada, 2011), but below the level of replacement—meaning that the population is shrinking without immigration. Despite this brief blip due to the high number of women at childbearing age, overall the fertility rate is still in decline (Vanier Institute of the Family, 2010a).

Recently the age of women with the highest fertility rate in Canada has shifted, from the 25 to 29 age group to the 30 to 34 age group. Thus, not only are women having fewer children today, they are also having their first child slightly later in life.

Entering Parenthood Today: Family Planning

Though improved birth control was not the reason for fertility decline, we should not underestimate its importance. In Canada, contraception is widely understood and widely practised (Balakrishnan, Lapierre-Adamcyk, and Krotki, 1993: 197). The widespread availability of effective contraception has not only allowed women to limit the total number of children they bear; it also allows them to space the children as desired. Even more important, contraception has allowed a separation of sexual intercourse from pregnancy, making sexual activity a form of self-expression, not merely a prelude to reproduction. As a result, most Canadians now see the entry into parenthood as a distinct choice, for good or bad.

Contraceptive use varies throughout the world, however. Knowledge, attitudes, and practices of contraception are not as thorough in less-developed countries as we find in

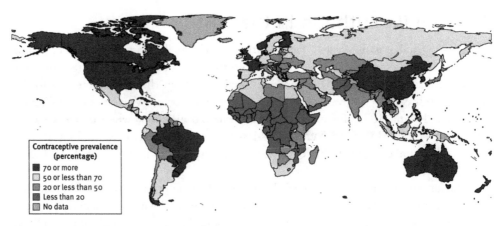

Figure 6.1 Modern Contraceptive Use

Source: Courtesy of United Nations Population Division.

Canada. Typically, contraception rates are higher where literacy is higher and women receive more education, social and economic opportunity, and general empowerment. The highest rates of contraceptive use are found in the People's Republic of China, with 84 percent of women of reproductive age using modern contraception, compared to Canada and the United States, where the percentages are 72 and 73 percent, respectively. No doubt, the high rates of use in China reflect the severely enforced one-child policy.

In Northern Europe, over three-quarters of women of reproductive age use contraception. By contrast, only 35.8 percent are using modern contraception in Western Asia, and just 22.4 percent are doing so in Africa (United Nations, 2001). Figure 6.1 shows the extent of contraception use in each country.

Contraceptive use also varies within Canada, with lower rates in some rural areas compared to cities, in part because accessing health care and contraceptive advice poses greater challenges in rural areas. In a study of women's experiences with maternity care in Ontario and Alberta, Sutherns and Bourgeault (2008) concluded that finding out about birth options in rural Canada is harder than in urban areas. Patients living nearer to care facilities have better health-care outcomes, thanks to more sophisticated technology; however, access to secondary care is also critical. A failure to provide this may result in a shift from rural neighbourhoods to areas with better access to medical care, as well as resulting in more troubled pregnancies and sickly infants.

Entering Parenthood Young

Increasingly, public concern has focused on "children having children." Yet the fertility rate of Canadian teenagers has dropped steadily since 1975. As a result, the proportion of Canadian live births accounted for by teenagers dropped from 6 percent in 1991 to 4.1 percent in 2009 (Statistics Canada, n.d.).

Teen fertility rates vary enormously across Organisation for Economic Co-operation and Development (OECD) countries. In 2009, Switzerland had the lowest rate and the United States had the highest, at 39.1 births per 1000 teenage girls (World Bank, 2011a). Even so, this figure marks a historic low for the United States, and the number has been declining for decades (Ventura and Hamilton, 2011). By contrast, Canada's teen birth rate in 2009 was 13 births per 1000 teenage girls (World Bank, 2011b).

How do we account for these large international variations? A study that interviewed pregnant or parenting adolescents found that four factors predict risky sexual behaviour that could lead to teenage pregnancy: presence of a family member with a drinking problem, physical assault by a family member, (early) age of first drunkenness, and (early) age of first wanted sexual experience (Kellogg, Hoffman, and Taylor, 1999). Comparative research (Jones et al., 1993) suggests that another source of the problem is cultural—namely, excessive sexualization of the mass media combined with a relative absence of sexual education in the schools and access to contraception in the community.

Adolescent parenting poses risks for both child and parent. Children born to teen mothers are more likely to have behavioural disorders, especially during preschool years, and to have poor listening vocabulary on entering school (Dahinten and Willms, 2002). As these children grow older (10–15 years old), they tend to have significantly lower math scores and commit more property offences than children born to older mothers (25–29 years of age) (Dahinten, Shapka, and Willms, 2007).

Teen mothers themselves face many obstacles. One in four teen mothers reports being depressed—twice the prevalence of mothers who had their first child in their late 20s. Teen mothers are more likely to be single parents and not work outside the home, which also puts them in a disadvantaged financial situation.

Teenage motherhood is not always the cause of low income; often, the opposite is the case. A compilation of studies (Ashcraft and Lang 2006; Levine and Painter, 2003; Klepinger et al., 1997, 1995; Ahn, 1994; Hoffman et al., 1993) showed that coming from a low-income background may cause both teenage motherhood and an increased risk of low income after childbearing (cited in Luong, 2008). Women from disadvantaged backgrounds are more likely to have low incomes even if they don't have children before the age of 20. That is because people from disadvantaged backgrounds get less education, on average. If they manage to get more education, they overcome this income hurdle, even if they had a first child as a teenager (Luong, 2008).

We know far less about the fathers of babies born to teen mothers. Using birth records, Millar and Wadhera (1997) found that more than three-quarters of births to teen mothers involved men who were older by an average of 4.1 years. Twenty-four percent of fathers were six or more years older than the teenage women they impregnated. Many of these fathers fail to stay around to raise and support the child. Likely, employment opportunities influence fathers to stay or leave: They are more likely to stay if they can find a job.

Teen pregnancy can be unexpected and unwanted, adding further complexity to the parenting situation. People who enter parenthood often unexpectedly find parenting more stressful and more difficult than other parents. This is particularly true of teen mothers, who are still forming their own identities. The result is greater stress associated with parenting. Fortunately, outside support often helps an adolescent mother to handle the demands her child poses. Researchers (Luster, Perlstadt, and McKinney, 1996) report that an intensive family support program can improve adolescent mothers' care of their infants.

Child Rearing Alone

According to the 2006 Census, lone parents and their children made up 15.9 percent of families in Canada. This followed a steady long-term increase from 11 percent in 1981(Vanier Family Institute, 2010b). Most (81 percent) of these lone-parent families were headed by women, but the percentage headed by men is increasing (Vanier Institute of the Family, 2010c). Some of these lone-parent families result from teen pregnancies or unwed (often unplanned) pregnancies; most result from the dissolution of a relationship.

Single mothers are of concern because they face a higher-than-average risk of physical and mental health problems. Their children also face an increased risk of social, academic, emotional, and behavioural difficulties. We will talk about this issue again later in the chapter.

The Decision Not to Have Children

Canadian couples who had no children living at home accounted for 38.4 percent of all families in 2006, up from 38 percent in 1991 and 34 percent in 1981 (Statistics Canada, 2007a). Some of these couples had children who had moved out upon reaching adulthood, and other couples had postponed their entry into parenthood and would eventually become parents. Many aspects of parenting are changing now, as is evident in "Canadian Trends in Parenting," below.

Canadian Trends in Parenting

- For the first time, more census families comprised couples *without* children than with children.

- With increases in education and the age of childbearing, a higher proportion of children age four and younger live with mothers in their forties.

- The upward trend for lone parents has stabilized, with more never-married lone parents and fewer widowed ones.

- Household size continues to decline, with a large increase in the number of one-person households.

- An increasing proportion of children age 14 and younger live with common-law parents.

- More young adults age 20 to 29 are living in the parental home because of extended education, or they are "boomerang children."

Source: Adapted from Anne Milan, Mireille Vézina, and Carrie Wells. 2006. Family portrait: Continuity and change in Canadian families and households in 2006: Findings. Demography Division, Statistics Canada. www12.statcan.ca/english/census06/analysis/famhouse/index.cfm.

Given traditional thinking about parenthood, some might assume that people who decide not to have children are more isolated or feel less fulfilled than parents. However, this is not necessarily the case. Childless people have no fewer friends than parents do, on average, though they may have fewer close relatives. In addition, childless people experience less stress than people with children (McMullin and Marshall, 1996), as we noted in the previous chapter, and their marital satisfaction is higher at all stages of the relationship.

Adoption

For a variety of reasons, some people choose to adopt children. With increases in cross-cultural and cross-national adoption, there has been an increased interest in the policies surrounding adoption.

Not long ago in North America, officials handled adoption in secrecy and kept their records secret from the child, the adoptive parent(s), and the biological parent(s). Many children were never even told they had been adopted. However, most family researchers today agree that it is better to tell children that they have been adopted when they are old enough to understand what it means. By openly talking to the child about his or her adoption, parents can make it a positive fact of the child's life.

Some people believe that open (i.e., non-secret) adoptions reassure the birth parents about their child's well-being and help adopted children form a secure identity. Others believe that contacts with birth parents interrupt and destabilize the adopted family and

Especially in Canada and the United States, adoptive parents may belong to a different ethnic or racial group from their adoptive child. This results in a blend of identities for the child.
Kathy Dewar/E+/Getty Images

confuse the child's sense of identity. More research is needed before we can say much with certainty about the conditions under which adopted children benefit from linking with their natural parents (Miall and March, 2005a).

Dramatic changes in the popular view of adoption are a natural result of changes in the modern family—especially in the growth of diversity in family forms. Indeed, there is even more tolerance today for cross-ethnic and cross-racial adoption than in the past. Especially in Canada and the United States, adoptive parents may belong to a different ethnic or racial group from their adoptive child. This results in a blend of identities for the child. An increased awareness of the value of the child's ethnic or racial identity encourages adoptive parents to go beyond their own community in search of their child's original community. Such parents generate a blend of identities for their children, often involving representatives of the child's original community.

Assisted Fertility

Most Canadian women expect to bear one or more children, but the norms about this are much weaker than one finds in other societies with higher rates of childbearing. In these *pronatalist* societies, people expect all women to bear children—indeed, many children—and stigmatize women who fail to produce them. In these high fertility cultures, most women fully internalize and support the pronatalist discourse (Remennick, 2000). Women who are infertile face stigma and, to cope with it, develop various strategies that include secrecy and selective disclosure about their "hidden disability."

Even in our society, infertility is often associated with lower levels of satisfaction with an intimate partner. Infertile women older than age 30 have an even more negative vision of the future than infertile women younger than age 30 (DeBoer, 2002). Many Canadian women regret their inability to become pregnant and seek medical help—often in the form of long-term and burdensome infertility treatments at high personal and financial costs.

Assisted human reproductive (AHR) technologies help couples who face infertility or sterility. According to information from the Canadian Fertility and Andrology Society (CFAS), rates of assisted reproduction in Canada are high and rising rapidly. However, the chance of success with many procedures is not high at all. In 2010, for example, the live birthrate for in vitro fertilization per cycle for women under 35 was only 38 percent—which translates to a 62 percent failure rate per attempt. This failure rate sharply increases as age increases (Orfali, 2010).

On the other hand, for some women, the new technology succeeds too well and they bear far more children than they had bargained for. Typically, births of three, four, or more children are a result of such assisted fertility.

It is worth noting that the success rates have steadily increased since the Canadian Assisted Reproductive Technologies Register's first annual report in 2001. Also, the number of multiple births has decreased at a less consistent rate (Gunby, 2010). However, a successful outcome is not the only factor affecting women's reaction to their experiences with assisted fertility. Some women, for example, resent the experience of male domination in fertility clinics (Birenbaum-Carmeli, 1998) or find the clinic experience humbling.

Sociologists and policy-makers have not yet thought through all the ethical issues presented by NRTs. They need to be more involved in the critical assessment process. We are only at the beginning of this new process and have much more to learn about the conditions under which assisted fertility succeeds socially as well as technologically.

HOW PARENTHOOD AFFECTS RELATIONSHIPS

Parenting has a negative effect on marital relationships, as we mentioned earlier. A meta-analysis of the literature on this topic by Twenge, Campbell, and Foster (2003) found that parents typically report lower marital satisfaction than childless couples. The researchers also found decreases in marital satisfaction with increases in the number of children. Children may be cheaper by the dozen (as a famous old book once claimed), but not better for the marital relationship.

New parents and couples with infants face a variety of new concerns: disappointed expectations, problems with returning to work, reductions in sexual intimacy, new intrusions by (and reliance on) in-laws, a reduction of sleep and leisure time, and problems communicating all these concerns to one's partner. Preserving closeness is critical to keeping marital satisfaction alive during the new transition to parenthood. Couples have trouble doing this, especially if they start out with low levels of attachment or have childhood memories of their parents lacking attachment (Curran, Hazen, Jacobvitz, and Feldman, 2005). Typically, these problems do not disappear as the children get older; often, parent–child conflicts introduce or intensify parent–parent conflict, reducing marital satisfaction even more (Hiotakis, 2005).

However, other factors affect marital satisfaction as much or more. For example, some couples start out parenthood with much higher levels of marital quality than others. Also, contextual factors—ethnic and religious beliefs, financial distress, chronic illness or disability, or social support, for example—affect the *rate* of satisfaction decline caused by parenthood. In general, people who hold traditional attitudes toward family and gender experience a smaller-than-average decline in marital satisfaction due to parenthood. People who value (less-traditional) individualism and independence experience a larger-than-average decline.

Some couples learn to re-calibrate their expectations and requirements so they can take more satisfaction from the new challenges they face. For example, couples who place a lower importance on sexuality intimacy and higher importance on building a future together are able to retain a high level of marital satisfaction. Having a sense of secure attachment also makes it easier for a couple to endure the strains and disruptions associated with new parenthood (Simpson, Rholes, Campbell, Tran, and Wilson, 2002), as does strong support from family and friends (Schulz, Cowan, and Cowan, 2006).

Life Course Concerns

Today, two incomes are often needed to ensure the financial well-being of a family (Vanier Institute of the Family, 2010d). Faced with the resulting challenge—a shortage of time and money—many women adopt strategies to time their education, career, marriage, and childbirth. Having a child later in life may be physically more risky for the mother and child, but it allows the mother to complete her education and secure employment (Taniguchi, 1999). Having a child earlier in life postpones higher education but gives the mother more time with her child when she has the most energy to enjoy it.

The parent–child relationship is arguably one of the most intense human relationships and has an almost permanent effect on people's lives. As children become adults and parents age, the relationship undergoes drastic changes. However, events—and the memory of events—that occur earlier in life can affect the future. For example, teenager problems in school, substance use, and disobedience are likely to produce prolonged and residual anger in elderly parents (Milkie, Norris, and Bierman, 2011). In part, this is because troubled teenagers are more likely to become troubled adults—a cause of continued concern for their elderly parents. However, often elderly parents are still angry about parent–child troubles experienced many decades earlier. For many parents, the teenage years are traumatic, causing permanent resentment.

Many parents worry about their adult children for a variety of reasons having to do with concerns about health, safety, finances, and workload (Hay, Fingerman, and Lefkowitz, 2008). The parental role of being responsible for all aspects of a child's life often carries through into later stages of the life course. By contrast, adult children are more likely to focus their worries about parents on health-related issues alone. That said, many carry resentments and negative memories about their parents into adulthood, leading to problems if and when the elderly parents rely on them for help and support in their infirmity.

Fingerman, Hay, Dush, Clichy, and Hosterman (2007) examined how the parent–child relationship changed when parents began to experience chronic illnesses and sensory impairments but were still leading independent lives. They proposed the name "transition to old age" for this stage of the parent's life course. Their study found that sensory impairments didn't lead to relationship changes unless vision loss meant the parent needed assistance from the adult child. Even then, many parents continued to receive the same assistance, or said they did. Often, parents minimized the effects of their disability on the relationship.

In some cases, both positive and negative feelings increased when the elderly parent required more assistance from his or her adult children (ibid). Mixed feelings such as these have been conceptualized as *ambivalence*. Connidis and McMullin (2002) state that such ambivalence is socially structured, in the sense that it results from conflicting social norms and expectations. Children have grown up expecting their parents to be competent and independent—indeed, providers of care to *them*. The loss of parental competence and independence, along with expectations that children will provide care to the parents, violates these expectations. Moreover, it often interferes with the adult child's other norms, expectations, and obligations: for example, to spouse, children, and job. When long-established norms around care and independence are disturbed (often by life transitions), they create conflict, uncertainty, and imbalance in relationships.

Elderly parents, for their part, are often reluctant or embarrassed to ask for more help from their children, and they understand why it may not be forthcoming. Many attribute the problem to the rushed pace of contemporary life. They want to see their children more often, but at the same time, they are proud of the success and responsibilities that keep their children so busy. Thus, the parents, too, felt ambivalent about this situation: As a study by Peters, Hooker, and Zvonkovic (2006) showed, parents had mixed feelings about their children's choices in life. However, given their child's age, a sense of what is appropriate in the relationship, and a reluctance to cause conflict, they hesitated to give advice.

Wilson, Shuey, and Elder (2003) found that ambivalence increased dramatically for women who acted as caregivers for their parents, but not for men who did so. That is because different gender norms regulate the lives of men and women. Women are popularly supposed to be the main providers of care and also to enjoy it (on the assumption that women are naturally more nurturing than men). Therefore, women who didn't enjoy caregiving felt conflicted; they felt as though they were unnatural or were violating the social rules. Men, by contrast, were normatively free to dislike caregiving. Despite the vast changes in women's lives over the past 50 years, these gender norms still exist in Canada today. Figure 6.2 shows only a slight gender imbalance in who provides care to

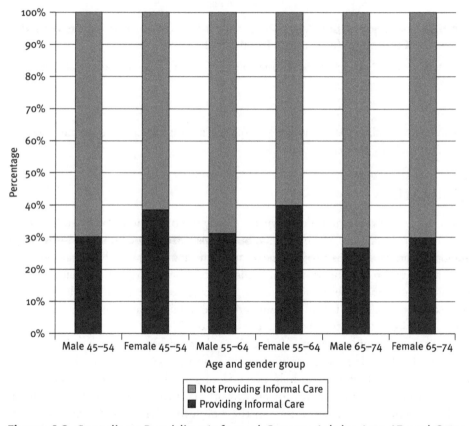

Figure 6.2 Canadians Providing Informal Care to Adults Age 45 and Over (Excluding Territories)

Source: Statistics Canada. 2009. (table). *2007 General Social Survey: Care Tables*. Statistics Canada Catalogue no. 89-633-X.

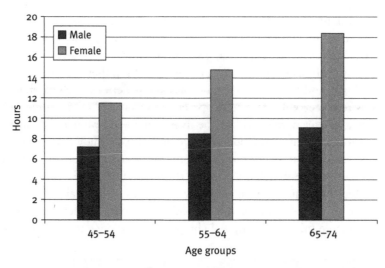

Figure 6.3 Hours Spent per Week Providing Informal Care to Adults Age 45 and Over by Canadians (Excluding Territories)

Source: Statistics Canada. 2009. (table). 2007 General Social Survey: Care Tables. Statistics Canada Catalogue no. 89-633-X.

aging adults in Canadian society, and Figure 6.3 reveals a significant gender imbalance in hours spent providing that care.

Socialization

As most people know, children do not arrive "ready to go" but must be carefully taught how to take part in families and in society. Sociologists define **socialization** as the social learning a person goes through to become a capable, functioning member of society. The **primary socialization** of children is usually the responsibility of the child's family. It has a deep impact on future life by helping to set the child's future values, goals, and, to a certain extent, personality. It is in the family that a child first learns how to gain rewards by doing set tasks and how to negotiate a consensus on rules.

Often parents decide how to socialize their children based on particular cultural or traditional values. Parents choose what skills and behaviours to teach their children based on what they feel will help them become healthy and successful members of society. Aboriginal families, for instance, work hard to promote high educational and achievement-oriented aspirations in their children (Cheal and Chirkov, 2008: 415). They rightly believe that education is a means of improving their children's social position and achieving success. Moreover, Aboriginal families work hard to make sure their children maintain a sense of cultural tradition and spirituality (Cheal and Chirkov, 2008: 415). Aboriginal mothers may give this particular priority because of historical attempts to assimilate the Aboriginal population into Canadian society. As this example shows, the socialization of children is a complex process that involves transmitting the parents' cultural and traditional beliefs to their children.

Equally important, children in well-functioning families learn that they are valued human beings. Thus, socialization is the beginning of social acceptance in the family and the community—and in this way, the beginning of self-esteem. The well-functioning family encourages each step in the child's physical, emotional, and moral development. In every aspect of this development, good communication plays an important part. Like the spousal relationship, the parental relationship relies on good communication. Talking to children helps them become social beings. See "Myths and Facts about Parent and Child Socialization" for illustrative examples of the complexity of this process.

Myths and Facts about Parent and Child Socialization

Myth: Major agents of socialization (family, peers, and mass media) reinforce gender-normative behaviour with little deviation or variation.

- Fact: A study by Lee and Troop-Gordon (2011) shows that gender socialization by peers can yield varying results. Consider boys who were harassed by their peers; how did they respond? Boys whose friends were mostly male were likely to respond in ways that society considers "masculine." Boys whose friends were mostly female, however, were more likely to respond to the harassment in ways that society would not consider masculine and might even consider feminine. Thus, children conform to the norms of their peer group. They are socialized by their peers, not by abstract notions of "maleness" or "femaleness."

Myth: Socialization is always a process of downward transmission, from parent to child.

- Fact: Wong and Tseng (2008), using in-depth interviews, showed that political socialization is often a bi-directional process in immigrant families. They found that many parents of immigrant families socialize their children politically through discussions about their country of origin. Children, by contrast, are more likely to socialize their parents by explaining the politics of the host country. Thus, socialization in this case, as in many others, is reciprocal, not one-way.

Myth: The effects of gendered socialization are always negative for girls, since gender roles are grounded in gender inequality.

- Fact: A study by Orr (2011) examined the effects of gender socialization on school performance in kindergarten children. The researchers found that, even by kindergarten, girls were likely to have positive attitudes toward school while boys were likely to have negative attitudes. These differences led to differences in grades: Positive attitudes led to better grades for girls, while negative attitudes led to lower grades for boys. As a result, the gender roles of girls—more cooperative and submissive, for example—predispose them to respond better to the school environment, while the male gender role can cause difficulty for boys.

Gender Socialization

Most children grow up securely attached to their family caregivers, and it is in this context that they begin to learn social roles, including their gender role. While sex is inborn, gender is not; people learn gender-based ways of behaving through **gender socialization**. The major agents of socialization—family, peer groups, schools, and the mass media—all serve to reinforce cultural and conventional definitions of masculinity and femininity. Gender socialization starts at birth and continues throughout life. Young children learn gender identities by watching others at nursery school or daycare, role-playing games, experimenting with hair and clothing styles, and body decoration (for example).

At home, parents routinely assign cleaning, child care, and meal preparation tasks to daughters and fixer-upper tasks to sons. Not surprisingly, children often form traditional, gender-based attitudes toward housework well before the end of high school. Men, older people, and less-educated people are especially likely to hold and teach traditional, gendered attitudes.

Learned gender differences also show up in our intimate relations—for example, in our communication practices, as we noted in an earlier chapter. For example, we teach women to behave in a demure, innocent, and disinterested fashion when sex is the topic of discussion with men. (Women are more forthcoming in discussions with other women.) Learned patterns of communication create and preserve distinctions between women and men, and reinforce social expectations between the sexes.

Ethnic Socialization

As mentioned earlier, many parents, especially those who raise their children outside their country of origin, want to ensure that later generations are aware of their culture and history. **Parental involvement** affects the identities children take on in later life. For example, among Australians of mixed Aboriginal and European heritage, children are more likely to call themselves Aboriginal if parents provide an upbringing rich in Aboriginal life experience (Ramsay, 2000).

Though other cultures may influence a child's final conception of himself or herself, how strongly children hold on to their ancestral cultural heritage depends on the efforts of their parents. Family rituals and routines play an important part in preserving a family's ethnic heritage. McCarroll (2000) finds they influence children's racial attitudes, for example. However, despite parents' best efforts, children still may choose to ignore ethnic traditions or identify with different groups. No child is just an empty vessel waiting to be filled with parental information but is an active participant in his or her own development. Of course, the effort to stray from parents' expectations may lead to conflict.

PARENTING PROCESSES

Parents differ in how they want their children to turn out. Some parents put a high value on obedience, for example. Other parents value independence. Some parents want their children to be cooperative and adaptable; others, to be competitive and ambitious. Some of these different perspectives on children are echoed in "Famous Quotations about Childhood," below.

However, most people would agree on what constitutes "good parenting." We can agree that all parents should aim to produce children who are healthy, law-abiding, and successful at school. When a child is failing, delinquent, or disturbed, this signals poor parenting. But poor parenting is not always the cause of the problem. Many factors besides parenting can increase the risks of childhood failure, delinquency, ill health, and depression. That being said, parents still play the largest part in creating the "right" conditions for a child's best emotional and cognitive development. These "right" parenting conditions include love and attachment, emotional stability, protection and control, and fair and moderate discipline.

Famous Quotations about Children

Of all the animals, the boy is the most unmanageable.

—Plato

If children grew up according to early indications, we should have nothing but geniuses.

—Goethe

Healthy children will not fear life if their elders have integrity enough not to fear death.

—Erik Erikson

What's done to children, they will do to society.

—Karl Menninger

Children are remarkable for their intelligence and ardour, for their curiosity, their intolerance of shams, the clarity and ruthlessness of their vision.

—Aldous Huxley

Children have never been very good at listening to their elders, but they have never failed to imitate them.

—James Baldwin

Children have no use for psychology. They detest sociology. They still believe in God, the family, angels, devils, witches, goblins, logic, clarity, punctuation, and other such obsolete stuff.

—Isaac Bashevis Singer

Source: www.famousquotesandauthors.com/topics/children_and_childhood_quotes.html.

Children's talent to endure stems from their ignorance of alternatives.

—Maya Angelou

Source: www.oxfordreference.com.myaccess.library.utoronto.ca/views/SEARCH_RESULTS.html?y=14&q=children&category=t93&x=19&ssid=308183164&scope=book&time=0.733832986209592.

Happiness is an imaginary condition, formerly often attributed by the living to the dead, now usually attributed by adults to children, and by children to adults.

—Thomas Szasz

Source: www.oxfordreference.com.myaccess.library.utoronto.ca/views/ENTRY.html?entry=t115.e3145&srn=25&ssid=236191040#FIRSTHIT.

Children begin by loving their parents; after a time they judge them; rarely, if ever, do they forgive them

—Oscar Wilde

Source: www.famousquotesandauthors.com/topics/children_and_childhood_quotes.html. and www.oxfordreference.com.myaccess.library.utoronto.ca

Love and Attachment

Most parents probably love their children, but problems can occur when parents do not know how to express this love—and many parents fall into this category. Children who *feel* unloved by their parents suffer emotional damage that may be long-lasting. Sometimes, children have difficulty receiving expressions of love from their parents. For example, autistic children may find a gentle, loving touch unpleasant. Depressed children may discount or distrust expressions of affection. And children with temperaments different from those of their parents may misunderstand their parents' efforts to express affection, viewing them instead as efforts to shame them or exert control. In addition, some parents and children may have higher relationship expectations than either party can meet. Relations between children and their fathers are especially problematic, since men are not supposed to express emotions as openly as women. Perhaps as a result, children usually remain closer to their mothers than to their fathers. At the same time, more children may feel ignored by their fathers than by their mothers.

Relations between parents and children, as well as relations between siblings, are subject to change as children and their parents age (Burholt and Wenger, 1998). Yet feelings of neglect or dislike are surprisingly resistant to change. That is because some of the most important bonds between parents and children are established in the first few months of life, around issues of attachment.

John Bowlby, a British psychoanalyst, was the first to state a formal theory of attachment (1969). While trying to understand the distress that some infants suffered after a separation from their parents, Bowlby noted that these infants would make great efforts to prevent separation from their parents or to re-establish closeness after a separation. Research showed that, far from being unusual, such behaviours were common to various mammals. In fact, they may be adaptive responses to separation from a primary attachment figure—someone who provides the support, protection, and care on which a helpless infant depends: That is, they may have significance for the evolution of human beings and other animal species.

According to Bowlby, infants often want to know whether the attachment figure is nearby, on hand, and attentive. If the answer is yes, the child feels loved, secure, and confident, and is likely to explore the environment, play with others, and be sociable. Otherwise, the child suffers anxiety and is likely to search for and call to the missing parent. These behaviours continue until the child is near the attachment figure again, or until the child "wears down." In the latter case, the child is likely to experience despair and depression.

To summarize, parental support and encouragement are important in creating a sense of attachment. Remember that children—indeed, people of all ages—form judgments about themselves by responding to how others—especially their parents—treat them. Children with kind, encouraging parents usually get higher grades at school, have more social competence, and get into less trouble with teachers. They have learned that people in authority—first their parents, then their teachers—are there to help them, not hold them back. Even in adolescence, often a time of big changes and doubts, children whose parents are encouraging do better. Adolescents with unsupportive parents are more likely than other adolescents to start smoking cigarettes and engage in other risky behaviours.

Emotional Stability and Family Cohesion

Emotional stability is also a key contributor to the healthy development of children. Without stable, consistent support from a parent, the child runs a higher risk of school problems, delinquency, low self-esteem, or diminished well-being. Factors that reduce the stability and cohesion of a family can include spousal conflict, addiction, depression, or chronic physical illness. For example, spousal conflict can cause parents to spend too little time with their children because they are depressed, stressed out, and distracted by their own problems. As well, marital conflict disrupts normal practices of discipline in the household. This can create uncertainty and decrease child–parent attachment.

On the other side, many practices help to strengthen express stability and cohesion. For example, family rituals are important—things like regular family meals and conversations, family outings, and vacations. **Family cohesion** is a sense of attachment among members of a family, preserved and represented by shared activities, self-identification as a family member, and signs of familiarity and liking. Take a simple example: family meals. Researchers report that children who live in families that have sit-down meals together at least three times a week are much less likely to become delinquents in their adolescence or turn to crime in adulthood. Family dinners are a sign of family cohesion that contribute to the healthy emotional development of children.

Protectiveness and Control

No less important than loving stability is parental **control and supervision**—how firmly, consistently, and fairly parents enforce rules for the child. Good rules guide and protect the child. They show the parents' concern and attachment. Children are less likely to become delinquents if their parents keep an eye on what they are doing, offer them support, and give them a chance to discuss whatever is bothering them. This is true of children in two-parent families, mother-only families, and mother–stepfather families. In forming and socializing healthy children, the quality of family relationships counts more than the number of parents.

The **authoritative parenting** style (high acceptance, high control) does best, turning out children who achieve the highest levels of academic performance and mental well-being. By comparison, other forms of parenting produce less desirable outcomes. For example, **authoritarian parenting** (low acceptance, high control) keeps the child from independence and learning to express herself. Children whose parents are authoritarian—controlling but not caring enough—are more likely than other children of authoritative parents to become delinquents, to use drugs (Man, 1996), to become depressed, and to fail in school (Radziszewska, Richardson, Dent, and Flay, 1996).

This does not argue in favour of lax parental control, however. **Unengaged parenting** (low acceptance/low control) can also be harmful. **Permissive parenting** (high acceptance, low control) may produce poor results, too. Permissive parenting produces poor grades, and low-achieving students are more likely to come from families with permissive parenting styles (Vergun, Dornbusch, and Steinberg, 1996; Bronstein, Duncan, and D'Ari, 1996; Radziszewska, 1996).

Naturally, many parents combine elements of the different styles, being more permissive of certain behaviours than others and more engaged in some circumstances than others. Far more important but less understood is the cross-cultural variation in parenting styles and their effects on children. Some believe that authoritarian parenting, a style that is common in many "traditional" parts of the world, carries less stigma and causes less harm in those areas than it does in Canada, where such parenting may be considered abusive.

Cultural factors mediate the effects of authoritarian parenting, as is shown in a study by Dwairy and Menshar (2006) of parenting in Egypt. There, the authors found that, among Arabs, the common types of parenting styles differ in rural and urban populations, and are also gender-specific. In rural communities, the authoritarian style is common, especially for the parenting of male adolescents. Parents are more likely to use an authoritative style with girls than with boys (Dwairy and Menshar, 2006). On the other hand, parents use an authoritarian parenting style with girls in urban communities, but not with boys (Dwairy and Menshar, 2006). Thus, parenting styles are adjusted to environment—whether rural or urban—and reflect variations in the need for control and obedience among sons and daughters in these contexts.

Whether authoritative or authoritarian, consistent discipline is better than inconsistent discipline, and consistency is more important than style of parenting. Moreover, the same authors can find no definitive proof that authoritarian parenting is harmful to Arab and Bedouin children, who are accustomed to such treatment. Perhaps, then, authoritarian parenting is harmful only when the child perceives it as unusual, abusive, or malevolent.

In short, one parenting style may not work well under all circumstances. However, in North America, researchers find that children whose parents are authoritarian, unengaged, or permissive are most likely to show problems of adjustment, poor academic achievement, or substance abuse. Here, the authoritative parenting style offers the best mixture of acceptance and control—not too much or too little of either.

Fair and Moderate Discipline

Related to control is the issue of discipline. Overzealous discipline may wipe out the benefits of control, as may lax discipline. The trick is to provide the right amount of discipline and provide it in the right way—that is, using the right technique.

Hoffman (1979) distinguishes between three basic types of disciplining technique: power assertion, love withdrawal, and induction. In using **power assertion**, a parent or other caregiver threatens a child with punishment for non-compliance. The child changes his or her behaviour to avoid punishment. The child's compliance is externally, not internally, motivated by a desire to avoid punishment. Similarly, in **love withdrawal**, a parent emotionally threatens a child, producing anxiety in the child over the possible loss of love. As with power assertion, the child complies with parental demands to avoid punishment.

Induction, on the other hand, teaches the possible benefits of a child's behaviour for others. When children raised inductively break the rules, they know they are contributing to another's distress and feel guilty. Feelings of guilt, unlike feelings of fear or anxiety, exercise an **internal moral control** over their behaviour. Inductive discipline—teaching good behaviour by setting a good example, then rewarding imitation—is better for the child than power assertion because it is internalized. Once rules are internalized, the child motivates himself to behave properly. Thus, inductive discipline fosters more consistent compliance (Hoffman, 1979).

However, inductive techniques are more time-consuming since they oblige parents to explain and model good behaviour. Not surprisingly, many parents continue to use some degree of physical punishment—a form of power assertion—as a disciplinary tool. Physical punishment and power assertion appeal to parents who were raised this way themselves or who do not have the time, patience, and inclination to teach rules inductively. In general, parents tend to raise children the way they were raised, often with the same unfortunate consequences—yelling, spanking, and fighting, among others (Barnett, Quackenbush, and Sinisi, 1996).

No wonder spanking and other forms of corporal punishment continue to be prevalent in Canada, as revealed in a review of the literature by the Global Initiative to End All Corporal Punishment (www.endcorporalpunishment.org).

Davis (1996) notes that when parents threaten physical punishment as a form of discipline, they typically want compliance with some simple demand. For example, the parent wants the child to sit still, be quiet, come with the parent, or stop touching things. Children typically respond by ignoring the parent. About half the adults making these threats also hit the children. What we learn from this scenario is that when parents use physical punishment routinely, it is routinely ineffective! At its extreme, harsh childhood discipline produces delinquency and low self-esteem (Peiser and Heaven, 1996). A broad range of studies has also found harmful outcomes in adulthood, including depression, alcoholism, aggressive behaviour, suicide, and a tendency to physically abuse one's family.

Caring for Sick Children

Providing parental care for sick children is particularly difficult and stressful, and researchers have given much attention to the stress caused by a severely ill child. Not surprisingly, the illness is stressful for the sick child: Many children who become chronically ill by age 15 also suffer from serious psychological and behavioural problems as a result. Often, other family members suffer health problems as well, or at least emotional and psychic depletion—most of all, the main caregiver. The more severe the decline of the caretaker parent and the longer the illness goes on, the more strain the entire family experiences and the more difficulty it has coping.

The problems that families face in coping with a severely ill child are often closely tied to problems that existed before the onset of illness (Ilze, Kalnins, Churchill, and Terry, 1980). In short, a family's capacity to cope under stressful conditions is correlated with its previous level of functioning (Steinhauer, Santa-Barbara, and Skinner, 1984).

Caregiving for the sick child, among other things, deprives other family members of care and attention that they crave, too. Fathers may feel estranged from their wives, healthy siblings estranged from their parents (Lademann, 1980; Larcombe, 1978). Often, siblings have a hard time giving voice to their feelings and wishes under these conditions. Serious behavioural problems at home and school may result, and often parents may be unaware of the reasons.

Most of the literature reflects a high rate of dysfunctional response to child illness, but sometimes illness strengthens family ties (Motohashi, 1978). For instance, through successful coping strategies, some families can thrive after the birth of a child with Down syndrome. And, though many parents react badly to the birth of a child with a disability, over time these parents can come to experience feelings of psychological well-being, personal growth, and increased satisfaction with parenting (Van Riper, 2007).

VARIATIONS ON A THEME

All families face obstacles from time to time, but some families face more obstacles than others—whether for reasons of time restraint, shortage of money, or social exclusion. However, as long as they follow the basic principles of good parenting mentioned above, they can function well, despite these obstacles.

Single Parents

Though most people emphasize the benefits of two-parent families, there is something to be said for single-parent families—especially those that have resulted from a divorce

---

Myths and Facts and Single Parenting

Myth: Since single mothers have significantly improved their financial condition in the past 30 years, they will continue to become more involved in the economy and other aspects of public life.

- Fact: It is true that between 1976 and 2007, the after-tax income of single mothers grew by 40.1 percent, and their poverty rate decreased from 53.9 to 23.6 percent. However, it is unclear whether these trends will continue. The lack of readily available community support and affordable child care limits how many women are able to pursue education, enter the labour market, and increase their working hours. Participation in the public sector may stall until these problems facing single parent families are addressed (Vanier Institute of the Family, 2010).

Myth: Financial resources are more important than effective parenting in preventing the problems that children in single-parent households tend to face.

- Fact: A study by Abada and Gillespie (2007) examined how parenting processes and family income mediate the relationship between family structure and child well-being. The study revealed that positive parenting practices played a larger role than financial resources in reducing emotional disorders in children from single parent households. Only hostile and ineffective parenting—not income—affected the risk of destructive and physically aggressive behaviour in children from single-parent households.

Myth: The main reason adolescents in single parent families are more likely than other teenagers to engage in drug use is that they have poor relationships with their parents.

- Fact: A study by Crawford and Novak (2008) confirmed earlier findings that adolescents in single-parent families are more likely to use substances than those from intact families. However, the same study showed that parental attachment may not be key to explaining this. Adolescents from single parent families have a higher risk of substance use because they have more opportunities to do so—mainly, a result of unsupervised interaction with peers who may encourage substance use. As well, it may reflect (to a lesser extent) a more permissive parenting style that is more common in single parent families (Crawford and Novak, op. cit.).

or separation. Here, typically, single-parent families provide children with a significant decrease in conflict, anxiety, and depression. This in turn may lead to better, more consistent parenting and a closer bond between the child(ren) and the custodial parent. "Despite their problems, these families can be viewed as representing a stage of one's life or a preference to marriage, rather than as a failure or a disaster … [and] a viable alternative to other ways of carving out a life for oneself and one's children" (Lynn, 2003).

However, single-parent families often have a harder time than two-parent families preserving a high quality of life for themselves and their children. Difficulties associated with single parenting are usually the result of lack of partner support, life distress, social isolation, and a shortage of money (Stern and Smith, 1995).

In large part, the problems result from a single parent having to do the earning and parenting work of two people—a nearly impossible job. As demonstrated in Figure 6.4, a significantly higher proportion of female-led lone-parent households occupy the

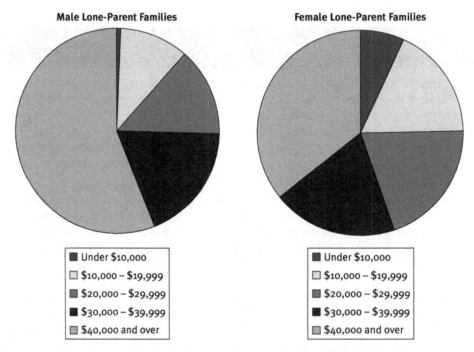

Figure 6.4 Income of Male and Female Lone-Parent Families

Source: Adapted from 2006 Census: Data Products on the Statistics Canada website, 2006 Census of Population. After-tax Family Income Groups (23A) and Census Family Structure (11) for the Census Families in Private Households of Canada, Provinces, Territories, Census Metropolitan Areas and Census Agglomerations, 2005—20% Sample Data (Topic-based tabulation). www12.statcan.gc.ca/census-recensement/2006/dp-pd/tbt/Rp-eng.cfm?LANG=E&APATH=3&DETAIL=0&DIM=0&FL=A&FREE=0&GC=0&GID=0&GK=0&GRP=1&PID=96427&PRID=0&PTYPE=88971,97154&S=0&SHOWALL=0&SUB=0&Temporal=2006&THEME=81-&VID=0&VNAMEE=&VNAMEF=

lower family income groups. What makes this gender imbalance more troublesome is that 80 percent of lone-parent families are headed by females (Statistics Canada, 2008). Female-headed lone-parent families, where a majority of children with lone parents live, are significantly more likely to experience financial hardship than male-headed lone-parent families.

Low income for many single mothers is a direct outcome of divorce (Duffy and Mandell, 2001). In turn, low income is likely to hinder the school performance of children in single-parent families. However, data from the National Longitudinal Survey of Children and Youth (Lipman, Offord, Dooley, and Boyle, 2002) shows that income disparities account for only a part of the variation in school readiness between children in single-parent families and those in two-parent families. Even controlling for (low) income, children in single-parent families are much more likely than children in two-parent families to present emotional, behavioural, and academic problems. Gender also plays a part, with boys in single-parent families being particularly prone to behaviour problems.

Parenting in Poverty

Because of limited financial and social resources, stress, and neighbourhood disadvantage, families that live in poverty face special challenges in raising healthy, successful children.

Often, parents who are unable to supply the basic needs for their family experience despair, depression, and social isolation and feel they are inadequate caregivers. They describe their financial situation "as a struggle, a fight, a daily preoccupation that consumed parental time, strength and patience" (Russell, Harris, and Gockel, 2008: 93). Under such circumstances, some families solve the problem by placing their children with other family members or even turning to temporary foster care until they can improve their financial situation.

Other things being equal, children who grow up in low-income families are at higher risk of behavioural and cognitive problems from preschool onward (Noel, Peterson, and Jesso, 2008). Poverty often deprives parents of access to educational resources and activities, and gives them less opportunity to pursue educational activities with their children (Ermisch, 2008). In some cases, this disadvantage can be overcome by particularly skillful parenting. For example, research shows that the effect of economic disadvantage on preschool child cognitive performance is mediated by parenting quality (Lugo-Gil and Tamis-LeMonda, 2008).

In this way, the disadvantages of poverty pass from one generation to the next (Scaramella et al., 2008). It's easy to trace the chain reaction. For example, economic disadvantage predicts a higher risk of mental health problems and maternal stress. In turn, this reduces the quality of parenting and decreases the child's life chances, thus perpetuating poverty (Mclanahan, 2009).

Social support may mitigate the negative effects of poverty to some extent by providing financial, child-care, or housing support (McLanahan, 2009). For example, by reducing parental stress, it improves the home environment for the child and therefore his or her school achievement. However, a literature review by Attree (2005) found that low-income single mothers have smaller support networks than mothers in two-parent families. As well, the most socially isolated women—women with the smallest support networks—are least likely to seek professional help in parenting. They are likely to feel the services do not cater to their specific needs and fear being labelled as "inadequate" parents.

The *duration* of poverty, and not only the extent, is a problem. Long-term poverty has especially harmful outcomes for children (Jones et al., 2002). Persistent poverty increases parental stress and family conflict. These, in turn, increase the likelihood of parental depression and hostile and ineffective parenting patterns—yelling, smacking, and providing no quality time or even time to help a child with homework. Poor parenting behaviours, in turn, produce undesirable child outcomes: reduced mental health (for example, more depression), worse physical health (for example, more physical injuries), and poorer school performance (for example, more school absences).

Poverty is worst in neighbourhoods characterized by high levels of violence, social disorder, and fear, where children experience greater risks of anxiety and depression (Caughy, Nettles, and O'Campo, 2008). Low-income families increasingly find themselves in these economically impoverished communities with a negative social climate. Positive parental involvement can mitigate the neighbourhood effects on behaviour problems to some degree. However, this puts an enormous burden on the shoulders of parents who are already stressed by poverty, unemployment, or underemployment.

Gay and Lesbian Families

As more countries accept or legalize gay and lesbian unions, the number of same-sex couples wishing to adopt or raise a child will naturally increase. A larger fraction of the public is coming to accept homosexuals, yet attitudes toward gay parents remain conservative, especially among older and rural people. Only around 20 percent of Canadians surveyed in Miall and March's (2005b) study, for example, were in favour of homosexuals adopting children, compared with the 92 percent who supported adoption by traditional married couples.

Research finds stereotypical views about homosexuality even among young, highly educated people. These views include the beliefs that homosexual parents create a dangerous environment for the child, provide a less secure home, and offer less emotional stability. Yet, contrary to popular belief, gay and lesbian parents appear to raise healthy, successful children just often as heterosexual families do (Wainwright, Russell, and Patterson, 2004).

With the legalization of gay marriage in 2005, 2006 marked the first time the Canadian Census included gay marriage in the definition of "family." The census in that year found that 9 percent of self-declared same sex couples—16.8 percent of lesbian couples and 2.9 percent of gay couples—had children under 25 in their households (Vanier Institute of the Family, 2010e).

According to the research literature, children raised by homosexual parents have the same behavioural and educational outcomes as children of heterosexual unions and feel just as loved and accepted by their parents (Mattingly and Bozick, 2001). Likewise, the self-esteem levels, the levels of functioning at home and in school, and the romantic lives of these adolescents are the same, regardless of family type (Wainwright, Russell, and Patterson, 2004). Finally, there is no more chance of children growing up gay or lesbian in a same-sex family than in a heterosexual family (Mooney-Somers and Golombok, 2000; Fitzgerald, 1999).

Aboriginal Families

Aboriginal or First Nations families face a different set of problems than we have discussed so far. Understanding the parenting of Aboriginal families means taking into account the long-term effects of conquest, colonization, and discrimination. Additionally, Frideres (in Cheal, 2007) has claimed that the familial organization of Aboriginal families has been profoundly altered on two separate occasions in the past hundred years.

First, from the late nineteenth century onward, many Aboriginal children were forcibly removed from their families and moved to residential boarding schools under a government policy of assimilation. During the process, Aboriginal children were no longer allowed to speak their own language or practise their spiritual values (Frideres, op. cit.). The teachers, often members of religious groups or orders, served as "parents" to the children, who did not see their natural parents for up to 10 months a year. In fact, for reasons of distance, some children never saw their parents during the years they attended residential schools.

These residential school "parents" were strict disciplinarians—perhaps best characterized as authoritarian parents who used techniques of power assertion to teach the children good behaviour. Harsh punishment was meted out to children who failed obey their school masters quickly enough (Bradbury, 2001). According to Frideres (op. cit.), this has led to an underdevelopment of good parenting skills in several generations of Canadian Aboriginals.

Not only did the government policy of forced assimilation destroy nearly three generations of Aboriginal families through forced separations and the forcible removal of children from their parents' care, the residential schooling also imposed European ideals of marriage, sexuality, and patriarchy (Bradbury, 2001: 71). The priests/teachers/school authorities sometimes even worked out arranged marriages for the children when they grew old enough (Fiske and Johnny, 1996). This "experiment" in cultural domination was a disaster for Aboriginal families and communities, who lost cultural traditions and social ties (Bradbury, 2001; Dickason, 2002). Survivors continue to make claims against the federal government for compensation for the abuse they suffered as a result of Canada's Native policy (see the Assembly of First Nations' website at www.afn.ca for details).

Second, during the 1960s and 1970s, another series of social service initiatives by provincial governments led to the removal of Aboriginal children from their homes to live with non-Aboriginal families (Frideres, op. cit.). This, too, has had a large, harmful effect on Aboriginal families and parenting practices. Cheal and Chirkov (2008: 407) note that the separation of Aboriginal children from their families has undermined traditional Aboriginal child-rearing patterns and hindered the spread of cultural knowledge from one generation to the next. In turn, some claim this has led to an increase in drug and alcohol dependency, and high rates of suicide among the Aboriginal population (ibid).

Custodial Grandparents

In some families, grandparents play a particularly important role. Many two-parent families (with both parents working) depend on retired grandparents for child care, for example. In this capacity, grandparents take some of the pressure off the parents and especially off the mothers. Often, the stress of daycare drop-off and pickup is reduced if children are left with the grandparents. And thanks to longer experience, grandparents can sometimes be more skilled caregivers than the children's parents. What's more, young mothers who live in three-generation households with their own mothers give their children better quality care than other young mothers (Cox, 2000) as a result of this accumulated experience close at hand.

Many immigrants to Canada place a high value on custodial grandparenting and—where available—parenting that is shared by extended families (e.g., by aunts and cousins). Caring for a second set of children can have its advantages. For example, research by Harrison, Richman, and Vittimberga (2000) found that grandparents report lower levels of parental stress than parents from both single- and two-parent families. They take it in their stride.

Cultural Variation

Immigration poses many difficulties for parenting attitudes and practices. In some instances, the problems are a result of economic difficulties the parents face on their arrival in North America. In other cases, the problem is cultural, owing to different ideas about parenting in Canada and the country of origin. This is particularly marked when cultural differences arise between the parents and their more acculturated child. Chinese mothers in a study by Buki, Ma, Strom, and Strom (2003) stated that the biggest challenge is the difference in adjustment to the new culture between them and their children.

One of the first major studies of immigration in North America was William I. Thomas and Florian Znaniecki's multi-volume *The Polish Peasant in Europe and America* (1918–1920). It examined the social and family lives of Polish immigrants—specifically why they often struggled and failed to overcome the challenges of assimilating into a new culture.

Many peasants came to America with expectations of success. Yet many immigrants had trouble altering their social customs—a necessity if they were to assimilate into American culture and achieve economic success. Social marginality resulted; the results of this marginality included poverty, delinquency, mental illness, marital conflict, and social isolation. Immigration demands prodigious change and adaptability from the immigrant, yet society provided none of the means needed to help bring this about. The stresses and difficulties—especially the conflicts between spouses, and between parents and children—that Thomas and Znaniecki described are still common among new immigrants to Canada today.

For their part, the children of immigrants are often challenged by the need to balance two cultures. If parents show understanding, the children's problem is solved more easily, but often parents are themselves struggling with a problem of cultural balance. Fathers can be particularly important in this regard Abad and Sheldon (2008).

As mentioned earlier, parenting styles are often different between Western and other cultures. Hispanic and Asian families have been shown to use authoritarian practices more readily than North Americans of European descent (Varela et al., 2004; Pong, Hao, and Gardner, 2005). As well, Chinese adolescents may report that their parents are warm but too controlling. In Shucksmith, Henry, and Glendinning's (1995) terms, we would characterize these Chinese parents as falling somewhere between authoritative and authoritarian.

Immigration affects family functioning and wellness in a variety of ways, influenced by the hardships encountered in the host country. For example, adolescent immigrants to Israel from the former Soviet Union have more psychological disorders and less family cohesion than native Israeli adolescents (Dwairy and Dor, 2009). They also report that their parents are less consistent and affectionate than before in their parenting. The causes of these psychological disorders are reportedly "immigration and cultural and social factors" (op. cit.: 416). These factors, as studied by Elias, Bar Ilan, and Sofer, and Portes and Borocz (cited Dwairy and Dor, 2009) include a decline in socio-economic status after immigration and a perception of the host country as being hostile toward immigrants.

In contrast, a smaller cultural gap between the home and host countries of immigrants and a small amount of perceived discrimination by immigrant adolescents minimize the effects of immigration to Portugal (Neto, 2006). Immigrants to Portugal often come from cultures that value family life over individualism, as in Portugal. Neto (op. cit.) found that the more immigrant youth complied with family obligations, the less likely they were to have mental health problems.

Often, when analyzing the effects of immigration on parenting processes, sociologists use the categories of *collectivist* and *individualist* cultures. A *collectivist* culture is one that values social bonds and obligations over personal autonomy and self-determination. As "Parenting Proverbs Across Time and Space" (on the next page) illustrates, the general distinctions made between collectivist and individualistic cultures do not always apply and do not address the unique characteristics of each culture. However, these categories prove useful as a way to distinguish generally between large groups of cultures. This is necessary if we want to understand the problems that immigrant families face, and how policy and cultural factors mediate the effects of these problems.

Immigrants to Canada face a variety of problems when they move here which affect their family relations. In general, cultural values related to parenting tend to persist after immigration due to efforts made by parents to retain their authority and promote traditional values. However, as with any area of sociology, it is important to remember that all generalizations are largely true and sometimes false: They are never meant to explain individual cases. Generalizations can help us understand the big picture, as long as we recognize that they are bound to give us a limited understanding.

So, for example, research suggests that South Asian mothers in North America often adapt their parenting styles to achieve their parenting goals of building a collective cultural identity for their children (Maiter and George, 2003). The mothers act as role models to build character and sometimes instill stricter moral and religious practices in their children—to create a sense of belonging to their cultural group—than they would have if they had remained in their home country.

Similarly, acculturation may erode some of the cultural values of Chinese immigrants while having little effect on their parenting beliefs and goals (Costigan and Su, 2008). A study by Su and Hynie (2011) showed the persistence of traditional parenting beliefs and goals despite external pressures for change. In fact, external pressures increased the tendency of Chinese Canadian mothers to practise authoritarian parenting. With less external pressure and more acculturation, they were more likely to practise authoritative parenting (ibid). Yet, despite their behavioural changes, cultural parental beliefs and goals did not fluctuate.

Parenting Proverbs across Time and Space

Every beetle is a gazelle in the eyes of its mother.
—Moorish proverb

God could not be everywhere and therefore he made mothers.
—Jewish proverb

A father is a banker provided by nature.
—French proverb

Source: www.famousquotesandauthors.com/topics/children_and_childhood_quotes.html.

Children are a poor man's riches.
—Danish Proverb

More precious than our children are the children of our children.
—Egyptian proverb

Source: http://creativeproverbs.com.

Do not confine your children to your own learning, for they were born in another time.
—Chinese proverb

It is the duty of children to wait on elders, and not the elders on children.
—Kenyan proverb

Source: http://creativeproverbs.com.

Respect for one's parents is the highest duty of civil life.
—Chinese proverb

Source: http://creativeproverbs.com.

The persistence of traditional cultural ideals about parenting can help see children through what is arguably one of the most difficult modes of immigration into Canada—the Domestic Worker Program. This mode of immigration separates children from their mothers until they, too, can come to Canada. However, sentiments gained from the experience itself, as well as the transmission of cultural values allowed by family cohesion, help protect youth from internalizing negative stereotypes against people who take part in the program (Pratt, cited in Rousseau et al., 2009). On the contrary, the prolonged separation in Filipino families reportedly creates appreciation for parents; once reunited, the children want to satisfy their parents' expectations of educational success. The result is family cohesion, positive attitudes toward school, and educational achievement.

As is evident in the proverbs about parenting, different cultures view parenting in somewhat different ways, but they all recognize its significance.

INFORMATION COMMUNICATION TECHNOLOGIES

Though parenting and parenting issues are ancient, many means of communication are new, and new communication technologies provide both new opportunities and new dangers for parent-child relationships. As we all know, information communication technologies (ICTs) give people the ability to communicate regardless of where they are. ICTs include mobile phones, social media, and various other forms of internet communication. As Ling and Yttri (2005) point out, mobile phones are a mode of communication that is under the control of adolescents, since most adolescents today own a mobile phone or have access to one, uncontrolled by their parents. This new element has many effects on parental authority and communication in the parent–child relationship.

Williams and Williams (2005) claim that mobile phone use by teens leads to an increased pattern of authoritative parenting, compared to authoritarian parenting. They argue that parent–child negotiation is the defining element of authoritative parenting and that mobile phones provide a new avenue for these negotiations to take place. Mobile phones allow parents to check up on where their children are, and this makes parents more likely to give their children more freedom. In this sense, mobile phones are a negotiation tool for the parent–child relationship.

But how do parents and adolescent children reach agreement about the use of this freedom and the use of these devices? According to Ling and Yttri (2005), most parents accept the consequences of children having control over their means of communication in exchange for an increased scope of monitoring opportunities. For their part, teens accept the need to be constantly accessible to their parents in exchange for the freedom that mobile phones allow.

However, mobile phones don't always guarantee that parents can know and supervise their child's whereabouts. A study by Weisskirch (2008) found that parental knowledge depends on the teens' willingness to initiate frequent phone calls. Conversely, a high frequency of parent-initiated phone calls is likely to result in the teens being secretive toward their parents.

Besides helping parents to monitor their children, mobile phones also help parents and children to maintain emotional connections. Blair and Fletcher (2011) found, for both mothers and children, mobile phones signify (or symbolize) emotional ties with other family members and adolescent autonomy. A study by Wei and Lo (2006) examining how college students use mobile phones found that affection was the most usual motivation for (and predictor of) mobile phone calls from students to their parents.

However, Ling and Yttri (2005) found that for teens, mobile phones may strengthen ties with peers at the expense of ties with parents. The fact that teens can communicate with their friends at any time means that they can be distracted at any time from family functions such as holidays and dinners. This increase in distraction can undermine the sense of family solidarity that normally results from these family rituals.

A similar pattern was found with the use of the internet for communication purposes among elementary school students. Lee and Chae (2007) noted that time spent online communicating was associated with a small decline in family communication. That is, online communication with friends appeared to replace or reduce the amount of communication with family members. However, uses of the internet for reasons other than communicating with friends didn't affect family communication.

ICTs take on a different role when families are separated. A study by Funston and Hughes (2006) found that teens whose parents had separated valued mobile phones more than teens from residentially intact families for purposes of private communication. For example, ITCs allowed them to talk easily to the non-residential parent without the residential parent knowing. However, teens of neither family structure valued the internet as a way to keep in touch with parents and tended to agree that face-to-face contact was better than internet communication. The exception was teens whose non-residential parents lived far away: They alone valued internet communication with parents, for the obvious reason that no other kind of communication was as easy.

Other studies have replicated this finding about the value of internet communication in long distance parent–child relationships. For example, Baldassar (2007) found that internet communicating, including social media and web video conferencing, allowed transnational families to provide each other with emotional support and advice (in Bacigalupe and Lambe, 2011). The authors note that, for us to fully appreciate the benefits of internet communication for families, we need to rethink our views on "proper" family communication, which (for many) is currently limited to face-to-face communication (ibid).

As online communication plays a greater role in many aspects of our lives, its effect on parent–child communication emerges as an important subject of study. Given the findings on their role in families with a parent residing far away, social media and internet video conferencing may be a promising avenue for parent–child communication in a variety of family forms.

CONCLUDING REMARKS

We learned in this chapter that parenting has changed and continues to change. The ways people become parents, the processes by which they begin parenting, and the kinds of families into which children are born and live have all changed in recent years. The need for good parenting, however, remains unchanged.

How well families raise their children affects the kind of adults those children will become and the world we will live in. How well parents have managed to balance discipline and freedom will affect how the children act and feel when they become teenagers. In Canada, teenagers who see their parents as accepting and warm and as less controlling have higher self-esteem than other children. The evidence shows they are healthier and perform better in school.

Childhood experiences resonate through adult life. For example, children punished physically by their parents are more likely to grow up to be aggressive toward other family members. Treating children this way dramatically increases their potential for violence as teenagers and, later, as parents of their own children. Nevertheless, not all family difficulties (or lucky breaks, for that matter) are the result of parental influences and choices.

As we saw in this chapter, parenting makes a difference to the ways that children grow up. In the next chapter, we further explore a topic with much significance for both parent–child relations and the family as a whole: the domestic division of labour.

CHAPTER SUMMARY

In this chapter, we examined parenthood from the perspective of societies, parents, and children. Today most people have fewer children, reproduce at a later age, and compress their parenting into a smaller time frame than in the past, allowing more time for careers and family. We can plan our families in this way because reliable contraceptive devices allow us to do so.

Reliable contraception, for example, has helped reduce the risk of teen pregnancy. As a result, the teen pregnancy rate is low in Canada, compared with the United States. Teen pregnancy can lead to many difficulties later. For example, many teenage mothers never make up their lost opportunities. They may also be unable to provide good parenting, so it is good this social risk has been reduced.

Once you have a child you must be a parent, and as a parent, you are responsible for primary socialization during your child's first years. Gender socialization begins as soon as the parent knows the sex of the child, sometimes even in utero. One of the jobs of the parent is to ready the child for entry into society, and some parents do it badly. Runaways are children who have judged their parents' parenting styles as so inadequate that they prefer life on the streets to life in the home of the parents. The research leaves us with little doubt about the difference between good parenting and bad.

Though class and cultural variation in styles of parenting remain, they are narrowing in many ways. The same principles of good parenting apply whatever the cultural group or class. Good parenting has social desirable results, while bad parenting has the opposite, at least in terms of North American cultural values.

Key Terms

authoritarian parenting Parenting characterized by low acceptance and high control, which can hinder the development of expressiveness and independence in children.

authoritative parenting Parenting characterized by high acceptance and high control, which produces the best results in children.

birth rate Number of births per 100 000 people in a given year.

control and supervision The extent to which parents oversee and censure their children's behaviour.

family cohesion A sense of attachment and relatedness among members of a family, both maintained and signified by shared activities, self-identification as a family member, and signs of familiarity and liking.

gender socialization The social learning process a person goes through to acquire gender roles and gender-based habits. This is done through family, peer groups, schools, and the mass media.

induction A form of discipline focused on using reason to encourage children to behave in certain ways in order to benefit themselves or others. For example, a child will be told to put away her toys so that others will not trip over them.

internal moral control An emotional feeling, such as guilt, that inhibits non-compliance.

love withdrawal A form of punishment to a child for non-compliance, where a child is denied the expression of love.

parental involvement Spending time with children, talking about them, and thinking about them.

permissive parenting A type of parenting with high acceptance and low control.

power assertion Threatening a child with punishment, usually in physical form, for non-compliance.

primary socialization Learning that takes place during childhood.

socialization The social learning process a person goes through to become a capable, functioning member of society; to prepare for life in society.

unengaged parenting A type of parenting with low acceptance and low control.

Critical Thinking Questions

1. Why and how might the ways a society defines *family* affect people's attitudes toward childbearing, contraception, adoption, and abortion?

2. Do the issues that arise with adoption and assisted fertility serve as evidence that the traditional idea of family is still influential in some ways? Explain.

3. How and why do parents socialize their children? How and why do children socialize their parents?

4. Research two distinctly different cultures. How might different styles of parenting yield the same results (i.e., adjustment, academic achievement, and not abusing substances) in these two cultures?

5. Can different kinds of families—for example, two-parent versus one-parent families, cohabiting versus married parent families, heterosexual versus homosexual families, native-born versus immigrant families—parent their children equally well? Explain your answer.

6. Research one key issue facing Aboriginal Canadians. How can you connect residential schools and non-Aboriginal foster families to this problem?

Weblinks

Planned Parenthood
www.plannedparenthood.com
For more than 90 years, Planned Parenthood has promoted a common-sense approach to women's health and well-being, based on respect for each individual's right to make informed, independent decisions about sex, health, and family planning.

Daily Strength
http://dailystrength.org/support-groups
/Childrens-Health-Parenting
This site offers parents free, anonymous online parenting advice from "people just like you," on topics that include children's mental and physical health and developmental and learning disorders. There are discussion groups designed for a wide variety of family types, including gay, military, single-dad, and adoptive families.

Dads and Moms of Michigan
www.dadsandmomsofmichigan.org/default
.aspx
Dads and Moms of Michigan (DMM) is a non-profit organization providing information, education, and the knowledge to effectively use available resources to all Michigan parents looking to remain actively involved in the lives of their children both during and after a divorce or separation.

Parenthoodkids.com
www.parenthoodkids.com
This site is "designed for kids of *any age*, and even for the young at heart! You will find resourceful information about homeschooling, recipes for fun foods that kids love to make and eat, games to play online, and birthday party game suggestions as well as games for everyday fun."

Health Canada: Healthy Living—Parenting
http://www.hc-sc.gc.ca/hl-vs/child-enfant
/parent/index-eng.php
Health Canada is the federal department responsible for helping Canadians maintain and improve their health, while respecting individual choices and circumstances. This webpage includes information on child development and effective parenting, healthy lifestyles, work-life balance, prenatal health, mental health, and more.

The Young Mommies Homesite
www.youngmommies.com
This website run by young mothers offers support and information to mothers and pregnant women in their teens and twenties. Teen pregnancy statistics, an article database, a resource directory for Canada and the United States, message boards, and chat rooms are just some of the resources offered.

Journal of Family Issues
http://jfi.sagepub.com
Journal of Family Issues (JFI), published monthly, provides up-to-date research, theory, and analyses on marriage and family life, including professional issues, research, and interdisciplinary perspectives on family studies, family violence, gender studies, social work, and sociology.

Family Relations
http://onlinelibrary.wiley.com/journal
/10.1111/(ISSN)1741-3729
An applied journal of family studies, *Family Relations* is mandatory reading for all professionals who work with families, including family practitioners, educators, marriage and family therapists, researchers, and social policy specialists. The journal's content emphasizes family research with implications for intervention, education and public policy, and publishing.

Journal of Marriage and Family
http://onlinelibrary.wiley.com/journal
/10.1111/(ISSN)1741-3737
For more than 70 years, the *Journal of Marriage and Family* (JMF) has been a leading research journal in the family field, featuring original research and theory, research interpretation and reviews, and critical discussion concerning all aspects of marriage, other forms of close relationships, and families.

Chapter 7
Work and Family Life

Jupiterimages/Pixland/Thinkstock

Chapter Outline

Learning Objectives

1 Explain how the gendered division of labour affects the value placed on housework by providing real-life examples.

2 Compare women's and men's work and recognize the disadvantages for women that are associated with gender stereotypes.

3 Define the "sandwich generation" and evaluate its effect on domestic work and paid work.

4 Describe factors affecting the work–family life balance and assess their impact on various family types.

5 Examine the role of culture in the family division of labour and identify changes to gender relations upon immigration to Canada.

6 Explain and provide examples of how the spillover of stress from work to home influences family interactions and cohesion.

7 Compare and contrast individual efforts and family efforts to manage the work-family balance.

8 Recognize the benefits of daycare for children and working parents.

9 Describe changes to the policies, employee benefits, and organizational culture of corporations and their effects on reducing work–family strain.

10 Compare the costs and benefits of telework and apply knowledge of this concept to real-world situations.

11 Differentiate between four types of welfare state strategies for alleviating poverty and determine their efficiency in addressing the problem of work–family tension.

This chapter will focus mainly on the **family work** done by intimate partners—for example, husbands and wives. We shall not consider the work of children or other family members—not because their contributions are unimportant but because of space considerations and limited data. In this chapter, we will return time and again to the stress caused by the conflicting demands of paid work, domestic work, and child care.

Housework and child rearing have not always been solely women's responsibility. In some past societies, men took a central role in caring for and raising children. The older idea of child rearing was that childhood should not be segregated from adulthood. Accordingly, fathers and mothers prepared their children for the real world by showing them adult work at an early age. As well, in the pre-industrial family, women were essential to market production. In a great many ways, women were an important part of economic production, just as fathers were an important part of domestic caregiving.

The terms *housework* and *women's work* came into being only with the rise of industrial capitalism, when people started to distinguish unpaid domestic labour from paid labour. Women could work for pay outside the home, but in the nineteenth century, skilled working-class men barred women from trade unions. *Housework* as we define it today is not a carry-over from pre-capitalist life: It is a result of the interaction between capitalism and patriarchy that allowed men to defend their privileges under new economic and social conditions (Jackson, 1992).

From the beginning, housework has been hard work for women. As historian Susan Strasser, author of the classic *Never Done: A History of American Housework*, has noted about colonial America,

> Women spun wool and flax, wove cloth, sewed it into clothing, grew food and prepared it for eating or storage, and made soap and candles. Other family members shared those tasks and (according to a gendered division of labor) worked in adjoining fields and small crafts shops. The colonial household, then, served as the central institution of economic production. (Strasser, 2006)

In Canada, too, women's work played an important part in settlement history. Within the agricultural communities of Alberta, for example, gender roles were restricted, with the expectation that women should be "caring, nurturing, and domestically proficient," whereas "the good male farmer is tough, hard-working, and in control of his environment" (Heather, Skillen, Young, and Vladicka, 2005: 89). Thus, in the late nineteenth and early twentieth centuries, men went out seeking work but women stayed home, acting as "community builders" and ensuring the survival of the family's farm.

Nineteenth-century farm families spent much of their time replenishing household supplies and repairing equipment. Upper- and middle-class families who could afford it hired domestic help, especially for tasks like laundry and work involving special skills (Strasser, 2006). In other homes, these household tasks were performed by the homemaker and her daughters. However, these tasks were not restricted to farms. Even non-farm women performed a significant economic role in household food production. The husband may have earned the wages, but female home support—wives and daughters—always made an important contribution to family finances (Armitage, 1979). And not only was the domestic work heavy in these households, it was never-ending. Nearly every chore meant building a fire and hauling water, for example.

The twentieth century saw a surge toward the industrialization of farming through the incorporation of technology, science, and global markets into agriculture (Heather et al., 2005). Even today, agriculture continues to modernize through the enlargement and intensification of farming operations (Smithers and Johnson, 2004). New farming methods have replaced traditional ones by increasing capital and technology. As well, much change has also resulted from new policies and rules around environmental sustainability and food quality (Smithers and Johnson, 2004). So even farms today are not what they were two centuries ago, nor are farm families.

As described in Chapter 2, industrialization changed the lives of rural families, and it also brought an influx of people into urban areas. With the arrival of the urban bourgeois family, the idea of "home" as a retreat from work emerged. This change came about through separation of home from the workplace, bringing new definitions of women as homemakers and full-time mothers, and a growing industry that catered to home efficiency. Compared to middle-class families, working-class families were least insulated from the workplace. Rather than serving as a refuge, working-class homes served mainly to reproduce the capitalist workforce, thus linking domestic and work life even more closely (Hareven, 1991).

Much of the change in family roles that we associate with modern life can be traced to the rise of urban, industrial society. New "labour-saving" appliances—the electric iron and the vacuum cleaner, for example—eased women's entry into paid work by making traditional housework less time-consuming. By the 1920s, the urban middle-class had access to many of our familiar household conveniences, including hot and cold running water, gas stoves, washing machines, refrigerators, and vacuum cleaners (Mintz, 2006). As mass-produced clothing became available and desirable and more women earned an income outside the home, fewer were obliged to sew clothing for their family members. Home sewing moved beyond its purely functional role to become a way of expressing personal tastes (Gordon, 2004).

Ironically, despite the spread of new household technology, the time spent on housework did not lessen for women. Time saved on cooking and cleaning was used instead for shopping, household management, and child care. The responsibility for these tasks still fell on individual households, and particularly on mothers, even as increased numbers of married women took paid work outside the home (Strasser, 2006). Oddly, the resulting stresses became personal problems and did not yield collective solutions.

Increasingly, with the spread of new technology, women were called on to learn and practise home economics—a form of education that many viewed as preparation for social reform (Apple and Coleman, 2003). Women's institutes tried to redefine domestic labour as skilled, giving women more status (Morgan, 1996). The professionalization of traditional domestic skills served to raise women's social standing largely through the application of Frederick Taylor's scientific management methods to housework (Turnbull, 1994; Strasser, 1978).

So, industrialization simplified many household tasks, allowing women to do more in less time. Yet, rather than enjoying spare time as a result, women devoted the same amount of time as ever to their housework. People came to expect women to make their homes attractive out of love, rather than any interest in market rewards. The work involved was thus viewed as a "labour of love," not work that deserves (and normally receives) payment. This merging of love with housework changed forever the relations between the sexes on the domestic front. Campaigns to promote the new household technologies highlighted the love ingredient of housework, lest women abandon their domestic work with the "mechanization" of the household (Fox, 1993: 151).

As mentioned earlier, home economists worked to raise the esteem of homemakers by promoting the idea that new home technologies needed skilled operators. High standards of cleanliness were thought to promote health and children's well-being. Concerns about the home being too dirty for curious young children led mothers to assume responsibility for cleaning as part of their identity as women and mothers (Fox, 2001). Thus, society charged homemakers with the duty of health promotion, a noble cause but unpaid and hugely undervalued. With this "scientization" of housework, women were assigned the role of preserving the home as their central lifework. In turn, this limited their access to markets outside the home they had enjoyed before industrialization. This limitation was evident, for example, in the influential writings of Charlotte Perkins Gilman, who, at the end of the nineteenth century, was imagining—or we should say, re-imagining—the future organization of work in households. Among other things, she imagined a more communal connection among families and households.

But Gilman's imaginings did not come to fruition. In response to a growing drive to consume, women began to take paid jobs outside the home to increase the family income. This need for outside work coincided with a growing demand for women workers in factories, especially during the Second World War, and for women workers in offices from the 1920s onward. The development of new office technology lessened the need for strength (and often skill) that had characterized earlier forms of work, making possible the vast movement of new female workers into the non-domestic, paid workforce.

It was in 1974 that British sociologist Ann Oakley published the first sociological study on this topic—her seminal book *The Sociology of Housework*. After that, housework began to emerge as a type of legitimate, difficult, and worthwhile work, not just a "labour of love." This classic work drew needed attention to domestic inequality and its relation to other forms of gender inequality. Since men rarely did housework, early sociologists and economists (almost exclusively male) had failed to consider it an important topic and, given its unpaid status, ignored its contribution to the economy. Oakley changed all that.

Oakley based her housework research on a small sample of British working- and middle-class homemakers. Social class, in her sample, made little difference: Both classes of women reported similar (negative) attitudes about housework and a similar (high degree of) identification with their homemaker role. All the women in Oakley's sample viewed housework as unpleasant. Despite this dislike, many of the informants viewed the role of homemaker as central to their identity; they felt mainly responsible for tending to the home and children. For this reason, most of these women swallowed their dissatisfaction with the monotony, isolation, and low social status that it provided them. They took it for granted as unavoidable.

Oakley concluded that women are disempowered and imprisoned by their beliefs about the proper role of women, especially of mothers, in a modern society. Despite their unhappiness, many housewives feel obliged by their culture to play a basically alienating and frustrating role. They have been socialized by a patriarchal gender ideology into accepting slavery in gilded cages. However mechanized the household or posh the suburban community, slavery remained slavery for these housewives.

THE WORTH OF HOUSEWORK

Today, housework hasn't disappeared and women continue to do most of it. As the twentieth century progressed, women became increasingly inclined to ask questions about the value of the domestic work they had been doing without payment. Some thought that mechanized homemaking could be valued like work outside the home and factored into calculations of the gross national product. Others argued, in contrast, that we could measure housework but still should not include it as a market exchange, since the work done by women at home ought to be freely provided (i.e., a labour of love.) Yet the amounts of work in question were and are enormous. In 1995, for example, the United Nations estimated that unpaid work by women around the world would cost $11 trillion if paid at fair market value (Nova Scotia Advisory Council on the Status of Women, 2000).

For the first time anywhere, in 1996 a government recognized unpaid work by including questions on it in the national Census. In the Census of Canada sample of one in five households, all respondents aged 15 and older, excluding full-time residents of institutions, were asked to report the number of hours spent in the previous week doing (1) unpaid housework, (2) unpaid child care, and (3) unpaid care or help to seniors. They were also invited to identify "periods when [they] were carrying out two or three of these activities at the same time."

Another important step in recognizing unpaid work was the payment of family allowances, discussed in Chapter 2. Family allowances (begun in Canada after World War II) were meant to buy needed items for children, and they were also a way to give women some small payment and recognition for child rearing. These monthly payments, based on the number of children at home, went to all women with children—but only to women, never to men. For many women who worked solely at home, this was their only independent income.

The federal government stopped its program of family allowances in 1992, replacing it with the Child Tax Credit program, which targets low- and middle-income families. Quebec intended its own program of baby bonuses both to increase the numbers of births and to provide support for women raising children. Of course, the amounts paid in no way compensate for the real costs involved in raising a child. However, they gave important recognition to the important, mainly unpaid work that Canadian women contribute to the economy.

The More Things Change

Today, women still do most of the housework, and this is true around the world. In none of the 20 countries Hook (2006) surveyed did the unpaid work by married men exceed 37 percent of the domestic total. Countries differ only in the extent of domestic inequality where the distribution of housework is concerned.

Because women have the primary responsibility for doing domestic work, many are undertaking a "double day" (Armstrong and Armstrong, 1994) when they enter the labour force—especially if they are mothers. (And today, most mothers of young children are in the paid labour force.) As a result, women tend to have little leisure time and certainly less leisure time than their husbands. "The ensuing exhaustion of women encourages dissatisfaction, especially when their partners do not share the responsibility of work in the home" (Armstrong and Armstrong, 1994: 227). In other words, the unequal distribution of household work promotes resentment and reduces marital satisfaction.

On farms, many women even work a "triple day," since they have to care for the household, the farm, and possibly hold a job outside the home as well (Martz, 2007). As Irish sociologist Patricia O'Hara (1998: 37) notes, it is no wonder farmwomen have been advising their daughters to leave the rural areas and especially agriculture. For all its difficulty, city life demands much less of women than farm life.

Men contribute to domestic work too, but their contribution is most notably on household maintenance and repairs. Often, they spend less time overall on these kinds of tasks than women spend on day-to-day housework and child care. As well, men can often postpone these sorts of household tasks until time allows: There is no urgency around trimming the hedge or repairing a lamp, for example. This means that men's work at home is less constraining than women's, which often must be done every single day (for example, meal preparation and bathing the children). Equally important from a psychological standpoint, no one sees men's work at home as defining them in the way that women's work does. Men who fix up and care for their homes are less often defined as "homemakers," though some people still define women as homemakers first and paid workers second.

Yet inequality in domestic work is not merely a result of patriarchal culture; we find a similar inequality in the arrangements of people in gay and lesbian relationships. The division of labour in gay and lesbian families is not based on gender, yet neither is it egalitarian (Oerton, 1998): Often a pattern of primary breadwinner/primary caregiver emerges in these families too. This suggests an inequitable division of household labour is likely to emerge in any family, regardless of its makeup. The inequality in heterosexual families is, therefore, not a result of patriarchal values and traditions

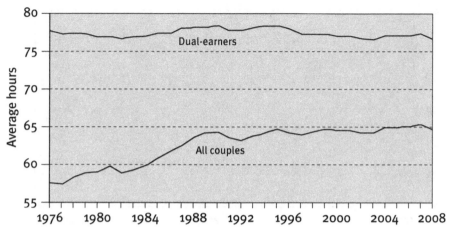

(a) The increase in total family work hours is due to more dual-earners, but the dual-earners' hours are stable.

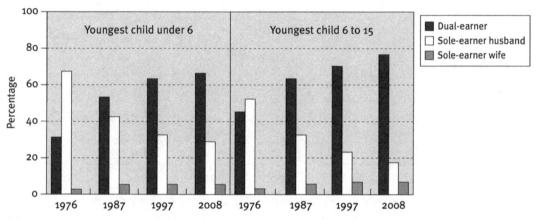

(b) Today the vast majority of couples with children are dual-earners.

Figure 7.1 The Changing Nature of the Family Workweek in Canada (*continued*)

alone, but of the demands of child rearing and an unequal time contribution to the paid labour force.

Figure 7.1 provides data from a recent Canadian report on the changing nature of the family workweek (Marshall, 2009). Several important trends in the past 30 years can be noted here. First, note the change in hours worked. In 1976, couples spent a total of 57.6 hours in paid work per week; and by 2008, this number had increased by 13 percent to 64.8 hours (Figure 7.1a). Household heads were not necessarily working longer; rather, there were more income contributors within the average family—usually, two adults.

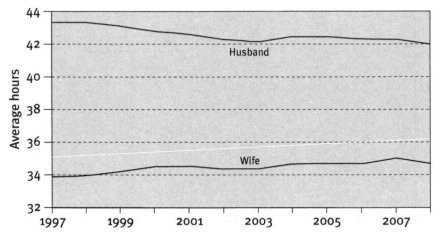

(c) Slight but steady narrowing of dual-earner hours since the late 1990s.

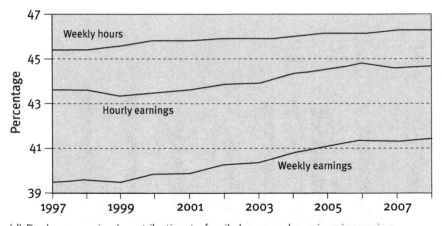

(d) Dual-earner wives' contribution to family hours and earnings increasing.

Figure 7.1 (*Continued*)

Source: Katherine Marshall. 2009. The family work week. *Statistics Canada Perspectives,* Catalogue no. 75-001-X. www.statcan.gc.ca/pub/75-001-x/2009104/pdf/10837-eng.pdf.

The problems we discuss in this chapter have been increasing with the number of dual-earner families, and the data in Table 7.1 show a large increase in the number of dual-earner families in the past three decades—a jump from just over one-third to three-quarters of all couples in 2008. **Dual-earner couples** work an average of 77 hours per week—nearly twice the number of hours of a **single-earner couple**. This suggests that, in most dual-earner couples, both spouses are working for pay close to full-time.

Table 7.1 The Degree of Labour Participation Varies by Age and Family Status

| | Age Groups | | | | |
Total	15+	15–24	25–54	55–64	65+
All members of economic families	69%	65%	86%	59%	9%
Family head	71	76	86	59	10
Spouse of head	71	81	88	61	11
Child of head	66	62	82	56	*
Other relative of head	53	65	80	52	4
Unattached individuals	60	77	86	56	6

Source: Data from Roger Sauvé. 2009. Family life and work life: An uneasy balance. Copyright (c) 2009 Vanier Institute of the Family. Retrieved from www.vifamily.ca/library/work/sauve/worklife.pdf. Reprinted with permission.

What's more, most of the families with children are dual-earners, a statistic that has been steadily rising since the mid-1970s (Figure 7.1b). This means that most families now have less time available to engage in unpaid work and leisure activities—for example, in housework, cooking, or child care, let alone unstructured fun. Parents are under more pressure these days to negotiate how they divide their time at home, especially their caregiving, and this pressure can be a source of stress and conflict, as we will see later in the chapter.

On a more positive note, it seems that the number of hours partners work is now starting to equalize (see Figure 7.1c). There may be several reasons for this, including "changes in the industrial and occupational structure, educational attainment and labour market opportunities, and individual and family preference and choice ... These trends are more likely to affect men's average hours since they have traditionally been more likely to work long hours." (Marshall, 2009: 8). But wives' earnings are also increasing (see Figure 7.1d), signalling the start of a change in breadwinning roles (Marshall, 2009).

Paid Work and Unpaid Work

Gendered work is slow to change, however. Despite a steady advance in gender equality—legal, political, social, and cultural—over the past several decades, discrimination against women remains an important problem in our society. Gender stereotyping and inequality continue in some workplaces. There, a *glass ceiling* results in earning differences between women and men. Because of stereotypes of women as nurturing and emotional, and of men as businesslike and rational, some women have been excluded from jobs that offer the biggest challenges and largest reward. Even today, women are still under-represented in leadership positions in business and government.

The work women do get to do—"women's work"—includes clerical jobs, sales, light manufacturing, and the catchall category of "service work" (which ranges from nurses' aides and grade-school teachers, to waitresses and welfare caseworkers—and pays poorly). In general, women's work not only pays less than men's but also is less inflation-proof. For men, poverty is often a result of unemployment and is curable by getting a job. But for women, concentrated in the low-wage stratum of the workforce, a job may not erase poverty; it may only reduce it. The low wages and job instability of women's work—the so-called secondary work sector—often mean that even full-time workers live in poverty.

Many families need women's wages to keep the family out of poverty. Without the contribution of women's wages, the number of families with low income would be very much higher than it is. Yet many continue to ignore the significance of this contribution. Armstrong and Armstrong (1994: 225) argue compellingly that the nature of women's work in the home and in the labour force reinforces and perpetuates the division of labour by gender. Heavy responsibilities at home often prevent women from taking on high-paying jobs with heavy responsibilities in the workplace and vice versa.

Of course, women enjoy many benefits from their paid work, despite the unfair workload. Some studies have shown that participation in the labour force can bring improved self-esteem and mental and physical health, as well as status and money (Tingey, Kiger, and Riley, 1996). Besides, as women do better economically, their families do, too. Cohen (1998) found that in families where women have higher incomes and occupational status, the families spend more money on housekeeping services and dining out. Though this choice to out-source domestic work is more popular (and feasible) among wealthier families, it is still one way that women can reduce the stress of the double day.

Women's participation in the paid workforce varies with age. Figure 7.1 shows that participation is at its peak for people age 25 to 55, when 86 percent of adult family members work for pay. Participation drops to 59 percent for people age 55 to 64, and then drops down to less than 10 percent among people more than 65 years old (Sauvé, 2009). This means that many of the problems we discuss in this chapter—especially the conflict between paid work, housework, and parenting—reach their peak during the ages of 25 to 55 years old. Life is easier before 25 and after 55, by this reckoning. However, as noted in "Canadian Workforce Trends," the aging of the baby boomers has led to an increased number of adults age 55 and over comprising the Canadian labour force.

- Dual-earner couples are now the dominant family form, comprising 7 out of 10 couples in 2008. With more contributors to the family income, the overall family work hours have increased and disposable family time has thus been reduced (Marshall, 2009).

- In 2010, employed Canadians were working fewer hours on average each week compared to 1976. Canadians worked 36.2 hours per week on average, a decrease from 38.0 hours per week in 1976 (Human Resources and Skills Development Canada, 2011).

- Sixty-three percent of single mothers with children younger than the age of six are taking part in the labour force, an increase from 44 percent in 1976 (Human Resources and Skills Development Canada, 2004).

- Women are still more likely than men to work part-time, drop out of the paid workforce, or hold two paid jobs to support the family. In 2006, 32 percent of female Canadians said they were working part-time to care for children or meet other personal or family responsibilities, but only 6 percent of males cited these reasons (Sauvé, 2009).

- The majority of Canadians are content with their occupations. Although 39 percent do not feel that they are paid enough for their work, 81 percent are happy with their jobs and 88 percent like their colleagues (*The Sudbury Star*, 2011).

- The aging of the baby boomers has altered the workforce's demographics. The proportion of Canadians in the labour force age 55 and over rose from 10 percent in 2001 to 17 percent in 2009. Projections suggest nearly one person in four in the labour force will be 55 years old or over by 2021 (Statistics Canada, 2011).

DOMESTIC WORK: CARING FOR FAMILY MEMBERS AND HOME

Child Care

As the work lives of women and men become more similar, child care becomes the great divide and source of conflict on the domestic scene. Baker and Lero (1996: 103) argue that "the gender-structured nature of the labour market, differential use of parental and child-rearing leave by men and women, and different gender expectations by families and communities preserve the unequal sharing of economic and social parenting."

Parents seldom share childcare equally (Wilson, 1996). Data from Statistics Canada (cited in Armstrong and Armstrong, 1994: 10) reveal that women are almost three times as likely as men to give physical care to children younger than the age of five and two-and-a-half times as likely to provide care for children between ages 5 and 18. The 2001 National Work-Life Conflict Study funded by Health Canada reported that 63 percent of female respondents had primary responsibility for child care, compared to 6 percent of male respondents (Higgins and Duxbury, 2002). These numbers have not changed much from the 1991 study.

More and more men have spent unpaid time caring for children younger than age 15, with 79.5 percent currently doing so—nearly comparable to the 86 percent of women who do so (Statistics Canada, 2006i: 31). Yet, women spend *longer hours* in unpaid child care than men, on average. For example, in 2006, nearly half of the women (47.3 percent) with a child younger than age 15 spent 30 or more hours a week caring for children, compared with just over one-fifth (21.8 percent) of men (Statistics Canada, 2006i: 31).

Women often must fulfill the family's nurturing, caring roles, especially toward family members who are ill or have disabilities. This is especially true in rural areas, where people have shorter life expectancies and higher rates of disability, and experience more accidents, poisonings, and incidents of violence than their urban counterparts (Edelman and Menz, 1996; Sutherns, McPhedran, and Haworth-Brockman, 2004).

Because of women's heavy family care responsibilities, some employers are reluctant to hire women with young children, especially single mothers. The National Childcare Study in Canada (cited in Armstrong and Armstrong, 1994: 106) found that each added child significantly lowers the chance that a single parent will be employed.

However, women are not free to take any job they are offered. A lack of access to quality, low-cost child care creates stress for all parents, but especially mothers, given their heavier responsibility for child care. Low-income single mothers are especially vulnerable because "without subsidies to help cover the costs of childcare, paid work may not be financially feasible for lone mothers earning minimum wage" (Mason, 2003: 49). The lone mothers who enter and remain in the labour market either receive assistance from mothers, sisters, or friends or they work in family-friendly environments (Mason, 2003).

An alternative to low-cost child care is grandparental care of the children. Whether this assistance from the older generation reduces the stress associated with child rearing and work demands, however, is unclear. In some instances, it may backfire. Consider a study of Taiwanese immigrants conducted in Vancouver. Sun (2008) finds that, where grandparental child care is concerned, mothers prefer help from their own mothers, not their mothers-in-law. (Fathers, on the other hand, are equally happy to receive help from their own parents and their parents-in-law.) As well, mothers are more likely than fathers to feel ambivalent about receiving the older generation's assistance. Perhaps they feel that accepting help creates conflict or creates obligations they would rather avoid.

On balance, however, child care improves with help from the older generation. The benefits go mainly to children and their mothers. In most families, fathers continue to serve mainly as economic providers, largely disconnected from issues of child care when the older generation is available. Mainly, help from paternal grandparents encourages mothers to play more active roles outside the home, while providing a nurturing environment for the children. At the same time, this support reinforces the traditional gendered division of child-care labour in the family.

In some cases, immigrant grandmothers who assist their children with child care also serve to sustain the patriarchal family structure of their home country. A study of Indo-Fijian immigrant women to Canada reveals this trend. Research has found that many grandmothers provide child care and perform household duties in exchange for care and support from their sons and daughters-in-law (Shankar and Northcott, 2009). Back home, the social and cultural norms of Fiji hold the husband responsible for the financial security of the family. Accordingly, none of the women in the study had ever worked in the paid labour force. Having been dependent for support on their husbands back home, they were dependent on their sons after immigrating to Canada.

However, the same study found that young Indo-Fijian women are less likely to adhere to traditional patriarchal norms than older Indo-Fijian women. They are reluctant to be dependent on husbands and less likely than women back home to develop submissive relationships with their mothers-in-law. The child care provided by paternal grandmothers allows younger daughters-in-law to obtain paid employment. In turn, their participation in the paid labour force makes them less dependent on their husbands for financial support and thus gives them more autonomy. This is how patriarchal relations tend to break down after immigration: gradually, and generation by generation.

Elder Work and Care: Emerging Challenges at Home

Aging poses problems both for elderly family members and for the younger people who care for them. Despite increased life expectancies for all Canadians, men die younger (on average) than women, and many women live on into widowhood, some for many decades. With the death of a spouse, the partner left behind has to not only deal with the pain and grief caused by the loss of their significant other, but must also reconstruct their identity as a newly single person. This, among other things, entails alterations in the daily tasks and routine responsibilities that the couple once shared.

Where one or both members of the couple survive into old age, caregiving becomes a major source of stress. Increased life expectancies among the old-old (that is, people older than age 85) have increased the demand for care. However, public funds for health and social services have been unable to keep up with this demand, limiting the choices available for care in a great many cases (Fast, Keating, Oakes, and Williamson, 1997). Thus, many Canadian families struggle to provide elder care that is not otherwise available or affordable. Usually, the burden of elder care falls on the shoulders of middle-aged women, most of whom are in the paid workforce.

Equally problematic is the shortage of caregiving children. Compared with decades (and centuries) past, fewer children are available to help take care of the elderly today because family sizes have shrunk over the past hundred years. This is especially pressing in Asian countries (for example, Japan, Korea) that follow the Confucian tradition of filial piety and among immigrants to Canada from these countries. The children's willingness to perform traditional elder-care tasks is compromised both by the demands of the modern workplace and by a growing shortage of siblings to help out.

Nowhere is this care shortage more marked than in China, owing in part to the Chinese one-child policy and also to the erosion of Confucian ideals under communism and with immigration. As a result, many Chinese children are less willing today to care

All of these issues—parenting, elder care, and paid work—cause high levels of stress, and in turn they hinder both work productivity and family functioning.

Monkey Business Images/Shutterstock

for their aging parents and also less willing to honour any of the traditional practices of an extended family. For example, they are less willing to live with grandparents and less willing to imagine sharing the same household with their parents when they become older (Zhan, 1998). Many of these children also fear that, on marrying, they may become long-term caregivers for as many as four older parents.

Similar problems arise in Canada for adult children whose parents have divorced and remarried. Their duty to care for elderly parents and step-parents (also grandparents and step-grandparents) is problem enough (Ganong-Coleman, 1998). Extra divorces add further strain, especially when these children are trying to build their careers, protect their own marriages, and raise their own children. Average households may be getting smaller but families are not getting any less complex!

With the large baby boom generation getting older, many families find themselves part of what is called the "sandwich generation"—they are caring for both dependent children and dependent older parents. The number of "sandwiched Canadians" is likely to grow as the population continues to age and young adults stay at home for longer periods of time (Statistics Canada, 2002i). Many dual-earner couples, facing these increased role demands, reduce their engagement in other roles so as to meet the increased demands on their time and energy (Cullen, Hammer, Neal, and Sinclair, 2009). The 2007 General Social Survey indicated that among caregivers age 45 and older, 34.7 percent cut back on social activities and 15.5 percent cut back on work hours to accommodate their other duties (Vanier Institute of the Family, 2010).

At the same time, today many older people are also responsible for caring for their grandchildren. Between 1991 and 2001, there was a 20 percent increase in the number of Canadian children under age 18 living solely with their grandparents. In 2006, this number stood at 28 200 for children age 14 and under (Statistics Canada, 2007f). Further, this arrangement is especially common in families of First Nations origin, including North American Indians, Métis, and Inuit, with one-third of First Nations Canadian grandparents raising two or more grandchildren. In comparison to other grandparent caregivers, First Nations caregivers are also more likely to be simultaneously caring for a senior and spending more than 30 hours each week on child-care and housework responsibilities (Fuller-Thomson, 2005).

Raising grandchildren often affects a couple's marital relationship, and doing so while raising one's own children also poses a challenge. Transitioning at an older age to a role that is not commonly held by older people—for example, becoming a parent again at the age of 60—or when the new responsibilities compete with existing responsibilities is difficult. Older grandparents may therefore find raising grandchildren stressful, particularly if they are retired or have exited the role of parent and entered that of grandparent. Whatever the cause, such a change in family structure is considerable and can influence a couple's relationship.

Matzek and Cooney (2009) studied the experiences of (two-generation) grandparents who cared for both their grandchildren and their own children, compared with grandparents who cared only for their grandchildren. Both sets of grandmothers reported higher levels of spousal strain than grandfathers, and two-generation grandmothers reported significantly less spousal support than the other grandparents. The researchers concluded that two-generation grandfathers may not have recognized that the added responsibility of caring for grandchildren posed a burden for their wives, since these grandmothers were already caring for their own children.

In the same study, employed caregivers reported stronger feelings of spousal support than unemployed caregivers; for them, paid work away from the home provided relief from their familial responsibilities as well as rewarding work relationships. Spouses, recognizing the strain of home and work demands, provided greater emotional and behavioural support to their working partners.

As noted, many grandparents today provide care for their grandchildren; as well, an increasing number of adult grandchildren are caring for their grandparents. Though many Botswanan grandchildren are traditionally expected to act as caregivers to their grandparents (Weibel-Orlando, 1997), elder care by grandchildren is new to many North Americans.

An American study found that grandchildren caregivers hold conflicting feelings about their new responsibility. On the one hand, many respondents report having a strong bond with their grandparents, a bond that (in many cases) is strengthened by the daily interactions around caregiving. On the other hand, many also expressed confusion and feelings of role reversal; it felt odd to be taking care of someone who had historically given them care. They also found they had to make sacrifices to fulfill their new commitments.

This sometime meant forgoing further education, employment opportunities, and personal goals (Fruhauf, Jarrott, and Allen, 2006).

Overall, caring for another family member—whether an older parent, a child, a grandchild, or a grandparent—is a major source of stress for Canadian families that compounds the stresses of domestic work, paid work, and personal development.

Economic Independence and Domestic Work

The movement toward greater household equality is a slow, complex process, as is any change of practices within a family. Sociologists have found that increases in women's paid work alter authority relations between husbands and wives, because women gain greater economic independence by holding a paid job. What, then, is the effect on children of having two parents holding paid jobs?

For example, does dual earning hinder the emotional and psychological development of children? Many adherents of traditional family life claim that it does, but the research findings are not in agreement. On the contrary, some research finds that school-aged children and adolescents with working mothers hold fewer stereotyped ideas about male and female roles, and daughters of these mothers are more ambitious. On the negative side, some research finds that children whose mothers work for pay are more likely than other children to experience "insecure attachment" to their mothers.

The issue of attachment is important, as we saw in the previous chapter. A child's insecurity is often correlated with the quality time he or she spends with parents, starting at an early age. Bonding develops over time and is based on long-term expressions of love, caring, communication, and active listening. All children need this love, supervision, and discipline. Whenever parents fail adequately to provide for these needs, their children will suffer. Setting aside time to attach and re-attach with children is important, especially for working parents.

However, children's overall adjustment depends not on the mother's employment alone, but also on the availability of the father and both parents' attitudes toward the mother working. Enjoyable features of work—such as the complexity of working with people, the challenge, and the stimulation—all contribute to good parenting (for example, gentler discipline, more warmth, and responsiveness). In short, happier parents produce happier children, and often, paid word contributes to a parent's happiness.

Thus, research shows that women with especially challenging, interesting, and complex jobs have less troubled or delinquent children—because the moms are happier with their lives and work. The economic benefits of employment and opportunities for workplace autonomy that improve parenting skills overshadow the disadvantages that stem from decrease in time working mothers can spend with their children (Cooksey, Menaghan, and Jekielelek, 1997: 658). Filling multiple roles—housework, paid work, and caregiving—does not *necessarily* cause people more stress. What determines whether a working mother feels stressed and whether this stress harms the family is whether the working mother feels she has control over her life (Tingey, Kiger, and Riley, 1996).

The Effects of Domestic Work on Paid Work

As we have seen, women are mainly responsible for the work—especially, the housework and caregiving—at home. As a result, many Canadians imagine that women will have weak connections with, and weak commitment to, paid jobs. And some evidence supports this supposition. Mothers, for example, take more advantage of parental and family leaves, **flextime**, and "family-friendly" workplace policies than do fathers, largely to care for dependent children. Women also more often turn down work that requires travel or decline promotions that require a geographical move because of their responsibilities for children and families.

Fathers are more likely than mothers to move from one job to another and one employer to another, because they view their family responsibility as maximizing income. Conversely, they are less likely than mothers to leave a job (or employer) or change to part-time work because of increased family responsibilities. Men still earn more, so it seems to make sense for women, who are typically paid less on average, to cut back hours if more caregiving is required. However, the result is continued occupational segregation, income inequality, and domestic inequality.

One result of their primary responsibility for domestic work means that women—by spending their adult lives caring for families and homes—are less likely to build up their own savings, pensions, contacts, and job status. This is why divorce and widowhood are harder on women than on men: Women have invested far more of themselves in their families than in the economy. Widows who have spent their adult lives in family work—including, increasingly, caring for a severely ill or dying spouse—typically find themselves without any pension. Wives who have spent their adult lives in family work may find it financially impossible, or nearly impossible, to leave an unhappy marriage or abusive relationship.

By contrast, participation in the paid workforce gives women more independence and, often, more confidence, too. This benefit has beneficial effects on marriage and also has beneficial effects after marriage. A history of workforce participation can improve the economic condition of divorced mothers, for example, by raising their income and sharing the costs of raising children through shared custody. This is why working mothers (whether full-time or part-time) are more likely to share their children's care with a former spouse (Juby, Le Bourdais, and Marcil-Gratton, 2005). Fathers are also more likely to gain full custody when their former wife is successfully integrated into the workforce, especially if these men were involved in the home during marriage.

WORK AND FAMILY LIFE

The Problem: Balancing Work and Family Life

Both paid work and family life make enormous demands on our time, energy, and emotions. Life often calls on us to make choices between work and family. People in widely

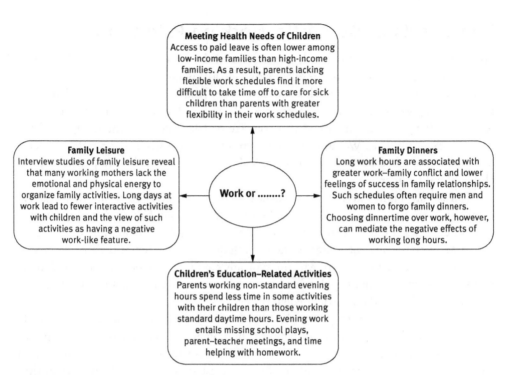

Figure 7.2 Choices faced by working parents

Sources: Clemans-Cope, L., et al., 2008. Access to and use of paid sick leave among low-income families with children. *Pediatrics* 122(2): 480–486.

Jacob, Jenet I., S. Allen, J. E. Hill, N. L. Mead, M. Ferris. 2008. Work interference with dinnertime as a mediator and moderator between work hours and work and family outcomes. *Family and Consumer Sciences Research Journal.* 36(4): 310–327.

Wight, Vanessa R., Sara B. Raley, and Suzanne M. Bianchi. 2008. Time for Children, One's Spouse and Oneself among Parents Who Work Nonstandard Hours. *Social Forces* 87(1): 243–271.

Shaw, Susan M. 2008. Family leisure and changing ideologies of parenthood. *Sociology Compass* 2: 1–16.

varying societies, doing different kinds of work, have tried to solve this problem in different ways. Today, for many Canadians the work–family problem has worsened, as many people have taken to working longer hours to make ends meet. (Figure 7.2 illustrates some of the choices faced by working parents in light of their demanding work schedules.)

Of course, by historical and comparative standards, most Canadians work relatively little. Due to extended full-time education, paid work today tends to start later in life and ends earlier in life (through retirement) than it did a century ago. Likewise, workweeks have shrunk from 38 hours in 1976 to 36.2 hours (Human Resources and Skills Development Canada, 2011).

Time Crunch

Why do people work longer hours if it means shortening the time they can spend with their families? Sociologists disagree about the answer to this question.

In her book *The Time Bind*, sociologist Arlie Hochschild (1997) shows that paid work gives women more rewards and less stress than does family life. Increasingly, workplaces are turning into home-like environments. And increasingly, the demands of family life are, for mothers, becoming less manageable and less egalitarian than the demands of paid work life. This, says Hochschild, accounts for some women spending so much time at work. (Also, full-time work receives more pay and more benefits than part-time work, and job-sharing arrangements are not widely available.) By contrast, more time off paid work means spending more time at home, doing more unpaid domestic work.

Besides this, employers demand more of our time. Even today, many women work longer hours because, like men, they are in jobs and careers where employers expect it. Many women value their careers and want to develop them, even though this often means working longer hours. Besides, many women understand that earning an independent income raises the likelihood of equal treatment in society and within the household.

Unfortunately, many workplaces seem to assume "that dedicated workers can free themselves from private duties, so nothing needs to interfere with the demands of their jobs" (Echtelt, Glebbeek, Lewis, Lindenberg, 2009: 190). Feminist sociologist Joan Acker argues that, in Western market economies, jobs already contain a gendered division of labour, despite what appear (on paper) to be "gender neutral" policies. The separation between the public and private spheres of life, and the corporate lack of responsibility for society's reproductive interests, "effectively denies women the opportunity to combine work and family life in a natural and optimal way" (Echtelt et al., 2009: 190).

Compare this with the situation of workers in Holland, where workplaces are characterized by more flexibility and autonomy than in North America. Employees there can decide when and where to work and thus effectively combine work and family life. In North America, a worker's success depends more heavily on peak performance, leading to time competition among workers, intensified work, longer hours, and more pressures to outperform oneself (Echtelt et al., 2009). Thus, the modern, supposedly gender-neutral workplace, with more overtime than the traditional workplace, may end up reproducing the traditional male model of work and worsening work–life conflict.

Adding to this, to some extent, is the technology we have produced to simplify work. The computer—at home and at the office—has revolutionized the pace of work by speeding up research (through the internet), communication (through email), and text production (through word processing.) The cell phone has made everyone available for work everywhere, always. By combining computer and cell phone—as with the BlackBerry—we have voluntarily made ourselves on call 24 hours a day. Because of these technological changes, we have come to expect near-instant responsiveness from the people we work with, and they expect it of us.

Descriptions of the resulting problem fall into several categories—overload, culturally induced stress, and spillover. By **overload**, we mean the excessive amount of work many people—especially mothers—have to do. By **culturally induced stress**, we mean the stress and guilt that people in our culture feel when they fail to get all the work done. Finally, by **spillover**, we mean the strains and demands that workers bring home from the workplace, and that family struggles are often unsuccessfully met.

Overload

As we have seen, the unequal division of domestic labour dumps much work on the shoulders of women—especially mothers—who also work for pay. Results include stress, resentment, lack of self-esteem, and poor health. As well, most women have to work longer hours to earn the same amount as men, due to their lower overall earning power—the **wage gap**.

Because women spend more combined time on paid work and domestic work than men, they experience more overload, especially during early parenthood, when they are still learning the new role of "parent." Not surprisingly, the extent of the overload varies over the family's life cycle. Especially when their children are young, women in dual-earner families report more overload and more symptoms of distress than men. Among dual-earner couples with children in the home, both wives and husbands also experience stress due to paid work. According to the data, only wives experience significant stress due to family life itself (Rwampororo, 2001).

Time management, by itself, is not enough to reduce the effects of strain on feelings of *stress* connected to overload. For both men and women, feeling in control is an important influence on the perception of overload. Without a sense of control at work or at home, both women and men risk developing depression and anxiety, and women are at the higher risk. Other things being equal, paid work stresses women more, and this causes women more absenteeism from work than it does men (Jacobson, Aldana et al., 1996). In part, this is because of the jobs that women hold. Women are more likely than men to hold paid jobs that are intrinsically stressful: for example, service jobs in which women have little control over the process. Many women's jobs—indeed, many marginal service jobs, like waitressing—combine heavy, continuing demands with a lack of decision-making authority (Karasek and Theorell, 1990). By contrast, women doctors, with more job autonomy than waitresses, experience fewer harmful effects of work overload.

So, overload in itself plays a role in people's feelings of dissatisfaction and frustration, but it is far from the whole story. Merely reducing the number of hours worked may not eliminate the sense of overload and the resulting dissatisfaction. That said, there are growing concerns about the dissatisfaction workers feel about their present work–life balance. Sometimes, we go too far for too long and our bodies let us know; our immune system is compromised, and we get colds, flu, and other infections easily. Both employers and employees now realize that this problem of overload affects not only the health of employees but their rates of absenteeism and the productivity of the company as a whole (Human Resources and Skills Development Canada, 2005a).

Cultural Sources of Distress

People react differently to overload and to stress generally. So, we cannot ignore the cultural context when discussing the family division of labour and its effects. In some cultures, where traditional conceptions of male and female are unyielding, working mothers who fail to live up to traditional standards may feel especially guilty or ashamed, whatever their level of overload. They may be working 15 hours a day and still feel as though they are failing to live up to cultural standards of womanhood or motherhood, for example.

For example, women Bulgarian and Israeli schoolteachers, in societies that favour a traditional division of household labour, report higher levels of home–work conflict than American, Australian, and Dutch schoolteachers, in societies that favour an egalitarian division of household labour (Moore, 1995). Both do similar amounts of work. However, the women who, for cultural reasons, aspire to the highest standards of domesticity experience the most conflict.

Sometimes the problem is normative uncertainty about how people are supposed to behave. For example, research suggests that Argentinian professional women ages 20 to 45 often feel they lack a clear definition of their roles as workers and mothers, and suffer especially high levels of stress as a result. The recent, rapid changeover from a male-dominated society to one where working women play an important social role has taken many couples by surprise.

Workload problems affect people differently, depending on their cultural or social group. In Canada, mothers from higher socio-economic backgrounds are more like to enter and stay in paid employment, even if they have responsibility for children. For a variety of reasons, high-income women are better able to deal with the dual burden of work and marriage than poorer women. This means the problem of work–family overload is greatest for women who are already the most socially vulnerable. The box "International Differences in Work–Life Balance" provides a look at how this problem is addressed in various countries.

Gender Relations, Housework, and Paid Work in Immigrant Families

Many women who immigrate to Canada have never done paid work before because of household responsibilities and strict gender roles that have limited their opportunities. Yet, after moving to Canada, some have no choice but to pursue employment to support their family (Remennick, 2007). Given the opportunity, some women are even tempted to seek economic independence, having only stayed with their husbands because of cultural ties and economic dependency (see Nissimi, 2007, for a description of this in the Mashhad immigrant community).

Some researchers argue that this economic opportunity for women can lead to a decrease in the prevalence of patriarchy, or at least a reconfiguration (Hyman, Guruge, and Mason, 2008). On the one hand, the change may be beneficial, with women from

International Differences in Work–Life Balance

- Taiwan—Taiwan has recently gone through a rapid modernization of work and lifestyles, so that more employees are now exposed to stressful Western and industrialized work situations. The rising female participation in paid work makes it even harder for families to maintain a work–life balance. In traditionally collective societies like Taiwan, Western-style flexible work options are not as effective as reductions in maximum work hours, monetary compensation for overtime, or training of managers to act as first-line counsellors for employees (Lu et al., 2009).

- Japan—The participation of the Komeito Party in Japan's coalition government influenced the introduction of three family-friendly policies— a child allowance, child-care services, and facilitation of the work–life balance—as means of lowering the fertility rate. A continued commitment to traditional gender roles and a lack of enforcement of family-related policies have undermined the effectiveness of these interventions (Roberts, 2005; Suzuki, 2008).

- France—Extensive state-sponsored child care means that nearly all children between the ages of three and six, and a minority of two-year-olds, attend state nursery schools. Even though French family policy favours higher rates of fertility, rather than increases in women's equality, the child-care policy has meant that more than 56 percent of women are employed, and a majority of these are working full-time (Crompton and Lyonette, 2006).

- Russia—Traditional gender role attitudes about housework still persist, but the Russian government has, for a long time, supported Russian women in their pursuit of full-time employment. Pregnant women are entitled to fully paid leave 10 weeks prior and 8 weeks after giving birth, followed by up to 70 weeks of partially paid leave. As a result, Russia even surpasses Sweden in the proportion of dual-earner and female-led families (Motiejunaite-Akvile and Kravchenko, 2008).

- Sweden—State policies recognize the importance of sharing care responsibilities and encouraging father involvement in the child-care process. Parental leave of 68 weeks is divided between both parents, with 8 weeks reserved for each of them individually. This arrangement, together with widely available, affordable, and high-quality child care, promotes dual-caring and flexible work arrangements for women (Motiejunaite-Akvile and Kravchenko, 2008).

- Britain—British women have the second-highest part-time employment (44 percent in 2001) in Europe, after the Netherlands, but the state provision for working mothers and caregivers has seen little growth. Working parents there are expected to make their own child-care arrangements, and the increase in child-care places has been largely a result of the involvement of the corporate private sector (Crompton and Lyonette, 2006).

traditionally patriarchal societies gaining more autonomy. On the other hand, this loss of power can cause insecurity in males who are used to domination, leading in turn to domestic conflict, and even violence (Hyman, Guruge, and Mason, 2008; Tang and Oatley, 2002; and Darvishpour, 2002).

The same problems arise whenever immigrants arrive from patriarchal societies. For example, a study of Korean immigrant couples in New York finds that the change in women's roles outside of the home is a source of marital tension (Min, 2001). The majority of married women in South Korea do not work in the paid labour force, but a significant number of women who immigrate seek employment. Working long hours, they are able to provide financial support and achieve a sense of independence. But while the wife's economic role in the family increases, the husband's role often decreases. Often, men's ability to find employment declines upon immigration, and so does their family status. The resulting clash between Korean men's patriarchal beliefs and their wives' increasing autonomy causes conflicts among these immigrant families.

According to Read (2004), the employment of immigrant Arab women remains rare. However, the employment of *native-born* women of Arab ancestry is comparable to that of other native-born North American women. Immigrant women tend to follow the traditional gender norms of their culture, which emphasize their responsibility primarily as mothers (Read, 2004; Williams and Vashi, 2007). Native-born women, acting against these traditional expectations, often cause serious tensions within the family that may even escalate to family violence, a topic to be discussed in a later chapter (Smith, 2008).

On the other hand, if a husband encourages more egalitarian gender roles and task-sharing, the wife's marital satisfaction and well-being increases greatly (van de Vijver, 2007). Some men from patriarchal societies are willing to encourage their wives to find a fulfilling job or even career. However, many are still reluctant to do so, since it might oblige them to take on roles traditionally associated with the female gender, for example, child-care obligations and housework.

Studies have found that class position can also influence men's attitudes toward gender roles (Espiritu, 1999). For example, Taiwanese immigrant men in the professional class often have more egalitarian views, and assist with child-care and housework more, than those in the working class.

In addition, men of transnational families are often more likely to assume the responsibilities of their working wives. A study of Canadian immigrants from Hong Kong and Taiwan highlights the choice of many couples to swap traditional gender roles (Walters, 2009). While the wives return to their home countries to pursue employment, the husbands remain in Canada and care for their children. These men willingly transition from distant breadwinners to single-parent homemakers, breaking the norms into which many were socialized. In such families, patriarchal attitudes that limit women's employment opportunities are absent, and with the passage of time in the host country, even more egalitarian views emerge. Many immigrants gradually find a sense of balance between the values of their old culture and the values they have adopted in their new one.

Spillover

Work-to-family *spillover* is the tendency for stressful jobs to have a negative impact on workers' family lives. The factors that cause work tensions to spill over into family life, and also undermine workers' health, include rigid work schedules and high levels of job responsibility with low control over how work is to be done.

The solution to problems of spillover is to provide more flexibility, both at home and at work. More job flexibility improves the work–family balance and benefits both individuals and businesses. Paid work may affect family life by dominating the thoughts and interactions of the spouses. Some workers feel their work keeps them from becoming intimately involved with another person. Other people report spending a lot of "leisure" time discussing their work with their partner. In nearly half of all couples (Miller and Gillies, 1996), the frequent discussion of work-related topics leads to conflict. Four respondents in ten tell researchers that their partner complains regularly that they are too absorbed in their work (Miller and Gillies, op. cit.).

The advancement of technology has increasingly blurred the line between work and family life. According to the International Data Corporation, businesses around the world will have bought 82 million personal digital assistants, "smartphones," and BlackBerry devices by 2011 (International Data Corporation, 2007). Such technologies tether employees to the work world and interfere with family relationships.

In a study of the use of BlackBerry phones for work related purposes, Middleton and Cukier (2006) identified positive effects, including increased productivity, but also negative effects on social interactions. Many respondents reported ignoring other people in the same room while attending to their Blackberry; others felt the device infringed on non-work related experiences. A study of the effect on the relationships between couples revealed similar findings. Couples using the device to communicate reported fewer face-to-face connections, spent less time together on average, and even used the BlackBerry to resolve personal conflicts via email (Czechowsky, 2009). This attachment to technology caused personal relationships to lose some of the intimacy they once had.

The spillover of stress from work to family occurs in different ways for men and women. Mothers who are stressed by their work are more likely to ignore their children, while fathers stressed by their work are more likely to pick fights with their children. Both child neglect and conflict increase the likelihood of adolescent problem behaviours. Such parent–adolescent conflict is most intense when work stresses *both* parents.

Spillover also affects children's views of work. Adolescents who witness their father's bad moods and hear about his stressful work experiences are likely to be influenced in their own work values (for example, in the value they attach to human-centred work). Views of mothers' work are less likely to influence adolescent work values, however (Galambos and Sears, 1998).

Spillover does not always harm people, of course; nor does the perception of spillover depend only on the hours worked. A Canadian study found that many lawyers who work 50 or more hours a week do not feel their work intrudes on other areas of their lives (Wallace, 1997). Often, the harmful effects of their long hours were offset by their interest in the work itself and the career rewards associated with success. Equally likely, they had adjusted their expectations of leisure and personal relations to accommodate the heavy workload they had experienced since entering the legal profession.

Spillovers in the other direction, from family to work, are also common and consequential. One in ten Canadians reported family-to-work interference in 2001, an increase from the 5 percent reported in 1991 (Higgins and Duxbury, 2003). Mothers are far more likely than fathers to report these family-to-work spillovers. Their most commonly cited reason for missing work, coming in late, or leaving early is having to care for a sick child.

Work-Related Stress

As we have noted, paid work produces stress—sometimes too much stress. In recent Statistics Canada data, more than one-third (34 percent) of respondents mentioned "too many demands and too many hours" as the main source of stress in the workplace. Other concerns included poor interpersonal relations (15 percent), the threat of layoff/job loss (13 percent), risk of injury/accident (13 percent), and learning new computer skills (11 percent; Sauvé, 2009). Stress of these kinds harms both family life and people's ability to function in the workplace. A high level of work–life conflict tends to lower people's levels of family and parental satisfaction (see Figure 7.3) and impair family functioning. Employers, in turn, report a higher turnover of employees, and high

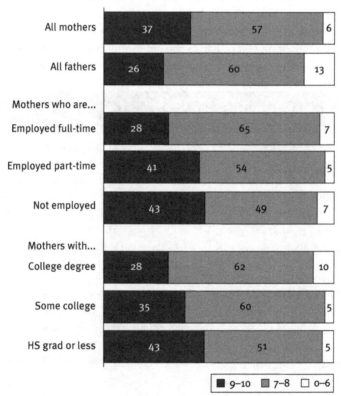

How good a job do you feel you've done so far as a parent?
(Self-ratings on a zero-to-ten scale)

Note: Mothers/fathers based on respondents with children under age 18.
Don't know responses are not shown.

Figure 7.3 Rate Your Own Parenting

Source: PEW Research Centre: Fewer Mothers Prefer Full-time Work, 2007. Reprinted with permission.

costs related to absenteeism and decreased worker motivation under these conditions (Sauvé, 2009).

As the information in "Six Key Findings about Work and Family Life" notes, supportive work environments are important because they affect the quality of mothers' parenting and the extent to which fathers contribute to child rearing. Workplace stress in low-income families decreases the quality of father–infant interactions and father parenting in general (Benjamin, Crouter, Lanza, and Cox, 2008). Likewise, workplace stress—in low-paying or part-time jobs, or jobs that require non-standard hours— reduces the well-being of children and youth in the households of single mothers (Lleras, 2008).

For both men and women, high levels of work-related stress, health-related stress, and depressive symptoms reduce the quality of job performance. When work stress increases, the likelihood of hostile marital interaction also increases. In that way and others, stress reduces the quality of marital and family functioning (Larson, Wilson, and Beley, 1994).

That said, as bad as it may be to have a stressful job, not having a job is worse because it means not having an income or social standing. Under conditions of unemployment, underemployment, and job insecurity, family conflict intensifies, as does the risk of domestic violence. Unemployment harms the emotional health of the spouses (especially for men), the quality of the marital relationship, the parent–child relationship, and family

Six Key Findings about Work and Family Life

- Our lives are far from leisurely—contrary to what some theorists expected a century ago. The average number of hours in the workweek for full-time employees rose between 1995 and 2005 (Statistics Canada, 2007d).

- There are disadvantages to mothers returning to work within a year of their child's birth, but there are also benefits. Mothers' mental health, well-being, and income all tend to increase, and there is a greater likelihood that children will receive high-quality child care (Collins, 2010).

- There has been a significant increase in the number of grandparents looking after their grandchildren in the absence of parents, especially in Aboriginal communities (Fuller-Thomson, 2005).

- Men do more hours of unpaid work in countries where "married, employed women work full-time hours, and when parental leave is short and available to men" (Hook, 2006: 653). But, when "married, employed women work few hours and men are ineligible to take parental leave, men's contribution to domestic work does not increase when children are born" (ibid).

- Senior Canadians' financial status has improved considerably over the past few decades, with the median after-tax income of married seniors rising by 34 percent, from $29 000 in 1980 to $38 900 in 2005. The income of seniors not living with family members saw even higher percentage increases during this period (Statistics Canada, 2007g).

- Less-supportive work environments, characterized by high levels of workplace stress and low levels of worker autonomy, result in lower levels of high-quality parenting by fathers in low-income families (Benjamin et al., 2008).

cohesion. Over time, job insecurity has a gradual, cumulative negative effect. For women, for example, job insecurity in one year increases job exhaustion and negative parenting a year later (Mauno and Kinnunen, 1999).

EFFORTS TO SOLVE PROBLEMS OF WORK–FAMILY BALANCE
Individual and Family Efforts

People have used various strategies to deal with the conflicting demands of paid work and housework (see Figure 7.4; Paden and Buehler, 1995; Wiersma, 1994). A common strategy has been for one parent, usually the mother, to stay at home and look after the young children. This is why women between the ages of 15 and 44 who have children at home are less likely than other women to work for pay.

Other strategies include one or both spouses working part-time, having fewer children, relying on extended family for help, and doing less housework. Some people

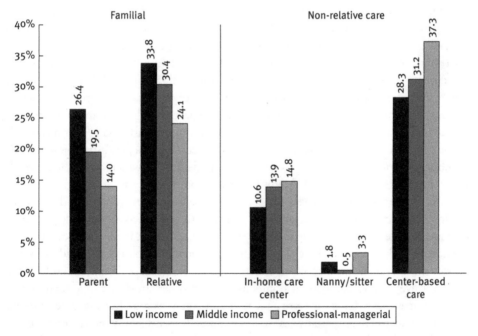

Figure 7.4 Taking Care of the Kids: Kinds of Child Care Used, by Family Group, 2004

Source: Heather Boushey and Ben Zipperer, 2004 Survey of Income and Program Participation, Center for Economic and Policy Research. www.americanprogress.org/issues/labor/report/2010/01/25/7194/the-three-faces-of-work-family-conflict.

redefine how much care their children need to lighten the care burden. Many families buy more services: for example, paying someone to clean the house, buying prepackaged dinners, or hiring sitters to look after the children.

Another way they deal with the problem is by redefining the domestic division of labour—specifically, by assigning more of the basic domestic tasks to male family members and more of the discretionary tasks to female members. Still, redefining the domestic division of labour to be more equal among family members may not always relieve women's distress within the household—if the problem lies elsewhere. Rivières-Pigeon, Saurel-Cubizolles, and Romito (2002), examining the domestic division of labour in France, Quebec, and Italy among new mothers, found that women's psychological distress was *not* associated with the unequal division of housework. Instead, it was associated with distress about the unequal division of child care. (See "Five Myths about Domestic Division of Labour" for other common misconceptions.)

Contrary to what Ann Oakley has reported, many women find housework to be mildly satisfying, since they enjoy a high degree of autonomy in doing household tasks. On the other hand, child care may be less gratifying, since it is largely driven by the needs and demands of the child. Caring for a young child can be exhausting, and many women report feeling unhappy when they do not receive significant help from their spouses. New mothers feel especially upset about the unequal division of child care if they consider their spouse's involvement in child care to be a form of support for their relationship and an important part of being a father (Rivières-Pigeon et al., 2002).

In short, redefining the domestic division of labour does not remove all conflict and distress from women's lives within the household, especially where children are present. It highlights the importance of reorganizing the division of child-care responsibilities within the family and reminds us that what is important is the ways people interpret their situation. Along those lines, it reminds us that what may matter most to marital satisfaction is not the equal distribution of work—more important is the perception of a *fair* distribution of work.

Self-employment is a form of work that offers flexibility, which makes it especially valuable for women (Carr, 1996). Many factors, including education, age, and past work experience, influence the willingness and capacity for self-employment, and market demand is also important. Self-employment can help women with valuable skills but little job experience and no credentials: for example, immigrant women with an inadequate knowledge of English, who work at home making clothes for large manufacturers. Though paid low wages, these women can organize their paid labour around the care needs of their families (Gringeri, 1995). However, doing the work at home also creates other stress and time management problems. It may mean doing the work after-hours and on weekends, leaving no leisure time; moreover, it may interfere spatially (as well as temporally) with family leisure activities.

Unlike paid work outside the home, paid work done inside the home often does not significantly reduce the number of hours the worker spends on domestic chores (Silver and Goldscheider, 1994). The result, some argue, is that home-based manufacturing reinforces women's lesser status both at work and at home. It gives an illusion of freedom, choice, and flexibility when, in fact, it is just another form of exploitation.

The home office provides another version of the same problem. New technologies, such as computers, smartphones, and email, allow many duties to be done just as efficiently at home as in a corporate workplace. As well, working from home saves the employer money, eliminating the need to pay for a workplace. A 2000 study of British teleworkers found that working from home improved relationships, support, and performance (Baruch, 2000). Yet, despite hopes to the contrary, **supplemental work at home (SWAH)** does not solve the problem of work/family spillover, as we will see later in this chapter.

New technology has made it easier for families to stay in touch during extended periods of separation due to work. For example, many parents who work abroad or travel abroad on business stay in touch with their children and spouses through a variety of technologies, including social media. A recent study of parents and children separated by work found that video conferencing is an effective way for family members to remain connected (Yarosh and Abowd, 2011). Eighty percent of the video-conference users expressed satisfaction with their ability to communicate with people at home, while just 33 percent of non-users were equally satisfied. Reportedly, video conferencing applications such as Skype and MSN Video Chat allowed families to be more expressive and intimate than they could over the regular telephone (let alone by email or regular mail).

Five Myths about Domestic Division of Labour

Myth: Child care becomes easier for working parents when their children start school.

- Fact: This is not always the case, for three reasons: Work hours are rarely the same as school hours; it is hard to predict, much less control, work schedules; and cuts in school funding make parents do more education work as well as paid work (De Wolff, 2003).

Myth: Stay-at-home men do not do their fair share of household work.

- Fact: This is not always the case, and some have suggested that many working women make this claim to compensate for the guilt they feel about being away from the home and shirking *their* duties (Hill, 2009).

Myth: An increasing number of children are living with their parents longer, and most are females.

- Fact: Young men are more likely than same-aged young women to be living at home.

Currently, 60 percent of young men between the ages of 20 and 24 and 26 percent between the ages of 25 and 29 still live at home (Vanier Institute of the Family, 2010).

Myth: Elder care by children is increasing because of rising poverty rates among the elderly.

- Fact: This is not true. In fact, poverty rates in elderly families have fallen considerably in the past few decades. The poverty rate for elderly people was just 1.5 percent in 2007 (Vanier Institute of the Family, 2010).

Myth: Care should be less problematic as Canadian employees have more flexible work schedules.

- Fact: It's true that more people have varied or non-standard work schedules, owing to contract, temporary, or part-time jobs. But often, their rate of pay is lower and their total working hours are longer, with more responsibilities and less security (De Wolff, 2003).

This improved communication is particularly important for young children, who sometimes experience cognitive, social, and motivational challenges when trying to communicate using only audio (Ballagas et al., 2009).

Some parents and children separated by work abroad play online games through websites such as Facebook. This long-distance interaction recreates family leisure activities that children would otherwise miss. Other ways of managing time away from the family include text messaging, instant messaging (IM), and email to facilitate conversation. These forms of social media make work-separation among families less alienating and reassure parents that their children are well.

The Daycare Debate

For obvious reasons, families today increasingly use daycare for their children. Among those who most need good quality daycare are the children of single parents. More than half of all the families with incomes below the poverty line are single-parent families headed by women (Statistics Canada, 2006a), and most do not receive enough financial support from the child's father. The continued increase in single-parent families has led to a continued increase in the demand for high quality, inexpensive child care so single mothers can support themselves and their children.

Today, more than half of Canadian children aged four and five spend part of their week in a care arrangement while their parents study or work outside the home (Statistics Canada, 2005e). Unregulated care outside the home, often by relatives or neighbours, is the most common form of care arrangement. Yet even unregulated child care can do children much good. For example, children from low-income families who are cared for in facilities outside the home, either regulated or unregulated, have superior vocabulary skills to those who do not take part in care arrangements.

Investments in public daycare for vulnerable children bring large returns over time because they help to reduce unemployment and dependency on social welfare, and increase tax revenues. Without high-quality affordable daycare, many working parents are unable to provide the care their children need. Parents with the most resources—the wealthiest 5 percent of parents—may hire nannies to provide at-home child care, if they wish. Other parents are able to leave their children with trusted relatives; in fact, one parent in six leaves their preschool children with a non-parental relative (for example, a grandmother; Statistics Canada, 2005e).

In corporate settings, on-site daycare is typically of high quality but it is still rare, and few children—especially, children from poor families—have access to it. Daycare centres provide the most common form of child care, but not all of these are good. Some are like large babysitting services, where the children do little more than play and rest; there is no educational input or creative stimulation. Poor-quality daycare results in, among other things, children becoming ill often (see, for example, Pruissen, 2006). This adds to lost paid time and adds stress to parents' lives.

Research based on the Canadian National Longitudinal Survey of Children and Youth (Kohen, Hertzman, and Willms, 2002) has identified three factors that make daycare most beneficial to children: low child-to-adult ratios, an educated staff with specialized training, and resources to provide stimulating activities. High-quality daycare centres increase children's linguistic, cognitive, and social competencies, and this has long-lasting benefits for children, especially those from low-income families.

The child's ability to benefit from daycare depends on at least three factors: the child's willingness to participate, the parents' attitude, and the staff's attitude. Most of all, children's adjustment to daycare, and their ability to benefit from it, depends on an interaction between these factors and a cooperative relationship between parents and centre staff (Sommer, 1992).

Maternal employment may produce acute problems when the mother experiences a great deal of stress at work and receives little support from friends and family. Videotaped interactions show that when highly stressed mothers reunite with their energetic preschoolers at the end of the workday, the mothers often withdraw emotionally and behaviourally. They speak less and offer the child fewer signs of affection than less stressed mothers. No doubt, their children pick up on this and struggle to make sense of it.

One popular family-friendly workplace initiative is on-site daycare for young children. This program does not change how parents have to work, but it relieves some anxieties. Collectively, services sponsored by employers, groups of employees, or unions are called *work-related child-care centres*. Daycares do not necessarily have to be on-site; any support to child care, whether community based or in the form of off-site, consortium centres, is helpful to working parents (see Barbeau, 2001).

Children do not receive worse parenting when both parents are working for pay, according to the research we have reviewed, so long as good quality daycare is available (see, for example, Paulson, 1996; Beyer, 1995). True, **parenting styles** may change when women start to work for pay, but it is still the parenting style, not maternal employment, that potentially causes a problem. The research suggests that all children need rich and stimulating experiences to support healthy development. Some get this at home, some at other people's homes, and some in well-regulated daycare facilities.

Today, there are not enough spaces at high-quality daycare facilities to care for every child who needs care, and long waiting lists are common. Various advocacy groups are pressing for better child care and fairer policies that will benefit all types of families. If the next generation of Canadians is to develop properly, quality care arrangements must be made available and affordable for all children, regardless of background, developmental level, or ability to pay.

Corporate Responses

Large corporations have, over the past 25 years, become more sensitive to the needs of families. As a result, many have provided new employee benefits and services, and even reformed their organizational cultures—the way they think and talk about work issues.

These changes and others like them have paid off. The more the organizations help employees meet their family responsibilities, the less strain employees experience between paid work and family roles. This reduces the work–family strain and increases work satisfaction (Warren and Johnson, 1995; Thomas and Ganster, 1995). And this, in turn, increases life satisfaction (Ezra and Deckman, 1996).

Employers have many reasons to do this. For example, doing so reduces employee turnover, hiring and training costs, and lost productivity. However, family-friendly workplace policies are available to only a minority of families so far. The 1999 Workplace and Employee Survey (WES) suggested that most companies' practices do not promote the integration of work and family. While roughly one-third of Canadian employees have flextime, access to other family-friendly work arrangements is rare.

Adoption of family-friendly practices is influenced by the company's size, industry, and the type of work performed, and within family-friendly companies, well-educated managers and professionals tend to gain the greatest benefits. In large companies, access to benefits is almost unrelated to the personal needs or family characteristics of its employees. Flextime and telework are most available in small companies with fewer than 10 employees (Statistics Canada, 2003a).

Unions have played a large part in pressing for more workplace benefits and gender equality. Overall, firm size and unionization are the most powerful determinants of family-friendly policies in North American, especially American, companies (Glass and Fujimoto, 1995). Corporate cutbacks and falling union membership in Canada do not bode well for family-friendly policies.

Since most people do not want the problems associated with home offices or self-employment, they increasingly value *flextime*. Flextime involves working the same number of hours but having some freedom to decide *when* to work these hours. Flextime is popular among parents, especially women, since (unlike part-time work) it does not lead to pay cuts or reduce chances for a promotion. Swapping shifts is another way to create flextime, but shift work carries costs to family life and personal health. Part-time work is a widely used policy for many reasons, and everywhere women with children are particularly likely to avail themselves of this option when other work options are lacking.

Organizations, for their part, like to put people on part-time work because they do not have to pay full benefits and can fire these employees at will. However, part-time status puts women who choose this for domestic reasons on a "**mommy track**." Employers see the women on this track as less committed to their work and to their career and thus less promotable.

Computerized Work and the Family

Technology and large-scale machinery have been changing the work process for the past two centuries, but computers have brought a new element to the mechanization of work. For one thing, they have eliminated many kinds of work—for example, secretarial typing and filing—that were common (especially for women) in the twentieth century. For another, they have further blurred the separation between home and workplace, intensifying the problems of overload, stress, and spillover we discussed earlier in this chapter.

The computerization of work and its transfer to a home setting—what is variously called telework, telecommuting, or computer-supported work at home (SWAH)—is still at an early stage, and research on this topic is still developing, but this much is known so far. First, telework blurs the boundaries between work and leisure, which complicates both work and leisure. Second, telework does not reduce the work done or the spillover from work life to family life. Third, telework does not appear to significantly change the gendering of domestic labour. Fourth, though telework may increase the time a parent spends near his or her spouse or child, there is no evidence that it improves (or increases) interactions between them.

A study by Scott Schieman and Paul Glavin (2012; using 2002 data from an American national study) shows that having more schedule control—that is, more control over the start and finish times of work—is associated with more frequent work–family role blurring, especially for men. And, for both women and men, more job autonomy is associated with more frequent work–family role blurring among both women and men. Such autonomy and control typically increases the amount of work-related contact outside of normal work hours; and for both genders, receiving work-related contact (for example, telephone calls) outside of normal work hours increases work-to-family conflict.

Thus, one disadvantage of the greater schedule control and autonomy associated with in-home work (and computerization of home work particularly) is blurred boundaries and increased conflict between work and family. And, as we have seen, more conflict between work and family predicts worse personal, health, social, and familial outcomes.

The effects of SWAH on individual workers are mixed. Without doubt, telework reduces travel from home to work and back. Teleworking also gives professional workers more freedom and control because they are less visibly supervised, although routine clerical work can be closely controlled through central keystroke checking. Employed parents who do SWAH report more task variety and job involvement than other parents. A study of fathers who work from home shows that telework can provide a change in family roles, as men acquire household responsibilities and emotional discourses that are typically characteristic of women and mothers (Marsh and Musson, 2008). On the other hand, teleworking passes the costs of workspace on to workers and gives workers more role overload, interference, and stress (Duxbury, Higgins, and Thomas, 1996).

A challenge for many employees doing computerized work has been to manage the distraction of social media. Websites such as Facebook and Twitter may increase the social cohesion of workers in the workplace, since people are more likely than ever to know each other's business by these means. However, social media (not to mention games, sports, and porn sites) are also potential distractions that detract from worker performance.

A study of Microsoft employees examined their attitudes toward social networking sites (SNS) such as Facebook and Twitter. Not surprisingly, the researchers found that "fun" was mentioned most often among employees age 26 and under. Some respondents viewed SNS as a plain waste of time, saying that it decreased productivity and contributed nothing to work-related communication (Skeels and Grudin, 2009). Thus, in principle,

SNS can be used for work-related purposes, but in practice they may be used much more often for illegitimate (i.e., non-work-related) personal functions (Wagman, 2010).

Family Policies: A Cross-National Outlook

Cross-national research on 15 industrial societies (Shaver and Bradshaw, 1995) found that people commonly apply three models to the relation between family and work. In the *traditional* model, the wife is economically dependent on her husband. In the *modern* model, the wife remains outside the labour market, but only while she has young children. In the *dual-breadwinner* model, the mother of young children is in full- or part-time employment. Most welfare states—for example, the Scandinavian societies of Sweden, Norway, Denmark, and Finland—typically embrace the dual-breadwinner model. They provide support to all women, whether or not they have young children and work for pay, though the levels of support vary among these welfare states.

Yet to be fully solved is the problem of low-income, single-parent families. Recall that single-parent households, especially those headed by women with young children, experience the highest levels of poverty. The question that arises then is what kinds of government policies are most effective in alleviating poverty among single mothers. Using Nancy Fraser's classification, Misra, Moller, and Budig (2007) identify four types of welfare state strategies that carry specific assumptions about the role of women and men in the household:

- *The carer strategy:* This is closest to the traditional model of family and work, where the husband is seen as the breadwinner and the wife as the caregiver. Policies of these welfare states encourage and reward women for providing care and reinforce traditional gender divisions. Caregiver allowances, parental leaves, and flextime may be provided, but part-time employment is considered the best way for women to combine employment and care. Here, women's caregiving is the primary source of provision of care. Countries in this category include the Netherlands, Germany, and Luxembourg.

- *The earner strategy:* This strategy is based upon the dual-breadwinner model, where men and women are equally encouraged to participate in the labour market, through policies against gender discrimination in employment and so on. However, little or no effort is made by the government to directly address the work–family tension described earlier in the chapter, and this questions the overall effectiveness of creating actual gender equality. Other countries that can be broadly classified in this category include Canada and the United Kingdom.

- *The choice strategy:* As the name suggests, these societies use a progressive strategy to provide women with more opportunity to exercise a choice to either provide care or engage in full-time employment. In France, for example, the state provides child care, generous parental leave, and home-care allowances that support parental care for two or more young children. France and Belgium exercise this strategy; however, there is little push here to equalize men's contribution to child care and housework.

- *The earner-carer strategy:* Welfare states employing this strategy envision a society where informal carework and employment is equally shared between men and women. Both are encouraged to take parental leave, and men's involvement in the household is promoted through paternity leaves that only men can take. Yet, the state also provides high-quality child care outside of the home to facilitate women's maintenance of full-time employment. Sweden, Norway, and Finland employ this paradigm.

CONCLUDING REMARKS

As we have seen, the increase in time spent away from home at work has created much stress within the family. Financial insecurity also increases stress within the family, and the past 20 years have provided many reasons for families to experience financial stress. For many people, the costs of family life are starting to outweigh the benefits. The results of family stress, bad parenting, and work disruption due to family concerns are significant public issues. To meet the ever-growing demands of paid work, family time has become increasingly regimented, with "quality time" scheduled and spooned out sparingly among family members.

Increasingly, dual-earner couples have developed behavioural strategies to solve work–home conflicts. These coping behaviours have transformed the way the family system works to reduce pressures on one or more of the family's members, without involving state expense. In truth, so far the Canadian state has done far too little to ease family–work tensions or improve the quality of life for women, children, or income earners. Currently in North America, irregular school schedules and lack of child-care services reflect a social and political belief in the full-time homemaker. Without adequate state support and social planning, women are still forced to make difficult choices between family and work.

For most of this chapter, we concentrated on the negative aspects of work—especially the stress that paid work causes families. We should not leave the topic without recognizing that work can also be a deeply rewarding experience, with many benefits for the family. For example, many studies of single mothers show that if the mother is in a job that she enjoys, the child often grows up unaffected by the absence of a father. Other studies show that professionals can sometimes apply to their family the problem-solving skills learned at work.

However, under the pressure to earn two incomes per family, and without adequate state support, husbands and wives need to cooperate better than ever to set up new domestic economies. Too many men still believe they are entitled to full domestic service from their wives. The whole question of what is fair in marriage—especially when both mates are working for pay and workers have children to care for—needs to be discussed. These discussions should take place in schools and universities, churches and temples, legislatures and courtrooms, workplaces, and the mass media.

All couples about to embark on a long-term relationship need to talk openly about their wishes and hopes with respect to housework, child care, and elder care. Doing so under pressure, when the problems have begun, is too late.

CHAPTER SUMMARY

This chapter looked at the intersection of what are arguably the two main aspects of an adult individual's life: family and work.

We showed family work to be just as important and valid as paid work, a major contributor to the socio-economic fabric of Canada. We examined child care, a major ingredient of domestic labour. Again, we found that mothers rather than fathers more often do this work. Satisfactory child care for working parents in Canada is lacking, with only 15 percent of children who need care having access to it. We also examined the growth in unpaid elder care, where family members care for their older and frail relatives.

The basic problem facing working parents is that both work and family life take up enormous amounts of their time, energy, and emotions; and it is difficult—but necessary—for adults to balance these often-conflicting demands. Imbalance, as we have seen, leads to stress and marital conflict.

Work–family problems fall into one of three categories: overload, culturally induced stress, and spillover. All work-related stress—whatever its type—is a major cause of marital problems in many families because it creates other problems, preoccupying the thoughts and interactions of the spouses and intensifying arguments over domestic responsibilities. These conflicts divert energy from child care and create unrest and anxiety in the household.

Both micro and macro solutions are needed. By *micro*, we mean personal and family solutions, such as postponing work to become a homemaker, restructuring work arrangements and schedules, or opting for daycare. By *macro*, we mean corporate responses, such as setting up flextime policies and on-site daycare services for the children of employees, and state responses, such as expanding parental leave policies and offering economic and social support for single parents.

Key Terms

culturally induced stress The stress and guilt people in our culture feel when they try to cope with the workload and their inability to get it all done.

dual-earner couples Both spouses or cohabitants are employed in full-time or part-time work.

family work Tasks involved in preserving a family, such as coordinating family activities with paid work and housework.

flextime Working the same number of hours but having some freedom to decide when to work these hours.

housework Tasks involved in maintaining a home, such as cleaning and cooking.

mommy track A term used to describe women who are seen as less committed to their work and to their career and thus less promotable.

overload The excessive amount of work many people, especially mothers, have to do.

parenting style The way in which a parent acts and communicates with children.

single-earner couples A union where only one spouse or cohabitant is employed, while the other is unemployed or not in the labour force.

spillover The situation in which concerns related to one part of one's life intrude on another part.

supplemental work at home (SWAH) Work in the home office that is aided by technological advances such as computers.

wage gap The differences between the sexes in number of hours spent working and average dollar earned per hour. Most women work longer hours to earn the same amount as men, due to women's lower overall earning power.

Critical Thinking Questions

1. There has been a shift in the role of women in rural and farming families from industrialization to modern time. Discuss the progression and identify barriers that continue to exist for women today with regard to the gendered division of labour.

2. Compare paid work for women and men and note the gender stereotypes with reference to the *glass ceiling*. What resources, tools, and strategies are available to women trying to gain equality in the public sphere?

3. Does the *sandwich generation* have an added benefit of in-home child care, or is a burden created for families? Discuss.

4. Examine the effect spillover can have on an immigrant woman working in the public sphere.

5. Identify the various efforts to solve problems of work–family balance. In your opinion, which is most effective and conducive to the different family types today?

6. Evaluate the responses of large corporations to address the needs of families. How effective are these strategies?

7. Discuss the pros and cons of telework. How does telework fare as a strategy to create work–family balance?

8. Assume the role of a government policy-maker. Which of the four types of welfare state strategies best suit the needs of your welfare state?

9. Immigrants often do not have their foreign credentials recognized upon immigrating, leaving providers to seek work in the service sector. Discuss the repercussions on family interaction and cohesion.

10. Compare the accessibility of child care for low-income families and more affluent families. How does the role of working women differ?

11. Identify the various strategies employers can implement to better address work-related stress.

Weblinks

Long Term Care Planning Network
www.ltcplanningnetwork.com
The Long Term Care Planning Network (LTCPN) is Canada's national resource centre for aging and care planning, education, and resources.

Reducing Work–Life Conflict: What Works? What Doesn't?
www.hc-sc.gc.ca/ewh-semt/pubs/occup-travail/balancing-equilibre/index-eng.php
This is a Health Canada site that contains a report on effective ways of reducing work–life conflict.

Managing Work | Life Balance International
www.worklifebalance.com.au/about.html
Managing Work | Life Balance International is a work–life consultancy that assists organizations to evaluate and implement effective solutions to work–life flexibility issues. Its goal is to help employees develop innovative responses to business challenges, creating a flexible corporate culture.

Help for Single Mothers
http://hfsm.org
This site provides resources aimed to help single mothers pursue their education, apply for financial assistance, and receive parenting and other advice.

Aboriginal and Indigenous Social Work
http://aboriginalsocialwork.ca/
This site contains an overview of social work conducted with First Nations, Native, Aboriginal, and Indigenous communities. It is a good source for general links, general social work links, and a range of valuable and useful information, especially if you are a social work educator, practitioner, researcher, or student.

Canada Immigration
www.canadaimmigrants.com
This site provides interdisciplinary information about discrimination against highly skilled immigrants in the Canadian job market and discourse on solutions to eliminate systemic racism.

Chapter 8
Stress and Violence
Realities of Family Life

Tatyana Gladskih/Fotolia

Chapter Outline

- Stress
  - Types of Stressors
  - Caregiving as a Source of Family Stress
  - The Effects of Family Illness
  - Coping with Caregiver Stress
  - Health Stressors and Supports
- Violence
  - Causes of Violence
  - Causes and Effects of Stress and Violence in Immigrant Families
  - Types of Abusive Relationships
  - Violence against Women in the Context of Poverty

- Effects of Violence
- Witnessing Violence

- Concluding Remarks

Learning Objectives

1. Use the ABCX family crisis model to identify why some families are better or worse at coping with stressors.

2. Identify how major upheavals, major life transitions, chronic stressors, and occasional stressors impact families.

3. Discuss how illness and health issues affect all members within the family.

4. Describe coping strategies that families can use to deal with the stressors they encounter.

5. Provide data about how common acts of intimate partner violence are in society.

6. Compare and contrast the potential causes of violence within families.

7. Discuss how issues of gender relate to the topic of marital violence.

8. Explain why the experience of immigration has the potential to cause violence within families.

9. List the types of abusive relationships that occur within families.

10. Describe how intimate partner violence impacts the mental health of victims.

11. Explain the traumatic effects that witnessing family violence has on children.

In earlier chapters we noted that close relations are hard work. Solving conflicts and communication problems, raising children effectively, earning necessary income, and getting all the household work done—these tasks are hard to do. They can be frustrating, draining, and upsetting. No wonder real people in real relationships can get exhausted, ill, and even depressed. Family life gives people a lot, but it also takes a lot; keep this in mind while reading this chapter.

In the mass media, families are often portrayed as havens in a heartless world, but in reality, families can also be danger zones. Family life is the site of our closest, most intimate relations. In the intimate family setting, people reveal their true selves, invest themselves, and leave themselves open to emotional, financial, and physical harm.

As we shall see, violence occurs too often in this vulnerable setting. The research on family life is full of attempts to explain why **domestic violence** is much more common than we would expect or hope. In this chapter we examine various forms of family stress and violence. We consider what it is about family life that often leads to stress and the ways that stresses affect family relationships. Finally, we examine the common forms of intimate or family violence, especially child abuse and wife battering.

By discussing stress and violence in the same chapter, we are *not* claiming that stress is the only or even the main cause of domestic violence. Stress does *not always* lead to violence, nor does violence *always* result from stress. In fact, stress is often an effect as well as a cause of family violence. However, what ties these two topics together is the simple fact that both stress and violence reveal the striking gap between an idealized, sentimental fantasy about family life and the way that flesh-and-blood families actually work.

Few people, when they form a family, imagine just how stressful family life is going to be at times, and for some families, a high degree of stress is recurrent or continuous. And few people, when they form a family, imagine there to be a risk of violence. Since family life is considered a private matter, family violence tends to be hidden. We rarely know when it is going on in other people's lives, and we try to keep other people from knowing if it is going on in our own lives.

Neither violence nor stress is part of the romantic ideal of family life that most of us have learned to imagine and embrace. So, for some readers, this chapter will be a shocking wake-up call. For others, it may simply confirm what they already know from their own first-hand experience. But it is important to remember—this can't be emphasized too often—that violence is not a normal, everyday result of stress. Stress is normal and common and can be coped with. Violence is abnormal and should not be coped with, but rather shunned and escaped.

STRESS

Family stress is "a state that arises from an actual or sensed imbalance between a **stressor** (that is, challenge, threat) and capability (that is, resources, coping) in the family's functioning" (Huang, 1991: 289). To explain the effect of stressor events on families, most current researchers employ a version of the **ABCX family crisis model** first elaborated by Hill (1949). In this model, A, which represents the stressor event, interacts with B, the family's crisis-meeting resources, and with C, the interpretation a family makes of the event, to produce X, the crisis.

This ABCX model focuses mainly on pre-crisis variables that make some families more or less able to cope with the impact of a stressor event. Researchers originally developed the model to study family adjustment to the crises of wartime separation and reunion (Hill, 1949). Sociologists have since used the model to examine differences in the ways families cope with a wide variety of difficult problems.

One factor that always influences stress is the nature of the stressor event itself, as measured by its severity, intensity, duration, and timing. We can evaluate stressor events both *objectively* and *subjectively*. An outsider, such as a researcher, using agreed-upon standards of measurements, can provide an objective evaluation of the stressor, which corresponds to A in the model. To do so, a researcher would measure how long the stressed period lasted and the frequency with which it recurred. Typically, the longer a stressor event lasts, the more severe its effects. The more often it occurs, the more it strains a family's resources, decreasing the family's ability to cope successfully.

Family members themselves also make a subjective evaluation of the stressor, which corresponds to C in Hill's model. How family members view and define that event controls the way they react to it. Their subjective evaluation of an event may not match the researcher's objective evaluation. However, what people believe about the event may even affect its outcome. Like any self-fulfilling prophecy, the family's belief in their ability to cope increases their actual ability to cope.

Since sociology is the study of social relationships and social institutions, sociologists are interested in learning how stress changes the roles and relationships that make up a family. For example, they study how stress changes the ways that spouses relate to each other, parents relate to children, children relate to parents, and siblings relate to one another. They study the ways stress affects patterns of communication and interaction, marital satisfaction, or parental competence within the family. How, they ask, does stress change the way that family members relate to extended kin, neighbours, community members, teachers, and employers? Finally, they find out how stress changes a family's ability to socialize children or to provide a stable and healthy workforce.

Often, extreme stress reduces a family's ability to act well in these respects. For that reason, sociologists are interested in how family members cope with and adjust to a long-term stressor. Finally, a family's success in coping with a stressor event will depend on the strength or quality of its crisis-meeting resources. As we will see, families that cope well with stresses are families that already possessed important resources—especially cohesion and flexibility—before the stresses began. We will find systemic differences between the families that pull together and the families that fall apart under the strains of stressor events.

Types of Stressors

Common causes of family stress fall into at least four categories:

- *Major upheavals,* such as war and natural disasters that affect many people simultaneously
- *Major life transitions*—acute disruptions because of events that may affect some family members simultaneously but not others—such as the birth of a child, the death of a parent, divorce, and retirement
- *Chronic stressors,* such as disability, severe physical or mental illness, drug and alcohol abuse, occupational problems, unemployment, or imprisonment of a family member

- *Occasional stresses,* which may be severe but go away without permanent change. Examples include a car accident, a burglary, a sudden illness of a family member, or even seemingly pleasant but stressful stimuli like a holiday trip. We will not discuss these occasional stresses in this chapter.

Major Upheavals For North American families, the Great Depression of the 1930s was a stressor causing widespread unemployment and poverty. A classic study of family life during the Depression (Cavan and Ranck, 1938) found that coping ability rests largely on a family's previous organization. Families reacted to the Depression in the same way as they had reacted to earlier problems. Thus, families that had been well organized before more readily recovered from the emotional strain caused early in the Depression. All families showed increasing strain as the Depression continued. However, families differed in the degree to which they felt this strain and the ways they dealt with it.

For North Americans, the Second World War both reduced and created stressors for families. It *reduced* some sources of family stress by providing jobs for people who had been unable to find work during the recent Depression. However, the dramatically increased wages that many teenagers brought home weakened parental control and increased delinquent behaviour. Also, the loss of a father to military service, or a mother's change of roles from homemaker to working woman, forced all members of the family to adjust (Levy, 1945). War, like unemployment, brought families closer together if they were already cohesive. They drove families apart if members were already enmeshed in conflict. Research today continues to examine the effects of war on family functioning and continues to find that families living under long-term war conditions suffer great stress.

Family Life Transitions Typically, we think of family life transitions as including only those events that are predicted and expected in average families: birth, death, marriage, perhaps divorce, retirement, the empty nest, and so on. They all have disruptive, stressful effects, even though they are common and foreseeable. It seems fitting now, in Canada and other societies with large immigrant populations, to include migration as a typical family transition—one that is common if not always foreseeable, and often likely to produce disruption and stress.

Like war and economic difficulty, migration has been a continuing source of family stress in Canada over the past 100 years. Immigrant families typically face **acculturative stress** because of the strains of adapting to a new society. These include a lack of local language skills, low employment and economic status, limited educational background, and broken social networks (Thomas, 1995). Prolonged stress of this kind can harm a family. Therefore, time spent in a new homeland may increase the anxiety and depression of both parents and children (Liebkind, 1993). Often, women are especially stressed because they are often more marginalized by migration than men.

Immigration into a new country affects the members of a family in different ways. In a sense, children have the easiest time of it, since they are the most adaptable. Yet children are more pressured to acculturate (if not assimilate) into their new surrounding cultures. Integration into a new culture may be stressful, as one culture replaces another. Thomas and Baek Choi (2002), who studied Indian and Korean adolescents, found their respondents had no or low acculturation stress if they had good social support from their peers—and especially their parents.

Since children of immigrants typically assimilate more rapidly than their parents, this sometimes creates conflict between parents and their children. For example, Southeast Asian adolescents in North America report experiencing much parent-induced stress due to parental expectations about academic performance (for example, the pressure to get good grades). They fear they will fail to meet family expectations. This extends to inter-personal relations as well, especially for adolescent women (Duong Tran, Lee, and Khoi, 1996). Often, there is a mismatch between parents' more traditional beliefs about how a young woman should act, especially toward dating, and views that daughters adopt from the new culture (Zhou and Bankston, 2001).

Chronic Stressors Chronic stressors confronting families may include poverty, inequality, and unemployment. They increase stress, reduce resilience, and hinder every part of a family's well-being, including its health. Taken as a package, economic stress—resulting from a lack of enough money, a fear of economic problems, job instability, and job insecurity—strongly influences family well-being.

Current research continues to examine the linkage between economic stress, poverty, and family dysfunction. Sociologists find that economic pressure on a family increases parental unhappiness and marital conflict. In a study by Fox and Chancey (1998), for example, both women and men sensed economic well-being was the strongest predictor of measures of individual and family well-being. A spouse's or partner's job variables were also important predictors for measures of family well-being. The respondent's own job instability and insecurity created stress and appeared more important to women than men, and more so for family than personal well-being outcomes.

Single mothers are especially vulnerable to economic and social stress. A longitudinal study of mothers from London, Ontario, by Avison, Ali, and Walters (2007) found that single mothers experience significantly higher levels of psychological distress than their married counterparts. The reasons for this are rooted in the structural disadvantage of being the sole breadwinner and caregiver, having to balance work and parenting strain. So, even though both married and lone mothers do not differ in their ability to *react to* and *cope with* stress, single parents are consistently *more exposed to* stressful life events and thus feel more stressed out.

Children and teenagers living with lone mothers are also more likely to experience times of temporary or persistent poverty, which can be harmful in itself. For instance, children who live in persistent poverty experience significantly higher levels of depressive symptoms when they enter adulthood (Mossakowski, 2008). The duration of poverty is important; the more extended the period of poverty, the stronger the relationship to men-tal health. The effect of past poverty remains significant when present socio-economic status and family background is controlled (Mossakowski, 2008).

At the same time, closer and more frequent contact between a lone mother and her adolescent child is likely to reduce stress from other sources. During early adolescence, closer watching by single mothers may increase their awareness of adolescent stress and in turn may buffer the negative effects of stress on adolescent adjustment (Hartos and Power, 2000).

Racism is another chronic source of stress for visible minorities—even for those who are economically successful. For those minorities who are less well off, like Aboriginal peoples, racism is the final insult. For such groups, community institutions such as churches, schools, newspapers, and voluntary associations help group members cope effectively with these and related problems.

Visible minorities in Canada rely on social supports to help them with problems of racism, isolation, and poverty. For example, among Somali immigrants, religious and cultural traditions help to promote family strength. Loyalty, respect, and stable hierarchical roles support spiritual unity. Beliefs in the sanctity of the family promote interdependence and sharing of resources for family survival. Community solidarity provides a context for values of peace and harmony that support psychological unity (Heitritter, 1999).

Caregiving as a Source of Family Stress

Caring for aging, infirm family members is often stressful, so it stands to reason that an aging, longer-living adult population, with an increase in caregiving responsibilities, will increase family stress.

In 2002, there were 670 000 Canadians aged 45 or older providing assistance and care to chronically ill seniors. A mere five years later, the number of caretakers had increased to 2.7 million. Among caregivers, the greatest increase was for women, with 22 percent of the female Canadian population providing care to seniors. By contrast, the percentage of men providing care remained at 19 percent. In roughly two out of three cases, people are caring for their elderly parents or parents-in-law (Vézina and Turcotte, 2010).

One result, as discussed in Chapter 7, is the so-called "sandwich generation": 42 percent of Canadian women ages 40 to 44 balance parental care, child care, and work outside the home. Stress builds as the caretaker devotes more time to the care recipient, whether the caregiver is working for pay or not. Stress is greatest where the caregiving needs are most numerous or intense. Most low-intensity caregivers experience little to no socio-economic consequences. However, high-intensity caregivers experience a higher degree of stress, and more than 50 percent of them suffer significant socio-economic consequences. The high demands for caregiving affect job performance for roughly 65 percent for women and 47 percent for men (Pyper, 2006).

Broader changes include a shift from institutional to community-based care, a growing ideological commitment (at least on paper) to elder care by the state, but also funding cuts by the federal government for such services (Canadian Centre for Policy Alternatives, 2004). Long-term care for older family members, people with disabilities, or the severely ill can put great strains on a family's functioning. As a result, caregivers often have to change their social activities or their sleep patterns, or give up holiday plans (Keating et al., 1999). The "caregiving family" in our North American culture contains both people who provide assistance and people who have some duty to provide help but who do not. An idealized view of family caregiving may be used to put pressure on families to provide more care, but it does not always work well (Keating et al., 1994).

For one, caregiving can be especially stressful for certain populations. Romanow suggests that rural communities are home to residents who have poorer health and more profound needs for primary health care, yet urban centres promote better access and quality of service (Ryan-Nicholls and Haggarty, 2007). Ryan-Nicholls and Haggarty (2007) also stress that recruitment and retention of health-care providers has contributed to this problem. Problems with access to health care in rural areas are obvious when examining the many difficulties parents face in raising children with special needs. Roberts, O'Sullivan, and Howard (2005) examine the technologies available for serving people with special needs in rural and northern communities. Open and distance learning (ODL) has bridged the gap for those who lack access to education, and information and communications technologies (ICT) play a critical role in offering services and education for children with special needs, their families, health-care providers, and teachers, especially in geographically isolated areas (Roberts et al., 2005).

Often most of the care responsibilities and the attendant strains fall on one family member, typically a woman (Keating et al., 1999). There has been a consistent trend in the direction of higher stress among women over the past few years. In 2003, Canadian Community Health Survey found that, at the age of 15, only 25 percent of males and females report high daily stress levels. Daily stress levels appear to peak when people reach the age range 35 to 54. These stress levels decrease by roughly 14 percent once people reach the age of 65 (see Figure 8.1).

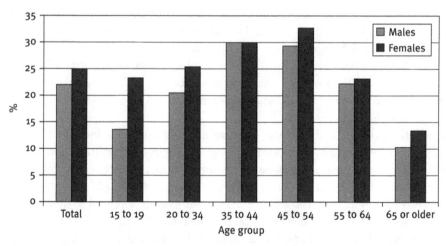

Figure 8.1 Percentage Reporting Most Days Quite a Bit or Extremely Stressful, Household Population Aged 15 or Older, by Age Group and Sex, Canada, 2010

Source: Park, Jungwee. "Health factors and early retirement among older workers." Statistics Canada. N.p., n.d. Web. 5 Oct. 2011.

Furthermore, the strain associated with caring for others increases the probability of developing physical health problems and emotional and mental distress (Vitaliano, et al., 2002). For instance, the risk of social or physical harm is especially associated with caring for someone with dementia (Gilliam and Steffen, 2006).

Elder care affects many aspects of family life. For example, sharing a household with elderly parents limits activities (Deimling, Nolker, and Townsend, 1989). Men sharing households with their mothers-in-law are more likely to report interference in their social lives, family vacation plans, time with wives and children, and relationships with other relatives (Kleban, Brody, Schoonover, and Hoffman, 1989).

Balancing caregiving and other responsibilities sometimes result in moments of "crisis." **Crisis episodes** in caregiving have been defined as significant events that are likely to lead to seeking help from professionals (Betts Adams, 2006), changing caregiving conditions (Usita, Hall, and Davis, 2004), or precipitating decision making (Taylor and Donnelly, 2006).

Sims-Gould, Martin-Matthews, Gignac, and Monique (2008) analyzed the nature of crisis episodes in employed caregivers' lives in a study of 5496 Canadian caregivers. They found that crisis episodes occur in two dimensions. First, crises can be enduring (chronic) or temporally bounded (acute), and second, they can be predictable or unpredictable (Sims-Gould et al., 2008). For instance, they classify a knee surgery required by the cared-for individual as temporally bounded and predictable, where a depression diagnosis was enduring and unpredictable. Similarly, events taking place in the caregiver's life can lead to crises.

The Effects of Family Illness

Severe illness is another source of stress because it requires prolonged caregiving. The extent, duration, and results of such family strains vary with the nature, severity, and duration of the illness. For example, informal caregivers for non-institutionalized parents with dementia report heightened feelings of burden and depression because of the care recipient's aimlessness, aggressive behaviours, forgetfulness, and restlessness (Chappell and Penning, 1996). Strains also vary according to the coping abilities and resources of the family and characteristics of the disease sufferer, whether a parent or child, old or young, male or female.

Poor health has forced many seniors to retire and rely on others for assistance. In 2006/2007, one in five Canadians stopped working for pay due to health-related issues. The high number of departures necessitated an increase in the number of caregivers required to provide adequate support for this ailing population (Park, 2010)

Many wives experience reduced anxiety when their mate is admitted to hospital for treatment. Many others suffer ambivalence: On the one hand, they feel relieved that they need no longer provide difficult home-based care and the husband is receiving excellent care; on the other hand, they feel guilty that they are failing to provide care themselves. As a result, in the first weeks after admission, wives often display poor physical health, low morale, and high levels of depression.

Longer stays often undermine patient self-care and increase depression among caregivers (Sulman, Rosenthal, Marshall, and Daciuk, 1996). Overall, wives with better social support and better psychosocial health are more satisfied with the care their spouse is receiving (Rosenthal and Dawson, 1991).

Coping with Caregiver Stress

As we have seen, family life is full of stresses. However, many families deal with them successfully; family functioning soon returns to normal, though the stressor may still be present. Families learn to cope by organizing their lives around handling their problems. Support from family, friends, and community agencies buffers the impact of caregiving, work, and family role strain. Overall, caregivers with larger support networks—especially, networks of women and kin—report lower levels of stress. Close relationships with people who are both personal supporters and caregivers lighten the load (Wright, 1994).

In this section, we will use caring for ill family members as an example of a family stressor. Like any stressor, it drains the resources of the family. Two broad categories of resources—material and emotional/psychological—are key in deciding which families can withstand crises successfully. Stressor events use up large amounts of all these resources. When a family member develops a severe illness, families may have to pay for costly medication and take time off from work to look after the ill person. Time and money ease these strains, but neither resource is equally available to all Canadians.

Psychological or emotional resources are the internal abilities to withstand misfortune. They may include coping skills that have been specifically learned and developed; they may also include aspects of personality such as self-confidence, calm, and bravery. Psychological/emotional resources also include feelings of trust and affection for other family members, an ability to communicate openly, and a willingness to risk change for the collective good.

Family members contribute to the emotional resources of others by listening well and offering encouragement. This role is especially important in the spousal relationship. Families with a good stock of psychological/emotional resources are better able to withstand stresses.

Health Stressors and Supports

Like other good things, good health is in part a product of social relationships. Social support is important in achieving and keeping good health. Social support includes information that diffuses through social channels, but it is more than that. To be useful, social support must give caregivers the right information and encouragement at the right time. It is social interaction and positioning in a network of relationships that grants meaning and value to health information. That is, the information is confirmed by acquaintances whom the listener trusts and respects.

Illness is partly a biological event and partly a socially performed drama, and family and friends play an important part in this culturally scripted drama. It is through interaction in social networks that people recognize (or admit) health problems, contact health facilities, and comply with medical advice. A key player in this drama is the sick person's primary caregiver—usually, the sick person's wife, mother, or daughter. The caregiver may have a full-time or part-time paid job besides domestic responsibilities. Whatever her other duties, the addition of primary caregiving drains a caregiver's time and energy. Often, however, the caregiver finds herself needing support.

Sometimes people can get this support from their doctor, and a doctor's time is limited. However, doctors remain primary advisers to resolve confusion over conflicting information, despite being sometimes averse to information from outside sources. Interpersonal trust depends on the degree to which patients see their doctors as competent, responsible, and caring. Continuities of care, meeting times that allow opportunities for response, patient instruction, and patient participation in decision making all encourage trust.

Online support groups, using social media websites, are becoming increasingly common. These groups help to establish virtual communities for people suffering from a chronic illness or for their caretakers. These relationships may be virtual, but they provide the same kinds of moral support as personal interactions. In one study, Chou, Hunt, Beckjord, Moser, and Hesse (2009) found that online support group users are mainly people with minimal education, poor health, a personal cancer experience, or psychological stress. The participants came together around a health-related problem. These communities provide support and useful information; they also help people build relationships over the internet and are an ideal outlet for caretakers. The percentage of people who used online support groups increased from 3.9 percent in 2005 to 4.6 percent in 2007 (Generations Online, 2010).

However, people get far more of the information and encouragement they need from their personal networks than from special-purpose support groups. Hundreds of empirical studies show that support from one's social network is a key factor in explaining resilience in dealing with life stresses and misfortune (Ganster and Victor, 1988).

Social relationships give people a *sense* that they are receiving social support, and this *sensed* social support is important to their well-being (Gottlieb, 1981, 1985). Strong social networks get people to address their medical needs and use health care regularly (Freidenberg and Hammer, 1998). It is through personal and interorganizational networks that people seek help with health problems (Pescosolido, 1996). Therefore, network characteristics make a difference to the care a sick person receives.

Large, cohesive networks typically promote higher levels of social participation, leading to higher levels of well-being and life satisfaction. So, membership in a large, cohesive social network is good for a person's health (Tennstedt and McKinlay, 1987; Wilson, Moore, Rubin, and Bartels, 1990).

Some health programs encourage forming new self-sustaining friendship networks. Women who take part in these programs improve their social networks and increase their quality of life and self-esteem (Anstorp and Benum, 1988). In Quebec, two out of every three older adults (ages 65 and older) provide support to others, making them important

Stress versus Rest

Take rest; a field that has rested gives a bountiful crop.

—Ovid

A crust eaten in peace is better than a banquet partaken in anxiety.

—Aesop, *Fables*

How beautiful it is to do nothing, and then to rest afterward.

—Spanish proverb

We live longer than our forefathers; but we suffer more from a thousand artificial anxieties and cares. They fatigued only the muscles; we exhaust the finer strength of the nerves.

—Edward George Bulwer-Lytton

One of the symptoms of an approaching nervous breakdown is the belief that one's work is terribly important.

—Bertrand Russell

There is more to life than increasing its speed.

—Mohandas K. Gandhi

It is impossible to enjoy idling thoroughly unless one has plenty of work to do.

—Jerome K. Jerome

Source: www.quotegarden.com/stress.html.

---

actors in their own informal support networks. Older adults who live alone or have small kinship networks receive less support than others (Martel and Légaré, 2001).

A key part of all case management is reconstructing social support networks damaged by illness or an inability to cope with severe illness (Pescosolido, Wright, and Sullivan, 1995). High levels of social support often reduce a primary caregiver's sense of a burden, but interaction with family and friends often declines after people become caregivers.

VIOLENCE

There is rich feminist and anti-racism literature on the topic of family violence, as well as research developing in disability, queer, and anti-oppression perspectives. Especially important is a structural feminist analysis, rooted in gendered inequalities. We will comment on this issue throughout the chapter. Due to space limitations, we have only the slightest opportunity to touch on these perspectives in this chapter and thereby risk omitting many significant recent findings.

That said, the theme that runs throughout this literature is that the victims and survivors of violence are not to blame, nor is violence a direct result of family stress. All families experience stress at one time or another, but not all families experience violence. So stress is not integrally related to violence and abuse. A second theme also needs mentioning. In light of new research, victims of violence are more likely to be seen as survivors of violence.

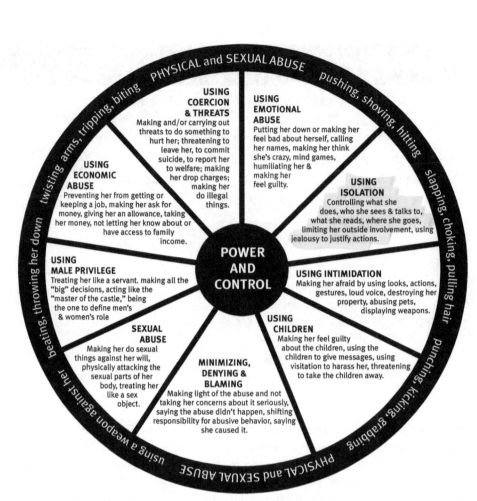

Figure 8.2 Power and Control Wheel

Source: Women's Safe Inc. www.theduluthmodel.org/pdf/PhyVio.pdf. The Power and Control Wheel was developed by the Domestic Abuse Intervention Project (DAIP), 202 E. Superior St., Duluth, Minnesota 55802. Reprinted with permission.

There is a growing literature on the ways abused and oppressed family members resist and fight back against abuse even while they remain locked in cycles of domestic violence they cannot escape and can scarcely avoid. There is a cycle of violence, as depicted in Figure 8.2.

However, we must avoid objectifying the victims of violence and begin to recognize the fight against abuse happens within family homes, as well as through legislation and other formal mechanisms.

So, how big a problem is family violence in our society? Discovering the exact statistics is difficult, partly for methodological reasons. To begin with, we have the problem of defining violence. What counts as violence varies from one culture to another and often from one family to another. Is female circumcision family violence? If so, what about infant male circumcision? Also lacking is a widely accepted definition of what exactly defines a family (Gelles, 1994). Students of family violence come at the issue from a host of disciplines that include anthropology, sociology, psychology, social work, medicine, and criminology. Within each discipline, there are competing definitions of what counts as family violence and various ways of measuring its extent. The term *family violence* did not even exist before 1930 (Busby, 1991: 336).

Family violence is an umbrella term covering different kinds of violence among different sets of family members. The oldest recognized form of violence is physical: the intentional use of physical force that one family member aims at hurting or injuring another family member (Busby, 1991: 335). In 2004, 94 police departments reported that, on average, 20 percent of children 18 years or younger were physically abused within their family, with girls experiencing almost twice the amount of abuse as boys (Brzozowski, 2004). It is estimated that family members, most commonly parents, carry out at least 20 percent of all physical assaults. Because of sexual violence's qualitatively different nature, researchers classify it separately from non-sexual physical violence and study it in its own right.

Macmillan and Gartner (1999) note a variety of types of violence in the literature: "(1) *interpersonal conflict* violence, which almost exclusively involves pushing, shoving, grabbing, and slapping; (2) *non-systematic abuse*, which involves a greater variety of violent acts, including threats, the throwing of objects, kicking and hitting; and (3) *systematic abuse*, which involves a high risk of all types of violent acts, including life-threatening violence such as beating, choking, and attacks with knives or guns" (p. 949). It is systematic abuse that most concerns researchers and policy-makers.

Data collection is problematic when trying to estimate the prevalence of family abuse in Canada. We usually lack access to hospital records and case files gathered by social workers. Violence typically takes place in private, as part of a continuing intimate relationship. Despite these difficulties, sociologists have developed better techniques for estimating its prevalence. "Spousal Violence in Canada" shows recent statistics on the prevalence of spousal violence in this country.

The first reliable and valid scale for measuring family violence, the **Conflict Tactics Scale**, measures verbal aggression and physical violence on a continuum. It looks at two dimensions. One is whether there have been three or more instances of violence in the previous year. The other is the severity of the act or acts. Factors included in the scale include the use of a weapon; injuries needing medical treatment; the involvement of a child, an animal, or a non-family member; drug or alcohol involvement; extreme dominance, violence, or surveillance; forced sex; extensive or repeated property damage; and police involvement (Straus, 1996).

How common is **intimate partner violence**? We use this term, rather than *marital* or *spousal* violence, since both married and unmarried couples inflict violence on each other. In fact, one study found consistently higher rates of violence among cohabiting couples (Brownridge and Halli, 2002). Findings from five studies hint that husband violence has occurred in up to *one-third* of couples who do not even report distress with their marriage and *one-half* of maritally distressed couples (Holtzworth-Munroe et al, 1992). On the other hand, some researchers have a tendency to inflate the number of events by using broad definitions (see Chapter 3).

Men and women are equally as likely to commit small acts of violence; the greatest predictor is previous experience of violence at the hands of a mate or spouse, a parent, or witnessing it.
Chris Rout/Alamy

Who commits intimate partner violence? Men and women are almost equally likely to commit small acts of verbal, psychological, and physical violence in intimate relationships. Statistics Canada reports that women kick, slap, or throw things, whereas men are more likely to punch, choke their partners, or use a weapon (Serran and Firestone, 2004). Men, however, are much more likely than women to commit the most physically and mentally harmful acts—for example, killing. Men are also more likely to engage in more prolonged violence than needed to kill their partners, often referred to as "over-kill," and the killing is also more likely to be sexualized than when women kill their partners (Gartner, Dawson, and Crawford, [2001] 1998).

Women who do kill a partner do so for different reasons than men. Men kill partners who have just left them or are planning to leave them. (Also, men are likely to kill themselves after killing their "property.") Women are most likely to kill their partner if they have been suffering continued abuse and are prevented from leaving the relationship. They are unlikely to kill themselves or their children.

One survey of self-reported domestic violence in Canada shows that (1) younger people are more violent to their spouses than older people; (2) unemployed people are more violent than employed people; but (3) lower-income and less educated people are no more violent than higher-income, highly educated people (Statistics Canada, 2005c).

These particular risk factors, and others, become increasingly obvious when examining intimate partner abuse among Aboriginals in Canada. Using survey data from 1999 and 2004, Brownridge (2008) found that Aboriginal women are four times more likely to experience intimate partner violence compared to non-Aboriginal women. More importantly, the high rate of violence against Aboriginal women has been linked to mental health problems, substance abuse, and an increase in HIV behaviour (ibid.).

Therefore, it seems that Aboriginal communities face particular social and situational factors that increase the likelihood of violence in intimate relationships. For one, the Aboriginal community tends to be younger than the rest of the general Canadian population; it also has lower educational attainment and higher rates of cohabitation, other factors that have been associated with partner violence (ibid.). Furthermore, Aboriginals have higher rates of unemployment, are more likely to live in rural areas, have higher rates of alcohol abuse, and have higher fertility rates than non-Aboriginal Canadians, also putting them at an increased risk for partner violence (ibid.).

However, much of the elevated risk of partner violence for Aboriginal women has been linked to the colonization of Aboriginal peoples, which has negatively affected the community and its members' health (ibid.), which will be discussed later in this chapter.

Spousal Violence in Canada

- Spousal violence reported to the police was more prevalent in Nunavut and Quebec (20 percent each) and lowest in British Columbia, Nova Scotia, and New Brunswick in 2005 (8 percent each; Statistics Canada, 2006e).

- Incidents of spousal violence were more common between current partners than former spouses in 2005 (69 percent versus 31 percent; Statistics Canada, 2006e).

- Common assault (61 percent) was the most frequently reported violent offence committed by a current or ex-spouse in 2005, followed by major assault (14 percent) and uttering threats (11 percent; Statistics Canada, 2006e).

- Over the past half decade, there has been an increase in the number of reports from female victims of family abuse. In 2009, roughly 34 percent of female victims reported severe abuse such as choking, use of weapons to threaten, or sexual assault, compared to the 10 percent of men who reported these incidences. As in 2004, women were twice as likely as men to report a crime in 2009. (Statistics Canada, 2011).

- Over the period 1997 to 2006, the largest proportion of spousal homicides involved victims living in common-law relationships (39 percent), while another one-third (36 percent) of spousal homicides occurred between married persons (Statistics Canada, 2006e).

- According to police reports from 2005, in the overall Canadian population, roughly 38 percent of women and 37 percent of men admitted to having victimized a family member (Kong and AuCoin, 2011).

Causes of Violence

Violence between intimate partners raises many questions. Why would a person abuse someone they have chosen to share their life with?

Researchers continue to debate the causes of family violence (for a text that reviews many controversies in the literature, see Gelles and Loseke, 1993). Possible contributors range from personal factors, such as stress level or a history of abuse, to cultural ideologies of families and "discipline." We will examine a few of the more obvious and influential variables.

Previous Experience of Violence Violence tends to breed more violence. The single best predictor of violent behaviour toward a partner is the experience of violence at the hands of a partner, or at the hands of a parent, or having witnessed partner violence as a child. Abused people often abuse others even more vulnerable than themselves. Thus, husbands may abuse wives, and wives abuse children or older parents.

People who abuse their spouses often abuse their children as well; the more often a person uses violence against a spouse, the more likely that person is to also use violence against a child. This relationship is especially strong for men. The likelihood of child abuse by a violent husband increases from 5 percent with one act of marital violence to near certainty with 50 or more such acts (Ross, 1996). Thus, children

International Differences in Attitudes toward Partner Violence

- In East Asian cultures, outside intervention in family disputes brings dishonour and shame. This attitude makes it difficult for women to seek help and for professionals to treat them (Weil and Lee, 2004).

- Battered women in many countries in Latin America and the Caribbean are required to undergo medical examinations and receive certificates before they can file an official domestic violence complaint with the police. Often, medical examiners under-report the injuries suffered or see them as being less serious (Creel, 2005).

- In Sub-Saharan Africa, women's refusal of sex is often cited as the cause of family violence. Fear of violence prevents many women from insisting on condoms for birth control or disease prevention (Watts and Mayhew, 2004).

- Many women in Russia are killed by their partners or relatives; however, the country has no law specifically addressing domestic violence (Amnesty International UK, n.d.). In many countries in the region, laws or enforcement patterns do not treat family violence as seriously as other forms of assault (Stop Violence Against Women, 2003).

- In Turkey, men have the choice of marrying the victims (through forced marriages) they sexually assaulted, raped, or abducted to reduce their punishment for these crimes (Amnesty International, 2004).

- In India, there is a high frequency of husbands physically abusing their pregnant wives. In one study, almost half of the sample experienced being kicked while pregnant (Jain, Sanon, Sadowski, and Hunter, 2004).

in abusive households are likely to both witness and experience domestic violence first-hand.

Children learn by observation to use violence to resolve disputes and vent frustration. Childhood experience doesn't explain all incidents of abusive behaviour, but it does account for many. According to Murray Straus (1992: 685), the more physical punishment a man experiences as a child, the higher is his likelihood of hitting a spouse. It is from their families that children learn to justify family violence.

However, many children who suffer or witness abuse never become abusive adults. Boys are more likely to respond with violence, whereas girls more often internalize their problems, resulting in depression and anxiety.

Patriarchal Attitudes Some view domestic violence as a defense of patriarchy by men who fear that women's increasing economic and social independence is eroding their dominance. For example, an income disparity between husband and wife predicts the occurrence of wife abuse (McCloskey, 1996), especially when it is the woman who has the higher income. Since employment is a symbolic resource in relationships—a source of status, power, and economic resources—spousal violence against women is most common when the wife has a job and the husband does not. Risks are low when neither partner is employed, or when only the husband has a job (Macmillan and Gartner, 1999).

Feminist theory proposes that patriarchal attitudes are an important source of domestic violence—that in patriarchal societies, domestic violence is intentional and strategically used by men to exert control over women (Peters, Shackelford, & Buss, 2002). This control over women by using violence in turn reinforces the traditional patriarchal family structure (Felson and Messner, 2000). In a modern variant of this approach, researchers have combined feminist theory with evolutionary theory to put patriarchy theory in more evolutionary terms. According to this revised feminist hypothesis, men use domestic violence especially to control the sexual behaviour of women. Doing so permits the husband to ensure the paternity of his offspring (Peters, Shackelford, and Buss, 2002). A statistical analysis of intimate partner violence by U.S. Department of Justice researchers Rennison and Welchans (2000) supports this hypothesis. It finds that higher rates of domestic violence are reported when women are in their reproductive years, with lower rates for women outside their reproductive years—that is, before puberty or after menopause.

Men who abuse their wives or partners often use elaborate excuses to justify their violence (Whiting, Oka, and Fife, 2012). For example, they often dehumanize and objectify their victims, thus minimizing the violence in their own eyes (Whiting, Oka, and Fife, 2012). Not surprisingly, male perpetrators of domestic violence hold more misogynistic attitudes toward women than non-violent men; and they also have more power over their partners (Holtzworth-Munroe et al., 2000). In relationships where women have control or power in the relationship, incidences of domestic violence perpetrated by men are much less common. This appears to hold true across different cultures. For example, a study in India found female ownership of a house or land acted as a deterrent against marital violence, since it gave the women bargaining power within the marriage (Panda and Agarwal, 2005). The same study found that women with steady jobs, and therefore control over personal resources, also had a lower-than-average risk of becoming victims of long-term physical violence.

Feminist theory proposes that marital violence is mainly the result of men trying to control women; however, many researchers have found that men and women commit roughly equal numbers of aggressive acts. This leads to the conclusion that both men and women have similar motivations for establishing control: that is, to influence their partner and establish power within the relationship. However, men and women differ in the methods they use to achieve control (Feltner and Outlaw, 2007). Studies have regularly found that women, compared to men, tend to commit acts of only moderate physical and emotional violence—for example, screaming and throwing things (Swan and Snow, 2002). Women are also more likely than men to escalate levels of aggression during intimate confrontations, while men are more likely to inhibit (or de-escalate) aggression (Winstok and Straus, 2011). Overall, men tend to commit fewer acts of violence against their partners; when they do so, they use more severe physical violence and higher levels of sexual abuse than their partners do (Swan and Snow, 2002).

In some degree, the difference between male and female aggressors may reflect the availability of support they receive in society. Compared to male aggressors, female aggressors lack the support of a patriarchal power structure, and this prevents them from establishing total control over their male partners (Swan and Snow, 2002). Men, on the other hand, receive at least some support in their quest for power; in the most traditional societies, they receive a great deal of support from a patriarchal ideology in society that views men as the heads of their home and family (Swan and Snow, 2002). That said, in any domestic relationship where one partner seeks to secure control over the other, violence is often the likely outcome (Felson and Outlaw, 2007).

Interactional Styles On occasion, both husbands and wives are violent. Some researchers argue that, in these cases, violence is an *interactional problem*—a result of marital dysfunction. For example, Brinkerhoff and Lupri (1988) state, on the basis of a survey conducted in Calgary, that husband-to-wife, wife-to-husband, and mutual violence occur in families at every socio-economic, educational, and income level. The strongest predictors of violence are interactional—meaning that they arise from relationship processes such as marital conflict, usual modes of expressing aggression, and stresses induced by work.

Psychologically abusive women show the same personality profiles as abusive men, characterized by jealousy, suspicion, immaturity, and insecurity. As to physical abuse, researchers report that more than 70 percent of these women have been physical to the point of shoving their husband or boyfriend or destroying their partner's possessions in anger (Stacey, Hazlewood, and Shupe, 1994: 124). Their spouses' superior strength kept them from more direct forms of assault, but many women nonetheless punched, slapped, kicked, or used a weapon against their partner. In such relationships violence is two-sided.

As Macmillan and Gartner (1999) have noted, "interpersonal conflict violence" is common and symmetrical, with equal numbers of male and female perpetrators. Battered women use more violence than women who are not battered, receive lower levels of social support, and experience higher levels of self-blame. Battered women, therefore, are more likely to use violence on their spouse when they feel they are receiving little social support, and even if they feel they are to blame for the conflict (Barnett, Martinez, and Keyson, 1996).

Most battered women in jail for killing their partner share a few distinctive characteristics. Typically, they were sexually assaulted during childhood, dropped out of high school, have an erratic work history of unskilled jobs, cohabited with their partner, experienced a drug problem, tried suicide by drug overdosing, and/or had access to the batterer's guns. These findings, based on interviews, help to explain why battered women kill their mates. After brutal, repeated assaults and death threats, and after failing in their attempts to escape through alcohol or drug abuse—even through attempted suicide—they see killing their abuser as the only way out (Roberts, 1996).

Women jailed for killing or assaulting their abusers are usually older, in the relationship longer, and have experienced a longer duration of violence in the relationship. They have also experienced more frequent and severe battering (including sex assaults) and suffered more injuries than a comparison group of battered women imprisoned for other offences. Further, battered women who killed or seriously assaulted their partners were more likely to believe that their lives were in danger. Often these women had no prior criminal record and had no history of violence before the killing (O'Keefe, 1997).

Status Inconsistency

Status inconsistency—the condition in which a person with a high rating on one dimension of status has a low rating on another—is another factor associated with increased risk of psychological and physical abuse, and an even greater risk of life-threatening violence. Violent men typically have lower levels of self-esteem due to their status inconsistency than non-violent men from either stressed or happy marriages (Murphy, Meyer, O'Leary, and Daniel, 1994). These men tend to be more jealous and possessive (Shackelford and Mouzos, 2005) and to consider their wives' behaviour toward them to be more damaging to their self-esteem.

Alcoholism and Drug Abuse

Excessive use of alcohol is a significant, though modest, predictor of both intimate-partner violence and child abuse (Merrill, Hervig, and Milner, 1996). Researchers have identified further variables that help explain the effects of alcohol on violence. Many drugs (including alcohol) are disinhibitors, causing people to relax their inhibitions, including inhibitions against violent behaviour. Other drugs increase adrenaline levels and, in this way, may cause anger or frustration levels to get out of control. Alcohol consumption is one of several high-risk behaviours that interact with poverty and stress to produce violence (Walters and Simoni, 1999).

In some couples, one or both partners excuse violence because of drinking or another extenuating circumstance. As a result, the violence has less of an impact on overall relationship satisfaction and thoughts of divorce (Katz, Arias, Beach, Brody, and Roman, 1995).

Lack of Coping Resources A lack of enough *coping resources* also increases the likelihood of violence in a family relationship. In one study, 90 percent of the violent families examined had serious problems such as financial difficulties and poor family cohesion. These families were also poorly integrated into society, with a resulting lack of social support (Bryant, Billingsley, and Kerry, 1963).

Social Isolation Lack of social support is a common predictor of physical child abuse. Mothers at the greatest risk of physically abusing their children are, typically, more socially isolated than others. Both practical support from work or school associates and emotional support from nurturing people help to decrease the potential for physical child abuse (Moncher, 1995).

Cultural Attitudes Attitudes that support violence as a whole, or violence against women and children in particular, also contribute to domestic violence. A society that overlooks violent behaviours may end up encouraging them. For example in certain cultures, it is legal for a husband to publically beat or kill his wife to "honour" his family. However, in a typical North American community, this is not considered acceptable, let alone legal (Beyer, 1999; Vandello and Cohen, 2003).

Aboriginal communities, for example, are diverse and varied. In some Aboriginal communities, male authority and socio-economic stress are associated with restriction of women's activities and violence against women, but the levels of these factors vary widely across Aboriginal groups. Some Aboriginal groups practise matrilineal descent, while others are patrilineal, and this diversity has far-reaching implications for the community context in which domestic violence occurs. An approach that integrates both feminist and community perspectives seems best suited to address the problem of domestic violence in Aboriginal North America.

Before the Aboriginal peoples were colonized, many communities were egalitarian and, as far as we can tell from records and reports, levels of intimate partner violence were low as a result. Violence in the home reportedly started when colonizers created hierarchies between men and women and used husbands to control women's sexuality. Violence by the state also helped create violence in the home. So, it should not be assumed that Aboriginal North Americans are prone to violence, nor that their culture promotes violence; this habit is something that was introduced or at least reinforced by colonizers.

Acculturation may also contribute to violence by increasing the stress level in a family. Acculturation is the "process of cultural and psychological change that results following meeting between cultures" (Berry and Sam, 2010). The progress of a person's acculturation process depends on his/her ability to change. Resisting behavioural and value change increases the immigrant's stress level as they are unable to adapt to their external environment. Emotions connected with stress often lead to social isolation and poor well-being.

Research shows that conservative immigrant families that feel culturally alienated or discriminated against often turn inward, to preserve the family's ethnic identity, values, and culture (Meetoo and Mirza, 2007). Their conservative values become amplified and, often, the male family members work harder to control the behaviour of female family members (ibid). Women in these families who do not behave according to the traditional value system may be violently punished—even killed—to maintain the family's "honour" (ibid). Such findings highlight the need for an improved understanding of acculturation stress.

Community violence—whether a result of patriarchal culture, substance abuse, warfare, poverty, or a combination of these—increases the likelihood of domestic violence. In Israel, Al-Krenawi, Slonim-Nevo, Maymon, and Al-Krenawi (2001) find levels of distress and symptomatic behaviour higher than Israeli norms among Arab adolescents who live under the threat of continuing blood vengeance. In 2006, the Journal of Pakistan Medical Association, studying 300 women admitted to hospital for childbirth, found 80 percent of the women had experienced some type of abuse within their marriage (Lahore, 2008). However, family functioning apparently mediated these effects and emerged as the major predictor for these women's mental health.

Likewise, Overstreet and Braun (2000) report that among African American children ages 10 to 15 living in or close to an inner-city public housing development, exposure to community violence produces perceptions of decreased neighbourhood safety and increased family conflict, which, in turn, leads to symptoms of post-traumatic stress disorder in the children.

It is unclear whether societies that overlook family violence have higher rates of violence than those that do not. However, societies that overlook violence offer less support to abuse victims. In the past, cultural myths prevented Canadian society from accepting domestic violence as a serious problem and therefore recognizing the need for laws and institutions to protect victims. These myths included the belief that women typically provoke violence and that family violence is a "private affair" and therefore police should stay out of it. To recognize "battered-wife syndrome" was a big step toward condemning domestic violence (Fineman and Mykitiuk, 1994).

To understand the prevalence of domestic violence in our society, we must understand ordinary people's attitudes toward intimacy, gender, and violence. Even those who are innocent of violent behaviour may unwittingly support violence by their ways of thinking.

Traditional Family Values Values of male dominance, gender-based division of labour, and overly strict parental discipline of children are associated with high levels of family violence, including child sexual abuse (Higgins and McCabe, 1994). A review of previous studies finds that assaultive husbands are likely to support a patriarchal ideology, including approval of marital violence and disapproval of gender equality. People in our society who hold egalitarian sex-role beliefs tend to be more sympathetic to battered women than are traditionalists (Coleman and Stith, 1997). Due to cultural conceptions of masculinity, men are generally more tolerant of domestic violence than women.

A belief in patriarchy is more common among lower-status, less educated men. One would expect, therefore, violence would be especially common among uneducated people. However, this does not appear to be so (Statistics Canada, 2005c).

In their analysis of data from the Canadian Violence Against Women Survey (Statistics Canada, 1993), Macmillan and Gartner (1996) examined the effects of proprietary or "coercively controlling" attitudes on domestic violence. Often, psychologically and physically abusive men fear the loss of their partner, whom they consider sexual and emotional property. These abusive men show a high degree of jealousy and always try to oversee their spouse or girlfriend. The jealous husband does not want his wife talking to other men. He tries to limit her contact with family or friends, insists on knowing who she is with and where she is at all times, and prevents her from knowing about or having access to the family income.

High levels of reported coercive control predict domestic violence and especially the most serious, systematic abuse (Macmillan and Gartner, 1996). Violence is used to gain power in the relationship (Schwartz, Waldo, and Daniel, 2005).

The effects of traditionalism on beliefs about domestic violence are even more obvious in recently industrializing countries. For example, residents of Singapore disapprove of wife beatings, even when extramarital affairs or child abuses by women are involved. However, beatings are more acceptable if people see the wife as violating her prescribed sex role, especially in failing to be the "good mother" and the "loyal wife" (Choi and Edleson, 1996). In traditional or recently industrialized societies, women themselves have a hard time escaping from these traditional notions.

Recent immigrants may hold on to such notions. For example, many Indian immigrant women in North America show the effects of patriarchal thinking in their acceptance of domestic violence.

Causes and Effects of Stress and Violence in Immigrant Families

For any family, immigration poses major life challenges. Therefore, it is the cause of stress for the families undergoing this significant change. More importantly, the stress of immigration may never completely diminish even after many years of being in the new country. A study done by Mirdal (2006) showed that, although the financial situation of immigrant women and their families had significantly improved in the years after immigration, the women still experienced a high level of stress regarding their immigrant status and the challenges of living in a county they still had some difficulty becoming accustomed to.

Many immigrants deal with this stress by choosing to live in areas that will be more familiar, both in language and culture, to their old communities. The many cultural neighbourhoods of the Greater Toronto Area illustrate this strategy. Here, immigrants find social support from other immigrants and are less distressed with acculturation and the challenges this poses. Immigrant parents, for instance, are then less pressured to fit in quickly and can in turn provide social support for their assimilating children (Thomas and Choi, 2006).

As a result, the children can go on to integrate smoothly with peers in school and pursue higher education and employment in the new country. Research has shown that good familial relationships are fundamentally important in the acculturation of immigrant children (see Birman and Taylor-Ritzler, 2007, on information about acculturation of adolescents from the former Soviet Union).

On the other hand, studies have also found that less acculturated children experience less discrimination and psychological distress (Buddington, 2002). This may be because they retain their cultural identity by befriending peers of the same cultural background or find other ways of being connected to their indigenous culture.

Not all stress escalates into familial conflicts resulting in domestic violence, but there is some evidence that stress related to immigration can do this readily, especially among families from traditionally patriarchal societies. For instance, a study by Kim-Goh and Baello (2008) found that immigrant men with low education attainment levels are most likely to approve of violence, especially toward non-compliant wives. Therefore, it seems the risk factors for abusive relationships in immigrant families include patriarchal authority, strict gender roles, lack of education, and women's financial dependence on partners especially related to immigration status (Morash, Bui, Zhang, and Holtfreter, 2007; Ammar, 2007; Hadas, Markovitzky, and Sarid, 2008). So, how are wives of such husbands to deal with this abuse, especially those who are economically and emotionally dependent?

Bui and Morash (2007) claim that social networks within immigrant communities are most helpful for these women. The support of family and friends is especially alleviating for distress associated with abuse. However, family and friends often discourage women from utilizing legal services to deal with abuse for various reasons, many of which relate to traditional gender roles and responsibilities. Also, closed networks limit opportunities for other sources of help available.

Types of Abusive Relationships

Child Abuse In 1946, the investigation of a child with an unexplained head injury led to the phrase **battered-child syndrome**. Before that, people often merely labelled beating a child "strict discipline." Systematic observation led researchers to find more cases. In 1962, Kempe, Silverman, Steel, Droegmueller, and Silver studied hospital patients and found 302 (known) cases of child abuse in one year. Of these children, 33 died and 85 suffered permanent brain injury. Mainly children under the age of three suffered from battered child syndrome. This study led to the first legislation that required professionals working with children to report suspected cases of abuse.

As we mentioned earlier, abused children often grow up to be abusive adults. Child abuse also contributes to a risk of delinquent behaviour. Most young delinquents have suffered childhood abuse of some kind.

It may not be possible to provide a valid estimate of the population affected by parent–child violence, but the true number is likely high. Child homicide by parents offers an extreme but well-documented version of child abuse. In the first few weeks of a child's life, the risk of being killed by a parent is about equal for males and females. From one week to 15 years, males are the victims in about 55 percent of all parent–child homicides. In the 16- to 18-year age group, this proportion increases to 77 percent (Kunz and Bahr, 1996). For a closer look at child and youth abuse in Canada, see "Six Key Findings on Child and Youth Abuse."

Cases of child abuse and elder abuse usually arise from attempts by the caregiver to control behaviour they find problematic. Male abusers typically use physical violence, whereas female abusers tend toward neglect or emotional manipulation (Penhale, 1993). Sometimes, adult children abuse the parents who abused them in childhood.

Note, finally, that lone mothers, although they are considerably more disadvantaged than partnered mothers, do *not* punish their children more frequently or more severely (Nobes and Smith, 2002). When fathers' actions are included, children from two-parent families are found to have been physically punished more frequently and severely (Nobes and Smith, 2002).

Elder Abuse **Elder abuse** receives less attention in our society than child abuse and spousal violence. For one thing, it is less common than other forms of domestic abuse. Most people would admit that children are our future, but many see older adults as burdens they must put up with until they pass on (Biggs, Phillipson, and Kingston, 1995). Another reason may be the economic prosperity of the past few decades, which allowed many seniors to provide for their own needs instead of being dependent on their children. However, with the aging of the baby boom population and the decrease of available pension funds, we may see an increased interest in the well-being of older adults.

Six Key Findings on Child and Youth Abuse

- In 2006, children and youth younger than aged 18 were most likely to be physically or sexually assaulted by someone they knew (Statistics Canada, 2006e).

- The rate of sexual assault committed by family members was four times higher for girls compared to boys in 2005 (Statistics Canada, 2006e).

- Boys were more likely to sustain physical injuries resulting from family violence in 2005 (Statistics Canada, 2006e).

- The rate of physical assault by a parent was more than three times higher than the rate of sexual assault in 2005 (Statistics Canada, 2006e).

- Six in ten homicides against children and youth were committed by family members in 2006 (Statistics Canada, 2006e).

- Infants (younger than one year of age) experienced higher rates of family-related homicide compared to older children in 2005, with baby boys being at a greater risk than baby girls (Statistics Canada, 2006e).

Abuse of older adults is sometimes described as a misuse of power and a violation of trust. Abusers may use many different tactics to exert power and control over their victims. Abuse may happen once, or it may occur in a repeated and intensifying pattern over months or years. The abuse may take many different forms, which may change over time. There are various types of abuse:

- **Emotional abuse** includes efforts to dehumanize or intimidate older adults. Any act that reduces their sense of self-worth or dignity and threatens their psychological and emotional integrity is abuse. This abuse may include, for example, threatening to use violence, threatening to abandon them, and intentionally frightening them.

- **Financial abuse** encompasses financial manipulation or exploitation including theft, fraud, forgery, or extortion. Anytime someone acts without consent in a way that financially or personally benefits one person at the expense of another it is abuse. Such acts may include stealing their money, pension cheques, or other possessions; selling their homes or other property without their permission; failing to use their assets for their benefit; and wrongfully using a power of attorney.

- **Physical abuse** includes any act of violence, whether or not it results in physical injury. Physical abuse may include, for example, beating, burning, or scalding, and pushing or shoving. Other forms of physical abuse may include tying older adults to furniture, using or misusing physical restraints, and excessively restraining them with alcohol, tranquilizers, or other medication.

- **Neglect** involves failing to care for older adults who are dependent and cannot meet their own needs. This type of abuse may include, for example, failing to provide enough nutrition; clothing, and other needs; satisfactory personal care; safe and comfortable conditions; and access to medical or health services, aids, or assistive devices or treatment for substance abuse.

- **Sexual abuse** includes behaving in a sexual way toward older adults without their consent or full knowledge. It includes all forms of sexual assault, sexual harassment, or sexual exploitation. (Adapted from Canada, Department of Justice, 2003).

Roughly 7 percent of the sample of more than 4000 adults 65 years of age and older who responded to the 1999 General Social Survey on Victimization (GSS) reported that they had experienced some form of emotional or financial abuse by an adult child, spouse, or caregiver in the five years prior to the survey, with the vast majority committed by spouses. (Other sources show more abuse by adult children.) Emotional abuse was more frequently reported (7 percent) than financial abuse (1 percent).

The two most common forms of emotional abuse reported were being put down or called names, or having contact with family and friends limited. Only a small proportion of older adults (1 percent) reported experiencing physical or sexual abuse. Almost 2 percent of older Canadians showed that they had experienced more than one type of abuse.

Since the 1999 General Social Survey on Victimization (CSS), there has been an increase from roughly 280 reported family cases of elder abuse to roughly 2400 reports in 2009. A Statistics Canada report, based on police statistics, revealed that about one-third of violent incidents against the elderly were committed by family members. Senior women were prone to abuse by both spouses and grown children, while senior men were mainly abused by grown children (Statistics Canada, 2011).

According to the incidence-based Uniform Crime Reporting (UCR2) Survey, in 2000 the largest category of police-reported violent crime committed against older adults by family members was assault—usually common assault, such as pushing, slapping, punching, and threats to apply force.

Older adults' experiences of abuse may be related to their living arrangement (living alone, with family members or others, or in an institution) and to their reliance on others for help and support in daily living (Canada, Department of Justice, 2003). For example, abuse in private homes may grow out of the older adult's financial or emotional dependence on family members or others, or vice versa. In long-term care facilities, abuse may emerge from the often-intimate processes in which staff and residents are involved, including feeding, bathing, dressing, moving, and providing medication and other treatments.

Therefore, it is important to educate older women on how to discourage violence against them and encourage them to actively participate in life and maintain their social support networks. This is especially true for those who live on lower incomes, have difficulty finding reliable transportation, and do not have someone to trust with the management of their money (Barnett, Buys, Lovie-Kitchin, Boulton-Lewis, Smith, and Heffernan, 2007).

Also, since immigration trends have contributed significantly to Canada's ethno-cultural diversity in the aging sector of the population, the issue of elder abuse has to be studied in different cultural environments. It is estimated that roughly one-third of the country's older citizens were born outside of Canada (Wasylkewycz, 1993, in Podnieks, 2008). When examining elder abuse in Canadian ethnic communities, Bergin (1995) finds that, much like the circumstances that lead to elder abuse in the general population, financial and emotional dependency, socio-economic factors, dysfunctional family dynamics, and caregiver stress may lead to elder abuse, or its perpetuation, in ethno-cultural communities.

Added to those risk factors in immigrant families are language barriers, social isolation, and socio-cultural factors. Often norms and values that are inconsistent with Canadian customs allow for the continuation of abuse into old age. For instance, issues of privacy, obligation, and unfamiliarity with formal services available to solve personal problems often prevent members of Asian families from seeking help (Yoshioka, Gilbert, El-Bassel, and Baig-Amin, 2003). Abused ethno-cultural older people may be unaware of their legal rights or about community resources. Unfortunately, the conditions of legal sponsorship, programs that reunify the family but reinforce elder dependence on the younger generations, may create circumstances that can lead to elder abuse.

When it comes to elder abuse in First Nations communities in Canada, the research is scarce. As already mentioned, there are overall higher rates of family violence in

Aboriginal communities than in the non-Aboriginal population in Canada. Whether this holds true for the incidence and prevalence of elder abuse both on- and off-reserve remains to be confirmed (Dumont-Smith, 2002). A 1997 report by the Native Women's Association of Canada on Aboriginal elder abuse revealed that elderly Aboriginal women were abused due to financial reasons, lack of respect due to loss of traditional roles, lower level of education, and drug and alcohol problems of abusers (Dumont-Smith, 2002).

More recently, a study on Aboriginal elders in the City of Toronto found that abuse is common and is of various types, including economic and social marginalization, neglect, and lack of emotional support from family and other caregivers (Cyr, 2005). To prevent future abuse of Aboriginal elders and to provide resources for coping, more research needs to be done in this area.

Sibling Abuse The most common form of domestic violence—between-sibling violence—is one that is considered natural and therefore most acceptable in our society (Steinmetz, 1977). We often excuse violence between children by saying they "don't know better." In general, the sibling relationship is less studied than the other spouse–spouse and parent–child relationships. We are far from knowing the full extent of sibling abuse, nor its long-term consequences.

Same-Sex Violence Partner violence seems to be as prevalent in the gay and lesbian community as in the heterosexual community. In a sample of 499 ethnically diverse gay men, lesbians, bisexuals, and transgendered people, physical violence was reported in 9 percent of current relationships and 32 percent of past relationships. One percent of participants had experienced forced sex in their current relationship and 9 percent in past relationships. Emotional abuse was reported by 83 percent of the participants. Women reported higher frequencies than men of physical abuse, coercion, shame, threats, and use of children for control. Ethnic differences in physical abuse and coercion emerged. Higher income was correlated with increased threats, stalking, sexual, physical, and financial abuses (Turell, 2000).

In another study, 283 white gay men and lesbians, ages 18 to 79, reported on their experiences both as victims and perpetrators of relationship violence by completing a modified version of the Conflict Tactics Scale. Almost half (47.5 percent) of the lesbians and 29.7 percent of the gays reported being victims of abuse. Thirty-eight percent of lesbians reported having perpetrated abuse, compared with 21.8 percent of gay men (Waldner-Haugrud, Gratch, and Magruder, 1997).

Internalized homophobia is a strong predictive factor for gay and lesbian partner violence. Other factors include violence in the family of origin, substance abuse, and dependency conflicts (West, 1998). As with heterosexuals, poor communication and social skills make it harder to solve problems peacefully, and thus make violence more likely (McClennen, 2005).

McClennen (2005) found *power imbalance* to be a significant factor in violence in lesbian and gay couples. However, violence can occur in egalitarian couples, too, as found in a study done on 52 psychologically abusive gay male couples (Landolt and Dutton, 1997). This may be because of other causes, for example, low self-esteem, secrecy due to not coming out, and lack of social support.

Same-sex violence challenges feminist theory on domestic violence. If patriarchal values and gender difference lead to partner violence, then why is it equally high among same-sex couples? Domestic violence theories that integrate a socio-political and psychological analysis of battering are better able to explain same-sex domestic violence (Klinger, 1995; Letellier, 1994) by focusing on power as something that is only *partly* predicted by gender.

Social media sites on the internet provide another means abusers sometimes use to target their partners. Just like other forms of abuse, abuse through social media sites is aimed at controlling and dominating a relationship (Fraser, Olsen, Lee, Southworth, and Tucker, 2010). That is why it mainly occurs among couples who have recently split up, where the abusing partner (usually a man) feels as though he is losing control of the relationship and wants to rectify that.

One common use of social media sites for abusive purposes is called *cyberstalking*, when people gather personal information on social media website about a former partner, then use the information to bully, threaten, or intimidate them (Southworth, Dawson, Fraser, and Tucker, 2005). This can include sending threatening messages or harassing the victimized partner. In some instances, cyberstalkers will impersonate the victim and post damaging information about the victim on social media sites (Fraser et al., 2010). Some websites are devoted entirely to abusing former partners, where people are able to post damaging information or photographs for a wide audience to see (ibid).

Research shows a strong relation between online stalking and future intimate partner violence; for this reason, stalking can be considered a warning sign for future abuse in other forms (e.g., physical or sexual; ibid). Occasionally, cyberstalkers use social media to gather information about their former partner or to locate a partner who has fled an abusive relationship (Southworth et al., 2005). That is why people who flee abusive relationships are cautioned against posting personal information that could reveal their new location (ibid.).

Violence against Women in the Context of Poverty

Violence against women is widespread and occurs in all segments of society. However, rates of intimate partner violence are especially high among low-income and homeless women both in Canada and the United States (Bassuk, Dawson, and Huntington, 2006; Morrow, Hankivsky, and Varcoe, 2004; Purvin, 2007). Among them, less educated, younger women with weaker social networks are even more likely to experience severe and recurring violence (Frias and Angel, 2007).

Seeming commitment to an abusive partner is strongest among women who have limited economic alternatives and are more heavily invested in their relationships. Thus, women with little education—and therefore little chance of achieving economic independence—and women with preschool children are more likely to stay. With practical help, these women could achieve economic independence and sever their ties with an abusive partner. Economic dependence on the partner or spouse, limited welfare assistance, and access to resources for coping with short-term and long-term effects of poverty restrict the available options.

Also, an interesting finding that calls for further research into this issue is the presence of significant ethnic variation among low-income women. Frias and Angel (2007) found that Hispanic women report the lowest lifetime rates of partner abuse than non-Hispanic white or African American women, and they also face lower risks of the initiation of abuse. In contrast, Hispanic and African American women are more likely than non-Hispanic white women to remain in an abusive relationship (Frias and Angel, 2007). Therefore, when it comes to intimate partner violence, we need to be wary of generalizations based on race, ethnicity, or income and realize that there are important differences in women's experience of domestic violence.

Effects of Violence

We know all too little about the thoughts and feelings of people involved in domestic violence. The victims of violence are less likely than average to verbalize their thoughts and feelings. In particular, female victims are much less aware of their emotional states and express many fewer positive feelings than the average adult woman (for a general review of this topic, see Jones, Hughes, and Unterstaller, 2001). This lack of emotional expression is likely an effect we spoke of earlier called *post-traumatic stress disorder* (PTSD).

More than four in five battered women meet the criteria for a diagnosis of PTSD, as do two in three verbally abused women (Kemp, Green, and Hovanitz, 1995). Compared with other battered women, those with PTSD have been the victims of more physical abuse, more verbal abuse, more injuries, a greater sense of threat, and more forced sex. Besides the battery itself, other factors contributing to PTSD are the experience of other distressing life events and a lack of sensed social support.

Not all violent events produce PTSD, but battered women are three times as likely to suffer from PTSD as are women who are maritally distressed but have not suffered battering. Women showing symptoms of PTSD—whether battered or not—are more likely to report having experienced childhood sexual abuse. They also report more previous traumas than women without PTSD.

Little research has been done on the linkage between spousal abuse and PTSD, but much research has documented other symptoms of domestic violence that are similar to symptoms of PTSD. For example, women subject to violence or forced sex have more fear of future assaults than other women (DeMaris and Swinford, 1996).

Abused women typically have lower self-esteem and less faith in their own efficacy than non-abused women. Another common result of domestic violence is depression. As physical abuse increases in severity, so does women's severity of depression (Orava, McLeod, and Sharpe, 1996). At a domestic violence shelter, more than four women in five are at least mildly depressed, and more than half remain depressed for six months or more after leaving the abusive home. Feelings of powerlessness, repeated abuse, and inadequate social support all contribute to persisting depression (Campbell, Sullivan, and Davidson, 1995).

Social and economic factors also conspire to make women fear their vulnerable and dependent condition. Typically, battered women live in "coercively controlling" environments and experience powerlessness and economic dependency (Forte, Franks, and Forte, 1996). To hide domestic conflict, abusive husbands often try to isolate their spouses, so that they also suffer from social isolation (Lempert, 1996).

Social media sites can sometimes help the survivors of abusive relationships by providing support and information for victims of abuse (Tucker, Cremer, Fraser, and Southworth, 2005). Instant messaging, for example, makes it easier for someone fleeing an abusive relationship to contact and communicate with family or friends. Equally, blogs or public forums allow survivors to share their personal stories or seek help from others with similar problems (ibid).

Jacobson, Gottman, Gortner, Berns, and Shortt (1996) found that only 38 percent of couples separate or divorce in the two years following an early assessment of severe husband-to-wife violence. Why do women remain in abusive relationships? Some have been taught to forgive and forget, and feel they ought to help their spouses be better people and support them through stresses. Also, abuse that is coercively controlling creates feelings of powerlessness and hopelessness (Aguilar and Nunez Nightingale, 1994).

Often women fear increased abuse, for themselves or their children, if they try to leave; blackmail and threats are not uncommon. Women may have few resources and believe they have nowhere to go. Some feel they deserve the abuse. Episodes of leaving or thinking about leaving are embedded in cycles of abuse (see Figure 8.3).

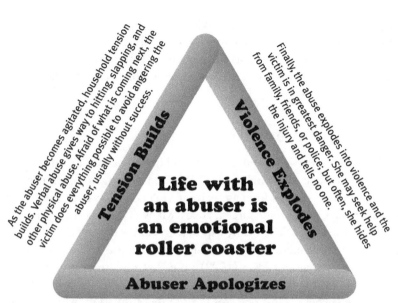

The abuser apologizes for past misbehavior, offering gifts and kind words; he promises to change, and often the victim believes him. She wants to believe that change is coming and she can trust the abuser.

Figure 8.3 The Cycle of Violence

Source: Adapted from Domestic Violence: Eastern Regional Committee Against Violence ISO-8859-1 http://www.ercav.ca/mwm_files/home/sys/media/1247162361.gif

Commonly, after an abusive episode, the perpetrator apologizes, showers the victim with gifts and affection, and promises it won't happen again. Abused wives are inclined to think it is the last time and the abusive husband has changed and didn't mean to be violent. Added to this is social pressure to be in a relationship: the common view that marriage is for better or for worse, and that one ought to stick it out because marriage and family is the bedrock of society. Preoccupation with the relationship is associated with more frequent previous separations from the relationship, continuing emotional involvement with the partner after separation, and more frequent sexual contact with the partner (Henderson, Bartholomew, and Dutton, 1997).

Heavily disabled women may also find it hard to leave a violent relationship. Hassouneh-Phillips and McNeff (2005) found that women with high degrees of physical impairments were more likely to feel they were unattractive and sexually inadequate than other women with mild impairments. Low self-esteem and a strong desire to be partnered, especially with non-disabled men, increased the likelihood that disabled women would enter and stay in abuse relationships over time (Hassouneh-Phillips and McNeff, 2005).

Battered women often lose the ability to decide about their relationship in their own best interest. However, some research (for example, Campbell, Miller, and Cardwell,

1994) rejects a "learned helplessness" model for most women experiencing abuse. These researchers believe that most abused women just need practical help and advice to be able to break with their past. They argue for supporting battered women seen in the health-care and social services systems so the women can more easily decide the status of their relationship.

Witnessing Violence

Witnessing violence between parents harms children's emotional and behavioural development (Kolbo, Blakely, and Engleman, 1996). Studies estimate that roughly 15.5 million children in America witness intimate partner violence every year (McDonald, Jouriles, Ramisetty-Mikler, Caetano, and Green, 2006). Many of these child witnesses are between birth and five years of age. Their early exposure to violence forces them to develop coping strategies, sometimes leading them to develop abnormalities in functioning as a result.

Clements, Oxtoby, and Ogle (2008) note that children exposed to violence at a young age may develop difficulties trusting others, making it hard for them to interact at school and elsewhere. This increases their sense of isolation, which may trigger more behavioural and emotional problems. Other effects of exposure to household violence include aggression, delinquency, feelings of anxiety and depression, lowered self-worth, and poor academic performance.

Children regularly exposed to violence at home are more likely to develop patterns of aggression and physical violence in their own daily behaviour. Family violence, along with exposure to violence elsewhere (for example, in interactive video games that are readily available to children), has dire effects on a child's development. In a study of factors contributing to youth violence, Ferguson, San Miguel, and Hartley (2009) examined the effect of external influences such as family, social media, and peers. They concluded that childhood delinquency and violence result mainly from family violence, more than from television, video games, or social media.

Baldry (2002) also found a positive correlation between exposure to parental violence and bullying among children. In a sample of Italian adolescents, Baldry's study showed that witnessing violence at home is one of the strongest influences on bullying behaviour. Interestingly, the effect of exposure to domestic violence was greater for girls than for boys: Their level of aggression, significantly higher than among children with little exposure to parental violence, is directed to mainly to bullying others.

Parent–child violence is also common in families where parent–parent violence occurs. Both are significant predictors of adolescent behaviour problems (O'Keefe, 1996). Exposure to physical abuse produces open hostility in children and a tendency to flare up in anger without a specific provocation. (Exposure to *emotional* abuse is more likely to produce shame, hostility, and anger—both expressed and unexpressed.) Often, the outcomes of domestic violence are gender-specific. Females tend to internalize their emotions, reporting higher levels of shame and guilt. Males are more likely to lash out or abuse alcohol.

Witnessing interparental violence is associated with more depression and PTSD symptomology, even when controlling for demographic variables, quality of parent–child relationships, personal victimization, and other life stressors. PTSD symptoms and depression increase with the frequency of incidents witnessed but not with the severity of the violence. These results contribute to the growing body of research that stresses the importance of treating exposure to interparental violence as a risk factor for youth.

Factors that influence the effects of witnessing violence include whether the child was also abused, child gender and age, and time since last exposure to violence (Edleson, 1999). Among college undergraduates, witnessing marital violence is associated with other family mental health risks, childhood physical and sexual abuse, and adult physical assaults by strangers (Feerick and Haugaard, 1999).

Like battered women, battered children show signs of PTSD (Wind and Silvern, 1994). Motta (1994) hints that a rise in family violence, violence within schools, and various other stressors are leading to the characteristic PTSD symptoms increasingly noted among children.

A reported one-quarter to one-third of all female children suffer *sexual abuse* before their eighteenth birthday, and at least one-half of all women with severe mental illness admit such events. An even higher percentage of mentally ill homeless women have a history of childhood victimization (Rosenberg, Drake, and Mueser, 1996). Among adolescent psychiatric patients, family dysfunction and trauma are more marked in those who have been sexually abused (Wherry et al., 1994). Sexual abuse, parental assault, and kidnapping experiences are especially strong predictors of depression and PTSD-related symptoms in 10- to 16-year-olds studied over a long period (Boney-McCoy and Finkelhor, 1996). Parental substance abuse, family conflict, and exposure to both child and adult abuse set in motion a vicious circle that predicts substance abuse and violence in later life (Sheridan, 1995).

In short, a **cycle of abuse** exists—a tendency for abused girls and daughters of abused mothers to become abused women and for male children of abusive fathers to become abusive fathers themselves. The connection between childhood abuse and adult abuse may lie in interpersonal functioning. Children who grow up in abusive families do not learn how to conduct their lives, or their marriages, in non-abusive ways, or how to prevent the escalation of violence or abuse (Weaver and Clum, 1996).

CONCLUDING REMARKS

We can learn a great deal from research about the best ways to intervene to solve problems of family stress and violence. First, we learn that violence is a major factor causing women to leave their marriages and children to leave their parents' home. Second, programs that try to address abuse directly—such as civil restraining orders, treatment programs for batterers, and policies requiring compulsory arrest and no dropped charges—are not usually effective in solving the problem of domestic violence (Davis and Smith, 1995). By contrast, treatments aimed at reducing alcohol and drug abuse may make a long-term difference to the likelihood of future violence (O'Farrell and Murphy, 1995; Brannen and Rubin, 1996).

Third, we must actively address problems like stress and violence. If we want to reduce family stresses, we must create a society that is family friendly with increased social support and practical help to working parents with small children. Fourth, research shows us the health and social service professions are, sadly, far behind the times. Fifth, research shows us that personal lives, and families, are increasingly diverse.

For example, because of language, cultural, and immigration issues, recently arrived immigrant and refugee women have needs that differ markedly from most battered women in the general population (Huisman, 1996). Along similar lines, lesbians are less likely than heterosexual women to use traditional battered women services that were designed for male–female relationships. Gay men face similar problems.

In the end, however, we must recognize there will be no major decline in the violence against family members until societies reduce the stresses on family members and increase the personal value of all people—especially children, women, older adults, the poor, immigrants, and sexual minorities. Societies must also reject the cultural justifications for domestic violence and deprive violent people of opportunities to hide or repeat their behaviour. Ending domestic violence must be a societal project, no less complex than dealing with unemployment, illiteracy, AIDS, or any of a dozen other recognized social problems.

CHAPTER SUMMARY

We have discussed two realities—stress and violence—that reveal the dark side of close relations. Stress, as we have noted, is a normal part of family life. We may have trouble coping with it, but stress can never be removed from our lives.

Common causes of family stress fall into at least four categories: major upheavals, such as wars and natural disasters; major life transitions, such as the birth of a child or divorce; chronic stresses, such as chronic illnesses, drug abuse, or unemployment; and occasional stresses, such as a car accident or the flu.

Violence is a potential outcome of family stress, but violence is never wholly the result of stress, nor is stress wholly the cause of violence. Domestic violence is widespread throughout society and diverse in nature. Family violence can take the form of physical, emotional, or psychological abuse. Stress does not always lead to violence, nor does violence always result from stress alone. However, stress is a common antecedent of violent behaviour and often mediates between violence and social conditions such as poverty and unemployment.

As we have seen, the experience of abuse in childhood or adulthood predicts more violence. Partner violence is also often associated with violence against children in the household. The perpetrators of violence are often men, but women also abuse their male partners. The motivation of the violence is different for each sex. Other types of violence include child abuse and elder abuse, which arise from attempts by the caregiver to control behaviour they find problematic.

We have also seen how certain populations in society such as immigrants, Aboriginals, and the poor are especially vulnerable to various forms of abuse. More importantly, by exploring the violence within these groups, it has become obvious that particular groups face unique dangers and factors that lead to and perpetuate violence.

Lastly, the effects of domestic violence are severe and widespread. They include depression, post-traumatic stress disorder, social isolation, and economic dependency. Children exposed to abuse are more likely to become abusers themselves, perpetuating the cycle of violence.

Key Terms

ABCX family crisis model A model of stress in which *A*, which represents the stressor event, interacts with *B*, the family's crisis-meeting resources, and with *C*, the family's interpretation of the event, to produce *X*, the crisis.

acculturative stress Stress originating from the challenges involved in adapting to a new society.

battered-child syndrome Physical injury due to abuse by parents or caregivers.

Conflict Tactics Scale An instrument developed by Murray Straus to measure the extent of domestic violence based on frequency and severity of incidents.

cycle of abuse A tendency for family violence to repeat itself from one generation to the next, as abused girls and daughters of abused mothers grow up to become abused women, and abused boys or sons of abusive fathers grow up to become abusive husbands or fathers.

crisis episodes Significant events that are likely to lead to seeking help from professionals,

changing caregiving conditions, and precipitating decision making.

domestic violence Family violence; violence against any member of the household, including a child, spouse, parent, or sibling.

elder abuse Physical violence, psychological cruelty, or neglect directed at an older person, usually by a caregiving family member.

intimate-partner violence Physical abuse between the members of a couple. It may be reciprocal ("common couple violence") or directed by one partner against the other, and may occur between cohabiters as well as legally married couples.

status inconsistency Lack of congruence between the various indicators of social class, such as education and occupation, or wealth and prestige.

stressor Something that causes stress; a challenge or threat.

Critical Thinking Questions

1. Why are some groups in society (for instance, single mothers or low-income families) especially vulnerable to chronic stress? Is their vulnerability based on larger structural problems inherent to their populations or rather due to a lack of coping resources?

2. Does the view of the elderly as burdensome and unproductive members of society make them more susceptible to abuse? Or are other factors more important in increasing their risk of violence?

3. What are the very most important reasons why women do not leave violent situations,

and how might the importance of these factors vary over a woman's life cycle?

4. How does abuse of the elderly differ from abuse of children in its causes and consequences? Explain.

5. How has modern technology changed the way abusive partners target and torment their victims?

6. Does a sharp increase in the amount of family stress automatically increase the risk and level of violence within the family? If not, why not?

Weblinks

Shelternet.ca
http://canada.wecanglobal.org/resouces
/shelternet
This site provides a wide range of information about abuse in a variety of languages, including a comprehensive listing of women's shelters across the country and information specifically geared for kids and teenagers suffering from abuse.

Ontario Women's Justice Network
www.owjn.org
This site offers legal information related to violence against women, specifically on justice and legal issues regarding rural, immigrant, transgender, and impoverished women.

Canadian Mental Health Association
www.cmha.ca
This site provides a wide range of information on mental health issues in Canada, including resources to better understand and prevent stress and violence.

Native Women's Association of Canada
www.nwac.ca/home
This site provides important resources for Aboriginal women in Canada, including a violence prevention kit that helps female Aboriginal youth recognize and leave abusive relationships at www.nwac.ca/programs/violence-prevention-toolkit.

Canadian Research Institute for the Advancement of Women
www.criaw-icref.ca
This site provides excellent and comprehensive information on the issues facing rural, immigrant, and low-income women.

Canadian Network for the Prevention of Elder Abuse
www.cnpea.ca
This wonderful source of information on elder abuse in English and French provides information on policy and practice for elderly issues in Canada, along with helpful links and resources to learn more about elder abuse prevention.

Ontario Women's Directorate
www.women.gov.on.ca/english/index.shtml
This site provides specific information on women's legal, wellness, and child issues, along with resources for young women about sexual harassment and equality issues.

Chapter 9
Divorce and Ending Relationships
Trends, Myths, Children, and Ex-Spouses

ZINQ Stock/Shutterstock

Chapter Outline

Learning Objectives

1 Understand different approaches to measuring divorce rates and what they mean for divorce risk.

2 Define and interpret micro-sociological, meso-sociological, macro-sociological causes of divorce.

3 Comprehend the causes and effects of divorce on the couple.

4 Understand of the effects of divorce and parental repartnering on children.

5 Evaluate the effects of divorce on society.

6 Analyze the relationship between immigration and divorce.

7 Dispel myths about divorce.

8 Explain the legal issues of divorce and cohabitation, both historic and current.

Divorce is often hard to understand. The factors leading to divorce are complex, as are the consequences for the individuals involved and for society. Adding another challenge is that close couple relations have changed so much recently, as we saw in Chapter 4, with the growing popularity of cohabitation. Cohabiting relationships that end are not counted as divorces. So, the greater the numbers of couples who cohabit, the lower the divorce rate will fall. Adding even more complexity, divorce rates are sometimes misleading, as we shall soon see. So, for divorce, as with much else about families, the numbers don't speak for themselves.

We often hear that one-half of all marriages end in divorce. It is certainly scary if people believe their own marriage stands only a 50-percent chance of surviving. However, this figure is misleading: Different methods of measurement lead to different statistical outcomes and sociological conclusions.

DIVORCE RATES

To explain why divorce rates are misleading at times, we must explain what the various indicators of divorce mean. There are several ways to compute divorce rates, and meanings depend very much on the method of calculation. The *crude divorce rate*, for example, is calculated as the number of divorces in a given year (say, 2013) divided by the mid-year population in 2013, multiplied by 100 000 (see Figure 9.1). This yields low rates because the denominator includes everyone in the population, many of whom are not at all at risk of divorce since they are children, single, or already divorced.

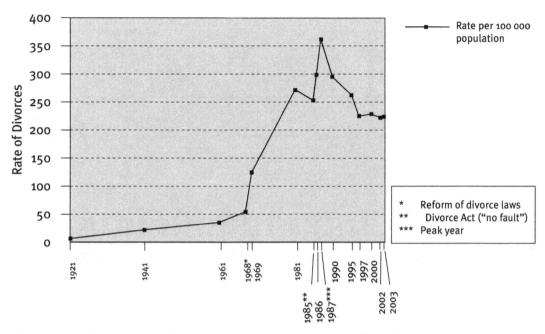

Figure 9.1 Divorce Rate per 100 000 Population in Canada, 1921–2003

Source: Data from Anne-Marie Ambert. 2005. Divorce: Facts, causes and consequences. The Vanier Institute of the Family. Data retrieved December 9, 2005, from www.vifamily.ca/library/cft/divorce_05.html.

By contrast, another measure of divorce is based on the number of marriages in a given year. By this calculation, the number of *divorces* in 2013 is divided by the number of *marriages* in 2013. This overestimates divorce risk and lends itself to attention-catching statements (for example, "One-half of all current marriages will end in divorce") that titillate but do not inform. Those married in 2013 are *not* those at risk of divorce in 2013! As well, if the number of marriages in any given year declines, as it has in the past decade in Canada, and the numbers of divorces stays the same (see Figure 9.2), it may appear as if the risk of divorce is rising when it is not. As you can see, this way of calculating divorce rate and risk is very misleading. It can be a "false fact" reported as true and then interpreted by couples as a serious risk. This is inappropriate and needlessly frightening.

Better measures of divorce risk, though too rarely provided for public discussion, consider the population at risk of a divorce and *only* that population. Thus, the population at risk of a divorce in 2013 are those (and only those) who are married at the beginning of 2013 *and earlier*. This estimate can be improved by standardizing for age and other social characteristics that are known to influence people's inclination to divorce. Since older people divorce less than younger people do, for example, we would do well to compute divorce rates on a "standard population" with the same supposed age structure at two

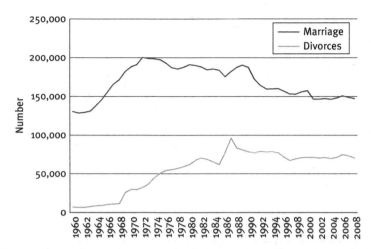

Figure 9.2 Number of Marriages and Divorces, Canada, 1960 to 2008

Source: Statistics Canada, 2012. Juristat Bulletin "Divorce cases in civil court, 2010/2011." Catalogue No. 85-002-X. Retrieved February 2013 from www.statcan.gc.ca/pub/85-002-x/2012001/article/11634-eng.htm.

points in time. Only in this way would we know whether divorce-proneness was increasing or whether changes in population makeup (such as population aging or immigration of young people) were causing the *appearance* of more divorce-proneness.

Yet another approach is to calculate a rolling divorce rate, which measures the number of people in the population ever divorced as a fraction of the population ever married. This method has advantages and disadvantages. One disadvantage is that this method is biased by cohort and period. Large cohorts (or generations) of people (like the baby boom generation) have an especially large effect on this kind of estimate. So, this approach, too, can be misleading.

The most refined method of measurement gives the closest approximation for the divorce rate in a lifetime. It looks at couples who married 30 years ago and what proportion of that population has since divorced. Since couples rarely divorce after 30 years of marriage (Ambert, 2005b)—although this is changing now, with more later-life divorces (Brown and Lin, 2012)—the actual divorce rate is significantly lower than the widely quoted "half of all marriages." According to the best estimate, the number of Canadian marriages that end before the thirtieth anniversary is just over one-third (Clark and Crompton, 2006). However, this method is not widely used.

One final measure, which to our knowledge is never used in official data, calculates the number of adult years lived outside marriage. If our purpose in computing divorce rates were to gauge people's desire to be married and stay married, nothing would show the societal rejection of marriage more than a continuous decline in the time people spent being married. Similarly, increases in person-years spent cohabiting could also be viewed as a rejection of traditional marriage. However, the goal of computing divorce rates is not only to measure the societal rejection of marriage. Divorce rates also help sociologists

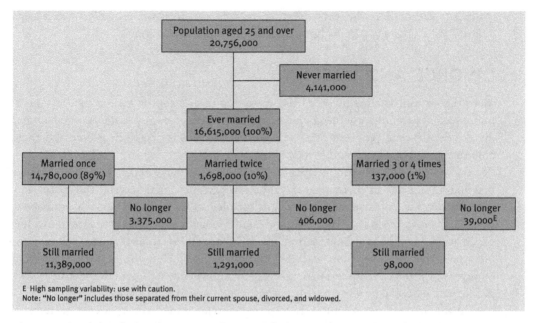

Population aged 25 and over
20,756,000

Never married
4,141,000

Ever married
16,615,000 (100%)

Married once
14,780,000 (89%)

Married twice
1,698,000 (10%)

Married 3 or 4 times
137,000 (1%)

No longer
3,375,000

No longer
406,000

No longer
39,000ᴱ

Still married
11,389,000

Still married
1,291,000

Still married
98,000

E High sampling variability: use with caution.
Note: "No longer" includes those separated from their current spouse, divorced, and widowed.

Figure 9.3 Risk of Marriage Dissolution after First, Second, and Third Marriages

Source: Warren Clark and Susan Crompton. 2006. Till death do us part? The risk of first and second marriage dissolution. Ottawa: Statistics Canada. Catalogue no. 11-008. *Canadian Social Trends.* p. 24.

develop and test theories about the factors that contribute to the survival and breakdown of marriages. In turn, this helps us understand something about the conditions that make for better and worse family functioning.

An interesting illustration of the advantage of organizing survey data in original ways to answer sociological questions comes from Canadian sociologists Clark and Crompton (2006). The authors analyzed data from the 2001 General Social Survey (GSS) to find out whether people face differential risks of divorce after their first, second, and third marriages. Figure 9.3 presents their breakdown of the data. Looking at divorce in this way, we first see that most ever-married Canadians (89 percent) only marry once (Clark and Crompton, 2006: 24). In addition, 69 percent of ever-married people remain with their first spouse, and people who do this, on average, remain married for 23.5 years. Only about 23 percent of people dissolve their first marriage after an average of 11 years together (Clark and Crompton, 2006: 23). This study has not been updated.

A lot more could be said about the challenges of divorce rates. Demographers spend a great deal of time perfecting these measures, and those who watch rates, like the readers of this text as well as policy-makers, should be careful to know what is being measured and how. Generally, the best rate is one that correctly measures the risks of experiencing something such as divorce by those who are most at risk for divorce. It is wise never to trust a rate without knowing what question you are trying to answer; equally, never accept a rate as valid unless you know how it was created and what it shows.

DIVORCE AND SOCIETY

Many questions involving divorce need answering in sociology as well as in allied disciplines such as psychology and economics, as divorce affects many people. As we shall see, divorce solves some problems and creates others—problems between people and their children, parents, siblings, and friends.

Sociologists hope to gain insights from research on divorce about the nature of social bonding, the effects of economy and culture on personal relations, and the causes and effects of divorce. At the micro-level, family sociologists try to understand why individual couples divorce. To do this, they examine family dynamics and interaction patterns, the expectations people have about married life, who they choose to marry and why, and people's subjective assessments of available alternative mates. They also examine the effects on divorcing spouses, their children, and other family members. Then, they consider how people may individually work to reduce the harmful effects of divorce.

At the macro-level, sociologists debate how to measure divorce, how to measure "a marriage or relationship breakdown," and how to measure the link between relationship breakdown and legal divorce. Often relationships break down long before divorce occurs, so separation may be a better indicator than divorce of marital problems. As we have noted, with dramatic increases in cohabitation, divorce rates are no longer reliable indicators of relationship breakdown. However, even in the past, they may not have been good indicators. And today's higher rates of cohabitation may lead to even higher rates of divorce in future—since cohabiters who then marry may be more likely to divorce (Le Bourdais, Neil, and Turcotte, 2000). However, higher cohabitation rates can also lead to lower divorce rates, since cohabiters are not at risk for legal divorce. And as cohabitation becomes more and more socially acceptable, the relation of cohabitation with divorce, as discussed by Le Bourdais, Neil, and Turcotte (2000), may become less apparent. For example, Kulu and Boyle (2010) found in a study relying on life history data from Austria that even though cohabiters who marry seem to have a higher risk of divorce, once controls are used for standard characteristics, risks for divorce diminish. Their conclusion: "[p]remarital cohabitation decreases the risk of marital separation …" (879).

Macro-sociologists have examined the social, cultural, economic, and political forces that shape marriage. Their goal has been to find out what accounts for the long-term increase in divorce rates over much of the twentieth century and the current stabilization and decline in divorce (Amato, 2010). To find out, they examine such large-scale processes as industrialization and urbanization, the increasing participation of women in the labour force, and changes in the societal norms regulating marriage and family life. They also study the macro-level effects of high divorce rates on family and social life, parenting, and the distribution of income.

Despite relatively high divorce rates, the family is still the most important and most fundamental institution in society, as we have argued in earlier chapters. Therefore, it is understandable that some may interpret high divorce rates as a sign of societal breakdown. This interpretation, favoured by political conservatives today, began with the work of nineteenth-century sociologist Émile Durkheim in works like *Suicide* and *The Division of Labor in Society*. Political conservatives are also more likely to see divorce rates as proof of the decreasing value of marriage in our society today. However, some have argued the opposite—namely, that we value "good" marriages more than ever (Houston, 2004). Today, we expect more of marriage than merely housekeeping and reproduction, for example. So, we are more likely today to hold off marrying or to leave relationships in which we find ourselves unhappy.

Conservative sociologists, sometimes called "marriage promoters," also note that, even today, high divorce rates are associated with high suicide rates, suggesting the divorce rate reflects distress or disorganization in the general population (see Popenoe, 1996, as a major proponent for this way of thinking). Positive correlations between divorce rates, suicide rates, and alcohol consumption per capita suggest a broad-based social characteristic—a **social pathology**, as early sociologists would have called it—that produces stress-related behaviours.

However, liberal sociologists deny that divorce rates necessarily show **social disorganization** (see Cherlin, 2004; Smart and Neale, 1999; Stacey, 1996, for example). Divorce may not hamper a healthy family and social life if clear social norms specify what is to happen to the husband, wife, and children after a divorce. In societies that handle divorce well, such as Sweden, children continue to live with their kin, often with their mother and her relatives. For this and other reasons, they may suffer less from the separation of their parents than North American children, for example. In Sweden, divorce produces fewer stress-related outcomes. And there are examples of smooth divorce arrangements in our own society. For example, the transition is easier when fathers remain involved with their children after divorce, or even become more involved (Smart and Neale, 1999).

People in our society have trouble thinking about divorce in a calm, dispassionate way, sometimes instead viewing it in dramatic terms, as evidence of a "pathology" or "societal breakdown." There may be two explanations for this way of thinking. First, divorce is both a personal (emotional) and religious (or ideological) matter. Leaders from many different religions argue that marriage is sacred and should not be dissolved. Politics also enter the debate, with socially conservative politicians and journalists debating more liberal people about the meaning of divorce and how societies ought to respond.

Second, we often have trouble remaining calm and dispassionate about divorce because we never prepare for divorce as we do for other major adult life experiences like education, employment, and marriage. Most young people, for example, say that they expect *never* to divorce (Vanier Institute of the Family, 2002). Although the odds favour marriages lasting, many do not. Yet people organize their lives and societal roles around the belief that long-term marriage is the most reasonable expectation (Beaupré, 2008). Some beliefs about marriage and divorce have not changed much in centuries, though historical and cross-national data show us that divorce practices surely have!

Separation and Divorce in the Immigrant Population

In general, marriage (as opposed to other intimate unions) is more common, and divorce is less common, in non-Western countries. There are exceptions such as Russia, where both marriage and divorce rates are high (Keenan et al., 2012), but Russia is a country that has been in turmoil since the end of the Soviet Union, with sharply reduced life expectancies and challenges with health, particularly prevalent alcoholism. But, overall it is the case that divorce is less common in the home countries of immigrants who come to Canada. This is because marriage is highly valued in traditional cultures. In these societies, women are often denied the right to divorce their mate on religious grounds, or they are permitted to do so but stigmatized afterward (see Ayyub, 2000, for an outline of divorce in the South Asian Muslim population). Immigrating to countries like Canada where the opportunity to divorce is more readily accessible gives many women the chance to exercise this choice that was unavailable before.

However, research shows that divorce is still not as common among immigrants as it is among the native-born in Canada (Se'ver, 2011). This is largely because of persisting traditional views of the process, which are mostly negative (Jaaber and Dasgupta, 2003). For example, some women view separation and divorce as a deliberate act of disobedience to their husband and an embarrassment to their family. On the other hand, immigration can be disruptive to identities and traditions, and can lead for some to higher risks of marital dissolution (Shirpak, Maticka-Tyndale, and Chinichian, 2011). Chang (2003), who studied differences in reported reasons for divorce among Korean immigrant and white non-immigrant women, found that most immigrants divorce for clear reasons. These include the ex-husband's use of violence, severe financial problems, or other highly negative circumstances. By contrast, white non-immigrant women base their reasoning on vaguer concerns like lack of emotional fulfillment. These different explanations reflect different cultural justifications for divorce.

No wonder immigrant women are clear and cautious: Immigrant women who do decide to divorce are at a higher risk of violence by their spouse than are native-born women in Canada (Spiwak and Brownridge, 2005). The increased risk is related to various factors: male dominance in patriarchical cultures, the financial dependence of women, and disagreement over various migration decisions (Spiwak and Brownridge, 2005; Morash, Bui, Zhang, and Holtfreter, 2007; and Katz, 2000). It should be noted, however, that underreporting of interpersonal violence by immigrant women tends to be high. Many are afraid to report to authorities—even more afraid than native-born women (see Tyyskä, 2011; Morton, 2011: 303-304).

A HISTORICAL, CROSS-NATIONAL OVERVIEW OF DIVORCE

In industrial societies, divorce rates hit a peak in the second half of the twentieth century. This peak occurred because of changes in the social, economic, and legal institutions that shape family life and individual expectations of marriage. Divorce is nothing new, however, nor is it limited to Western industrial societies (see Phillips, 1988). What follows is a thumbnail sketch of the relevant socio-historical processes.

Social Changes

In pre-industrial times, as we discuss in Chapter 2, most families were rural, land-based, self-sufficient units. They produced most of what they needed to feed, clothe, and house their own members. The division of labour was simple. Tasks and responsibilities were allocated according to age and gender. *Social differentiation* beyond that was slight, except for royalty and the aristocracies in some parts of the world.

With the onset of the Industrial Revolution about two hundred years ago (mid-nineteenth century in Canada), however, the modern Western family lost its main economic function. Most production moved out of the household and into factories and (later) offices. These changes affected the strength of family ties and the family's ability to control its members. People's lives became more individuated and governed by market forces.

In the past hundred years, other functions of the family, such as the education and training of the young, increasingly have become the responsibility of the state. In Canada, compulsory education was the state response to unruly youth of the early industrial period. This meant the family was no longer the only source of personal security. Of course, that period of state expansion is now at an end. With increasing job and policy insecurity (in pensions, social assistance, and so on), families may once again be becoming a crucial source of security for individuals (McDaniel, 2002; McDaniel, Gazso, and Um, 2013).

To be sure, the family was always, and is still, important. Especially today, it is only by pooling their members' incomes that many families keep themselves out of poverty and off social assistance (McDaniel, Gazso, and Um, 2013). Immigrant family members, in particular, pool their resources to achieve upward mobility.

Nonetheless, since the second half of the twentieth century, the family has been much less necessary for educational and other social purposes. As a result, people may invest less of themselves in the family. And the looser their ties become, the easier it is to sever them when problems arise or attractive alternatives beckon. So, divorce rates rise (South, Trent, and Shen, 2001). Figure 9.4 shows the trends in marital status of Canadians at the end of the twentieth century, while Figure 9.5 charts the trends nearly up to the present. Since 1971, the proportion of married people continued slowly to fall, while the proportion of divorced, cohabiting, and single people rose. By 2005, divorced people comprised 5.9 percent of the population aged 15 years and older, compared to only 1.7 percent in 1975 (Statistics Canada, 2006a: 9). Also signalling the changed

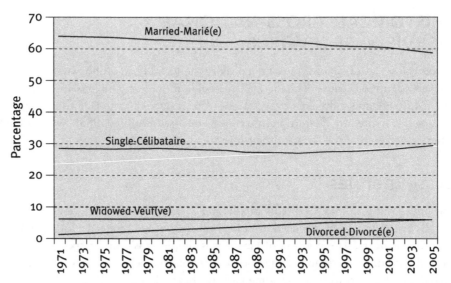

Figure 9.4 Population Changes in Marital Status, Canada, 1971 to 2005

Source: Statistics Canada. 2006. Annual Demographic Statistics, 2005. Ottawa: Statistics Canada. Catalogue no. 91-213: 8.

evaluation of family life, "the proportion of single people has been rising steadily since 1991 (27.1 percent), and by July 1, 2005, it had reached 29.3 percent" (Statistics Canada, 2006a: 8). There is a small change in the proportion of the population who are married, from 40.5 percent in 2008 to 39.7 percent by 2012. Also the number of

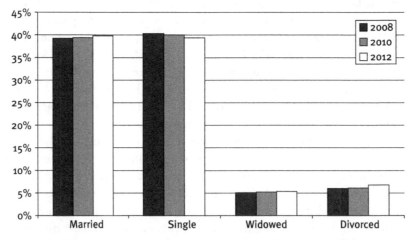

Figure 9.5 Population changes in marital status, Canada, 2008 to 2012

Sources: Statistics Canada, 2013. CANSIM table 051-0042. Retrieved February 2013 from www5.statcan.gc.ca/cansim/a26?lang=eng&retrLang=eng&id=0510042&paSer=&pattern=&stByVal=1&p1=1&p2=-1&tabMode=dataTable&csid=.

single people has seen an increase (from 29.3 percent in 2008 to 39.5 percent in 2012), although it shows a slight decrease in the past few years. The percentage of the population who are divorced increased slightly from 5.9 percent in 2008 to 6.8 percent in 2012, showing a stabilizing of the rate of divorce when compared to the more rapid rises over other periods (see Figure 9.4; Statistics Canada, 2013).

By this historical, and more current, reckoning, higher divorce rates are the result of a change in the ties that bind family members to one another. Where family ties once rested on life-and-death economic dependence and co-dependence, today they rest more often on fragile emotions of love and liking. Since emotional ties are by their nature more fickle than ties of economic dependence, we more easily sever them. However, not every couple that falls out of love gets a divorce, since divorce is a legal process and not a social or emotional one. Some couples, as we shall see, may not wish to end their marriages publicly at all. Others do.

Legal Changes

To understand divorce as a legal process, we must understand the laws governing divorce and how they have changed. Divorce laws in Canada and other Western countries have gradually loosened over the past two centuries. For example, during the colonial period in North America, divorce was illegal in the southern United States and Quebec. It was granted elsewhere only under narrowly defined circumstances such as adultery or after proof of seven years of desertion. Until the mid-twentieth century, Canadian law required an Act of Parliament for each divorce to be granted (Snell, 1983). Not surprisingly, divorces were granted most often to well-to-do and influential people. Before the 1968 Divorce Act (which accepted separation as a legitimate ground for divorce), most marriages "dissolved by taking other options, such as separation, desertion, or maintaining an 'empty shell' relationship by minimizing communication between partners" (McVey, 2008: 190).

There was a strong sense in the early 1900s in Canada that divorce was a moral and political issue, with bad implications for the country. Snell (1983: 113) quotes E.A. Lancaster, the Conservative Member of Parliament for Lincoln, Ontario, 1900–1916: "Where will this country come to in twenty-five years if we are going to grant divorces because some woman has been disappointed in regard to her husband ... The whole social fabric of the country would go to pieces."

Increasingly over the twentieth century, North American governments granted divorces on ever-widening grounds, such as marital cruelty, marital rape, sodomy, bestiality, homosexuality, and adultery. As divorce laws become more lenient, there was an accompanying rise in divorce rates. A turning point occurred in the late 1960s and early 1970s with the introduction of **no-fault divorce** laws in Canada and some jurisdictions in the United States. In Canada, the 1968 Divorce Act first enlarged the "fault grounds" under which a divorce could be granted, but also allowed divorce without accusations of wrongdoing in the case of "marital breakdown," which required three years of living apart, or five if both spouses did not agree to divorce.

The 1985 Divorce Act considers marriage breakdown to be the only ground for divorce, though the older grounds such as adultery or cruelty are considered evidence of breakdown. It is no longer necessary for one spouse or the other to accept moral blame for the breakdown of the marriage. This change in approach reflects a gradual societal redefinition of divorce.

No longer does divorce have to be a stigmatizing process where one party is held responsible under the law. On the contrary, we now may be more likely to look critically at marriages that survive even though they are emotionally dead. These are marriages that we now think could end, freeing their participants to find emotional fulfillment in another union, or living singly.

No-fault divorce laws implicitly define marriages in which couples are "incompatible" or have "irreconcilable differences" as grounds for divorce. Divorce, according to no-fault laws, then, could end marriages that are "irretrievably broken." The grounds for no-fault divorce are not inherently adversarial; they are based almost entirely on the loss of emotional connections. In earlier times, many marriages may have broken down emotionally or may never have been emotionally secure in the first place. It is only recently the legal system has come to view this as reason enough to end a marriage.

In December 2002, the Government of Canada announced a new approach to divorce in Canada (Douglas, 2006). The purpose of proposed changes to the 1985 Divorce

Major Canadian Divorce Statistics

- The divorced population in Canada in 2012 was 4.83 percent of the population, although this number did not include those living common-law. There was no significant change from 2008 (Statistics Canada, 2013).

- More than one-third of marriages in Canada will end in divorce before the thirtieth wedding anniversary (Clark and Crompton, 2006). In 2011, the Vanier Institute, using data from Statistics Canada, published "Four in Ten Marriages End in Divorce" (see Figures 9.6a and 9.6b).

- Men between the ages of 20 and 64 are six times as likely to suffer from depression if they are divorced or separated than if they stay married. The figure is 3.5 times as likely for divorced or separated women (Rotermann, 2007).

- Forty-three percent of women who have undergone a marital breakup (divorce or separation) had a substantial decrease in household income in 2006 while 15 percent of separated or divorced men had a financial decline (Rotermann, 2007).

- In 1951, divorce accounted for only 3 percent of lone parents, but the proportion of divorced lone parents had increased tenfold, to 31 percent, by 2001 (Beaujot and Ravanera, 2008). In 2011, there were more than 1.5 million lone parent families—16.3 percent of all census families—in Canada, an increase from 8 percent in 2006 (Statistics Canada, 2012a).

- Among seniors (age 65 and older), the proportion of divorced people tripled from 1.7 per cent in 1981 to 5.1 percent in 2001 (Turcotte and Schellenberg, 2006: 139).

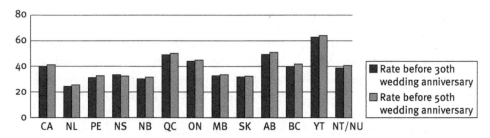

Figure 9.6a Percentage of Couples Who Can Expect to Divorce before their Thirtieth and Fiftieth Anniversaries

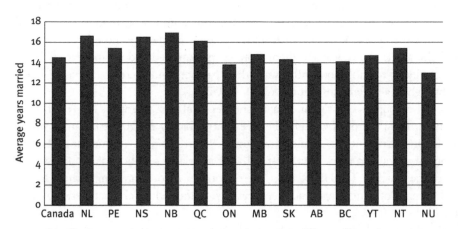

Figure 9.6b Average Duration of Marriage for Divorced Persons, Canada, 2011

Source: Reprinted with permission from Vanier Institute of the Family, 2011. Fascinating Families, Issue 41. "Four in Ten Marriages End in Divorce." www.vanierinstitute.ca/include/get.php?nodeid=132.

Act was, according to then Minister of Justice Martin Cauchon, to focus on children's needs primarily. Bill C-22, an Act to amend the Divorce Act, et al., would have replaced the terms "custody" and "access" in the Divorce Act with "parental responsibility" and "contact." It also would have provided courts with a new list of factors to apply to decisions surrounding the post-separation parenting of children whose parents divorce (Douglas, 2006). Regrettably, the bill made no headway.

However, on May 1, 2006, amended Federal Child Support Guidelines came into force, which clarified the term "extraordinary expenses" to respond to judicial disagreement over the significance of the term. The guidelines also provided for education-related and extracurricular-activity extraordinary expenses to be added to child support amounts payable. They included new tables for setting child support levels, which reflected changes in tax structures in the provinces (Douglas, 2006).

CAUSES OF DIVORCE

In the discussion that follows, we speak of "causes," but we might as well use the words **determinants** or **predictors**. Many supposed causes of divorce intertwine with other causes. Their distinct, separate influence is hard to discover. The most we can say with certainty is that these are predictors—correlates that typically precede divorce and influence its likelihood in sometimes complicated ways.

Although underplayed in sociological discussion about the "cause" of divorce, a couple's emotional interaction and personal characteristics, such as being naturally more caring, compromising, or compassionate, can also play a role in marriages and subsequent divorces. This means that, although the importance of communication for the success of relationships is paramount (see Chapter 5), *knowing* how to communicate or problem solve may be still be inadequate if the marriage is not founded on mutual respect and admiration (Houston, 2004: 955). For instance, happy couples are more likely to have individual characteristics that make them more even-tempered and warm-hearted. They are also more likely to show goodwill toward their partners and therefore are more likely to work through any differences (Houston, 2004: 952).

Moreover, a couple's emotional climate and personal characteristics may clash from the beginning. Most people (wrongly) believe that unhappy marriages began as happy relationships and that conflicts developed during the marriage that were unknown before. On the contrary, Houston found that most unhappy marriages fell short of happiness from the onset of the marriage (2004: 952). So, the reasons for divorce are complicated by the emotional climate of a marriage and the interplay of individual characteristics as well (Putnam, 2011).

We also distinguish among three levels of causal explanation: the micro-, macro-, and meso-levels. By **micro-level** causes, we mean something close to the lived experience of people who divorce: attitudes, perceptions, sentiments, beliefs, and the like. We include the experiences of rejection, infidelity, and marital dissatisfaction in this category. By **macro-level** causes, we mean societal changes like increased social tolerance of divorce, women's involvement in the workforce, and changes in divorce laws.

Finally, middle-range or **meso-level** causes of divorce are, typically, demographic predictors—that is, characteristics of people who are at a high risk of divorce. In this area, it is unclear whether these characteristics are causes, determinants, or merely predictors. For example, people who marry at an early age, or after only a short relationship, run an especially high risk of divorce, due to the stress, conflict, and dissatisfaction that arise when two immature people who do not know each other well try to work out a life together.

Precisely what we call the "cause" in the situation will vary from one analyst to another. Let us begin with the micro-sociological causes of divorce. They are the easiest causes to understand intuitively. However, they may not be the major factors leading to divorce—or, at least, predicting them.

Micro-sociological Causes

We commonly cite two kinds of micro-sociological "reasons." The first are grounds that people use when they file for divorce. These "grounds" may have value in a court of law, but sociologists find them largely unrevealing. We learn more from the personal accounts of individuals who have undergone divorce. They tell us a lot about the state of mind of the divorcing people and the ways they make sense to themselves of what has happened. However, people often do not understand the reasons for their own behaviour. As well, "(b)ecause these studies only include divorced respondents, they can tell us little about the extent to which these factors predict divorce" (White, 1990).

The second kind of micro-sociological reasons people cite to explain divorce typically describes the dynamics of the marriage relationship. As we said in Chapter 5, the quality of a relationship largely determines the stability of a marriage. Marriages likely to end in divorce have a typical profile. Usually, they are characterized by poor communication and poor conflict-resolution skills as well as a lack of commitment to the spouse and/or to the institution of marriage. The spouses may have few shared values and interests, and there is often a perceived inequity between spouses, and limited respect, love, and affection on the part of one or both spouses. These are overall average traits and will not characterize each situation. We can imagine people in such relationships wanting and getting a divorce. However, because these are common problems of relationships, they are not good predictors. Even those on the inside of the relationship often cannot make that prediction.

Consider, instead, some life course (demographic) variables that make certain people more divorce-prone than others. These are better than micro-sociological variables at identifying conditions that produce tensions and unhappiness—which, in turn, increase the likelihood of divorce. Even if they do not seem to explain divorce as well, they are better at predicting it.

Meso-sociological Causes

Not everyone who marries gets divorced. In fact, the majority stay married, as discussed earlier. Moreover, the probability of divorce is spread unevenly throughout the population. Thus, to understand the causes of divorce we must look at who gets divorced.

Major life course and demographic variables correlated with a high divorce risk include young age at marriage, cohabitation before marriage, second or subsequent marriage, parental divorce, premarital pregnancy and/or child-bearing, childlessness—or conversely having a large number of children—early stage of marriage, urban residence, residence in British Columbia or Alberta (or in Quebec), absence of religious belief or affiliation, and low socio-economic status.

Age at Marriage Young age at marriage is probably the strongest predictor of divorce in the first five years of marriage (Amato, 2010; Ambert, 2002). Risks are especially high for people who marry in their teens. Various explanations for this have been ventured: Young people lack the emotional maturity needed for marriage, and they have ill-founded expectations of what married life holds in store. They are more likely to become disappointed and disillusioned with marriage, especially when they come upon plentiful alternatives to their current spouse (South, Trent, and Shen, 2001). As well, early marriage tends to reduce educational achievement. Young marriers divorce more often because they have less education, therefore a lower income, and fewer communication skills—which, in turn, can result in more misunderstandings and marital conflict.

Ironically, though young marriers in our own society have high rates of divorce, young-marrying societies, in which the average age at marriage is low, have low rates of divorce. Typically, countries with low average ages of marriage have other features—for example, high rates of child-bearing, strongly institutionalized religion, extended families, and restrictive divorce laws—that keep the divorce rates low for people of all ages. Latin American and Islamic societies share these features, as do some cultures in Africa and Asia (Emery, 2013).

Cohabitation Cohabitation before marriage has, as we've said in earlier chapters, also been correlated with a higher risk of divorce. However, this fact needs careful interpretation. Societal and family pressures may push cohabiting people into marriage before they are ready, even if they are unsuited for marriage or for each other. Cohabitation, by hastening marriage, may increase the risk of separation and divorce (Ambert, 2002). On the other hand, couples in happy cohabiting relationships who succumb to societal pressures to marry may find their relationship changed adversely by the social policies that shape expectations about wives and husbands and supposedly encourage stability. Couples, in other words, may not be separating as much from each other as from the socially scripted roles and expectations that legal marriage entails. It would be interesting to find out how many couples who previously cohabited and subsequently marry actually go back to living in a cohabiting relationship. Much has been learned about intimate unions from gay and lesbian couples, some of whom saw the reality that they could not legally marry in the past (in most jurisdictions) as strengthening their relationships (see Lehr, 1999; Rothblum, Balsam, and Solomon, 2011). In other words, couples are creating their own ways to be couples rather than working to fit into legally prescribed roles and obligations which some find constraining. Feminist sociology has found that legal marriage is often too constricting for women. Of course, that changed with the option for legalized gay and lesbian marriages in Canada beginning in 2005 and now in many other countries.

Still another possible explanation for this finding is **adverse selectivity**—that is, that the people who choose to cohabit are different from those who choose to marry without first cohabiting. However, as more people—and more varied people—cohabit, cohabitation may no longer predict a high risk of divorce. Therefore, cohabitation as a predictor variable for divorce risk is likely on the way out of sociological theories, although not all sociologists agree.

Second Marriages Other things being equal, second marriages are more likely than first marriages to end in divorce. The risk in Canada is estimated to be about 10 percent higher than in first marriages (Ambert, 2002; 2005b). Data on marriages and divorces in Canada has not been collected recently. The probability that third marriages will end in divorce is higher still. (As well, remarriages that end in divorce end more quickly than first marriages.) Yet people still get married after a divorce. Approximately 70 percent of men and 58 percent of women in Canada (excluding Quebec) marry again following separation. Remarriages are also more common among immigrants than among Canadian-born citizens (Ambert, 2005b; Wu, 1994).

This finding defies our common sense. One would expect remarriages—like cohabiting relationships—to have a lower divorce rate. People who had already gone through one divorce would, we imagine, be more careful choosing their next mate. They would try harder to make their marriage work, to avoid the problems and costs associated with divorce. Some, in fact, do just this. When a second marriage endures, it often outlasts the first (Ambert, 2002; 2005b; Wu, 1994). Moreover, when remarriages work out, it is typically because the remarried people are older than average. Older people are less likely to divorce (although as we have seen, this is changing). Young people who remarry are more likely to divorce than older people who remarry.

Another viable explanation is that people who have already been married choose cohabitation as a substitute to marriage the second time around. For these adults, cohabitation is a union in itself, one that will not end in marriage and that has a similar level of commitment as marriage (Ambert, 2005; Beaupré, 2008). In this case, older cohabiters experience higher levels of happiness and stability than younger ones (King and Scott, 2005). Despite their success, these relationships are not counted as remarriages and as such do nothing to decrease the perceived overall risk of divorce in second marriages.

Adverse selectivity may *again* be the explanation for the higher divorce tendency in second and third marriages. People who experience a first divorce may be more willing to get a second. They may more readily see divorce as a solution to marital problems.

A competing theory argues that the stresses and strains of a remarriage are greater than those of first marriages. Second marriages may bring "baggage" from the first marriage/divorce, the (difficult) integration of stepchildren into reconstituted families, or the challenges of ongoing interactions with ex-spouses. Furthermore, fewer norms guide second marriages, although that is changing with their greater frequency. This makes remarriages more challenging. Both theories are compelling. We need more research to decide which explanation is better or whether both sets of factors come into play, with other factors still not well understood (Amato, 2010; Putnam, 2011).

Parental Divorce People whose parents divorced are more likely to divorce. They also have a greater tendency not to marry. However, the mechanism that transmits this inheritance is unclear. Perhaps people whose parents divorced are less likely to believe that marriages can last. That makes them more likely to opt for divorce when things get tough. They may have married before they were ready, out of fear that they would be

Myths and Facts about Divorce

Myth: Families where children live with their biological mothers are more stable across all situations.

- **Fact:** When a resident stepfather is present, the family is less stable than a family where the child is living with his/her biological father and a resident stepmother (Ambert, 2005b).

Myth: Higher divorce rates among children are a result of the conflict they saw in their families.

- **Fact:** This is not always true. Higher divorce risks also occur among adult children where their divorced parents had low levels of conflict. A sense of less commitment to each other may have been passed on to the children (Ambert, 2005b).

Myth: Stepparents have little connection with stepchildren.

- **Fact:** Many children enjoy the presence of a stepparent and benefit from the affection. Where stepfamilies endure, young adults are strongly attached to the reconstructed family (Ambert, 2005b).

Myth: With divorce, spouses are not concerned with what the ex-partner thinks.

- **Fact:** Perceptions of a former spouse can still have a powerful impact. Ex-wives' approval

of the quality of fathering plays a role in how satisfied divorced fathers are (Cohen and Finzi-Dottan, 2005).

Myth: People with lower socio-economic status are least able to afford to leave their marriage and thus have lower risk of marital dissolution.

- **Fact:** People with less than high school education at the time of their first marriage face a 38 percent greater risk of divorce than those who completed high school. University graduates, on the other hand, are at 16 percent less risk for marital dissolution, suggesting that people with higher social status are happier and less likely to divorce (Clark and Crompton, 2006: 24).

Myth: Second marriages are more likely to end in divorce than first marriages.

- **Fact:** In reality, remarriages made after the age of 40 are more stable than first marriages, due to the partners' increased maturity. For example, the risk for marital dissolution of Canadians who remarried in their forties is half that of those who were younger than 30 (Clark and Crompton, 2006: 25).

---

alone (like their parents). They may have married before they understood what marriage was all about, because their parents' marriage did not last long enough for them to find out. On the other hand, they may be the victims of optimism. This does not mean, however, that if your parents are divorced your risks of divorce are automatically high. They are not. Many children of divorced parents marry well and live happily.

One Canadian study (Corak and Heisz, 1999) compared children whose parents divorced with those who lost a parent to death. The researchers found, interestingly, that children who lose a parent to death have the same likelihood of marrying and of divorcing as anyone else.

The correlation of parental divorce with heightened divorce risk may be due again to adverse selectivity. People whose parents divorced were once a small minority. Today, they are not. Their parents' divorce stigmatizes them less and leaves them less ignorant about the variety of possible adaptations to marital conflict. They know that people survive divorce and that many people are better for doing so. If this explanation is so, we might expect that more people will have "learned how to divorce" from their parents. However, demographically speaking, as the average age of the population increases, and as older people remarry less often and cohabit more often, we may see a decline in divorce.

Child-bearing, Before and After Marriage Evidence documenting the relationship between premarital child-bearing and the likelihood of divorce is overwhelming. For people who marry after having a child, the risk of divorce is high. Couples who marry after discovering that they are expecting a child may marry under extreme pressure to legitimate the birth of their child. This is not the best motivation to marry. The good news is that shotgun weddings (marrying quickly because of pregnancy) are less common than they used to be.

Stepfamily Parents

According to Statistics Canada, "one characteristic of stepfamily parents is that they are more likely to be in a common-law union. According to data from the 2011 General Social Survey, 48 percent of parents aged 20 to 64 living in stepfamilies were living common-law. For parents in intact families, the proportion was 14 percent. Among parents in common-law relationships, those in stepfamilies were more likely than intact-family parents to want to marry.

When asked 'Do you think you will ever marry (or marry again)?', 42 percent of stepfamily parents living common-law said yes. For intact-family parents, the proportion was 32 percent."

Source: Statistics Canada, 2011. General Social Survey: Overview of Families in Canada – Being a parent in a stepfamily: A profile" Catalogue No. 89-650-X – No. 002. http://www.statcan.gc.ca/pub/89-650-x/89-650-x2012002-eng.pdf (accessed 27-02-2013)

The relationship between the birth of children within marriage and the likelihood of divorce is strong but not straightforward. Couples who end up divorcing tend to have no children or have fewer on average than those who stay married (Ambert, 2002). The reasons may be unrelated to child-bearing; it may be that most divorces occur within the early years of marriage. It is also likely that people who have no children may see themselves as freer to divorce than couples with children. Again, adverse selectivity is operating here.

However, children are quickly becoming less of a deterrent to divorce. The number of children affected by divorce and the fraction of divorces involving children have increased in recent years (Amato, 2010). Today, couples are less likely to stay together for the children.

Stage of Marriage Duration of marriage is strongly negatively correlated with a propensity to divorce. That said, the lowest risk of divorce is in the first year of marriage (Statistics Canada, 2002a). The rate follows an inverted-U shape that is skewed toward the left. Before the first anniversary, divorce occurs in less than one in every 1000 marriages. After the first anniversary, the rate goes up to 4.3, and then jumps to 18.0 the following year. The peak occurs at around the third and the fourth year, with 25.0 and 25.7 divorces, respectively. The curve goes down slowly each year after the fourth anniversary (Statistics Canada, 2004a). After 15 years of marriage, couples are less likely to divorce. The explanation is that the more time and energy people invest in their marriage, the higher the costs of abandoning the marriage and starting a new life. Couples are more aware of being badly matched early in the marriage since the factors responsible for divorce (for example, emotional satisfaction) carry more weight in the early years. As well, people think when a mistake has been made, it should be changed before it is too late. After about three years, relationships stabilize and many partners adjust.

On the other hand, with increases in longevity and more women having careers and means of living on their own, the rates of later life divorce are increasing substantially. Brown and Lin (2012) estimate based on U.S. national data that the divorce rate among those aged 50 plus doubled between 1990 and 2010. This suggests that people may be less willing to live out their later years in an unhappy marriage than they used to be. No similar studies have been done in Canada. Also, the longer a marriage goes on, the older the spouses tend to be, and the more likely they are to have grown up with cultural values in which marriage had much greater normative pull than it does today. We must wait another few decades before we find out the strength of this **cohort effect**—something that influences everyone of roughly the same age.

Place of Residence People living in urban centres are much more likely to divorce than people in rural areas. In some cases, these findings reflect a higher probability of divorce under the demands and stresses of urban life. However, in part these statistics also reflect adverse selectivity—specifically, the tendency for rural people to migrate to urban areas before, during, or after a divorce, or for younger people to migrate to cities for work or education and find themselves marrying there. A family farm or a rural small town can be a difficult place for divorced people, especially divorced women.

The effect of urban living is sometimes confounded by the divorce-increasing role of migration. When we control for many possible explanatory factors, rates of union instability are strongly related to recent and lifetime migration experience. Many immigrants come from cultures with strong family sanctions for lasting marriages. An alternative explanation is that when immigrants from countries in which marriage is seen primarily as a practical arrangement come to Canada and encounter the expectation that marriage should be based on passion and companionship, they may look at their own marriage from a different point of view and may become dissatisfied. A third possibility is that selectivity explains the finding. People who take the initiative of moving to a new country are risk takers, willing to confront challenges and make changes in their lives. They may be more willing to consider divorce than the more cautious people who stay behind. Alternatively, they may experience greater stresses, which can cause even firmly based marriages trouble.

Religion Finally, the ethnic and religious composition of the population has something to do with the patterns of divorce. The risk of divorce is lower for foreign-born Canadians. Interestingly, the risk of divorce is no higher in Quebec, where cohabitation is much more common than it is in other provinces. That of course, could be the reason since cohabiters are not counted as divorced when the unions end. Wu (2000) noted that the risk of divorce is lower among Catholics and Protestants than among those with other or no religious affiliation. The more religious people are, the less likely they will be to opt for divorce, even if they are unhappy in their marriages. Couples in which the spouses belong to different religions are more likely to divorce than couples who belong to the same religion. (Goode, 1993: 320; McDaniel, Boco, and Zella, 2013). But, in analyzing generational data in California, it is found that, once controlling for socio-economic status and other basic characteristics, the effects of religion (both affiliation and religiosity) on divorce disappear (McDaniel, Boco, and Zella, 2013).

Related to this is the overall **secularization** of societies such as Canada. With the massive move away from religion as a dominant social institution have come new norms. Among these, individual choice and liberalization of sexual beliefs and behaviours loom large. Marriage has become, for many, an individual choice rather than a covenant taken before God and extended family. Even couples who marry in churches tend to believe less in the religious covenant aspect now. Divorce, then, is seen more as a choice rather than the breaking of a larger spiritual commitment, or of an extended family network.

Socio-Economic Status Class, or **socio-economic status** (SES), is strongly correlated with probability of divorce. The divorce rate increases as one moves down the socio-economic ladder. Study after study confirms that, whatever the index of socio-economic status used—income, occupation, or education—we observe an inverse correlation between SES and divorce rates.

Economic stresses produce marital stresses. Moreover, the poor have less (economically) to lose from divorce and less to gain from staying married. However, differences in divorce rates by SES tend to be decreasing. This is in part a function of an increase in the divorce rate among middle- and upper-class people.

Goode (1993) suggests that this change is the result of a shift in the strongest variable in this pattern: the discrepancy between the husband's and the wife's incomes. Women with employment and incomes similar to that of their husbands can afford to divorce. This explanation assumes that women are more likely to want out than men. The more economically independent women become, the more likely they will be to leave their marriages when they want. Along similar lines, some argue that marriage, though seemingly about love or emotional union, is still a way for women to gain economically, even in the second and third decades of the twenty-first century. Women's desires for marriage to work reflect their economic needs for support and their wish to avoid poverty, according to this reasoning. Of course, to confirm this hypothesis, we would have to look further at who initiates separation or files for divorce, and why. But that could be misleading too.

An unexpected finding is the opposite link between class and divorce for women and for men. Evidence shows that the higher a man's income, the less likely he is to divorce. On the other hand, the higher a woman's income, the more likely she is to divorce (Wu and Schimmele, 2005b). The latter suggests that marriage represents economic dependence for women, though not for men. However, this theory doesn't explain why men are reluctant to divorce if they earn a high income.

On this topic, the findings are confusing. Some research finds that increases in wives' SES and labour-force participation increase the probability of marriage disruption. For example, Wu (2000) found that for women, having a job outside the home or being in school is associated with higher rates of divorce. When the wife's work status is higher than her husband's, the relationship can become unstable (Tzeng and Mare, 1995). This, however, is a growing trend and may now be stabilizing unions (Glynn, 2012). Most research finds that marital happiness and well-being increase as women's income increases. This happiness, in turn, decreases the likelihood of divorce (Rogers and DeBoer, 2001).

Couples with more education and a stronger attachment to the workforce generally have more stable marriages. In addition, these couples are most likely to be egalitarian. Given the importance of work in stabilizing marriage, it is no surprise that unemployed people have higher divorce risks than employed people. The receipt of family-support income also increases the likelihood a married woman will become divorced (Hoffman and Duncan, 1995; Davies and Denton, 2001). This does not mean that social transfers cause marital instability, but only that economic and other instabilities may be correlated.

Macro-sociological Causes

It should be clear by now that although the decision to divorce is one made by an individual couple, the decision is influenced strongly by large processes in the structure of society over which people have little, if any, control (Emery, 2013).

The institution of the family has changed a great deal over the past two centuries and even more so in recent decades. The ties of authority and economic dependence that bind family members together have weakened considerably. In addition, the legal structure forcing people to remain together has loosened, making divorce an attainable option for many people. Other important macro-level determinants of divorce include wars and migrations, economic cycles, gender roles, social integration, and cultural values. We will look at each of these factors in turn.

Economic Cycles People are less likely to divorce during recessionary periods than during periods of economic prosperity (Hellerstein and Morrill, 2011). People feel freer to strike out on their own when economic opportunities exist. They are more wary of leaving a familiar home or relationship, even if it is unpleasant, in times of economic uncertainty. And they may need the advantage of pooling resources in couples or families to get by in tough economic times.

Moreover, divorce is costly. It requires establishing separate households, dividing the property, and establishing specific terms for the support of children. Legal costs can also be high. These expenses tax most people's financial resources even during prosperity and often become prohibitive in bad times. If this happens, the effect is short-lived. Or couples may opt to live separately in the same house for a period until they can afford separate homes. Although divorce rates drop during depressions, they rise rapidly when the depression ends.

On the other hand, according to White's (1990: 905) review of the sociological literature on divorce, "(t)he most sophisticated analysis of American time series data ... finds that the effect of prosperity is to reduce divorce." Although prosperity may make divorce more feasible, the *benefits* of prosperity outweigh this effect on personal relationships (South, 1985). Thus, divorce rates may fall because financial security adds stability to personal relationships. At the least, the evidence on this is inconclusive.

Gender Expectations The evidence regarding the influence of gender expectations is difficult to interpret. Researchers have examined two hypotheses. First, when social structures allow women more economic independence from men and families, women have more freedom to divorce (Hetherington and Kelly, 2002; Popenoe, 1996; Stacey, 1996). Feminist theories enable us to see women's options in larger social and policy contexts, so that challenges such as discrimination against divorced lone mothers, particularly among women of colour or newer immigrants, lack of child-care options, problems with credit ratings, and so on can come into play as women consider divorce (Se'ver, 2011: 251–252). Second, a growing similarity of women's and men's lives may produce less marital cohesion than complementary, reinforcing roles do. Both of these imply that the more women become financially secure, the higher the divorce rate will be. Yet, as women marry men of similar socio-economic status, it may be that the divorce gap between higher SES couples and others widens.

Evidence suggests the most satisfying marriages (for both spouses) are those in which women's and men's roles in the household are more egalitarian, with men more sensitive and nurturing, and where husbands and wives share equally in making the decisions that affect their lives (Stacey, 1996). Antill and Cotton (1987) studied 108 couples and found that when both spouses are high on "feminine" characteristics such as nurturance, sensitivity, and gentleness, couples are happier than when one or both spouses is low on this cluster of characteristics. "**Femininity**" of both wives and husbands is positively associated with a smooth marital adjustment (Kalin and Lloyd, 1985). The explanation is that many of these qualities and characteristics are conducive to good interpersonal relationships. Relationships that both spouses view as equitable have the best marital adjustment. The greater the perceived inequity, the poorer the marital adjustment, and thus the higher the risks of divorce (Mahoney and Knudson-Martin, 2009). Of course, equality in intimate relationships is hard to define by couples who may often disagree about whether they have equality in their relationships (Mahoney and Knudson-Martin, 2009).

The nature of the relationship between gender expectations and divorce-proneness is unclear. Historical and cross-cultural research is addressing the issues of (1) whether divorce rates and rates of female participation in paid work are intrinsically related; (2) whether the observed relationship is a passing effect of the tension between changing social expectations and lagging societal understandings of these changes; and (3) whether the divorce rate is as high as in countries that have had a longer history of female participation in the labour force (Emery, 2013; Se'ver, 2011).

Cultural Values and Social Integration Since the mid-twentieth century, the cultural value placed on marriage has been declining. Many scholars argue that formal marriage has lost much of its normative support and social appeal. Distinctions between marital and non-marital child-bearing, between marriage and cohabitation, have lost their normative force. Marriage and divorce are seen as formalities or sets of family options. That said, many couples will live together until they decide to have children, at which point they marry. Today, it is argued, we invest less, or at least differently, in family commitments, whether to parents, spouses, or children.

Another macro-level determinant of divorce is a society's degree of **social integration**. The higher the social integration, the lower the divorce rate. In a stable, highly integrated community, which could be a religious community or perhaps an ethnic community, consensus on social rules is strong and rule breakers are shunned. This happens especially when the rules broken bear on social institutions as central to the community life as "the family." The highly integrated community typically supports various "pro-family" ideals bearing on marriage, premarital or extramarital sexuality, or child obedience. In Canada, Muslim and some South Asian communities are particularly protective of their daughters. Girls are seen as holding a special place in the communities as "cultural vessels" (Tysskä, 2011: 104). This can lead to girls in these communities leading double lives, with a foot in mainstream Canadian culture, where they seek acceptance, and a foot in their families' traditions. By getting a divorce, people, particularly women, risk incurring social stigma for flouting social norms and tearing the social fabric of their community. In these highly integrated communities, this is scary stuff and can be a definite deterrent to divorce.

EFFECTS OF DIVORCE

Divorce, like the breakup of any important relationship, can be messy and painful. Most couples decide to divorce only reluctantly over a long period. For many of them, considerable trauma is involved. Some may experience discrimination and may be, for a time, almost without friends. Some, notably women, suffer serious economic deprivation (Gazso and McDaniel, 2010).

In such a high conflict time, outside intervention may become necessary to reduce the risk of harmful and potentially long-standing escalations. This is especially important when children are involved in a separation. The parents must make decisions about the children, child support, maintenance, and the division of marital assets, and must negotiate liabilities. Family therapists or marriage counsellors can provide short-term or continuing support and insight to couples going through separation.

More recently, mediation has gained popularity among family therapists and divorcing couples (Emery, 2012). The main purpose of mediation is not to have the counsellor discuss with clients what they should do. Rather, the emphasis is on drawing "on the resources and knowledge of its participants to allow for creative solutions to the needs of the families who engage in this process" (Katz, 2007: 106). In other words, the role of the mediator is to promote an effective discussion between family members, who, in the process, will discover the unique resources they have available and come up with solutions on their own.

The main differences between traditional therapy and mediation, according to Katz (2007), are the role played by the counselor, the process engaged in, and the intended outcomes. Mediation always involves both parties with clearly defined goals while therapy tries to understand the past and feelings are often worked through. Traditional therapy works with multigenerational genograms where the focus of mediation is only the relevant parties. In traditional therapy, the therapist intervenes to resolve mental health behavior and relationship concerns as opposed to mediation where it is the clients who are assisted by a counselor to use direct talk to negotiate and make decisions. Furthermore mediation, as it emphases improving communication, helps both parties move to common underlying interests from their previous fixed bargaining positions with the overlying goal of creating a legally binding contract.

Effects on Both Spouses

One of the major effects of divorce is economic: For men and women, but especially women, incomes decrease. Economic distress is a large contributor to generalized psychological distress and to social-policy challenges (Davies, McMullin, and Avison with Cassidy, 2001; Gazso and McDaniel, 2010). However, economic distress is only one aspect of divorce and its aftermath. The other side is the emotional stress of interpersonal conflict. But of course, emotional distress can be made worse by financial worries. This begins well before the divorce and may reach its peak then. In the years immediately preceding divorce, people experience higher-than-usual levels of distress. However, conflict does not end with divorce. The effects of divorce on the divorcing adults, both material and emotional, can be surprisingly long-lasting for some (Gustafson, 2009; Mastekaasa, 1995). In a review of studies of divorce, Amato (2010) finds that pre-divorce marital discord conditions the effects of divorce on children.

Former spouses often disagree on the involvement of non-custodial parents in co-parenting. An overwhelming majority of residential parents feel they have problems with the issue of visitation rights. A smaller but still large percentage of non-residential parents do, too. In addition, these problems do not go away quickly. For residential parents, visitation problems may be connected to feelings of hurt and anger about the divorce. They are also connected with concerns about the ex-spouse's parenting abilities, child support, and sometimes about abuse of the child. In some countries, there is less conflict over custody as custody arrangements are less variable (see Kalmijn, 2010).

After divorce, most couples or parents find themselves unprepared for the new challenges they face and the inadequacy of counselling and support services. Even in the best post-divorce circumstances, many factors challenge a parent's efforts to maintain closeness with their children. A study by Yarosh, Chew, and Abod (2009) found that parents and children faced communication challenges when children were away from the residential parent's home and visiting at the other parental house. Children found it difficult to carry on conversations about activities they did at the other parent's home and found phone conversations awkward. It was also difficult for them to think of meaningful topics for discussion. Ex-spouses were also hesitant to call their child while visiting for fear they would interrupt the flow of activities at the other house. Remarriage or a new partnership also added further complexity to interactions between ex-spouses as well as with children (Shaff et al., 2008; Weiss, 1996).

Remarriage is associated with less frequent co-parental interaction, less reported parenting support from the former spouse, and more negative attitudes about the other parent for both women and men. For men, remarriage predicts lower levels of parenting satisfaction and involvement in children's activities (Christensen and Retting, 1995). But some research is finding that there are more benefits for children in remarried families than previous studies have indicated (Shaff et al., 2008).

Non-custodial fatherhood has increased due to increases in divorce and births outside of unions. The standard divorce—the mother with custody, the father with child-support responsibilities and visiting rights—is the reality in most cases involving longer duration marriages, higher male income, and younger children. That said, joint or shared custody is becoming the norm in divorces where dependent children are involved (Bauserman, 2012). Access to the children is seen as essential to some, but not all, non-custodial parents, and visiting is important to the quality of the subsequent father–child relationship (Peters and Ehrenberg, 2008). Access and child support are complementary, and joint custody tends to improve father–child relations, reduce parenting stress and conflict, and improve compliance (Bauserman, 2012). Most mothers are willing to allow visitation even if the father does not pay child support, thus acknowledging the importance of father–child relationships (Laakso, 2004).

International Findings about Divorce

- As in Western societies, educational level in Japan is associated with divorce risk, which is lower among mothers with a university degree (Raymo, Iwasawa, and Bumpass, 2004). Divorced mothers in Japan have full custody of children. The parent without custody typically has no access to the child and is out of the child's life (Morely, n.d.).

- Russia has one of the world's highest divorce rates. Divorced Russian women with children have little likelihood of remarrying. One major reason for this is the shortage of men: Workers' mortality rates are high. There is a significantly higher proportion of women in their thirties than there are men (Nesterov, 2004).

- Though divorce is allowed, it is not widely practised in India. Where most marriages are arranged, women gain their social status from their husbands. When divorce occurs, the wife moves out. Her social connections break down too, as she is discouraged from befriending men and from socializing with married couples. The worry is that a divorced woman might be a marriage wrecker (Sonawat, 2001).

- Political and cultural resistance to divorce is strong in Italian society, where traditional family is deeply rooted. Italy has the lowest divorce rate in Europe, followed by Ireland, at 0.73 per 1000 population in 2003 (*United Nations Demographic Yearbook, 2003*). Yet separations occur, suggesting that unhappy married couples remain separated rather than taking legal steps to divorce (De Rose, 2001).

- In the Netherlands, adults who choose to remarry after a divorce are younger on average (42–47 years) than those who choose living apart together (59–64 years; De Jong Gierveld, 2004).

- Divorce in China is rare, at only 10 percent to 15 percent of the population. Society and neighbourhood groups become mediators when marriages fail, often preventing divorce. Divorced Chinese women are more likely to remarry than men and to remarry sooner (Dong, Wang, and Ollendick, 2002), unlike in the West.

China's divorce rate rises for seventh year in a row

No wonder Chinese singles fear getting married: the country's divorce rate continued to rise in 2012, for the seventh year in a row, according to a survey by Tsinghua University and the CPC's Xiaokang magazine. Compared to 2011, the number of divorces was more than 7.5 percent higher in 2012. Currently, China's divorce rate is 2.3 percent overall, but that figure masks dramatic differences between the city and countryside; like elsewhere, the divorce rates are highest in major cities. For example, Beijing—the nation's capital—has China's highest divorce rate at 39 percent, with Shanghai–the nation's economic powerhouse–following closely at 38 percent. These rates are somewhat higher than are found in Hong Kong and Taipei, with rates of 34 and 35 percent respectively.

—Adapted from Michael Evans

Adapted from http://shanghaiist.com/2013/02/25/chinas_divorce_rate_rises_for_seven.php

Divorce affects non-custodial fathers' views of their parental role. Common themes among non-custodial fathers include divorce-related emotional distress; dissatisfaction with custody, visitation, and child support arrangements; perception of divorce proceedings as unfair; and ongoing conflicts with former spouses (Dudley, 1996; Kruk, 2010). Moreover, his disempowerment, loss of legal custody, and relegation to the role of an economic provider has a profound impact on his masculine identity (Kruk, 2010; Mandell, 1995). Fathers often have limited contact with their children after divorce, and this contact decreases over time. They are more likely to see preschool-age children every week than school-age children (Stephens, 1996).

Why do so many fathers have reduced contact and visitation? Researchers offer many explanations. One is that non-residential fathers feel less competent and less satisfied in the role of father (Kruk, 2010). Typically, fathers of all kinds who identify strongly with the role of father are more frequently involved with their children. Non-residential fathers identify less strongly with the role (Minton and Pasley, 1996). Overall, fathers who do not want contact with their children are more apt to have been less involved with child rearing, to feel indifferent about their children, or to have been in an abusive or violent relationship (Smart and Neale, 1999; Greif, 1995).

In contrast to many non-custodial fathers, nine men studied by Arendell (1995) and more studied by Smart and Neale (1999) have developed strategies more congruent with their aim to parent their children actively. Their accounts and actions are child-centred. Each of these men has established, with their former wives, some type of parenting partnership. They actively seek to create "best case scenarios" post-divorce and become absorbed with family relationships. Unlike most divorced fathers, these men are satisfied, even pleased with their parenting. Simultaneously, they see themselves as defying the norms of masculinity. Thus, self-confidence and uncertainty coexist for these innovative fathers.

Effects on Women

This section emphasizes the adverse effects of divorce. However, we will begin by acknowledging that divorce may also have benefits. For example, divorced mothers whose marriages were difficult, and sometimes abusive, are typically relieved when their marriages are over. However, even among those who are happy to be out of a bad or intolerable relationship, a majority expresses concern about the situations they face after divorce. They tend to face diminished opportunities and perceived second-class treatment (Kurz, 1995; Warrener, Koiveunen, and Postmus, 2013).

Because women and men have different experiences after a divorce, they behave differently. For example, separated men are six times as likely as married men to commit suicide, especially in the younger age groups (Barrett and Turner, 2005). However, separated women do not have much higher suicide rates than married women. After divorce, both male and female suicide rates rise. Thus, as Durkheim said, marriage protects both sexes, but it does so differently. Women with more children have lower suicide rates than women with fewer children, for example. It is possible that their child-rearing responsibilities protect women against suicide. This protection erodes as their children become independent.

Divorce depresses both women and men, but not always and not in the same ways. But, of course, causality can work the other way too: Depression can pose challenges for a union and contribute to divorce (Davila, Stroud, and Starr, 2008). However, women undergoing divorce show greater increases in rates of depression. Men whose marriages are breaking up typically show higher rates of alcohol problems but not of distress (Felix, Robinson, and Jarzynka, 2013; Wu and Hart, 2002). Women report more distress but not more alcohol problems. These findings support the idea that men externalize their problems in response to circumstances that lead women to internalize. Women also show more symptoms of distress before the separation, whereas men display more symptoms after the final separation. Researchers must measure men's and women's well-being differently, and therapists need to help them in gender-appropriate ways. Feminist research has found that therapy is not always sensitive to gender needs and differences (Calixte, Johnson, and Motapanyane, 2010).

After divorce, women suffer a decline in their standard of living. A classic American study by Lenore Weitzman (1985) estimated a decline of 73 percent in women's standard of living, compared to a 42-percent decline for men in the first year after divorce. (For comparable Canadian data, see Finnie, 1993, which is discussed below. For more recent analyses, see Gadalla, 2009). This drop in living standard occurs even among less advantaged subgroups, such as African American and Hispanic low-income adults. Most young minority men fare poorly after divorce in absolute economic terms. However, young minority women fare even worse, a disparity that stems, either directly or indirectly, from women's roles as primary child caretakers (Smock, 1994).

Finnie's (1993) Canadian research also demonstrates that both men's and women's income drops as a result of divorce, but women's income drops twice as much, on average. Men tend to recover lost income more quickly than women in the aftermath of divorce. As well, since men have higher income, they are less likely to be poor (Ambert, 2005b). The poverty-triggering of marital dissolution is less likely to affect men than women (Vandecasteele, 2011). Thus, divorce is much more likely to plunge divorced women into poverty and keep them there for longer. This is especially true if they have children for whom they are solely or largely responsible.

Also, women get custody of the children, which means that fewer dollars have to support more people. And women with children may have stepped away from paid employment to work at home with the children while they are young, thus reducing their years of income and work experience. This also means reduced contributions to pension plans and risks of lower income in the older years, too (LaRochelle-Côté, Myles, and Picot, 2012). Low income is the cause of higher levels of life strains reported by separated women, according to a six-year longitudinal study (Nelson, 1994). On the other hand, some researchers find that "fathers are better off after divorce, for they can now spend most of their money on one person, themselves ..." (Goode, 1993: 166). Some divorced fathers dutifully provide child support for their children after divorce, and researchers like Finnie (1993) have found that those fathers' incomes drop, though not as much as women's.

Women's economic disadvantage after divorce is largely due to the traditional practice of investing male human capital in the wage labour market and female human capital in the family and home. This is a structural circumstance that feminist research has shown disadvantages women throughout their life courses, particularly if they withdraw from the paid labour force to raise children (Se'ver, 2011). The latter greatly disadvantages women after divorce, when women are likely to receive inadequate compensation for time spent out of the wage labour market. Even women with almost the same educational background as men are at a considerable disadvantage over time.

The impact of divorce is often lifelong; the healing and recovery processes take time. Healing is influenced by such variables as age of the woman and child(ren), potential for employment, remarriage, coping skills, social networks, and income changes. Having a steady, satisfying job is associated with higher self-esteem and lower distress among divorced women. A good job provides meaning, social interaction and support, productivity, positive distraction, and, fundamentally important, income. Spiritual practice helps some women. Others change their behaviours to reduce stress. They may take up exercise or otherwise focus on nurturing a healthy body; they may take classes or take up hobbies to improve their mental well-being; they may revamp their personal appearance to give themselves a boost. (For more on this theme, see Wallerstein and Blakelee, 1990.) We will discuss more about life after divorce in Chapter 11, when we consider fresh family starts.

Effects on Children

In the past, many couples avoided divorce and stayed together "for the sake of the children." Their concern was, in some respects, justifiable. Divorce can have harmful effects for the children involved. However, research shows repeatedly that the effects of divorce on children as well as on parents depend very much on what is happening in the family before divorce and the quality of family relationships during and after the divorce (Amato and Booth, 1996; Amato, Loomis, and Booth, 1995; Smart and Neale, 1999; Stacey, 1996). If the family is violent or family relationships are abusive and hostile, for example, then divorce might provide relief. The effects on children also depend on the society or community's values. If, for example, a community believes that divorce is bad under almost all circumstances, the negative effects for all involved, including children, will be worse (Kalmijn, 2010).

Hetherington and Kelly (2002) suggest that the negative long-term effects of divorce on children may have become so exaggerated that it has become a self-fulfilling prophecy. For example, children of divorced parents can display poorer social and psychological

Children who have witnessed divorce, on average, show higher levels of depression, anxiety, and loneliness. Some children may even blame themselves for the divorce and may have particular difficulty in adjusting to new circumstances.
Pixland/Thinkstock

adjustment than children from non-divorced homes (Kunz, 1992:352). More recent research, however, shows that mother's education and income are crucial factors in the effects of divorce on children's achievements (Shaff et al., 2008).

But if schools, counsellors, and parents are taught to look for these outcomes, that could account, in part, for why they find them more often. When the children grow up, they are much more likely than those from intact families to think their own marriages may be in trouble. Were there other differences in these children prior to divorce? Are their subsequent expectations about their own marriages a result of childhood experience or of much-hyped research showing negative outcomes?

Research (Statistics Canada, 2005f) has found that the tension and turmoil leading up to the divorce are more harmful to children's mental health than the divorce itself. If most of the damage is done to children who live in families where there is constant fighting, then staying together, especially for the sake of the children, may not be the wisest choice.

Parental divorce can increase the risk of adolescent depression in two ways. First, it may be a source of many secondary problems and stresses that cause depression. Second, it can alter youths' reactions to these stresses, sometimes increasing the depressive effects (Davila, Stroud, and Starr, 2008). Economic hardships, a common outcome of divorce for children, also increase the risk of depression, thus accounting for the greater vulnerability of youths in single-parent families to depression (Amato and Sobolewski, 2001; Aseltine, 1996). That these factors go together makes it challenging for researchers to sort out the independent effects of divorce per se.

On the other hand, separation and divorce can improve family functioning (Statistics Canada, 2005f), especially if custody rules are clear and agreed upon, civility is maintained, and peaceful order is beneficial to both parents. Mothers with joint custody report lower levels of parenting stress and better co-parental relations than sole-custody mothers (Bauserman, 2012). But joint custody is known to be more probable as well as more workable for couples that get along better in the first place and put their children's interests above their own (Bauserman, 2012; Smart and Neale, 1999). This produces a happier set of parents, which will no doubt lead to better parenting.

Other things being equal, marriage or living in a stable, caring, long-term relationship is better for children than divorce. Children living in lone-mother families with no parental conflict and with continuing contact with the non-residential father still have lower levels of well-being, on average, than children who live in two-parent families without parental conflict. However, the well-being of children living in peaceful single-mother families is higher than that of children living in two-parent families with a lot of parental conflict. The degree of parental conflict after divorce is more important for the well-being of children than contact with the absent father. That is to say, it is better for the children of divorce if the father doesn't come around if parental arguments break out when he does (Dronkers, 1996; Peters and Ehrenberg, 2008).

Beyond the effects on thinking and feeling, divorce is correlated with variations in children's behaviour. So, for example, in a family that is not abusive, divorce can be related to deterioration in children's school performance; increased proneness to crime, suicide, and out-of-wedlock births; lesser adult work performance; and likelihood of the children themselves becoming divorced later in life (Galston, 1996; Shaff et al., 2008). The experience of divorce may weaken trust in people and institutions, and impede the capacity to form stable, enduring relationships.

Parental divorce and remarriage have strong effects on children's attitudes toward premarital sex, cohabitation, marriage, and divorce, even after controlling for parental attitudes (Axinn and Thornton, 1993). Thus, children do not merely replicate their parents' values and attitudes toward non-marital sex, marriage, and divorce, but develop an approach that incorporates their life course experience. Kozuch and Cooney (1995) as well as Amato (2010) note, however, that results from studies using parental marital status to predict young adults' attitudes have been inconsistent. In Kozuch and Cooney's survey of young adults from a variety of backgrounds, parental marital status predicted only two of five attitudes toward marriage and family. By contrast, level of parental disagreement predicted four of the five.

Children of divorce often marry earlier, are more likely to cohabit, achieve less economically, and hold more pro-divorce attitudes. All these factors account for some intergenerational transmission of divorce. However, holding these constant, behaviour problems play the largest part in this transmission of divorce. Children witnessing their parents' divorce are more likely than other children to learn behaviours that interfere with the maintenance of stable intimate relationships (Amato, 1996)—for example, to learn how conflict works but not how cooperation works. All of these findings, however, have become less and less common in children of divorce as divorce has become more common. In fact, children whose parents have divorced are now as diverse as children from intact families.

Divorce has been associated in the past with less formal schooling, possibly because young people with divorced parents may have less family financial support for pursuing post-secondary education. The support they receive is much more likely to come from their custodial than non-custodial parent (Grissett and Furr, 1994). Thus, the lower educational and occupational attainment of children of divorce is more likely associated with reduced financial support than with a loss of confidence in higher education. Students who are excellent can easily find financial support for higher education, however, through scholarships or student loans.

Despite these seemingly negative outcomes for children of divorce, recent research does not support the fear that divorce will produce problem behaviours. Neither exposure to parental divorce nor exposure to parental conflict affects the quality of attachment to adult intimates, nor the quality of parenting (Amato, 2010; Tayler, Parker, and Roy, 1995). Adolescence and early adulthood may present challenges—more to women than to men—but challenges in adolescence are common, whatever kinds of families one comes from. Coming from a divorced family may add to those pressures. However, coming from a divorced family does not, in the end, diminish an individual's ability to cope with new challenges (Dunlop and Burns, 1995). In fact, it might contribute to resilience.

Relations with Parents

Since divorce often results in the departure of the biological father from the family, father–child relationships are often most affected (Peters and Ehrenberg, 2008). In a study by Dunn, Cheng, O'Connor, and Bridges (2004), positive relationships between children and non-resident fathers were correlated with ongoing contact between child and father, the quality of the mother–child relationship, and the frequency of contact between the mother and her former partner. Increasingly, children and fathers do preserve a continuing relationship after the divorce. However, on average, adolescents in divorced families get less advice from their fathers and feel less satisfied with paternal support. Adolescents from intact families say they have more positive emotional relationships with their fathers than do adolescents

Causes and Effects of Divorce

- In general, marriage is less likely to result in divorce for people who marry later, who did not live common-law before the wedding, have children, attend religious services, are university educated, and believe that marriage is important if they are to be happy (Clark and Crompton, 2006).

- According to data from the National Population Health Survey (NPHS), men and women who go through a divorce tend to have a higher risk of being depressed in the two years following the end of the relationship. The risk is especially great for divorced men, who are six times more likely to be depressed than those who remain married (Davila, Stroud, and Starr, 2008; Rotermann, 2007).

- Problems in the realm of work and household labour as well as emotional and psychological relationship problems have become more important motives for a divorce, especially for women. This is consistent with the increase in emancipatory attitudes in the past decades

(de Graaf and Kalmijn, 2006; Mahoney and Knudson-Martin, 2009).

- Older women who are divorced are more likely to live in low income than older women who are widowed. With the rising older population, more older women are at risk for entering poverty in the future (LaRochelle-Côté, Myles, and Picot, 2012; Turcotte and Schellenberg, 2006).

- Changes in father–child contact are more closely linked to the mother's subsequent remarriage than to the father's. Non-resident fathers sometimes reduce frequency of visits when their children acquire a stepfather, but they are not significantly reduced after the birth of a child in the father's new union (Juby, Billette, Laplante, and Le Bourdais, 2007).

- Divorce may be associated with increased levels of anxiety and depression in children. However, child anti-social behaviour decreases when marriages in highly dysfunctional families are dissolved (Strohschein, 2005).

from divorced or remarried families. Adolescents who live with both parents may fight their fathers to achieve independence. However, this can be a good thing, related to the development of more self-esteem and a stronger ego identity (McCurdy and Scherman, 1996).

Amato and Booth (1996) used data from a 12-year longitudinal study of marital instability to examine the effects of divorce on parent–child relationships. The quality of the parents' marriage has both direct and indirect implications for later parent–child affection. Problems in the parent–child relationship before divorce, and low quality in the parents' marriage when children were (on average) 10 years old, led to low parental affection for the children when they were (on average) 18 years old. Divorce continued to undermine affection between fathers and children, although not between mothers and children. Thus, when there is a long history of turbulence and indifference, the break in a father–child relationship may predate divorce. Departure may reduce the child's access to his or her father. However, those fathers who maintain contact remain important people in their children's lives and an important source of support in times of stress (Munsch, Woodward, and Darling, 1995; Peters and Ehrenberg, 2008; Smart and Neale, 1999).

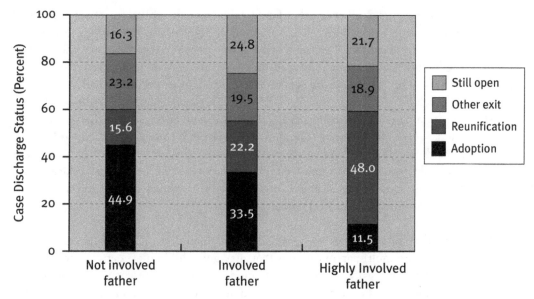

Figure 9.7 Discharge Outcome by Level of Non-resident Father Involvement

Source: More about the Dads: Exploring Associations between Nonresident Father Involvement and Child Welfare Case Outcomes. 2008. Prepared for U.S. Department of Health and Human Services et al. Washington, D.C. http://aspe.hhs.gov/hsp/08/moreaboutdads/.

As we have seen in previous chapters, there is a substantial amount of research on the lives of single mothers and the difficulties they face raising children. There is much less literature on father involvement in child rearing following a parental split. Edin, Tach, and Mincy (2009) used data from the Fragile Families and Child Wellbeing Study and from interviews with 150 unmarried fathers to understand contemporary non-marital father involvement. The authors found that "father involvement drops sharply after the parents' relationships end, especially when they enter subsequent relationships and have children with new partners" (Edin et al., 2009: 149).

As seen in Figure 9.7, father involvement is important not only for the welfare of the child(ren) involved but also because it affects the outcome of important delibera-tions about child custody and family reunification. For various reasons, unknown father cases rarely result in parent–child reunification. Mothers who are unable or unwilling to identify their child's likely father may have other characteristics that are related to the likelihood of an adoption outcome. The uncertainty about a father's identity may point to a broader family dysfunction, for example. And, if an initial placement with a relative works out well, the caseworker may be reluctant to seek contact even with an identified father.

Compared with those who grew up in two-parent families, the adult children of divorced parents perceive their relationships with both mothers and fathers to be of lower quality. The quality is two or three times lower for fathers than for mothers. Usually, memories of parental conflict or other family problems can explain the effect of parental divorce on relationship quality. Adult children of divorce also have much less current contact with their parents than adults from two-parent families (Webster and Herzog, 1995). Children evaluate their relationships with mothers more positively than those with fathers. They evaluate pre-separation relationships more positively than post-separation relationships, with some recovery after the passage of time. A positive relationship with one parent contributes negatively to the evaluation of the other parent after separation, suggesting that separation typically polarizes loyalties (Hoffman and Ledford, 1995). As divorce had become much more common in generations earlier, this means that fewer older people now may have close relations with their adult children, with implications for care as they age. This may also be true for parents of adult immigrants whose older parents may live in the homeland.

Stepfamilies Stepfamilies, often formed by the remarriage of biological parents after their divorce, are multi-parent families that may give children as many as two full sets of parents (and siblings), and four sets of grandparents. The presence of loving parents and grandparents can be a real plus for a child, under the right circumstances. However, stepfamilies can pose problems too, for a variety of reasons. Stepfamilies are formed after divorce, and marital conflict precedes the divorce. So, there are problems to solve—bad feelings between the former spouses—even before the new families begin. These feelings can affect the relationship between children and the stepparent. Portrie and Hill (2005) found that a mother's conflicts with the former spouse have negative effects on children and their stepfathers. But other research finds that a parent's remarriage and stepfamilies provide benefits to children (Shaff et al., 2008)

Chiefly, however, the problems associated with stepfamilies are due to the number and rapidity of changes a child must make. This is especially true if the remarriage occurs within a few years of the divorce.

Stepfamilies

Stepfamilies can be classified as either *simple* or *complex*. In a simple stepfamily, all children are the biological or adopted children of one and only one married spouse or common-law partner. A complex stepfamily consists of any of the following:

- families in which there is at least one child of both parents and at least one child of only one parent

- families in which there is at least one child of each parent and no children of both parents

- families in which there is at least one child of both parents and at least one child of each parent.

In the 2011 census, of the 3 684 675 couple families with children, 87.4 percent were intact families and 12.6 percent were stepfamilies.

Statistics Canada, 2012a

Adapting to new parent(s) and potentially more siblings may cause confusion and stress for the child. Even a child who likes his or her new siblings may feel in competition with step-siblings for the affection of his or her parent.

Moreover, remarriages are problematic if they create an unstable environment for the child. As we have seen, remarriages have a higher failure rate than first marriages. But, when they work, they last for a long time. Research also shows that changes in parenting can significantly affect a child. These changes increase the likelihood that a child will suffer poor grades, poor health, low self-esteem, drug abuse, peer rejection, and lower self-reported well-being. At the extreme, a succession of divorces and remarriages presents an unstable environment, especially since expectations change with each new parent. We'll talk more about remarriage and stepfamilies in Chapter 11.

In sum, for children, parents, and other relatives, divorce, like other major life events, can be stressful. However, we must be careful not to exaggerate the extent or permanence of harm done. Developing resources and protections can reduce the effects of these stressors and indeed build resilience and character. Higher levels of coping resources support a greater optimism about the future, fewer financial problems, more confidence in parenting ability, and a more satisfactory relationship with the former spouse (O'Leary, Franzoni, and Brack, 1996).

Factors that reduce the adverse effects of divorce on children include a strong and clear sense that both parents still love them, an understanding that they are not to blame for the divorce, and regular visits with the non-custodial parent. Parental conflict, as we have said often, has a negative effect in both intact and divorced families (Weiner, Harlow, Adams, and Grebstein, 1995).

The impact of divorce on children varies enormously, depending on many factors, including the responsiveness of parents, schools, and communities. Overall, young adults are optimistic about marriage, and their parents' divorce does not have a large impact on their attitudes toward marriage and divorce (Landis-Kleine, Foley, Nall, Padgett, and Walters-Palmer, 1995).

Though divorce may sometimes cause problems, it sometimes also solves problems. Divorce spares many children serious problems. It may even bring benefits. People whose parents divorced during their adolescent years display a much higher level of moral development than those whose parents did not divorce (Kogos and Snarey, 1995). Underlying the development of moral judgment is an increased perspective-taking, necessary for children of divorce who witness differences in opinions between their parents. But, of course, witnessing differences of opinion is not limited to parents who divorce.

Effects on the Elderly

We have seen that today's older generation has more diverse family networks than previous generations. For example, older people today are more likely than previous cohorts to have experienced divorce. (For a look at the average age of Canadians who divorce,

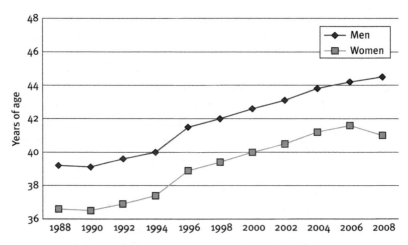

Figure 9.8 Average Age at Divorce, Canada, 1988 to 2008

Note: Average age at divorce is calculated using data from actual divorces occurring in a particular year.

Source: Human Resources and Skills Development Canada, 2012. "Indicators of well-being in Canada." Retrieved February 2013 from http://www4.hrsdc.gc.ca/.3ndic.1t.4r@-eng.jsp?iid=76&bw=1. For 1986 to 1996, Statistics Canada: Vital statistics compendium, 1996. Ottawa: Statistics Canada, Heath Statistics Division, 1999 (Cat. No. 84-214-XPE); for 1997 to 2003: Statistics Canada. Divorces. Shelf tables. Ottawa: Statistics Canada, 1999-2005; for 2004: 30 and 50 year total divorce rates per 1,000 marriages, Canada, provinces and territories, annual (rate per 1,000 marriages) (CANSIM Table 101-6511). Ottawa: Statistics Canada, 2008; and for 2006-2008: Statistics Canada, Health Statistics Division, Canadian Vital Statistics, Divorce Database and Marriage Database. Ottawa: Statistics Canada, 2011.

see Figure 9.8, and for the trend in the United States for those 50 years of age and older. So it is important to understand how trends in family life and partnership dissolution may affect future support and care for older adults, given that their social networks are largely composed of family members (Askham, Ferring, and Lamura, 2007; LaRochelle, Myles, and Picot, 2012).

On the one hand, there is the belief the experience of divorce weakens family ties, thereby reducing family support. There is evidence that divorce can have negative effects on support at older ages (Curran, McLanahan, and Knab, 2003; Kalmijn, 2007; Shapiro, 2003). It has been suggested that older people who have gone through divorce experience decreased contact and relationship quality with adult children as well as perceived support from children when compared with those in intact marriages (Curran et al., 2003; Kalmijn, 2007). Further, a Canadian study has shown that divorce followed by remarriage among older couples is accompanied by decreased support from networks of friends (Schlesinger and Schlesinger, 2009).

On the other hand, it has been suggested that the deleterious effects of partnership dissolution for support in later life may be disappearing (Thornton and Young-DeMarco, 2001). For instance, Glaser, Stuchbury, Tomassini, and Aksham (2008) found that partnership dissolution did not have a detrimental association with late-life support. In fact, separated older parents (age 70 and older) were significantly more likely to receive help from their adult children than married older parents. This research also found that the level of family support increased with increasing age and the health needs of the older person, regardless of family history (Glaser et al., 2008). Thus, a changing notion of the definition of "family," a greater acceptance of divorce, and an increasing tolerance of different family forms could be contributing to the stability of intergenerational support relationships.

CONCLUDING REMARKS

As we have seen, divorce is both a micro- and a macro-level phenomenon, with both micro- and macro-level effects. Little synthesis between macro- and micro-level analyses has been achieved. We are still far from having a comprehensive theory that predicts who will divorce and why, but our sociological insights are increasing.

The past 30 years have not fulfilled legislators' objectives in adopting no-fault divorce, although it is more prevalent now. Family lives have improved with expanded choice and happiness. Some have remarked on how the combined effect of increased divorce rates and increasing levels of child-bearing in cohabiting relationships have ensured that more than half the children born in the 1980s will be raised in single-parent families or in families where parents are not married for all or part of their lives. The decline of marriage has also led to paternal disinvestments in children. Divorced men are less likely to support children financially than men who live in intact families. Increased maternal earning capacity or improved public investment has not compensated for the decline in paternal support (Whitehead, 1996).

The conservative approach, largely found south of the border, to the problems of divorce, teen pregnancy (a problem in the United States but not in Canada), suicide, violence, and substance abuse is to blame the emerging culture of tolerance and the welfare state, contending that they undermine the benefits of self-reliance and community standards. The conservative definition of family values tends to be far too narrow. However, the perspective rightly emphasizes the role of family in child-rearing, whatever form it takes.

Liberals tend to recognize that increased unemployment, rising competition, and the need for dual-earner households have threatened the traditional family in some ways, or at least posed challenges. However, they may overemphasize the extent to which government services can replace effective family bonds (Giele, 1996). Among socially conservative people, strategies to encourage the reinstitutionalization of the traditional family would include restricting the legal benefits of family life and of marriage. These would begin with tighter controls on entry into marriage, more difficulties in leaving a marriage through divorce, and legally defining marriage as a moral duty between partners, rather than a personal contractual decision (Schneider, 1996). Some conservatives even suggest that marriage is the best solution to poverty for women.

Though it is not the job of sociologists to favour one side or the other, it is part of our responsibility to collect and examine evidence that would support one side or another. Here, sociology has an important role to play in the process by which a democratic society makes the policies and laws that govern family life.

The evidence shows us that divorce tends to be correlated with unhappiness and trouble. The question is, does divorce cause the unhappiness and trouble or do unhappiness and trouble cause divorce? Further, does divorce prolong unhappiness and trouble or cut it short? While it is foolhardy to generalize about all divorces, there is no evidence to show that divorce is the cause of most family-related unhappiness. Though it is true that people benefit from stable family lives when those families are functioning well, it is also true that people suffer from family lives when those families function badly.

For better or worse, it is up to the participants to decide whether their family life works well or badly. Outsiders' impressions count for little. What counts is a person's individual experiences in families. If the people involved think their family is working well, then to all intents and purposes, it is. If not, and efforts to correct the situation don't work, then divorce makes good sense—for the sake of the children as well as the spouses themselves, and sometimes for the extended family. After all, a child can experience good parenting without father and mother living together. On the other hand, conditions of stress, violence, unhappiness, and depression make good parenting almost impossible. We must assume that most parents take these factors into account when they decide to stay together or divorce. This being so, the conservative viewpoint on divorce has little to offer us. The traditional family they crave may never have existed and may not have been the happiest of families in any case, particularly for women.

CHAPTER SUMMARY

In this chapter we looked at the rise and now stability in divorce experienced since the middle of the twentieth century in most industrial societies. As social scientists, we look at the nature of social bonding, and our discussions on divorce cover not only some of the reasons behind increased divorce rates, we also examine the effects of divorce prevalence on individuals and society as a whole. Although these trends show a dramatic change in family structure and the functions the family plays in our lives, research has shown that our beliefs and attitudes about the role of the family have not kept pace. This makes the task of assessing the real impacts of divorce a bit more difficult, yet all the more needed.

Historically, divorce has worried social scientists and policy-makers alike. This concern has grown with the increase of divorce rates worldwide. Divorce rates have now stabilized or declined in Canada and the United States as well as in other parts of the world. Social, legal, and cultural changes have all played a part in divorce trends.

Generally, causes of divorce should more accurately be called predictors, since it is easier to note relationships between variables than to pin down a clear cause-and-effect relationship. Factors influencing the likelihood of divorce are found at the micro-, meso-, and macro-levels. Micro-level factors include poor communication, poor conflict-resolution skills, lack of commitment, lack of shared interests, and perceived inequity. Meso-level factors include age at marriage, marital duration, location, religiosity, class, and race. Macro-level factors include war, economic cycles, and cultural values.

The effects of divorce were then considered. Divorce can be a time of stress for spouses and children. Both men and women suffer a decline in standard of living, but men's incomes drop less and rebound faster. This effect is especially important for women, since they are most commonly the prime caregivers of the children after a divorce. Typically, fathers gradually disengage from children, though some do remain closely involved in parenting. Children tend to be distressed immediately after a divorce but gradually adjust. Finally, with a growing senior population in Canada, it is important to understand the trends and effects of separation and divorce in this population, especially how this affects intergenerational relationships in families. Women in particular who are divorced later in life are more apt to be poor in their later years.

The harmful effects of divorce are often talked about. Yet it is important to recognize that many of the harmful effects observed stem not from divorce per se but from poor family interactions prior to, during, and after the divorce. Hence, it may be important and helpful for families to seek professional help during this emotionally stressful time. Family therapy and mediation are just two examples of options available for people going through separation and divorce.

We concluded with a look at some popular political viewpoints on divorce. There is a movement in the United States urging legal and policy changes to discourage divorce, in an attempt to alleviate some of the social burdens that divorce produces. We find many of the proposed solutions incomplete and ineffective because of the narrow interpretations of the problem, which labels divorce as the culprit rather than poor family interactions.

Key Terms

adverse selectivity A tendency for people who choose to engage in a given behaviour to be, by nature of the kind of people they are, also at risk for a given outcome; selectivity may create the appearance of cause-and-effect relationships where they do not exist.

cohort effect The accumulated experience of going through life in the same set of years. For example, people born in the period 1924–1928 experienced World War II as teenagers and the postwar economic boom as young marrieds, and may have certain views or attitudes in common because of these experiences.

determinant A factor that contributes to an outcome (such as divorce) without necessarily being the direct or principal cause.

femininity A cluster of characteristics, such as nurturance, sensitivity, and gentleness, traditionally considered natural to women but that can be found in men or women.

macro-level The broad level of examining a social phenomenon, focusing on changes that affect society as a whole.

meso-level A middle range at which a social phenomenon may be examined, focusing on demographics—the characteristics of the people affected.

micro-level The smallest level at which a social phenomenon may be examined, the level of interactions between individuals and effects on individuals.

no-fault divorce Divorce granted because of marital breakdown rather than of specific wrongdoing (for example, adultery) on the part of one spouse or the other.

predictor A characteristic that is correlated with and precedes an outcome but may not be a direct cause.

secularization A move away from religion as an organizing principle of society.

social disorganization A breakdown of societal functioning.

social integration The state of societies that are closely knit and stable, in which people hold similar world views and there is a strong consensus on social rules.

social pathology A broad-based distress or disorganization within society.

socio-economic status Class; standing in society in terms of income, education, and prestige.

Critical Thinking Questions

1. In this chapter, you learned the importance of understanding the variation in divorce rates. (a) Formulate a sociological research question about divorce and propose how you would gather and analyze data on divorce rates. (b) Discuss how changes in the legal aspects of divorce may make it difficult to study the history of family breakdown and analyze divorce trends.

2. Discuss possible interventions that would lessen the negative impacts of divorce. For each approach, specify whether it addresses the micro-level, meso-level, or macro-level causes of divorce.

3. Children can be greatly affected by divorce. When parents repartner, children can find themselves living with more than one set of parents and in different homes with different rules. Discuss effective ways that stepfamilies can organize themselves to reduce conflict and stress.

4. The population of older adults in Canada is undoubtedly growing. Can you think how this may contribute to novel challenges faced by families or the society at large, when either the parents or grandparents divorce?

5. "Divorce rates are no longer a useful way of studying relationship dissolution, since so many people don't even bother getting married when they form a relationship." Do you agree with this statement: Why or why not?

Weblinks

Service Canada: Getting Divorced
www.servicecanada.gc.ca/eng/lifeevents/divorce.shtml
This site provides a list of links and information to help understand the legal issues and the process of divorce in Canada.

Ontario Association for Marriage & Family Therapy
www.oamft.on.ca
This site is a resource for marriage and family therapists, as well as for the public interested in finding a therapist in Ontario or finding out about the profession in general.

Canadian Divorce Laws
www.canadiandivorcelaws.com
This site is a guide to the legal situation in Canada, written by a lawyer. It provides access to a library of articles on issues such as child support, child custody, spousal support, property division, divorce procedure, and more.

Ministry of the Attorney General—Family Law
www.attorneygeneral.jus.gov.on.ca/english/family
This site provides the public with comprehensive information about family law, the family court system, and legislation in Ontario.

Stepfamily Network
www.stepfamily.net
This online forum and social networking site supports stepfamilies through sharing and discussion.

Organisation for Economic Co-operation and Development and (OECD) Family Database
www.oecd.org/els/social/family/database
This OECD database includes cross-national information on family outcomes and policies as categorized under four broad headings: the structure of families, the labour market position of families, public policies for families and children, and child outcomes.

Families Change
www.familieschange.ca
This site, developed by the Province of British Columbia, provides easy-to-understand pamphlets and information about separation and divorce for kids, teens, and adults.

Chapter 10
Family Transitions and Innovations
Second Families, Empty Nests, Cluttered Nests, and New Kinds of Families

Marc Debnam/Digital Vision/Thinkstock

Chapter Outline

Learning Objectives

1   Identify different types of family transitions and understand the factors behind them.

2   Characterize the risks involved in family transitions for children, women, men, and lone parents.

3   Understand the risks involved in family transitions for older people.

4   Describe how broader social factors and family characteristics influence various transitions.

5   Understand what role technology plays in family transitions and innovations.

6   Discuss aspects of society that contribute to the development of today's families, sandwich families, cluttered nest families, and others.

7   Describe how social policies contribute to the development of today's families, sandwich families, cluttered nest families, and others.

8   Identify a working definition of *family* that encompasses transitions and innovations.

The transition into parenthood is a perplexing and momentous moment in an individual's life and in the life cycle of families. Transitions to different family situations can be just as challenging and momentous, if not more so. The term *transition* can mean a happy shift to a new family life. Yet some transitions are not fresh starts, but are a stale repetition of an old pattern without much that is new. Some transitions prove impossible. Family transitions can involve reinventing close relations or customizing social ideals about families to best fit one's particular needs and situation.

In Chapter 9, we explored the many challenges posed by family dissolution. In this chapter, we focus on life *after* separation, divorce, or widowhood. We also examine what is possible and what we can learn from the multiple ways in which people make transitions from one kind of family to another as they experience family dissolution, as they age, and as they invent new ways to be familial.

FAMILY TRANSITIONS IN THE PAST

We often think of family transitions as a recent phenomenon. In reality, making fresh starts is nothing new, as we saw in Chapter 2. With the massive flows of refugees and immigrants from strife-torn and, in some cases, poverty-stricken regions in Europe through the first half of the twentieth century, many people started families afresh in North America. And immigrants and refugees are still coming, and they have been joined by people from Africa, Asia, Latin America, and the Caribbean who are fleeing an old life or seeking new opportunities in Canada, Australia, or the United States. Once in Canada, new ways to live in families are worked out, as are ongoing relations with family in the homeland. This is sometimes called living in transnational families.

Fresh starts were more characteristic of families in the past than we sometimes acknowledge today. Higher mortality rates often meant that families experienced the death of one or both spouses or parents while children were still young, creating the need for new living arrangements. Remarriage after the death of a first spouse was frequent, as were stepfamilies, adoption, and fostering children. In some ways, widows in the past were similar to lone mothers today in the economic vulnerability they and their children faced and in the social challenges they posed (Gordon and McLanahan, 1991).

WHAT IS A FAMILY TRANSITION?

A family transition can be characterized by hope and dreams for a wonderful shared future. The strength of this hope is evidenced in social research that shows that most young people expect never to be divorced. This may be indicative of their sense of commitment to a lifelong relationship, but their hopeful expectations may blind them to the known risks of divorce. Any happy young couple on the brink of establishing themselves, whether married or cohabiting, gay/lesbian or heterosexual, is making a fresh start.

In this chapter we discuss second or subsequent starts at families and familial relationships. The processes through which transitions come about are various. It can be a flight from violence, an escape from an abusive practice sanctioned by the prevailing culture, a mutually agreed upon separation or divorce, a death, or myriad other family changes over the life course. It can be a rediscovery of roots and a new basis on which to found and maintain a family, or even a discovery of cultural origins in a new setting or country. It can also involve a personal reinvention to meet an individual's needs.

Family transitions are possible when things do not work out as expected or hoped for the first time around. They provide an adventure through which to explore the complex ways in which people make families afresh and establish close relations.

One of the themes in this text is that families are immensely varied. Perhaps at no point is this clearer than when families experience transition. The multiple pathways of transition include the shrinking of family to its smallest unit—a single-person household with non-household-based families—or to a parent with child. It can also involve non-residential parenting and the development of intricate and large extended-kin or non-kin networks. Another theme is that *family processes* rather than *family types or forms* provide the rewarding focus of family studies. In considering family transitions and innovations, we observe families and individuals actively engaging in family as a process, in designing families anew, in negotiating family, and in striking bargains with former family members on how to endure. Our emphasis here is on family dynamics, wherein lies the active development of new solutions to family challenges.

Multiple Family Starts

With long life expectancies and rapidly changing family dynamics, people may expect to make not one but multiple family transitions over the course of their lives. Think of those who marry or cohabitate after having lived alone or as an adult in the parental home. They have already experienced two kinds of transitions: first, the new ways of being family when they became adults living with parents, and second, marriage or cohabitation. And family transitions are likely to continue throughout their lives, with possible separation, divorce, cohabitation, perhaps remarriage, then possibly widowhood, and maybe another later-life relationship or marriage.

Within each of these family states, phases can mark other kinds of transitions—into parenthood, into or out of working parenthood, from being in a two-earner to a one-earner (or no-earner) family, to grandparenthood, to step-parenthood, and so on. In families today, diversity is the norm, with almost endless possibilities. The **standard North American family (SNAF)** no longer exists. (

[handwritten margin note: -nuclear family)]

Living Solo

Many people who experience the end of a marriage or committed relationship become single before establishing any new family. Some may move directly from one relationship to another, and some stay single with no intimate relationship. Living solo is an option growing in popularity. In 2011, 5 587 165 people age 15 years and over did not live in Census families, representing about one-fifth (20.5 percent) of adults, up slightly from a decade earlier (18.8 percent in 2001). The largest category of non-family living arrangements was living alone, which accounted for 13.5 percent of the population age 15 and over, up from 12.5 percent in 2001 (Statistics Canada, 2012a). The largest proportion living alone was found among respondents age 65 and older; 31.5 percent of women in this age group lived alone in 2011 compared with 33.7 percent in 1981. For men age 65 and older, 16 percent lived alone in 2011. The proportion of older men and women living alone increases with advancing years, but more so for women, who live longer than men and are more likely to be widowed in old age (Statistics Canada, 2012a).

Is singlehood an aspect of family life? Some might respond that a single person living alone is not a family. True enough, but a single person is not necessarily without a family. Most of us have families somewhere, even if we live alone, separated from our spouses or partners. *Family* is not equivalent to *household*. Families and close relations can and do exist, and even thrive, across households. And those households may be spread across the world.

For some, living alone is a transitional stage to a new committed relationship (we will discuss that in a moment). For increasing numbers of North Americans, however, living alone is a life choice, a preference, or better than other alternatives. That said, the diversity of solo living prevents us from making any solid generalizations about it.

Lone-Parent Families

Marital or relationship dissolution can be the start of lone parenthood, but it is not the only pathway. There has been growth in the numbers of people having children without being in a committed couple relationship, either married or cohabitating. Here, we will focus on the more common pathway to lone parenthood—as a result of marriage or relationship breakdown.

Before discussing lone parenthood as a family transition, it is important to shed some light on the perplexing problem of defining lone parents. Typically, estimates of the number of lone parents are based on a one-time sample, such as a census or a survey, and are looked at from the viewpoint of adults. The research question typically asked is this: What proportion of adults at this moment are living in lone-parent families? Four problems, at least, are apparent in this approach.

The first is that it often remains unknown whether the parents surveyed are indeed living on their own or are cohabiting. For example, common-law families are rapidly increasing in number. Between 2006 and 2011, the number of common-law couples in Canada rose 13.9 percent, more than four times the 3.1 percent increase for married couples (Statistics Canada, 2012a). By 2006, the percentage of children aged 15 and younger who lived with lone parents reached 18.3 percent, and from 2006 to 2011 lone-parent families increased 8.0 percent (Statistics Canada, 2012a).

Second, without considering lone parenthood from a life course perspective, it is not possible to see it as a process rather than a state, to see how the experience affects adults and children, and to distinguish between transitional and permanent arrangements. Third, and importantly, examining single parenthood in terms of adult relationships tends to overlook the ways lone parenthood affects children. In Canada, the percentage of children aged 15 and younger who lived with lone parents was 12.4 percent in 1986, 16.0 percent in 1996, and 18.3 percent in 2006, and in 2011 census, lone-parent families represented 16.3 percent of the population (Statistics Canada, 2012a)—a steady increase in the number of children growing up in single-parent households. Women make up the overwhelming majority (80 percent) of lone parents in Canada and are also the most economically disadvantaged families in the country. Female lone-parent families in 2011 accounted for 12.8 percent of all Census families, while male lone-parent families represented 3.5 percent (Statistics Canada, 2012a).

Fourth, and significantly, because the Census collects data on a household basis, rather than by families, it may be that lone-parent households are joint or shared custody families. In these cases, the children may live with both parents, having the benefits of two parents, but not live with them at the same time. This is one of the complexities of *family* not being the same as *household.*

Lone parenthood has increased dramatically in North America in recent decades. This pace of change is not seen in all Western countries, however. In the United States in 2009, single-parent families accounted for 27.3 percent of all families, with 23.6 percent being mother only (U.S. Census Bureau, 2011). The overwhelming majority of lone parents in both Canada and the United States are mothers, although the fastest-growing family type in Canada between 1990 and 2000 was lone-father families (Sauve, 2002: 3). Between 2006 and 2011, lone-father households in Canada increased by 16.2 percent, compared with only a 6 percent jump in those headed by women (Statistics Canada, 2012a). The United States has also seen a growth in single-father families, with the proportion increasing from 2 percent in 1980 to 3.7 percent in 2009 (U.S. Census Bureau, 2011).

The incidence of poverty remains high among lone parents, particularly lone mothers. In 2010, the national median income for lone-parent families was $29 310 (Statistics Canada, 2012b). In Canada in 2008, 21 percent of lone-mother families were below the low-income cutoff, making these families the group with the highest incidence of family poverty in the country (Statistics Canada, 2011). This compares with only 7 percent of lone-father families, and with a poverty rate of 7.4 percent among husband–wife families with children younger than age 18 living at home (Statistics Canada, 2002h: 5). Dooley (1993: 117) found that poverty among lone-mother families is most resistant to remedy. The good-news part of this story is that low income among lone-mother families in Canada dropped from 54 percent in 1976 to 21 percent in 2008 (Statistics Canada, 2011) A drop has also occurred among two-parent families with children, but these families are the least likely to experience poverty (Statistics Canada, 2002h; 2011). Lone mothers experienced a significant increase in employment between 1990 and 2000 and are now more likely to be employed than are wives with children (Sauve, 2002: 3–4).

But the news on lone mothers in poverty is not all good. Among lone mothers still in poverty, the depth of their poverty may have increased. Affordable housing shortages over recent decades and changes in work options have posed big problems. "Among the surging number of single mothers who have taken refuge in temporary shelters [recently] are an entirely new class of homeless—formerly secure career women," notes Gadd (1997: D1). Statistics Canada does not collect data on homelessness, but studies done by others such as the Canadian Homelessness Research Network (2013) suggest that women with children, particularly lone mothers, may be the fastest growing group of the homeless.

Many women with dependent children tumble into poverty when their marriage or union ends. This occurs for a number of interconnected reasons. Marriage, in our society, is still a presumed economic alliance between a man who can earn more and a woman who is economically subordinate or dependent while devoting herself to child-bearing and child rearing (Townsend, 2002). Or, marriage enables the pooling of incomes of two adults, thereby raising the family income considerably. What Townsend calls "the package deal" of marriage, however, is still prevalent. Evidence of this can be found in women's emphasis on dating sites on their appearance, while men's self-descriptions focus more on their economic security or job. When the marriage ends, women find (as noted in Chapter 9) that the initial disparity between income and potential income has widened. As well, a woman with young dependent children and perhaps less work experience, less training or education, and sole responsibility for children may not seem like a good prospect to an employer. And on separation, the considerable benefits of having the combined incomes of two earners no longer exist.

With the added challenge of finding affordable housing, lone mothers can quickly become poor, and tend to remain so, with disadvantages both for themselves and for their children (Gazso and McDaniel, 2010b). Not surprisingly, the consequences to men of divorce are seldom as financially bleak.

As discussed in Chapter 6, children in lone-parent families are known to suffer both directly from the disadvantage of their family situations—particularly poverty—and from society, which stigmatizes them and expects less from them. Of course, the bigger impact issue for children in lone-parent families is poverty, not the family form itself. The two forces of stigma (which is decreasing as the numbers of lone-parent families increase) and poverty work together to create lower achievement prospects that can become self-fulfilling. These factors, though powerful, are not deterministic. Many children from lone-parent families achieve at high levels indeed, among them Barack Obama and Barbara Streisand, to cite but two world-famous examples. Other successful achievers from lone-parent families surround us every day. Nonetheless, making opportunities and countering lingering stigmas is often not easy for mothers, the children themselves, or society.

The benefits of living in a lone-parent family, for both mothers and their children, are not to be discounted. Among other things, they may learn the value of independence, invention and innovation, self-reliance, and mutual interdependence, and they may learn to value women in a world that too often fails to do so (Ferri, 1993). Children from disadvantaged situations where love persists can learn to persevere, to aim high in their expectations, and to deny short term gratification for long-term gain. A very interesting international comparative study (Bradshw et al., 2011) found that well-being of children is associated with material and housing circumstances, and not family structure.

Latchkey children is a term used to refer to children who are regularly left for some part of the day without adult supervision, epitomizing both the best and the worst of resilience. Not all latchkey children are from lone-parent families. Many are from two-income families where no one is home when they return from school each day. Both good and bad consequences were found for latchkey children in one study (Leung, Robson, Cho, and Lim, 1996). Benefits include learning to be independent and responsible (Nicholas, 2009), as well as acquiring useful life skills such as how to start dinner for the family or how to grocery shop. Among the drawbacks are loneliness, fear, boredom, underachievement in school, and perhaps an increased likelihood of drug or alcohol abuse.

In recent decades, lone mothers in the United States, and even in Canada, have been the targets for cutbacks to social assistance (welfare in the United States) and vicious public labels such as "welfare queens." Lone-parent families have continued to pose perplexing problems for policy-makers because of the persistent poverty of some—particularly lone-mother—families (Mather, 2010). It is, in large part, because the rise in lone-mother families has contributed to increased poverty that policy light has been focused on lone mothers. One of the most prevalent misconceptions is the presumption that children in lone-mother families are parented only by their mothers. Increasingly, children who are listed in official data such as censuses as living in lone-mother households have regular contact with fathers in joint custody arrangements. Families in these situations stretch across two households, but parenting is shared and contact with fathers maintained. As well, a growing share of children in what are counted as lone mother households actually have parents living in the home common-law (Mather, 2010).

The mosaic of lone-parent families—with different ethnic mixes, some parents divorced or separated and others never married or cohabiting, some long-term and others transitory lone parents—is challenging for policy-makers. Policy needs to acknowledge the very different pathways to lone motherhood and the particular needs of both mothers and children in different types of lone-parent families.

Many countries, including Canada and the United States, have had long-standing policies that explicitly or implicitly treat women and children as the responsibilities of husbands and fathers (Baker, 1995: 13; Korpi, Ferrarini, and Englund, 2013; Mather, 2010). This persists, and actually has gained in strength recently, as governments downsize and expect families to do more and more. Only when family support fails do states believe they must act, reluctantly and under pressure. Most often, fathers with low income themselves simply cannot provide child support. In the United States, where there are very high incarceration rates of young African American men, additional problems with child support arise. State family policies have ranged from providing incentives to lone mothers to parent full-time, as in the Netherlands, to offering incentives for them to work in the paid labour force, as in Sweden and Australia (Baker, 1995; Korpi, Ferrarini, and Englund, 2013), to apprehending children at risk in Aboriginal families (Castellano, 2002). In the United States there are explicit policies aimed at strengthening and promoting marriage as a solution to poverty among lone-mother families (Mather, 2010). Generally, policies in European countries are more generous to lone-parent families, as a result of greater gender equality in the workforce and more accessible and affordable child-care support for working mothers (Crompton and Lyonette, 2006; Korpi, Ferrarini, and Englund, 2013). This, in turn, enables parents to maintain a better work–life balance.

Behind social policies oriented to lone-parent families are three models. The first is the *private family approach*, characterized by the United Kingdom and the United States, where family is believed to be a private institution that ought to look after itself, with the state stepping in only on a casualty basis (Korpi, Ferrarini, and Englund, 2013; Lesemann and Nicol, 1994: 117). This contrasts with the *family-oriented model* (France and Quebec), which sees the government as having a public interest in families. The third is the *state-based model* (Sweden and Nordic countries), which sees state intervention as important not to help families but to promote socio-economic participation and gender equality as fully as possible. Canada is caught between these models, using a little of each in its approach to policies for lone parents.

Much recent attention has been devoted to moving lone mothers away from social assistance (Gazso and McDaniel, 2010b). An interesting and innovative Canadian study of 150 single mothers on social assistance found that lone mothers on social assistance in Canada are actively involved in an extensive range of social and economic strategies to exit social assistance. They are realistic and hopeful about the possibilities but feel that they could benefit from useful supports and information. Indeed, the main predictors of successful exits are social supports, including information, and the women's aspirations (Gorlick and Pomfret, 1993). Other research has found that there are negatives to welfare-to-work programs for those who participate in them on a mandatory basis (Gazso and McDaniel, 2010b).

A study of women on social assistance in Niagara Falls, Canada, provides a different understanding of poverty from the perspective of those who are poor. The participants described life on social assistance alike to "living under a giant microscope" (Collins, 2005: 22), where the perception of constant surveillance translates into feelings of guilt about "every little" purchase or action and also means the loss of many freedoms. "Freedom to spend, freedom to have a good time, freedom to voice an opinion, freedom to work and freedom to make sensible decisions ('sometimes have to go against good budgeting sense to follow the rules') are all identified" as sacrifices that must be made in order to live on social assistance. For these families, the successful exit out of poverty is impeded by their loss of autonomy, lowered self-esteem, and the cyclical nature of stress and money shortage (Collins, 2005).

Seeking Parenthood on One's Own

The largest growth in child-bearing outside of marriage or cohabiting relationships in Canada is occurring among women in their early thirties (Statistics Canada, 2013). Overall rates of never married women in Canada have risen substantially in Canada, with an 8 percent increase from 2010 to 2011 (Statistics Canada, 2013). The exception is the rate of births to teens, which in Canada had been falling (Dryburgh, 2001; Statistics Canada, 2013), but between 2010 and 2011 saw a modest increase. The teen pregnancy rate in the United States is also decreasing, but remains more than double that of Canada: In 2008, the rate of teenage births in Canada was 4.2 percent (Statistics Canada, 2012c) compared with the U.S. rate of 10.4 percent (US Census Bureau, 2012).

If mature women are having births without being in couple relationships as they are in Canada, several factors could be at work. There could be accidental pregnancies, as there always are. More women who accidentally become pregnant now choose to keep and raise their babies instead of giving them up for adoption. This is a deliberate choice in favour of motherhood, even if the conception itself may not have been planned. There is also evidence that some women are seeking motherhood on their own without the traditional step of marriage or being in a committed relationship.

Few studies have looked at unmarried lone mothers—women who *begin* single parenthood without being married or in a union at all. This is a subject of greater research interest in the United States than in Canada since the rate of never-married lone mothers is much higher there and takes place at earlier ages. One study (Clark, 1993) found that the social and economic costs of unmarried single motherhood are evident 10 years after the first child is born. Although there are no effects on likelihood of marrying, the risks of poverty are greater than for married mothers (Dryburgh, 2001). As well, there is lessened opportunity to pursue education, thus further disadvantaging the unmarried mothers (Mather, 2010). As the children grow, however, the initial discrepancies between unmarried and married mothers decrease. The woman's age at first unmarried motherhood matters greatly: The younger she is, the greater the disadvantage and the less likely she is to catch up later on. Children born to younger unattached mothers do less well in school and on IQ tests than other children.

In deliberately seeking motherhood alone, options exist today that did not exist previously. Some of these options were introduced in Chapter 3. With the stigma lessened of having a child outside marriage, it may not be surprising that some women are opting for it. This may be a generation of women who have been taught to get what they aim for in life, rather than waiting for all their dreams to fall into place by luck or chance. Some are successful, educated career women who know their own minds and have the resources to raise a child on their own. Others may have been infertile earlier in their lives or not in situations where they wanted to have children, but had not given up their dreams of motherhood. Options include the reproductive technologies of **artificial insemination** and **in vitro fertilization**, informal means to access sperm for conception, private adoptions, and foreign adoptions.

Let's look first at adoption, although in reality women often look at adoption only after considering the option of giving birth. Not long ago, adoption was carefully controlled by churches and the government. For good or for bad, it was thought that adoptive parents should be married and matched in religion, region, and ethnicity/race as much as possible to the adopted child. This left out single women, single men, cohabiting couples, and lesbians and gays. It also often left out the non-religious. Adoption has opened up considerably in recent years, most notably in private adoptions whereby the birth mother (or parents) can know and sometimes select the adoptive family for the baby/child. More single people have been able to adopt children too, although the waiting lists are lengthy and the screening tight and sometimes judgmental about lifestyle.

A new option that has provided opportunities for couples and single women and men wishing to adopt is foreign adoptions. These occur for numerous reasons. Strife and disruption in various world regions have created unwanted babies and children, either as war orphans or as a result of policies, such as the forbidding of birth control and abortion in Romania a few years ago. The one-child policy in China has led to numbers of babies, primarily girls, being adopted by Canadians and others, as many Chinese choose, for cultural reasons, to have a boy if they can have only one child (Dorow, 2002). There is concern that some babies or children are being taken from their parents for the lucrative foreign adoption market or brought into the world for the purposes of the adoption market. It is not fully known whether this occurs and, if so, to what extent.

Foreign adoption has meant that more Canadians and Americans can adopt if there are fewer babies and children available for adoption within their own country. Motivation for seeking foreign adoption can be humanitarian. International adoption can be costly and time-consuming, with lengthy screening and often frustrating international negotiations, but it is possible for people to become the adoptive parent of a child born elsewhere.

The number of children adopted from international agencies in 2010 was slightly lower than previous years. Figures released by Citizenship and Immigration Canada (CIC) show that in 2010, 1946 children from abroad found homes in Canada compared to 2122 the year before (see Figure 10.1). This 8 percent drop is still within the long-term average of 2000 children per year who find a family in Canada. China continued to provide the highest number of adoptees in 2010 with 472 children (Hilborn, 2011)

New reproductive technologies (NRTs) have also opened possibilities for single people, as well as gay and lesbian couples, to have children of their own. For example,

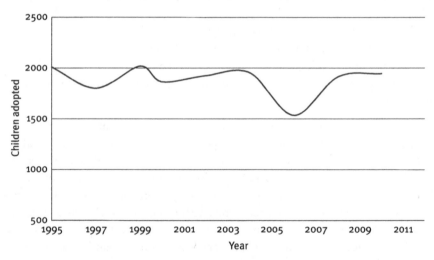

Figure 10.1 Canadians Go Abroad to Adopt, 2010

Source: Robin Hilborn, ed., 2011. "Canadians go abroad to adopt 1,946 children in 2010." Retrieved December 2012 from Family Helper www.familyhelper.net, www.familyhelper.net/news/111027stats.html.

artificial insemination has been used for a long time. It has not been routinely discussed until recently, however. In 2004, Canadian legislation made surrogate motherhood for pay illegal. It still occurs, though, with surrogates hired outside Canada. India is a favoured country for surrogates (Deomampo, 2013). *In vitro fertilization*, or test-tube conception, has a low success rate but has been used to help women and couples conceive if one or both has fertility problems. These technologies have created new families and challenged the bases on which nuclear families have traditionally been built. NRTs have also led to legal wrangles about parenthood and citizenship rights and responsibilities (Kr/>løkke, Foss, and Pant, 2012).

Feminists have long been concerned about the implications of NRTs for women (see McDaniel, 1988, for example). Many issues have been raised, from exploitation of poor women as reproducers, to issues of citizenship, to rights and parental responsibilities. Fertility, it has been suggested, becomes commodified with NRTs (Krøløkke, Foss, and Pant, 2012), with bioethical implications as well as questions of what are called "fragmentary bodies": Egg donors, gestational mothers, sperm donors, and legal mothers and fathers may not be clearly defined, so that parenting becomes contested territory.

Changing families and reproductive technologies have led to new types of fatherhood, too. Eichler (1997: 72) notes that there are now nine kinds of fathers, perhaps more:

- biological, social, exclusive, full fathers
- non-biological but social, exclusive, full fathers
- biological but not social fathers
- biological, social, exclusive, partial fathers (where the father is non-custodial)
- biological, social, non-exclusive (where the mother has a new partner), partial fathers
- non-biological but social, exclusive, partial fathers
- non-biological but social, non-exclusive, partial fathers
- gay co-fathers, non-biological, social, non-exclusive fathers
- post-mortem biological fathers (where the man's sperm is taken for impregnation after his death)

Gay and lesbian couples, who have been able to legally marry in every province in Canada since 2005, can legally adopt in Canada (Davis, 2013). They can also adopt children in some U.S. states, such as Florida (Goldberg et al., 2010). The evidence shows that children adopted by gays and lesbians do pretty well the same as other adopted children (Sullivan, 2012). Such families have values similar to those of heterosexual couples and raise their children in accordance with those values. Of course, some outside of gay and lesbian families may discriminate or have trouble with gay families. The bulk of the evidence suggests that most people accept and come around to approve of these families with children.

Not much is known about men seeking fatherhood outside marriage or committed relationships. It is not known how many men, on their own, are seeking fatherhood. It might be anticipated, however, that as men's self-images with respect to families and fatherhood change, more men might seek to have children outside of marriage or a committed relationship. It also might be predicted that, even with contemporary social changes, fewer men than women would deliberately seek single parenthood (Townsend, 2002). Practices such as surrogate motherhood (whereby a woman agrees to conceive and gestate a baby for a fee), where available, are more readily accessible to men, given their greater average purchasing powers. As mentioned above, paid surrogacy is illegal in Canada.

PARENTING WITHOUT LIVING TOGETHER

When spouses separate, divorce, or part ways, the important question arises of who will assume responsibilities for the children in the new families that emerge. Custody decisions are often amicable and made by the couple without resort to the courts, but also can be the basis for immensely heated emotions, nasty court battles, and highly charged policy forums. The latter have been seen in Canada far too often. Successful fresh starts following divorce or separation can depend on custody arrangements being satisfactory for all family members involved. Custody involves the children's entire well-being, including day-to-day care, control, and protection, instilling of values, and future opportunities. Custody issues often connect to, and overlap with, issues of access to children by the non-custodial parent as well as issues of child support.

Joint custody (also called co-parenting) is rapidly increasing in both Canada and the United States. Some feminists (Drakich, 1993; Eichler, 1997, for example) think, however, that it is unlikely to work successfully except in those cases where the marriage breakdown was amicable. Joint custody requires ongoing negotiations in good faith by both partners, and the capacity of each to have the best interests of the children at heart. The child(ren) can continue to be socially parented by both parents, which can help their development and their adjustment to the disruption of the separation and divorce. However, if the mother and father have different standards of living (as they often do), the kids may blame one or the other for the relative deprivation the child endures in that household. If Mom and Dad live in different regions, there can be a lot of travel back and forth, creating a sense of rootlessness for the child. And if the child has regular contact with both parents but the parents don't coordinate their parental roles well, the child can play one parent against the other. A major challenge for divorced families is that there is no clear model for non-residential parenting. The relation of parenting to custody issues is, in part, what makes custody such a political hot button, particularly for men's rights groups.

REMARRIAGE OR COHABITATION

Most divorced people remarry (Baker, 1996, Richardson, 2001) or form a new union. As mentioned in Chapter 9, in Canada, excluding Quebec, approximately 70 percent of men and 58 percent of women marry again following divorce (Ambert, 2005b). (The most recent data on marriages collected by Statistics Canada is for 2004.) Remarriage of divorced people is so common now that some see it as normative. Called "conjugal succession," "recycling the family" (Richardson, 2001: 231), or serial monogamy, it seems here to stay.

In the United States, more people marry, divorce, and remarry than in Canada (Richardson, 2001; Statistics Canada, 2002a). Although still popular, the overall rate of remarriage has declined a little in Canada recently, corresponding with the lower marriage rate. In fact, in 2006, more than half of divorced Canadians did not have intentions to remarry (see Figure 10.2; Beaupré, 2008). One explanation is that people are opting for cohabitation over remarriage.

When cohabitation is taken into account, the number of fresh starts at intimate unions may be even higher. It is difficult to determine levels of cohabitation, since, unlike marriage, cohabitation has no clear start and finish date. Language is also elusive: These unions may be described as common law, living together, trial marriage, in French as **"union libre,"** or by slang terms such as "shacking up." Whether these terms connote similar kinds of living arrangements is far from clear. No matter how definitions are spelled out on surveys and census forms, people's own self- and social definitions of what is and is not cohabitation come into play in their responses. In 2006, about 30 percent of divorced people were living in common-law unions. Further, data show that intentions to remarry decrease with age (Beaupré, 2008). The trend is toward a preference for common-law unions after the marital dissolution, reflecting an overall increase in this form of union.

More divorced men than women remarry (see Figure 10.2b), and the likelihood of remarrying following divorce is reduced if one has children, particularly for women. Children limit the time available for searching for a marriage partner and may also deter potential partners. It seems that men may be uncomfortable with taking on the stepfather role or are unwilling to provide financially for someone else's child (Goldscheider, Kaufman, and Sassler, 2009). That said, one of 10 children in Canada in 2011 lived in stepfamilies, measured for the first time on the 2011 short-form census (Statistics Canada, 2012a).

But regardless of the form, most people do enter a new intimate partnership. More than anything else, the extent of new unions after divorce underlines people's desire to have committed, emotionally involving relationships. Divorce rates would mark a decline in family only if most divorced people stayed single. Of course, some do stay single—in increasing numbers, in fact.

Less is known about remarriage after widowhood, but generally it is less common than remarriage after divorce (Connidis, 2001: 108). In large part, this may simply be that divorce tends to occur earlier in life than widowhood. One Canadian study (Wu, 1995), using event history analysis, found that men are almost twice as likely to remarry as women, with particularly high rates for high-income men. This is not surprising given that women tend to outlive men. Men who are widowed would have a larger pool of potential mates than women who are widowed. Prospects for remarriage of widows and widowers have dropped recently, particularly for young widowers (Nault and Belanger, 1996: 11). The drop was less for young widows. Nault and Belanger (1996: 13) conclude,

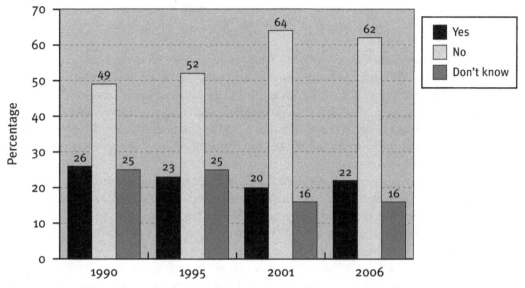

(a) More than half of divorced Canadians stated that they do not intend to remarry.

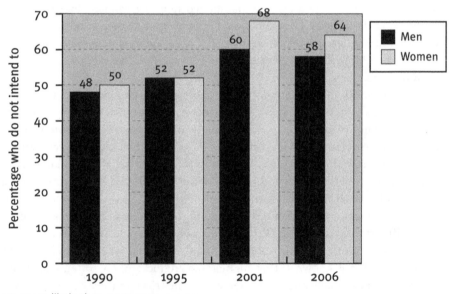

(b) Men are more likely than women to remarry.

Figure 10.2 Changes in Intentions to Remarry Among Divorced Canadians

Source: Pascale Beaupré. 2008. "I do . . . Take two? Changes in intentions to remarry among divorced Canadians during the past 20 years," *The General Social Survey: Matter of Fact no. 5.* Ottawa: Statistics Canada. Catalogue no. 89-630-X.

"The chances of widowed persons remarrying are consequently much lower, in particular for women who at older ages find themselves facing a marriage market strongly slanted against them."

Second marriages, as we noted in Chapter 9, have a higher risk of divorce than do first marriages. The reasons for this could be many. When couples marry or form a committed relationship, they begin a process of "social construction of marriage," by which they create together their own shared traditions and memories. Over time, they create a new definition of themselves in relation to the world around them. When a marriage ends, this social construction of self-identity in relation to marriage becomes shaky but it is not forgotten.

In remarrying, new and different social constructions must be developed through negotiation of new social roles and divisions of labour. The shadow of the past relationship always provides implicit comparisons. When children are involved, the increased number of relationships and the need to maintain an ongoing relationship with the ex-spouse can make remarriage even more challenging.

Little is known about the extent to which obligations to extended family members remain after divorce and remarriage. One of the few studies that has looked at this found that the divorce of either younger or older generations in families tends to magnify the gendered nature of family responsibilities (Connidis, 2001). Contacts with extended family members continue but are maintained more by women than by men. Another study found that among 190 women and 93 men who divorced and remarried, most feel that they are obligated to help family members in need, if possible (Coleman, Ganong, and Cable, 1997). They perceive their obligations to the younger generation as stronger than those to elders.

The majority of couples succeed in meeting the challenges of a second marriage (Birditt and Antonucci, 2012). What works is, not surprisingly, similar to what works in a successful first marriage: good communication, realistic expectations, honesty, and a shared sense of humour. Meyerstein (1997) suggests that advance preparation is highly useful in a good second marriage. It helps to recognize that a second marriage is not the same as a first and that the first marriage cannot be repressed and forgotten but should be mined for lessons learned. Beyond these sensible approaches, the couple needs to work to develop the marital relationship and to establish and maintain the new loyalties to each other (Birditt and Antonucci, 2012; Kheshgi-Genovese and Genovese, 1997).

The transitions and innovations of immigrant families is an understudied field in sociology. What is known is that immigrants are more likely to remarry than are non-immigrants, most likely due to a preference for marriage in their culture, as well as other factors such as financial dependency (Berger, 2000). However, King (2007) recently found that children from immigrant families are significantly less close to their step-mothers than are non-immigrant children, although the reasons are unclear. Perhaps immigrant children also hold cultural values regarding sustained marriage and may therefore negatively view remarriage and their father's new spouse.

- In 2005, almost one-third (31 percent) of children between the ages of 10 and 17 in Canada experienced the separation of their parents (Robinson, 2009).

- In 2011, married-couple families made up 67 percent of all families in Canada, while common-law couples rose 13.9 percent to represent 16.7 percent, and lone parents increased 8 percent, representing 16.3 percent of all families (Statistics Canada, 2012a).

- Between 2006 and 2011, the number of male-headed lone-parent families increased by 16.2 percent in Canada, compared with 6 percent among those headed by women. However, lone mothers still make up 78.9 percent of lone parents in Canada (Statistics Canada, 2012a).

- In 2011, 59.3 percent of all young adults aged 20 to 24 lived with their parents, about the same as in 2006 (59.5 percent) but higher than the 41.5 percent who did so in 1981. For 25- to 29-year-olds, one-quarter (25.2 percent) lived with their parents in 2011, up slightly from 24.7 percent in 2006, and more than double the 11.3 percent in 1981 (Statistics Canada, 2012d).

- Senior men are much more likely to live with a spouse. This was the most common type of living arrangement for senior men aged 85 and older (38 percent) in Canada in 2011, while it was the least frequent for senior women of the same age (7 percent; Turcotte and Schellenberg, 2006).

- Cohabiting couples who experience an increase in earnings have greater odds of subsequent marriage. Cohabiting couples who become poor, on the other hand, are associated with a 37 percent decrease in marriage likelihood (Gibson-Davis, 2009).

- From the 2011 Canadian Census, it was possible for the first time to classify Census families comprised of couples with children as either intact families or stepfamilies. Of the 3 684 675 couple families with children in 2011, 87.4 percent were intact families and 12.6 percent were stepfamilies (Statistics Canada, 2012a).

The Challenges of Blended/Stepfamilies

Blended families are remarried or cohabiting families in which one or both partners brings children into the new relationship (Statistics Canada, 2002a: 6; 2012a). The terminology of blended families is as challenging as that for cohabiting couples. The terms *blended* or *reconstituted* make new families sound almost strange, in contrast to "regular" families. One suggestion is the term **binuclear family** (Church, 1996: 83), which also has drawbacks.

Making stepfamilies is not easy or straightforward (Allan, Crow, and Hawkers, 2011). Even the language is perplexing: What should a child call step-parents? How should a child refer to the children of the step-parent? There is also the contemporary reality of biological fathers and mothers who are often a continuing part of the child's life. The child may make comparisons between the two "mothers" or "fathers," or play one against the other, or deny that the step-parent is really a parent after all. Step-parents, too, may make comparisons, experience self-doubts about their parenting, or find that the necessary ongoing relationship with the absent parent is challenging.

With the trend toward joint custody—or co-parenting responsibilities—children may be shuffled back and forth between the homes of parents (Ackerman, 1996; Allan, Crow, and Hawkers, 2011). This can create a sense of rootlessness and possibly insecurity. It can also make for a mad rush as children fit in living in different homes along with all the many other demands of childhood (school, sports, music lessons, often language or religious classes, and so on). Children can also resent that one stepsibling gets to go off for what may appear as a holiday for a period while he or she cannot. Or the child may resent the presence of a stepsibling in what they consider "their" domain (Richardson, 2001: 233).

A particular challenge of life in blended families is the sharing of children at special family events, such as Christmas, Chanukah, or Ramadan (Allan, Crow, and Hawkers, 2011). Children we may think of as ours are away at the other parent's place for some holidays, which creates the need for regular negotiations and close collaboration among the various parents and their other family members. Some parents, too, may deeply feel the absence of their children at important family times.

Family research is helpful in identifying what works successfully in blended families. A popular research strategy is to compare second families with so-called "intact" families. This research design has its problems in that the two kinds of families may not be comparable. Using intact families as an implicit standard may lead to inappropriate and pre-judicial comparisons. Members of blended families may have been through family disruption and, for good or bad, have learned strategies for dealing with problems, while intact families may not have had such lessons. In addition, while first families may follow the examples of their own families of origin, blended or stepfamilies may be breaking new territory, making up the rules as they live through experiences.

Nonetheless, the findings of what works well bear sharing. A significant predictor of success is the degree of focus on the children themselves. Another important factor is the consensus on parenting between the new spouse and the child's parent (Allan, Crow, and Hawkers, 2011; Saintjacques, 1995). Preparation for the step-parent role is also important. Accept the reality that both the new spouse and stepchildren had a previous family life that did not, and never can, include the step-parent (Allan, Crow, and Hawkers, 2011; Richardson, 2001: 232). Step-parents also need to recognize that they ultimately have limited control over whether the child(ren) accept them. Trying too hard can be a mistake.

Step-parenting can be stressful, and stepmothering is more challenging than step-fathering (Allan, Crow, and Hawkers, 2011; Morrison and Thompson-Guppy with Bell, 1986). We all seem to have a vivid image of the wicked stepmother from fairy tales. In addition, women have traditionally borne the major responsibilities for child care and child rearing, meaning more contact with stepchildren and more points at which to encounter tender feelings on both sides.

Two forces tend to draw lone parents to remarry: First, there is the desire to escape from the "cheerless life" of the lone parent; and second, "the widespread view in Western societies that the nuclear family is the proper setting in which to bring up children" (Allan, Crow, and Hawkers, 2011; Collins, 1991: 159), or what Church (1996: 87) refers to as filling the "kin vacuum." Recognition in the light of day that lone parenthood has distinct advantages, and that the nuclear family is not all that it is deemed to be for children or for anyone else, gets crowded out by the power of ideological beliefs that "order" must be restored to what is seen as a deviant family form. In deciding whether to make the transition to step-parenthood or blended family, lone mothers must balance the roles of mother and woman, and are influenced by the "herd" notion that marriage or being part of a couple relationship must be good because most people do it.

From the child's viewpoint, there may be a need to establish new relationships with the step-parent, and perhaps with stepsiblings, but also with both the custodial and non-custodial parent, as all the relationships adjust to the new family arrangement.

Famous Quotes on Marriage

Marriage is the triumph of imagination over intelligence. Second marriage is the triumph of hope over experience.

—Oscar Wilde

A successful marriage requires falling in love many times, always with the same person.

—Mignon McLaughlin

As to marriage or celibacy, let a man take the course he will. He will be sure to repent.

—Socrates

When people get married because they think it's a long-time love affair, they'll be divorced very soon, because all love affairs end in disappointment. But marriage is a recognition of a spiritual identity.

—Joseph Campbell

I have yet to hear a man ask for advice on how to combine marriage and a career.

—Gloria Steinhem

Sir, if you were my husband, I would poison your drink.

—Lady Astor to Winston Churchill

Madam, if you were my wife, I would drink it.

—Churchill's reply

I've sometimes thought of marrying, and then I've thought again.

—Noel Coward, 1956

Men marry women with the hope they will never change. Women marry men with the hope they will change. Invariably they are both disappointed.

—Albert Einstein

After marriage, husband and wife become two sides of a coin; they just can't face each other, but still they stay together.

—Hemant Joshi

Bigamy is having one wife too many. Monogamy is the same.

—Oscar Wilde

Love is blind, marriage is the eye-opener.

—Pauline Thomason

By all means, marry. If you get a good wife, you'll become happy; if you get a bad one, you'll become a philosopher.

—Socrates

I was married by a judge. I should have asked for a jury.

—Groucho Marx

Source: www.etni.org.il/quotes/marriage.htm.

The development and ultimate success of these relationships depend on conceptions of who is family and who is not. Shared parenting can produce a broader and sometimes more accepting view of what family is and can be. Where there is a distinct difference in socio-economic status between the homes of the two parents, there can be ambivalence and even guilt, which can cause the child to wonder about families and gender, but can also expand the child's horizons.

Discontinuity of relationships between children in blended families and their grandparents has been the subject of research recently. It is of growing policy and legal importance as grandparents increasingly assert rights to access. Studies show that grandparents (mostly paternal grandparents) are most at risk of losing contact with their grandchildren (Kruk, 1995; Ahrons and Tanner, 2003). Low rates of contact occur when the grandparent is related to the children's non-resident parent, or when the children live with a step-parent (Lussier, Deater-Deckard, Dunn, and Davies, 2002). The primary mediators in ongoing grandparent/grandchild relationships are the daughters-in-law. Disrupted contact is found to have adverse consequences for the grandparents. The consequences for grandchildren are less known. Yet a continuous relationship with grandparents can be of benefit, particularly when the grandparents themselves have a stable relationship. They can set positive examples and serve as a source of stability (Milan and Hamm, 2003).

WIDOWHOOD

Widowhood is an expectable life event. Given the difference between men's and women's life expectancies, a woman who marries or establishes a lasting relationship can realistically anticipate that she will be left a widow. The good news, however, is that widowhood is occurring later than it used to (Connidis, 2001: 93; Moore and Rosenberg, 1997: 31). In Canada, almost 80 percent of women age 85 and older are widowed, while even at age 70 to 74, 40 percent are widowed. In contrast, 39.5 percent of men age 85 and older are married, compared to only 7.2 percent of women the same age.

Older women, mainly widows, are much more likely than men to change their living arrangements late in life. Usually, these changes are related to health status, but they also relate to family. A man with health problems more often has a built-in caregiver at home, his wife, while a woman with health problems, even at the same age, is less likely to have that benefit. Hence, she is more likely to move in with relatives or into an institution.

Myths abound about widows. Mainly they are seen as sad and depressed. Depression does strike some, and at times it is debilitating. But it is not the only reality for widows. Eighteen months or so after the spouse's death, most widows are ready to start life over for themselves (Gee and Kimball, 1987: 90). Most often this means reaching out to friends, siblings, adult children, and others such as clergy or even lawyers. Some develop active new hobbies or interests. Contact with their peers seems to provide the most satisfaction for widows. Some even note that this is the first time that they have felt independent and that they enjoy it (Connidis, 2001: 96).

The death of a long-term partner for gay and lesbian couples poses different problems. The sense of loss may be similar, but the lack of institutionalized acceptance of gay and lesbian relationships may make for less strong support (Connidis, 2001: 96). On top of this challenge is the prevalence of AIDS among gay men, the stigma involved, and the reality that more bereaved partners will be left behind. There can also be losses of others in the gay network, intensifying the sense of loss and grief.

FAMILY TRANSITIONS IN MID- AND LATER LIFE

Most research on family transitions focuses on people younger than age 50. But with increasing life expectancy and divorce likelihood, the proportions of those older than age 65 who are divorced has risen. In 2001, approximately 6 percent of both men and women aged 65 and older in Canada were divorced, compared with 1 percent for both in 1971 (Statistics Canada, 2002j). People older than 50 remarry with increasing frequency and establish new cohabiting families as well. In Canada, a relatively small percentage of older people remarry or enter their senior years remarried. However, among those divorced or widowed at younger ages, a majority of men and a substantial minority of women eventually remarry (Connidis, 2001: 111).

Some older couples who are alone after widowhood or divorce may choose to cohabit but keep separate households in order to maintain continuity in their living arrangements and to avoid fuss by their offspring about loyalties and inheritance (Borell and Karlsson, 2002). A study in France (Caradec, 1997: 65) of conjugal arrangements among those age 60 and older found "a great diversity of conjugal lifestyles: some couples live together in marriage, some outside marriage (showing that cohabitation is not reserved for the young in age), and others have adopted more novel forms of union, intermittent or alternating cohabitation." Borell and Karlsson (2002) found similar innovative living arrangements among older people in Sweden. And similar diversity of living arrangements among older people in Canada is apparent (Statistics Canada, 2012a).

Another family transition found in later life may be when grandparents take on a custodial or a near-parental role of their grandchildren (Thomas, 2012). This transition can be extremely stressful for both grandparents and grandchildren. Most grandparents become caregivers of their grandchildren during a divorce, teen pregnancy, drug abuse, health concerns, or incarceration of parents. Grandparents may resent the fact that in their later years they must once again deal with parenting young children, but also may have the added stress of dealing with the problems of their own children as well (Lumpkin, 2008: 358; Thomas, 2012). Lumpkin found that grandparents who serve as primary or near-custodial parents experienced more stress, more financial problems, poor physical health, limitations on activities, and depression (Lumpkin, 2008: 359). More research is needed as custodial and near-custodial grandparents become part of a bigger trend for dual-income families and grandparents who are healthier, more independent, and living longer.

Living apart together (LAT) is growing in popularity in Canada (Statistics Canada, 2013). LATs are not only for high-powered couples but also for those who wish companionship without the traditional arrangement of sharing a home full-time. When LAT relationships were discussed in a large family sociology class by one of your authors (McDaniel) in fall 2002, several students mentioned that one of their parents had arrangements with a partner similar to those found in France and Sweden by researchers. And the students thought that these were happy and clever ways to be a couple. LATs may catch on as the current university-age generation ages and as partners in close relationships cannot find jobs in the same area.

This may suggest two things: first, as Caradec (1997: 65) argues, an **intergenerational contagion** whereby non-marital unions have become diffused from young to old; and second, the need for different people—in this case, people at different stages in the life course—to customize relationships to fit their particular needs. Available statistical data routinely collected by censuses, vital statistics, or social surveys may not truly capture the immense diversity possible in family living arrangements, much as they work to do so.

GAY/LESBIAN FAMILIES

There have always been gay fathers and lesbian mothers. In the past with attitudes being very different than today, gay or lesbian people often became parents in a heterosexual marriage or relationship, then came out subsequently as gay or lesbian. What is newer is

Diversity among gay and lesbian families exists as well. Whether they are publicly open about their relationship is a significant step.
BananaStock/Thinkstock

gay and lesbian *families*, increasingly accepted by society (Sullivan, 2012), with policy entitlements and protections under family law (Goldberg et al., 2013). Gay and lesbian couples more often now decide to have children together and raise them as a family unit. Gay and lesbian couples that form after the end of a heterosexual relationship or marriage are also living as a family with the children of one or both partners. At present in Canada, a majority of gay/lesbian families with children had these children with a heterosexual ex-spouse (Arnup, 2012). However, more gay/lesbian couples are deciding to have children through adoption or various other means. Lesbian couples deciding to give birth to a child must negotiate which one will become pregnant and then agree on the process. For our purposes, we discuss gay and lesbian parents raising children in families, however they formed, as well as gay and lesbian couples in committed relationships.

The significance of these new kinds of families cannot be underestimated. They are transforming the ways families are measured, as witnessed by the change in definition of family on the 2001 Census of Canada to include same-sex common-law unions (Statistics Canada, 2002c). And family laws and policies in Canada, as well as workplace policies, have largely been widened to include same-sex families.

Same-sex families have transformed thinking about families theoretically. An entirely new way to theorize close relations, *queer theory*, has grown out of this line of inquiry. Identities, relationships, even politics are seen as less fixed and more social (Lehr, 1999). Queer theory argues that we *perform* gender, like a concert by Michael Jackson or Madonna, on a social stage, and in doing so, we change ourselves and society (Walters, 1999: 250). This gives both power and insight to people and to family theorists and researchers. In this way, same-sex families are really an engine of both social and sociological change, and a way to see how the two are linked.

Diversity exists among gay and lesbian families, as among all families. With respect to gay and lesbian families, there are several added dimensions. One is whether they are "out" as a family, or, in other words, open about their relationship with people they know and meet. Miller (2003: 104), in describing his own gay family, said:

> The family I live in as a father is also the family I live out in as a gay man. I call it an "out family" for three reasons: its openness to homosexual membership; its opposition to heterosexist conformity (the prejudicial assumption of heterosexuality as normal and proper); and its overtness within the contemporary lesbian and gay movement. ... Mine is a family that opens out, steps out, and stands out. It opens out to people traditionally excluded from the charmed circle of Home; it steps out beyond the police and policed borders of the Normal; and it stands out as a clear new possibility on the horizon of what used to be called ... the Just Society.

Not all gay and lesbian families are "out" in this or any other sense. Some, particularly older couples, still remain cloaked in secrecy, out of fear for the children or themselves (Connidis, 2001).

Lesbian families with children have been seen as a contradiction: women having children without heterosexual relations. Or they are seen as threats: women without the need for men. Lesbian mothers became more visible in the 1970s and 1980s, according to Epstein (1996: 109), because they chose to claim their identities as both mothers and lesbians. She notes, with sadness, that the claiming often occurred in courtrooms in custody hearings, where lesbians were typically defined as unfit mothers. Recall the example of "Ms. T," discussed in Chapter 6, who was denied foster children despite years of successful foster parenting. The risk of losing custody of their children still gives lesbian mothers a strong motivation to conceal their orientation.

Same-gender families are becoming more of a cultural norm, and from a rural perspective, they tend to be more normative than within an urban context. Bell's paper discusses the symbolism of "farm boys" and "wild men" and homosexual relationships in an agricultural setting (2000). He mentions that the focus has been on the urban context as the prime site for sexual identity exploration and community formation; however, the rural context has also been eroticized in much media and film (Bell, 2000). The author suggests that the countryside seems to be a way to become a man and that the natural environment causes homosexuality to take on a slant closer to nature rather than "against" it (Bell, 2000: 559).

Gay and lesbian families offer innovative models of family in several fundamental ways, according to family research. First, both gay and lesbian families may provide important developmental learning for children in the possibilities of resisting confining gender-role expectations (Epstein, 1996: 111).

Second, lesbians can teach daughters, in particular, how not to compete with other women but to bond with them to work together. Third, both gay men and lesbians force a questioning of the assumptions and values of heterosexist nuclear families. Fourth, gay families raise vital questions about the presumptions we make about masculinity in families and in society. And fifth, gay and lesbian families are an effective force of change in family policies.

The challenges involve rethinking what families are, what spouses are and do, and what parenting is. These are profoundly important sociological endeavours at reconceptualizing families. It was in large part this sort of rethinking that has led, in recent years, away from defining family by form and instead defining families broadly on the basis of processes: what families *do* rather than what they *are*.

Gay and lesbian families, not being structured hierarchically by gender, do not have the same divisions of labour by gender that many heterosexual families have. They are chosen families, characterized by fluid boundaries, new roles, and little institutionalized symbolism. They can be creative in making families and in devising new ways to be familial. Although this may be seen as a positive aspect of same-sex relationships, the absence of gender roles can make for complications when deciding to raise a family. A study on lesbian families by Fiona Nelson (1996) found that one of the problems associated with same-sex families was societies reluctant to see this as a real family, which in turn made it difficult for the lesbian parents to feel like a true family (Nelson, 1996, in Fox: 442). The women in Nelson's study found that many places did not offer family admission rates or discounts to lesbian families (Nelson, 1996, in Fox: 453). Furthermore, while the gay community may be a strong network of support for couples, the study found that there was a frequent lack of understanding within the lesbian community because of the relatively recent practice of lesbian couples deciding to start a family, and so the couples often felt that their friends did not understand what it meant to have a child and how this changed life (Nelson, 1996, in Fox: 452).

Furthermore, Epstein (1996) refers to parenting roles in lesbian couples being based on personality attributes rather than gender, so one parent is the funny one, or the hard-liner, or the one pushing academics. One of Epstein's (1996: 119) respondents puts it well: "We're not modelling male-female power dynamics, we're modelling women doing everything that needs to be done in order to maintain life."

Yet, there are tensions in lesbian and gay families, emanating in part from the linger-ing lack of acceptance and the absence of blueprints on how to be.

Relationships in which gender forms no part of the household or the domestic division of labour may be described as **post-gender families**. This kind of relationship raises important questions about gender and about the social concept of "coupledom." Oerton (1997) explored these issues among lesbian couples in an article she evoca-tively titled "Queer Housewives?" Her conclusion was that gendering processes may so intertwine with all domestic labour and all that we are in families that inventing family without these processes is challenging, but not impossible. She argued that creative new solutions to family processes, particularly divisions of labour, might be found in closer study of lesbian and gay couples. Risman (1998) argued that some of these new solutions can be found among heterosexual couples as well.

Risman and Johnson-Sumerford (1998) examined heterosexual "post-gender" marriages in which the partners share equally in paid and unpaid family work without regard for gender. They found that there are four pathways to such relationships: a dual-career household, a dual-nurturer relationship, a post-traditional relationship, and external forces that open relationships to egalitarianism. Egalitarianism is likely to affect both the power balance and the emotional quality of the relationship, Risman and Johnson-Sumerford suggest, for the good.

Gay and lesbian parents often create a network of "chosen" family (friends, former partners, and willing relatives) in addition to their kin for social and emotional support as well as to offer their children adult role models of the other sex. This support system may include other gay or lesbian families, or may not (Arnup, 2012). Gay and lesbian parents also have access to mainstream community organizations that are supportive of same-sex families.

From an urban standpoint, many organizations and support groups exist for gay and lesbian families. However, for those living in more geographically isolated areas, supports may be less available. McCarthy touched on this in her research discussing the challenges lesbians face in a non-urban environment due to a shortage of support groups and social arenas for sharing of experiences (2000). This hinders social group identity, which in turn may cascade into psychological problems. Unfortunately, research done on rural life usually overlooks gay and lesbian residents. In McCarthy's study, evidence indicated that

- Second union formation occurs faster following the disruption of a first union among cohabiters than among the divorced (Wu and Schimmele, 2005a).

- Non-marital child-bearing is adversely associated with the ability to marry economically attractive men and maintain long-term marital unions (Graefe and Lichter, 2008).

- Young adults are more likely to leave home at an earlier age (younger than 21 years) if they grow up in a non-traditional family, have more than two siblings, have a Canadian-born mother, did not attend religious services during adolescence, live in a region outside Quebec, and grow up in a smaller town (population less than 5000; Beaupre, Turcotte, and Milan, 2006a).

- Preschool children have a stabilizing effect on parental partnership, whether married or cohabiting, but the effect is weak for older children. Although pregnancy precipitates marriage among cohabiters, the odds of marriage decline to pre-pregnancy levels following the birth (Steele, Kallis, Goldstein, and Joshi, 2005).

- Older couples fare better when they are both retired. Married seniors, where both spouses are working or are looking for work, report the lowest relationship quality (Chalmers and Milan, 2005).

- In 2011, there were just over 64 000 same-sex couples in Canada, up 42.2 percent from 2006. Of those, 32.5 percent were married couples, reflecting the first five-year period in which same-sex marriage was legal across the country (Statistics Canada, 2012a).

rural lesbians felt isolated and uncertain of social identity development (2000). It is known that gay and lesbian families follow daily routines much like those of heterosexual families (Arnup, 2012; Nelson, 1996; Sullivan, 2012). All children need love and supervision. They all need to be sheltered, fed, taken to school, and so on. As well, the family life cycle is similar for both same-sex and opposite-sex-parent families: Children arrive, grow up, go through stages, and parenting continues accordingly (Arnup, 2012; Ambert, 2005c).

TRANSITIONS OUT OF PARENTING: EMPTY NESTS

Even without marital dissolution, transitions in family life occur. Many families experience the empty nest, and increasing numbers of others may wish to. An empty nest occurs when children grow up and move away.

When the children do decide to leave the parental home, it is usually a significant transition for their parents as well. For many parents, the move is accompanied by feelings of relief, pride in having fulfilled their parental role, and joy at seeing their children successfully transitioning toward greater independence. For the young adults, "the first departure is a symbolic marker as they make the transition from youth to adulthood" (Beaupré et al., 2006a).

In the past, getting a secure job and getting married to start a family were the two main reasons why young people left their parental home. Today, most young adults move out to pursue educational or employment opportunities or simply in order to gain independence from their parents (Beaupré et al., 2006a). However, research consistently shows that children who leave home for these reasons are "more likely to boomerang than those who leave to marry and set up their own conjugal household" (Beaupré et al., 2006a: 10).

Many young adults are increasingly reluctant to leave the parental home. The 2011 Census of Canada found that 42.3 percent of the 4 318 400 young adults aged 20 to 29 lived in the parental home, either because they never left it or because they returned home after living elsewhere (Statistics Canada, 2012d). Although there was little change in this from 2006, a big change is evident if we compare with 1981, for example, when 26.9 percent of young adults lived with their parents. There are many reasons why young adults live at home with their parents in such large numbers. Among those reasons, they may see the parents as a source of emotional or financial support; they may not be part of a couple as yet, or be on the rebound from a relationship breakdown; they may find that supporting a place of their own is prohibitively costly; and there may be cultural preferences involved (Mitchell, 2006).

Young adults are more likely to leave the parental home when they live in stepfamilies than when they live in either lone-parent or two-parent biological families (Beaupré et al., 2006a). This raises the important question of long-term implications for social inequalities (Mitchell, 1994; 2006). If some young adults increase their disadvantage by leaving the family home earlier than others, then the ultimate outcome will be widening social inequalities. If combined with early pregnancies, early family starts, or leaving school to support oneself, the long-term consequences are magnified. This is especially true for young people who find themselves in unstable family situations or who have to cope with difficult relationships in the family. Interestingly, women who live with a stepfamily have a much higher probability (57 percent risk) of leaving home before the age of 18 as compared with men (30 percent risk; Mitchell, 1994: 11; 2006).

Retirees are another large and rapidly growing group in Canadian society. According to a Statistics Canada report entitled A *Portrait of Seniors in Canada*, the number of seniors living in Canada is predicted to rise from 4.2 million to 9.8 million between 2005 and 2036 (Turcotte and Schellenberg, 2006). Figure 10.3 provides a breakdown of living arrangements of seniors by age group in 2011.

The overwhelming majority of seniors in Canada live alone or with a spouse (Statistics Canada, 2012e). So, empty nests are a reality for most Canadians, even if occurring later than in the past. A minority of older adults feel that there is no one, or only one person, on whom they can rely for help (Moore and Rosenberg, with McGuinness, 1997: 47). Most, however, rely on a number of friends and family, both close and far. In fact, apart from spouses, close friends are often the main source of emotional support for older individuals (Turcotte and Schellenberg, 2006).

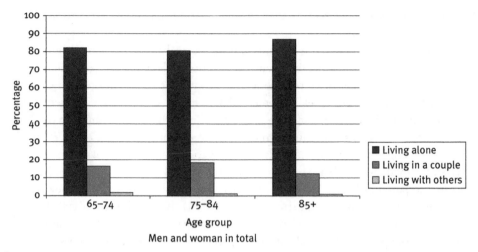

Figure 10.3 Living Arrangements of Men and Women over 65, Canada, 2011

Source: Statistics Canada, 2012e. Census of Population, 2011. Retrieved December 2012 from www12.statcan.gc.ca/census-recensement/2011/as-sa/98-312-x/2011003/tbl/tbl3_4-1-eng.cfm.

SANDWICHED FAMILIES AND CLUTTERED NESTS

Recently, there has been a shift in living arrangements and family lives that in some ways constitutes a new kind of family. It takes two forms. One is the return to the family home of adult children, as well as the presence of adult children who have never left, discussed above. This has become a very prevalent living arrangement. In fact, some researchers argue that "[i]t is now commonly understood that midlife parenthood often comprises prolonged periods of coresidence with grown adults" (Mitchell, 1998: 2; 2006). The other is older parents living with mid-life children (Rosenthal, Martin-Matthews, and Matthews, 1996), or mid-life offspring living with their aging parents.

People in midlife who live with or have responsibilities for both the young and the old are sometimes called the "sandwich generation." It is rare for three or more generations to share living quarters, but it is far from rare for them to be interdependent on each other in a variety of ways, even when they maintain separate households. Some view refilled nests as a crisis for mid-life people struggling to work, care for older parents, and look after themselves, their homes, and their communities. This may be a particular struggle in what was called the Great Recesssion of 2008+.

Children are still growing up, but they are moving away with less and less frequency, as can be seen in Figure 10.4. In fact, data from the 2011 Census show that 42.3 percent of young adults aged 20 to 29 were living with parents, up considerably from the past (Statistics Canada, 2012d). Even older young adults, between the ages of 25 and 29, are increasingly staying home; in 2006, just over a quarter (26 percent) of them lived with

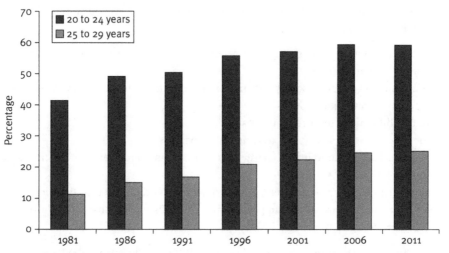

Figure 10.4 Young Adults Living in the Parental Home, Canada, 1981 to 2011

Source: Statistics Canada, 2012d. Censuses of Population, 1981 to 2011. Retrieved February 2013 from www12.statcan.gc.ca/census-recensement/2011/as-sa/98-312-x/2011003/fig/fig3_3-1-eng.cfm.

parents, a substantial increase from 15.6 percent in 1986. This, suggests Statistics Canada, is one reason for the overall decline in the proportion of households headed by people younger than age 30 in Canada.

According to Beaupré et al. (2006a: 9), most of the increase took place in "the early 1980s and early 1990s, years during which Canada endured two of the most severe labour recessions since the 1930s." Of course, we experienced the 2008+ recession, which added to the phenomenon of some families sharing households and resources out of need. Together with the fact that today's young people are more highly educated and attend school for more years than their parents did (Clark, 2007; Statistics Canada 2012d), it makes sense financially to remain at home. As Clark (2007: 14) points out, "The transitions of today's young adults are both delayed and elongated: delayed, because young adults take more time to complete their first major transition (leaving school), thus postponing all subsequent transitions; and elongated, because each subsequent transition takes longer to complete and stretches the process from their late teens to their early 30s."

Another growing trend is the emergence of the **"boomerang kid,"** a young adult who, after living away from the parental home for a period of time, returns to live with his or her parents (Mitchell, 2006). In the past, this was a rare event, but it has become more common with each generation. For example, only 1 in 10 early baby boomers born between 1947 and 1951 returned home within five years of first leaving, but 3 in 10 **generation X** young adults (born between 1972 and 1976) do so today (Beaupré et al., 2006b).

According to Statistics Canada, factors that explain this trend, in addition to those noted above, include the following:

- growing acceptance of common-law relationships, which are more likely to end in dissolution than marriage
- higher numbers of young adults pursuing post-secondary education, which leaves graduates with heavy student debts
- financial difficulties incurred with losing jobs
- reduced social stigma attached to living with parents
- wanting a higher standard of living that is not financially feasible when living on your own
- the emergence of new and different roles of parents and children in families
- needing a parent's emotional support during the stressful transition to adulthood and independence (Beaupre et al., 2006b: 28)

The common perception seems to be that young people are layabouts sponging off parents. Research by Mitchell (1998; 2006) shows that this presumption is incorrect. Generations living together in families provide mutual support and generally get along well. Middle generations receive valued companionship and the satisfaction of facilitating their child's transition into adulthood.

For their part, adult children receive a number of valuable services, such as free or low-cost housing, food, and perhaps access to a car. In other research (Mitchell and Gee, 1996a), even marital satisfaction is unaffected by the presence at home of adult children, provided the kids do not leave and return home multiple times.

In terms of social policy, it seems that the family home is becoming a kind of safety net for youth who cannot establish themselves in independent residences (Mitchell, 2006; Mitchell and Gee, 1996b; Statistics Canada, 2012d). Some researchers call this transition stage in young adulthood "semi-autonomous living," where the home is a refuge from financial and emotional difficulties (Beaupré et al., 2006b). Families that cannot afford, in economic or social terms, to take adult children into their homes may be forced to cut the net for their children. In times of sharp reductions in social safety nets, this may force the young people to seek low-wage employment rather than education or training in order to support themselves. "Not being able to return to the security and comforts of home could have a devastating effect on the lives of young adults who are not psychologically prepared to be launched as adults" (Mitchell and Gee, 1996b: 68).

With respect to older relatives living with those in midlife, or the other way around, the issues are remarkably similar. It should be noted, however, that this kind of living arrangement is not common among Canadians. Most older Canadians in 2011 lived in couples or alone (Statistics Canada, 2012e). In 2002, approximately 27 percent of Canadians in midlife were part of the sandwich generation (Williams, 2005). This proportion is growing for a number of reasons (Schroeder, MacDonald, and Shamian, 2012): First, population aging means more older family members. It is projected that by 2036, one in five Canadians will be 65 years or older (Statistics Canada, 2010). Second, the

Six Myths about the Sandwich Generation

Myth: People who are part of sandwich generation are often extremely stressed, and finding balance is challenging.

■ Fact: According to the 2002 Statistics Canada General Social Survey, a large proportion of people who worked at the same time as providing care for their child(ren) and parents were generally satisfied with the balance they had achieved (Williams, 2005). Yet, Statistics Canada (2011) found from the 2010 General Social Survey that 27 percent of working Canadians were under great stress.

Myth: Most children who have experienced a disruption in their family structure are unhappy.

■ Fact: It is true that a disruption can cause unhappiness; however, the majority of children (72 percent) who experience family disruption remain happy or find ways of being happy. And 92 percent of children who lived with both of their parents until age 15 felt that they had a very happy childhood (Williams, 2001).

Myth: It is mainly women who provide care both to young and old.

■ Fact: Though more women (32 percent) provide care to both their parents and their children, the portion of men who are "sandwiched" is not that far behind (25 percent;

Schroeder, MacDonald, and Shamian, 2012; Williams, 2005).

Myth: When grandparents live with the family, financial stress on the family increases.

■ Fact: Grandparents are sometimes financial contributors. In multigenerational households where the middle generation is a couple, 16 percent of the grandparents were primary financial providers. And when the middle generation was a lone parent, 50 percent of grandparents were financial supporters (Milan and Hamm, 2003).

Myth: Living apart together (LAT) occurs mostly among the young.

■ Fact: A significant portion (44 percent) of LAT occurs among people age 30 and older: 19 percent are in their thirties, 14 percent in their forties, and 11 percent are aged 50 and older (Milan and Peters, 2003; Statistics Canada, 2013b).

Myth: Adult children with children of their own increase contact with their parents after a marital disruption because they need support.

■ Fact: Interestingly, marital status has no significant impact on the frequency of contact of adult children with their parents (Townsend-Batten, 2002).

pattern of low fertility rates means there will be fewer in mid-life available to take care of older people in the future (Olazabal, 2010; Williams, 2005). And last, today's adults are delaying forming unions and parenthood. All three trends together mean more situations where older family members require care while young children are still at home.

Finally, reductions in Canadian health-care services mean those who are hospitalized return home "quicker and sicker." This often means, for older relatives, temporary or permanent reliance on their adult children. Nevertheless, older parents living in the home are not always a burden on the family; rather, they can be an asset, even financially (see "Six Myths about the Sandwich Generation").

NEW KINDS OF CLOSE RELATIONS

In addition to the types of relationships already discussed, other forms of family are emerging. The definition of *family* is becoming more fluid and dependent on circumstances. For example, a crisis, such as a life-threatening illness, can challenge one's idea of family and precipitate new kinds of close relations. When people living with HIV/AIDS were asked who or what they considered to be family, the results were surprising (Wong-Wylie and Doherty-Poirier, 1997).

For this group, family as process was paramount. To be considered family, an individual must have a *reciprocal relationship* with the respondent and must be *accepting, supportive*, a source of *health and wellness resources*, and an *inspirational influence*. What kinds of people met these criteria for the respondents? They listed seven categories of people as comprising their created families (not every respondent had family from each category): families of origin, health-care professionals, friends, other people with HIV/AIDS, deceased friends, family caregivers, and valued material objects.

One man included his physician in his self-defined family in an equal place with his wife and son. In his case, all but one of the friends included in his family definition also had HIV/AIDS. Significantly, he specifically excluded some members of his blood family, such as his mother, from his family definition. Yet another defined his family as consisting of computers, bridge, his ex-partner, and the "gay world" writ large, only incidentally noting his mother, brother, and sister.

These findings emphasize the limitations of assuming we know what family is. We all possess the power to define family for ourselves. Most importantly, this study shows that family, however we define it, is becoming more rather than less important. This is a point we have made throughout this text in a variety of ways and with numerous examples.

It need not take the crisis of HIV/AIDS for us to create new kinds of families. Many of us create families for ourselves—in a new land, in situations where we have lost our families through war or time, when we have irresolvable disputes with families, or when our memories of our families of origin are too horrid to forgive. In these cases and endless others, we make families of our friends, neighbours, communities, those with whom we share something important, and even our pets, plants, work, computers, and sporting equipment.

CONCLUDING REMARKS

We explored multiple and varied transitions and innovations in family in this chapter. With family being placed increasingly into the realm of ideology and politics, it sometimes seems as if different approaches to family are in competition for our hearts. The transitions and new kinds of close relations discussed here are not the full list of possible ways that family life changes and that we change family for ourselves. Nor are they arranged like a smorgasbord for us to choose what we like best. For most of us, the kinds of families we live in choose us. Sometimes, as the old phrase has it, life happens. We do not necessarily make informed and deliberate choices about the ends of marriages or relationships. Sometimes the choice is not ours, but our partner's or spouse's. Sometimes we flee from violence or an intolerable situation to something unknown but safer.

Within our various kinds of families, however, we do make choices. We engage in and develop processes that define us as families. We try to do our best within the opportunities and constraints society offers. It is these choices, not the shape our families take, that matter most to our happiness and the happiness of our children.

In the contest over which kind of family is preferable, we can lose track of the reality that all of us in families are sharing and caring for each other. The similarities in daily family living far outweigh the differences.

CHAPTER SUMMARY

This chapter discusses transitions to different family situations of many sorts: singlehood, one-parent families, second relationships or remarriage, stepfamilies, empty nests, and the invention of new kinds of families. Some transitions can bring new ways to behave and to live in close relations, or fresh starts. Others could better be called stale starts, since they merely lead to a repetition of old patterns and of old relational problems.

Family transitions and new families are not new phenomena in human society. With large-scale immigration and high death rates in the past in North America, many single-parent families and orphans existed.

The perils of some transitions in family, such as to lone parenthood, include high risks of poverty for single mothers and their children after separation and divorce. Similar risks exist for women who choose to have children on their own without partners, a phenomenon growing in popularity. Adoption of children from other countries can have perils as well: The children face the cultural challenges of adapting to the new family's customs and the lingering effects of possible trauma experienced in early childhood.

Becoming a parent without a partner as a deliberate choice is a new kind of family,

one that makes for multiple kinds of parenthood and families. Parenting arrangements on separation and divorce also create new kinds of parents, most notably in shared parenting situations in which a non-residential parent is involved in active parenting. The good news here is that families can extend beyond the walls of a household.

Remarriage is more common for men than for women; for both, the risks of divorce are higher with a second marriage. Social pressures toward remarriage are sometimes more ideological than material; people want to be like other couples in society and to avoid stigma. Cohabitation after divorce is growing as the family of choice in Canada, particularly in Quebec.

Blended families are increasing in Canada and pose challenges to the ways we think of families. As the number of relationships both within and outside the household multiply, new vocabularies must be invented.

We learned that not all family transitions are choices. Some people flee from abuse or from culturally sanctioned violence into new lives, in the process creating new families.

Living solo is a growing option for many people who maintain close family ties but not in their own households. Counter to this is the sandwich family, which involves both youth and older parents living together with the middle generation, or cluttered nests, a variant on this theme where youth either never leave the family home or return home to live.

With aging, families change and family transitions are made. Changing times have enabled post-gender families to develop and some same-sex families to live more openly.

Key Terms

artificial insemination A process of introducing semen into a woman's body without sexual intercourse; can be a medical process but may not be.

binuclear family A term used to describe a blended family, or a family where the spouses each bring children and non-residential parents into a new family.

blended family Typically describing a family comprising two previously married spouses, with children, who marry each other and bring their children together in a new family.

boomerang kid A young adult who returns to the parental home after a period of living independently.

generation X According to Statistics Canada, this is the cohort born between 1967 and 1976.

in vitro fertilization Commonly known as test-tube fertilization; conception that occurs

by bringing together ova and sperm in medical procedures.

intergenerational contagion A process by which trends that begin in one generation may be adopted by other generations. An example is cohabitation, which was mostly a youthful phenomenon but has now been adopted by people of all generations.

latchkey children Children who are regularly left for some part of the day without adult supervision.

post-gender families Families in which the division of labour is not based on gender.

Standard North American Family (SNAF) Mother, father, two kids, and usually a dog or a cat.

union libre Widely used term for common-law union in Quebec.

Critical Thinking Questions

1. Discuss how immigration can produce new ways to be family. In your opinion, is change only limited to immigrant groups? Discuss how demographic changes in Canada can affect family life and transitions.

2. Not only are lone mothers the most economically disadvantaged, but their poverty is also the most resistant to remedy. Create a cause-and-effect flowchart to illustrate the factors involved in the perpetuation of poverty among single mothers.

3. In this chapter, three social policy approaches to lone-parent families were discussed: the private family model, the family-oriented model, and the state-based model. Discuss which approach(es) Canadian policy-makers

should adopt in light of the recent trends and changes in family life.

4. In this chapter we learned that young adults are more likely than in the past to remain in the parental home longer and to "boomerang" back. Thinking about the issues they involve, what kinds of policies can the government introduce to enable young adults to successfully transition into adulthood and independence?

5. What effect are new communications media (e.g., Skype) likely having on the formation and maintenance of new kinds of families? Are they simply permitting people to do the same old things in new ways?

Weblinks

The Future of Children
www.futureofchildren.org
This collaborative research undertaking by Princeton University and the Brookings Institution seeks to promote effective policies and programs for children. This site is a great resource for research publications that focus on policy changes.

Families in Transition (FIS)
www.fsatoronto.com/programs/families.html
This Family Service Toronto branch provides specialized services for separating, divorcing, and remarrying families that focus on supporting children.

Empty Nest Moms
http://emptynestmoms.com
An online support group for single mothers facing the challenges associated with their children moving out or heading to college or university.

Lesbian & Gay Parenting
www.apa.org/pi/parent.html
This online publication by the American Psychological Association contains highlights of research findings on lesbian mothers, gay fathers, and their children, an annotated bibliography, and additional resources.

Transition Magazine
www.vanierinstitute.ca/transition_magazine#.UnA8eiQTFz8
An online publication from the Vanier Institute of the Family in Canada that provides up-to-date information on the trends in family life and policy affecting Canadians.

TroubledWith
www.troubledwith.com
TroubledWith.com is a collection of articles, resources, and referrals organized by topic around family issues and concerns.

National Stepfamily Resource Center
www.stepfamilies.info
This site provides information, resources, and support for stepfamily members. Topics include counselling, finances, co-parenting, co-grandparenting, and more.

Chapter 11
A Glimpse into the Future
Where Do Families Go from Here?

Gladskikh Tatiana/Shutterstock

Chapter Outline

Learning Objectives

1 Demonstrate an understanding of the role of technology in our personal relationships.

2 Describe the crucial role technology plays in children's lives and families.

3 Examine the changes in reproduction due to technology and the policy challenges these changes pose.

4 Analyze how technology is used in creating and maintaining romantic relationships.

5 Recognize the challenges technology creates for our intimate relationships.

6 Assess future trends in family roles and transitions.

7 Assess the changing social and personal expectations for relationships.

8 Describe the policy challenges faced by society as we strive to meet the needs of changing families.

In this chapter, we wonder what the future holds for families. Methodically predicting the future has important practical value, as thinking about the future in useful ways can help us avoid the mistakes of the past. This is not to say that we can predict perfectly. A record of many inaccurate past predictions proves this cannot be done. Besides, no matter how good our predictions may be, we can never prepare completely. However, where social organization is concerned, preparation is always better than being taken by surprise.

Our close relations—especially our family relations—are intricate, varied, and always changing. We end this text by addressing the likely changes to family life in the future, and the forces—especially technological forces—behind those changes.

Some family problems of the present will likely persist, and new problems will emerge. A future of families without problems is unthinkable, if only because we continue to create new problems as we go along. Like much else in the past hundred years, the problems of the future will probably involve science and technology, travel and communication, and war and intergroup conflict. Since we will likely continue to live in a global society, humanity's problems will be progressively global in scope. Though human health is continually improving, concerns about health and health risks will continue to grow. Medical technology will improve, but new illnesses will also develop, and new disasters will force us to cope in different ways.

Most important, since we increasingly rely on information and technology, our problems will increasingly be concerned with information flow, and with the use, abuse, and malfunction of technology. Our ability to solve family problems—and, in this way, to improve society—will need better social science and more social science–based policies.

FAMILY LIFE IN THE TWENTY-FIRST CENTURY

The pace of technological change in the past decade has been daunting to even the most technologically aware people. Many social theorists think technological changes bring about social changes (for example, Castells, 1996). In their theories, the presumed impacts of technological changes and innovations on societies, social institutions, and individuals result in various ethnic, cultural, and social concerns. People and societies are always having to react to, adjust to, or repair a change caused by technology. This is only partly true. While technology does influence culture, it alone does not drive the process of social change; a society's search for change does. Social change is the co-production of economic and political imperatives, social values, and technical and social inventions.

One of the most fundamental understandings to emerge from the new sociology of technology is that technology is more than hard wires and virtual buttons. Technologies have not transformed us or our families' communications. Instead, we use the technologies because social life in families has changed so much that, for many, direct communication is not as possible as it once was. The technological boom itself is created more by the demands of a changing society than by any inherent aspect of the technologies themselves (Brown and Lauder, 2001; McDaniel, 2000). Sociological research finds that technologies and social changes, in gender for example, are mutually reinforcing (Wajcman, 2010).

Yet the technological explosion is changing families in multifaceted ways. Reproductive technologies that allow clinically infertile people to become parents raise many questions. Equally challenging are questions posed by medical technology that extends lives and close relations for longer than ever before.

Other concerns arise from the cultural effects of technology. For example, routines such as family dinners—an important part of identity development—are becoming less common with the use of microwave ovens and prepared fast or frozen foods to ease the time pressure so many families experience today. And with texting on mobile devices, family members may be physically together but really not interacting. Rather than sharing time together, family members may eat alone, standing in the kitchen, before racing off to the next activity.

Information and communication technologies (ICT) have helped some individuals to jump off the so-called hamster wheel of work and set their own hours at home, away from the hubbub of commutes, office gossip, and the nine-to-five regime. Individuals must make choices regarding the creation and maintenance of the work–family boundary and their transitions between work and family roles. Factors that influence these choices include the degree to which the individual identifies with the institutional ideal of nine-to-five work. Do culture and a sense of duty both in the workplace and at home come into play? Does the location of the job have any bearing on the role of work and family in life satisfaction? "Teleworkers use various cues and rituals to segment their work and home roles and to manage the tension between the flexibility afforded by the telework arrangement and the need to maintain structure in order to accomplish tasks, protect role responsibilities and aid transitions between role domains" (Fonner and Stache, 2012: 255). Telework can create a sense of gratification, both professionally and personally, and give the individual a better sense of control with greater levels of autonomy and power as they determine their boundaries. It can also be challenging to manage to care for families and work in the same space at the same time. It might be many years before we learn what implications such changes in work will have for families.

Today, technologies offer families new ways to start and prolong close relations, but they also pose new challenges to our relationships. In this chapter, we focus on information technology as one example.

Just as earlier social inventions—the development of cities, factories, automobiles, telephones, and television—changed families in earlier times, information technologies—especially smartphones, social media, tablets, and email—have already changed, and will continue to change, families and family lives. We cannot tell precisely how much or in what ways these technologies will affect family life (see Silva, 2010).

However, it is already obvious that computers and other ICT affect families in several ways (Hughes, Ebata, and Dollahite, 1999). First, ICT affects the culture as a whole and thus affects families. Second, ICT affects the ways family members communicate with one another and with others. Since communication is a central aspect of family life, new communication technology has changed family lives greatly. Third, ICT is a means of teaching and providing therapy, giving people unequalled access to information and advice about families and family life, both good and bad.

Technology and Canadian Families

- 52 percent—Canadians aged 18 to 24 who are friends with their parents on Facebook.

- 37 percent—Canadians aged 18 to 24 who agree that "growing up with technology sets me up for more success than my parents' generation."

- 23 percent—Canadians aged 18 to 24 who agree that "technology helps me have a better relationship with my parents."

- 42 percent—Canadian parents who agree that "technology allows me to stay closer to my kids."

- 21 percent—Canadian parents who "use social media like Facebook to keep track of [their] kid(s)."

- 35 percent—Canadian parents who agree that "technology keeps my family closer together."

Source: Rogers Innovation Report: 2012 Trend Watch, August 2012 slidesha.re/NiMl421 is: http://www.slideshare.net/Rogers/rogers-innovation-report-parents-youth-study (accessed 24-10-2012)

FAMILIES IN THE CONNECTED SOCIETY

Today, any discussion of close relations must consider *virtual communities*, especially close relations that exist in cyberspace. These relations are characterized by rare face-to-face contact and regular electronic contact. Because of the country's vast geography, Canada's researchers have often been at the forefront of theorizing about long-distance communication technologies. As a nation of vast distances and sparse population, Canada has always relied on transport and communication technology to make social organization possible. As such, Canada has been a "connected" nation for many years, with usage rates of basic telephone, internet, and cable services among the highest in the world (see Figure 11.1 for information about current internet use). Contributing to these networks of communication is the fact that Canada is an immigrant society. Many immigrants retain active connections with relatives and friends in their homelands and in other parts of the world through communication technologies.

A few simple statistics tell the tale. In 2006, more than 99 percent of Canadian households had landline or mobile telephone service, almost 80 percent owned a computer, and nearly 70 percent had home internet access (Statistics Canada, 2008b). These numbers were significantly higher than in previous years and continue to increase quickly, reflecting the willingness of Canadians to remain connected in virtual communities. Figure 11.1 paints the picture of the rapid evolution of connectivity.

As a result, ever-speedier delivery of information, goods, and services has become a social fixation. Smartphones, PDAs, tablets, and laptops connect ever more people, making them continuously available. Since 1999, Canadians have seen an increase from 11.1 percent to 80.5 percent in home internet access (see Figure 11.2). As for the effects of being "wired," the jury is still out—some argue that electronic connectedness makes censorship and information management possible on a scale never before imagined. Others argue that connectedness weakens elite control over information and enables ordinary people to air their political, social, and cultural views more freely.

So how do internet and social media use affect close relations? Researchers disagree about the overall effect of ICT on family and community life. On the one hand, the new connectivity may intrude on family life, disturbing family rituals and cohesion. Early research highlighted the tendency of computers and other ICT to isolate families, individuate family members—separate them from one another in individual activities—and even produce addictive behaviour. For instance, Nie and Hillygus (2002) found that frequent internet use is associated with less time spent with family and friends and on social activities in general, as well as increased depression and loneliness.

On the other hand, increased connectivity makes it easier to contact friends, neighbours, acquaintances, spouses, children, parents, and siblings. This is exactly what a three-year study by University of Toronto sociologists Barry Wellman and Keith Hampton (1999) found. Wellman and Hampton surveyed residents moving into and living in a community they nicknamed Netville.

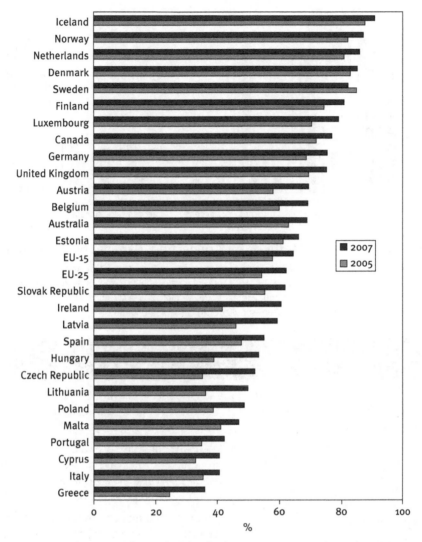

Figure 11.1 Internet Use by Individuals, by Country, 2005 and 2007

Note: Data refer to individuals aged 16 to 74. For Canada, 2005 data refer to individuals aged 18 to 74, and 2007 data refer to individuals aged 16 to 74. For Australia, 2005 data refer to individuals aged 18 or older for the reference period 2004 to 2005, and 2007 data refer to individuals aged 15 or older for the period 2006 to 2007. The EU-15 and EU-25 values refer to European Union 15-country and 25-country aggregate averages, respectively.

Sources: Eurostat, *Community Survey on ICT Usage in Households and by Individuals,* 2005 and 2007; Statistics Canada, *Canadian Internet Use Survey,* 2005 and 2007; and Australian Bureau of Statistics, *Multi-Purpose Household Survey,* 2004 to 2005 and 2006 to 2007.

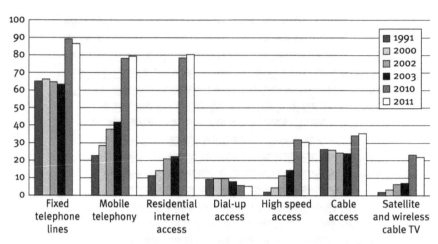

Figure 11.2 Diversity of Methods for Connecting, Canada, by Percentage

Sources: Statistics Canada. 2005 and 2013. Table 1: Connections by Type. *Innovation Analysis Bulletin.* Catalogue no. 88-003-XIE. Vol. 7, No. 2. p. 13, www.statcan.gc.ca/pub/88-003-x/88-003-x2005002-eng.pdf, and "Dwelling characteristics and household equipment," CANISM, table 203-0027 and Catalogue No. 62F0026M. http://www.statcan.gc.ca/tables-tableaux/sum-som/l01/cst01/famil133a-eng.htm.

Trends in Canadian Internet Use

■ Internet use can take time away from other activities. For instance, more than 25 percent of Canadian internet users spend less time watching television once they start using the internet; 15 percent of internet users take time away from reading; 11 percent from sleeping; 11 percent from doing leisure activities at home; and 10 percent from doing household chores (Dryburgh, 2001).

■ Conversely, internet use can improve interaction with family and friends. For example, some Canadians report that their communications with friends (5 percent) and family (3 percent) increased as a result of their using the internet (Dryburgh, 2001).

■ Canada is a wired nation. Currently, it ranks as the second most wired of all OECD countries (after South Korea) for high-speed access (Statistics Canada, 2005h).

■ Cell phone subscriptions increased from 98 000 in 1987 to more than 18 million by the end of 2006. Currently, there are almost as many wireless phones as landlines in Canada (Moscovitch, 2007).

■ In Canada, long-distance calling increased as a proportion of total calling, with long-distance minutes almost tripling from almost 20 billion in 1995 to 56 billion in 2002 (Sciadas, 2006).

■ Although information and communications technology (ICT) prices decreased significantly between 1997 and 2003, average Canadian household spending on all ICT (including telephones and television) increased from $2118 to $2780 during that time (Sciadas, 2006).

■ Almost 7 million Canadians aged 18 and older placed an order online in 2005, while more than 9 million logged on to browse or, in other words, to do some "window shopping." The people who made an online purchase represented about 41 percent of all adults who used the internet in 2005 (Statistics Canada, 2005h).

Residents varied from beginner to expert in their degree of computer and internet experience. Of the 109 homes in Netville, 64 were connected to the local network. The researchers found that residents with access to the high-speed local network recognized, talked, and visited with many more of their neighbours than did residents without this technology. A neighbourhood email list increased in-person socializing, as residents organized parties, barbecues, and other local events online. Wired residents also had more contact and exchanged more help with friends and relatives living *outside* their neighbourhood. Far from destroying social life, Wellman and Hampton found that virtual relations improve it.

Reinforcing the positive effects of virtual relations on social life, a separate study by the Media Awareness Network, *Young Canadians in a Wired World*, concluded that "a wired kid is a social kid" (Moscovitch, 2007). The study found that the internet is a crucial part of adolescents' social environment, allowing them to connect with friends, explore social roles, learn about their interests, and express themselves. Overall, for most adolescents, the internet contributes to increasing their confidence about making friends. Most new friends, however, still come from schools, sports, and parties (Moscovitch, 2007).

So, overall, communication technologies have had different effects on social life and will continue to have unpredictable effects, at least for a while.

Information technology is becoming more and more necessary from an academic standpoint. In 2005, more than one-quarter of adult Canadians—an estimated 6.4 million—used the internet for education, training, or school work (McKeown and Underhill, 2005). By 2009, usage had increased substantially, with many courses, both post-secondary and training, being offered online and many individuals seeking information via the internet (Statistics Canada, 2010).

Table 11.1 shows the number of Canadians who used the internet for educational purposes by province in 2005. Despite its growing popularity, ICT access varies in different regions for different people. Looker and Thiessen (2003) analyzed the difference between urban and rural dwellings, and access to information technology within residential neighbourhoods as well as schools. Gender, socio-economic status, and location play a major role in access to ICT. This study illustrated that despite being less likely to have access to computers at home, the use and competency levels of rural youth are not compromised because of increased use of computers at school (Looker and Thiessen, 2003). Also, female youth and youth from families with low parental education have a lesser chance of accessing a computer in the home. This is sometimes referred to as the digital divide. Interestingly, the data showed that rural schools have been able to provide resources for students who may not have access at home, and therefore 60 percent of youth (rural) versus 40 percent (urban) first learned to use ICT for academic purposes. On the contrary, rural schools have less educational software and use less specialized software (Looker and Thiessen, 2003). Addressing this issue through strategies for fund allocation for rural institutions may improve educational prospects for students.

Adding to the growing debate about information technology, Bowers, Vasquez, and Roaf (2000) examined the use of computers in First Nations reservation schools across North America. While educators, linguists, and tribal leaders have highlighted the positive

Table 11.1 Purpose of Internet Use, 2005

Province	Education Users	Other Users	Non Users
	Percent		
Newfoundland and Labrador	20	30	50
Prince Edward Island	24	33	43
Nova Scotia	28	37	36
New Brunswick	20	34	46
Quebec	21	37	42
Ontario	32	38	30
Manitoba	28	35	37
Saskatchewan	26	37	37
Alberta	30	38	32
British Columbia	29	38	33

Source: Statistics Canada. 2005. Canadian Internet Use Survey. www.statcan.gc.ca/pub/81-004-x/2007004/10375-eng.htm.

aspects of allowing Aboriginal youth to access computers in schools, others are less sure. On the one hand, computer access in schools will allow First Nations youth to engage in various forms of networking, increase their employment opportunities, and allow them to learn more about their cultural traditions (Bowers et al., 2000). Conversely, computer use can be seen as culture-transforming technology and may negatively contribute to First Nations people's sense of identity by exposing them to the dominant Western culture and challenging their local values, knowledge, and traditions (Bowers et al., 2000). The need for teachers to educate their students on the appropriate and inappropriate uses of information technology is crucial for First Nations youth to gain the benefits of computer access while avoiding the negative outcomes of culture loss.

Intimacy and Technology

The effects of technology on intimacy depend on the *type* of close relationship.

Haythornthwaite (Haythornthwaite, Kazmer, Robins, and Showmaker, 2000; Haythornthwaite 2001a, 2001b) has shown that among strongly tied (that is, closely related) people, easy, cheap technologies such as email or Skype do not replace traditional communication means–for example, face-to-face meetings or telephone calls. Closely related communicators use new as well as old technologies and communicate often. More frequent, and more varied, communication strengthens a relationship. By contrast, weakly tied communicators rely on one medium and are less motivated to explore new technologies. Their relationships remain distant as a result.

Technology and Relationships

- Over the last few decades, the internet has lured us into a virtual new world where people do old-fashioned things—get acquainted, fall in love, and break up in brand new ways.

- In India, marriages have been arranged for centuries—even millennia—so online dating services represent a profound challenge to ancient traditions.

- In China, many have started to participate in *wang hun*, where people get to role-play at marriage online. Sometimes the games go too far, however, some married couples have divorced on the grounds of emotional adultery—even though no face-to-face meetings took place between the online lovers.

- Some new websites (GeneTree.com and Ancestry.com) combine genealogy, medical technology, and social networking making use of inexpensive cheek-swab DNA tests to help people with similar DNA link up around the world.

- Technology doesn't just bring people together; it makes it easier for them to break up too. Breaking up via email or text message is much easier and less painful than doing so face to face, researchers are finding.

Source: Brown, Arnold, 2011. "Relationships, Community and Identity in the New Virtual Society," The Futurist. 45(2)29-34.

Connectedness has a huge impact on people's lives. In a post-industrial, information-based economy, connectivity affects people's employability—their chances of getting a good job or any job at all. Indirectly, this has an impact on family life, since, as we have stressed in other chapters, the demands of work (including schoolwork) always influence the quality of close relations. Canadians' unequal access to the internet and social media, and their unequal computer literacy, may affect people's educational and occupational attainment and, indirectly, the class structure.

We cannot predict how quickly the digital divide will shrink. In the longer run, ICT may provide traditionally disadvantaged and isolated families with new opportunities to improve their social condition. This will improve family life, as well as change the face of work and community life. However, we are far from seeing this happen as yet.

Technology and Family Development

Changes in technology that simplify contact among family and friends are likely to contribute to the quality and cohesion of relationships. Over the past 150 years, changes in communications and transport technologies have made contact among kin and friends, whether they live near one another or great distances apart, less expensive, faster, and easier. As email and internet use spreads, geographic constraints on social relationships continue to lessen (Silva, 2010).

The spread of easy communication shrinks distances, and we can expect this shrinking of distances to continue. Yet, despite the constant changes in the technological context of social relationships, most social theory continues to assume that people will form and preserve close relationships mainly through face-to-face interaction (Adams, 1998; Farrell, VandeVusse, and Ocobock, 2012). It was not until recently that people could travel or communicate often enough with close relations who lived at a distance to maintain those relationships. So, researchers who studied close relations focused on people who were geographically as well as emotionally close. Psychologists who studied interpersonal attraction, for example, focused on the importance of visual cues: how physical appearance plays a role in attraction, and what gestures and facial expressions people use to show involvement (see Short, Williams, and Christie, 1976). In the internet age, we need a new inventory of the ways people signal their characteristics, preferences, and qualities. So much of the internet experience is now visual–Skype, uploading photos and videos, video chats—that it enables families and friends to interact in real-time (or nearly) as if they were in the same room. Through use of these technologies, the "millennial generation" report feeling closer, during adolescence, to their parents than previous generations (Pew, 2010).

Comparing Communication Technologies

One strategy for studying the future of close relations and technology is to examine how technology has affected close relations in the past. New technologies rapidly cross traditional social barriers and achieve wide adoption (Fischer, 1992; Silva, 2010). Here we review the history of two recent communication technologies: the telephone and email.

Why a Cellphone May be Better than a Toilet if You're Very Poor

21 March 2013–United Nations Deputy Secretary-General Jan Eliasson today launched a call for urgent action to end the crisis of 2.5 billion people without basic sanitation, and to change a situation in which more people worldwide have mobile phones than toilets.

Of the world's seven billion people, six billion have mobile phones. However, only 4.5 billion have access to toilets or latrines—meaning that 2.5 billion people, mostly in rural areas, do not have proper sanitation. In addition, 1.1 billion people still defecate in the open.

The countries where open defecation is most widely practiced are the same countries with the highest numbers of under-five child deaths, high levels of under-nutrition and poverty, and large wealth disparities.

"We can reduce the cases of diarrhoea in children under five by a third simply by expanding the access of communities to sanitation and eliminating open defecation," ... [said the Deputy Executive Director of the UN Children's Fund (UNICEF), Martin Mogwanja] ...at the launch of the call to action at UN Headquarters. "In fact, diarrhoea is the second largest killer of children under five in the developing world and this is caused largely by poor sanitation and inadequate hygiene."

"This can also improve the safety of women and girls, who are often targeted when they are alone outdoors. And providing safe and private toilets may also help girls to stay in school which we know can increase their future earnings and help break the cycle of poverty.

Source: Reproduced by permission of United Nations, Department of Public Information.

The Telephone Social histories of the telephone (Pool, 1977; Fischer, 1992) show that, from the beginning, telephones were used mainly for long-distance calling. Commercial interests advertised the telephone as a means to link family and friends; women were shown using it for "kin-keeping."

The telephone allowed people to express their views in their own voice, it was simple to use, and, once the private line replaced the party line, it was as private as face-to-face communication. As a result, the telephone was adopted by everyone and widely used to preserve close relations, even at a distance. People quickly became dependent on this new communication instrument.

Yet surprisingly, the effects of the telephone on social life have been modest. At most, the telephone has helped them by keeping people in touch between face-to-face meetings.

Note that the telephone—like other forms of communication—has had both positive and negative effects on close relations. Applewhite and Segal (1990) studied the ways peace-keeping troops in the Sinai (in Israel) use telephones on the frontlines. Talking to parents and spouses preserves social support systems while on duty. However, a large minority report feeling sad after a phone call, or angry about being in the Sinai, or anxious after receiving disturbing news from home. Yet, given the opportunity, people use telephones and other communication technology, all of which have the capacity to make them happy, anxious, or sad.

Along similar lines, a study of the U.S. military (Pincus, House, Christenson, and Alder, 2004) found that many spouses are frustrated with the unidirectional phone contact initiated only by the soldier, which makes them feel "trapped" at home waiting for a call. And when soldiers call home and no one answers, they may feel forgotten, which can lead to anger and resentment—especially if this occurs frequently. "Now that Internet and e-mail are widely available," the study notes, "spouses report feeling much more in control as they can initiate communication and do not have to stay waiting by the phone. Another advantage of e-mail, for both Soldier and spouse, is the ability to be more thoughtful about what is said and to 'filter out' intense emotions that may be unnecessarily disturbing. This is not to say that military couples should 'lie' to protect each other, but rather it helps to recognize that the direct support available from one's mate is limited during the deployment."

Email The advantages of email are sometimes similar to those of the telephone. Email is even cheaper than telephone communication and much cheaper than long-distance travel. It allows people to avoid being seen by the message recipient, yet it creates "symbolic proximity."

Like the telephone, email allows escape from continued contact if that is desired. It gives one time to think and reflect. Email is not as interruptive as the telephone, nor is it dependent on both people being available at the same time. Unlike the telephone, email is strictly a print medium. However, email carries a variety of dangers of its own. Faceless anonymity poses the risk of indiscretion, misunderstanding, and misquoting. The shield of visual and vocal anonymity may encourage blunt disclosure and self-misrepresentation. On the other hand, some studies have found that the greater self-disclosure made possible by this shield outweighs any negative outcomes.

Relationships with online communicators are possible for people formerly prevented from socializing—for example, people housebound by illness or child care. However, the community feeling gained from cyber relations is often illusory. At this point, we have no idea what net effect email will have on close relations.

Communication Technology and the Family Cycle

What effect will newer technologies—smartphones, social media, direct communication that combines sight and sound—have on family life? Research on the topic is just beginning; so far, the most plentiful information concerns parental fears about children's safety online.

However, an existing theory can be used to consider the likely effects of innovations. Adams and Stevenson (2002) looked at technology from the viewpoint of family development theory.

The basic premise of this theory is that families continuously change with changes in social expectations, environmental constraints, and the demands of family members (for example, biological, psychological, and social needs). As families change and restructure, they engage in *developmental tasks*, or activities that prepare them for coming stages.

Traditional "stages" include marriage without children, marriage with various-aged children (for example, infant, preschool, school-age, adolescent, young adult), marriage with children who live outside the household, grandparenting, and marriage in late life.

Research regarding the effects of communication technologies on family life is ongoing. With decreasing privacy, on-line safety is of most concern at this time.
Pavel Losevsky/Fotolia

White (1998) expanded these traditional stages to include divorce and remarriage, stages that people previously classified as "non-normative," or not widely accepted, but are now considered normative, as we saw in Chapter 2. Also, the growth of cohabitation, the rise of child-bearing as a "discretionary option," and legalization of same-sex marriages have increased the variety of family lives, as we have seen in earlier chapters. With so many different kinds of family experiences, it makes no sense to speak of "the average family." The primary research question offered by family development theory is: How does technology influence family change over time? Specifically, how does the use of ICTs influence the norms and roles of family members? How do families use technology in the developmental tasks that contribute to life course transitions? In what ways is the use of technology different across various stages of development? Does technology affect or contribute to the experience of *off time*, or non-normative stage transitions? Finally, how does family development differ in families with continuous access to technology and in families without such access? Note that we could pose parallel questions about the development of friendship groups or networks—indeed, any networks of close relations.

Home use of the computer and of smartphones will likely affect some stages more than others. For example, it could harm "early marriages"—newly formed couples and couples with no children or young children—more than long-established relationships. Usually, families with preschool children need to invest much time in preserving cohesion and solving new problems. They cannot afford to devote much time to texting or email (unless it is work-related and unavoidable), or parenting and marital quality could suffer. Smartphones, however, seem to be connected to almost every hand now, whatever they are doing as well.

Busy working couples in settled, loving relationships rely on ICTs to keep in touch with each other. Technologies then are helping relationship connections. Communication technologies also allow parents to keep in touch with their children when they are away from home, or at college or university. Increasingly, email, texting, and Skype can be an important means of staying in touch with relatives in different parts of the world, as well as with aging parents.

Communication Technology and the Forming of Relationships

As mentioned earlier, technology not only helps maintain relationships, it increasingly helps create them. While dates and romantic relationships were traditionally initiated via face-to-face interaction, people now rely to a large degree on launching romantic relationships via Facebook or online dating sites (Sautter, Tippett, and Morgan, 2010). A study that investigated how gender influences the choice of communication means suggests that males and females differ in their pattern of preference for communication in making the first move. Women initiate more first moves through texting than by telephone (Byrne and Findlay, 2004). The increasing popularity of texting in recent years is contributing to changes in dating scripts.

Traditional courtship—picking up the telephone and asking someone on a date—required courage, strategic planning and a considerable investment of ego (by telephone, rejection stings). Not so with texting, e-mail, Twitter or other forms of "asynchronous communication," as techies call it. In the context of dating, it removes much of the need for charm; it's more like dropping a line in the water and hoping for a nibble.

"I've seen men put more effort into finding a movie to watch on Netflix Instant than composing a coherent message to ask a woman out," said Anna Goldfarb, 34, an author and blogger in Moorestown, N.J. A typical, annoying query is the last-minute: "Is anything fun going on tonight?" More annoying still are the men who simply ping, "Hey" or " 'sup."

Source: Williams, 2013.

Online dating is experiencing an incredible boom. Most online daters seek, or say they seek, long-term partners, and list the advantages of internet dating as convenience, privacy and confidentiality, and the opportunity to meet people they would otherwise never meet (Brym and Lenton, 2001; Kang and Hoffman, 2011). Online romantic relationships are thus rapidly becoming commonplace for many Canadians. It is not as common among recent immigrants or particular ethnic groups, such as Muslims or southern Asians, as it is for native-born Canadians and Americans (Sautter, Tippett, and Morgan, 2010).

By referring to millions of users, science, and math, online dating sites suggest that meeting romantic partners online is not only different from, but also better than, searching for partners in conventional ways. Despite being scarce, the research on the extent of

Online Dating

- Online dating sites typically emphasize that their services are unique intended to assist dating through the Internet.

  - The homepage of PlentyOfFish, for example, claims that membership on the site gets you access to "145 million monthly visitors" and that "you are not going to find any other site that has more singles looking to meet new people" (PlentyOfFish.com, 2011).

- Online dating sites also claim that people do better forming relationships using their services than they do dating offline.

- The Web site for eHarmony, for example, asserts that the services the site offers "deliver more than just dates"; instead, it promises connections to "singles who have been prescreened on . . . scientific predictors of relationship success" (eHarmony.com, 2011b, para. 1).

- The OkCupid Website also implies access to knowledge unavailable to the layperson with the straightforward claim, "We use math to get you dates" (OkCupid.com, 2011).

(Finkel, Eastwick, Kamey, et al., 2012)

involvement of older adults in internet dating reveals that older adults do use the internet to meet potential romantic partners. A Canadian study (Brym and Lenton, 2001), for instance, found that 1.6 percent of online daters are age 60 and older, and a number of online dating sites now cater exclusively to clientele over 50. Niche sites exist for every kind of subgroup and preference.

The online relationships of older adults reflect those of their younger counterparts. For instance, Malta (2007) found that older Australian adults (ages 61 to 85) develop intimate, meaningful, and long-lasting relationships online. Further, for a majority the relationships become sexual very quickly, in all cases at the first face-to-face meeting; and for some of the participants, cybersex is an integral part of their relationship. Such results illustrate that the desire for love and intimacy remains very important regardless of age.

The long-term outcomes of relationships formed through internet dating are not known. Given the expanded possibility of meeting people, the types of relationships formed will be more diverse. Future research will need to address several questions: Are these relationships more or less prone to breakups and divorces than relationships formed in other ways? Will spouses feel insecure or suspicious that their partner might be meeting someone else on-line? Will parents who met online have different attitudes to their children's dating? Will they be more open to internet use by their children?

Cyberspace offers people unparalleled opportunities to meet and grow emotionally close to people who may be at a great distance (Kang and Hoffman, 2011; Merkle and Richardson, 2000). Nearness and physical attraction are key in starting a conventional relationship. However, physical attraction may play a less immediate part in the plunge into intimate, sometimes highly sexualized, and self-disclosing cyber-relationships. Many people report adopting bogus names and identities for their interactions online. Deception can be part of the fun of cyberspace, a type of social gaming.

A sense of distance and seeming anonymity reduce the anxiety some people feel about showing their feelings or fears in face-to-face relationships. Usually, people reveal themselves fully only in the deepest and most intimate relationships—typically in those relationships that have survived a test of time. However, in computer-mediated relationships (CMRs), people come to know each other intimately much more quickly than they do in face-to-face relationships. This rapid intimacy may pose a threat to established relationships. Collins (1999) asks, "Should we regard cyber sexual affairs as a species of adultery, an impermissible form of sexual betrayal, and cyber-romances as a comparable species of emotional infidelity?" Computer-mediated relationships, by largely erasing the sexual aspect of betrayal and stressing the emotional aspect, may redefine how our culture thinks about fidelity.

By now, many of us know people who met their mates, or left their spouses, because of cyber-romance. In her classic work on divorce, Diane Vaughan (1985) stresses that a key stage in the breakdown of a marriage is the establishment, by one partner, of an alternate social world. Their partners feel betrayed by internet intimacy because they feel that all intimacy must remain within the boundaries of the marital relationship. However, for some, cybersex or online affairs may not be considered a form of infidelity. Some have suggested that couples may feel a sense of betrayal by a partner's internet relationship. However, a study by Whitty and Quigley (2008) discovered that cybersex or falling in love online may not yet be considered the most upsetting infidelity. In fact, they found that not everyone in their sample was convinced cybersex or online relationships were considered real infidelity, although they did consider them transgressions away from the relationship (Whitty and Quigley, 2008: 465). Cyberspace allows various forms of sexual stimulation without the complications involved with buying porn from book/video stores, prostitutes, and street exhibitionism and voyeurism (Schneider, 2003). Pornography can be accessed or purchased easily, inexpensively, and privately in one's own home. In extreme cases, the activities change from mere browsing to sharing in cybersex with online chat partners. The online infidelity sometimes turns into real-life infidelity for seriously involved users. Schneider's study showed that cybersex or internet pornography can be addictive, affecting relationships with real-life partners. As the user spends less time with the real-life spouse, cybersex can be a major contributor to separation and divorce.

Technology for Family Caregiving

Cyberspace is not only a place for meeting and mating with people, or keeping in touch with family and friends. It is also a storehouse of useful information for people facing challenges. Increasingly, people look to cyberspace for answers to questions about health, jobs, and family relations. In recent years, researchers have paid particular attention to the possible uses of the telephone and internet as means of delivering social support to caregivers. Researchers provided taped informational lectures over the telephone for some subjects and a peer telephone network for others. After three months, caregivers in *both* programs showed less psychological distress, more perception that they were receiving social support, and more satisfaction with the support they were receiving. However, after six months, the gains had levelled off or declined; caregiver burden and social conflict increased again (Goodman, 1990).

Some health professionals have set up telephone support groups for AIDS caregivers. Use of the telephone gives people a sense of confidentiality not always possible in face-to-face groups. It also supports people who are isolated because of the stigma associated with HIV/AIDS and the lack of support networks in their communities (Wiener, Heilman, and Battles, 1998). In one program, caregivers in semi-structured groups made eight conference calls to exchange information about resources and coping strategies. Participants reported feeling satisfied with the group experience (Meier, Galinsky, and Rounds, 1995). They felt less isolated and more personally effective, but their sense of social support and coping did not improve (Rounds, Galinsky, and Despard, 1995).

The internet can also be a source of support for caregivers, and others in need of support. Online chat groups eliminate time and distance barriers and limits on group size; they increase variety and diversity of support, anonymity, pre- and post-group support, opportunity for expression through written communication, and potential training experiences for group leaders (Finn, 1995). Furthermore, the internet connections can have positive effects on caregiver well-being through various support groups and programs. For instance, a study that set out to evaluate the efficacy of a multimedia support program delivered over the internet to employed family caregivers of persons with dementia found that 30 days post-exposure, participants displayed more positive perceptions of caregiving (Beauchamp et al., 2005). The caregivers also showed significant improvements in depression, anxiety, and the level and frequency of stress and caregiver strain. Such interactive multimedia interventions delivered over the internet thus have the potential to provide low-cost, effective social support for caregivers. And today, family caregiver support is much needed, as elder care is becoming a central part of many people's lives.

Potential disadvantages of going online include the chance of destructive interactions, a lack of clear and accountable leadership, limited access to non-computer-using populations, and a lack of research about benefits and user satisfaction (Finn, 1996; Finn and Lavitt, 1994). There are other worries as well, about cyberbullying, about exploitation and violence—the list is very long and concerning (Kowalski, Limber, and Agatson, 2012).

The internet also has a role to play in family therapy, especially in treating families that are isolated or whose members are geographically separated. It is also a valuable source of information on travel, leisure activities, health, and other areas of interest for older adults, who are the fastest-growing group of internet users (Hogeboom et al., 2010; Silver, 2003). Figure 11.3 shows the different areas that attract older surfers to the internet.

Use of computer monitoring can allow older adults who need care to live by themselves—a preference of an increasing number of people of all ages (Klinenberg, 2012). Older adults want to choose who will provide necessary care. Websites provide health-care information for specific conditions to help them make informed decisions on the care they receive, who provides it, and the costs involved.

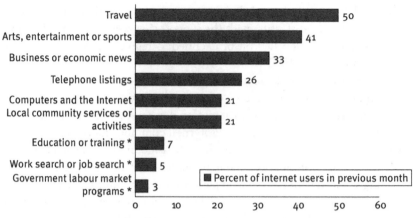

Figure 11.3 What Attracts Older Surfers to the Internet?

Source: Cynthia Silver. 2003. Older surfers. *Canadian Social Trends*. Ottawa: Statistics Canada.
www.statcan.gc.ca/pub/11-008-x/11-008-x2001003-eng.pdf.

Internet access can provide people with illnesses with quick feedback on how their lives and medical condition are affected by their compliance with medication, exercise, and diet. This type of information can lighten the burden on family members who act as caregivers and, at the same time, help older adults retain the sense of autonomy so important to well-being.

Age Differences in Internet Use

- Although the young are the most avid users of ICTs, little difference exists between young and middle-aged adults in Canada with respect to internet use. In 2009, 82.9 percent of Canadians under age 34 used the internet at home at least once a day, compared to 71.9 percent of people aged 35 to 54, 69.1 percent of those 55 to 64, and 65.9 percent of those 65 and older (Statistics Canada, 2010b).

- Of the younger users, nearly half (44.1 percent) used the internet to search for employment opportunities in a typical month. Interestingly, 43.6 percent of young Canadians who were already employed searched for additional employment opportunities online in 2009 (Middleton and Leith, 2007).

- The proportion of surfers aged 16 to 25 who download music in Canada (73.5 percent) is almost double the proportion of those in their late twenties or thirites, and almost six times the proportion of those older than age 50 (Middleton and Leith, 2007).

- Instant messaging programs found on the internet are especially popular among the young, a reflection of a generation that more and more wants to "reach" and "be reached" with immediacy (Middleton and Leith, 2007).

- Older surfers are more likely to search for certain types of information through the internet, including government and health information (Middleton and Leith, 2007).

Electronic bulletin boards can play a similar role, helping caregivers at home to develop problem-solving skills and providing counselling to prevent physical, emotional, and social crises (Bucher, Houts, Mezy, and Maguth Nezy, 1996).

THE NEW REPRODUCTIVE TECHNOLOGIES

New reproductive technologies make it possible to separate fertilization from child-bearing and parenting. In this way, they have the potential to revolutionize family life. Often, however, technologies are used to advance traditional goals by traditional social means— through families, kinship networks, communities, churches, schools, and other ways.

Research by Maureen Baker (2002) illustrates this point. Many cultures link heritage and status to "biological" children—children who are genetically related to their parents. So, in most parts of the world, "blood ties" are central to kinship. As a result, infertility causes people great anxiety, self-doubt, and depression, especially in societies that consider having children equivalent to entering normal adulthood. There, fertility clinics increasingly offer hope. This is a large part of the reason why some ethnic groups curtail women's freedom to the extent they do. Women are seen as the vessels of culture transmission.

More low-fertility couples can now reproduce. This helps to perpetuate the ideal of the "normal" family with biological children, and reinforces, to some degree, the social pressure on all couples to reproduce. For example, many women who have undergone successful fertility treatment want to stay home from work to care for their child after spending so much time and effort trying to reproduce. Rather than challenging traditional views of family, these new technologies appear merely to reinforce them. The wish to create a "normal" and socially accepted family unit remains strong in modern societies.

The same can be said of selective abortion of female fetuses by some ethnic groups whose culture and ethnic practice prefers boys. Fetus sex is determined by ultrasound, a technology typically used to assess the health of the fetus.

Such practices support our argument that technology tends to be a co-producer of social change. Often, technology is merely the handmaiden of human ambitions, however forward or backward those may be. If technology is to be understood in terms of social values and social organization, changes in family life must also be understood in those terms. As shorthand, we can think of recent changes in family life as a growth of *individualization*.

THE GROWTH OF INDIVIDUALIZATION

With industrialism and post-industrialism came a package of changes that had the net effect of allowing people to lead more separate yet interdependent lives. This has had a major impact on family life. Let us focus on one aspect of this change—what we call the *individualization* of people's lives (Jones, Marsden, and Tepperman, 1990; Beck-Gernsheim, 1983; Schultz, 1983; Herlyn and Vogel, 1989). With individualization, there is more variety, fluidity, and idiosyncrasy in all the major demographic processes: in migration, marriage, divorce, child-bearing, family decision making, and the relation of work life and family life. We expect people to be self-sufficient actors in their economic, household, leisure, and intimate relationships.

Individualization of social roles means the empowerment of women through higher levels of formal education and more participation in the paid labour force. The rise of a service economy creates more employment opportunities for women and thus speeds up this process. Any growth in jobs that free people from family dependency and control increases the variety, fluidity, and idiosyncrasy of people's private lives. Nevertheless, they still need and want the emotional attachments of family life.

When people are able to choose their own lives—for example, their mate, their living arrangement, or the number of children they will bear—they exercise this choice. This produces heightened satisfaction—at least, at the time of the decision—but also social changes.

More choice also produces more confusion and ambivalence about how, and when, to limit choice. Do we tolerate or celebrate the marriages of same-sex couples? Support or oppose birth control awareness among teenagers? Allow abortion after the occurrence of sexual abuse or violent sexual assault but not in other cases when women seek it?

The outcome of struggles for and against change in family life is hard to predict. However, it seems likely that anything that (1) slows the growth of opportunities after an earlier growth, (2) increases the individualization of lives faster than the creation of new cultural meanings and norms, or (3) otherwise produces uncertainty and confusion (for example, a war or environmental disaster) will increase support for a backward-looking mythology of the family.

How do people cope with the ambivalence and confusion of intimacy and close relations these days? Typically, they develop new social forms and invent new lifestyles to deal with the doubts they face. *Formal* changes include laws and policies such as new legislation to define marriage and its rights and duties, to support gender equity and affirmative action for women, to improve daycare, and to encourage fertility control. *Informal* changes include efforts people make in their own lives to negotiate new social roles and norms. For example, people work out new ways of disciplining the children of their spouse's first marriage, interacting with their mother's new boyfriend, or getting to know a co-worker's same-sex spouse.

A New Conception of Care

- We were more spoiled than the previous generations from the point of view of education, health . . . we are better at getting services. Plus there is the fact that we have gotten an education, so we know how to formulate our demands (p. 213).

- You have to be fulfilled, you have to have an interesting job; the family comes afterwards. So, you have to establish these things before thinking of others. You have to be fulfilled before thinking of others. I would say that this is what most characterizes the values of the Baby-Boomers (p. 214).

- I told her: "no, that I can't do." Or: "that, I can." Or if she told me: "I need to go to the hospital." Well, I tell her: "Look . . ." I give her my schedule, and I slot her into it, if you will. Sometimes I have changed my schedule; often, even. But when I felt that it was going to be a "No," then . . . But if my mother asks me to do her housework, to wash her fridge every week, to change her bedclothes, etc., I don't want to deal with that, because . . . I just don't want to do it! There are limits that I have to set and it is those limits that I need to negotiate with my mother because I am not ready to drop all my activities (p. 215).

- Someone who does not work, and then goes to help their parents, their expenses should be accounted for. Someone who is working and is obliged to leave their job then finds that they are having a hard time getting social assistance because they are caring for a parent, well they should probably get paid a salary (p. 216).

Source: Guberman, Nancy, Jean-Pierre Lavoie, Laure Blein, and Ignace Olazabal, 2012. "Baby Boom Caregivers: Care in the Age of Individualization," The Gerontologist, 52(2) 210-218. http://0-gerontologist. oxfordjournals.org.darius.uleth.ca/content/52/2/210. full.pdf+html (accessed 21-11-2012).

A new way of understanding the role of intergenerational caregiving, particularly the care of the elderly, has become increasingly vital.

> [Caregivers] object to being confined to the sole identity of caregiver at the expense of the other aspects of their lives. Being a caregiver no longer seems to be something normal, to be taken for granted in one's trajectory. What appears normal… is having a professional life, an active social life, and regular activities that allow them to take care of themselves, and this, even if they are caregivers. In a social context where identity is profoundly marked by the values and social imperatives of productivity, personal growth, and self-realization, Baby Boom family caregivers are continually admonished to fulfill themselves in all spheres of life: as a worker, a lover, a parent, a grandparent, a friend, or a volunteer. This leads to the development of many identities that must be maintained in order to confer a feeling of success. (Guberman, Lavoie, Blein, et al., 2012: 216)

A NEW CULTURE OF INTIMATE LIFE

Out of all these changes, a new culture of intimate life emerges. Social and cultural changes, in turn, bring pressure for further changes by government and business. For example, the growth in part-time work, work sharing, and workplace child care all reflect, in part, new ideas about the necessary relationship between work and family life.

In turn these changes further increase choice, confusion, and cultural change, so the cycle of family change continues. With few exceptions, this cycle works similarly in all societies. Bearing that in mind, what kinds of families are likely to result from this continuing process of individualization? At least four main kinds of nuclear family are likely to appear, which differ along two main dimensions: (1) role separability and (2) personal interchangeability (Jones et al., 1990).

Role separability in families refers to the separation of being a spouse from being a parent. Many North American households are made up of cohabiting couples with children, or reconstituted or blended families, where spouses may or may not parent one another's children. A second dimension, **personal interchangeability**, refers to the choice of a spouse based on his or her ability to fill certain roles rather than for the individual's unique characteristics. People who marry for love choose a mate for his or her unique characteristics. People who marry for instrumental reasons are more interested in a mate who is a good provider, or who can produce healthy offspring. Personal interchangeability is well suited to societies with high rates of mortality. By contrast, purely romantic marriages are unpredictable and unstable.

Now we can cross-classify nuclear families along these two dimensions. Doing so yields four possibilities: We call them (1) corporate, (2) collected, (3) concatenated, and (4) cyclical families.

Inseparable family roles and personal interchangeability characterize the **corporate family**. In this kind of family people can come and go without changing the essential structure of the family. The husband serves as father to the younger generation in the household—children, apprentices, and household servants—and the wife serves as mother, whoever the natural parents of these children may be.

It is only in a society dominated by this kind of family that people can think and speak of "the family" as a well-defined social institution. The state protects the institution of "the family." In culture and by law, "the family" has social importance, enjoys its own resources, and commands its members' loyalties. This kind of family underlines its members' duty to the group. As Sacks (1991) says, such families exist because of choices people do *not* make: To be a child is to accept the authority of parents one did not choose. To be a parent is to accept responsibility for a future one may not live to see (Sacks, 1991: 56–7).

This kind of family is best suited to a theocratic, undifferentiated social structure. There, the state, the law, and religion are closely tied together and lean the same way on family matters. In societies where the corporate family dominates, competing models of life—for example, notions that individuals have rights and liberties—and competing institutions (like the secular school) hold little sway. The "corporate family" existed among the nineteenth- and early twentieth-century European and North American middle classes. It is a patriarchal family in which a double standard prevails and in which men are dominant. Today, the corporate family—once the dominant model in Western societies—has lost its support in law and public opinion, at least in Canada. In the more religious United States, such a patriarchal model of the family still prevails in traditional circles, despite the mass culture's commitment to romantic choice. An attempt to combine the two notions of marriage is evident in the popular HBO series about polygamy in Utah, *Big Love*.

By contrast, separable roles and interchangeable performers characterize the **collected family**. It is similar to Duberman's (1975) "reconstituted" family, which follows the remarriage of partners who have children from previous unions. Like the corporate family, the collected family needs family members to conform to traditional notions of husband, wife, father, mother, and child. However, given the complexities of remarriage, family members concede the impossibility of compelling mates to be both good spouses *and* good parents to the resident children.

In these families, it is not the family as a whole but the unit roles that are the locus of loyalty, meaning, and resources. Children are allowed to feel close to their mother, for example, without feeling obliged to love her intimate partner or call him "Daddy." Societies like our own—with growing numbers of reconstituted families—are beginning to recognize the odd character and special needs of collected families. For example, the state increasingly delivers benefits to partners *or* parents *or* children, not to the "family head" of earlier days. In this system, one cannot assume the family has a "head," or even that the traditional idea of "family head" has any meaning today.

A third kind of family, the **concatenated family**, is exactly opposite to the corporate family, since separable roles and unique performers characterize it. From the outside, the concatenated family looks like a chance event, a slow collision of individuals in time and space. The concatenated family is nothing more than a household at a particular moment.

Here, family members vest meanings, loyalties, and resources in particular individuals, not roles. Families exist only through sharing these meanings and resources. As a result, family members must constantly affirm and renegotiate the bases for this sharing.

Here, the meaning of *intimate partner* or *parent* is no longer certain. Occasionally definitions will mesh for long periods. In any event we cannot assume, in these families, that members will have a permanent commitment to "the family" or even to their current partner and children. The concatenated family is an extreme version of radical individualism. It assumes that people ought to have continuous, unlimited free choice in their living arrangements. This freedom is subject only to the legal protection of minors from the results of a family breakdown and the protection of all family members from household violence. Supporters of this family type see family life as a lifestyle or individual choice—so far as the adults are concerned, a supermarket for intimate relations.

In this system, mating is motivated by considerations of the spouse's unique characteristics, which may not continue to allure. Child-bearing is motivated by a biological drive to reproduce or by self-expression—a form of psychic consumption of children for personal pleasure. Under these conditions, marital dissolutions will likely be frequent. Not surprisingly, this family system creates many potential kinship connections—for example, many sets of grandparents (Gross, 1987). However, more mothers than fathers will remain with their children in case of a divorce. So in practice, concatenated families (with children) are more matrifocal. Women and children remain in the household, while men come and go. In North America and Europe, concatenated families are still far from the average.

Like the corporate family, the **cyclical (or recycled) family** features traditional (inseparable) roles. Still, unlike the corporate family, there is no interchangeability in the cyclical one. Each is a "return engagement" occurring *because of* the unique relationship of the members. This return engagement may be a second marriage of the same people, which is rare but occurs. More often, it is a second parenthood, during which people are called on to parent their now-adult children (occasionally called "boomerang kids") a second time.

For example, in Canada since 1981 the percentages of men and women between the ages of 20 to 34 living with parents have risen significantly. The result is a complex household that *looks* like a corporate family but has none of the predictability or normative power of that older arrangement. Many reasons account for the return of adult children: unemployment, inadequate income for accommodation, or the need for extra education or babysitting help. Unique family situations result from an interaction between the reasons for return and the expectations of the children and parents.

We can wonder whether the change from corporate families to collected, concatenated, and cyclical families is as certain as it seems. Some wishful thinkers want (and some policy-makers encourage) mothers of preschool children to leave the workforce and devote their adult lives to family. If they did, family incomes would drop significantly. For illustration, in 2000 women contributed 35.6 percent to the total household income in the United States (Boushey, 2009) and 42 percent in Canada in 2008 (Statistics Canada, 2009).

Even after considering the costs that they would not incur, such as daycare and other work-related expenses, families would still suffer a net loss of income. The loss would be greatest for those dual-income families in which the wife earns more than the husband—25.3 percent of dual-earner families in the United States (Selvin, 2007) and 29 percent in Canada (Statistics Canada, 2006i). However, there are no signs suggesting a return to old, restrictive family forms—at least not in Canada.

LIKELY CHANGES IN THE FUTURE

When Canadians discuss family today, they talk about two things. They stress that families, and what happens with families, matter to them. They also talk about the diversity of families today in comparison to the past. We hear about married couples with or without children, common-law or cohabiting couples with or without children, female- or male-headed single-parent families, adoptive families, foster families, empty nesters, gay or lesbian families, and the list goes on. At times the impression might be that a smorgasbord of choices about how to live in families exists.

Viewing diverse families only as varied structures may be deceptive in other ways. We may overlook or underestimate diversity *within* various family forms, suggesting that

Major Findings about Families

- In 2003, 30 percent of women primary bread-winners had a university degree compared with 21 percent of secondary-earner wives and 25 percent of primary-earner husbands. Moreover, more than one-third of primary-earner wives had more education than their husbands (Statistics Canada, 2006i).

- Canada is one of the developed countries with the lowest rates of communication between young people and their parents, with fewer than 50 percent of Canadian teens talking with their parents on a regular basis (Bernard, 2008).

- Family meals are most common in Italy (93.8 percent), France (90.4 percent), and Switzerland (89.9 percent). Canada lags behind, with only 72 percent of Canadian 15-year-olds saying they sit down with their parents to eat the main meal of the day "several times a week" (Bernard, 2008).

- In Canada, the 2011 census revealed that 20.9 percent of households headed by lesbian couples had children, versus 3.96 percent among male same-sex households (Statistics Canada, 2012a).

- Forty-four percent of Canadians feel that their work has a negative impact on their family and interferes with the amount of time they spend with their children (Duxbury and Higgins, 2003).

- Employees with a serious work–family conflict miss an average of 13.2 days of work a year versus 5.9 days missed for those without a conflict. This results in financial losses of $2.7 billion a year in direct costs and $10 billion in indirect costs in Canada (Barette, 2009).

families are more uniform than they are. The term *family* itself may be too restrictive, ignoring everyone to whom we are not related by conventional notions of blood or marriage. This restrictive idea of family, which suggests a clear distinction between family and friends, takes away from us other ways to care for those we like. For example, we may parcel out our love and caring cautiously, thinking that family has a monopoly on caring. Yet, as discussed in Chapter 10, people may define many different kinds of people as family (McDaniel, 1994).

People are inventing new ways to be family. **Other-mothering** is one such family innovation, which allows extended relations or friends to mother children and moves beyond the nuclear, biological family. Other-mothering is

> . . . revolutionary in American society because it takes place in opposition to the ideas that parents, especially mothers, should be the only child rearers . . . This kind of shared responsibility for child care can only happen in small community settings where people know and trust one another. It cannot happen in those settings if parents regard their children as their 'property,' their possession. (hooks, 1984: 144)

The Vanier Institute of the Family (2004) lists the "top 10 trends for Canadian families" as follows:

1. Fewer couples are getting legally married.

2. More couples are breaking up.

3. Families are getting smaller.

4. Children experience more transitions as parents change their marital status.

5. Canadians are satisfied with life.

6. Family violence [continues to be] under-reported.

7. Multiple-earner families [have become] the norm.

8. Women [continue to do] most of the juggling involved in balancing work and home.

9. [Socio-economic] inequality [between families] is worsening.

10. The future will have more aging families.

Not all of these items are truly "trends." For example, items 5, 6, 7, and 8 make no statement about change over time, so they are not trends. However, the other items identify continuing changes—trends—in Canadian family life that we have discussed in this text.

As social scientists and as citizens, we have several ways of responding to these stated trends. First, we can continue to watch the data and report whether these trends are continuing. Second, we can make and test theories about the reasons for these trends. Third, we can propose and evaluate social policies that will increase the benefits and decrease the harms associated with these trends. Fourth, we can lead public discussions about the ways we can promote the trends we favour and slow down the trends we dislike.

We have argued throughout this text that inevitably more people will cohabit and divorce and bear fewer children (items 1–3 on p. 380), and by implication that children will experience more transitions as parents change their relationships (item 4). Not only are these trends universal in industrial societies, they are unlikely to reverse themselves and they result from the growth of human freedom—a quality most of us would want to promote. Also, families and populations will continue to age (item 10); this is a sure result of the decline in child-bearing.

It is hard to imagine social conditions that would lead Canadians to return to low rates of cohabitation or divorce or to high birth rates. It is therefore important for us to think about the problems these conditions create, and the ways we can reduce the associated harm. Consider, for example, the changes associated with the rise to dominance of the multiple-earner family, a family form that is likely to become even more common in the future.

Dual-Income Families

Dual-income families are important harbingers of family change. As discussed earlier, the proportion of women with families who work outside the home has grown steadily. This pattern is not likely to change. The economy needs the wages and skills of women too much, and governments need the taxes women contribute. Career and job commitments may lead to postponed weddings and to more commuting relationships in the future. Women may delay child-bearing, but the emotional value placed on children will still mean that most couples will have children at some point.

In years to come, life with children and two incomes will continue to challenge both work and family for both men and women. With changes in the global marketplace, men's work may not be as privileged as it was in the past, when men were viewed as *primary* family providers. Women increasingly are taking on the role of provider, even where a man is present, as men's work becomes more precarious and insecure. More husbands may follow their spouses' career or job opportunities. This means changes in the roles and expectations of spouses and in the ways children come to see what mothers and fathers are and do.

Refilled Nests

For a time it was the common pattern that children grew up and left the family home when they could make their own way in the world. However, as discussed in Chapter 10, couples who thought that their children had grown up and "flown away" soon experience a **refilled nest** with adult children who are returning to school (or have never left school), having trouble finding or keeping jobs, getting separated or divorced, or even having children of their own (Boyd and Pryor, 1989).

The future may be, then, like the past: Some families live in refilled nests only out of necessity and see themselves as merely pooling housing and resources to survive. Others, however, may see huge creative possibilities in refilled nests—grandparents providing child care while parents work; sharing housework among more family members; reducing environmental problems by having fewer accommodations; developing new ways of intergenerational caring for elders. In her book *The Boomerang Age*, Canadian sociologist Barbara Mitchell notes that today's young people often move through a larger variety of family-related roles, statuses, and living arrangements.

Mitchell also notes that public issues such as globalization, the decline of the welfare state, and various forms of social inequality affect the circumstances of young adulthood, resulting in an increased need for social policy reforms related to education, housing, child care, and gender equality. However, increased individualization in the pursuit of social goals makes the problems associated with boomerang kids almost unavoidable, for we are unlikely to see a permanent return to the traditional, extended family.

Nominal and Virtual Families

In the future, we are also likely to see an increase in the number of non-standard "virtual" families, and increased confusion about how these families should be treated, relative to what we are calling "nominal" families. *Nominal families* are those empowered (by law) to care for their members—in particular, for children, older adults, and people with disabilities or severe illnesses. *Virtual families* do the actual work of caring for these family members. To be sure, in many households, virtual families *are* nominal families—that is, the working family unit coincides in structure with the legal definition of family. But as domestic arrangements continue to diversify, family responsibilities are increasingly being taken up by a broad and non-traditional range of caregivers. Virtual families may include grandparents, aunts, uncles, cousins, friends, and even neighbours.

To understand the difference, consider Kay, a 24-year-old university student. Kay lived in Toronto for the past seven years with her younger brother, her mother's mother, Bea, and Bea's second husband, Harold. Kay's younger sister, Jo, lives in a group home in Oshawa; she attends school only sporadically and periodically gets into trouble with the law. Bea has refused to let her come home, because Jo has stolen money from Bea in the past to buy drugs. Kay's estranged mother, a drug addict, lived in Sudbury until last spring, when she died of a drug overdose. Kay has met her father only once, though he lives in Toronto with a wife and young children. Kay is emotionally closest to her grandmother, her sister, and an aunt—her mother's sister—who lives in Ottawa. Kay has recently moved to Montreal, where she will live with a close friend from high school and attend a different university. Question: Who are the members of Kay's "family"? Answer: It's hard to say. Gazso and McDaniel (2014) have studied a number of what they call "families by choice," finding that many people, perhaps particularly those in low income, make families for themselves.

Canadian policy-makers tend to think in terms of nominal families. Virtual families, in contrast, reflect the true diversity of our nation's family landscape. Only after we have adequately defined "families" can we study the formation and dissolution of "families." With virtual families, this may mean studying the formation and dissolution of intimate, long-lived support groups or support networks—networks of kin and friends who care for Canada's children, older adults, and people with disabilities or severe illnesses.

How does this notion of nominal versus virtual family connect with shifting patterns of family structure, formation, and dissolution, and what are the policy implications? Take, as an example, the issue of custody rights following divorce. In most jurisdictions, when a couple divorces, only they—as heads of a nominal family—have automatic rights to child custody and access. Yet in Canada's increasingly diverse family landscape, new partners, grandparents, uncles and aunts, friends, older siblings, fictive kin, and others— potential members of a virtual family—may play at least as big a role as one or both biological parents in caring for those children. While current legal and social policies assign to parents the default right to these children, other people who have accepted responsibility for them may be refused rights to custody or access.

The policy challenges, then, are to recognize the limits of traditional legal and social definitions in capturing the modern diversity of family structures; to better document the practical and often inventive networks of caregiving that families create to promote their own well-being; and to ensure that social programs and services are delivered with these realities of Canadian family life in mind.

There are a great many things we need to learn about virtual and nominal families in Canada. For example,

■ What is the (empirical) *overlap* between nominal families and virtual families in Canada today? For example, what proportion of families is both nominal and virtual? How does this overlap (or congruence) vary regionally, and by various groupings (age, ethnicity, and so on)? If we don't know, how could we find out (since this pattern identifies the most vulnerable families)?

■ *How well do people do* in virtual families, compared with people in nominal families? Are we right to assume that people in well-functioning virtual families (whether or not these families are also nominal) are the happiest and healthiest Canadians? If we don't know, how could we find it out?

■ What factors affect the *well-being of people in virtual families*? In particular, are virtual families hampered by not enough income or not enough rights to perform their family-like roles? If we don't know, how could we find it out?

■ What factors affect the *formation, maintenance, and dissolution of virtual families*? What factors influence members of these families to continue supporting one another? And, for virtual families, what defines "formation," and what defines "dissolution"? If we don't know, how could we find out?

■ How are virtual families—their formation, dissolution, and well-being—affected by any of the following *trends*: increases in cohabitation; immigration; poverty and unemployment, especially among the young (for example, boomerang generation);

globalization and increased LAT; improved new communications technology for holding family together at a distance; in-home work; young mothers working outside the home; increased longevity; prolonged survival of people with disabilities or severe illness; same-sex union formation; individualization of women's lives? What effects do these trends have on family problems, such as domestic violence? If we don't know, how could we find out?

The Future of Immigrant Families

Previous chapters have noted that Canada faces a future of increased immigration and interaction between cultures from all over the world. Simultaneously, the country will witness further modifications to family forms. According to Bourne and Rose (2001), these are two of the most important transformations already occurring in Canadian society. We can foresee increased diversity in metropolitan areas as well as shifts in social attitudes regarding work and gender relations (Bourne and Rose, 2001: 107). These changes will occur in combination with each other to change both the future of immigrant families and of our country. No doubt, they will affect the variety of family lives in this country.

Diversity Across the Life Course

Immigration is not the only source of increased variety. The trend toward diversity in close relations across the life cycle reveals a clear pattern of individualization of family life. People live longer now than ever before. In the lifetime allotted to each of us, we can—and likely will—live in many kinds of families. This is true even if our family lives

---

Challenges of Immigrant Fathers

- We do not have opportunities to gain good jobs despite our educational credentials. It seems we are relegated to secondary status because of the color of our skin. This causes considerable stress on us as individuals and our families. (p. 149)

- As long as you are underpaid, you do not feel good and all the things that you need for your children you do not get so you are really under pressure and one can get distressed. (p. 149)

- We share the kitchen. I do not wait when I come home from work...[at home] that [did] not happen. A man [did] not go into the kitchen. (p. 150)

- The tough part is that it is only me who... [cares for] my family...But if we were back home, I do not see anything...tough in taking care of the family because the responsibility of the family is not mine alone. All relatives are part of this process. (p. 150)

Source: Este, David C. and Admasu A. Tachble, 2009. "The Perceptions and Experiences of Russian Immigrant and Sudanese Refugee Men as Fathers in an Urban Center in Canada," The ANNALS of the American Academy of Political and Social Science, 624(1)139-155. http://ann.sagepub.com/content/624/1/139.full.pdf+html (accessed 27-11-2012)

---

are stable and secure. Children grow up and leave home eventually—even if it takes them a longer time to do so! Couples find themselves in different family situations by living year after year. The longer we live, the more family diversity we will face. The life-cycle perspective offers a different view of diversity and one well worth considering, if for no other reason than to promote tolerance of other ways of being close in families.

Policy Challenges

Societies are not especially good at guessing the challenges that will face them in a few years. Growing family inequalities pose major policy challenges today (McDaniel, Gazso, and Um, 2013).

Between 1990 and 2010, the richest 1 percent of Canadian tax filers accounted for 10.6 percent of the national income, down from a peak of 12.1 percent in 2006 (Statistics Canada, 2013), while incomes remained stagnant for the poorest 20 percent. The result is increasing family income inequality in Canada, a trend obvious since 1980. Using data from the terminated Survey of Consumer Finances (SCF) and its replacement, the Survey of Labour and Income Dynamics (SLID), Picot and Myles (2004) reported a 6 percent increase in the inequality in incomes of Canadian families between 1990 and 2000, which has widened further since. That said, income inequality has always been greater in Canada than it is in Europe, though considerably lower than in the United States.

The most recent available statistics, for 2008, show a Gini index (measuring the inequality of family incomes) of 32.1 in Canada compared with 45.0—more than a third higher—in the United States (CIA World Factbook, 2008).

This inequality, of course, is not evenly spread around the population. Statistics Canada reports that a few Canadian groups are especially subject to long-term or persistent economic deprivation: "Persistent low income tends to be concentrated among five groups: single parents, recent immigrants, people with work disabilities, unattached people aged between 45 and 64, and Aboriginal people" (Statistics Canada, 2005g).

Traditionally, government support and tax policies have reduced family income inequalities. However, transfer payments did less in the 1990s and 2000s to mitigate the market effects of income inequality than they did in the 1980s (Frenette, Green, and Milligan, n.d.).

Will continuing declines in government support for low-income families further increase inequality? Research evidence suggests that this is a significant problem, not only for low-income families, but for all of society. In pioneering research, Wilkinson (1994) demonstrated that mortality rates and life expectancies in the industrialized world are more closely related to income inequality than to per capita income or per capita economic growth. Despite an overall increase in Canadian life expectancies, shorter life expectancies are found in poorer neighborhoods—and the poorer, the shorter (Statistics Canada, 2002k).

McDaniel (1998) showed how meanings given to relative deprivation filter through families. Poor children in wealthy societies feel bad about themselves and often blame their families. This has severe implications for their life chances and potential to contribute to society. Cheal (1996: xv) adds that two factors—the higher risks of being poor while a child and the shortage of government programs for low-income families with children—pose a huge cause for concern about future families. Poor children often grow up to be poor adults.

A second major policy challenge is child care, as discussed earlier. If mothers of young children continue to work for pay in the numbers they currently do, and if "mother work" remains mainly a woman's domain, some solutions to caring for children must be found. In the lengthy public deliberation on the pros and cons of daycare, children are not getting the care they need.

This issue is central to the future of families, since without some solution, couples may have little choice but to restrict their child-bearing even further or forgo parenthood altogether. All society would suffer as a result. Child care is also important to gender equality, since affordable child care makes it easier for women to contribute to society in ways equal to their talents and education.

We openly admit the centrality of families to our individual lives and happiness and to our collective future and yet we seem reluctant to meet the needs of families in developing creative solutions. Lesemann and Nicol (1994: 124) noted that, "It is paradoxical that the family seems simultaneously to be recognized and supported by the government . . . and abandoned by it."

The authors of an analysis of data from the National Longitudinal Survey of Children and Youth (NLSCY) end with a "blueprint for a family-enabling society." The first recommendation is constructive collaboration among all levels of government, parents, teachers, and children themselves to set the conditions for improving outcomes for children. The Early Childhood Development (ECD) Accord between the provinces and the federal government in 2000 identified four areas of co-operation: promoting healthy pregnancy, birth, and infancy; improving parenting and family supports; strengthening early childhood development, learning, and care; and strengthening community supports.

The second is investment in human capital, based on lifelong learning. To achieve this, we need seamless and universal support for families, from conception to kindergarten. Older children, strongly influenced by classroom and school environments, need continuing educational and social supports to stay in school.

The third is social inclusion. Successful communities bolster outcomes for their least advantaged children. Finally, we need an increased capacity for program evaluation, oversight, and research. We need to examine policies to see if they are making the intended difference.

The United Nations Convention on the Rights of the Child was confirmed by Canada in 1991. Respect for children is implicit in the research collected and in the conclusions of the NLSCY study. However, respect for children must be put into practice to build a family-enabling society and to have positive results for vulnerable children. Children must be viewed as having inherent rights as human beings. They must also be seen as individuals with a growing need for autonomy.

CONCLUDING REMARKS

Two views of history are directly useful for our glimpse into the future of families. First, there is the image of the present as the peak of progress; according to this view, the future advances in the same direction. A contrasting view, equally prevalent, is that we used to have, or be, something wonderful, but with time what was good slipped away and was replaced by a society with fewer clear values, more social problems, less stability, and less certainty.

We consider both views simplistic. We end this text with a call for modest optimism about the future of the family. In all likelihood, the future holds new and unforeseen problems that will challenge many families and their members—in addition to all the problems we can already expect.

So far, no one has found a technological fix for the kinds of organizational, interpersonal, and emotional problems that normally arise in ordinary family life—indeed, in all close relations. We do not foresee an easy solution to the problems of family life through genetic engineering, artificial intelligence, faster computers, smarter houses, better electrical appliances, or little white pills that can satisfy our human needs for love, meaning, belonging, attachment, and communication. However, families themselves will continue to largely meet these needs. And through continuing study we can hope to learn more about how healthy families work and how to help other families do the same.

CHAPTER SUMMARY

In this chapter, we mulled over the future of close relations, beginning with a clear understanding that social prediction is far from a perfect science or art. Contesting visions of families in the future are considered.

We began with an examination of the new communication technologies, virtual communities, and the role of families in the "connected society." We noted that new technologies increase the reach of family life, instead of limiting it, as critics had feared. While it is difficult to predict the likely effects of cyberspace on family life, we noted that two major communication technologies— telephone and email—did not transform family life as drastically as people had expected. On the contrary, they allowed people to pursue their most cherished goals more efficiently.

ICTs pose problems with sexuality, specifically cybersex and the potential for online infidelity and cyberbullying. Mating and dating online create new ethical issues and may force families to rethink what they mean by commitment in the face of extended sexual opportunities. The same technology that extends the reach of mating and dating also extends the reach of caregiving. So, just as technology lures people away from their families, it also allows them to pay closer attention to their family members' needs, if they wish.

The new reproductive technologies also show the importance of human agency. Though these new technologies offer new opportunities and new ethical challenges, they are being used to further traditional pro-natalist agendas.

The most dramatic future changes to family life are extensions of a change that has been in process for centuries: the individualization of family life. More families are rethinking spousal and parental roles and shifting away from uniform corporate family structures to a wide variety of collected, concatenated, and cyclical family structures.

We noted various trends in this chapter; for example, families continue to get smaller, children experience more transitions as parents change their marital status, family violence continues to be under-reported, multiple-earner families have become the norm, socio-economic inequality between families is worsening, and the future will have more aging families.

Dual-income families will continue to be important carriers of family change. In years to come, life with children and two incomes will continue to challenge both work and family for both men and women.

Family nests can refill readily when adult children bring their own children and possibly spouses back to the family home. The increase in boomerang families will place new demands on parents and children alike. In short, the longer we live, the more family diversity we will face.

Growing family inequalities pose a major policy challenge today. In the past 20 years, income inequalities have widened in Canada. The concern for the future is whether continuing declines in government support for low-income families will further increase family inequality in Canada. Family policy challenges are complex and diverse and their solution may be central to the future of families and of us all.

Key Terms

collected family A structure that requires family members to conform to traditional notions of husband, wife, father, mother, and child. However, given the complexities of remarriage, family members concede the impossibility of compelling mates to be both good spouses *and* good parents to the resident children.

concatenated family A family exactly opposite to the corporate family, characterized by separable roles and unique performers. The concatenated family is nothing more than a household at a particular moment in time.

corporate family A family in which people can come and go without changing the essential structure of the family. The husband serves as father to the younger generation in the household—children, apprentices, and household servants—and the wife serves as mother, whoever the natural parents of these children may be.

cyclical (or recycled) family A family form featuring traditional (inseparable) roles, but no role interchangeability. Instead, the performances of its members are unique. Each is a "return engagement" occurring *because of* the unique relationship of the members.

other-mothering Close parental-type care by extended relations or friends.

personal interchangeability Choosing a spouse based on his or her ability to fill certain roles rather than for the individual's unique characteristics.

refilled nests Family homes to which adult children have returned, possibly bringing their own children and/or spouses.

role separability The separation of being a spouse from being a parent.

Critical Thinking Questions

1. What is the impact on intimacy of always being connected to the world via one electronic medium or another? Is there a difference in using ICTs to maintain relations with people who are at a distance compared to people with whom we share a close environment?

2. Consider two stereotypes: first, that older adults do not use computers—especially, not the internet—and, second, that older adults do not have sex. How do these stereotypes influence research and hence knowledge about computer-mediated communication and the nature of online romantic relationships for older adults?

3. Generally, how do computer-mediated relationships (CMRs) compare to face-to-face

relationships in terms of intimacy and gender roles? Are the dating scripts different for CMRs, in your opinion?

4. The percentage of women in the labour force in Canada rose from 33 percent in 1971 to more than 50 percent in 2008, and of this number, 69 percent were mothers with a child younger than three years old. How can women today balance work–family conflict without returning to traditional family forms?

5. Why does one have to keep in mind the distinction between nominal versus virtual family, and what are the policy implications? Discuss how closing the gap between virtual and nominal families will change family life in the future.

Weblinks

References

Abad, Neetu S., & Kennon M. Sheldon. 2008. Parental autonomy support and ethnic culture identification among second-generation immigrants. *Journal of Family Psychology* 22: 652–657.

Abbott, Douglas A., & Glenna Slater. 2000 Spring. Strengths and stresses of Omaha Indian families living on the reservation. *Great Plains Research* 10(1): 145–168.

Abe, Namiko. 2005. Getting married in Japan. *Japanese Language*. Retrieved November 4, 2005, from **http://japanese.about.com/library/weekly/aa080999.htm**

Abu-Laban, Sharon McIrvin, & Susan A. McDaniel. 1998. Beauty, status and aging, pp. 78, 102. In Nancy Mandell (Ed.), *Feminist Issues: Race, Class and Sexuality* (2nd edition). Scarborough, ON: Prentice-Hall Allyn and Bacon.

Abu-Laban, Sharon, & Susan A. McDaniel. 2004. Aging women and standards of beauty. In Nancy Mandell (Ed.), *Feminist Issues: Race, Class and Sexuality* (4th edition). Toronto: Prentice-Hall.

Ackerman, Marc J. 1996. *Does Wednesday Mean Mom's House or Dad's? Parenting Together While Living Apart*. Toronto: Wiley & Sons.

Adams, Rebecca G. 1998. The demise of territorial determinism: Online friendships, pp. 153–162. In Rebecca G. Adams and Graham Allan (Eds.), *Placing Friendship in Context*. UK: Cambridge University Press.

Adams, Rebecca G., & Michelle Stevenson. 2002. A lifetime of relationships mediated by technology. In F. Lang and K.L. Fingerman (Eds.), *Growing Together: Personal Relationships Across the Lifespan*. New York: Cambridge University Press.

Aguilar, Rudy J., & Narina Nunez Nightingale. 1994 March. The impact of specific battering experiences on the self-esteem of abused women. *Journal of Family Violence* 9: 35–45.

Ahmadi, Khodabakhsh, & Fateme Hossein-abadi. 2009. Religiosity, marital satisfaction and child rearing. *Pastoral Psychology* 57: 211–221.

Ahrons, Constance R., & Jennifer L. Tanner. 2003. Adult children and their fathers: Relationship changes 20 years after parental divorce. *Family Relations* 52(4): 340–351.

Aida, Yukie, & Toni Falbo. 1991. Relationships between marital satisfaction, resources, and power strategies. *Sex Roles* 24(1–2): 43–56.

Ajrouch, Kristine J., Kathryn M. Yount, Alba M. Sibai, and Pia Roman. 2013. "A Gendered Perspectives on Well-Being in Later Life." In Susan A. McDaniel and Zachary Zimmer (Eds.), *Global Ageing in the Twenty-First Century: Challenges, Opportunities and Implications*. (pp. 49–78). Farnham, Surrey, UK: Ashgate.

Alam, S.S., Yeow, P., & Loo, H.S. (2011). An Empirical Study on Online Social Networks Sites Usage: Online Dating Sites Perspective. *International Journal of Business and Management*, 6(10), 155–161.

Alberta Justice. 2002. Alberta's Adult Interdependent Relationship Act and you. Retrieved August 5, 2005, from **http://www.justice.gov.ab.ca/home/default.aspx?id=3550**

Alexander, Christopher. 1997. Factors contributing to the termination of long-term gay male relationships. *Journal of Gay & Lesbian Social Services* 7(1): 1–12.

Al-Krenawi, A., V. Slonim-Nevo, Y. Maymon, & S. Al-Krenawi. 2001. Psychological responses to blood vengeance about Arab adolescents. *Child Abuse & Neglect* 25(4).

Allan, Graham, Graham Crow, and Sheila Hawkers, eds. 2011. *Stepfamilies*. Basingstoke: Palgrave.

Alterovitz, Sheyna, & Mendelsohn. 2009. Partner preferences across the life span: Online dating by older adults. *Psychology and Aging* 24(2): 513–517.

Amato, Paul R. 1996 August. Explaining the intergenerational transmission of divorce. *Journal of Marriage and the Family* 58.

Amato, Paul R. 2010. "Research on Divorce: Continuing Trends and New Developments," *Journal of Marriage and Family* 72 (3): 650–666.

Amato, Paul R., & Alan Booth. 1996 May. A prospective study of divorce and parent–child relationships. *Journal of Marriage and the Family* 58: 356–365.

Amato, Paul R., & J.M. Sobolewski. 2001. The effects of divorce and marital discord on adult children's psychological well-being. *American Sociological Review* 66: 900–921.

Amato, Paul R., David R. Johnson, Alan Booth, & Stacy J. Rogers. 2003. Continuity and change in marital quality between 1980 and 2000. *Journal of Marriage and the Family* 65: 1–22.

Amato, Paul R., Laura Spencer Loomis, & Alan Booth. 1995. Parental divorce, marital conflict and offspring well-being during early adulthood. *Social Forces* 73(3): 895–915.

Ambert, Anne-Marie. 2002. *Divorce: Facts, causes, and consequences*. Ottawa: Vanier Institute of the Family.

Ambert, Anne-Marie. 2005a. Cohabitation and marriage: How are they related? Ottawa: Vanier Institute of the Family. Retrieved November 15, 2005, from **http://www.vifamily.ca/library/cft/cohabitation.html**

Ambert, Anne-Marie. 2005b. Divorce: Facts, causes and consequences. Ottawa: Vanier Institute of the Family. Retrieved December 9, 2005, from **www.vifamily.ca/library/cft/divorce_05.html**

Ambert, Anne-Marie. 2005c. Same-sex couples and same-sex-parent families: Relationships, parenting, and issues of marriage. Ottawa: Vanier Institute of the Family. Retrieved January 10, 2006, from **http://www.vifamily.ca/library/cft/samesex_05.html#FAMILIES**

Ammar, Nawal H. 2007. Wife battery in Islam: A comprehensive understanding of interpretations. *Violence Against Women* 13: 516–526.

Amnesty International. 2004, June 2. Turkey: Women confronting family violence. Retrieved July 14, 2005, from **http://web.amnesty.org/library/Index/ENGEUR440132004?open&of=ENG-TUR**

Amnesty International UK (n.d.). A global outrage: Global and UK statistics. Retrieved July 14, 2005, from **http://www.amnesty.org.uk/svaw/vaw/global.shtml**

Andersson, B.E. 1996. Children's development related to day-care, type of family and other home factors. *European Child & Adolescent Psychiatry 5*, supplement 1, 73–75.

Andersson, Gunnar. 2004. Childbearing after migration: Fertility patterns of foreign-born women in Sweden. *International Migration Review* 38: 747–775.

Angus Reid Group. 1999. *Family Matters: A Look at Issues Concerning Families and Raising Children in Canada Today*. Toronto: Angus Reid Group.

Anstorp, Trine, & Kirsten Benum. 1988. Social network stimulation as preventive method among middle-aged women in a neighborhood in Oslo. *International Journal of Family Psychiatry* 6(2): 177–187.

Anthony, E.J. 1970. The impact of mental and physical illness on family life. *American Journal of Psychiatry* 127: 138–145.

Antill, John K., & Sandra Cotton. 1987. Self disclosure between husbands and wives: Its relation to sex roles and marital happiness. *Australian Journal of Psychology* 39(1): 11–24.

Antonucci, T., & Akiyama, A. 1995. Convoys of social relationships: Family and friendships within a life span context, pp. 355–371. In R. Blieszner & V.H. Bedford (Eds.), *Handbook of Aging and the Family* (4th edition). Westport, CT: Greenwood Press.

Applbaum, Kalman. 1995 Winter. Marriage with the proper stranger: Arranged marriages in metropolitan Japan, *Ethnology* 34: 37–51.

Apple, R.D., & J. Coleman. 2003. As members of the social whole: A history of social reform as a focus of home economics, 1895–1940. *Family and Consumer Sciences Research Journal*, 32(2): 104–126.

Applewhite, Larry W., & David R. Segal. 1990 Fall. Telephone use by peacekeeping troops in the Sinai. *Armed Forces and Society* 17(1): 117–126.

Arditti, Joyce A. 1997. Women, divorce, and economic risk. *Family and Conciliation Courts Review* 35(1).

Arendell, Terry J. 1995. *Fathers in Divorce: Best Case Scenarios*. American Sociological Association.

Ariss, Rachel. 2007. Intimacy, commitment, and family formation, pp. 44–63. In David Cheal (Ed.), *Canadian Families Today: New Perspectives*. Toronto: Oxford University Press.

Armitage, Susan H. 1979 April. Household work and childrearing on the frontier: The oral history record. *Sociology and Social Research* 63(3): 467–474.

Armstrong, Pat, & Hugh Armstrong. 1985 Summer. Political economy and the household: Rejecting separate spheres. *Studies in Political Economy* 17: 167–177.

Armstrong, Pat, & Hugh Armstrong. 1994. *The Double Ghetto: Canadian Women and Their Segregated Work* (3rd edition). Toronto: McClelland & Stewart.

Arnup, Katherine. 2012. "Out in this World: The Social and Legal Context of Gay and Lesbian Families." In T. Richard Sullivan (Ed.). 2012. *Queer Families, Common Agendas: Gay People, Lesbians and Family Values*. New York: Routledge, pp. 1–26.

Aseltine, Robert H. Jr. 1996 June. Pathways linking parental divorce with adolescent depression. *Journal of Health and Social Behavior* 37.

Askham, J., Ferring, D., & Lamura, G. 2007. Personal relationships in later life, pp. 186–208. In J. Bond, S. Peace, F. Dittmann-Kohli, and G.J. Westerhof (Eds.), *Ageing in Society*. Sage, London.

Ataca, B., & J.W. Berry. 2002. Psychologcial, sociocultural and martial adaptation of Turkish immigrant couples in Canada. *International Journal of Psychology* 37: 13–26.

Attané, Isabelle. 2012. "Being a Woman in China Today: A Demography of Gender," *China Perspectives* 5–15. **http://chinaperspectives.revues.org/6013**

Attree, Pamela. 2005. Parenting support in the context of poverty: A meta-synthesis of the qualitative evidence. *Health & Social Care in the Community* 13(4): 330–337.

Avison, William R., Jennifer Ali, & David Walters. 2007. Family structure, stress, and psychological distress: A demonstration of the impact of differential exposure. *Journal of Health and Social Behavior* 48(3): 301–317.

Axinn, William G., & Arland Thornton. 1993. Mothers, children, and cohabitation: The intergenerational effects of attitudes and behavior. *American Sociological Review* 58(2): 233–246.

Ayyub, Ruksana. 2000. Domestic violence in the South Asian Muslim immigrant population in the United States. *Journal of Social Distress & the Homeless* 9: 237–248.

Baines, C.T., P.M. Evans, & S.M. Neysmith. 1998. Women's caring: Work expanding, state contracting, pp. 3–22. In C.T. Baines, P.M. Evans, & S.M. Neysmith (Eds.), *Feminist Perspectives on Social Welfare*. Oxford University Press, Toronto.

Baker, A. 2007. Expressing emotion in text: Email communication of online couples. In *Online matchmaking* (pp. 97–111). Hampshire, England: Palgrave Macmillan.

Baker, Maureen. 1996. Introduction to family studies: Cultural variations and family trends, pp. 3–34. In Maureen Baker (Ed.), *Families: Changing Trends in Canada* (3rd edition). Toronto: McGraw-Hill Ryerson.

Baker, Maureen. 2001. *Families: Labour and Love, Family Diversity in a Changing World*. Vancouver: University of British Columbia Press.

Baker, Maureen. 2002. *Medically Assisted Fertility, Gender and the Future of Family Life*. International Sociology Association Paper, Brisbane, July 7–13, 2001.

Baker, Maureen. 2005a. Definitions, cultural variations and demographic trends. In Maureen Baker (Ed.), *Families: Changing Trends in Canada* (5th edition). Toronto: McGraw-Hill Ryerson.

Baker, Maureen. 2005b. Families, the state and family policies, pp. 259–276. In Maureen Baker (Ed.), *Families: Changing Trends in Canada* (5th edition). Toronto: McGraw-Hill Ryerson.

Baker, Maureen. 2009. *Families: Changing Trends in Canada*, 6th edition. Toronto: McGraw-Hill Ryerson.

Baker, Maureen, & Donna Lero. 1996. Division of labour: Paid work and family structure, pp. 78–103. In

Maureen Baker (Ed.), *Families: Changing Trends in Canada* (3rd edition). Toronto: McGraw-Hill Ryerson.

Bala, Nicholas. 2009. "Why Canada's Prohibition of Polygamy is Constitutionally Valid and Sound Social Policy," *Canadian Journal of Family Law* 165. **http://heinonline.org/HOL/LandingPage?collection=journals&handle=hein.journals/cajfl25&div=11&id=&page=**

Balakrishnan, T.R., Evelyne Lapierre-Adamcyk, & Karol J. Krotki. 1993. *Family and Childbearing in Canada: A Demographic Analysis.* Toronto: University of Toronto Press.

Barbeau, Carole. 2001. Work-related child-care centres in Canada—2001. Retrieved May 22, 2005, from Human Resources Development Canada Labour Program: **http://www.hrsdc.gc.ca/en/lp/spila/wlb/pdf/child_care_en.pdf**

Barer, M.L., R.G. Evans, & C. Hertzman. 1995. Avalanche or glacier? Health care and demographic rhetoric. *Canadian Journal on Aging* 14(2): 193–224.

Barette, J. 2009. Work/family balance: What do we really know? *Contemporary Family Trends.* Ottawa: Vanier Institute of the Family. Retrieved June 11, 2009, from **http://www.vifamily.ca/library/cft/barrette/work_family_balance.pdf**

Barnett, Karen, Laurie Buys, Jan Lovie-Kitchin, Gillian Boulton-Lewis, Dianne Smith, & Maree Heffernan. 2007. Older women's fears of violence: The need for interventions that enable active ageing. *Journal of Women & Aging* 19(3–4): 179–193.

Barnett, Mark A., Steven W. Quackenbush, & Christina S. Sinisi. 1996. Factors affecting children's, adolescents', and young adults' perceptions of parental discipline. *Journal of Genetic Psychology* 157(4): 411–424.

Barnett, Ola W., Tomas E. Martinez, & Mae Keyson. 1996 June. The relationship between violence, social support, and self-blame in battered women. *Journal of Interpersonal Violence* 11: 221–233.

Barraket, Jo, & Millsom S. Henry-Waring. 2008. Getting it on(line): Sociological perspectives on e-dating. *Journal of Sociology* 44: 149–65.

Barrett, Anne E., & R. Jay Turner. 2005. Family structure and mental health: The mediating effects of socioeconomic status, family process, and social stress. *Journal of Health and Social Behavior* 46(2): 156–169.

Barrett, Michele, & Mary McIntosh. 1980. *The Anti-Social Family.* London: Verso.

Basavarajappa, K.G. 1998. Living arrangements and residential overcrowding among older immigrants in Canada. *Asian Pacific Migration Journal* 7(4): 409–432.

Bassuk, Ellen, Ree Dawson, & Nicholas Huntington. 2006. Intimate partner violence in extremely poor women: Longitudinal patterns and risk markers. *Journal of Family Violence* 21(6): 387–399.

Bastida, Elena. 2001. Kinship ties of Mexican migrant women on the United States/Mexico border. *Journal of Comparative Family Studies* 32: 549–569.

Bauserman, Robert. 2012. "A Meta-Analysis of Parental Satisfaction, Adjustment, and Conflict in Joint Custody and Sole Custody Following Divorce," *Journal of Divorce and Remarriage* 53(6): 464–488.

Bawin-Legros, Bernadette. 2004. "Intimacy and the new sentimental order," *Current Sociology* 52(2):241–250.

Baxter, L., & West, L. 2003. Couple perceptions of their similarities and differences: A dialectical perspective. *Journal of Personal and Social Relationships,* 20(4): 491–514.

Beauchamp, N., A.B. Irvine, J. Seeley, & B. Johnson. 2005. Worksite-based internet multimedia program for family caregivers of persons with dementia. *The Gerontologist* 45(6): 793–801.

Beaujot, Rod. 2000. *Earning and Caring in Canadian Families.* Peterborough, Ontario: Broadview Press.

Beaujot, Roderic, & Zenaida Ravanera. 2008. Family change and implications for family solidarity and social cohesion. *Canadian Studies in Population* 35(1): 73–101.

Beaupré, Pascale. 2008. I do... Take Two? Changes in Intentions to Remarry among Divorced Canadians during the Past 20 Years, Ottawa: Statistics Canada. **http://www.statcan.gc.ca/pub/89-630-x/2008001/article/10659-eng.htm**

Beaupre, Pascale, Pierre Turcotte, & Anne Milan. 2006a. When is junior moving out? Transitions from the parental home to independence. *Canadian Social Trends.* Ottawa: Statistics Canada. Catalogue no. 11-008: 9–15.

Beaupre, Pascale, Pierre Turcotte, & Anne Milan. 2006b. Junior comes back home: Trends and predictors of returning to the parental home. *Canadian Social Trends.* Ottawa: Statistics Canada. Catalogue no. 11-008: 28–34.

Beck-Gernsheim, Elisabeth. 1983. From living for others to a life of one's own: Structural changes in women's lives. *Soziale Welt* 34(3): 307–340.

Beeby, Dean. 2006. End polygamy ban, report urges Ottawa. *Globe and Mail,* January 13. Retrieved January 14, 2006, from **http://www.theglobeandmail.com/servlet/Article=News/TPStory/LAC/20060113/POLYGAMY13/TPNational/?query=polygamy**

Behnke, Andrew O., Brent A. Taylor, & Taylor Ruben Parra-Cardona. 2008. I hardly understand English, but . . . : Mexican origin fathers describe their commitment as fathers despite the challenges of immigration. *Journal of Comparative Family Studies* 39: 187–205.

Belgrave, Faye Z., Barbara Van Oss Marin, & Donald B. Chambers. 2000. Cultural, contextual, and interpersonal predictors of risky sexual attitudes among urban African American girls in early adolescence. *Cultural Diversity & Ethnic Minority Psychology* 6(3): 309–322.

Bell, David. 2000. Farm boys and wild men: Rurality, masculinity, and homosexuality. *Rural Sociology* 65(4): 547–561.

Belsky, J., S. Woodworth, & K. Crnic. 1996. Troubled family interaction during toddlerhood. *Development and Psychopathology* 8: 477–495.

Bengston, Vern L., Timothy J. Biblarz, and Robert E. L. Roberts. 2002. *How Families Still Matter: A Longitudinal Study of Youth in Two Generations.* Cambridge, U.K. Cambridge University Press.

Benjamin, W., Ann C. Crouter, Stephanie T. Lanza., & Martha J. Cox. 2008. Paternal work characteristics and father-infant interactions in low-income, rural families. *Journal of Marriage and Family* 70(3): 640–653.

Bennett, Neil G., Ann K. Blanc, & David E. Bloom. 1988. Commitment and the modern union: Assessing the link between premarital cohabitation and subsequent marital stability. *American Sociological Review* 53: 127–138.

Bennun, Ian. 1997. Systemic marital therapy with one partner: A reconsideration of theory, research and practice. *Sexual and Marital Therapy* 12(1).

Berger, R.M. 1990. Passing: The impact on the quality of same-sex couple relationships. *Social Work* 35: 328–332.

Berger, Roni. 2000. When remarriage and immigration coincide: The experience of Russian immigrant stepfamilies. *Journal of Ethnic & Cultural Diversity in Social Work* 9: 75–96.

Bergin, B. 1995. *Elder Abuse in Ethnocultural Communities: An Exploratory Study with Suggestions for Intervention and Prevention.* Ottawa, ON: Canadian Association of Social Workers.

Bernard, Jessie. 1973. *The Future of Marriage.* New York: Bantam.

Bernard, R., & Petipas J. 2008. Rediscovering the family meal. *Contemporary Family Trends.* Ottawa: Vanier Institute of the Family. Retrieved June 12, 2009, from **http://www.vifamily.ca/library/cft/food/food_eng.pdf**

Bersamin, M.M, D.A. Fisher, S. Walker, D.L. Hill, & J.W. Grube. 2007. Defining virginity and abstinence: Adolescents' interpretations of sexual behaviours. *Journal of Adolescent Health* 41: 182–188.

Betts Adams, K. 2006. The transition to caregiving: The experience of family members embarking on the dementia caregiving career. *Journal of Gerontological Social Work*, 47(3/4): 3–29.

Beyer, Sylvia. 1995. Maternal employment and children's academic achievement: Parenting styles as mediating variable. *Developmental Review* 15(2): 212–253.

Bianchi, S.M., & L.M. Casper. 2000. American families. *Population Bulletin: Washington* 55(Part 4).

Bibby, Reginald. 2001. Canada's teens: A national reading on family life. *Transition Magazine* 31(3). Ottawa: Vanier Institute of the Family. Retrieved August 15, 2002, from **http://www.vifamily.ca**

Bibby, Reginald W. 2009. *The Emerging Millennials: How Canada's Newest Generation is Responding to Change and Choice.* Lethbridge, AB: Project Canada Books.

Bibby, Reginald W. 2011. *Beyond the Gods and Back: Religion's Demise and Rise and Why it Matters.* Lethbridge, AB: Project Canada Books.

Biggs, Simon, Chris Phillipson, & Paul Kingston. 1995. *Elder Abuse in Perspective.* Taylor & Francis.

BioPortfolio. 2006. Retrieved from **http://www.bioportfolio.com/cgi-bin/acatalog/info_996.html**

Bird, Chloe E., & Michelle Rogers. 1998. *Parenting and Depression: The Impact of the Division of Labor within Couples and Perceptions of Equity.* Society for the Study of Social Problems (SSSP).

Birditt, Kira S., and Toni C. Antonucci. 2012. "Till Death Do Us Part: Contexts and Implications of Marriage, Divorce and Remarriage Across Adulthood." *Research in Human Development* 9(2): 103–105.

Birenbaum-Carmeli, Daphna. 1998. Reproductive partners: Doctor-woman relations in Israeli and Canadian IVF contexts, pp. 75–92. In Nancy Scheper-Hughes and Carolyn Sargent (Eds.), *Small Mall Wars: The Cultural Politics of Childhood.* Berkeley: University of California Press.

Birman, Dina, & Tina Taylor-Ritzler. 2007. Acculturation and psychological distress among adolescent immigrants from the former soviet union: Exploring the mediating effect of family relationships. *Cultural Diversity & Ethnic Minority Psychology* 13: 337–46.

Blackmon, Amy Dixon. 2000. Empathy in marriage: Implications for marital satisfaction and depression. *Dissertation Abstracts International: Section B: The Sciences and Engineering* 61(5-B), 2746.

Blanchet, T. Bangladesh girls sold as wives in north India. 2005. *Indian Journal of Gender Studies* 12: 305–344.

Blando, J.A. 2001. Twice hidden: Older gay and lesbian couples, friends, and intimacy. *Generations* 25(2): 87–89.

Bogle, K. 2008. *Hooking Up: Sex, Dating and Relationships.* New York: NYU Press.

Boies, S.C. 2002. University students' uses of and reactions to online sexual information and entertainment: Links to online and offline sexual behaviour. *Canadian Journal of Human Sexuality* 11: 77–89.

Bolovan, I., & S.P. Bolovan. 2008. From tradition to modernization: Church and the Transylvanian Romanian family in the modern era. *Journal for the Study of Religions and Ideologies* 7: 107–133.

Boney-McCoy, Sue, & David Finkelhor. 1996 December. Is youth victimization related to trauma symptoms and depression after controlling for prior symptoms and family relationships? A longitudinal, prospective study. *Journal of Consulting and Clinical Psychology* 64: 1406–1416.

Borell, Klas, & Sofie Ghazanfareeon Karlsson. 2002. Reconceptualising intimacy and ageing: Living apart together. Paper presented at International Symposium, *Reconceptualising Gender and Ageing,* Centre for Research on Ageing and Gender, University of Surrey, 25–27 June.

Bourne, Larry S., & Damaris Rose. 2001. The changing face of Canada: The uneven geographies of population and social change. *The Canadian Geographer* 45 (2001): 105–119.

Boushey, H. 2009. Infographic: The importance of women breadwinners. Washington, D.C.: Center for American Progress. Retrieved June 11, 2009, from **http://www.americanprogress.org/issues/2009/04/women_breadwinners.html**

Bowers, C.A, Miguel Vasquez, & Mary Roaf. 2000. Native people and the challenge of computers: Reservation schools, individualism and consumerism. *American Indian Quarterly* 24(2): 182–199.

Bowlby, J. 1969. *Attachment and Loss: Vol. 1. Attachment.* New York: Basic Books.

Boyce, Cheryl A., & Andrew J. Fuligni. 2007. Issues for developmental research among racial/ethnic minority and immigrant families. *Research in Human Development. Special Issue: Social context, cultural processes and mental health across the life span among ethnically diverse populations* 4: 1–17.

Boyce, William, Maryanne Doherty, Christian Fortin, & David MacKinnon. 2003. Canadian youth, sexual health and HIV/AIDS study: Factors influencing knowledge, attitudes and behaviours. Ottawa: Council of Ministers of Education, Canada. Retrieved November 4, 2004, from http://www.cmec.ca/publications/aids/CYSHHAS_2002_EN.pdf

Boyd, Monica, & Anne Li. 2003. May–December: Canadians in age-discrepant relationships. *Canadian Social Trends* 70: 29–33.

Boyd, Monica, & Edward T. Pryor. 1989. The cluttered nest: The living arrangements of young adult Canadians. *Canadian Journal of Sociology* 14(4): 461–477.

Boyd, Monica, & Elizabeth Grieco. 2003. Women and migration: Incorporating gender into international migration theory. Retrieved September 12, 2008, from http://www.migrationinformation.org/issues_mar03.cfm

Bradbury, Bettina. 1984. Pigs, cows and boarders: Non-wage forms of survival among Montreal families, 1861–1891. *Labour/Le Travail* 14: 9–46.

Bradbury, Bettina. 2001. Social, economic, and cultural origins of contemporary families, pp. 69–95. In Maureen Baker (Ed.), *Families: Changing Trends in Canada* (4th edition). Toronto: McGraw-Hill Ryerson.

Bradshaw, Jonathan, Antonia Keung, Gwyther Rees, and Haridhan Goswami. 2011. "Children's Subjective Well-Being: International Comparative Perspectives." *Children and Youth Services Review* 33(4): 548–556.

Brannen, Stephen J., & Allen Rubin. 1996. Comparing the effectiveness of gender-specific and couples groups in a court-mandated spouse abuse treatment program. *Research on Social Work Practice* 6(4): 405–424.

Brinkerhoff, Merlin B., & Eugen Lupri. 1988. Interspousal violence. *Canadian Journal of Sociology* 13(4): 407–434.

Brison, Robert J., William Pickett, Richard L. Berg, James Linneman, Jamie Zentner, & Barbara Marlenga. 2006. Fatal agricultural injuries in preschool children: Risks, injury patterns and strategies for prevention. *Canadian Medical Association Journal* 174(12): 1723–1726.

Bronstein, Phyllis, Paula Duncan, & Adele D'Ari. 1996 October. Family and parenting behaviors predicting middle school adjustment: A longitudinal study. *Family Relations* 45: 415–426.

Bronte-Tinkew, Jacinta, Kristin A. Moore, Randolph C. Capps, & Jonathan Zaff. 2006. The influence of father involvement on youth risk behaviors among adolescents: A comparison of native-born and immigrant families. *Social Science Research* 35: 181–209.

Brotman, S. 1998. The incidence of poverty among seniors in Canada: Exploring the impact of gender, ethnicity and race. *Canadian Journal on Aging* 17(2): 166–185.

Broude, Gwen J. 1996 Fall. The realities of daycare. *Public Interest* 125: 95–105.

Brown, Arnold. 2011. "Relationships, Community and Identity in the New Virtual Society." *The Futurist* 45(2): 29–34. http://encore.uleth.ca:50080/ebsco-web/ehost/pdfviewer/pdfviewer?vid=5&hid=123&sid=647efacc-3b0c-459e-9e5a-ce2b7f7df512%40sessionmgr114

Brown, S.L., J.R. Bulanda, & G.R. Lee. 2005. The significance of nonmarital cohabitation: Marital status and mental health benefits among middle-aged and older adults. *The Journal of Gerontology: Social Sciences* 60B: S21–S29.

Brown, Jennifer S.H. 1980. *Strangers in Blood: Fur Trade Company Families in Indian Country*. Vancouver: University of British Columbia Press.

Brown, Jennifer S.H., 1992. A Cree nurse in the cradle of Methodism: Little Mary and the Egerton R. Young family at Norway House and Berens River, pp. 93–110. In Bettina Bradbury (Ed.), *Canadian Family History: Selected Readings*. Toronto: Copp Clark Pitman.

Brown, Phillip, & Hugh Lauder. 2001. *Capitalism and Social Progress: The Future of Society in a Global Economy*, pp. xvi, 338. Basingstoke, Hampshire; New York: Palgrave.

Brown, Susan L. 2004. Moving from cohabitation to marriage: Effects on relationship quality. *Social Science Research* 33: 1–19.

Brown, Susan L., and I-Fen Lin. 2012. "The Gray Divorce Revolution: Rising Divorce Among Middle-Aged and Older Adults, 1990–2010," *The Journals of Gerontology* 67 (6):731–741. http://psychsocgerontology.oxford-journals.org/content/67/6/731.full.pdf+html

Brownridge, Douglas A. 2008. Understanding the elevated risk of partner violence against Aboriginal women: A comparison of two nationally representative surveys in Canada. *Journal of Family Violence* 23: 353–367.

Brownridge, Douglas A., & Shiva S. Halli. 2002. Understanding male partner violence against cohabiting and married women: An empirical investigation with a synthesized model. *Journal of Family Violence* 17(4): 341–361.

Bruhn, J.G. 1977. Effects of chronic illness on the family. *Journal of Family Practice* 4: 1057–1067.

Brumer, Anita. 2008. Gender relations in family-farm agriculture and rural-urban migration in Brazil. *Latin American Perspectives* 35: 11–28.

Bryant, H.D., A. Billingsley, & G.A. Kerry. 1963. Physical abuse of children: An agency study. *Child Welfare* 42: 125–130.

Brym, Robert J., & Rhonda L. Lenton. 2001. *Love Online: A Report on Digital Dating in Canada*. www.msn.ca. Retrieved June 14, 2009, from http://www.nelson.com/nelson/harcourt/sociology/newsociety3e/loveonline.pdf

Bucher, Julia A., Peter S. Houts, Arthur M. Nezu, & Christine Maguth Nezu. 1996 January. The prepared family caregiver: A problem-solving approach to family caregiver education. *Patient Education & Counseling* 27(1), 63–73.

Buddington, Steve A. 2002. Acculturation, psychological adjustment (stress, depression, self-Esteem) and the academic achievement of Jamaican immigrant college students. *International Social Work* 45: 447–464.

Bui, Hoan N., & Merry Morash. 2007. Social capital, human capital, and reaching out for help with domestic violence: A case study of women in a Vietnamese-American community. *Criminal Justice Studies: A Critical Journal of Crime, Law and Society* 20: 375–390.

Buki, Lydia P., Tsung-Chieh Ma, Robert D. Strom, & Shirley K. Strom. 2003. Chinese immigrant mothers of adolescents: Self-perceptions of acculturation effects on parenting. *Cultural Diversity & Ethnic Minority Psychology* 9: 127–140.

Bulcroft, R, & Bulcroft, K. 1991. The nature and functions of dating in later life. *Research on Aging*, 13(2): 244–260.

Bumpass, Larry, & Hsien-Hen Lu. 2000. Trends in cohabitation and implications for children's family contexts in the United States. *Population Studies* 54(1): 29–41.

Bumpus, Matthew F., Ann C. Crouter, & Susan M. McHale. 1999 May. Work demands of dual-earner couples: Implications for parents' knowledge about children's daily lives in middle childhood. *Marriage and the Family* 61(2): 465–475.

Bumpus, Matthew Franklin. 2001 February. Mechanisms linking work-to-family spillover and parents' knowledge of their children's daily lives. *Dissertation Abstracts International, A: The Humanities and Social Sciences* 61(8), 3368–A.

Burholt Vanessa, & Clare G. Wenger. 1998 September. Differences over time in older people's relationships with children and siblings. *Ageing and Society* 18(5): 537–562.

Busby, Dean M. 1991. Violence in the family, pp. 335–385. In Stephen J. Bahr (Ed.), *Family Research: A Sixty-Year Review, 1930–1990, Volume 1*. New York: Lexington Books, Maxwell Macmillan International.

Buss, D., & Schmitt, D. 1993. Sexual strategies theory: An evolutionary perspective on human mating. *Psychology Review*, 100: 204–232.

Byrne, R., and Findlay, B. 2004. Preference for SMS versus telephone calls in initiating romantic relationships. *Australian Journal of Emerging Technologies and Society* 2(1): 48–61.

Caldwell, John C., P.H. Reddy, & Pat Caldwell. 1984. The determinants of family structure in rural south India. *Journal of Marriage and the Family* 46(1): 215–229.

Calixte, S.L.L., J.L. Johnson, and J.M. Motapanyane. 2010. "Liberal, Socialist and Radical Feminism." In Mandell, Nancy (Ed.), *Feminist Issues*, 5th edition. Toronto: Pearson, pp. 1–39.

Calliste, Agnes. 2001. Black families in Canada: Exploring the interconnections of race, class and gender, pp. 401–419. In Bonnie J. Fox (Ed.) *Family Patterns, Gender Relations* (2nd edition). Toronto: Oxford University Press.

Campbell, Jacquelyn C., Paul Miller, & Mary M. Cardwell. 1994 June. Relationship status of battered women over time. *Journal of Family Violence* 9: 99–111.

Campbell, Rebecca, Cris Sullivan, & William S. Davidson. 1995 June. Women who use domestic violence shelters: Changes in depression over time. *Psychology of Women Quarterly* 19: 237–255.

Canada, Department of Justice. 2003. *Abuse Is Wrong in Any Language*. Ottawa: Dept of Justice Canada. Catalogue no. J2-131/1995E.

Canada, Department of Justice. 2005a. Dating violence: A fact sheet from the Department of Justice Canada. Family Violence. Retrieved November 4, 2005, from http://canada.justice.gc.ca/en/ps/fm/datingfs.html#head2

Canada, Department of Justice. 2005b. Civil marriage and the legal recognition of same-sex unions. Retrieved January 13, 2006, from http://www.canada.justice.gc.ca/en/fs/ssm/index.html

Canada, Department of National Defence. 2006. Retrieved February 25, 2006, from http://www.forces.gc.ca/site/operations/current_ops_e.asp

Canadian Centre for Policy Alternatives. 2004. Medicare still on life support: Health care accord flawed by poor accountability and enforcement. Retrieved April 18, 2006, from http://www.policyalternatives.ca/index.cfm?act=news&do=Article&call=983&pA=BB736455

Canadian Homelessness Research Network. 2013. *The Study of Homelessness in Canada 2013*. Toronto: York University.

Canada Revenue Agency. 2013. "Marital Status." http://www.cra-arc.gc.ca/bnfts/mrtl/menu-eng.html?=slnk

Cann, A. 2004. Rated Importance of Personal Qualities across Four Relationships. *The Journal of Social Psychology*, *144* (3), 329.

Cannon, Bethany. 1999 December. Marriage and cohabitation: A comparison of adult attachment style and quality between the two types of relationships. *Dissertation Abstracts International B: The Sciences & Engineering* 60(5–B), 2332.

Caradec, Vincent. 1997. Forms of conjugal life among the young elderly. *Population: An English Selection* 9: 47–74.

Carolan, M. 1999. Contemporary Muslim women and the family. In H. McAdoo (Ed.), *Family Ethnicity: Strength in Diversity*. Newbury Park, CA: Sage, 213–221.

Carr, D. 2004. The desire to date and remarry among older widows and widowers. *Journal of Marriage and Family* 66(4): 1051–1068.

Carr, Deborah. 1996. Two paths to self-employment? Women's and men's self-employment in the United States, 1980. *Work and Occupations* 23(1): 26–53.

Carstensen, Laura L., John M. Gottman, & Robert W. Levenson. 1995 March. Emotional behavior in long-term marriage. *Psychology and Aging 10*.

Cashdan, Elizabeth. 1993. Attracting mates: Effects of paternal investment on mate attraction strategies. *Ethology and Sociobiology* 14(1): 1–23.

Castellano, Marlene Brant. 2002. *Aboriginal Family Trends: Extended Families, Nuclear Families, Families of the Heart*. Ottawa: Vanier Institute of the Family. Accessed December 30, 2002, from http://www.vifamily.ca.

Castells, Manuel. 1996 March. The net and the self: Working notes for a critical theory of the informational society. *Critique of Anthropology* 16(1): 9–38.

Caughy, Margaret O'Brien, Saundra Murray Nettles, & Patricia J. O'Campo. 2008. The effect of residential neighbourhood on child behavior problems in first grade. *American Journal of Psychology* 42: 39–50.

Cavan, R., & K.R. Ranck. 1938. *The Family and the Depression*. Chicago: University of Chicago Press.

CBC News Online. 2005 June 29. The Supreme Court and same-sex marriage. Retrieved from http://www.cbc.ca/news/background/samesexrights

CBC News Online. 2008. Retrieved from http://www.cbc.ca/news/background/census/mixed-marriages.html

CBC News. 2005, March 9. Marriage by the Numbers. *CBC News Online*.

CBC. 2013. "Unmarried Quebec couples have no right to alimony, court rules: Supreme Court rules on Eric vs. Lola case involving woman seeking $56K monthly. http://www.cbc.ca/news/canada/montreal/story/2013/01/25/supreme-court-ruling-eric-vs-lola-quebec-civil-code.html

CBS News Online. 2003 September 2. Rape debate in Japan. Retrieved November 4, 2005, from http://www.cbsnews.com/stories/2003/09/02/world/main571280.shtml

Central Intelligence Agency. 2008. Distribution of family income: Gini index 2008 country ranks. *CIA World*

Factbook. Washington, D.C.: Central Intelligence Agency, Office of Public Affairs. Retrieved from **http://www.cia.gov/library/publications/the-world-factbook/rankorder/2172rank.html**

Cha, Heung Bong. 2004. Public policy on aging in Korea. *Geriatrics and Gerontology International* 4: 45–48.

Chalmers, Lee, & Anne Milan. 2005. Marital satisfaction during the retirement years. *Canadian Social Trends*. Ottawa: Statistics Canada. Catalogue no. 11-008.

Chang, Janet. 2003. Self-reported reasons for divorce and correlates of psychological well-being among divorced Korean immigrant women. *Journal of Divorce & Remarriage* 40: 111–28.

Chant, Sylvia. 2000 December. Men in crisis? Reflections on masculinities, work and family in North-West Costa Rica. *European Journal of Development Research* 12(2): 199–218.

Chappell, Neena. 2013. "The Cultural Context of Social Cohesion and Social Capital: Exploring Filial Caregiving." In Susan A. McDaniel and Zachary Zimmer (Eds.), *Global Ageing in the Twenty-First Century: Challenges, Opportunities and Implications*. (pp. 235–252). Farnham, Surrey, UK: Ashgate.

Chappell, Neena L., & Margaret Penning. 1996 January. Behavioural problems and distress among caregivers of people with dementia. *Ageing and Society* 16(1): 57–73.

Cheah, Charissa S.L., & Valery Chirkov. 2008. Parents' personal and cultural beliefs regarding young children. *Journal of Cross-Cultural Psychology* 39(4): 402–423.

Cheal, David. 1991. *Family and the State of Theory*. Toronto: University of Toronto Press.

Cheal, David. 1996. *New Poverty: Families in Postmodern Society*. Westport, CT: Greenwood Press.

Cheal, David. 1997. *Hidden in the Household: Poverty and Dependence at Different ages*. Paper presented at the Conference, Intergenerational Equity in Canada, 20–21 February. Statistics Canada, Ottawa.

Cheal, David. 2002. *Sociology and Family Life*. London: Palgrave.

Cherlin, A. J. 2004. "The Deinstitutionalization of American Marriage." *Journal of Marriage and the Family* 66: 848–861.

Cherlin, Andrew J. 2005. American marriage in early twenty-first century. *Marriage and Child Wellbeing* 15(2).

Cheung, Maria. 2008. Resilience of older immigrant couples: Long-term marital satisfaction as a protective factor. *Journal of Couple & Relationship Therapy* 7: 19–38.

Chibber, Karuna S., Karl Krupp, Nancy Padian, and Purnima Madhivanan. 2012. "Examining the Determinants of Sexual Violence Among Young, Married Women in Southern India." *Journal of Interpersonal Violence*, 27(12):2465–2483.

ChildStats.gov. 2005. America's children: Key national indicators of well-being 2005. Retrieved January 10, 2006, from **http://childstats.ed.gov/americaschildren/pop6.asp**

Choi, Alfred, & Jeffrey L. Edleson. 1996. Social disapproval of wife assaults: A national survey of Singapore. *Journal of Comparative Family Studies* 27(1): 73–88.

Christensen, Donna-Hendrickson, & Kathryn D. Rettig. 1995. The relationship of remarriage to post-divorce co-parenting. *Journal of Divorce and Remarriage* 24: 1–2.

Church, Elizabeth. 1996. Kinship and stepfamilies, pp. 81–106. In Marion Lynn (Ed.), *Voices: Essays on Canadian Families*. Scarborough, ON: Nelson.

Clark, Susan M. 1993. Support needs of the Canadian single parent family, pp. 223–238. In Joe Hudson & Burt Galaway (Eds.), *Single Parent Families: Perspectives on Research and Policy*. Toronto: Thompson.

Clark, Warren, & Susan Crompton. 2006. Till death do us part? The risk of first and second marriage dissolution. *Canadian Social Trends*. Ottawa: Statistics Canada. Catalogue no. 11-008: 23–32.

Clark, Warren. 2007. Delayed transitions of young adults. *Canadian Social Trends*. Ottawa: Statistics Canada. Catalogue no. 11-008. Retrieved June 9, 2009, from **http://www.statcan.gc.ca/pub/11-008-x/2007004/10311-eng.htm**

Clemans-Cope, L., Cynthia D. Perry, Genevieve M. Kenney, Jennifer E. Pelletier, & Matthew S. Pantell 2008. Access to and use of paid sick leave among low-income families with children. *Pediatrics* 122(2): 480-486.

Clifford, Janice Elizabeth. 1998 February. The effects of single-mother families on adult children's marital stability. *Dissertation Abstracts International, A: The Humanities and Social Sciences* 58(8), 3320–A.

Cohan, Catherine L., & Stacey Kleinbaum. 2002. Toward a greater understanding of the cohabitation effect: Premarital cohabitation and marital communication. *Journal of Marriage and Family* 64(1): 180–192.

Cohen, Orna, & Ricky Finzi-Dottan. March 2005. Parent-child relationships during the divorce process: From attachment theory and intergenerational perspective. *Contemporary Family Therapy* 27(1): 81–99.

Cohen, Philip N. 1998. Replacing housework in the service economy: Gender, class, and race-ethnicity in service spending. *Gender & Society* 12(2): 219–231.

Coleman, Jean U., & Sandra M. Stith. 1997 June. Nursing students' attitudes toward victims of domestic violence as predicted by selected individual and relationship variables. *Journal of Family Violence* 12: 113–138.

Coleman, Marilyn, Lawrence Ganong, & Susan M. Cable. 1997 February. Beliefs about women's intergenerational family obligations to provide support before and after divorce and remarriage. *Journal of Marriage and the Family* 59: 165–176.

Collins, Andrew. 2010. Monographs of the Society for Research in Child Development. *Developmental Psychology* 75.

Collins, Louise. 1999 Summer. Emotional adultery: Cybersex and commitment. *Social Theory and Practice* 25(2): 243–270.

Collins, Randall. 1985. *Sociology of Marriage and the Family: Gender, Love, and Property*. Chicago: Nelson-Hall.

Collins, Stephanie Baker. 2005. An understanding of poverty from those who are poor. *Action Research* 3(1): 9–31.

Coltrane, Scott. 1998. *Gender and Families*. Thousand Oaks, California: Pine Forge Press.

Comeau, Tammy Duerden, & Anton L. Allahar. 2001. Forming Canada's ethnoracial identity: Psychiatry and the history of immigration practices. *Identity* 1: 143–160.

Confer, J. C., Perilloux, C., & Buss, D. 2010. More than just a pretty face: men's priority shifts toward bodily attractiveness in short-term versus long-term mating contexts. *Evolution and Human Behavior* 31 (5): 348–353.

Connidis, Ingrid Arnet. 2001. *Family Ties and Aging.* Thousand Oaks, CA: Sage.

Cooksey, Elizabeth C., Elizabeth G. Menaghan, & Susan M. Jekielek. 1997. Life course effects of work and family circumstances on children. *Social Forces* 76(2): 637–667.

Coontz, Stephanie. 1997. Working with what we've got: The strengths and vulnerabilities of today's families, pp. 157–171. In Stephanie Coontz, *The Way We Really Are.* New York: Basic Books.

Coontz, Stephanie. 2005. *Marriage, a History: From Obedience to Intimacy, or How Love Conquered Marriage.* New York: Viking.

Corak, Miles, & Andrew Heisz. 1999. *Death and Divorce: The Long-Term Consequences of Parental Loss on Adolescents.* Analytical Studies Branch Research Paper Series. Ottawa: Statistics Canada. Catalogue no. 11F0019MIE999135.

Couch, Danielle, & Pranee Liamputtong. 2008. Online dating and mating: The use of the internet to meet sexual partners. *Qualitative Health Research* 18: 268–279.

Courts, N.F., A.N. Newton, & L.J. McNeal. 2005. Husbands and wives living with multiple sclerosis. *Journal of Neuroscience Nursing* 37(1): 20–27.

Cowan, Ruth Schwartz. 1979 January. From Virginia Dare to Virginia Slims: Women and technology in American life. *Technology and Culture* 20(1): 51–63.

Cox, Christine E. 2000. *The Contributions of Grandmothers to Perceived Competence in Young Children.* Southern Sociological Society (SSS).

Cox, Martha, J., & Jeanne Brooks-Gunn (Eds.). *Conflict and Cohesion in Families: Causes and Consequences.* Mahwah, NJ: Lawrence Erlbaum.

Creel, Liz. 2005. Domestic violence: An ongoing threat to women in Latin America and the Caribbean. Population Reference Bureau. Retrieved July 12, 2005, from http://www.prb.org/Template.cfm?Section =PRB&template=/ContentManagement/Content Display.cfm&ContentID=4744

Crohan, Susan E. 1996 November. Marital quality and conflict across the transition to parenthood in African American and white couples. *Journal of Marriage and the Family* 58.

Crompton, Rosemary, & Clare Lyonette. 2006. Work–life "balance" in Europe. *Acta Sociologica* 49(4): 379–393.

Cronk, Lee, & Dunham Bria. 2007. Amounts spent on engagement rings reflect aspects of male and female. *Human Nature* 18(4): 329–333.

Cross, Gary, & Richard Szostak. 1995. Women and work before the factory, pp. 37–51. In Gary Cross & Richard Szostak (Eds.), *Technology and American Society: A History.* Englewood Cliffs, NJ: Prentice Hall.

Crossley, Thomas F., & Lori J. Curtis. 2006. Child poverty in Canada. *Review of Income and Wealth* 52(2): 237–260.

Cullen, Jennifer C., Leslie B. Hammer, Margaret B. Neal., & Robert R. Sinclair. 2009. Development of a typology of dual-earner couples caring for children and aging parents. *Journal of Family Issues* 30(4): 458–483.

Cunningham, M., & A. Thornton. 2004. *The Influence of Parents' and Childrens' Union Transitions on Attitudes toward Cohabitation.* Annual meeting of the Population Association of America.

Curran, Melissa, Nancy Hazen, Deborah Jacobvitz, & Amy Feldman. 2005. Representations of early family relationships predict marital maintenance during the transition to parenthood. *Journal of Family Psychology* 19(2): 189–197.

Curran, S., McLanahan, S., & Knab, J. 2003. Does remarriage expand perceptions of kinship support among the elderly? *Social Science Research* 32(2): 171–190.

Curtis, Kristen Taylor, & Christopher G. Ellison. 2002. Religious heterogamy and marital conflict: Findings from the national survey of families and households. *Journal of Family Issues* 23(4): 551–576.

Cyr, R., 2005. Breaking the cycle of violence: Preventing violence against seniors in the Aboriginal community. Retrieved May 20, 2009, from http://www .web.net/~ocsco/downloads/abuse_of_aboriginal_ seniors.pdf

Dahinten, V. Susan, Jennifer D. Shapka., & J. Douglas Willms. 2007. Adolescent children of adolescent mothers: The impact of family functioning on trajectories of development. *Journal Youth and Adolescence* 36: 195–212.

Dahinten, V. Susan, & J. Douglas Willms. 2002. The effects of adolescent child-bearing on children's outcomes, pp. 243–258. In J. Douglas Willms (Ed.), *Vulnerable Children: Findings from Canada's National Longitudinal Survey of Children and Youth.* Edmonton: University of Alberta Press, and Ottawa: Human Resources Development Canada, Applied Research Branch.

Dakin, John, & Richard Wampler. 2008. Money doesn't buy happiness, but it helps: Marital satisfaction, psychological distress, and demographic differences between low- and middle-income clinic couples. *American Journal of Family Therapy* 36(4): 300–311.

Daley, Suzanne. 1999 October 14. France gives legal status to unmarried couples. *New York Times.*

Darvishpour, Mehrdad. 2002. Immigrant women challenge the role of men: How the changing power relationship within Iranian families in Sweden intensifies family conflicts after immigration. *Journal of Comparative Family Studies* 33: 271–296.

Dasgupta, Shamita Das. 1998. Gender roles and cultural continuity in the Asian Indian immigrant community in the U.S. *Sex Roles* 38(11–12): 953–974.

Davidson, Kate. 2001. Late life widowhood, selfishness and new partnership choices: A gendered perspective. *Ageing and Society* 21(3): 297–317.

Davidson, Kate, Sara Arber, & Jay Ginn. 2000. Gendered meanings of care work within late life marital relationships. *Canadian Journal on Aging* 19(4): 536–553.

Davies, Lorraine, & Patricia Jane Carrier. 1998. The importance of power relations for the division of household labour. *Canadian Journal of Sociology* 23(4).

Davies, Lorraine, Julie Ann McMullin, William R. Avison, with Gale L. Cassidy. 2001. *Social Policy, Gender Inequality and Poverty.* Ottawa: Status of Women Canada.

Davies, Sharon, & Margaret Denton. 2001. *The Economic Well-Being of Older Women Who Become Divorced or Separated in Mid and Later Life.* Social and Economic Dimensions of an Aging Population Research Papers, Number 66. Hamilton, ON: McMaster University.

Davila, Joanne, Catherine B. Stroud, and Lisa R. Starr. 2008. "Depression in Couples and Families." In Gotlib, Ian H., and Constance L. Hammen (Eds.), *Handbook of Depression*, 2nd edition. New York: Guildford Press, pp. 467–491.

Davis, Phillip W. 1996. Threats of corporal punishment as verbal aggression: A naturalistic study. *Child Abuse and Neglect* 20(4): 289–304.

Davis, Mary Ann. 2013. "Demographics of Gay and Lesbian Adoption and Family Policies." In A. K. Baumle (Ed.), *International Handbook on the Demography of Sexuality*. Dorhrecht: Springer, pp. 3–19.

Davis, Robert C., & Barbara Smith. 1995 October. Domestic violence reforms: Empty promises or fulfilled expectations? *Crime and Delinquency* 41: 541–552.

Deal, James E., Karen Smith Wampler, & Charles F. Halverson Jr. 1992 December. The importance of similarity in the marital relationship. *Family Process* 31(4): 369–382.

Dearing, Eric. 2004. The developmental implications of restrictive and supportive parenting across neighborhoods and ethnicities: Exceptions are the rule. *Applied Developmental Psychology* 25: 555–575.

DeBoer, Danelle D. 2002 December. The effect of infertility on individual well-being. *Dissertation Abstracts International, A: The Humanities and Social Sciences* 62(6), 2249–A.

De Graaf, Paul M., & Matthijs Kalmijn. 2006. Divorce motives in a period of rising divorce. *Journal of Family Issues* 27(4): 483–505.

Deimling, Gary T., Noelker, Linda S., & Aloen L. Townsend. 1989. *A Comparative Analysis of Family Caregivers' Health and Well-Being*. North Central Sociological Association (NCSA).

De Jong Gierveld, Jenny. 2004. Remarriage, unmarried cohabitation, living apart together: Partner relationships following bereavement or divorce. *Journal of Marriage and the Family* 66(1): 236–243.

DeKeseredy, Walter S., & Katharine D. Kelly. 1995. Sexual abuse in Canadian university and college dating relationships: The contribution of male peer support. *Journal of Family Violence* 10(1): 41–53.

DeLamater, J., & M. Sill. 2005. Sexual desire in later life. *Journal of Sex Research* 42: 138–149.

DeLongis, Anita, & Darrin R. Lehman. 1989 March. The usefulness of a structured diary approach in studying marital relationships. *Journal of Family Psychology* 2(3): 337–343.

DeMaris, Alfred. 2007. The role of inequity in marital disruption. *Journal of Social and Personal Relationships* 24(2): 177–195.

DeMaris, Alfred, & Steven Swinford. 1996 January. Female victims of spousal violence: Factors influencing their level of fearfulness. *Family Relations* 45: 98–106.

de Munck, V. C., and Korotayev, A. V. 2007. Wife-Husband Intimacy and Female Status in Cross-Cultural Perspective. *Cross-Cultural Research*, 41 (4), 307–308, 329.

Deomampo, Daisy. 2013. "Gendered Geographies of Reproductive Tourism." *Gender and Society*. May 8, online pre-publication. **http://gas.sagepub.com/content/early/2013/05/08/0891243213486832.1.full**

De Rose, Alessandra. 2001. Separation and divorce: Effect on family structures and life conditions. *Labour* 14(1): 145–160.

De Valk, Helga A.G., & Aart C. Liefbroer. 2007. Parental influence on union formation preferences among Turkish, Moroccan, and Dutch adolescents in the Netherlands. *Journal of Cross-Cultural Psychology* 38: 487–505.

De Wolff, Alice. 2004. Working and having a life in Canada: a ten year review, pp. 1–19. In *Bargaining for work and life*. Retrieved May 27, 2005, from **http://ofl.ca/index.php/library/index_in/C41**

Dickason, Olive. 2002. *Canada's First Nations: A History of Founding Peoples from Earliest Times*. Don Mills, ON: Oxford University Press.

Diez-Bbolanos, A.M., & Perez Rodrigues. 1989 July. Effects of inequality on the female's marital adjustment and satisfaction. *Revista de Psicologia General y Aplicada* 42(3): 395–401.

Ding, Shijun. 2004. The rural elderly support in China and Thailand. *Geriatrics and Gerontology International* 4: 56–59.

Dinkmeyer, Don, & Robert Sherman. 1989 March–June. Brief Adlerian family therapy. *Individual Psychology: Journal of Adlerian Theory, Research & Practice. Special Issue: Varieties of Brief Therapy* 45(1–2): 148–158.

Divale, William, & Albert Seda. 2001. Modernization as changes in cultural complexity: New cross-cultural measurements. *Cross-Cultural Research* 35: 127–153.

Dong, Qi, Yanping Wang, & Thomas H. Ollendick. 2002. Consequences of divorce on the adjustment of children in China. *Journal of Clinical Child and Adolescent Psychology* 31(1): 101–110.

Dooley, Martin. 1993. Recent changes in the economic welfare of lone mother families in Canada: The roles of market work, earnings and transfers, pp. 115–132. In Joe Hudson & Burt Galaway (Eds.), *Single Parent Families: Perspectives on Research and Policy*. Toronto: Thompson.

Doosje, Bertjan, Krystyna Rojahn, & Agneta Fischer. 1999. Partner preference as a function of gender, age, political orientation and level of education. *Sex Roles* 40(1–2): 45–60.

Dorow, Sara. 2002. China R us? Care, consumption and transnationally adopted children. In D. Cook, (Ed.), *Symbolic Childhood*. New York: Peter Lang.

Douglas, Kristen. 2006. *Divorce Law in Canada*. Ottawa: Government of Canada, Law and Government Division. Retrieved from **http://www.parl.gc.ca/information/library/PRBpubs/963-e.html**

Doust, Janet L. 2008. Two English immigrant families in Australia in the 19th century. *The History of the Family* 13: 2–25.

Drakich, Janice. 1993. In whose best interest? The politics of joint custody, pp. 331–341. In Bonnie Fox (Ed.), *Family Patterns, Gender Relations*. Toronto: Oxford University Press.

Dronkers, Jaap. 1996. *The Effects of Parental Conflicts and Divorce on the Average Well-Being of Pupils in Secondary Education*. American Sociological Association.

Dryburgh, H. 2001. Changing our ways: Why and how Canadians use the internet. Retrieved June 11, 2009, from **http://www.statcan.gc.ca/bsolc/olc-cel/olccel?lang=eng&catno=56F0006X**

Dryburgh, Heather. 2001. Teenage pregnancy. *Health Reports* 12(1): 1–9. Ottawa: Statistics Canada. Catalogue no. 82–003.

Dua, Enakshi. 1999. Beyond diversity: Exploring the ways in which the discourse of race has shaped the institution of the nuclear family, pp. 237–260. In Enaskshi Dua (Ed.), *Scratching the Surface: Canadian Anti-Racist Feminist Thought*. Toronto: Women's Press.

Duberman, Lucile. 1975. *The Reconstituted Family: A Study of Remarried Couples and their Children*. Chicago: Nelson-Hall Publishers.

Dudley, James R. 1996. Noncustodial fathers speak about their parental role. *Family and Conciliation Courts Review 34*(3).

Duffey, T.H., H.R. Wooten, & C.A. Lumadue. 2004. The effect of dream sharing on marital intimacy and satisfaction. *Journal of Couple & Relationship Therapy 3*: 53–68.

Duffy, Anne, & Nancy Mandell. 2001. The growth in poverty and social inequality: Losing faith in social justice, pp. 77–114. In Dan Glenday & Ann Duffy (Eds.), *Canadian Society: Meeting the Challenges of the Twenty-First Century*. Toronto: Oxford University Press.

Dumont-Smith, C. 2002. Aboriginal elder abuse in Canada. Retrieved May 20, 2009, from **http://www.ahf.ca/ pages/download/28_37**

Dunlop, Rosemary, and Ailsa Burns. 1995. The sleeper effect: Myth or reality? *Journal of Marriage and the Family 57*(2): 375–386.

Dunne, Gillian A. 1997. *Lesbian Lifestyles: Women, Work and the Politics of Sexuality*. Toronto: University of Toronto.

Dunne, Gillian A. 2001. Opting into motherhood: Lesbians blurring the boundaries and transforming the meaning of parenthood and kinship. *Gender and Society 14*(1): 11–35.

Duong Tran, Quang, Serge Lee, & Sokley Khoi. 1996 December. Ethnic and gender differences in parental expectations and life stress. *Child and Adolescent Social Work Journal 13*: 515–526.

Durkheim, Émile. 1951. *Suicide, étude de sociologie*. (English Title) *Suicide: A Study in Sociology*. Translated by John A. Spaulding and George Simpson. Glencoe, Ill: Free Press.

Dush, Claire M. Kamp, & Paul R. Amato. 2005. Consequences of relationship status and quality for subjective well-being. *Journal of Social and Personal Relationships 22*(5): 607–627.

Duxbury, L., & Higgins, C., 2003. *Work–Life Conflict in Canada in the New Millennium: A Status Report*. Ottawa: Healthy Communities Division, Health Canada.

Duxbury, Linda Elizabeth, Christopher Alan Higgins, & D. Roland Thomas. 1996. Work and family environments and the adoption of computer-supported supplemental work-at-home. *Journal of Vocational Behavior 49*(1): 1–23.

Dwairy, Marwan, & Kariman E. Menshar. 2006. Parenting style, individuation, and mental health of Egyptian adolescents. *Journal of Adolescence 29*: 103–117.

Eastwick, Paul W. & Eli J. Finkel. 2008. Sex differences in mate preferences revisited: Do people know what they initially desire in a romantic partner? *Journal of Personality and Social Psychology 94*(2): 245–264.

Eaton, Linda Carole. 2000 August. A study of the correlation between the coming-out process and the first long-term homosexual relationship between gay males.

Dissertation Abstracts International, A: The Humanities and Social Sciences 61(2): 782–A-783–A.

Echenberg, Havi, James Gauthier, & André Léonard, 2011. Current and Emerging Issues, Some Public Policy Implications of an Aging Population, 41st Parliament, 16-17. Retrieved from **http://parl.gc.ca/Content/LOP/ ResearchPublications/CurrentEmergingIssues-e .pdf#page=18**

Echtelt, Patricia Van, Arie Glebbeek, Suzan Lewis, & Siegwart Lindenberg. Post-Fordist work: A man's world? Gender and working overtime in the Netherlands. *Gender & Society 23*(2): 188–214.

Edelman, M.A., & B.L. Menz. 1996. Selected comparisons and implications of a national rural and urban survey on health care access, demographics, and policy issues. *Journal of Rural Health 12*: 197–205.

Edin, Kathryn, and Rebecca Joyce Kissane. 2010. "Poverty and the American Family: A Decade in Review," *Journal of Marriage and the Family 72*(3): 460–479.

Edin, Kathryn, & Joanna M. Reed. 2005. Why don't they just get married? Barriers to marriage among the disadvantaged. *The Future of the Children 15*(2): 117–137.

Edin, Kathryn, Laura Tach, & Ronald Mincy. 2009. Claiming fatherhood: Race and the dynamics of paternal involvement among unmarried men. *The ANNALS of the American Academy of Political and Social Science 162*(1): 149–177.

Edleson, Jeffrey L. 1999 August. Children's witnessing of adult domestic violence. *Journal of Interpersonal Violence 14*(8): 839–870.

Edmonds, P., B. Vivat, R. Burman, E. Silber, & I.J. Higginson. 2007. Loss and change: experiences of people severely affected by multiple sclerosis. *Palliative Medicine 21*: 101–107.

Eells, Laura Workman, & Kathleen O'Flaherty. 1996. Gender perceptual differences in relation to marital problems. *Journal of Divorce and Remarriage 25*(2).

Eichler, Margrit. 1997. *Family Shifts: Families, Policies and Gender Equality*. Toronto: Oxford University Press.

Eichler, Margrit. 2001. Biases in family literature, pp. 51–66. In Maureen Baker (Ed.), *Families: Changing Trends in Canada* (4th edition). Toronto: McGraw-Hill Ryerson.

Eisikovits, Rivka A. 2000. Gender differences in cross-cultural adaptation styles of immigrant youths from the former U.S.S.R. in Israel. *Youth and Society 31*: 310–331.

Elder, Glen H. Jr. 1992. Models of the life course. *Contemporary Sociology 21*: 632–635.

Elder, Glen H. Jr., Monica Kirkpatrick Johnson, & Robert Crosnoe. 2004. The emergence and development of life course theory, pp. 3–19. In Jeylan T. Mortimer and Michael J. Shanahan (Eds.), *Handbook of the Life Course*. New York: Kluwer.

Elgar, Frank J., Christine Arlett, & Renee Groves. 2003. Stress, coping, and behavioural problems among rural and urban adolescents. *Journal of Adolescence 26*(5): 574–585.

Elgar, Frank J., John Knight, Graham J. Worrall, & Gregory Sherman. 2003. Attachment characteristics and behavioural problems in rural and urban juvenile delinquents. *Child Psychiatry and Human Development 34*(1): 35–48.

El-Ghannam, Ashraf R. 2001. Modernisation in Arab societies: The theoretical and analytical view. *International Journal of Sociology and Social Policy* 21: 88–131.

Ellison, Nicole B. 1999 Fall. Social impacts: New perspectives on telework. *Social Science Computer Review* 17(3): 338–356.

Emanuels-Zuurveen, Lineke, & Paul M.G. Emmelkamp. 1997. Spouse-aided therapy with depressed patients. *Behavior Modification* 21(1).

Emery, Robert E. 2012. *Renegotiating Family Relationships: Divorce, Child Custody and Mediation*, 2nd edition. New York: Guildford Press.

Emery, Robert E. 2013. *Cultural Sociology of Divorce: An Encyclopedia*. Thousand Oaks, CA: Sage.

Emmers-Sommer, Tara M. 2003. Couple relationships, pp. 327–332. In James J. Ponzettie, Jr. (Ed.), *International Encyclopedia of Marriage and Family* (2nd edition), Vol. 1. New York: Macmillan Reference USA.

Engels, Frederick. [1884]1972. *The Origin of the Family, Private Property and the State*. New York: Pathfinder.

Engle, Patrice L., Sarah Castle, & Purnima Menon. 1996. Child development: Vulnerability and resilience. *Social Science and Medicine* 43(5): 621–635.

Epstein, Rachel. 1996. Lesbian families, pp. 107–130. In Marion Lynn (Ed.), *Voices: Essays on Canadian Families*. Toronto: Nelson Canada.

Ermisch, John. 2008. Origins of social immobility and inequality: Parenting and early child development. *National Institute Economic Review* 205: 62–71.

Esping-Andersen, G. 1999. *Social Foundations of Post Industrial Economics*. Oxford University Press, New York.

Espiritu, Yen Le. 2001. "We don't sleep around like white girls do": Family, culture, and gender in Filipina American lives. *Signs* 26(2): 415–440.

Este, David C., and Admasu A. Tachble. 2009. "The Perceptions and Experiences of Russian Immigrant and Sudanese Refugee Men as Fathers in an Urban Center in Canada." *The ANNALS of the American Academy of Political and Social Science*. 624(1): 139–155. http://ann.sagepub.com/content/624/1/139.full .pdf+html

Estrada, Ana Ulloa, & Julianne M. Holmes. 1999 April–June. Couples' perceptions of effective and ineffective ingredients of marital therapy. *Journal of Sex & Marital Therapy* 25(2): 151–162.

Evans, Michael, 2013. "China's divorce rate rises for seventh year in a row." http://shanghaiist.com/2013/02/25/ chinas_divorce_rate_rises_for_seven.php

Ezra, Marni, & Melissa Deckman. 1996 March–April. Balancing work and family responsibilities: Flextime and child care in the federal government. *Public Administration Review* 56: 174–179.

Farhood, Laila, Huda Zurayk, Monique Chaya, Fadia Saadeh, Garbis Meshefedjian, & Thuraya Sidani. 1993. The impact of war on the physical and mental health of the family: The Lebanese experience. *Social Science and Medicine* 36(12): 1555–1567.

Farrell, Betty, Alicia VanderVusse, and Abigail Ocobock. 2012. "Family Change and the State of Family Sociology." *Current Sociology* 60(3): 263–301.

Fast, Janet E., Norah C. Keating, Leslie Oakes, & Deanna L. Williamson. 1997. *Conceptualizing and Operationalizing the Costs of Informal Elder Care*. NHRDP Project No. 6609–1963–55. Ottawa: National Health Research and Development Program, Health Canada.

Fawcett, Matthew. 1990. Taking the middle path: Recent Swedish legislation grants minimal property rights to unmarried cohabitants. *Family Law Quarterly* 24: 179–202.

Feerick, Margaret M., & Jeffrey J. Haugaard. 1999 December. Long-term effects of witnessing marital violence for women: The contribution of childhood physical and sexual abuse. *Journal of Family Violence* 14(4): 377–398.

Feingold, Alan. 1995. Physical appearance and gender: Sociobiological and sociocultural perspectives, review of Linda A. Jackson. *Archives of Sexual Behavior* 24(5): 580–581.

Feldman, Shirley S., Lawrence Fisher, & Laura Seitel. 1997. The effect of parents' marital satisfaction on young adults' adaptation: A longitudinal study. *Journal of Research on Adolescence* 7(1): 55–80.

Felix, Daniel S., W. David Robinson, and Kimberly J. Jarzynka. 2013. "The Influence of Divorce on Men's Health." *Journal of Men's Health*. 18 January 2013. http://www.sciencedirect.com/science/article/pii/ S1875686712000954

Ferri, Elsa. 1993. Socialization experiences of children in lone parent families: Evidence from the British National Child Development Study, pp. 281–290. In Joe Hudson & Burt Galaway (Eds.), *Single Parent Families: Perspectives on Research and Policy*. Toronto: Thompson.

Fincham, Frank D., & Steven R.H. Beach. 2006. Relationship satisfaction, pp. 579–594. In Anita L. Vangelisti and Daniel Perlman (Eds.), *The Cambridge Handbook of Personal Relationships*. New York: Cambridge University Press.

Fineman, Martha Albertson, & Roxanne Mykitiuk (Eds.) 1994. *The Public Nature of Private Violence: The Discovery of Domestic Abuse*. New York, NY: Routledge.

Fingerson, Laura. 2000. *Do Parents' Opinions Matter? Family Processes and Adolescent Sexual Behavior*. Paper presented to the American Sociological Association (ASA).

Finkel, Eli J., Paul W. Eastwick, Benjamin R. Karney, Harry T. Reis, and Susan Sprecher. 2012. "Online Dating: A Critical Analysis From the Perspective of Psychological Science." *Psychological Science in the Public Interest*. 13(1): 3–66. http://www.psych. rochester.edu/faculty/reis/documents/Psychological ScienceinthePublicInterest-2012-Finkel-3-66.pdf

Finn, Jerry. 1996. Computer-based self-help groups: On-line recovery for addictions. *Computers in Human Services* 13(1): 21–41.

Finn, Jerry, & Melissa Lavitt. 1994. Computer-based self-help groups for sexual abuse survivors. *Social Work with Groups* 17(1–2): 21–46.

Finnie, Ross. 1993. Women, men, and the economic consequences of divorce: Evidence from Canadian longitudinal data. *Canadian Review of Sociology and Anthropology* 30(2): 205–241.

Firestone, Juanita M., Linda C. Lambert, & William A. Vega. 1999 June. Intimate violence among women of Mexican origin: Correlates of abuse. *Journal of Gender, Culture, and Health* 4(2): 119–134.

Fischer, Claude S. 1992. *America Calling: A Social History of the Telephone to 1940*. Berkeley, CA: University of California Press.

Fisher, H. 1992. *Anatomy of Love: A Natural History of Mating, Marriage and Why We Stray*. New York: Fawcett.

Fisher, S., A. Allan, & M.M. Allan. 2004. Exploratory study to examine the impact of television reports of prison escapes on fear of crime, operationalised as state anxiety. *Australian Journal of Psychology* 56(3): 181–190.

Fiske, Jo-Anne, & Rose Johnny. 1996. The Neduten family: Yesterday and today, pp. 225–241. In Marion Lynn (Ed.), *Voices: Essays on Canadian Families*. Toronto: Nelson.

Fisman, Raymond, & Sheena Iyengar. 2008. Racial preferences in dating. *Review of Economic Studies* 75: 117–132.

Fitzgerald, B. 1999. Children of lesbian and gay parents: A review of the literature. *Marriage and Family Review* 29(1): 57–76.

Flandrin, J-L. 1979. *Families in Former Times: Kinship, Household and Sexuality in Early Modern France*. Cambridge: Cambridge University Press.

Fleras, Augie, & Jean Leonard Elliott. 2003. *Unequal Relations: An Introduction to Race and Ethnic Dynamics in Canada* (4th edition). Toronto: Prentice Hall.

Fleury, Dominique. 2008. "Low Income Children," Perspectives on Labour and Income 9(5):14-23, Statistics Canada. **http://www.statcan.gc.ca/pub/75-001-x/2008105/pdf/10578-eng.pdf**

Follette, William C., Neil S. Jacobson, Dirk Revenstorf, Donald H. Baucom, Kurt Hahlweg, & Gayla Margolin. 2000 June. Variability in outcome and clinical significance of behavioral marital therapy: A reanalysis of outcome data. *Prevention & Treatment* 3: unpaged.

Fonner, Kathryn L., and Lara C. Stache. 2012. "All in a day's work, at home: teleworkers' management of micro role transitions and the work-home boundary." *New Technology, Work and Employment* 27(3): 242–257. **http://onlinelibrary.wiley.com/doi/10.1111/j.1468-005X.2012.00290.x/pdf**

Forsdick Martz, Diane J. 2006. *Canadian Farm Women and Their Families: Restructuring, Work and Decision Making* [Dissertation].

Forsyth, Craig, & Robert Gramling. 1998. Socio-economic factors affecting the rise of commuter marriage. *International Journal of the Sociology of the Family* 28(2): 93–106.

Forte, James A., David D. Franks, & Janett A. Forte. 1996 January. Asymmetrical role-taking: Comparing battered women. *Social Work 41*: 59–73.

Forthofer, Melinda S., Howard J. Markman, & Martha Cox. 1996 August. Associations between marital distress and work loss in a national sample. *Journal of Marriage and the Family 58*.

Foshee, Vangie A., Katherine J. Karriker-Jaffe, Heathe Luz McNaughton Reyes, Susan T. Ennett, Chirayath Suchindran, Karl E. Bauman, & Thad S. Benefield. 2008. *Journal of Adolescent Health 42*: 596–604.

Fox, Bonnie J. 1993. The rise and fall of the breadwinner-homemaker family, pp. 147–157. In Bonnie J. Fox (Ed.), *Family Patterns, Gender Relations*. Toronto: Oxford University Press.

Fox, Bonnie J. 2001. The formative years: How parenthood creates gender. *La Revue Canadienne de Sociologie et d'Anthropologie/The Canadian Review of Sociology and Anthropology* 38(4): 373–390.

Fox, Bonnie J., & Meg Luxton. 2001. Conceptualizing family, pp. 22–33. In Bonnie J. Fox (Ed.), *Family Patterns, Gender Relations* (2nd edition). Toronto: Oxford University Press.

Fox, Greer Litton, & Dudley Chancey. 1998 November. Sources of economic distress: Individual and family outcomes. *Journal of Family Issues* 19(6): 725–749.

Fredriksen, Karen. 1996. Gender differences in employment and the informal care of adults. *Journal of Women & Aging* 8(2): 35–53.

Freiband, David M. 1996. The fulfillment of marital ideals: A study of marital satisfaction and personal well-being. *Dissertation Abstracts International: Section B: The Sciences and Engineering* 56(12-B), 7092.

Freidenberg, Judith, & Muriel Hammer. 1998 Spring. Social networks and health care: The case of elderly Latinos in East Harlem. *Urban Anthropology* 27(1): 49–85.

French, Maggie. 1991. Becoming a lone parent, pp. 126–142. In Michael Hardy & Graham Crow (Eds.), *Lone Parenthood: Coping with Constraints and Making Opportunities in Single-Parent Families*. Toronto: University of Toronto Press.

Frenette, Marc, David A. Green, & Kevin Milligan. n.d. The tale of the tails: Revisiting recent trends in Canadian after-tax income inequality using Census data. Retrieved April 24, 2006, from **http://www.econ.ubc.ca/kevinmil/research/centax6.6.pdf**

Frias, Sonia M., & Ronald J. Angel. 2007. Stability and change in the experience of partner violence among low-income women. *Social Science Quarterly* 88(5): 1281–1306.

Frideres, J.S. 2007. Building bridges: Aboriginal, immigrant, and visible minority families in the twenty-first century, pp. 195–212. In David Cheal (Ed.), *Canadian Families Today: New Perspectives*. Toronto: Oxford University Press.

Fu, Xuanning. 2008. Interracial marriage and family socioeconomic well-being: Equal status exchange or caste status exchange? *Social Science Journal* 45: 132–155.

Fuller-Thomson, E. 2005. Canadian First Nations grandparents raising grandchildren: A portrait in resilience. *International Journal of Aging and Human Development* 60(4): 331–342.

Gadalla, T. M. 2009. "Impact of Marital Dissolution on Men's and Women's Incomes: A Longitudinal Study." *Journal of Divorce and Remarriage* 50(1):55–65.

Gadd, Jane. 1997. The drift to the bottom. *Globe and Mail*, 21 June: D1, D2.

Galambos, Nancy L., & Heather A. Sears. 1998 November. Adolescents' perceptions of parents' work and adolescents' work values in two-earner families. *Journal of Early Adolescence* 18(4): 397–420.

Galston, William A. 1996. Braking divorce for the sake of children, The American Enterprise 7 (May/June). *Globe and Mail*, 2000, 49.

Ganong-Coleman, Lawrence H. 1998 Fall. Attitudes regarding filial responsibilities to help elderly divorced parents and stepparents. *Journal of Aging Studies* 12(3): 271–290.

Ganster, Daniel C., & Bart Victor. 1988 March. The impact of social support on mental and physical health. *British Journal of Medical Psychology* 61(1): 17–36.

Gartner, Rosemary, Myrna Dawson, & Maria Crawford. 2001 (1998). Women killing: Intimate femicide in Ontario, 1974–1994. In Bonnie J. Fox (Ed.), *Family Patterns, Gender Patterns* (2nd edition). Toronto: Oxford University Press, 473–490.

Gaunt, Ruth. 2006. Couple similarity and marital satisfaction: Are similar spouses happier? *Journal of Personality* 74(5): 1401–1420.

Gazso, Amber, & Susan McDaniel. 2009. *The Risky Business of Being a Lone Mother on Income Support in Canada and the U.S.* Paper presented at the Pacific Sociological Association meetings, San Diego, April 2009.

Gazso, Amber, and Susan A. McDaniel. 2010. "The Risks of Being a Lone Mother on Income Support in Canada and the United States." *International Journal of Sociology and Social Policy*, 30(7/8): 368–386.

Gazso, Amber, and Susan A. McDaniel. 2010a. "The Great West 'Experiment:' Neo-Liberal Convergence and Transforming Citizenship in Canada." *Canadian Review of Social Policy*, 63/64: 15–35.

Gazso, Amber, and Susan A. McDaniel. 2010b. "The Risks of Being a Lone Mother on Income Support in Canada and the United States." *International Journal of Sociology and Social Policy*, 30(7/8): 368–386.

Gazso, Amber, and Susan A. McDaniel. 2014. "Families by Choice and the Management of Low Income through Social Supports." *Journal of Family Issues*, forthcoming.

Gee, Ellen M. 1986. The life course of Canadian women: An historical and demographic analysis. *Social Indicators Research* 18: 263–283.

Gee, Ellen M., & Meredith M. Kimball. 1987. *Women and Aging*. Toronto: Butterworths.

Gelles, R., & D. Loseke (Eds.). 1993. *Current Controversies on Family Violence*. Newbury Park, CA: Sage.

Gelles, Richard J. 1994 Spring. Introduction: Part of a special issue on family violence. *Journal of Comparative Family Studies* 25: 1–6.

Ghimire, Dirgha J., William G. Axinn, Scott T. Yabiku, & Arland Thornton. 2006. Social change, premarital nonfamily experience, and spouse choice in an arranged marriage society. *American Journal of Sociology* 111: 1181–1218.

Gibbs, Jennifer L., Nicole B. Ellison, & Rebecca D. Heino. 2006. Self-presentation in online personals: The role of anticipated future interaction, self-disclosure, and perceived success in internet dating. *Communication Research* 33: 152–177.

Gibson-Davis, Christina M. 2009. Money, marriage, and children: Testing the financial expectations and family formation theory. *Journal of Marriage and Family* 71(1): 146–160.

Giddens, Anthony. 1992. *The Transformation of Intimacy: Sexuality, Love, and Eroticism in Modern Societies*. Cambridge: Polity Press.

Giele, Janet Zollinger. 1996. Decline of family: Conservative, liberal and feminist views. In David Popenoe, Jean Bethke Elshtain, and David Blankenhorn (Eds.), *Promises to Keep: Decline and Renewal of Marriage in America*. Lanham, MD: Rowman and Littlefield Publishers, Inc.

Gilliam, C.M., & A.M. Steffen. 2006. The relationship between caregiving self-efficacy and depressive symptoms in dementia family caregivers. *Aging and Mental Health* 10(2): 79–86(8).

Gillian, A.D. 2001. The lady vanishes? Reflections on the experiences of married and divorced non-heterosexual fathers. *Sociological Research Online* 6(3). Retrieved May 25, 2009, from **http://www.socresonline.org .uk/6/3/dunne.html**

Gim Chung, R.H. 2001. Gender, ethnicity, and acculturation in intergenerational conflict of Asian American college students. *Cultural Diversity and Ethnic Minority Psychology* 7: 376–386.

Gladstone, J.W. 1995. The marital perceptions of elderly persons living or having a spouse living in a long-term care institution in Canada. *The Gerontologist* 35(1): 52–60.

Glaser, K., R. Stuchbury, C. Tomassini, & J. Askham. 2008. The long-term consequences of partnership dissolution for support in later life in the United Kingdom. *Ageing & Society* 28(3): 329–351.

Glass, Jennifer, & Tetsushi Fujimoto. 1995. Employer characteristics and the provision of family responsive policies. *Work and Occupations* 22(4): 380–411.

Glavin, Paul, and Scott Schieman. 2012. "Work-Family Role Blurring and Work-Family Conflict: The Moderating Influence of Job Resources and Job Demands." *Work and Occupations* 39: 7–98.

Glick, Susan. 1997 April. Examining the relationship between perceived emotional expressiveness and marital adjustment. *Dissertation Abstracts International: Section B: The Sciences & Engineering* 57(10–B), 6648.

Glynn, Sarah Jane. 2012. "The New Breadwinners: 2010 Update, Rates of Women Supporting Their Families Economically Increased Since 2007." Center for American Progress. **http://www.americanprogress .org/wp-content/uploads/issues/2012/04/pdf/ breadwinners.pdf**

Godard, J. 2007. PACS seven years on: Is it moving towards marriage? *International Journal of Law, Policy and the Family* 21(3): 310–321.

Goldberg, Abbie E, April M. Moyer, Elizabeth R. Weber, and Julie Shapiro. 2013. "What Changed When the Gay Adoption Ban was Lifted?: Perspectives of Lesbian and Gay Parents in Florida." *Sexuality Research and Social Policy* 10(2): 110–124.

Goldscheider, Frances, Gayle Kaufman, & Sharon Sassler. 2009. Navigating the "new" marriage market: How attitudes toward partner characteristics shape union formation. *Journal of Family Issues* 30(6): 719–737.

Goldstein, Marion Z. 1990. The role of mutual support groups and family therapy for caregivers of demented elderly. *Journal of Geriatric Psychiatry* 23(2): 117–128.

Goode, William. 1993. *World Changes in Divorce Patterns*. New Haven: Yale University Press.

Goodman, Catherine. 1990 November. Evaluation of a model self-help telephone program: Impact on natural networks. *Social Work* 35(6): 556–562.

Goossens, Frits A., Geertruud Ottenhoff, & Willem Koops. 1991. Day care and social outcomes in middle childhood: A retrospective study. *Journal of Reproductive and Infant Psychology* 9(2–3): 137–150.

Gordon, Linda, & Sara McLanahan. 1991. Single parenthood in 1900. *Journal of Family History* 16(2): 97–116.

Gordon, Sarah A. 2004. Boundless possibilities: Home sewing and the meanings of women's domestic work in the United States, 1890–1930. *Journal of Women's History* 16(2): 68–91.

Gorlick, Carolyne A., & D. Alan Pomfret. 1993. Hope and circumstance: Single mothers exiting social assistance, pp. 253–270. In Joe Hudson & Burt Galaway (Eds.), *Single Parent Families: Perspectives on Research and Policy.* Toronto: Thompson.

Gott, M., & S. Hinchliff. 2004. How important is sex in later life? The views of older people. *Social Science and Medicine* 56: 117–128.

Gottlieb, B.H. (Ed.). 1981. *Social Networks and Social Support.* Beverly Hills, CA: Sage.

Gottlieb, Benjamin H. 1985 Spring. Social networks and social support: An overview of research, practice, and policy implications. *Health Education Quarterly* 12(1): 5–22.

Gottman, John M., with Nan Silver. 1999. *The Seven Principles for Making Marriage Work.* New York: Random House.

Gottman, John Mordechai. 1995. *Why Marriages Succeed or Fail: And How You Can Make Yours Last.* New York: Fireside Books, 1995.

Government of Canada. 2005. News Release, 18 April. Retrieved November 30, 2005, from **http://www.cic.gc.ca/english/press/05/0511-e.html**

Government of Canada. 2012. Citizenship and Immigration Canada, News Release "Canada welcomes largest number of parents and grandparents in almost twenty years." **http://www.cic.gc.ca/english/department/media/releases/2012/2012-11-05.asp**

Government of Canada. 2012. "Canada Post Group of Companies reports pre-tax loss of $75 million in the third quarter." *Canada News Centre.* **http://news.gc.ca/web/article-eng.do;jsessionid=ac1b10 5430d75adb0983ebcf4af3ba86aafadafb0aea.e34 Rc3iMbx8Oai0Tbx0SaxmPbxv0?mthd=tp&crtr .page=1&nid=708919&crtr.tp1D=1**

Grable, John E., Sonya Britt, & Joyce Cantrell. 2007. An exploratory study of the role financial satisfaction has on the thought of subsequent divorce. *Family and Consumer Sciences Research Journal* 36: 130–50.

Graefe, Deborah Roempke, & Daniel T. Lichter. 2007. When unwed mothers marry: The marital and cohabiting partners of midlife women. *Journal of Family Issues* 28(5): 595–622.

Graefe, Deborah Roempke, & Daniel T. Lichter. 2008. Marriage patterns among unwed mothers: Before and after PRWORA. *Journal of Policy Analysis and Management* 27(3): 479–497.

Graham, Carolyn W., Judith L. Fischer, Duane Crawford, Jacki Fitzpatrick, & Kristan Bina. 2000 October. Parental status, social support, and marital adjustment. *Journal of Family Issues* 21(7): 888–905.

Grahame, Kamini M. 2006. Shifting arrangements: Indo-Trinidadian women, globalization, and the restructuring of family life. *Sociological Spectrum* 26: 425–452.

Grant, Bruce. 2005. The traffic in brides. *American Anthropologist* 107: 687–689.

Gray-Little, Bernadette, Donald H. Baucom, & Sherry L. Hamby. 1996. Marital power, marital adjustment and therapy outcomes. *Journal of Family Psychology* 10(3).

Greaves, Kathleen Marie. 2001 May. The social construction of sexual interaction in heterosexual relationships: A qualitative analysis. *Dissertation Abstracts International, A: The Humanities and Social Sciences* 61(11), 4565–A-4566–A.

Green, Alan G., & David Green. 2004. The goals of Canada's immigration policy: A historical perspective. *Canadian Journal of Urban Research* 13: 102–139.

Green, R.J., P.L. Williams, C.S. Johnson, & I. Blum. 2008. Can Canadian seniors on public pensions afford a nutritious fiet? *Canadian Journal on Aging* 27(1): 69–79.

Greenland, K., & R. Brown. 2005. Acculturation and contact in Japanese students studying in the United Kingdom. *Journal of Social Psychology, 145:* 373–389.

Greif, Geoffrey L. 1995. When divorced fathers want no contact with their children: A preliminary analysis. *Journal of Divorce and Remarriage* 23(1–2).

Grimm-Thomas, Karen, & Maureen Perry-Jenkins. 1994 April. All in a day's work: Job experiences, self-esteem, and fathering in working class families. *Family Relations* 43: 174–181.

Gringeri, Christina. 1995. Flexibility, the family ethic, and rural home-based work. *Affilia* 10(1): 70–86.

Grissett, Barbara, & Allen L. Furr. 1994. Effects of parental divorce on children's financial support for college. *Journal of Divorce and Remarriage* 22(1–2).

Gross, Penny. 1987. Defining post-divorce remarriage families: A typology based on the subjective perceptions of children. *Journal of Divorce* 10(1, 2): 205–217.

Groves, Melissa, & Diane Horm-Wingerd. 1991. Commuter marriages: Personal, family and career issues. *Sociology and Social Research* 75(4): 212–217.

Gruber, James E., & Susan Fineran. 2007. The impact of bullying and sexual harassment on middle and high school girls. *Violence Against Women* 13(6): 627–643.

Guberman, Nancy, Jean-Pierre Lavoie, Laure Blein, and Ignace Olazabal. 2012. "Baby Boom Caregivers: Care in the Age of Individualization." *The Gerontologist* 52(2): 210–218. **http://0-gerontologist.oxfordjournals .org.darius.uleth.ca/content/52/2/210.full.pdf+html**

Gündüz-Hosgör, Ayse, & Jeroen Smits. 2008. Variation in labor market participation of married women in Turkey. *Women's Studies International Forum* 31: 104–117.

Gustafson, Kaaryn. 2009. "Breaking Vows: Marriage Promotion, the New Patriarch, and the Retreat from Egalitarianism." *Stanford Journal of Civil Rights and Civil Liberties* 269–277. **http://heinonline.org/HOL/ LandingPage?collection=journals&handle=hein .journals/stjcrcl5&div=13&id=&page**

Guttman, Joseph. 1993. *Divorce in Psychosocial Perspective: Theory and Research.* Hillsdale, NJ: Lawrence Erlbaum Associates.

Haas, Stephen M., & Laura Stafford. 1998 December. An initial examination of maintenance behaviors in gay and lesbian relationships. *Journal of Social and Personal Relationships* 15(6): 846–855.

Hadas, Doron, Gila Markovitzky, & Miri Sarid. 2008. Spousal violence among immigrants from the former Soviet Union—general population and welfare recipients. *Journal of Family Violence* 23: 549–555.

Hadjistavrolous, Thomas, & Myles Genet. 1994. The underestimation of the role of physical attractiveness in dating preferences: Ignorance or taboo? *Canadian Journal of Behavioural Science* 26(2): 298.

Hagan, John, & Bill McCarthy. 1998. *Mean Street: Youth, Crimes and Homelessness*. Cambridge, MA: Cambridge University Press.

Haimes, Erica, & Kate Weiner. 2000 July. "Everybody's got a dad ... ": Issues for lesbian families in the management of donor insemination. *Sociology of Health and Illness* 22(4): 477–499.

Handrahan, Lori. 2004. Hunting for women: Bride-kidnapping in Kyrgyzstan. *International Feminist Journal of Politics* 6: 207–33.

Hannah, Mo Teresa, Wade Luquet, & Joan McCormick. 1997 Spring. COMPASS as a measure of the efficacy of couples therapy. *American Journal of Family Therapy* 25.

Hareven, Tamara K. 1991 Spring. The home and the family in historical perspective. *Social Research* 58(1): 253–285.

Harris, Colette. 2006. Bride kidnapping in Kyrgyzstan. *Slavic Review* 65: 153–54.

Harris, Marvin. 1997. *Culture, People, Nature: An Introduction to General Anthropology* (7th edition). New York: Longman.

Harrison, Deborah. 2002. *The First Casualty: Violence Against Women in Canadian Military Communities*. Toronto: Lorimer.

Harrison, Deborah, Karen Robson, Patrizia Albanese, Chris Saunders, and Christine Newburn-Cook. 2011. "The Impact of Shared Location on the Mental Health of Military and Civilian Adolescents in a Community Affected by Frequent Deployments." *Armed Forces & Society* 37(3):550–560.

Harrison, Kelley A., Gina S. Richman, & Glenda L. Vittimberga. 2000 March. Parental stress in grandparents versus parents raising children with behavior problems. *Journal of Family Issues* 21(2): 262–270.

Hartos, Jessica L., & Thomas G. Power. 2000 September. Relations among single mothers' awareness of their adolescents' stressors, maternal monitoring, mother-adolescent comunication, and adolescent adjustment. *Journal of Adolescent Research* 15(5): 546–563.

Hassebrauck, Manfred. 1996. Relationship concepts and relationship satisfaction: The importance of real and perceived similarity in couples. *Zeitschrift für Sozialpsychologie* 27(3), 183–192.

Hassouneh-Phillips, Dena, & Elizabeth McNeff. 2005. I thought I was less worthy: Low sexual and body esteem and increased vulnerability to intimate partner abuse in women with physical disabilities. *Sexuality and Disability* 23(4): 227–240.

Haythornthwaite, Caroline. 2001a January. *Tie Strength and the Impact of New Media*. Proceedings of the 24th Hawaii International Conference of System Sciences.

Haythornthwaite, Caroline. 2001b November. Introduction: The Internet in everyday life. *American Behavorial Scientist* 45(3): 363–382.

Haythornthwaite, Caroline, M.M. Kazmer, J. Robins, & S. Showmaker. 2000. Community development among distance learners: Temporal and technological dimensions. *Journal of Computer-Mediated Communication* 6(1).

Heaphy, B., A.K.T. Yip, & D. Thompson. 2004. Ageing in a non-heterosexual context. *Ageing and Society* 24(6): 881–902.

Heather, Barbara, Lynn Skillen, Jennifer Young, & Theresa Vladicka. 2005. Women's gendered identities and the restructuring of rural Alberta. *Sociologia Ruralis* 45(1–2): 86–97.

Heimdal, Kristen R., & Sharon K. Houseknecht. 2003. Cohabiting and married couples' income organization: Approaches in Sweden and the United States. *Journal of Marriage and Family* 65(3): 525–538.

Heitritter, Dianne Lynn. 1999 November. Meanings of family strength voiced by Somali immigrants: Reaching an inductive understanding. *Dissertation Abstracts International, A: The Humanities and Social Sciences* 60(5), 1782–A-1783–A.

Helbig, Sylvia, Thomas Lampert, Michael Klose, & Frank Jacobi. 2006. Is parenthood associated with mental health? Findings from an epidemiological community survey. *Social Psychiatry and Psychiatric Epidemiology* 41(11): 889–96.

Hellerstein, Judith K., and Melinda Sandler Morrill. 2011. "Booms, Busts, and Divorce." *The Berkeley Electronic Journal of Economic Analysis and Policy* 11(1):1935–1682.

Henderson, A.J.Z., K. Bartholomew, & D.G. Dutton. 1997. He loves me; he loves me not: Attachment and separation resolution of abused women. *Journal of Family Violence* 12 (June): 169–191.

Henningsen, David Dryden, Mary Braz, & Elaine Davies. 2008. Why do we flirt?: Flirting motivations and sex differences in working and social contexts. *Journal of Business Communication* 45.4: 483–502.

Henry, Ryan G., & Richard B. Miller. 2004. Marital problems occurring in midlife: Implications for couples therapy. *American Journal of Family Therapy* 32: 405–417.

Hequembourg, A.L. 2007. Becoming lesbian mothers. *Journal of Homosexuality* 53(3): 153–180.

Herlyn, Ingrid, & Ulrike Vogel. 1989 July. Individualization: A new perspective on the life situation of women. *Zeitschrift fur Sozialisationsforschung und Erziehungssoziologie* 9(3): 162–178.

Hetherington, E. Mavis, & John Kelly. 2002. *For Better or for Worse: Divorce Reconsidered*. New York: W. W. Norton.

Hilborn, Robin, (Ed.). 2011. "Canadians go abroad to adopt 1,946 children in 2010." *Family Helper*, October 27. **http://www.familyhelper.net/news/111027stats.html**

Higgins, Chris, & Linda Duxbury. 2002. The 2001 national work-life conflict study: Report one. Retrieved May 25, 2005, from Public Health Agency of Canada: **http://www.phacaspc.gc.ca/publicat/work-travail/report1**

Higgins, Daryl J., & Marita P. McCabe. 1994. The relationship of child sexual abuse and family violence to adult adjustment: Toward an integrated risk-sequelae model. *Journal of Sex Research* 31(4): 255–266.

Hill, Amelia. 22 Nov 2009. "'Useless stay-at-home men' a female myth." *The Guardian*. 22. **http://www.guardian.co.uk/lifeandstyle/2009/nov/22/working-women-husbands-housework**

Hill, R. 1949. *Families Under Stress: Adjustment to the Crises of War Separation and Reunion*. New York: Harper and Bros.

Hiotakis, Samantha. 2005. An investigation of familial variables associated with marital satisfaction. *Dissertation Abstracts International: Section B: The Sciences and Engineering* 66(5-B), 2877.

Hochschild, A. 2001 (1997). The third shift. In Bonnie J. Fox (Ed.), *Family Patterns, Gender Relations* (2nd edition). Toronto: Oxford University Press, 338–51.

Hochschild, Arlie Russell. 1997. *The Time Bind: When Work Becomes Home and Home Becomes Work*. New York: Metropolitan Books.

Hoem, Britta, & Jan M. Hoem. 1988 September. The Swedish family: Aspects of contemporary developments. *Journal of Family Issues* 9(3): 397–424.

Hofferth, Sandra L. 1996. Effects of public and private policies on working after childbirth. *Work and Occupations* 23(4): 378–404.

Hoffman, Charles D., & Debra K. Ledford. 1995. Adult children of divorce: Relationships with their mothers and fathers prior to, following parental separation, and currently. *Journal of Divorce and Remarriage* 24(3–4).

Hoffman, Martin L. 1979. Development of moral thought, feeling, and behavior. *American Psychologist* 34(10): 958–966.

Hoffman, Saul, & Greg Duncan. 1995 Winter. The effect of incomes, wages and AFDC benefits in marital disruption. *Journal of Human Resources* 30.

Hogeboom, David L., Robet J. McDermott, Karen M. Perrin, Hana Osman, and Bethany A. Bell-Ellison. 2010. "Internet Use and Social Networking among Middle-Aged and Older Adults." *Educational Gerontology* 36(2): 93–111.

Holtzworth-Munroe, Amy, Jennifer Waltz, Neil S. Jacobson, Valerie Monaco, Peter A. Fehrenbach, & John M. Gottman. 1992. Recruiting nonviolent men as control subjects for research on marital violence: How easily can it be done? *Violence and Victims* 7(1): 79–88.

Hook, Jennifer L. 2006. Care in context: Men's unpaid work in 20 countries, 1965–2003. *American Sociological Review* 71: 639–660.

hooks, bell. 1984. *Feminist Theory: From Margin to Centre*. Boston: South End Press.

Horowitz, Allan V., Julie McLaughlin, & Helene Raskin White. 1998. How the negative and positive aspects of partner relationships affect the mental health of young married people. *Journal of Health and Social Behavior* 39(2): 124–136.

Howell, Nancy, with Patricia Albanese & Kwaku Obosu-Mensah. 2001. Ethnic families, pp. 116–142. In Maureen Baker (Ed.), *Families: Changing Trends in Canada* (4th edition). Toronto: McGraw-Hill Ryerson.

Huang, Frederick Y., & Salman Akhtar. 2005. Immigrant sex: The transport of affection and sensuality across cultures. *American Journal of Psychoanalysis* 65: 179–188.

Huang, I-Chiao. 1991. Family stress and coping, pp. 289–334. In Stephen J. Bahr (Ed.), *Family Research: A Sixty-Year Review, 1930–1990, Volume 1*. New York: Lexington Books, Maxwell Macmillan International.

Huck, Barbara. 2001 February/March. Love in another world. *The Beaver: Canada's History Magazine*: 12–19.

Hughes, R., A.T. Ebata, & D. Dollahite. 1999. Introduction: Family life in the information age. *Family Relations* 48: 5–6.

Huisman, Kimberly A. 1996. Wife battering in Asian American communities: Identifying the service needs of an overlooked segment of the U.S. population. *Violence Against Women* 2(3): 260–283.

Human Resources and Skills Development Canada. 2004. Archived: The Changing Face of Canadian Workplaces. **http://www.hrsdc.gc.ca/eng/labour/ employment_standards/fls/resources/resource01 .shtml**

Human Resources and Skills Development Canada. 2005a. Addressing work-life balance in Canada. Retrieved May 27, 2005, from **http://www.hrsdc.gc.ca/asp/ gateway.asp?hr=/en/lp/spila/wlb/awlbc/01table_of_ contents.shtml&hs=wnc**

Human Resources and Skills Development Canada. 2005b. Work-related child-care centres in Canada–2001. Retrieved May 27, 2005, from **http://www.hrsdc .gc.ca/asp/gateway.asp?hr=/en/lp/spila/wlb/ wrccc/02table_of_contents.shtml&hs=wnc**

Humphreys, Terry, & Ed Herold. 2007. Sexual consent in heterosexual relationships: Development of a new measure. *Sex Roles* 57: 305–315.

Huston, Ted L., & Heidi Melz. 2004. The case for (promoting) marriage: The devil is in the details. *Journal of Marriage and Family* 66(4): 943–958.

Hwang, Wei-Chin. 2006. Acculturative family distancing: Theory, research, and clinical practice. *Psychotherapy: Theory, Research, Practice, Training* 43 (2006): 397–409.

Hyman, Ilene, Sepali Guruge, & Robin Mason. 2008. The impact of migration on marital relationships: A study of Ethiopian immigrants in Toronto. *Journal of Comparative Family Studies* 39: 149–163.

Hynie, Michaela, Richard N. Lalonde, & Nam Lee. 2006. Parent-child value transmission among Chinese immigrants to North America: The case of traditional mate preferences. *Cultural Diversity and Ethnic Minority Psychology* 12: 230–44.

Ibarra, Maria de la Luz. 2010. "Creating Intimate Boundaries: Culture and Social Lives." In Eileen Boris and Rhacel Salazar Perrenas (Eds.). *Intimate Labors: Cultures, Technologies and the Politics of Care*. Stanford, CA: Stanford University Press.

Illig, Diane S. 1999 October. Instrument development for assessing the task allocation by lesbian and gay couples with regard to household and familial tasks. *Dissertation Abstracts International, A: The Humanities and Social Sciences* 60(4), 1347–A.

Jaaber, R., & S. Das Dasgupta. 2003. Assessing social risks of battered women. *Praxis International* 10: 14. Available at **http://www.praxisinternational.org/ library_frame.html** under "Library: Advocacy."

Jackson, Stevi. 1992. Towards a historical sociology of housework: A materialist feminist analysis. *Women's Studies International Forum* 15(2): 153–172.

Jacob, Jenet I., S. Allen, J.E. Hill, N.L. Mead, M. Ferris. 2008. Work interference with dinnertime as a mediator and moderator between work hours and work and family outcomes. *Family and Consumer Sciences Research Journal* 36(4): 310–327.

Jacobson, Bert H., Steven G. Aldana, R.Z.Goetzel, K.D. Vardell, T.B. Adams TB, R.J. Pietras 1996 September–October. The relationship between perceived stress and self-reported illness-related absenteeism. *American Journal of Health Promotion* 11(1): 54–61.

Jacobson, N.S., J.M. Gottman, E. Gortner, S. Berns, & J.W. Shortt. 1996. Psychological factors in the longitudinal course of battering: When do the couples split up? When does the abuse decrease? *Violence and Victims* 11: 371–392.

Jacoby, A.P., & J.D. Williams. 1985. Effects of premarital sexual standards and behavior on dating and marriage desirability. *Journal of Marriage and the Family* 47: 1059–1065.

Jaffe, Dena H., Orly Manor, Zvi Eisenbach, & Yehuda D. Neumark. 2007. The protective effect of marriage on mortality in a dynamic society. *Annals of Epidemiology*, 17(7): 540–547.

Jain, D., S. Sanon, L. Sadowski, & W. Hunter. 2004. Violence against women in India: Evidence from rural Maharashtra, India. *Rural and Remote Health 4*, article number 304.

Jambunathan, Saigeetha, Diane C. Burts, & Sarah Pierce. 2000. Comparisons of parenting attitudes among five ethnic groups in the United States. *Journal of Comparative Family Studies* 31: 395–406.

James, Spencer J., and Brett A. Beattie. 2012. "Reassessing the Link between Women's Premarital Cohabitation and Marital Quality," *Social Forces*, 91(2): 635–662.

Jamieson, Lynn. 1999. Intimacy transformed? A critical look at "the pure relationship." *Sociology* 33(3): 477–494.

Jeffrey, Kirk. 1975. Marriage, career, and feminine ideology in nineteenth-century America: Reconstructing the marital experience of Lydia Maria Child, 1828–1874. *Feminist Studies* 2: 2–3, 113–130.

Jepson, Lisa K., & Christopher A. Jepson. 2002. An empirical analysis of the matching patterns of same-sex and opposite-sex couples. *Demography* 39(3): 435–453.

Jin, Xiaochun, Morris Eagle, & Marianne Yoshioka. 2007. Early exposure to violence in the family of origin and positive attitudes towards marital violence: Chinese immigrant male batterers vs. controls. *Journal of Family Violence* 22: 211–222.

Johnson, Susan, and Jay Lebow. 2000. The "coming of age" of couple therapy: A decade in review. *Journal of Marital and Family Therapy* 26(1): 23–38.

Johnston, C. 2008. The PACS and (post-)queer citizenship in contemporary republican France. *Sexualities* 11(6): 688–705.

Jones, Charles L., Lorna Marsden, & Lorne Tepperman. 1990. *Lives of Their Own: The Individualization of Women's Lives*. Toronto: Oxford University Press.

Jones, D. N., & Figueredo, A., Jose. 2007. Mating Effort as a Predictor of Smoking in a College Sample. *Current Research in Social Psychology*, 12(13):186–195.

Jones, Elise F., Jacqueline Darroch Forrest, Noreen Goldman, Stanley Henshaw, Richard Lincoln, Jeannie Rosoff, Charles F. Westoff, & Deidre Wulf. 1993. *Teenage Pregnancy in Industrialized Countries*. New Haven: Yale University Press.

Jones, Loring, Margaret Hughes, & Ulrike Unerstaller. 2001. Post-traumatic stress disorder (PTSD) in victims of domestic violence: A Review of the research. *Trauma, Violence and Abuse* 2(2): 99–199.

Jones, Melanie. 2010. "Systemic/Social Issues Aboriginal Child Welfare." *Relational Child & Youth Care Practice*, 23(4): 17–30. http://encore.uleth.ca:50080/ebsco-web/ehost/pdfviewer/pdfviewer?sid=b97fd556-b536-460a-beef-cc17aa7bac1e%40sessionmgr114&vid=2&hid=123

Jordan, Karen M., & Robert H. Deluty. 2000. Social support, coming out, and relationship satisfaction in lesbian couples. *Journal of Lesbian Studies* 4(1): 145–164.

Juby, Heather, Celine Le Bourdais, & Nicole Marcil-Gratton. 2005. Sharing roles, sharing custody? Couples' characteristics and children's living arrangements at separation. *Journal of Marriage and the Family* 67: 157–172.

Juby, Heather, Jean-Michel Billette, Benoit Laplante, & Celine Le Bourdais. 2007. Nonresident fathers and children. *Journal of Marriage and Family* 28(9): 1220–1245.

Judge, Sharon Lesar. 1998 July. Parental coping strategies and strengths in families of young children with disabilities. *Family Relations* 47(3): 263–268.

Kahana, Eva, Boaz Kahana, & Jennifer Kinney. 1982. Coping among vulnerable elders, pp. 64–85. In Zev Harel, Phyllis Ehrlich et al. (Eds.), *The Vulnerable Aged: People, Services, and Policies*. New York: Springer Publishing Co.

Kalin, Rudolf, & Carol A. Lloyd. 1985. Sex-role identity, sex-role ideology and marital adjustment. *International Journal of Women's Studies* 8(1): 32–39.

Kallivayalil, Diya. 2007. Feminist therapy: Its use and implications for South Asian immigrant survivors of domestic violence. *Women & Therapy* 30: 109–127.

Kalmijn, M. 2007. Gender differences in the effects of divorce, widowhood, and remarriage on intergenerational support: does marriage protect fathers? *Social Forces* 86(3): 1079–1104.

Kalmijn, Matthijs. 1991. Shifting boundaries: Trends in religious and educational homogamy. *American Sociological Review* 56(6): 786–800.

Kalmijn, Matthijs. 1993. Spouse selection among the children of European immigrants: A comparison of marriage cohorts in the 1960 Census. *International Migration Review* 27(1): 51–78.

Kalmijn, Matthijs. 2010. "Country Differences in the Effects of Divorce on Well-Being: The Role of Norms, Support and Selectivity." *European Sociological Review* 26(4): 475–490.

Kalnins, Ilze V., M. Pamela Churchill, & Grace E. Terry. 1980. Concurrent stresses in families with a leukemic child. *Journal of Pediatric Psychology* 5(1): 81–92.

Kang, Tanya, and Lindsay H. Hoffman. 2011. "Why Would You Decide to Use an Online Dating Site? Factors that Lead to Online Dating." *Communication Research Reports* 28(3): 205–213.

Karasek, Robert, & Tores Theorell. 1990. *Healthy Work: Stress, Productivity, and the Reconstruction of Working Life*. New York: Basic Books.

Karlsson, S.G., & K. Borell. 2002. Intimacy and autonomy, gender and ageing: Living apart together. *Ageing International* 7(4): 11–26.

Karney, Benjamin R., & Thomas N. Bradbury. 1995. Assessing longitudinal change in marriage: An introduction to the analysis of growth curves. *Journal of Marriage and the Family* 57(4): 1091–1108.

Karriker-Jaffe, Katherine J., Vangie A. Foshee, Susan T. Ennett, & Chirayath Suchindran 2008. The development of aggression during adolescence: Sex differences in trajectories of physical and social aggression among youth in rural areas. *Journal of Abnormal Child Psychology* 36: 1227–1236.

Kashyap, Lina. 2004. The impact of modernization on Indian families: The counselling challenge. *International Journal for the Advancement of Counselling* 26: 341–350.

Katz, Elana. 2007. A family therapy perspective on mediation. *Family Process* 46(1): 93–107.

Katz, Jeanne, Sheila M. Peace and Sue Spurr (Eds.). 2012. *Adult Lives: A Life Course Perspective.* Bristol, UK: Policy Press.

Katz, Jennifer, & Laura Myhr. 2008. Perceived conflict patterns and relationship quality associated with verbal sexual coercion by male dating partners. *Journal of Interpersonal Violence* 23.6: 798–814.

Katz, Jennifer, & Vanessa Tirone. 2009. Women's sexual compliance with male dating partners: Associations with investment in ideal womanhood and romantic well-being. *Sex Roles* 60(5–6): 347–356.

Katz, Jennifer, Ileana Arias, Steven R.H. Beach, Gene Brody, & Paul Roman. 1995. Excuses, excuses: Accounting for the effects of partner violence on marital satisfaction and stability. *Violence and Victims* 10(4).

Keating, Norah, Janet Fast, Judith Frederick (Statistics Canada), Kelly Cranswick (Statistics Canada), & Cathryn Perrier. 1999. *Eldercare in Canada: Context, Content and Consequences.* Ottawa: Statistics Canada, Housing, Family and Social Statistics Division.

Keenan, K., E. Grundy, M.G. Kenward, and D.A. Lyon. 2012. "Alcohol and Harm to Others in Russia: Longitudinal Analysis of Couple Drinking and Subsequent Divorce," *Journal of Epidemiology and Community Health* 66. **http://jech.bmj.com/content/65/Suppl_1/A23.3.short**

Kellogg, Nancy D., Thomas J. Hoffman, & Elizabeth R. Taylor. 1999 Summer. Early sexual experiences among pregnant and parenting adolescents. *Adolescence* 34(134): 293–303.

Kelly, Mary Bess. 2010. "The Processing of Divorce Cases through Civil Court in Seven Provinces and Territories." *Juristat.* Ottawa: Statistics Canada, Cata no. 85-002-X.

Kemp, Anita, Bonnie L. Green, & Christine Hovanitz. 1995 March. Incidence and correlates of post-traumatic stress disorder in battered women: Shelter and community samples. *Journal of Interpersonal Violence* 10: 43–55.

Kemp, C.L., & M. Denton. 2003. The allocation of responsibility for later life: Canadian reflections on the roles of individuals, government, employers and families. *Ageing & Society* 23: 737–760.

Kempe, C.H., F.N. Silverman, B.F. Steele, W. Droegmueller, & H.K. Silver. 1962. The battered-child syndrome. *Journal of the American Medical Association* 181: 17–24.

Kennedy, M.A., & B.B. Gorzalka. 2002. Asian and non-Asian attitudes toward rape, sexual harassment, and sexuality. *Sex Roles* 46: 227–38.

Kerr, Don, & Roderic Beaujot. 2003. Child poverty and family structure in Canada, 1981–1997. *Journal of Comparative Family Studies* 34(3): 321–335.

Kerr, Don, Melissa Moyser, & Roderic Beaujot. 2006. Marriage and cohabitation: demographic and socio-economic differences in Quebec and Canada. *Canadian Studies in Population* 33(1): 83–117.

Kesner, John E., & Patrick C. McKenry. 2001 March–April. Single parenthood and social competence in children of color. *Families in Society* 82(2): 136–144.

Keyfitz, Nathan. 1988. On the wholesomeness of marriage. In L. Tepperman & J. Curtis (Eds.), *Readings in Sociology: An Introduction.* Toronto: McGraw-Hill Ryerson.

Kheshgi-Genovese, Zareena, & Thomas A. Genovese. 1997. Developing the spousal relationship within stepfamilies. *Families in Society: The Journal of Contemporary Human Services* 78(3): 255–271.

Kiecolt-Glaser, Janice K., & Tamara L. Newton. 2001. Marriage and health: His and hers. *Psychological Bulletin* 127(4): 472–500.

Kiko-Net (2002). White Paper on the Internet in Japan. Retrieved July 28, 2005, from **http://www.kiko-net. com/Foreigners/White_Paper/White_Paper.php?year=2002#PersonalService**

Kim-Goh, Mikyong, & Jon Baello. 2008. Attitudes toward domestic violence in Korean and Vietnamese immigrant communities: Implications for human services. *Journal of Family Violence* 23: 647–654.

Kimuna, Sitawa R., Yanyi K. Djamba, Gabriele Ciciurkaite, and Suvana Cherkuri. 2012. "Domestic Violence in India: Insights from the 2005–2006 National Family Health Survey." *Journal of Interpersonal Violence,* 28(4): 773–807.

King, Rosalind Berkowitz, & Kathleen Mullan Harris. 2007. Romantic relationships among immigrant adolescents. *International Migration Review* 41: 344–370.

King, Thomas. 2012. *The Inconvenient Indian: A Curious Account of Native People in North America.* Toronto: Doubleday Canada.

King, V. 2007. When children have two mothers: Relationships with nonresident mothers, stepmothers, and fathers. *Journal of Marriage and the Family* 69: 1178–1193.

King, V., & M.E. Scott. 2005. A comparison of cohabiting relationships among older and younger adults. *Journal of Marriage and Family* 67: 271–285.

Kinnunen, Ulla, Jan Gerris, & Ad Vermulst. 1996 October. Work experiences and family functioning among employed fathers with children of school age. *Family Relations* 45: 449–455.

Kirchler, Erich. 1989 March. Everyday life experiences at home: An interaction diary approach to assess marital relationships. *Journal of Family Psychology* 2(3): 311–336.

Kissane, Rebecca Joyce, & Richard Krebs. 2007. Assessing welfare reform, over a decade later. *Sociology Compass* 1–2: 789–813.

Kleban, Morton H., Elaine M. Brody, Claire B. Schoonover, & Christine Hoffman. 1989 May. Family help to the elderly: perceptions of sons-in-law regarding parent care. *Journal of Marriage and the Family* 51(2): 303–312.

Klein, David M., & James M. White. 1996. *Family Theories: An Introduction.* Thousand Oaks, California: Sage.

Klinenberg, Eric. 2012. *Going Solo: the Extraordinary Rise and Surprising Appeal of Living Alone.* New York: Penguin.

Klinger, Rochelle L. 1995. Gay violence. *Journal of Gay & Lesbian Psychotherapy* 2(3): 119–134.

Kluwer, Esther S., Jose Heesink, & Evert Van de Vliert. 1996 November. Marital conflict about the division of household labor and paid work. *Journal of Marriage and the Family* 58.

Korpi, Walter, Tommy Ferrarini, and Stefan Englund. 2013. "Women's Opportunities under Different Family Policy Constellations: Gender, Class and Inequality Tradeoffs in Western Countries Re-examined." *Social Politics* 21(1): 1–40.

Knee, Raymond C., Cynthia Lonsbary, Amy Canevello, & Heather Patrick. 2005. Self-determination and conflict in romantic relationships. *Journal of Personality and Social Psychology* 89: 997–1009.

Knox, David, Marty Zusman, & Andrea McNeely. 2008. University student beliefs about sex: Men vs. women. *College Student Journal* 42(1): 181–185.

Knox, David. 2005. *Choices in Relationships: Introduction to Marriage and Family* (with Infotrac). Belmont: Thomson Wadsworth. Retrieved November 4, 2005, through Google Print Publisher Program.

Kobayashi, A. 1992. The Japanese-Canadian redress settlement and its implications for "race relations." *Canadian Ethnic Studies* 24(1): 1–19.

Kogos, Jennifer L., & John Snarey. 1995. Parental divorce and the moral development of adolescents. *Journal of Divorce and Remarriage* 23(3–4).

Kohen, Dafna, Clyde Hertzman, & J. Douglas Willms. 2002. The importance of quality child care, pp. 261–276. In J. Douglas Willms (Ed.), *Vulnerable Children: Findings from Canada's National Longitudinal Survey of Children and Youth*. Edmonton: University of Alberta Press, and Ottawa: Human Resources Development Canada, Applied Research Branch.

Kohli, M., M. Rein, A. Guillemard, & H. Van Gunsteren. 1991. *Time for Retirement: Comparative Studies of Early Exit from the Labour Force*. Cambridge: Cambridge University Press.

Kohli, Martin. 1986. Social organization and subjective construction of life course, pp. 271–292. In A.B. Sorenson, F.E. Weinhert, & L.R. Sharrod (Eds.), *Human Development and the Life Course*. Hillsdale, CA: Erlbaum.

Kolbo, Jerome R., Eleanor H. Blakely, & David Engleman. 1996 June. Children who witness domestic violence: A review of empirical literature. *Journal of Interpersonal Violence* 11: 281–293.

Koskinen, S., K. Joutsenniemi, T. Martelin, & P. Martikainen. 2007. Mortality differences according to living arrangements. *International Journal of Epidemiology* 36: 1255–1264.

Kowalski, Robin M., Susan P. Limber, and Patricia W. Agatson. 2012. *Cyberbullying: Bullying in the Computer Age*. Chichester, Sussex: Wiley.

Kozuch, Patricia, & Teresa M. Cooney. 1995. Young adults' marital and family attitudes: The role of recent parental divorce, and family and parental conflict. *Journal of Divorce and Remarriage* 23(3–4).

Kroløkke, Charlotte, Karen A. Foss, and Saumya Pant. 2012. "Fertility Travel: The Commodification of Human Reproduction." *Cultural Politics* 8(2): 273–282.

Kronby, Malcolm C. 2010. *Canadian Family Law* (10th edition). Mississauga, ON: J. Wiley.

Kruger, Helga, & Rene Levy. 2001. Linking life courses, work and the family: Theorizing a not so visible nexus between women and men. *Canadian Journal of Sociology* 26(4): 145–166.

Kruk, E. 1995. Grandparent grandchild contact loss: Findings from a study of grandparent rights members. *Canadian Journal on Aging* 14(4): 737–754.

Kruk, Edward. 2010. "Parental and Social Institutional Responsibilities to Children's Needs in the Divorce Transition: Fathers' Perspectives." *The Journal of Men's Studies* 18(2): 159–178.

Kulu, Hill, and Paul J. Boyle. 2010. "Premarital Cohabitation and Divorce: Support for the 'Trial Marriage' Theory?" *Demographic Research* 23(31):879–904.

Kumar, Pramod, & Jayshree Dhyani. 1996. Marital adjustment: A study of some related factors. *Indian Journal of Clinical Psychology* 23(2): 112–116.

Kunz, J. 1992. The effects of divorce on children. In S.J. Bahr (Ed.), *Family Research: A Sixty-Year Review, 1930–1990, Volume 2*. New York: Lexington Books, pp. 325–376.

Kunz, Jennifer, & Stephen J. Bahr. 1996. A profile of parental homicide against children. *Journal of Family Violence* 11(4): 347–362.

Kurz, Demie. 1995. *For Richer or For Poorer: Mothers Confront Divorce*. New York: Routledge.

La Rose, Lauren. CBC News In Depth. 2008 April 2. Census: Mixed-race taboo drops away. Retrieved April 15, 2009, from **http://www.cbc.ca/news/background/census/mixed-marriages.html**

Laakso, Janice. 2004, Spring. Key determinants of mothers' decisions to allow visits with non-custodial fathers. *Fathering*.

Lademann, A. 1980. The neurologically handicapped child. *Scandinavian Journal of Audiology* 10 (suppl.): 23–26.

Laermans, Rudi, & Carine Meulders, 1998. Washing practices, cleanliness and social identity. A historical-sociological interpretation in the light of the private/public distinction [original title: Waspraktijk, properheid en sociale identiteit. Een historisch-sociologische interpretatie in het licht van het onderscheid prive/publick]. *Tijdschrift voor Sociologie* 19(3): 281–299.

Lai, D., & Leonenko, W. 2007. Correlates of living alone among single elderly Chinese immigrants in Canada. *International Journal of Aging and Human Development* 65(2): 121–148.

Lai, D.W.L. 2005. Cultural factors and preferred living arrangements of aging Chinese Canadians. *Journal of Housing for the Elderly* 19(2): 71–86.

Lampard, Richard. 2007. Couples' places of meeting in late 20th century Britain: Class, continuity and change. *European Sociological Review* 23.3: 357–371.

Landis, Dana, Noni K. Gaylord-Harden, Sara L. Malinowki, Kathryn E. Grant, Russel A. Carleton., & Rebecca E. Ford. 2007. Urban adolescent stress and hopelessness. *Journal of Adolescence* 30(6): 1051–1070.

Landis-Kleine, Cathy, Linda Foley, Loretta Nall, Patricia Padgett; & Leslie Walters-Palmer. 1995. Attitudes toward marriage and divorce held by young adults. *Journal of Divorce & Remarriage* 23(3&4): 63–74.

Landolt, Monica A., & Donald G. Dutton. 1997 September. Power and personality: An analysis of gay male intimate abuse. *Sex Roles* 37(5–6): 335–359.

Landry, Yves. 1992. Les filles duroi au xviie siècle: Orphelines en France. *Pioniéres au Canada*. Montreal: Lemeac.

Lapierre-Adamcyk, Evelyne. 1987 May. *Mariage et politique de la famille*. Paper presented at the Association des Demographiques du Québec, Ottawa.

Larcombe, E.S. 1978. A handicapped child means a handicapped family. *Journal of the Royal College of General Practice* 28: 46–52.

LaRochelle-Côté, Sebastien, John Myles, and Garnett Picot. 2012. "Income Replacement Rates among Canadian Seniors: The Effect of Widowhood and Divorce," Ottawa: Statistics Canada, Catalogue no. 11F0019M, no. 343. **http://www.statcan.gc.ca/ pub/11f0019m/11f0019m2012343-eng.htm**

LaRochelle-Côté, Sebastien, John Myles, and Garnett Picot. 2012. "Income Replacement Rates Among Canadian Seniors: The Effect of Widowhood and Divorce." *Canadian Public Policy* 38(4): 471–495.

LaRossa, Ralph. 2004. The culture of fatherhood in the fifties: A closer look. *Journal of Family History* 29(1): 47–70.

Larson, Jeffrey H., Stephan M. Wilson, & Rochelle Beley. 1994 April. The impact of job insecurity on marital and family relations. *Family Relations* 43: 138–143.

Larson, Reed W., & Sally Gillman. 1999 February. Transmission of emotions in the daily interactions of single-mother families. *Journal of Marriage and the Family* 61(1): 21–37.

Lau, Anna S., David T. Takeuchi, & Margarita Alegria. 2006. Parent-to-child aggression among Asian American parents: Culture, context, and vulnerability. *Journal of Marriage and Family* 68: 1261–1275.

Lauer, Robert H., Jeanette C. Lauer, & Sarah T. Kerr. 1990. The long-term marriage: Perceptions of stability and satisfaction. *International Journal of Aging and Human Development* 31(3): 189–195.

Laumann, E.O, J.H. Gagnon, R.T. Michael, & S. Michaels. 1994. *The Social Organization of Sexuality: Sexual Practices in the United States*. Chicago: University of Chicago Press.

Lavoie, F., M. Hebert, R. Tremblay, F. Vitaro, L. Vezina, & P. McDuff. 2002. History of family dysfunction and perpetration of dating violence by adolescent boys: A longitudinal study. *Journal of Adolescent Health* 30: 375–383.

Lavoie, Francine, Line Robitaille, & Martine Herbert. 2000. Teen dating relationships and aggression: An exploratory study. *Violence Against Women* 6: 6.

Lawrence, Erika, Alexia D. Rothman, Rebecca J. Cobb, Michael T. Rothman, & Thomas Bradbury. 2008. Marital satisfaction across the transition to parenthood. *Journal of Family Psychology* 22(1): 41–50.

Le Bourdais, Celine, Evelyne Lapierre-Adamcyk, & Philippe Pacaut. 2004. Changes in conjugal life in Canada: Is cohabitation progressively replacing marriage? *Journal of Marriage and the Family* 66: 929–942.

Le Bourdais, Celine, & Nicole Marcil-Gratton. 1994. Quebec's pro-active approach to family policy, pp. 103–116. In Maureen Baker (Ed.), *Canada's Changing Families: Challenges to Public Policy*. Ottawa: Vanier Institute of the Family.

Le Bourdais, Celine, & Nicole Marcil-Gratton. 1996. Family transformations across the Canadian/American border: When the laggard becomes the leader. *Journal of Comparative Family Studies* 27(3): 415–436.

Le Bourdais, Celine, G. Neil, & Pierre Turcotte. 2000. The changing face of conjugal relationships. *Canadian Social Trends* 56: 14–17.

Lee, Sharon M., and Edmonston, Barry. 2013. "Canada's Immigrant Families: Growth, Diversity and Challenges." *Population Change and Lifecourse Strategic Knowledge Cluster Discussion Paper Series/Un Réseau stratégique de connaissances Changements de population et parcours de vie Document de travail*: Vol. 1: Iss. 1, Article 4. Available at **http://ir.lib.uwo.ca/pclc/vol1/iss1/4**

Légaré, Jacques, Laurent Martel, Leroy O. Stone, & Hubert Denis. 2000. *Living Arrangements of Older Persons in Canada: Effects on Their Socio-Economic Conditions*. UN Economic Commission for Europe [ECE]: Geneva, Switzerland. United Nations Population Fund [UNFPA]: New York.

Lehmiller, J. J., and Agnew, C. R. 2008. Commitment in Age-Gap Heterosexual Romantic Relationships: A Test of Evolutionary and Socio-cultural Predictions. *Psychology of Women Quarterly*, 32, pp. 74–82.

Lehr, Valerie. 1999. *Queer Family Values: Debunking the Myth of the Nuclear Family*. Philadelphia: Temple University Press.

Leiter, Michael P., & Marie-Josette Durup. 1996. Work, home, and in-between: A longitudinal study of spillover. *Journal of Applied and Behavioural Science* 32(1): 29–47.

Lempert, Lora Bex. 1996. Language obstacles in the narratives of abused women. *Mid-American Review of Sociology* 19(1–2): 15–32.

Lesemann, Frederic, & Roger Nicol. 1994. Family policy: International comparisons, pp. 117–125. In Maureen Baker (Ed.), *Canada's Changing Families: Challenges to Public Policy*. Ottawa: Vanier Institute of the Family.

Lester, David. 2003. The regional correlates of suicide in Canada: Changes over time. *Archives of Suicide Research* 7: 145–148.

Letellier, Patrick. 1994 Summer. Gay and bisexual male domestic violence victimization: Challenges to feminist theory and responses to violence. *Violence and Victims* 9(2): 95–106.

Leung, A.K.C., W.L.M. Robson, H. Cho, & S.H.N. Lim. 1996. Latchkey children. *Journal of the Royal Society of Health* 116(6): 356–359.

Lever, Janet, Christian Grov, Tracy Royce, & Brian Joseph Gillespie. 2008. Searching for love in all the "write" places: Exploring internet personals use by sexual orientation, gender, and age. *International Journal of Sexual Health* 20.4: 233–246.

Levin, Irene. 2004. Living apart together: A new family form. *Current Sociology* 52(2): 223–240.

Levy, D.M. 1945. The War and Family Life: Report for the War Emergency Committee, 1944. Reprinted in *American Journal of Orthopsychiatry* 15: 140–152.

Li, P.S. 1996. *The Making of Post-war Canada*. Toronto: Oxford University Press.

Lichter, D.T., & Z. Qian. 2008. Serial cohabitation and the marital life course. *Journal of Marriage and Family* 70(4): 861–878.

Lichter, D.T., Z. Qian, & L. Mellott. 2006. Marriage or dissolution? Union transitions among poor cohabiting women. *Demography* 43: 223–240.

Lichter, Daniel T., & Julie H. Carmalt. 2009. Religion and marital quality among low-income couples. *Social Science Research* 38: 168–187.

Liebkind, Karmela. 1993. Self-reported ethnic identity, depression, and anxiety among young Vietnamese refugees and their parents. *Journal of Refugee Studies* 6(1): 25–39.

Lipman, Ellen L., David R. Offord, Martin D. Dooley, & Martin H. Boyle. 2002. Children's outcomes in differing types of single-parent families, pp. 229–242. In J. Douglas Willms (Ed.), *Vulnerable Children: Findings from Canada's National Longitudinal Survey of Children and Youth*. Edmonton: University of Alberta Press, and Ottawa: Human Resources Development Canada, Applied Research Branch.

Liu, J.H., S.H. Ng, A. Weatherall, & C. Loong. 2000. Filial piety, acculturation, and intergenerational communication among New Zealand Chinese. *Basic & Applied Social Psychology* 22: 213–223.

Lleras, Christy. 2008. Employment, work conditions, and the home environment in single-mother families. *Journal of Family Issues* 29(10): 1268–1297.

Lloyd, Eva. 2008. The interface between childcare, family support and child poverty strategies under New Labour: Tensions and contradictions. *Social Policy & Society* 7(4): 479–494.

Logan, John Allen, Peter Hoff, & Michael Newton. 2008. Two-sided estimation of mate preferences for similarities in age, education, and religion. *Journal of the American Statistical Association* 103.482: 559.

Looker, Diane E., & Victor Thiessen. 2003. Beyond the digital divide in Canadian schools: From access to competency in the use of information technology. *Social Science Computer Review* 21(4): 475–490.

Lu, Luo, Shu-Fang Kao, Cary L. Cooper, Tammy D. Allen, Laurent M. Lapierre, Michael O'Driscoll, Steven A.Y. Poelmans, Juan I. Sanchez., & Paul E. Spector. 2009. Work resources, work-to-family conflict, and its consequences: A Taiwanese-British cross-cultural comparison. *International Journal of Stress Management* 16(1): 25–44.

Lugo-Gil, Julieta, & Catherine S. Tamis-LeMonda. 2008. Family resources and parenting quality: Links to children's cognitive development across the first 3 years. *Child Development* 79(4): 1065–1085.

Lumpkin, James R. 2008. Grandparents in a parental or near-parental role: Sources of stress and coping mechanisms. *Journal of Family Issues* 29(3): 357–372.

Luo, Shanhong, & Eva C. Klohnen. 2005. Assortive mating and marital quality in newlyweds: A couple-centered approach. *Journal of Personality and Social Psychology* 88(2): 304–326.

Lupri, Eugen. 1993. Spousal violence: Wife abuse across the life course. *Zeitschrift fnr Sozialisationforschung und Erziehungssoziologie* 13(3): 232–257.

Lussier, Gretchen, Kirby Deater-Deckard, Judy Dunn, & Lisa Davies. 2002. Support across two generations: Children's closeness to grandparents following parental divorce and remarriage. *Journal of Family Psychology* 16(3): 363–376.

Luster, Tom, Harry Perlstadt, & Marvin McKinney. 1996 July. The effects of a family support program and other factors on the home environments provided by adolescent mothers. *Family Relations* 45: 255–264.

Luxton, Meg (Ed.). 1997. *Feminism and Families: Critical Policies and Changing Practices*. Halifax: Fernwood.

Luxton, Meg. 2001. Conceptualizing "families": Theoretical frameworks and family research, pp. 28–50. In Maureen Baker (Ed.), *Families: Changing Trends in Canada* (4th edition). Toronto: McGraw-Hill Ryerson.

Lye, Diane N., & Timothy J. Biblarz. 1993. The effects of attitudes toward family life and gender roles on marital satisfaction. *Journal of Family Issues* 14(2): 157–188.

Lynn, Marion. 2003. Single-parent families, pp. 6–54. In Marion Lynn (Ed.), *Voices: Essays on Canadian Families* (2nd edition). Toronto: Thomson Nelson.

Macmillan, R.I., & R. Gartner. 1999. When she brings home the bacon: Labour force participation and spousal violence against women. *Journal of Marriage and the Family* 61: 947–958.

Madathil, Jayamala, & James M. Benshoff. 2008. Importance of marital characteristics and marital satisfaction: A comparison of Asian Indians in arranged marriages and Americans in marriages of choice. *The Family Journal* 16: 222–230.

Mahoney, Anne Rankin, and Carmen Knudson-Martin. 2009. "Gender Equality in Intimate Relationships." In Mahoney, Anne Rankin and Carmen Knudson-Martin (Eds.), *Couples, Gender and Power*. New York: Springer, pp. 3–16.

Malta, S. 2007. Love actually! Older adults and their romantic internet relationships. *Australian Journal of Emerging Technologies and Society* 5(2): 84–102.

Man, Guida. 2001. From Hong Kong to Canada: Immigration and the changing family lives of middle-class women from Hong Kong, pp. 420–438. In Bonnie J. Fox (Ed.), *Family Patterns, Gender Divisions* (2nd edition). Toronto: Oxford University Press.

Mandell, Deena. 1995. Fathers who don't pay child support: Hearing their voices. *Journal of Divorce and Remarriage* 23(1–2).

Mandell, Nancy. 2011. "Portraying Canadian Families." In Nancy Mandell and Ann Duffy (Eds.), *Canadian Families: Diversity, Conflict and Change* (4th edition). Toronto: Nelson, pp. 3–32.

Manning, W.D., M.A. Longmore, & P.C. Giordano. 2007. The changing institution of marriage: Adolescents' expectations to cohabit and to marry. *Journal of Marriage and Family* 69(3): 559–575.

Manning, W.D., P.J. Smock, & D. Majumdar. 2004. The relative stability of cohabiting and marital unions for children. *Population Research and Policy Review* 23: 135–159.

Manning, Wendy D. 2004. Children and the stability of cohabiting couples. *Journal of Marriage and the Family* 66(3): 674–689.

Marano, Hara-Estroff. 1997 March–April. Love lesson: Six new moves to improve your relationship. *Psychology Today* 30.

March, James G., & Herbert A. Simon. 1958. *Organizations*. New York: Wiley.

Marcil-Gratton, Nicole. 1993. Growing up with a single parent: A transitional experience? Some demographic measurements, pp. 73–90. In Joe Hudson and Burt Galaway (Eds.), *Single Parent Families: Perspectives on Research and Policy*. Toronto: Thompson Educational Publishing.

Marcil-Gratton, Nicole, Céline Le Bourdais, & Évelyne Lapierre-Adamcyk. 2000 Autumn. The implications of parents' conjugal histories for children. *Isuma* 1(2): 32–40.

Marshall, Katherine. 2009. The family work week. *Statistics Canada Perspectives*. Ottawa: Statistics Canada. Catalogue no. 75-001-X. Retrieved from **http://www.statcan.gc.ca/pub/75-001-x/75-001-x2009104-eng.htm**

Marshall, T. 2008. Cultural Differences in Intimacy: The Influence of Gender-Role Ideology and Individualism-Collectivism. *Journal of Social and Personal Relationships*, 25(1), 143, 155.

Martel, Laurent, & Jacques Légaré. 2001. Avec ou sans famille proche à la vieillesse: une description du réseau de soutien informel des personnes âgées selon la présence du conjoint et des enfants. *Cahiers québécois de démographie* 30(1): 89–114.

Martinengo, Giuseppe, Jenet I. Jacob, and E. Jeffrey Hill. 2010. Gender and the Work-Family Interface: Exploring Differences Across the Family Life Course. *Journal of Family Issues* 31(10): 1363–1390.

Martz, Diane J. Forsdick. 2007. Canadian farm women and their families: Restructuring, work and decision making. *Dissertation Abstracts International, A: The Humanities and Social Sciences*. 67(10): 3932.

Mason, Mary Ann, Arlene Skolnick, & Stephen D. Sugarman (Eds.). 2003. *All Our Families: New Policies for a New Century* (2nd edition). New York: Oxford University Press.

Mason, Robin. 2003. Listening to lone mothers: Paid work, family life, and childcare in Canada. *Journal of Children & Poverty* 9(1): 41–54.

Mastekaasa, Arne. 1995. Divorce and subjective distress: Panel evidence. *European Sociological Review* 11(2).

Mather, Mark. 2010. U.S. Children in Single-Mother Families, Data Brief, Population Reference Bureau **http://www.prb.org/Publications/PolicyBriefs/singlemotherfamilies.aspx**

Matthews, Lisa S., Rand D. Conger, & K.A.S. Wickrama. 1996. Work-family conflict and marital quality: Mediating processes. *Social Psychology Quarterly* 59(1): 62–79.

Matthey, Stephen, Bryanne Barnett, Judy Ungerer, & Brent Waters. 2000. Paternal and maternal depressed mood during the transition to parenthood. *Journal of Affective Disorders* 60(2), 75–85.

Mattingly, Marybeth J., & Robert N. Bozick. 2001. *Children Raised by Same-Sex Couples: Much Ado about Nothing.* Southern Sociological Society (SSS).

Mauno, Saijo, & Ulla Kinnunen. 1999 August. Job insecurity and well-being: A longitudinal study among male and female employees in Finland. *Community, Work & Family* 2(2): 147–171.

McCabe, M. 2006. A longitudinal study of coping strategies and quality of life among people with multiple sclerosis. *Journal of Clinical Psychology in Medical Settings* 13: 369–379.

McCabe, Marita P. 1999. The interrelationship between intimacy, relationship functioning, and sexuality among men and women in committed relationships. *Canadian Journal of Human Sexuality*, 8(1): 31–38.

McCarroll, Linda Diane. 2000 August. Family Rituals: Promoting the ethnic identity of preschoolers. *Dissertation Abstracts International, A: The Humanities and Social Sciences* 61(2), 783–A.

McCarthy, Linda. 2000. Poppies in a wheat field: Exploring the lives of rural lesbians. *Journal of Homosexuality* 39(1): 75–94.

McClennen, Joan C. 2005. Domestic violence between same-gender partners: Recent findings and future research. *Journal of Interpersonal Violence* 20(2): 149–154.

McCloskey, Laura A. 1996 August. Socio-economic and coercive power within the family. *Gender and Society*: 449–463.

McCormack, Arlene, Ann Wolbert Burgess, & Peter Gaccione. 1986. Influence of family structure and financial stability on physical and sexual abuse among a runaway population. *International Journal of Sociology of the Family* 16(2): 251–262.

McCurdy, Susan J., & Avraham Scherman. 1996. Effects of family structure on the adolescent separation-individuation process. *Adolescence* 31(122).

McDaniel, S.A. 1997. Serial employment and skinny government: Reforming caring and sharing among generations. *Canadian Journal on Aging* 16(3): 465–484.

McDaniel, S.A. 2005. The family lives of the middle-aged and elderly in Canada. In Maureen Baker (Ed.), *Families: Changing Trends in Canada* (5th edition). Toronto: McGraw-Hill Ryerson, 181–199.

McDaniel, Susan A. 1988. A New Stork Rising? Women's Roles and Reproductive Changes. *Transactions of the Royal Society of Canada*, V(3): 111–122.

McDaniel, Susan A. 1996a. The family lives of the middle-aged and elderly in Canada, pp. 195–211. In Maureen Baker (Ed.), *Families: Changing Trends in Canada* (3rd edition). Toronto: McGraw-Hill Ryerson.

McDaniel, Susan A. 1996b. Toward a synthesis of feminist and demographic perspectives on fertility. *The Sociological Quarterly* 37(1): 83–104.

McDaniel, Susan A. 1998. Towards healthy families, pp. 3–42. In *National Forum on Health, Determinants of Health: Settings and Issue, Vol. 3*. Ste.-Foy, Quebec: Editions Multimodes.

McDaniel, Susan A. 1999. Untangling love and domination: Challenges of home care for the elderly in a restructuring Canada. *Journal of Canadian Studies* 34(3): 191–213.

McDaniel, Susan A. 2000. Capturing the elusive social impacts of technology: Towards a research agenda, pp. 109–121. In John de la Mothe and Gilles Paquet (Eds.), *Information, Innovation, and Impacts*. One of a series on Economics of Science, Technology, and Innovation, from Kluwer Academic Publishers.

McDaniel, Susan A. 2001. "Born at the right time": Gendered generations and webs of entitlement and responsibility. *Canadian Journal of Sociology* 26(2): 193–214.

McDaniel, Susan A. 2002. Women's changing relations to the state and citizenship: Caring and intergenerational relations in globalizing western democracies. *Canadian Review of Sociology and Anthropology* 39(2): 1–26.

McDaniel, Susan A., and Paul Bernard. 2011. "Life Course as a Policy Lens." *Canadian Public Policy*, 37, Supplement, (April): S1–S13.

McDaniel, Susan, Adebiyi Germain Boco, and Sara Zella. 2013. "Changing patterns of religious affiliation, religiosity and marital dissolution: A 35-year follow-up study of members of three generation families." Working manuscript.

McDaniel, Susan A., Amber Gazso, Hugh McCague, and Ryan Barnhart. 2013. "Les disparités en matière de santé au fil du vieillissement: une comparaison du parcours de vie des premiers baby-boomers et des pré-babyboomers au Canada (Health Disparities as We Age: A Life Course Comparison of Canadian Early Boomers with Pre-Boomers)." *Sociologie et Societies*, XLV(1): 43–65.

McDaniel, Susan A., Amber Gazso, and Seonggee Um. 2013. "Generationing Relations in Challenging Times: Americans and Canadians in Mid-Life in the Great Recession." *Current Sociology*, 61 (3): 301–321.

McDaniel, Susan A., & Robert Lewis. 1998. Did they or didn't they? Intergenerational supports in families past: A case study of Brigus, Newfoundland, 1920–1945, pp. 475–497. In Lori Chambers & Edgar-Andre Montigny (Eds.), *Family Matters: Papers in Post-Confederation Canadian Family History*. Toronto: Canadian Scholars Press.

McDaniel, Susan A., & Erica van Roosmalen. 1991. Sexual harassment in Canadian academe: Explorations of power and privilege. *Atlantis: A Women's Studies Journal* 17(1): 1–19.

McDaniel, Susan A., and Zachary Zimmer. "Global Ageing in the Twenty-First Century: Where to from here?" In Susan A. McDaniel and Zachary Zimmer (Eds.), *Global Ageing in the Twenty-First Century: Challenges, Opportunities and Implications*. (pp. 309–318). Farnham, Surrey, UK: Ashgate.

McDonald, H. 2011, February 15. Travelers attack Channel 4 over My Big Fat Gypsy Wedding. *The Guardian*, pp 12.

McDonald, Ted, Elizabeth Ruddick, Arthur Sweetman, and Christopher Worswick (Eds). 2010. *Canadian Immigration: Economic Evidence for a Dynamic Policy Environment*. Montreal and Kingston: Queen's Policy Studies Series, McGill-Queen's University Press.

McElroy, Ann. 1975. Canadian arctic modernization and change in female Inuit role identification. *American Ethnologist* 2(4): 662–686.

McGlone, J. 1980. Sex differences in human brain asymmetry: A critical survey. *The Behavioral and Brain Sciences* 3: 215–223.

McIntosh, Scott, Dawson, & Locker. 2011. What do older adults seek in their potential romantic partners? Evidence from online personal ads. *International Journal of Again and Human Development*, 72(1): 6–82.

McKeown, Larry, & Cathy Underhill. 2005. Learning online: Factors associated with use of the Internet for education purposes. *Education Matters*. Ottawa: Statistics Canada. Catalogue no. 81-004-XIE. Retrieved from **http://www.statcan.gc.ca/pub/81-004-x/2007004/10375-eng.htm**

McLanahan, Sara. 2009. Fragile families and the reproduction of poverty. *The Annals of the American Academy* 621: 111–131.

McLanahan, Sara, & Julia Adams. 1987. Parenthood and psychological well-being. *Annual Review of Sociology* 13: 237–257.

McLanahan, Sara, & Julia Adams. 1989. The effects of children on adults' psychological well-being: 1957–1976. *Social Forces* 68.

McLean, Lorna. 2004. To become part of us: Ethnicity, race, literacy and the Canadian Immigration Act of 1919. *Canadian Ethnic Studies/Etudes Ethniques au Canada* 35: 1–28.

McMahon, Martha. 1995. *Engendering Motherhood: Identity and Self-Transformation in Women's Lives*. New York: Guilford.

McMullin, Julie Ann, & Victor W. Marshall. 1996 Fall. Family, friends, stress, and well-being: Does childlessness make a difference? *Canadian Journal on Aging/La Revue Canadienne du Vieillissement* 15(3): 355–373.

McVey, Wayne W. Jr. 2008. Is separation still an important component of marital dissolution? *Canadian Studies in Population* 35(1): 187–205.

Meier, Andrea, Maeda J. Galinsky, & Kathleen A. Rounds. 1995. Telephone support groups for caregivers of persons with AIDS. Social Work with Groups. *Special Groups: Current Perspectives on Theory and Practice* 18(1): 99–108.

Melby, Janet N., Shu-Ann Fang, K.A.S. Wickrama, Rand D. Conger, & Katherine J. Conger. 2008. Adolescent family experiences and educational attainment during early adulthood. *Developmental Psychology* 44(6): 1519–1536.

Merkle, Erich R., & Rhonda A. Richardson. 2000 April. Digital dating and virtual relating: Conceptualizing computer-mediated romantic relationships. *Family Relations* 49(2): 187–192.

Merrill, Lex L., Linda K. Hervig, & Joel S. Milner. 1996. Childhood parenting experiences, intimate partner conflict resolution, and adult risk for child physical abuse. *Child Abuse and Neglect* 20(11): 1049–1065.

Metz, Michael E., & Norman Epstein. 2002. Assessing the role of relationship conflict in sexual dysfunction. *Journal of Sex & Marital Therapy* 28: 139–64.

Meyerstein, Israela. 1997. The problem box ritual: Helping families prepare for remarriage. *Journal of Family Psychotherapy* 8(1): 61–65.

Miall, Charlene E., & Karen March. 2005a. Open adoption as a family form: Community assessments and social support. *Journal of Family Issues* 26(3): 380–410.

Miall, Charlene E., & Karen March. 2005b. Social support for changes in adoption practice: Gay adoption, open adoption, birth reunions, and the release of confidential identifying information. *Families in Society* 86(1): 83–92.

Middleton, Catherine, & Jordan Leith. 2007. *Intensity of Internet Use in Canada: Exploring Canadians' Engagement with the Internet*. Paper for the Statistics Canada 2007 Socio-Economic Conference. Retrieved from **http://www.broadbandresearch.ca/ourresearch/middleton_leith_STC2007.pdf**

Milan, Anne, & Brian Hamm. 2003 Winter. Across the generations: Grandparents and grandchildren. *Canadian Social Trends*: 2–7. Retrieved January 11, 2006, from **http://dsp-psd.pwgsc.gc.ca/Collection-R/Statcan/11-008-XIE/0030311-008-XIE.pdf**

Milan, Anne, & Brian Hamm. 2004 Summer. Mixed unions. *Canadian Social Trends*: 1–8. Statistics Canada Catalogue no. 11-008.

Milan, Anne, & Alice Peters. 2003. Couples living apart. Statistics Canada: Canadian Social Trends. Retrieved June 4, 2005, from **http://64.233.161.104/search?q=cache:bB5S6r-666QJ:www.statcan.ca/english/studies/11-008/feature/star2003069000s2a02.pdf+living+apart+together,+canada&hl=en**

Mileham, Beatriz Lia Avila. 2007. Online infidelity in Internet chat rooms: An ethnographic exploration. *Computers in Human Behavior* 23(1): 11–31.

Milikian, Levon H., & S. Al-Easa Juhaina. 1981. Oil and social change in the Gulf. *Journal of Arab Affairs* 1(1): 79–98.

Millar, Nancy. 1999. *Once Upon a Wedding*. Calgary: Bayeaux Arts.

Millar, Paul, & Anne H. Gauthier. 2002. What were they thinking? The development of child support guidelines in Canada. *Canadian Journal of Law and Society* 17(1): 139–162.

Millar, Wayne, & Surinder Wadhera. 1997. A perspective on Canadian teenage births, 1992–1994: Older men and younger women? *Canadian Journal of Public Health* 88: 333–336.

Miller, David, & P. Gillies. 1996. Is there life after work? Experiences of HIV and oncology health staff. *AIDS Care* 8(2): 167–182.

Miller, James. 2003. Out family values. In Marion Lynn (Ed.). *Voices: Essays on Canadian Families*. Scarborough, ON: Thomson.

Miller, Kim S., Rex Forehand, & Beth A. Kotchick. 1999. Adolescent sexual behavior in two ethnic minority samples: The role of family variables. *Journal of Marriage and the Family* 61(1): 85–98.

Mills, T.L., Z. Gomez-Smith, & J.M. De Leon. 2005. Skipped generation families: Sources of psychological distress among grandmothers of grandchildren who live in homes where neither parent is present. *Marriage & Family Review* 37(1–2): 191–212.

Mincieli, L., J. Manlove, M. McGarrett, K. Moore, & S. Ryan. 2007. *The relationship context of births outside of marriage: The rise of cohabitation* (Child Trends Research Brief No. 2007-13). Washington, D.C.: Child Trends. Retrieved May 20, 2009, from **http://www .childtrends.org/Files//Child_Trends-2007_05_14_ RB_OutsideBirths.pdf**

Minton, Carmelle, & Kay Pasley. 1996. Fathers' parenting role identity and father involvement: A comparison of nondivorced and divorced, nonresident fathers. *Journal of Family Issues* 17(1).

Mintz, Steven. 2006. Housework in late 19th century America, on Digital History.com. Retrieved July 19, 2006, from **http://www.digitalhistory.uh.edu/ historyonline/housework.cfm**

Mirdal, Gretty M. 2006. Stress and distress in migration: Twenty years after1. *The International Migration Review* 40: 375–389.

Misra, Joya, Stephanie Moller, & Michelle J. Budig. 2007. Work-family policies and poverty for partnered and single women in Europe and North America. *Gender & Society* 21(6): 804–827.

Mistry, Rashmita S., Edward D. Lowe, Aprile D. Benner, & Nina Chien. 2008. Expanding the family economic stress model: Insights from a mixed-methods approach. *Journal of Marriage and Family* 70(1): 196–210.

Mitchell, Barbara Ann. 2006. *The Boomerang Age: Transitions to Adulthood in Families*. New Brunswick, NJ: Transaction Books.

Mitchell, Barbara A., & Ellen M. Gee. 1996a. Boomerang kids and midlife parental marital satisfaction. *Family Relations* 45: 442–448.

Mitchell, Barbara A., & Ellen M. Gee. 1996b. Young adults returning home: Implications for social policy, pp. 61–71. In Burt Galaway & Joe Hudson (Eds.), *Youth in Transition: Perspectives on Research and Policy*. Toronto: Thompson Educational Publishing.

Mitchell, Barbara. 1998. *The Refilled Nest: Recent Canadian Trends and Their Implications*. Paper presented at the 9th Annual John K. Friesen Conference, The Overselling of Population Aging, Simon Fraser University, 14–15 May 1998.

Mitchell, Barbara. 2005. *The Boomerang Age: Transitions to Adulthood in Families*. Somerset, NJ: Transactions Books.

Mock, R. 2011. August 22. The Top 5 "Myths and Truths" About Online Dating for the 50-Plus Singles. *PR Newswire*, pp. 6.

Mofina, Rick. 2003. Gay families no longer rejected. *Edmonton Journal*, 3 January: A5.

Molassiotis, A., O.B.A. Van Den Akker, & B.J. Broughton. 1997 February. Perceived social support, family environment and psychosocial recovery in bone marrow transplant long-term survivors. *Social Science & Medicine* 44(3): 317–325.

Moncher, Frank J. 1995 September. Social isolation and child-abuse risk. *Families in Society* 76: 421–433.

Mongeau, P.A., & C.M. Carey. 1996. Who's wooing whom: An experimental investigation of date initiation and expectancy violation. *Western Journal of Communication* 60(3): 195–213.

Montgomery, James C. 2003. The issues shared by professionals living and working in rural communities in British Columbia. *Canadian Journal of Rural Medicine* 8(4): 255–260.

Monzo, Lilia D., & Robert Rueda. 2006. A socio-cultural perspective on acculturation: Latino immigrant families negotiating diverse discipline practices. *Education and Urban Society* 38: 188–203.

Mooney-Somers, F., & S. Golombok. 2000. Children of lesbian mothers: From the 1970s to the new millennium. *Sexual and Relationship Therapy* 15(2): 121–126.

Moore Lappé, Frances. 1985. *What to Do After You Turn Off the TV? Fresh Ideas for Enjoying Family Time*. New York: Ballantine Books.

Moore, Dahlia. 1995. Role conflict: Not only for women? A comparative analysis of 5 nations. *International Journal of Comparative Sociology* 36(1–2): 17–35.

Moore, Eric G., & Mark W. Rosenberg, with Donald McGuiness. 1997. *Growing Old in Canada: Demographic and Geographic Perspectives*. Toronto & Ottawa: Nelson & Statistics Canada. Catalogue no. 96-321-MPE, no. 1.

Moorman, S.M., A. Boodi, & K.L Fingerman. 2006. Women's romantic relationships after widowhood. *Journal of Family Issues* 27(9): 1281–1304.

Morash, Merry, Hoan Bui, Yan Zhang, & Kristy Holtfreter. 2007. Risk factors for abusive relationships. *Violence Against Women* 13: 653–675.

Morely, Jeremy D. n.d. *Japanese Family Law—or The Lack Thereof!* Retrieved on December 9, 2005, from **http:// www.international-divorce.com/d-japan.htm**

Morgan, Debra G., Karen M. Semchuk, Norma J. Stewart, & Carl D'Arcy. 2002. Rural families caring for a relative with dementia: Barriers to use of formal service. *Social Science and Medicine* 55(7): 1129–1142.

Morgan, Maggie. 1996. Jam making, Cuthbert rabbit and cakes: Redefining domestic labour in the Women's Institute, 1915–60. *Rural History* 7(2): 207–219.

Morrison, Kati, & Airdrie Thompson-Guppy, with Patricia Bell. 1986. *Stepmothers: Exploring the Myth.* Ottawa: Canadian Council on Social Development.

Morrow, Marina, Olena Hankivsky, & Colleen Varcoe. 2004. Women and violence: The effects of dismantling the welfare state. *Critical Social Policy* 24(3): 358–384.

Morton, Mavis. 2011. "Violence in Canadian Families Across the Life Course." In Nancy Mandell and Ann Duffy, Eds., *Canadian Families: Diversity, Conflict and Change,* 4th edition. Toronto: Nelson, 277–322.

Morton, Suzanne. 1992. The June bride as the working-class bride: Getting married in a Halifax working-class neighbourhood in the 1920s, pp. 360–379. In Bettina Bradbury (Ed.), *Canadian Family History: Selected Readings.* Toronto: Copp Clark Pitman.

Moscovitch, A. 2007. *Good Servant, Bad Master? Electronic Media and the Family.* Ottawa: Vanier Institute of the Family. Retrieved June 13, 2009, from **http://www.vifamily.ca/library/cft/media07.html**

Mossakowki, Krysia N. 2008. Dissecting the influence of race, ethnicity, and socioeconomic status on mental health in young adulthood. *Research on Aging* 30(6): 649–671.

Motiejunaite, Akvile, & Zhanna Kravchenko. 2008. Family policy, employment and gender-role attitudes: A comparative analysis of Russia and Sweden. *Journal of European Social Policy* 18(1): 38–49.

Motohashi, S. 1978. A record of a mother of a handicapped child. *Japanese Journal of Nursing* 42: 968–970.

Motta, Robert W. 1994. Identification of characteristics and causes of childhood post-traumatic stress disorder. *Psychology in the Schools* 31(1): 49–56.

Moustgaard, H., & Martikainen, P. 2009. Nonmarital cohabitation among older Finnish men and women: Socioeconomic characteristics and forms of union dissolution. *Journal of Gerontology: Social Sciences.* 10.1093/geronb/gbp024. Retrieved May 13, 2009, from **http://psychsocgerontology.oxfordjournals.org/cgi/reprint/gbp024v1**

Muncer, Steven, Roger Burrows, Nicholas Pleace, Brian Loader, & Sarah Nettleton. 2000. Births, deaths, sex and marriage ... but very few presents? A case study of social support in cyberspace. *Critical Public Health* 10(1): 1–18.

Munsch, Joyce, John Woodward, & Nancy Darling. 1995. Children's perceptions of their relationship with coresiding and non-coresiding fathers. *Journal of Divorce and Remarriage* 23(1–2).

Murdock, George. 1949. *Social Structure.* New York: MacMillan.

Murphy, Christopher M., Shannon-Lee Meyer, Daniel K. O'Leary. 1994. Dependency characteristics of partner assaultive men. *Journal of Abnormal Psychology* 103(4): 729–735.

Musick, Kelly, and Larry Bumpass. 2012. "Reexamining the Case for Marriage: Union Formation and Changes in Well-Being," *Journal of Marriage and Family,* 74(1):1–18.

Myers, Jane E., Jayamala Madathil, & Lynne R. Tingle. 2005. Marriage satisfaction and wellness in India and the United States: A preliminary comparison of arranged marriages and marriages of choice. *Journal of Counseling & Development* 83(2): 183–190.

Myers, Scott M. 2006. Religious homogamy and marital quality: Historical and generational patterns, 1980–1997. *Journal of Marriage and Family* 68(2): 292–304.

Myers, Scott M., & Alan Booth. 1996. Men's retirement and marital quality. *Journal of Family Issues* 17(3).

Naiman, Sandy. 2005, June 7. Marriage: Take the plunge ... or run away? Retrieved June 6, 2005, from **www.canoe.ca/LifewiseHeartLove01/0110_marriage_sun.html**

Nakhaie, M.R. 1995. Housework in Canada: The national picture. *Journal of Comparative Family Studies* 26(3): 409–425.

National Child Benefit. 2009. NCB: A unique partnership of the Government of Canada, provinces and territories and First Nations. Retrieved April 19, 2009, from **http://www.nationalchildbenefit.ca/eng/06/ncb.shtml**

Nault, Francois, & Alain Belanger. 1996. *The Decline in Marriage in Canada, 1981–1991.* Ottawa: Statistics Canada. Catalogue no. 84–536-XPB.

Naumann, Pamela D., et al. 2007. My grandfather would roll over in his grave: Family farming and tree plantations on farmland. *Rural Sociology* 72(1): 111–135.

Nelson, F. 2001 (1996). "Lesbian Families." In Bonnie J. Fox (Ed.), *Family Patterns, Gender Relations* (2nd edition). Toronto: Oxford University Press, 441–457.

Nelson, Fiona. 1996. *Lesbian Motherhood: An Exploration of Canadian Lesbian Families.* Toronto: University of Toronto Press.

Nelson, Geoffrey. 1994 January. Emotional well-being of separated and married women: Long-term follow-up study. *American Journal of Orthopsychiatry* 64: 150–160.

Nesterov, Andrey. 2004, June 25. Eighty percent of marriages in Russia end up in divorce. Pravda, 25 June. Retrieved December 9, 2005, from **http://english.pravda.ru/main/18/90/359/13194_divorce.html**

Newell, Lloyd David. 1999 October. A qualitative analysis of family rituals and traditions. *Dissertation Abstracts International, A: The Humanities and Social Sciences* 60(4), 1348–A.

Ng, Kok-mun, Johnben Teik-cheok Loy, Clinton G. Gudmunson, & Winnee Cheong. 2009. Gender differences in marital and life satisfaction among Chinese Malaysians. *Sex Roles* 60: 33–43.

Niaz, U. 2003. Violence against women in South Asian countries. *Archives of Women's Mental Health* [Wien] 6: 173–84.

Nicholas, A. J. 2009. "Generational Perceptions: Workers and Consumers." *Journal of Business and Economics Research* 7(10): 1–7.

Nie, Norman H., & D. Sunshine Hillygus. 2002. The impact of Internet use on sociability: Time-diary findings. *IT & Society,* 1(1): 1–20.

Nielsen, Mark R. 2002. Are all marriages the same? Marital satisfaction of middle-class couples. *Dissertation Abstracts International, A: The Humanities and Social Sciences* 63(11), 4108–A-4109–A.

Nielsen//Net Ratings. 2005. 21st century dating: The way it is. Retrieved November 4, 2005, from **http://www.netratings.com/pr/pr_050802_uk.pdf**

Nielsen//NetRatings. July 2005. Online Dating Survey. UK: MegaPanelo.

Nissimi, Hilda. 2007. From Mashhad to New York: Family and gender roles in the Mashhadi immigrant community. *American Jewish History* 93: 303–328.

Nobes, Gavin, & Marjorie Smith. 2002 April. Family structure and the physical punishment of children. *Journal of Family Issues* 23(3): 349–373.

Noel, Melanie, Carole Peterson, & Beulah Jesso. 2008. The relationship of parenting stress and child temperament to language development among economically disadvantaged preschoolers. *Journal of Child Language* 35(4): 823–843.

Noller, Patricia. 1996. What is this thing called love? Defining the love that supports marriage and family. *Personal Relationships* 3(1): 97–115.

Nova Scotia Advisory Council on the Status of Women. 2000, March. Unpaid work: Some selected statistics. Retrieved May 25, 2005, from **http://www.gov.ns.ca/staw/unpaidw.htm**

O'Donohue, William, & Julie L. Crouch. 1996 January. Marital therapy and gender-linked factors in communication. *Journal of Marital and Family Therapy* 22.

O'Farrell, Timothy J., & Christopher M. Murphy. 1995 April. Marital violence before and after alcoholism treatment. *Journal of Consulting and Clinical Psychology* 63: 256–262.

O'Keefe, M. 1998. Factors mediating the link between witnessing interparental violence and dating violence. *Journal of Family Violence* 13: 39–57.

O'Keefe, Maura. 1996. The differential effects of family violence on adolescent adjustment. *Child and Adolescent Social Work Journal* 13(1): 51–68.

O'Keefe, Maura. 1997 March. Incarcerated battered women: A comparison of battered women who killed their abusers and those incarcerated for other offenses. *Journal of Family Violence* 12(1): 1–19.

Olazabal, J. Ignace. 2010. "Intergenerational Relations in Aging Societies: Emerging Topics in Canada." *Journal of Intergenerational Relationships* 8(1): 105–107.

O'Leary, Micky, Janet Franzoni, & Gregory Brack. 1996. Divorcing parents: Factors related to coping and adjustment. *Journal of Divorce and Remarriage* 25(3–4): 85–103.

Oakley, Ann. [1974]1985. *The Sociology of Housework*. London: Martin Robertson. Reprinted with new Introduction. Oxford: Basil Blackwell.

Oerton, Sarah. 1997. Queer housewives? Some problems in theorising the division of domestic labour in lesbian and gay households. *Women's Studies International Forum* 20(3): 421–430.

Oerton, Sarah. 1998. Reclaiming the "housewife"? Lesbians and household work. *Journal of Lesbian Studies* 2(4): 69–83.

O'Hara, Patricia. 1998. *Partners in Production? Women, Farm and Family in Ireland*. CI, New York: Berghahn Books.

Oliver, Mary Beth, & Constantine Sedikides. 1992. Effects of sexual permissiveness on desirability of partner as a function of low and high commitment to relationship. *Social Psychology Quarterly* 55: 321.

Ontario Association for Marriage and Family Therapy (1996). Marriage and family therapy fact sheet. Retrieved June 7, 2005, from **http://www.oamft.on.ca/about.htm**

Orava, Tammy A., Peter J. McLeod, & Donald Sharpe. 1996 June. Perceptions of control, depressive symptomatology, and self-esteem of women in transition from abusive relationships. *Journal of Family Violence* 11: 167–186.

Orbuch, T.L., J. House, R.P. Mero, & P.F. Webster. 1996. Marital quality over the life course. *Social Psychology Quarterly* 9(2): 162–171.

Orodenker, Sylvia Z. 1990 February. Family caregiving in a changing society: The effects of employment on caregiver stress. *Family & Community Health* 12(4): 58–70.

Oropesa, R.S., & Nancy S. Landale. 2004. The future of marriage and hispanics. *Journal of Marriage and Family* 66: 901–920.

Oswald, Ramona Faith. 2002. Resilience within the family networks of lesbians and gay men: Intentionality and redefinition. *Journal of Marriage and the Family* 64(2): 374.

Overstreet, Stacy, & Shawnee Braun. 2000 April. Exposure to community violence and post-traumatic stress symptoms: Mediating factors. *American Journal of Orthopsychiatry* 70(2): 263–271.

Owen, Michelle K. 2001. "Family" as a site of contestation: Queering the normal or normalizing the queer? pp. 86–102. In Terry Goldie (Ed.), *In Queer Country: Gay and Lesbian Studies in the Canadian Context*. Vancouver: Arsenal Pulp Press.

Paden, Shelley, & Cheryl Buehler. 1995. Coping with the dual-income lifestyle. *Journal of Marriage and the Family* 57: 101–110.

Pagnini, Deanna, & S. Philip Morgan. 1990. Intermarriage and social distance among U.S. immigrants at the turn of the century. *American Journal of Sociology* 96: 405–432.

Pandy, Shanta, & Jeoung–hee Kim. 2008. Path to poverty alleviation: Marriage or postsecondary education? *Journal of Family and Economic Issues* 29: 166–184.

Parr, Joy (Ed.). 1990. *Childhood and Family in Canadian History*. Toronto: McClelland & Stewart.

Paulson, Sharon E. 1996 April. Maternal employment and adolescent achievement revisited: An ecological perspective. *Family Relations* 45: 201–208.

Pecchioni, Loretta L. 2001 April. Implicit decision-making in family caregiving. *Journal of Social and Personal Relationships* 18(2): 219–237.

Peiser, Nadine C., & Patrick C.L. Heaven. 1996 December. Family influences on self-reported delinquency among high school students. *Journal of Adolescence*: 557–568.

Penhale, Bridget. 1993. The abuse of elderly people: Considerations for practice. *British Journal of Social Work* 23(2): 95–112.

Peplau, Letitia Anne, & Adam W. Fingerhut. 2007. The close relationships of lesbian and gay men. *Annual Review of Psychology* 58: 405–424.

Perunovic, Mihailo, & John G. Holmes. 2008. Automatic accommodation: The role of personality. *Personal Relationships* 15: 57–70.

Pescosolido, Bernice A. 1996. Bringing the "community" into utilization models: How social networks link individuals to changing systems of care. *Research in the Sociology of Health Care*, 13(Part A): 171–197.

Pescosolido, Bernice A., Eric Wright, & William Patrick Sullivan. 1995. Communities of care: A theoretical perspective on case management models in mental health. *Advances in Medical Sociology* 6: 37–79.

Peters, Brad, and Marion F. Ehrenberg. 2008. "The Influence of Parental Separation and Divorce on Father-Child Relationships." *Journal of Divorce and Remarriage* 49(1–2):78–109.

Peterson, B.D., M. Pirritano, U. Christensen, & L. Schmidt. 2008. The impact of partner coping in couples experiencing infertility. *Human Reproduction* 23(5): 1128–1137.

Pew Internet and American Life Survey, **http://www .pewsocialtrends.org/2010/02/24/millennials-confident-connected-open-to-change**

Pflieger, Jacqueline C., & Alexander T. Vazsonyi. 2006. Parenting processes and dating violence: The mediating role of self-esteem in low- and high-SES adolescents. *Journal of Adolescence* 29: 495–512.

Phillips, Lisa. 1995. The family in income tax policy. *Policy Options/Options Politiques* 16(10): 30–32.

Picot, Garnette, & John Myles. 2004. *Income Inequality and Low Income in Canada*. Retrieved March 20, 2006, from **http://policyresearch.gc.ca/page.asp?pagenm=v7n2_art_03**

Pina, Darlene L., & Vern L. Bengston. 1995 June. Division of household labor and the well-being of retirement-aged wives. *The Gerontologist 35*.

Pincus, Simon H., Robert House, Joseph Christenson, & Lawrence E. Adler. 2004. The emotional cycle of deployment: A military family perspective. U.S. Army. Retrieved at **http://www.hooah4health.com/deploymentFamilymatters/emotionalcycle.htm**

Pittaway, Kim, 2011. "Single is the new married." **http:// kimpittaway.com/2011/02/13/single-is-the-new-married**

Plambech, Sine. 2005. "Mail order brides" in northwestern Jutland: Transnational marriages in the global care economy. *Dansk Sociologi* 16: 91–110.

Podnieks, E. 2008. Elder abuse: The Canadian experience. *Journal of elder abuse and neglect* 20(2): 126–150.

Pong, Suet-ling, Lingxin Hao, & Erica Gardner. 2005. The roles of parenting styles and social capital in the school performance of immigrant Asian and Hispanic adolescents. *Social Science Quarterly* 86: 928–950.

Pool, Ithiel de Sola (Ed.). 1977. *The Social Impact of the Telephone*. Cambridge, MS: MIT Press.

Popenoe, David. 1993. American family decline, 1960–1990: A review and appraisal. *Journal of Marriage and the Family* 55(3): 527–542.

Popenoe, David. 1996. Modern marriage: Revising the cultural script, pp. 247–270. In David Popenoe, Jean Bethke Elshtain, & David Blankenhorn (Eds.), *Promises to Keep: Decline and Renewal of Marriage in America*. Lanham, MD: Rowman and Littlefield Publishers, Inc.

Popenoe, David. 1988. *Disturbing the Nest: Family Change and Decline in Modern Societies*. New York: A. de Gruyter.

Portelli, Christopher J. 2004. Economic analysis of same sex marriage. *Journal of Homosexuality* 47(1): 95–109.

Portrie, Torey, & Nicole R. Hill. 2005. Blended families: A critical review of the current research. *The Family Journal: Counseling and Therapy for Couples and Families* 12(4): 445–451.

Prentice, Susan. 2007. Less access, worse quality: New evidence about poor children and regulated child care in Canada. *Journal of Children & Poverty* 13(1): 57–73.

Pruissen, Catherine M. 2006. Reducing illness in child care. The Resource Centre: Child Care Online. Retrieved April 18, 2006, from **http://www.childcare .net/library/reduceillness.shtml**

Purvin, Diane. 2007. At the crossroads and in the crosshairs: Social welfare policy and low-income women's vulnerability to domestic violence. *Social Problems* 54(2): 188–210.

Putnam, Richard R. 2011. "First Comes Marriage, Then Comes Divorce: A Perspective on the Process." *Journal of Divorce and Remarriage* 52(7): 557–564.

QMI Agency. 2011. February. Canadians happy with their jobs, not so with their pay: Study. *The Sudbury Star*. **http://www.thesudburystar.com/ArticleDisplay .aspx?e=2959389**

Quach, Andrew S., & Elaine A. Anderson. 2008. Implications of China's open-door policy for families: A family impact analysis. *Journal of Family Issues* 29: 1089–1103.

Quirk, Gregory J., & Leonel Casco. 1994. Stress disorders of families of the disappeared: A controlled study in Honduras. *Social Science and Medicine* 39(12): 1675–1679.

Rabin, Claire, & Giora Rahav. 1995. Differences and similarities between younger and older marriages across cultures: A comparison of American and Israeli retired nondistressed marriages. *American Journal of Family Therapy* 23(3).

Raffaelli, M., & L.L. Ontai. 2001. 16 years old and there are boys calling over to the house: An exploratory study of sexual socialization in Latino families. *Culture, Health, and Sexuality* 3: 295–310.

Ram, Bali. 1990. *New Trends in the Family: Demographic Facts and Features*. Ottawa: Statistics Canada. Catalogue no. 91–535E.

Ramsay, Guy M. 2000. The family and cultural identity in Aborigines and Torres Strait Islanders of Chinese ancestry: A rural–urban divide. *Journal of Family Studies* 6(2): 199–213.

Rankin, Elizabeth Anne DeSalvo. 1993. Stresses and rewards experienced by employed mothers. *Health Care for Women International* 14(6): 527–537.

Ravanera, Zenaida R., & Fernando Rajulton. 1996. Stability and crisis in the family life course—findings from the 1990 General Social Survey, Canada. *Canadian Studies in Population* 23(2): 165–184.

Ravanera, Zenaida R., Fernando Rajulton, & Thomas K. Burch. 1998. Early life transitions of Canadian women: A cohort analysis of timing, sequences, and variations. *European Journal of Population* 14(2): 179–204.

Ray, JoAnn. 1990. Interactional patterns and marital satisfaction among dual-career couples. *Journal of Independent Social Work* 4(3): 61–73.

Raymo, James M., Miho Iwasawa, & Larry Bumpass. 2004. Marital dissolution in Japan: Recent trends and patterns. *Demographic Research* 11: 396–419.

Read, Jen'nan Ghazal. 2004. Cultural influences on immigrant women's labor force participation: The Arab-American case. *International Migration Review* 38: 52–77.

Regnerus, Mark D. 2006. The parent-child relationship and opportunities for adolescents' first sex. *Journal of Family Issues* 27(2): 159–183.

Regmi, P. R., van Teijlingen, E. R., Simkhada, P., & Acharya, D. R. 2011. Dating and sex among emerging adults in Nepal. *Journal of Adolescent Research*, 26(6): 675.

Reimann, Renate. 1999. *Becoming Lesbian Mothers: Lesbian Couples' Transition to Parenthood*. American Sociological Association (ASA).

Reisner, Ellin. 2000 October. Work/family spillover: A qualitative study of public transportation operators. *Dissertation Abstracts International, A: The Humanities and Social Sciences 61*(4), 1637–A.

Reiter, Michael, Jaimie Krause, & Amber Stirlen. 2005. Intercouple dating on a college campus. *College Student Journal 39.3*: 449–455.

Remennick, Larissa. 2000 December. Childless in the land of imperative motherhood: Stigma and coping among infertile Israeli women. *Sex Roles 43*(11–12): 821–841.

Remennick, Larissa. 2005. Cross-cultural dating patterns on an Israeli campus: Why are Russian immigrant women more popular than men? *Journal of Social and Personal Relationships 22*: 435–454.

Remennick, Larissa. 2007. "Being a woman is different here": Changing perceptions of femininity and gender relations among former Soviet women living in Greater Boston. *Women's Studies International Forum 30*: 326–341.

Ren, Xinhua Steve. 1997 January. Marital status and quality of relationships: The impact on health perception. *Social Science and Medicine 44*(2): 241–249.

Renaud, Philip J. 2004. Adult interdependent partners and farm estate planning. *Ag-Succession Factsheet* (Alberta Ministry of Agriculture, Food, and Rural Development). Retrieved May 13, 2009, from http://www1.agric.gov.ab.ca/$department/deptdocs.nsf/all/agdex8649/$file/812-20.pdf?OpenElement

Rhoades, G.K., S.M. Stanley, & H.J. Markman. 2009. Couples' reasons for cohabitation: Associations with individual well-being and relationship quality. *Journal of Family Issues 30*(2): 233–258.

Richard, Madeline. 1991. *Ethnic Groups and Marital Choices: Ethnic History and Marital Assimilation*. Vancouver: University of British Columbia Press.

Richardson, C. James. 2001. Divorce and remarriage. In Maureen Baker (Ed.), *Families: Changing Trends in Canada* (4th edition), pp. 206–237. Toronto: McGraw-Hill Ryerson.

Richer, Shawna. 2002, June 8. Abstinence, Inc., *Globe and Mail*.

Riches, Gordon, & Pamela Dawson. 1996. An intimate loneliness: Evaluating the impact of a child's death on parental self-identity and marital relationships. *Journal of Family Therapy 18*(1).

Richmond, Virginia P. 1995. Amount of communication in marital dyads as a function of dyad and individual marital satisfaction. *Communication Research Reports 12*(2): 152–159.

Rishi, W.R. 1970. *Marriages of the Orient*. Singapore: Chopmen.

Risman, Barbara. 1998. *Gender Vertigo: American Families in Transition*. New Haven: Yale University Press.

Risman, Barbara J., & Danette Johnson-Sumerford. 1998. Doing it fairly: Study of postgender marriages. *Journal of Marriage and the Family 60*: 23–40.

Rivières-Pigeon, Catherine des, Marie-Josèphe Saurel-Cubizolles, & Patrizia Romito. 2002. Division of domestic work and psychological distress 1 year after childbirth: A comparison between France, Quebec and Italy. *Journal of Community and Applied Social Psychology 12*: 397–409.

Roberts, Albert R. 1996 September. Battered women who kill: A comparative study of incarcerated participants with a community sample of battered women. *Journal of Family Violence 11*: 291–304.

Roberts, Glenda S. 2005. Balancing work and life: Whose work? whose life? whose balance? *Asian Perspective 29*(1): 175–211.

Roberts, Judy, Julia O'Sullivan, & Joan Howard. 2005. The roles of emerging and conventional technologies in serving children and adolescents with special needs in rural and northern communities. *Journal of Distance Education 20*(1): 84–103.

Robinson, Paul. 2009. Profile of child support beneficiaries. *Juristat 29*(1). Ottawa: Statistics Canada. Catalogue no. 85-002-X.

Rodrigues, James R., & Tricia L. Park. 1996. General and illness-specific adjustment to cancer: Relationship to marital status and marital quality. *Journal of Psychosomatic Research 40*(1).

Rogers Innovation Report. 2012. Trend Watch, August 2012. **http://www.slideshare.net/Rogers/rogers-innovation-report-parents-youth-study**

Rogers, Stacy J., & Danelle D. DeBoer. 2001. Changes in wives' income: Effects on marital happiness, psychological well-being, and the risk of divorce. *Journal of Marriage and the Family 63*(2): 458–472.

Roschelle, Anne R. 2008. Welfare indignities: Homeless women, domestic violence, and welfare reform in San Francisco. *Gender Issues 25*(3): 193–209.

Rosen, Larry D., Nancy A. Cheever, Cheyenne Cummings, & Julie Felt. 2008. The impact of emotionality and self-disclosure on online dating versus traditional dating. *Computers in Human Behavior 24*: 2124–2157.

Rosenberg, Stanley D., Robert E. Drake, & Kim Mueser. 1996. New directions for treatment research on sequelae of sexual abuse in persons with severe mental illness. *Community Mental Health Journal 32*: 387–400.

Rosenthal, Carolyn J., & Pam Dawson. 1991. Wives of institutionalized elderly men: The first stage of the transition to quasi-widowhood. *Journal of Aging and Health 3*: 315–334.

Rosenthal, Carolyn J., Anne Martin-Matthews, & Sarah H. Matthews. 1996. Caught in the middle? Occupancy in multiple roles and help to parents in a national probability sample of Canadian adults. *Journal of Gerontology 51B*(6): S274–S283.

Rosenthal, Carolyn. 1985. Kinkeeping in the familial division of labor. *Journal of Marriage and the Family 47*: 965–974.

Ross, Susan M. 1996. Risk of physical abuse to children of spouse-abusing parents. *Child Abuse and Neglect 20*(7): 589–598.

Rotermann, M. 2007. Marital breakdown and subsequent depression. *Health Reports 18*(2): 33–44.

Rothblum, Esther D., Kimberly F. Balsam, and Sondra E. Solomon. 2011. "Narratives of Same-Sex Couples

Who Had Civil Unions in Vermont: The Impact of Legalizing Relationships on Couples and on Social Policy." *Sexuality Research and Social Policy* 8:183–191.

Rounds, Kathleen A., Maeda J. Galinsky, & Mathieu R. Despard. 1995 October. Evaluation of telephone support groups for persons with HIV disease. *Research on Social Work Practice, Special Issue: A Festchrift in Honor of Edwin J. Thomas, Vol.* 5(4): 442–459.

Rowland, D.T. 1991 Spring. Family diversity and the life cycle. *Journal of Comparative Family Studies* 22(1): 1–14.

Russell, Mary, Barbara Harris, & Annemarie Gockel. 2008. Parenting in poverty: Perspectives of high-risk parents. *Journal of Children and Poverty* 14(1): 83–98.

Rwampororo, Rosern Kobusingye. 2001 March. Social support: Its mediation of gendered patterns in work-family stress and health for dual-earner couples. *Dissertation Abstracts International, A: The Humanities and Social Sciences* 61(9), 3792-A-3793-A.

Ryan-Nicholls, Kimberley D., & John M. Haggarty. 2007. Collaborative mental health care in rural and isolated Canada. *Journal of Psychosocial Nursing* 45(12): 37–47.

Sabourin, Teresa Chandler. 1995. The role of negative reciprocity in spouse abuse: A relational control analysis. *Journal of Applied Communication Research* 23(4).

Sacks, Jonathan. 1991. The *Persistence of Faith: Religion, Morality and Society in a Secular Age.* The 1990 Reith Lectures. London: Weidenfeld and Nicolson.

Saewyc, Elizabeth M., Darlene Taylor, Yuko Homma, & Gina Ogilvie. 2008. Trends in sexual health and risk behaviours among adolescent students in British Columbia. *Canadian Journal of Human Sexuality* 17: 1–13.

Saintjacques, M.C. 1995. Role strain prediction in stepfamilies. *Journal of Divorce and Remarriage* 24(1–2): 51–72.

Salisbury, D.L. 1997. Retirement planning and personal responsibility: The changing shape of the three-legged stool. *Generations* 21(2): 23–26.

Salvadori, Marina, J.M. Sontrop, A.X. Garg, J. Truong, R.S. Suri, F.H. Mahmud, J.J Macnab, W.F Clark. 2008. Elevated blood pressure in relation to overweight and obesity among children in a rural Canadian community. *Paediatrics* 122(4): 821–827.

Sanchez, Laura, & Elizabeth Thomson. 1997. Becoming mothers and fathers: Parenthood, gender and the division of labour. *Gender and Society* 11(6): 747–772.

Saroglou, V., C. Lacour, and M.E. Demeure. (2010). Bad humour, bad marriage: Humour styles in divorced and married couples. *Europe's Journal of Psychology*, 3, pp. 94–121.

Saunders, Doug, 2011. "Why a Cellphone May be Better than a Toilet if You're Very Poor." **http://dougsaunders. net/2011/03/poverty-mobile-phone-cellphone-toilet**

Sauve, Roger. 2002. *Job, Family and Stress among Husbands, Wives and Lone Parents 15–64 from 1990 to 2000.* Ottawa: Vanier Institute of the Family. Accessed December 30, 2002, at **http://www.vifamily.ca**.

Sauve, Roger. 2009. *Family Life and Work Life: An Uneasy Balance.* Ottawa: Vanier Institute of the Family. Retrieved from **http://www.canadiansocialresearch .net/work_life_balance.htm**

Sautter, Jessica M., Rebecca M. Tippett, and S. Philip Morgan. 2010. "The Social Demography of Internet Dating in the United States." *Social Science Quarterly* 91: 554–575.

Sayer, Liana C., Anne H. Gauthier, & Frank F. Furstenberg, Jr. 2004. Educational differences in parents' time with children: Cross-national variations. *Journal of Marriage and the Family* 66: 1152–1169.

Scanzoni, John. 2000. *Designing Families: The Search for Self and Community in the Information Age.* Thousand Oaks, CA: Pine Forge Press.

Scanzoni, John. 2001. From the normal family to alternate families to the quest for diversity with interdependence. *Journal of Family Issues* 22(6): 688–710.

Scaramella, Laura V., Tricia K. Neppl, Lenna L. Ontai, & Rand D. Conger. 2008. Consequences of socioeconomic disadvantage across three generations: parenting behavior and child externalizing problems. *Journal of Family Psychology* 22(5): 725–733.

Schlesinger, R.A., and B. Schlesinger. 2009. Canadian-Jewish seniors: Marriage/cohabitation after age 65. *Journal of Gerontological Social Work* 52(1): 32–47.

Schneider, Carl E. 1996. The law and the stability of marriage: The family as a social institution, pp. 187–213. In David Popenoe, Jean Bethke Elshtain, & David Blankenhorn (Eds.), *Promises to Keep: Decline and Renewal of Marriage in America.* Lanham, MD: Rowman and Littlefield Publishers, Inc.

Schneider, Jennifer P. 2003. The impact of compulsive cybersex behaviours on the family. *Sexual and Relational Therapy* 18(3): 329–354.

Schroeder, Bonnie, Jane MacDonald, and Judith Shamian. 2012. "Older Workers with Caregiving Responsibilities: A Canadian Perspective on Corporate Caring." *Ageing International* 37: 39–56.

Schultz, Wolfgang. 1983. From the institution of the family to differentiated relationships between men, women, and children: On structural changes of marriage and the family. *Soziale-Welt* 34(4): 401–419.

Schulz, Marc S., Carolyn Pape Cowan, & Philip A. Cowan. 2006. Promoting healthy beginnings: A randomized controlled trial of a preventive intervention to preserve marital quality during the transition to parenthood. *Journal of Consulting and Clinical Psychology* 74(1): 20–31.

Schwartz, Christine, & Robert Mare. 2005. Trends in educational assortative marriage from 1940 to 2003. *Demography* 42.4: 621–646.

Schwartz, Jonathan P., Michael Waldo, & David Daniel. 2005. Gender-role conflict and self-esteem: Factors associated with partner abuse in court-referred men. *Psychology of Men & Masculinity* 6(2): 109–113.

Schwartz, Pepper, & Virginia Rutter. 1998. *The Gender of Sexuality.* Thousand Oaks, California: Pine Forge Press.

Sciadas, G. 2006. Our lives in digital times. Connectedness Series 14: 5–23. Retrieved June 11, 2009, from **http://www .statcan.gc.ca/pub/56f0004m/56f0004m2006014- eng.pdf**

Scott, Katherine. 1996. *The Progress of Canada's Children.* Ottawa: Canadian Council on Social Development.

Selvin, M. 2007. More wives becoming primary breadwinners. *Los Angeles Times.* Retrieved June 12, 2009, from **http://www.mcall.com/business/yourmoney/ sns-yourmoney-0211pay,0,7399103.story**

Senn, C.Y., S. Desmarais, N. Verberg, & E. Wood. 2000. Predicting coercive sexual behavior across the lifespan in a random sample of Canadian men. *Journal of Social and Personal Relationships* 17: 95–113.

Serewicz, Mary, Claire Morr, & Elaine Gale. 2008. First-date scripts: Gender roles, context, and relationship. *Sex Roles* 58(3–4): 149–164.

Serran, Geris, & Philip Firestone. 2004. Intimate partner homicide: A review of the male proprietariness and the self-defense theories. *Aggression and Violent Behavior*, 9: 1–15.

Se'ver, Aysan. 1990. Mate selection patterns of men and women in personal advertisements. *Atlantis: A Women's Studies Journal* 15(2): 70–76.

Se'ver, Aysan. 2011. Marriage go-round: Divorce and remarriage in Canada. In Nancy Mandell and Ann Duffy (Eds.). *Canadian Families: Diversity, Conflict and Change*, 4th edition. Toronto: Nelson, 243–274.

Shackelford, T.K., & J. Mouzos. 2005. Partner killing by men in cohabiting and marital relationships: A comparative, cross-national analysis of data from Australia and the United States. *Journal of Interpersonal Violence* 10: 1310–1324.

Shadish, William R., Kevin Ragsdale, & Renata R. Glaser. 1995. The efficacy and effectiveness of marital and family therapy: A perspective from meta-analysis. *Journal of Marital and Family Therapy* 21(4).

Shaff, Kimberly Anne, Nicholas H. Wolfinger, Lori Kowaleski-Jones, and Ken R. Smith. 2008. Family Structure Transitions and Child Achievement. *Sociological Spectrum: Mid-South Sociological Association* 28(6):681–704.

Shapiro, A. 2003. Later-life divorce and parent-adult child contact and proximity. *Journal of Family Issues* 24(2): 264–285.

Shaver, Sheila, & Jonathan Bradshaw. 1995. The recognition of wifely labour by welfare states. *Social Policy and Administration* 29(1): 10–25.

Shaw, Susan M. 2008. Family leisure and changing ideologies of parenthood. *Sociology Compass* 2:1–16.

Shek, Daniel T.L. 1995 June. Gender differences in marital quality and well-being in Chinese married adults. *Sex Roles* 32.

Sheldon, Kennon. 2007. Gender differences in preferences for singles ads that proclaim extrinsic versus intrinsic values. *Sex Roles* 57(1–2): 119–129.

Sheridan, Michael J. 1995. A proposed intergenerational model of substance abuse, family functioning, and abuse/neglect. *Child Abuse and Neglect* 19(May): 519–530.

Shi, Liping. 2000 February. The communication structure of intercultural married couples and their marital satisfaction. *Soshioroji* 44(3): 57–73.

Shirpak, Khosro Refaie, Eleanor Maticka-Tyndale, and Maryam Chinichian. 2011. "Post Migration Changes in Iranian Immigrants' Couple Relationships in Canada." *Journal of Comparative Family Studies* 42(6): 751–770.

Short, J., E. Williams, & B. Christie. 1976. *The Social Psychology of Telecommunications*. London; New York: Wiley.

Silva, Elizabeth. 2010. *Technology, Culture and Family: Influences on Home Life*. Basingstoke; Palgrave.

Silver, Hilary, & Frances Goldscheider. 1994 June. Flexible work and housework: Work and family constraints on women's domestic labor. *Social Forces* 72: 1103–1119.

Simon, R.W. 1995. Gender, multiple roles, role meaning, and mental health. *Journal of Health and Social Behaviour* 36: 182–194.

Simpson, Jeffry A., W. Steven Rholes, Lorne Campbell, Sisi Tran, & Carol L. Wilson. 2003. Adult attachment, the transition to parenthood, and depressive symptoms. *Journal of Personality and Social Psychology* 84(6): 1172–1187.

Sims-Gould, J., A. Martin-Matthews, Monique A.M. Gignac. 2008. Episodic crises in the provision of care to elderly relatives. *Journal of Applied Gerontology* 27(2): 123–140.

Singer, Merrill C., Pamela I. Erickson, Louise Badiane, Rosemary Diaz, Dugeidy Ortiz, Traci Abraham, & Anna Marie Nicolaysen. 2006. Syndemics, sex and the city: Understanding sexually transmitted diseases in social and cultural context. *Social Science & Medicine* 63: 2010–2021.

Sitrin, Allison Gayle. 2001 September. The impact of the quality of marital adaptation on prenatal maternal representations and postnatal satisfaction with social support. *Dissertation Abstracts International: Section B: The Sciences & Engineering* 62(3–B), 1599.

Skinner, Kevin B., Stephen J. Bahr, D. Russell Crane, & R.A. Call Vaughn. 2002. Cohabitation, marriage, and remarriage: A comparison of relationship quality over time. *Journal of Family Issues* 23(1): 74–90.

Skinner, N.F., and Iaboni, K.B. 2009. Personality implications of adaption-innovation: IV. Cognitive style as a predictor of marital success. *Social Behaviour and Personality*, 37 (8), 1111–1113.

Skultety, K.M. 2007. Addressing issues of dexuality with older couples. *Generations* 31(3): 31–37.

Smart, Carol. 2007 *Personal Life:New Directionsin Sociological Thinking*, Cambridge: Polity Press.

Smart, Carol, & Bren Neale. 1999. *Family Fragments?* Cambridge, UK: Polity Press.

Smith, Andrea. 2008. Transnationalism and the immigrant: Continuity or paradigm shift? *Identities: Global Studies in Culture and Power* 15: 462–481.

Smith, Jane E., V. Waldorf, & D. Trembath. 1990. Single white male looking for thin, very attractive... *Sex Roles* 23(11–12): 675–683.

Smith, Richard B., & Robert A. Brown. 1997. The impact of social support on gay male couples. *Journal of Homosexuality* 33(2): 39–61.

Smithers, John, & Paul Johnson. 2004. The dynamics of family farming in North Huron County, Ontario. Part I: Development trajectories. *The Canadian Geographer* 48(2): 191–208.

Smithers, John, Paul Johnson, & Alun Joseph. 2004. The dynamics of family farming in North Huron County, Ontario. Part II: Farm-community interactions. *The Canadian Geographer* 48(2): 209–224.

Smock, P., P. Huang, W. Manning, & C. Bergstrom. 2006. *Heterosexual Cohabitation in the United States: Motives for Living Together among Men and Women*. Working Paper. Ohio: Center for Family and Demographic Research.

Smock, Pamela J. 1994 September. Gender and the short-run economic consequences of marital disruption. *Social Forces* 73.

Snell, James G. 1983. The white life for two: The defence of marriage and sexual morality in Canada, 1890–1914. *Histoire sociale/Social History* 16(31): 111–128.

Sommer, Dion. 1992. A child's place in society: New challenges for the family and day care. *Children and Society* 6(4): 317–335.

Sonawat, Reeta. 2001. Understanding families in India: A reflection of societal changes. *Psicologia: Teoria e Pesquisa* 17(2): 177–186.

Song, Jung Ah, Betsy M. Bergen, & Walter Schumm. 1995. Sexual satisfaction among Korean-American couples in the Midwestern United States. *Journal of Sex and Marital Therapy* 21(3): 147–158.

South, S.J., K. Trent, and Y. Shen. 2001. Changing partners: Toward a macrostructural opportunity theory of marital dissolution. *Journal of Marriage and the Family* 63: 743–754.

South, Scott. 1985. Economic conditions and the divorce rate: A time-series analysis of the children. *Journal of Marriage and the Family* 47(1): 31–42.

Spanking poll backs ruling. 2004, February 1. *Winnipeg Sun.*

Spiegel, Hans M.L., & Donna C. Futterman. 2009. Adolescents and HIV: Prevention and clinical care. *Current HIV/AIDS Reports* 6(2): 100–107.

Spillane-Grieco, Eileen. 1984. Characteristics of a helpful relationship: A study of empathic understanding and positive regard between runaways and their parents. *Adolescence* 19(73): 63–75.

Spiwak, Rae, & Douglas A. Brownridge. 2005. Separated women's risk for violence: An analysis of the Canadian situation. *Journal of Divorce and Remarriage* 43: 105–117.

Sprecher, S. 2009. Relationship Initiation and Formation on the Internet. *Marriage & Family Review* 45(6-8): 761–782.

SPRY Foundation (2004). Computer-based technology and caregiving of older adults: What's new, what's next. Retrieved July 28, 2005, from **http://www.spry.org/new_publications/CBTCOA_English.pdf**

Srinivasan, S. 2001. Being Indian, being American: A balancing act or a creative blend? *Journal of Human Behavior in the Social Environment* 3: 135–158.

Stacey, J., & Biblarz, T. 2001. (How) Does the sexual orientation of parents matter? *American Sociological Review* 66: 159–183.

Stacey, Judith. 1990. *Brave New Families.* New York: Basic Books.

Stacey, Judith. 1996. *In the Name of the Family: Rethinking Family Values in the Postmodern Age.* Boston: Beacon.

Stacey, William A., Lonnie R. Hazlewood, & Anson D. Shupe. 1994. *The Violent Couple.* Westport, CN: Praeger.

Stack, C. 2001 (1974). Swapping: What goes round comes round. In Bonnie J. Fox (Ed.), *Family Patterns, Gender Relations* (2nd edition). Toronto: Oxford University Press, 393–400.

Stafford, Laura, Susan L. Kline, & Caroline T. Rankin. 2004. Married individuals, cohabiters, and cohabiters who marry: A longitudinal study of relational and individual well-being. *Journal of Social and Personal Relationships* 21(2): 231–248.

Stanley, S.M., G.K. Rhoades., & H.J. Markman. 2006. Sliding versus deciding: Inertia and the premarital cohabitation effect. *Family Relations* 55(4): 499–509.

Stanton, Glenn T. 1996 May–June. The counterrevolution against easy divorce: New rumbling in the states. *The American Enterprise* 7.

Statistics Canada, Censuses of Population, 1961 to 2011, Statistics Canada Catalogue No. 98-312-X-2011003.

Retrieved from **http://www12.statcan.gc.ca/census-recensement/2011/as-sa/98-312-x/2011003/fig/desc/desc3_1-4-eng.cfm**

Statistics Canada. 1993. Violence against women survey. *The Daily*, 18 November.

Statistics Canada. 1996a. *Life Events: How Families Change, Labour and Income Dynamics* 5(1). Ottawa: Statistics Canada.

Statistics Canada. 1996b. Dual-earner families. *The Daily*, 6 June.

Statistics Canada. 1997c. *Income Distributions by Size in Canada, 1996.* Ottawa: Statistics Canada. Catalogue no. 13-207-XPB.

Statistics Canada. 1998b. Marriages and Divorces, 1996. *The Daily*, 29 January.

Statistics Canada. 2001a. Marriages. *The Daily*, Thursday, 15 November.

Statistics Canada. 2002a. Changing conjugal life in Canada. *The Daily*, 11 July. Retrieved December 9, 2005, from **http://www.statcan.ca/Daily/English/020711/d020711a.htm**

Statistics Canada. 2002b. 2001 Census: Profile of Canadian families and households: Diversification continues. Census release 22 October 2002, **http://www.statcan.ca**

Statistics Canada. 2002c. *General Social Survey–Cycle 15: Family History.* Ottawa: Statistics Canada. Catalogue no. 89-575-XIE. Retrieved July 11, 2002, from **http://www.statcan.ca**

Statistics Canada. 2002d. Divorces, 1999 and 2000. *The Daily*, 2 December.

Statistics Canada. 2002e. *The Daily*, 26 September. Retrieved April 25, 2006, from **http://www.statcan.ca/Daily/English/020926/d020926c.htm**

Statistics Canada. 2002f. *2001 Census of Canada: Profile of Canadian Families and Households: Diversification Continues.* Ottawa: Statistics Canada. Catalogue no. 96F0030XIE2001003. Retrieved October 22, 2002, from **http://www.statcan.ca**

Statistics Canada. 2002g. 2001 Census: Marital status, common-law status, families, dwellings and households. *The Daily*, October 22. Retrieved from **http://www.statcan.gc.ca/daily-quotidien/021022/dq021022a-eng.htm**

Statistics Canada. 2002h. Family income, 2000. *The Daily*, 30 October.

Statistics Canada. 2002i, November 6. 2001 Census. Retrieved May 13, 2005, from **http://www12.statcan.ca/english/census01/Products/Analytic/companion/fam/canada.cfm**

Statistics Canada. 2002j. *2001 Census of Canada.* Legal marital status, age and sex, Canada. Retrieved January 12, 2006, from **http://www12.statcan.ca/english/census01/products/standard/themes/RetrieveProductTable.cfm?Temporal=2001&PID=55525&APATH=3&GID=355313&METH=1&PTYPE=55496&THEME=38&FOCUS=0&AID=0&PLACENAME=0&PROVINCE=0&SEARCH=0&GC=0&GK=0&VID=0&FL=0&RL=0&FREE=0**

Statistics Canada. 2002k. Impact of income on mortality in urban Canada. *The Daily*, 26 September. Retrieved July 28, 2005, from **http://www.statcan.ca/Daily/English/020926/d020926a.htm**

Statistics Canada. 2002l. Changing conjugal life in Canada. *General Social Survey*. Retrieved May 13, 2009, from http://www.statcan.gc.ca/pub/89-576-x/89-576-x2001001-eng.pdf

Statistics Canada. 2002m. Profile of Canadian families and households: Diversification continues. Retrieved May 24, 2009, from http://www12.statcan.ca/english/census01/Products/Analytic/companion/fam/pdf/96F0030XIE2001003.pdf

Statistics Canada. 2003a, February 24. 2001 Census: Where Canadians work and how they get there: Work at home stable while working outside the country increases. Retrieved May 27, 2004, from http://www12.statcan.ca/english/census01/Products/Analytic/companion/pow/home.cfm

Statistics Canada. 2003b. Couples living apart. *Canadian Social Trends*. Retrieved May 13, 2009, from http://www.statcan.gc.ca/pub/11-008-x/2003001/article/6552-eng.pdf

Statistics Canada. 2004a. Divorces. *The Daily*, 4 May. Retrieved August 5, 2005, from http://www.statcan.ca/Daily/English/040504/d040504a.htm

Statistics Canada. 2004b. Births. *The Daily*, 19 April. Retrieved October 16, 2005, from http://www.statcan.ca/Daily/English/040419/d040419b.htm

Statistics Canada. 2004c. 2001 Census: Profile of Canadian families and households. Retrieved November 30, 2005, from http://www12.statcan.ca/english/census01/Products/Analytic/companion/fam/canada.cfm#same_sex_common_law

Statistics Canada. 2004d. 2001 Census: Profile of Canadian families and households. Retrieved November 30, 2005, from http://www12.statcan.ca/english/census01/Products/Analytic/companion/fam/canada.cfm#children

Statistics Canada. 2004e. June 28. 2001 Census: Families and household profile–Canada. Retrieved May 27, from 2005, http://www12.statcan.ca/english/census01/Products/Analytic/companion/fam/canada.cfm#seniors

Statistics Canada. 2004f. Family Income. *The Daily*, 26 May. Retrieved January 12, 2006, from http://www.statcan.ca/Daily/English/040526/d040526d.htm

Statistics Canada. 2005. *Chart 1*. http://www.statcan.gc.ca/pub/11-008-x/2006007/c-g/4097833-eng.htm

Statistics Canada. 2005a. Births. *The Daily*, 12 July. Retrieved October 16, 2005, from http://www.statcan.ca/Daily/English/050712/d050712a.htm

Statistics Canada. 2005b. Canada's Aboriginal population in 2017. *The Daily*, 28 June. Retrieved October 16, 2005, from http://www.statcan.ca/Daily/English/050628/d050628d.htm

Statistics Canada. 2005c. *Family Violence in Canada: A Statistical Profile*. Ottawa: Statistics Canada. Catalogue no. 85-224-XIE.

Statistics Canada. 2005d. Study: Mature singles who don't expect to marry. *The Daily*, 7 June. Retrieved November 18, 2005, from http://www.statcan.ca/Daily/English/050607/d050607a.htm

Statistics Canada. 2005e. *The Daily*, 7 February. Retrieved from http://www.statcan.ca/Daily/English/050207/d050207b.htm

Statistics Canada. 2005f. Divorce and the mental health of children. *The Daily*, 13 December. Retrieved December 14, 2005, from http://www.statcan.ca/Daily/English/050309/d050309b.htm

Statistics Canada. 2005g. Trends in income inequality in Canada from an international perspective. *The Daily*, 10 February. Retrieved July 28, 2005, from http://www.statcan.ca/Daily/English/050210/d050210c.htm

Statistics Canada. 2005h. E-commerce: Shopping on the internet. *The Daily*, 1 November. Retrieved from http://www.statcan.gc.ca/daily-quotidien/061101/dq061101a-eng.htm

Statistics Canada. 2006. Child care: An eight-year profile. *The Daily*. http://www.statcan.gc.ca/daily-quotidien/060405/dq060405a-eng.htm

Statistics Canada. 2006a. *Annual Demographic Statistics, 2005*. Ottawa: Statistics Canada. Catalogue no. 91-213.

Statistics Canada. 2006b. *Canada's Changing Labour Force*. Ottawa: Statistics Canada. Catalogue no. 97-559-X.

Statistics Canada. 2006c. *The Daily*, 7 March. Retrieved April 18, 2006, from http://www.statcan.ca/Daily/English/060307/d060307a.htm

Statistics Canada. 2006d. *The Daily*, 30 March. Retrieved from http://www.statcan.ca/Daily/English/060330/d060330a.htm

Statistics Canada. 2006e. *Family Violence in Canada: A Statistical Profile*. Ottawa: Statistics Canada. Catalogue no. 85-224-X.

Statistics Canada. 2006f. The Internet experience of younger and older Canadians. *Information Analysis Bulletin* 8(1): 8–10.

Statistics Canada. 2006g. Survey of 2005 household expenditures. *The Daily*, 12 December. Retrieved http://www.statcan.ca/Daily/English/061212/d061212b.htm

Statistics Canada. 2006h. *Telecommunication Statistics*. Retrieved June 11, 2009, from http://www.statcan.ca/Daily/English/070514/d070514d.htm

Statistics Canada. 2006i. Wives as primary breadwinners. *The Daily*, 23 August. Retrieved from http://www.statcan.gc.ca/daily-quotidien/060823/dq060823b-eng.htm

Statistics Canada. 2007. Seniors. *CYB Overview 2007*. http://www41.statcan.ca/2007/70000/ceb70000_000-eng.htm

Statistics Canada. 2007a. 2006 Census: Families, marital status, households and dwelling characteristics. *The Daily*, 12 September. Retrieved May 13, 2009, from http://www.statcan.gc.ca/daily-quotidien/070912/dq070912a-eng.htm

Statistics Canada. 2007b. Census snapshot of Canada: Families. *Canadian Social Trends*. Ottawa: Statistics Canada. Catalogue no. 11-008: 39–40.

Statistics Canada. 2007c. *Family Portrait: Continuity and Change in Canadian Families and Households in 2006*. Ottawa: Statistics Canada. Catalogue no. 97-553-XIE.

Statistics Canada. 2007d. *Labour*. Ottawa: Statistics Canada. Retrieved from http://www41.statcan.ca/2007/2621/ceb2621_000_e.htm

Statistics Canada. 2007e. Marriages. *The Daily*, 17 January. Retrieved May 13, 2009, from http://www.statcan.gc.ca/daily-quotidien/070117/dq070117a-eng.htm

Statistics Canada. 2008a. Births. *The Daily*, 26 September. Retrieved from http://www.hc-sc.gc.ca/sr-sr/pubs/hpr-rpms/bull/2005-10-chang-fertilit/intro-eng.php

Statistics Canada. 2008b. *Information and Communications Technology*. Retrieved June 13, 2009, from http://www41.statcan.gc.ca/2008/2256/ceb2256_000-eng.htm

Statistics Canada. 2008c. Life after teen motherhood, *The Daily*, 23 March.

Statistics Canada. 2009. *Study: Hours and Earnings of Dual-Earner Couples*. Retrieved June 13, 2009, from http://www.statcan.gc.ca/daily-quotidien/090424/dq090424beng.htm

Statistics Canada. 2010a. Population Projections for Canada, 2009–2036. Ottawa: Statistics Canada, Cata. No. 91-520-X. http://www.statcan.gc.ca/pub/91-520-x/91-520-x2010001-eng.htm

Statistics Canada. 2010a. Internet use by individuals, by type of activity. Statistics Canada. http://www.statcan.gc.ca/tables-tableaux/sum-som/l01/cst01/comm29a-eng.htm

Statistics Canada. 2010b. Internet use by individuals, by selected frequency of use and age. http://www.statcan.gc.ca/tables-tableaux/sum-som/l01/cst01/comm32a-eng.htm

Statistics Canada. 2011. Sources of Stress among Workers. *The Daily*. 13 October 2011.

Statistics Canada. 2011. Labour force survey estimates (LFS), by total and average usual and actual hours worked, main or all jobs, type of work, sex and age group, annual (CANSIM Table 282-0028). Ottawa: Statistics Canada. http://www.statcan.gc.ca/pub/71-001-x/2011012/related-connexes-eng.htm

Statistics Canada. 2011. Women in Canada: A Gender-Based Statistical Report. Ottawa: Statistics Canada. http://www.statcan.gc.ca/pub/89-503-x/2010001/article/11388-eng.htm#a4

Statistics Canada, 2011. General Social Survey: Overview of Families in Canada—Being a parent in a stepfamily: A profile. Catalogue No. 89-650-X – No. 002. http://www.statcan.gc.ca/pub/89-650-x/89-650-x2012002-eng.pdf

Statistics Canada. 2011. Study: Projected trends to 2031 for the Canadian labour force. *The Daily*. 17 August. http://www.statcan.gc.ca/daily-quotidien/110817/dq110817b-eng.htm

Statistics Canada. 2011. Census Family, 2011 Census Dictionary. Ottawa: Statistics Canada, Cata no. 98-301-XWE. http://www.statcan.gc.ca/census-recensement/2011/ref/dict/fam004-eng.cfm

Statistics Canada, 2011. Canada Vital Statistics, Marriage Database and Demography Division (population estimates), Ottawa: Statistics Canada. http://www4.hrsdc.gc.ca/.3ndic.1t.4r@-eng.jsp?iid=78

Statistics Canada, 2011a. Families, Living Arrangements and Unpaid Work. Catalogue No. 89-503-X. http://www.statcan.gc.ca/pub/89-503-x/2010001/article/11546-eng.pdf

Statistics Canada. 2012a. Portrait of Families and Living Arrangements in Canada (from the 2011 Census of Canada short form). http://www12.statcan.gc.ca/census-recensement/2011/as-sa/98-312-x/98-312-x2011001-eng.cfm#a1

Statistics Canada. 2012b. CANISM 111-0020. Family characteristics, single-earner and dual-earner families, by number of children. http://www5.statcan.gc.ca/cansim/pick-choisir?lang=eng&p2=33&id=1110020

Statistics Canada. 2012b. Years to retirement, 1998 to 2009. Retrieved from http://www.statcan.gc.ca/daily-quotidien/121204/dq121204b-eng.htm

Statistics Canada. 2012c. Low Income in Canada–A Multi-line and Multi-index Perspective. Catalogue no. 75F0002M—No. 001. Retrieved from http://www.statcan.gc.ca/pub/75f0002m/75f0002m2012001-eng.pdf

Statistics Canada, 2012d. Visual Census. Catalogue No. 98-315-XWE. Retrieved from http://www12.statcan.gc.ca/census-recensement/2011/dp-pd/vc-rv/index.cfm?LANG=ENG&VIEW=C&TOPIC_ID=3&GEOCODE=01&CFORMAT=jpg#f3_1

Statistics Canada. 2012a. Portrait of Families and Living Arrangements in Canada (from the 2011 Census of Canada short form). http://www12.statcan.gc.ca/census-recensement/2011/as-sa/98-312-x/98-312-x2011001-eng.cfm#a1

Statistics Canada, 2012b. Fifty years of families in Canada: 1961 to 2011; Families, households and marital status, 2011 Census of Population. http://www12.statcan.gc.ca/census-recensement/2011/as-sa/98-312-x/98-312-x2011003_1-eng.pdf

Statistics Canada, 2012c. CANSIM, Table 051-0042. http://www.statcan.gc.ca/tables-tableaux/sum-som/101/cst01/famil01-eng.htm

Statistics Canada. 2012c. CANSIM 102-4507. Live births, by age and marital status of mother, Canada. http://www5.statcan.gc.ca/cansim/a47

Statistics Canada. 2012d. Living arrangements of young adults aged 20 to 29. Catalogue No. 98-312-X-2011003 http://www12.statcan.gc.ca/census-recensement/2011/as-sa/98-312-x/98-312-x2011003_3-eng.cfm

Statistics Canada, 2012d. Census of Population, 2011, Living arrangements of seniors and Living arrangements of young adults aged 20 to 29 Catalogue No. 98-312-X2011003. http://www12.statcan.gc.ca/census-recensement/2011/as-sa/98-312-x/98-312-x2011003_4-eng.cfm

Statistics Canada. 2012e. Living arrangements of seniors. Catalogue No. 98-312-X-2011003. http://www12.statcan.gc.ca/census-recensement/2011/as-sa/98-312-x/98-312-x2011003_4-eng.cfm

Statistics Canada, 2012e. 2011 Census of Population, Catalogue No. 98-312-XCB2011024 (Quebec / Québec, Code24). http://www12.statcan.gc.ca/census-recensement/2011/dp-pd/prof/index.cfm?Lang=E

Statistics Canada,2012f. 2011 Census of Population, Statistics Canada catalogue no. 98-312-XCB2011024 (Canada, Code01). http://www12.statcan.gc.ca/census-recensement/2011/dp-pd/tbt-tt/Rp-

Statistics Canada. 2013. Aboriginal Peoples in Canada—National Household Survey 2011. http://www12.statcan.gc.ca/nhs-enm/2011/as-sa/99-011-x/99-011-x2011001-eng.cfm#a1

Statistics Canada. 2013. High Income Trends among Canadian Taxfilers, 1982–2010. *The Daily*. January 28, 2013.

Statistics Canada. 2013. Measuring Violence against Women: Statistical Trends, Ottawa; Statistics Canada, Cata no. 85-002-X. http://www.statcan.gc.ca/pub/85-002-x/2013001/article/11766/hl-fs-eng.htm

Statistics Canada. 2013a. National Household Survey 2011. Aboriginal Peoples in Canada: First Nations People, Métis and Inuit. Retrieved from http://www12.statcan.gc.ca/nhs-enm/2011/as-sa/99-011-x/99-011-x2011001-eng.cfm#a1

Statistics Canada. 2013a. Births by Marital Status and Age, CANSIM table 102-4507, Ottawa: Statistics Canada. http://www5.statcan.gc.ca/cansim/a47

Statistics Canada. 2013b. Living Apart Together. *The Daily*, March 5, 2013.

Statistics Canada. 2013b. National Household Survey 2011. Immigration and Ethnocultural Diversity in Canada. Retrieved from http://www12.statcan.gc.ca/nhs-enm/2011/as-sa/99-010-x/99-010-x2011001-eng.cfm#a4

Steele, Fiona, Constantinos Kallis, Harvey Goldstein, & Heather Joshi. 2005. The relationship between childbearing and transitions from marriage and cohabitation in Britain. *Demography* 42(4): 647–673.

Steinberg, Laurence, Susie D. Lamborn, Nancy Darling, Nina S. Mounts, & Sanford M. Dornbusch. 1994. Over-time changes in adjustment and competence among adolescents from authoritative, authoritarian, indulgent, and neglectful families. *Child Development* 65(3): 754–770.

Steinhauer, Paul D., Jack Santa-Barbara, & H. Skinner. 1984. The process model of family functioning. *The Canadian Journal of Psychiatry/La Revue canadienne de psychiatrie* 29(2): 77–88.

Steinmetz, S.K. 1977. *The Cycle of Violence: Assertive, Aggressive, and Abusive Family Interaction*. New York: Praeger.

Stephens, Linda S. 1996. Will Johnny see Daddy this week? An empirical test of three theoretical perspectives of post-divorce contact. *Journal of Family Issues* 12(4).

Stern, Susan B., & Carolyn A. Smith. 1995. Family processes and delinquency in an ecological context. *Social Service Review* 69(4): 703–731.

Stiffman, Arlene Rubin. 1989a. Physical and sexual abuse in runaway youths. *Child Abuse and Neglect* 13(3): 417–426.

Stohs, Joanne Hovan. 1995. Predictors of conflict over the household division of labor among women employed full-time. *Sex Roles* 33(3–4).

Stop Violence Against Women. 2003, September 10. Prevalence of domestic violence. Retrieved on July 14, 2005, from http://www.stopvaw.org/Prevalence_of_Domestic_Violence.html

Story, Nathan T., Cynthia A. Berg, Timothy W. Smith, Ryan Beveridge, Nancy J. M. Henry, & Gale Pearce. 2007. Age, marital satisfaction, and optimism as predictors of positive sentiment override in middle-aged and older married couples. *Psychology and Aging* 22: 719–727.

Strasser, Susan M. 1978. The business of housekeeping: The ideology of the household at the turn of the twentieth century. *The Insurgent Sociologist* 8(2–3): 147–163.

Strasser, Susan. 2006. Housework, on Answers.com. Retrieved July 19, 2006, from http://www.answers.com/topic/housework

Straus, M. 1992. Family violence. In Edgar F. Borgatta & Marie L. Borgatta (Eds.), *Encyclopedia of Sociology*, Vol. 2. New York: Macmillan Publishing Co.

Straus, Murray A. 1996. *Identifying Offenders in Criminal Justice Research on Domestic Assault*. Beverley Hills, CA: Sage Publications.

Strohnschein, Lisa. 2005. Parental divorce and child mental health trajectories. *Journal of Marriage and Family* 67(5): 1286–1300.

Strong-Boag, Veronica. 2000. Long time coming: The century of the Canadian child? *Journal of Canadian Studies* 35(1): 124–261.

Stutzer, Alois, & Bruno S. Frey. 2006. Does marriage make people happy, or do happy people get married? *Journal of Socio-Economics* 35(2): 326–347.

Sudarkasa, N. 2001 (1997). African-American families and family values. In Bonnie J. Fox (Ed.), *Family Patterns, Gender Relations* (2nd edition). Toronto: Oxford University Press, 377–392.

Sugiman, P. 1983. Socialization and cultural duality among aging Japanese Canadians. *Canadian Ethnic Studies* 15(3): 17–35.

Sugiman, P., & H.K. Nishio. 1983. Socialization and cultural duality among aging Japanese Canadians. *Canadian Ethnic Studies* 15(3): 17–35.

Suitor, Jill J., & Karl Pillemer. 1988 November. Explaining intergenerational conflict when adult children and elderly parents live together. *Journal of Marriage and the Family* 50(4): 1037–1047.

Sullivan, T. Richard (Ed.). 2012. *Queer Families, Common Agendas: Gay People, Lesbians and Family Values*. New York: Routledge.

Sulman, Joanne, Carolyn J. Rosenthal, Victor W. Marshall, & Joanne Daciuk. 1996. Elderly patients in the acute care hospital: Factors associated with long stay and its impact on patients and families. *Journal of Gerontological Social Work* 25(3–4): 33–52.

Sun, S.H. 2008. "Not just a business transaction": The logic and limits of grandparental childcare assistance in Taiwan. *Childhood* 15(2): 203–224.

Sunahara, A.G. 1981. *The Politics of Racism: The Uprooting of Japanese Canadians during the Second World War*. Toronto: James Lorimer & Company.

Sundie, J. M. 2003. Conspicuous consumption as a mating strategy. *ProQuest Information & Learning* 64(3): 123–139.

Sussman, D., & S. Bonnell. 2006. Wives as primary breadwinners. *Perspectives on Labour and Income* 7(8). Retrieved June 10, 2009, from http://www.statcan.gc.ca/pub/75-001-x/10806/9291-eng.htm

Sutherns, Rebecca, & Ivy Lynn Bourgeault. 2008. Accessing maternity care in rural Canada: There's more to the story than distance to the doctor. *Health Care for Women International* 29: 863–883.

Sutherns, Rebecca, Marilou McPhedran, & Margaret Haworth-Brockman (Eds). 2004. *Summary Report: Rural, Remote and Northern Women's Health: Policy and Research Directions*. Winnipeg: Centres of Excellence for Women's Health.

Suwal, Juhee Vajracharya. 2003. *Aspects of Demographic and Epidemiological Transitions in Nepal*. Ph.D. thesis in Sociology, University of Alberta.

Suzuki, Kenji. 2008. Politics of the falling birthrate in Japan. *Japanese Journal of Political Science* 9(2): 161–182.

Swahn, Monica, Thomas Simon, Ileana Arias, & Robert Bossarte. 2008. Measuring sex differences in violence, victimization and perpetration. *Journal of Interpersonal Violence* 23.8: 1120–1138.

Sydie, Rosalind A. 1987. *Natural Women, Cultured Men: A Feminist Perspective on Sociological Theory*. Toronto: Methuen.

Tang, T.N., & K. Oatley. 2002. *Transitions and Engagement of Life Roles among Chinese Immigrant Women*. American Psychological Association Annual Convention.

Taniguchi, Hiromi. 1999. The timing of childbearing and women's wages. *Journal of Marriage and the Family* 61(4), 1008–1019.

Tannen, Deborah. 1993. *Gender and Conversational Interaction*. New York: Oxford University Press.

Tastsoglou, E., and A. Dobrowolsky (Eds). *Women, Migration, and Citizenship: Making Local, National, and Transnational Connections*. Ashgate Publishers, 2006.

Tayler, Lyn, Gordon Parker, & Kay Roy. 1995. Parental divorce and its effects on the quality of intimate relationships in adulthood. *Journal of Divorce and Remarriage* 24(3–4).

Taylor, B.J., & M. Donnelly. 2006. Professional perspectives on decision making about the long-term care of older people. *British Journal of Social Work* 36: 807–826.

Teachman, Jay D., & Karen A. Polonko. 1990. Cohabitation and marital stability in the United States. *Social Forces* 69(1): 207–220.

Teare, John F., Karen Authier, & Roger Peterson. 1994. Differential patterns of post-shelter placement as a function of problem type and severity. *Journal of Child and Family Studies* 3(1): 7–22.

Tennstedt, Sharon L., & John B. McKinlay. 1987. *Predictors of Informal Care: The Role of Social Network Characteristics*. American Sociological Association (ASA).

Ternikar, Farha Bano. 2004. Revisioning the ethnic family: An analysis of marriage patterns among Hindu, Muslim, and Christian South Asian immigrants. *Dissertation Abstracts International*, 65(8), 3176–A-3177–A. (UMI No. 3143927).

Thies, K., & Travers, J. 2006. *Handbook of human development for health care professionals*. Sudbury, MA: Jones & Bartlett.

Thomas, Linda Thiede, & Daniel C. Ganster. 1995 February. Impact of family-supportive work variables on work-family conflict and strain: A control perspective. *Journal of Applied Psychology* 80: 6–15.

Thomas, Madhavappallil, & Jong Baek Choi. 2006. Acculturative stress and social support among Korean and Indian immigrant adolescents in the United States. *Journal of Sociology and Social Welfare* 33: 123–143.

Thomas, Tania N. 1995. Acculturative stress in the adjustment of immigrant families. *Journal of Social Distress and the Homeless* 4(2): 131–142.

Thompson, L.W., J.N. Breckenridge, D. Gallagher, & J. Peterson. 1984. Effects of bereavement on self-perceptions of physical health in elderly widows and widowers. *Journal of Gerontology* 39(3), 309–314.

Thompson, Suzanne C., Louis J. Medvene, & Debra Freedman. 1995. Caregiving in the close relationship of cardiac patients: Exchange, power and attribution perspectives on caregiver resentment. *Personal Relationships* 2(2).

Thomson, Elizabeth Jean, & Min Li. 1992. *Family Structure and Children's Kin*. Madison: University of Wisconsin Center for Demography and Ecology.

Thomson, Elizabeth, Maria Winkler-Dworak, and Sheela Kennedy. 2013. The Standard Family Life Course: An Assessment of Variability in Life Course Pathways. In Ann Evans and Janeen Baxter (Eds.), *Negotiating the Life Course: Stability and Change in Life Pathways*. Dordrecht: Springer.

Thornton, A., & L. Young-DeMarco. 2001. Four decades of trends in attitudes toward family issues in the United States. *Journal of Marriage and the Family* 63(4): 1009–1037.

Tingey, Holly, Gary Kiger, & Pamela J. Riley. 1996. Juggling multiple roles: Perceptions of working mothers. *Social Science Journal* 33(2): 183–191.

Tjaden, P., & N. Thoennes. 2000. *Prevalence, Incidence, and Consequences of Violence Against Women: Findings from the National Violence Against Women Survey*. Research Report. Washington, D.C., and Atlanta, G.A.: U.S. Department of Justice, National Institute of Justice, and U.S. Department of Health and Human Services, Centers for Disease Control and Prevention.

Todd, Sheri. 2004. *Improving Work-Life Balance: What Are Other Countries Doing?* Retrieved May 22, 2005, from Human Resources and Skills Development Canada & Labour Program. **http://www.hrsdc.gc.ca/en/lp/spila/wlb/pdf/improving-work-life-balance.pdf**

Torppa, Cynthia Burggraf. 2002. Gender Issues: Communication Differences in Interpersonal Relationships fact sheet. Ohio State University Extension. Retrieved from **http://ohioline.osu.edu/flm02/FS04.html**. Reprinted with permission.

Townsend, John Marshall. 1990. Effects of partners' physical attractiveness and socio-economic status on sexuality and partner selection. *Archives of Sexual Behaviour* 19(2): 149–164.

Townsend, Nicholas W. 2002. *The Package Deal: Marriage, Work and Fatherhood in Men's Lives*. Philadelphia: Temple University Press.

Townsend-Batten, Barbara. 2002 Spring. Staying in touch: Contact between adults and their parents. *Canadian Social Trends* 64: 9–12. Retrieved January 12, 2006, from **http://dsp-psd.pwgsc.gc.ca/Collection-R/Statcan/11-008-XIE/0040111-008-XIE.pdf**

Trovato, Frank. 2013. *Aboriginal Populations: Social, Demographic and Epidemiological Perspectives*. Edmonton, AB: University of Alberta Press.

Trudel, Gilles, Lyne Landry, & Yvette Larose. 1997. Low sexual desire: The role of anxiety, depression and marital adjustment. *Sexual and Marital Therapy* 12(1).

Tucker, M. Belinda, & Claudia Mitchell-Kernan. 1995. *The Decline in Marriage among African Americans: Causes, Consequences, and Policy Implications*. New York: Russell Sage Foundation.

Turcotte, Martin, & Grant Schellenberg. 2006. *A Portrait of Seniors in Canada*. Ottawa: Statistics Canada. Catalogue no. 89-519-XIE.

Turcotte, Martin. 2013. Living Apart Together. Ottawa: Statistics Canada, catalogue no. 75-006X. **http://www.statcan.gc.ca/pub/75-006-x/2013001/article/11771-eng.htm#a1**

Turnbull, Annmarie. 1994. An isolated missionary: The domestic subjects teacher in England, 1870–1914. *Women's History Review* 3(1): 81–100.

Turell, Susan C. 2000. A descriptive analysis of same-sex relationship violence for a diverse sample. *Journal of Family Violence* 13: 281–293.

Twenge, Jean M., W. Keith Campbell, & Craig A. Foster. 2003. Parenthood and marital satisfaction: A meta-analytic review. *Journal of Marriage and the Family* 65: 574–583.

Tyyskä, Vappu. 2011. "Immigrant and Racialized Families." In Nancy Mandell and Ann Duffy, Eds. *Canadian Families: Diversity, Conflict and Change*, 4th edition. Toronto: Nelson, 86–122.

Tzeng, Jessie M. 2000. Ethnically heterogamous marriages: The case of Asian Canadians. *Journal of Comparative Family Studies* 31(3): 321–337.

Tzeng, Jessie, & Robert Mare. 1995 December. Labor market and socioeconomic effects on marital stability. *Social Science Research 24*.

United Nations Demographic Yearbook 2003. Table 25: Divorces and Crude Divorce Rate by Urban/Rural Residence. Retrieved January 12, 2006, from **http://unstats.un.org/unsd/demographic/products/dyb/dyb2.htm**

United Nations Secretariat. 2003, May. Partnership and reproductive behaviour in low-fertility countries. ESA/P/WP.177. Retrieved November 30, 2005, from **http://www.un.org/esa/population/publications/reprobehavior/partrepro.pdf**

United Nations, Department of Economic and Social Affairs, Population Division. 2004. World Contraceptive Use 2003. Retrieved April 26, 2006, from **http://www.un.org/esa/population/publications/contraceptive2003/wcu2003.htm**

United Nations. 1991. *Building the Smallest Democracy at the Heart of Society*. Vienna: United Nations International Year of the Family Secretariat.

USA: National Health Statistics Reports, Number 49, Table 1, March 22, 2012. **http://www.cdc.gov/nchs**

U.S. Census Bureau. 2011. 2008 Survey of Income and Program Participation, Wave 2 **http://www.census.gov/hhes/socdemo/children/data/sipp/living2009/tab02.pdf**

U.S. Census Bureau. 2012. Statistical Abstract, Births, Deaths, Marriages, & Divorces. **http://www.census.gov/compendia/statab/cats/births_deaths_marriages_divorces.html**

Usita, P.M., S.S. Hall, & J.C. Davis. 2004. Role of ambiguity in family caregiving. *Journal of Applied Gerontology*, 23: 20–39.

Uskul, Ayse, Richard Lalonde, & Lynda Cheng. 2007. Dating among Chinese and European Canadians: The roles of culture, gender, and mainstream cultural identity. *Journal of Social and Personal Relationships* 24.6: 891.

Utz, R.L., E.B. Reidy, D. Carr, R. Nesse, & C. Wortman. 2004. The daily consequences of widowhood: The role of gender and intergenerational transfers on subsequent housework performance. *Journal of Family Issues* 25(5): 683–712.

Vaijayanthimala, K., K. Bharati Kumari, & Bharati Panda. 2004. Socio-economic heterogamy and marital satisfaction. *Journal of Human Ecology* 15(1): 9–11.

Valdivia, Corinne, & Jere Gilles. 2001. Gender and resource management: Households and groups, strategies and transitions. *Agriculture and Human Values* 18(1): 5–9.

Valens, E.G. 1975. *The Other Side of the Mountain*. New York: Warner Books.

Van de Vijver, & J.R. Fons. 2007. Cultural and gender differences in gender-role beliefs, sharing household task and child-care responsibilities, and well-being among immigrants and majority members in the Netherlands. *Sex Roles* 57: 813–24.

Vandercasteele, Leen. 2011. "Life Course Risks or Cumulative Disadvantage? The Structuring Effect of Social Stratification Determinants and Life Course Events on Poverty Transitions in Europe." *European Sociological Review* 27(2): 246–263.

Van Kirk, Sylvia. 1980. *"Many Tender Ties": Women in Fur-Trade Society, 1670–1870*. Winnipeg: Watson & Dwyer.

Van Kirk, Sylvia. 1992. The custom of the country: An examination of fur trade marriage practices, pp. 67–92. In Bettina Bradbury (Ed.), *Canadian Family History: Selected Readings*. Toronto: Copp Clark Pitman.

Van Riper, Marcia. 2007. Families of children with Down syndrome: Responding to a "change in plans" with resilience. *Journal of Pediatric Nursing* 22(22): 116–128.

Vanier Institute of the Family. 1994. *Profiling Canada's Families*. Ottawa: Vanier Institute of the Family.

Vanier Institute of the Family. 2000. *Family Facts*. Retrieved May 12, 2005, from **http://www.vifamily.ca/library/facts/facts.html**

Vanier Institute of the Family. 2002. *Profiling Canada's Families II*. Ottawa: Vanier Institute of the Family.

Vanier Institute of the Family. 2004. *Profiling Canada's Families III*. Ottawa: Vanier Institute of the Family.

Vanier Institute of the Family. 2010. *Families Count–Profiling Canada's Families IV*. Ottawa: Vanier Institute of the Family.

Vanier Institute of the Family. 2010. "Forming Unis—Again." **http://www.vanierinstitute.ca/modules/news/newsitem.php?ItemId=152#.UR1MY_LCTTo**

Vanier Institute of the Family, 2011. Fascinating Families, October 26, Issue 41. Four in Ten Marriages End in Divorce. **http://www.vanierinstitute.ca/include/get.php?nodeid=132**

Vanier Institute of the Family. 2012. Families Count: Profiling Canada's Families IV. **http://www.vanierinstitute.ca/families_count_-_profiling_canadas_families_iv#.UaUlsdjm98**

Vanier Institute of the Family. 2013. Our Approach to Family. **http://www.vanierinstitute.ca/our_approach_to_family**

Vanier Institute of the Family. 2013. Definition of Family. **http://www.vanierinstitute.ca/definition_of_family#.UdyJfFT4Dcc**

Vansteenwegen, Alfons. 1996a. Individual and relational changes seven years after couples therapy. *Journal of Couples Therapy* 6(1–2).

Vansteenwegen, Alfons. 1996b. Who benefits from couple therapy? A comparison of successful and unsuccessful couples. *Journal of Sex and Marital Therapy* 22(1).

Vansteenwegen, Alfons. 1998 April–June. Divorce after couple therapy: An overlooked perspective of outcome research. *Journal of Sex & Marital Therapy* 24(2): 123–130.

Varela, Enrique R., Juan Jose Sanchez-Sosa, Angelica Riveros, Eric M. Vernberg, Montserrat Mitchell, & Joanna Mashunkashey. 2004. Parenting style of Mexican, Mexican American, and caucasian-non-

Hispanic families: Social context and cultural influences. *Journal of Family Psychology* 18: 651–57.

Vaughan, Diane. 1985. *Uncoupling: Turning Points in Intimate Relationships*. New York: Oxford University Press.

Verberg, N., E. Wood, S. Desmarais, & C. Senn. Gender differences in survey respondents' written definitions of date rape. 2000. *Canadian Journal of Human Sexuality* 9: 181–190.

Vergun, Pamela Bea, Sanford M. Dornbusch, & Laurence Steinberg. 1996. *"Come All of You Turn to and Help One Another": Authoritative Parenting, Community Orientation, and Deviance Among High School Students*. American Sociological Association paper.

Vinokur, Amiran D., Richard H. Price, & Robert D. Caplan. 1996. Hard times and hurtful partners: How financial strain affects depression and relationship satisfaction of unemployed persons and their spouses. *Journal of Personality and Social Psychology* 71.

Vitaliano, Peter P., James M. Scanlan, Jianping Zhang, Margaret Savage, Irl Hirsch, & Ilene Siegler. 2002. A path model of chronic stress, the metabolic syndrome, and coronary heart disease. *Psychosomatic Medicine* 64: 418–435.

Wadsby, Marie, & Gunilla Sydsjoe. 2001 December. From pregnancy to parenthood: A study of couples' relationship. *Frangraviditet till foeraeldraskap: En studie av parrelationen. Nordisk Psykologi* 53(4): 275–288.

Wainwright, Jennifer L., Stephen T. Russell, & Charlotte J. Patterson. 2004. Psychosocial adjustment, school outcomes, and romantic relationships of adolescents with same-sex parents. *Child Development* 75(6): 1886–1898.

Waite, Linda J. 1999. Reviewed work: *Marriage in Men's Lives* by Steven L. Nock. *American Journal of Sociology* 105(3): 866–868.

Waite, Linda J. 2000. The family as a social organization: Key ideas for the twenty-first century, *Contemporary Sociology* 29(3): 463–469.

Wajcman, Judy. 2010. "Feminist Theories of Technology." *Cambridge Journal of Economics* 34(1): 143–152.

Walczynski, Pamela Theresa. 1998 April. Power, personality, and conflictual interaction: An exploration of demand/withdraw interaction in same-sex and cross-sex couples. *Dissertation Abstracts International: Section B: The Sciences & Engineering* 58(10–B), 5660.

Waldner-Haugrud, Lisa K., Linda Vaden Gratch, Brian Magruder. 1997 Summer. Victimization and perpetration rates of violence in gay and lesbian relationships: Gender issues explored. *Violence and Victims* 12(2): 173–184.

Wallace, Jean E. 1997 April. It's about time: A study of hours worked and work spillover among law firm lawyers. *Journal of Vocational Behavior* 50(2): 227–248.

Waller, Maureen R., & Sara S. McLanahan. 2005. His and her marriage expectations: Determinants and consequences. *Journal of Marriage and the Family* 67(1): 53–67.

Wallerstein, J., & S. Blakelee. 1990. *Second Chances: Men, Women, and Children a Decade After Divorce*. New York: Ticknor and Fields.

Wallerstein, Judith S. 1996 April. The psychological tasks of marriage: Part 2. *American Journal of Orthopsychiatry* 66.

Wallerstein, Judith S., & Julia M. Lewis. 2004. The unexpected legacy of divorce: Report of a 25-year study. *Psychoanalytic Psychology* 21(3): 353–370.

Walters, Karina L., & Jane M. Simoni. 1999 August. Trauma, substance use, and HIV risk among urban American Indian women. *Cultural Diversity & Ethnic Minority Psychology* 5(3): 236–248.

Walters, Suzanna Danuta. 1999. Sex, text and context: (In)between feminism and cultural studies. In Myra Marx Ferree, Judith Lorber, and Beth B. Hess (Eds.), *Revisioning Gender*. Thousand Oaks, CA: Sage.

Ward, C. & Terence J. 2004. Relation of shyness with aspects of online relationship involvement. *Journal of Social and Personal relationships*, 21(5): 611–623.

Warren, Jennifer A., & Phyllis J. Johnson. 1995 April. The impact of workplace support on work–family role strain. *Family Relations* 44: 163–169.

Warrener, Corinne, Julie M. Koivunen, and Judy L. Postmus. 2013. "Economic Self-Sufficiency among Divorced Women: Impact of Depression, Abuse, and Efficacy." *Journal of Divorce and Remarriage* 54(2): 163–175.

Wasylkewycz, M.N. 1993. The elder abuse resource centre, a coordinated community response to elder abuse: One Canadian perspective. *Journal of Elder Abuse and Neglect* 5(4): 21–33.

Wathen, C. Nadine, & Roma H. Harris. 2007. "I try to take care of it myself": How rural women search for health information. *Qualitative Health Research* 17(5): 639–651.

Watts, Charlotte, & Susannah Mayhew. 2004. Reproductive health services and intimate partner violence: Shaping a pragmatic response in sub-Saharan Africa. *International Family Planning Perspectives* 30(4): 207–213.

Weaver, Terri L., & George A. Clum. 1996. Interpersonal violence: Expanding the search for long-term sequelae within a sample of battered women. *Journal of Traumatic Stress* 9(4): 783–803.

Webster, Pamela S., & Regula A. Herzog. 1995 January. Effects of parental divorce and memories of family problems on relationships between adult children and their parents. *Journal of Gerontology, Series B: Psychological Sciences and Social Sciences* 50B.

Weil, Jennifer M., & Hwayun H. Lee. 2004. Cultural considerations in understanding family violence among Asian American Pacific Islander families. *Journal of Community Health Nursing* 21(4): 217–227.

Weiner, Jennifer, Lisa Harlow, Jerome Adams, & L. Grebstein. 1995. Psychological adjustment of college students from families of divorce. *Journal of Divorce and Remarriage* 23(3–4): 75–95.

Weinfeld, Morton. 2001. *Like Everyone Else ... but Different: The Paradoxical Success of Canadian Jews*. Toronto: McClelland and Stewart.

Weiss, Robert S. 1996. Parenting from separate households, pp. 215–230. In David Popenoe, Jean Bethke Elshtain, & David Blankenhorn (Eds.), *Promises to Keep: Decline and Renewal of Marriage in America*. Lanham, MD: Rowman and Littlefield Publishers, Inc.

Weitzman, Lenore. 1985. *The Divorce Revolution: The Unexpected Social and Economic Effects for Women and Children in America*. New York: Free Press.

Wellman, Barry, & Keith Hampton. 1999 November. Living networked on and offline. *Contemporary Sociology* 28(6): 648–654.

West, Carolyn M. 1998. Leaving a second closet: Outing partner violence in same-sex couples, pp. 163–183. In Jana L. Jasinski, & Linda M. Williams (Eds.), *Partner Violence: A Comprehensive Review of 20 Years of Research.* Thousand Oaks, CA: Sage.

Wharton, Amy S., & Rebecca J. Erickson. 1995. The consequences of caring: Exploring the links between women's job and family emotion work. *Sociological Quarterly 36*(2): 273–296.

Wheaton, Blair. 1999. The nature of stressors. In Allan V. Horwitz and Teresa L. Scheid (Eds.), *A Handbook for the Study of Mental Health.* New York: Cambridge University Press, 176–197.

Wherry, Jeffrey N., John B. Jolly, John F. Aruffo, Greg Gillette, Lela Vaught, & Rebecca Methony. 1994. Family trauma and dysfunction in sexually abused female adolescent psychiatric and control groups. *Journal of Child Sexual Abuse 3*(1): 53–65.

Whisman, Mark A., & Neil S. Jacobson. 1989. Depression, marital satisfaction, and marital and personality measures of sex roles. *Journal of Marital and Family Therapy 15*(2): 177–186.

White, James M. 1998. The normative interpretation of life course event histories. *Marriage and Family Review 27*(3–4): 211–235.

White, Lynn. 1990. Determinants of divorce: A review of research in the eighties. *Journal of Marriage and the Family 52*(4): 904–912.

Whiteford, Peter. 2009. *Family Joblessness in Australia.* Australia: Document prepared for the Social Inclusion Unit, Department of the Prime Minister and Cabinet. Retrieved June 2, 2009, from **http://74.125.113.132/ search?q=cache:FdSvSrx4KPwJ:www.social-inclusion.gov.au/Documents/Family%2520Job lessness%2520in%2520Australia2%2520(3) .rtf+lone+parenthood+international+data&cd=12 &hl=en&ct=clnk&gl=ca&client=firefox-a**

Whitehead, Barbara Dafoe, & David Popenoe. 2001. Who wants to marry a soul mate? New survey findings on young adults' attitudes about love and marriage. In *The State of Our Unions: The Social Health of Marriage in America.* Retrieved June 6, 2005, from **http://marriage.rutgers.edu./Publications/SOOU/ TEXTSOOU2001.htm**

Whitehead, Barbara Dafoe. 1996. The decline of marriage as the social basis of childbearing, pp. 3–14. In David Popenoe, Jean Bethke Elshtain, & David Blankenhorn (Eds.), *Promises to Keep: Decline and Renewal of Marriage in America.* Lanham, MD: Rowman and Littlefield Publishers, Inc.

Whitty, Monica T., & Laura-Lee Quiqley. 2008. Emotional and sexual infidelity offline and in cyberspace. *Journal of Marital and Family Therapy 34*(4): 461–468.

Wiegerink, D. J., Roebroeck, M. E., Van, D. S., Stam, H. J., & Cohen-Kettenis, P. 2010. Importance of peers and dating in the development of romantic relationships and sexual activity of young adults with cerebral palsy. *Developmental Medicine & Child Neurology, 52*(6), 576–582.

Wiener, Lori S., Nancy Heilman, & Haven B. Battles. 1998. Public disclosure of HIV: Psychosocial considerations for children, pp. 193–217. In Valerian J. Derlega, & Anita P. Barbee (Eds.) *HIV and Social Interaction.* Thousand Oaks, CA: Sage.

Wienke, Chris, & Gretchen J. Hill. 2009. Does the "marriage benefit" extend to partners in gay and lesbian relationships? *Journal of Family Issues 30*(2): 259–289.

Wiersma, Uco J. 1994 February. A taxonomy of behavioral strategies for coping with work-home conflict. *Human Relations 47*: 211–221.

Wight, Daniel, Lisa Williamson, & Marion Henderson. 2006. Parental influences on young people's sexual behaviour: a longitudinal analysis. *Journal of Adolescence 29*: 473–494.

Wight, Vanessa R., Sara B. Raley, and Suzanne M. Bianchi. 2008. Time for children, one's spouse and oneself among parents who work nonstandard hours. *Social Forces 87*(1): 243–271.

Wilkinson, Richard G. 1994. From material scarcity to social disadvantage. Daedalus: *Journal of the American Academy of Arts and Sciences 123*(4): 61–77.

Williams, Cara. 2005 Summer. The sandwich generation. *Canadian Social Trends 77*: 16–21. Retrieved January 10, 2006, from **http://dsp-psd.pwgsc.gc.ca/Collection-R/ Statcan/11-008-XIE/0010511-008-XIE.pdf**

Williams, Alex, 2013. "The End of Courtship?" **http://www .nytimes.com/2013/01/13/fashion/the-end-of-courtship .html?src=me&ref=general&pagewanted=all&_r=0**

Williams, John D., & Arthur P. Jacoby. 1989. The effects of premarital heterosexual and homosexual experience on dating and marriage desirability. *Journal of Marriage and the Family 51*(2): 489–497.

Williams, L., M. Kabamalan, & N. Ogena. 2007. Cohabitation in the Philippines: Attitudes and behaviors among young women and men. *Journal of Marriage and Family 69*(5): 1244–1256.

Williams, Rhys H., & Gira Vashi. 2007. Hijab and American Muslim women: Creating the space for autonomous selves. *Sociology of Religion 68*: 269–87.

Williamson, Deanna L., & Fiona Salkie. 2005. Welfare reforms in Canada: implications for the well-being of pre-school children in poverty. *Journal of Children & Poverty 11*(1): 55–76.

Willms, J. Douglas (Ed.). 2002. *Vulnerable Children: Findings from Canada's Longitudinal Survey of Children and Youth.* Edmonton: University of Alberta Press.

Wills, C. 2001. Women, domesticity and the family: Recent feminist work in Irish cultural studies. *Cultural Studies 15*: 33–57.

Wilson, Paul A., Stephen T. Moore, Dana S. Rubin, & Pamela K. Bartels. 1990. Informal caregivers of the chronically ill and their social support: A pilot study. *Journal of Gerontological Social Work 15*(1–2): 155–170

Wilson, S.J. 1996. *Women, Families and Work* (4th edition). Toronto: McGraw-Hill Ryerson.

Wilson, Sue J. 2005. Partnering, cohabitation and marriage, pp. 145–162. In Maureen Baker (Ed.), *Families: Changing Trends in Canada* (5th edition). Toronto: McGraw-Hill Ryerson.

Winch, Robert F. 1962. *The Modern Family.* New York: Holt.

Wind, Tiffany Weissmann, & Louise Silvern. 1994 May. Parenting and family stress as mediators of the long-term effects of child abuse. *Child Abuse and Neglect 18*: 439–453.

Winfield, Idee, & Beth Rushing. 2005. Bridging the border between work and family: The effects of supervisor-employee similarity. *Sociological Inquiry* 75(1): 55–80.

Wong, Yin-Ling, Irene Wong, & Irving Piliavin. 2001. Stressors, resources, and distress among homeless persons: A longitudinal analysis. *Social Science & Medicine* 52: 1029–1042.

Wong-Wylie, Gina, & Marianne Doherty-Poirier. 1997. *Created Families: Perspectives From Persons Living with HIV/AIDS*. Paper presented at the Canadian Home Economics Association, Victoria, B.C.

Wright, Eric Reaney. 1994 August. Caring for those who "can't": Gender, network structure, and the burden of caring for people with mental illness. *Dissertation Abstracts International, A: The Humanities and Social Sciences* 55(2), 380–A.

Wu, Zheng. 1994. Remarriage in Canada. A Social Exchange Perspective. *Journal of Divorce and Remarriage* 21 (3–4), 191–224.

Wu, Zheng, & Christoph M. Schimmele. 2005a. Repartnering after first union disruption. *Journal of Marriage and the Family* 67(1): 157–172.

Wu, Zheng, & Christoph Schimmele. 2005b. Divorce and Repartnering, pp. 202–228. In Maureen Baker (Ed.), *Families: Changing Trends in Canada* (5th edition). Toronto: McGraw-Hill Ryerson.

Wu, Zheng, & R. Hart. 2002. The effects of marital and non-marital union transition on health. *Journal of Marriage and the Family* 64: 420–432.

Wu, Zheng. 1995. Remarriage after widowhood: A marital history study of older Canadians. *Canadian Journal on Aging* 14(4): 719–736.

Wu, Zheng. 2000. *Cohabitation: An Alternative Form of Family Living*. Don Mills, ON: Oxford University Press.

Wu, Zheng, & T.R. Balakrishnan. 1995. The dissolution of premarital cohabitation in Canada. *Demography* 32: 521–532.

Wylie, Mary Lou. 2000. Halving it all: How equally shared parenting works. *Gender & Society* 14(3): 485–487.

Xiaohe, Xu, & Martin King Whyte. 1990. Love matches and arranged marriages. *Journal of Marriage and the Family* 52(3): 709–722.

Xu, Anqi, Xiaolin Xie, Wenli Liu, Yan Xia, & Dalin Liu. 2007. Asia: Chinese family strengths and resiliency. *Marriage & Family Review* 41(1–2): 143–164.

Yaffee, Jennifer Beth. 2003. The role of perceived attitude similarity in relationship satisfaction among heterosexual and lesbian couples. *Dissertation Abstracts International: Section B: The Sciences and Engineering* 63(12-B): 6148.

Yarosh, Svetlana, Yee Chieh "Denise" Chew, & Gregory D. Abowd. 2009. Supporting parent-child communication in divorced families. *International Journal of Human-Computer Studies* 67: 192–203.

Yeh, H.-C., F. Lorenz, K.A.S. Wickrama, R.D. Conger, & G.H. Elder. 2006. Relationships among sexual satisfaction, marital quality, and marital instability at midlife. *Journal of Family Psychology* 20: 339–343.

Yick, Alice G. 2001. Feminist theory and status inconsistency theory: Application to domestic violence in Chinese immigrant families. *Violence Against Women* 7: 545–62.

Yick, Alice G., & Jody Oomen-Early. 2008. A 16-year examination of domestic violence among Asians and Asian Americans in the empirical knowledge base: A content analysis. *Journal of Interpersonal Violence* 23: 1075–1094.

York, Glyn Y. 1987 Summer. Religious-based denial in the NICU: Implications for social work. *Social Work in Health Care* 12(4): 31–45.

Yoshioka, M.R., L. Gilbert, N. El-Bassel, & M. Baig-Amin. 2003. Social support and disclosure of abuse: Comparing South Asian, African American, and Hispanic battered women. *Journal of Family Violence* 18(3): 171–180.

Young, C., & Boyd, S. 2006. Losing the feminist voice? Debates on the legal recognition of same sex partnerships in Canada. *Feminist Legal Studies* 14(2): 213–240.

Yousif, Ahmed F. 1994. Family values, social adjustment and problems of identity: The Canadian experience. *Journal Institution of Muslim Minority Affairs* 15.1: 108–120.

Yum, Y. & Hara, K. 2005. Computer-mediated relationship development: A cross-cultural comparison. *Journal of Computer-Mediated Communication*, 11(1): 133–152.

Zachariah, Rachel. 1996. Predictors of psychological well-being of women during pregnancy; replication and extension. *Journal of Social Behavior and Personality* 11(1).

Zhan, Gao. 1998 June. The sojourning life as problematic: Marital crises of Chinese students who are studying in the U.S. *Dissertation Abstracts International, A: The Humanities and Social Sciences* 58(12), 4825–A.

Zhang, S.Y., & S.L. Kline. 2009. Can I make my own decision? A cross-cultural study of perceived social network influence in mate selection. *Journal of Cross-Cultural Psychology* 40: 3–23.

Zhenchao, Qian, & Daniel T. Lichter. 2007. Social boundaries and marital assimilation: Interpreting trends in racial and ethnic intermarriage. *American Sociological Review* 72: 68–94.

Zhou, Min, & Carl L. Bankston III. 2001. Family pressure and the education experience of the daughters of Vietnamese refugees. *International Migration* 39(4): 133–151.

Zick, Cathleen D., & Jane L. McCullough. 1991 April. Trends in married couples' time use: Evidence from 1977–78 and 1987–88. *Sex Roles* 24 (7–8): 459–487.

Zur Institute. 2013. "Cybersex Addiction & Internet Infidelity: Clinical Update." **http://www.zurinstitute .com/cybersex_clinicalupdate.html**

Index